THE
DUFF COOPER DIARIES
1915–1951

THE
DUFF COOPER DIARIES
1915–1951

Edited by

JOHN JULIUS NORWICH

Weidenfeld & Nicolson

LONDON

First published in Great Britain in 2005
by Weidenfeld & Nicolson

1 3 5 7 9 10 8 6 4 2

A CIP catalogue record for this book
is available from the British Library.

ISBN 0 297 84843 7

Typeset, printed and bound in Great Britain
by Butler and Tanner Ltd, Frome and London

Weidenfeld & Nicolson

The Orion Publishing Group Ltd
Orion House
5 Upper Saint Martin's Lane
London, WC2H 9EA

www.orionbooks.co.uk.

CONTENTS

ILLUSTRATIONS

Sections of illustrations appear between pages 178 & 179 and 338 & 339. All photographs are provided courtesy of Duff Cooper's family, with the exception of the portrait of Duff Cooper in the Paris Embassy (Cecil Beaton collection, by kind permission of Sotheby's). If any copyright has failed to be acknowledged, the publishers would welcome details for inclusion in any subsequent editions.

INTRODUCTION

My father, Duff Cooper, has now been dead for half a century: a period of time not long enough for his diary to be a historical treasure like those of Samuel Pepys or John Evelyn, nor short enough for it to be required reading for students of current affairs. Why then, it may be asked, is it being published now? Why, indeed, should it be published at all?

The answer to the first question is simple. My father did not leave his diary to me. Those seventeen handwritten volumes, as he was well aware, contained a remarkably frank record of his life – and in particular of his extremely *mouvementé* sex life. Understandably enough, he did not want them to pass directly into my hands, or indeed those of my mother (which would have amounted to much the same thing). A more suitable recipient, he felt, would be his nephew and publisher, Rupert Hart-Davis. This choice very nearly led to disaster: Rupert, profoundly shocked by what he had read, decided to destroy them. Fortunately he told me of his intention, and I was able to persuade him to do no such thing; he finally agreed – though with some reluctance – to hand them over to me. For the next few years they remained in our attic, during which time they were seen only by my parents' respective biographers, John Charmley and Philip Ziegler. Some years later my daughter Artemis and my son-in-law Antony Beevor drew on the years 1944–9 for their book *Paris After the Liberation*; then in 2002, when the release by the Public Record Office of further papers concerning the abdication of King Edward VIII reawakened interest in that period, the relevant section of the diary was published in the *Sunday Telegraph*. With these exceptions, no one to my knowledge has seen the diary since my father's death, apart from my wife Mollie and myself. It is barely two years ago that Mollie completed the enormous task of putting the whole thing on to a computer. Only then did I myself read it for the first time from end to end.

The answer to the second question is a good deal more important. Essentially, it is that my father was a first-rate witness of – and often a first-hand participant in – just about every significant political development that occurred between 1914 and his death forty years later. But there is more to it than that. As a man-about-town, married to one of the most famously beautiful and remarkable women of her day, a lover of parties and good company and, finally, the author of a brilliant biography of Talleyrand – which in fifty years has never once been out of print – he was also ideally placed to report on the social and literary life of England during the first half of the twentieth century. Winston Churchill and General de Gaulle, Edward VIII and Mrs Simpson, Neville Chamberlain and Lloyd George, Hilaire Belloc and Evelyn Waugh – these are only a few of the names that people his pages.

And then, of course, there is my father himself. To those few who were immune to his intelligence and his charm he was a drinker, a gambler and a shameless pursuer of beautiful women; nor, as the diary makes clear, were they entirely wrong. He was in no sense an alcoholic; indeed, I only once saw him seriously drunk – after a nightmare evening at the Soviet Embassy in Paris, an incident recorded as fully as he was able to remember (which was not very fully) in the pages that follow. Nevertheless, as he readily admitted in his autobiography *Old Men Forget*, he consistently drank more than most people would have said was good for him. He certainly gambled recklessly in his youth – in one evening in 1914 he lost almost four times his annual salary – but the habit fortunately left him in later life. He might still play from time to time at the tables of Deauville or Monte Carlo; there was also plenty of bridge and backgammon for lowish stakes and the occasional bet on a horse. But after his marriage his playing was never remotely compulsive; and although he left virtually no money at his death, this was due more to his natural extravagance than anything else. Where women were concerned, on the other hand, he would certainly have entered a plea of guilty; but I shall return to that later.

He was born on 22 February 1890 and died on 1 January 1954. His father, Sir Alfred Cooper, was a distinguished surgeon originally from Norwich (hence the title): the recognized leader in his special field – which was, it must be recorded, venereal disease and piles. His mother was the great-granddaughter of King William IV, who had no less than nine illegitimate offspring by Mrs Dorothy Jordan, the leading *comédienne* of her day. One of their countless grand-children married – curiously enough, at the British Embassy in Paris – James, the 5th Earl Fife. The youngest of the Fifes' four children, Lady Agnes, was in her youth more than a little flighty: at the age of twenty-eight, with two elope-ments and a divorce behind her, she had been disowned by her family, was practically penniless and – despite the fact that her brother had married the eldest daughter of the future King Edward VII – no longer received in polite society. In the hopes of becoming a nurse, she took a menial job in one of the major London teaching hospitals, and it was there in 1882 that she caught the eye of Dr Cooper. The two of them – together they were said to know more than anyone else about the private parts of the English aristocracy – married, and eventually, after four daughters, produced a son – my father.

After his education at Eton and Oxford – where, according to John Charmley, 'he trailed clouds of dissipation' – he joined the Foreign Office, and con-sequently in 1914 found himself in what was known as a 'reserved profession', which kept him, much to his disgust, in London for the first three years of the war. Only in 1917, when the holocaust of young officers – including nearly all his closest friends – had left the Army seriously depleted, was he released for service. Thus it was not till early in 1918 that he went to France. He made up for lost time by promptly winning the DSO (Distinguished Service Order), an award considered second only to the Victoria Cross.

In June 1919, despite the furious opposition of her parents, he married Lady Diana Manners now, at the age of twenty-seven, a celebrity. She was, first of all, startlingly beautiful; secondly, she was a member of the aristocracy – in those days still an advantage, rather than the millstone that it so often proves today – who had been brought up in one of England's most spectacular country houses, Belvoir Castle, as the youngest daughter of the 8th Duke of Rutland. (Her adoring public would have been horrified to know that she was in fact the result of a long and passionate love affair between the Duchess and the Hon. Harry Cust, poet, man of letters and editor of the *Pall Mall Gazette*.) Ever since her presentation at Court in 1911 she had been the darling of the society and gossip columns; when she married my father – a penniless commoner of whom no one had ever heard – at St Margaret's Westminster on 2 June 1919 – a body of mounted police had to be summoned to control the crowds outside.

Ever since my father's return from France he had been increasingly bored by the Foreign Office. He longed for a political career; but money was short, and he knew that in throwing up his job he would be taking a serious financial risk. Fortunately my mother had recently played the leading role in two silent films, and had thus caught the eye of Europe's greatest theatrical producer, the Austrian Max Reinhardt. He promptly cast her as the Madonna in *The Miracle*, his adaptation of a medieval mystery play, which opened in New York in 1924 and thereafter toured first America, then Eastern Europe and finally England.

While she acted, he campaigned. In 1924 he was elected Conservative Member for Oldham and remained in Parliament for the next twenty years, serving as Secretary of State for War and First Lord of the Admiralty. He resigned from the latter post in 1938 in protest against the Munich agreement with Hitler, but returned to the Cabinet in 1940 when Winston Churchill succeeded Neville Chamberlain as Prime Minister and made him his Minister of Information. In 1941 he spent six months in Singapore, and in January 1944 went to Algiers as Churchill's representative to the French Committee for National Liberation and its leader General Charles de Gaulle. This led automatically to the Embassy in Paris, where he was Ambassador from September 1944 to December 1947.

Reading his diary, I have learned much about my father and feel that I understand him now a good deal better than I did before. He was not only a statesman and – at the end of his career – a diplomat. He was a scholar, a wit and a poet, with a genuine passion for literature; he could – and did – recite poetry by the hour, and since he was as happy in French as he was in English there were few great novels in either language that he had not read. He never underestimated the importance of pleasure, and much of the diary – some might say too much – is concerned with this side of his life: the food he ate, the wine he drank – and, not least – since he was a romantic through and through – the women he loved.

It is this last aspect, not surprisingly, that has caused me the greatest concern. My father was obviously every bit as attractive to women as they were to him, and his love affairs were legion. (Many of his successes may have been due to his habit of bombarding his quarries with sonnets, for which he had a quite extraordinary facility.) Most – I hesitate to say all – of these affairs are described in detail in the diary, a fact which leaves little doubt in my mind that, unlike many diarists, he never intended it for any eyes but his own. I would have written 'no doubt', but for a few lines written on 30 September 1948:

> 'Why do people keep diaries? asked Rupert, and I found it difficult to answer. 'Is it because you look forward to re-reading them?' I don't think so. I don't enjoy re-reading mine. 'Are you thinking of posterity reading them?' I don't think I am, but I may be. I don't want Diana to read my diary and she is closer to me than any human being – nor should I particularly like John Julius to. There is much that I shouldn't mention if I wanted them to read it. Perhaps the answer is that people who love life as much as I do want to keep some record of it – because it is all they can keep.

The last thing I wish to do is to betray him, or indeed my mother, though her own behaviour was immaculate in comparison. Astonishingly, too, she hardly ever minded. (Gloria Rubio was an exception, though even she later became a friend.) Louise de Vilmorin – as the diary makes abundantly clear – she loved almost as much as my father did himself; I even remember, when the affair was at its height, going on a hilarious week's trip à trois through south-west France with Louise and my mother (as always at the wheel), while my father remained in Paris. As for Susan Mary Alsop, the two corresponded regularly; when my mother went to Washington it was with Susan Mary that she stayed. Once, shortly before she died, I asked her how she had managed to be so devoid of jealousy. 'Oh,' she said, 'they were all the flowers. I knew I was the tree.'

To have published the diary in its present form much before the beginning of the twenty-first century would none the less have been out of the question. Today, however, my father has been dead for over fifty years, my mother for nearly twenty; and the other ladies concerned have also been long in their graves. Moreover all the major affairs and a good many of the minor ones have already been chronicled by John Charmley and Philip Ziegler, and if this diary is to be worth reading at all it must provide a portrait of the many-faceted man that my father was: I have no wish to create a plaster saint. This is not to say that we have not made any cuts – had we not done so, the book would have been many times its present length – but the vast majority of these have been on the grounds of interest rather than prudery.

There is a distinct possibility, on the other hand, that my father may during the later years of the Second World War and after have wielded the blue pencil himself. The handwritten volumes are untouched, but for the years 1944 and 1945 and the first five months of 1947 we possess only typescripts. Were these sections originally dictated? We have no means of telling, but there is an unmistakable change of tone.

In the task of editing, we have not had political historians primarily in mind. They will, I believe, find plenty of grist for their particular mills, but for me at least the social mores reflected in the diary are every bit as fascinating. My father writes, for example, of the atmosphere of London during the First World War, the life of young officers in the trenches, the country house weekends, the servants (he had a personal valet till the day he died), the reading aloud, the importance of the theatre (he would go at least once a week, occasionally even to two plays on the same evening). The abdication and the Munich crisis are covered in detail, most of the Second World War, alas, rather less so – often because he was simply too busy – but he picks up the threads again in a brilliant account of the 1945 Foreign Ministers' Conference and the years at the Paris Embassy.

One thought only continues to trouble me: will average readers, when they put this book down, actually *like* my father? I am not sure that they will; I can only hope they will remember that good diaries are almost by definition introspective. Though some of the following entries strike me as very funny indeed, soul-searching is seldom a fertile field for humour or charm – and few of us go around telling our friends our innermost secrets. (If they did, would we like them as much?) What diaries never tell us is how the writer struck those around him, or how much fun he was. Speaking personally, I believe that no one could ever have had a better father, or one who could have left me with happier memories: the reading aloud, the poetry, the plays we saw, the enthusiasm for everything (except music), the long walks through Paris and Venice, the shared love of history, the lightly-worn erudition and above all the unfailing capacity for enjoyment and the sheer love of life itself – never, never was there a dull moment. His friends of both sexes were legion because, as Bob Boothby said at his memorial service, 'he was absolute for friendship'. He was also absolute for generosity and warmth of heart. He always had time. He was greatly loved.

In the Prologue to his biography, John Charmley described my father as 'a statesman who composed sonnets over the gaming-tables; a wit whose patriotism impelled him to sacrifice all for honour; a *bon viveur* and London clubman whose integrity and courage made him beloved by his many friends'. All these aspects are reflected in the diary. The figure that emerges is more intelligent than intellectual, and a good deal more sybarite than saint. But he makes no attempt to conceal his failings and, above all, he never takes himself too seriously. He loved every moment of his life, and his sense of humour never let him down.

John Julius Norwich

PART ONE
1915–1919
The First World War, Courtship and Marriage

Duff had gone up to New College, Oxford, in 1908 and in 1913 passed the Foreign Office examination. In that same year he had first met Lady Diana Manners. With the outbreak of war in 1914, most of his friends immediately enlisted; members of the Foreign Office, however, were not permitted to do so. Duff therefore remained in London, as did his great friend Alan Parsons who was excused military service on medical grounds and was also working in Whitehall. The diary begins in 1915 when Duff was twenty-five. At that time he was living with his mother, Lady Agnes Cooper, in a flat at 9 Berkeley House, Hay Hill, but after a brief interval in the Stafford Hotel he moved into rooms at 88 St James's Street on 11 October.

1915

April 14, 1915. Norton Priory

On Sunday evening I was at Stanway [home of the Charteris family in Gloucestershire] and Cynthia[1] and I settled that we would both start diaries and see who went on the longest.

On Tuesday morning I bought this book and one more beautiful for Cynthia.

April 15, 1915

After dinner I had to do some difficult negotiation work between Sibbie[2] and Richard as regards their future and ended up having an awkward quarter of an hour with Mother on the subject of the bottle. All due to Evelyn Fitzgerald[3] who talked nonsense to Steffie[4] which she unkindly and unwisely reported to Mother.

Friday April 16, 1915

I dined at the Carlton. A large party, including Diana, Lady Cunard[5], Hugo[6],

---

[1] Lady Cynthia Asquith, née Charteris (1887–1960). Married 1910 Herbert 'Beb' Asquith, son of H. H. Asquith by his first wife. Her diaries for 1914–18 were published in 1968.

[2] Sybil Hart-Davis (1886–1927), Duff's third sister, married Richard Hart-Davis, a stockbroker, in 1904.

[3] The Hon. Evelyn Fitzgerald (1874–1946). In 1923 he married Helen Drury, sister of Lord Beaverbrook.

[4] Stephanie (1885–1918), Duff's eldest sister, married first, Arthur Levita (d. 1910) and second, in 1916, Tolly Wingfield. In 1915 she was living at Norton Priory, West Sussex.

[5] Maud, later Emerald, Cunard (1872–1948), American wife of Sir Bache Cunard and one of the great political and society hostesses of the period. She was in love with Beecham.

[6] Hugo Rumbold (1884–1932), stage designer.

Thomas Beecham[1] and Bonham Carter.[2] After dinner they all went to a play but I went to the Ambassadors to pick up M.T.[3] and go and have another dinner with her at the Savoy. At 12 o'clock we both went to a small supper party at the Cavendish consisting of Diana, Nancy,[4] Iris,[5] Hugo, Hallam[6] and ourselves. It was great fun and everyone was very drunk at the end especially me. As Diana was going off with Hallam and I with Marjorie, Diana said to me in the hall that although we both had our stage favourites we really loved each other best, and kissed me divinely, which nobody noticed though they were all standing by.

Saturday April 17, 1915

The last day of my week's holiday. I went in the morning to see Letty[7] and Mary[8] off to Egypt. I gave them both a large box of strawberries. Diana was at the station. I drove back from Liverpool Street with Diana and spent the rest of the morning with her. We picked up Nancy and Iris and went and had oysters and plovers' eggs and chablis at Wilton's and later, with the addition of Hugo we lunched at the Cavendish. Diana went down to Belvoir in the afternoon. I went out with M.T. and we finished up at Fitzroy Street where we lay almost platonically in one another's arms torn between desire and fatigue – at least I was, but fear and fatigue had the upper hand with her. Tomorrow I return to the Foreign Office.

Monday April 19, 1915

On Sunday morning I went back to the Foreign Office, arriving there at 8.30 a.m. How I hated getting up. I began cold baths this morning. Everything seems to be getting on better with Foreign Affairs since I was there last. All the difficulties which Russia was making about Italian cooperation [with the Allies] which nearly caused negotiations to be broken off have been got over,

---

[1] Sir Thomas Beecham (1879–1961), conductor. He mounted Covent Garden opera seasons 1910–20.

[2] Sir Maurice 'Bongie' Bonham Carter (1880–1960), PPS to Asquith 1910–16, married Lady Violet Asquith, Asquith's daughter, in 1915.

[3] Marjorie Trefusis (d. 1937), actress. Daughter of Sir Henry Graham, Clerk of Parliaments, hence her residence in the House of Lords. Married Capt. the Hon. Walter Alexander Trefusis in 1911, divorced 1919 and married Capt. John Craigie.

[4] Nancy Cunard (1896–1965), daughter of Lady Cunard, briefly married Sydney Fairbairn in 1916. A poet and an intellectual and political activist, she lived an expatriate life in Paris from 1925.

[5] Iris Tree (1897–1968), daughter of Sir Herbert Beerbohm Tree (1852–1917), the actor-manager and founder of RADA, sister of Viola Parsons. Actress and poet.

[6] Basil Hallam (1889–1916). A music-hall performer, he joined the Balloon Corps and was killed in 1916.

[7] Violet 'Letty' Manners (1888–1971), Diana's sister, married first Hugo 'Ego' Charteris, Lord Elcho (1884–1916) in 1911 and second Guy Benson (1888–1975) in 1921.

[8] Lady Mary Charteris (1895–1960), Ego's sister, married first Tom Strickland in December 1915 and second Maj. John (Jock) Lyon in 1943.

and the only thing now is that Russia insists on Italy fixing a date which Italy is very unwilling to do.

I lunched with Marjorie at the Carlton, went back to the Foreign Office for an hour and then went and fetched her from the House of Lords. We dined at the Carlton and then went to Fitzroy Street. Marjorie wanted more to drink when we got there so I came home and took her back a bottle of champagne. We couldn't open it and at last in desperation I tried to knock its head off against the wall. The result was that the whole bottle broke to fragments, and every drop was spilt on the floor and I cut my hand. The room was covered with blood and wine. I loved Marjorie more than ever, she goes to Southsea for a week tomorrow to act her silly play.

Monday morning at the Foreign Office we had the longest telegram I ever saw, 1100 groups. It took three hours to decypher, type etc. It was from Petrograd – all about various rather quibbling alterations which Russia wants to make in the terms of the agreement with Italy.

I lunched with Miss Lowenthal who now calls herself Miss Lynn[1] and who was very angry at my calling her by the other. She is under four feet high, known to be a German Jewess and suspected of being a Sapphist. Iris and Diana were at lunch. It was a beautiful, warm spring day and I ordered three new suits. Dined with Edwin Montagu[2] – Katharine and Raymond[3] and Diana and Bonham Carter were there. We went to see Constance Stewart-Richardson[4] perform at the Empire and afterwards went on to His Majesty's and saw the last act of the first night of the revival of *Oliver Twist*.

Tuesday April 20, 1915

The difficulties Russia is making about the date of Italy's joining seem serious. We sent off two telegrams to Petrograd about it today, one private one from the King to the Czar begging him to give way.

I had tea with Ruby,[5] just back from France. Hazel[6] was there. I drove Hazel home. She asked me whether I loved her best which was awkward. I asked her whether she loved me best and she said she did, which was more awkward still. It is an extraordinary thing, but nobody begins to be

[1] Olga Lynn, 'Oggie', (1882–1961), a professional singer and singing teacher.

[2] Edwin Montagu (1879–1924), married Venetia Stanley in 1915. A Liberal politician, he was Financial Secretary to the Treasury and briefly Minister of Munitions 1914–16, and Secretary of State for India 1917–22, when he was compelled to resign from office.

[3] Katharine Asquith, née Horner (1885–1976), sister of Edward Horner, she married Raymond Asquith in 1907. Close friend of Diana Manners. Raymond Asquith (1878–1916), a barrister, was Asquith's son by his first wife.

[4] Lady Constance Stewart-Richardson, née Mackenzie (1882–1932), a dancer, was married to Sir Edward Stewart-Richardson Bt. (d. 1914) and the daughter of the 2nd Earl of Gomartie.

[5] Ruby Peto (1909–51), daughter of Col. Walter James Lindsay and cousin of Diana's mother, Violet Rutland. In 1909 she married Ralph Harding Peto, divorced 1923.

[6] Hazel Lavery (1887–1935), American wife of Sir John Lavery (1856–1941), the Irish portrait painter.

really fond of me until just the moment when I cease being quite so fond of them.

The Russians have given way about Italy though very unwillingly. Sazonov[1] says he considers our not holding Italy down to a definite and early date a diplomatic defeat for us. He also says that people in Russia are beginning to criticize unfavourably the way in which the war is being carried on in the west, and to compare the inaction of the French with Russia's desperate advance in the Carpathians. Some people think that Sazonov was right and that if we had been firmer with the Italians they would have given way. However the great thing was to get them in and there now seems no danger of failing in that. Bulgaria too seems suddenly coming round. We heard also today that Turkey is short of ammunition and the Dardanelles will not be able to withstand two more attacks similar to the one they have already had. They want to get ammunition through Roumania, which, especially when Roumania hears of Italy's action, she is sure to prevent.

Dined with the Laverys. Winston Churchill[2] and Mrs Winston were there, Lady Randolph,[3] Nellie Hozier[4] and Edwin Montagu. Winston was very tired but cheered up under the influence of wine. His mother bored him terribly and would ask him a thousand questions. He had to sit to Lavery after dinner and Hazel, Nellie and I went to the Chelsea Palace. We had to drive Nellie home in a hansom as we couldn't get a taxi and then I drove Hazel from the Admiralty to her home. She was looking so beautiful and was so sweet and loving.

April 24, 1915

After dinner I went to the Cavendish [Hotel] where I had a row with Diana. She hit me so hard on the face that she made my mouth bleed and I eventually gave her the gentlest tap on the cheek on which she left the room and the hotel. I ran after her and apologized humbly but she wouldn't speak to me and I left Raymond trying to persuade her to return. I was rather glad of the excuse to get home early to bed.

---

[1] Sergei Sazonov (1816–1927), Russian Foreign Minister under Tsar Nicholas II 1910–16, when he was forced to resign. Russian Ambassador to London, 1916–17, where he remained after the Revolution.

[2] Sir Winston Churchill (1874–1965) married Clementine Hozier (1885–1977) in 1908. First Lord of the Admiralty under Asquith 1911–15; Minister of Munitions under Lloyd George 1917–18; Secretary of War and Air 1918–21; Colonial Secretary 1921–2; Chancellor of the Exchequer under Baldwin 1924–9; First Lord of the Admiralty 1939–40; Prime Minister 1940–5 and 1951–5.

[3] Lady Randolph Churchill (1854–1921), born Jennie Jerome, an American, was the mother of Winston Churchill.

[4] Nellie Hozier (1888–1925), sister of Winston Churchill's wife, Clementine. She married Col. Bertram Romilly in 1915.

Monday April 26, 1915

Saw in the paper this morning that Rupert Brooke[1] had died of sunstroke at Lemnos. Terribly sad. I knew him very little, but he was a very good poet and a very beautiful man. I wrote some verses and sent them to Eddie Marsh[2] who was devoted to him.

> Hushed is the music of the sweetest voice
> That filled the shambles of our world with song,
> Still is the heart that beat so brave and strong,
> The heart that bids us mourn not but rejoice,
> Because we know that his high soul, at peace,
> Went singing down the dark and silent way,
> And that there lives forever from today
> A piece of England in the Isles of Greece.

Today the Treaty with Italy[3] was signed. The next thing seems to be to get Bulgaria in, which I believe would not be difficult if it were not for the King.

April 28, 1915

Went to see Diana in the afternoon. She has quite forgiven me and likes me better than ever. She has had all the letters I ever wrote her typewritten and carries them about with her like a book. They look beautiful in print.

April 30, 1915

My day off from the Foreign Office. Had the old Priest[4] to lunch with me at the Junior Carlton. He told me that someone, whom he wouldn't name, said to him the other day what a pity it was I got drunk every night. It really is monstrous that everyone should say this about me. The end of April and I make as usual a resolution to drink less and read more during the coming month.

May 4, 1915

Went to the first night of *The Right to Kill*. Went to the Rutlands' box. We all went to the room behind the Trees' box in the middle. Lloyd George[5] was

---

[1] Rupert Brooke (1887–1915). After a brilliant career at Cambridge he settled at the Old Vicarage, Grantchester. His first volume of poems was published in 1911. In 1914 he joined the Royal Naval Division and died of blood-poisoning in the Dardanelles in 1915. *1914 and Other Poems* was published posthumously.

[2] Sir Edward Marsh (1872–1953), civil servant, scholar and patron of the arts and a close friend of Rupert Brooke. Churchill's Private Secretary almost continuously 1905–28.

[3] The Treaty of London, by which Italy came into World War I, allied to Britain, France and Russia.

[4] The Rev. H. B. Allen, curate at Stanway for many years and close friend of the Charteris family.

[5] David Lloyd George, 1st Earl Lloyd George (1863–1945). Minister of Munitions 1915; Secretary of State for War 1916; Prime Minister Dec. 1916–Oct. 1922.

there and Rufus Isaacs.[1] The former I had never seen before – a common, ugly, uninteresting looking little man.

May 7, 1915

The *Lusitania* sunk [*a British cargo and passenger ship, on which many American lives were lost*]. People seem very worried about it, as though it were a defeat for us, whereas of course it makes not the faintest difference to the war and only helps to stir up America against Germany. People differ as to whether the cooperation of America would be a help or a hindrance to us. We should of course get no more ammunition from her and her army and navy would be of little value. Hazel tells me that Winston said it would be a bad thing for us were America to make war on Germany but I don't agree with him. It certainly has looked lately as though Germany wanted to provoke America instead of trying to conciliate her as at first.

Dined with Edwin. Diana was there, she goes to France tomorrow to see about her hospital.[2] Raymond and Katharine, Bongy, Venetia Stanley,[3] Nancy, Ruby and Alan[4] were also there. Alan has been made one of McKenna's[5] private secretaries. How I wish I had something interesting to do instead of everlasting office boy work.

May 8, 1915

Edward[6] has been seriously wounded. Katharine and Sir John and Lady Horner went to France today to see him. I do pray he may recover.

May 12, 1915

The feeling in America is so strong that they may be forced to go to war. If they do they will simply be playing into Germany's hands and we are most anxious to prevent it. It is a pity that the mass of the people both here and in America don't seem to realize this, but our press is very restrained and

---

[1] Rufus Isaacs, 1st Marquess of Reading (1860–1935). Attorney-General 1910–13; Lord Chief Justice 1913–21; Viceroy of India, 1921–6.

[2] Diana Manners worked as a VAD (voluntary nurse) at Guy's Hospital in 1914–15. She and her mother then planned to open a hospital near Boulogne. The plan fell through and eventually their home in Arlington Street, St James's, was turned into a hospital for officers where Diana assisted the trained nurses.

[3] Venetia Stanley (1887–1948), a lifelong friend of Diana's, married Edwin Montagu in 1915. Before her engagement she had been a close confidante of the Prime Minister, H. H. Asquith.

[4] Alan Parsons (1887–1933) began his career in the Civil Service and was Private Secretary to Edwin Montagu when the latter was Secretary of State for India. From 1925–9 he was dramatic critic and gossip columnist for the *Daily Sketch*, and he worked on the *Daily Mail* 1929–33. He was married to Viola Tree, Iris Tree's sister and Diana's oldest friend.

[5] The Rt. Hon. Reginald McKenna (1863–1943), Chancellor of the Exchequer 1915–May 1916 Chairman of Midland Bank, 1919–43.

[6] Edward Horner (1818–1917), son of Sir John and Lady Horner and brother of Katharine Asquith. Friend of Duff's at Oxford.

sensible for once. Here is another instance of the truth that it is not statesmen and diplomats who are responsible for wars but the people themselves, a truth that socialists and democrats refuse to recognize. The disadvantage to us if America joins in will be immediate and military, but I cannot help feeling that in the long run neutral nations and even the more thoughtful of the Germans could not fail to be impressed by the spectacle of all the most civilized nations in the world joined in alliance against one enemy.

May 13, 1915

America's note to Germany today looks as though war is inevitable. Germany probably will refuse compensation for the people drowned on the *Lusitania* and certainly will not promise not to do it again, so that America can hardly with dignity avoid war. President Wilson is anxious to avoid it and does not believe that the people really want it, but fears they may be dragged in. It seems absurd that a country like America should be forced to go to war against its will.

I dined with Mrs Astor,[1] a party of twenty. I sat between Ruby and Lady G. Churchill.[2] The latter told me that the other day at the Admiralty Lady Essex[3] said to Winston that she heard it was alright about Italy and Winston asked who had told her so. She said that I had, and apparently after she had gone Winston was furious about people letting out secrets. It is really very unlucky as all I did say to Lady E. when she asked me 'How about Italy?' was that I didn't think she need worry about that. I had it out with her after dinner and we both exonerated ourselves. She told me that Colonel House[4] told her at dinner that he thought America would go to war and that Germany was calculating on her not being able to go on supplying England with ammunition, but that here Germany was once more out in her calculations as America would still continue to supply us with ammunition and not less than before. Germany could not hurt America unless she brought her fleet out and that she dared not do. I hope he is right. He ought to know.

May 14, 1915

Early this morning we learned that the Italian Government resigned last night. At first we were depressed at the Foreign Office, thinking it meant that Italy was going to shuffle out after all. But then people began to say that this was only a strategical move on the part of the Government designed to dish

---

[1] Ava Astor, divorced wife of John Jacob Astor. In 1919 she became the second wife of the 4th Baron Ribblesdale.

[2] Lady Gwendoline Churchill, 'Goonie', née Bertie (1885–1941), married Major John 'Jack' Churchill, DSO, in 1908.

[3] Adela Grant (d. 1922). An American, she married the 7th Earl of Essex in 1893.

[4] Edward Mandell House (1858–1938), colonel in name only. An American politician, he was President Woodrow Wilson's closest confidant 1914–18. He was in London Jan.–June 1915 and again Jan.–Mar. 1916.

Giolitti[1] and strengthen their own hands. This view seems to be the true one. Just before I left the Foreign Office at 4 this afternoon a telegram came in from Rome saying that the Government would probably be recalled, and that the Milan *Corriere della Sera* would announce this evening that Italy had denounced the Triple Alliance and had signed an agreement with the Triple Entente. It said also that Rome was practically in a state of siege and that the German Embassy was protected by a large force including cavalry.

May 15, 1915

I lunched at Arlington Street [London home of Diana's parents, the Duke and Duchess of Rutland]. The Duchess and Diana returned last night from Boulogne and John Granby[2] had suddenly appeared on two days leave from the front. He was terribly pessimistic about the war, especially our part of it. Said the 10th had been wiped out. The Duke was so childishly happy at having John back, he was quite pathetic.

   That same evening George Moore[3] came in after dinner and sat and talked to Raymond and me. He is interesting about the war because one can take it that he is voicing French's[4] opinion. As regards the present differences of opinion between French and Kitchener[5], he said he didn't believe the theory that Kitchener was starving French for men and ammunition now because he wished to finish the war with his own New Army[6] later on led by himself. He said that Kitchener knew his own inability to command an army in the field which I should doubt. He also talked a lot of rot about America, saying that if they once went to war they would never quit until they had hung the Kaiser.

In May, Asquith formed a war coalition government with the Conservatives. Churchill left the Admiralty and became Chancellor of the Duchy of Lancaster.

May 22, 1915

Went down to Sutton to stay with Mrs Lindsay.[7] Venetia and Edwin who had come down for the day dined with us and went back to London after dinner. They are supposed to be engaged and she must become a Jewess which she has always looked.

---

[1] Giovanni Giolitti (1842–1928), Italian Prime Minister 1911–14. Opposed Italian participation in WWI.

[2] The Marquess of Granby, later 9th Duke of Rutland (1886–1940), Diana's brother, married Kathleen Tennant (Kakoo) in 1916.

[3] George Gordon Moore, American railway millionaire, was famous for his lavish parties and a great admirer of Diana. He was a great friend and confidant of Field Marshal Sir John French.

[4] Field Marshal Sir John French (1852–1925). GOCIC British Expeditionary Force in France.

[5] Field Marshal Lord Kitchener, 1st Earl Kitchener (1850–1916). Secretary of State for War.

[6] Kitchener's New Army consisted of volunteer recruits who enlisted after the outbreak of war.

[7] Norah Burke married Henry Lindsay, Diana's uncle, in 1895.

May 23, 1915

Heavenly weather and everything looking too beautiful 'to one who has been long in city pent'. Mrs Asquith[1] came over to tea and raged about the *Daily Mail* and *The Times*. It is settled that Arthur Balfour[2] goes to the Admiralty. Raymond [Asquith] says that all the other ministers refuse to have F. E. Smith[3] in the Cabinet.

May 31, 1915 (London)

Buchanan[4] telegraphed today that he hadn't dared approach Sazonov officially on the subject of giving way to Roumania's demands. Sazonov is more confident than ever. We are now making overtures to Bulgaria. We haven't had their answer yet but when Des Graz[5] approached the Serbian Prime Minister as to whether Serbia would be prepared to make any cession of territory to Bulgaria the Prime Minister replied that it was out of the question and that he would resign rather than consent to it. There is no limit to the hatred of the Serbs for the Bulgars, who they say committed every atrocity in the recent raid on Serbia, burning the wounded alive. The Bulgars are brutes, but they ought to have most of Macedonia because they certainly got less than they deserved out of the Balkan War, though it was their own fault and the population of eastern Macedonia is chiefly Bulgar. If only all those damned little states could be persuaded to pull together.

The end of May. Have kept my resolution well about not drinking much and have read a good deal but not enough.

June 2, 1915

I had tea with Cynthia. Her diary is already more than half full. I can't think what she writes in it. Her life can't be as interesting as mine though mine's dull enough. She was looking very pretty and taking things very seriously, Beb [Asquith] being at the war etc. She said she wouldn't like to see war abolished from the world which made me argue. I can't understand how any sane civilized person can think such things. She had seen Winston lately whom she described as very depressed but very dignified. He told her that if he had to appoint a First Sea Lord again he would appoint Fisher,[6] which was rather

---

[1] Margaret (Margot) Tennant (1864–1945) married H. H. Asquith as his second wife in 1894.

[2] Arthur Balfour, 1st Earl Balfour (1848–30). Conservative Prime Minister 1902–5; First Lord of the Admiralty under Asquith 1915–16; Foreign Secretary under Lloyd George 1916–19; Lord President of the Council 1919–22.

[3] Frederick Edwin (F. E.) Smith K. C., 1st Lord Birkenhead (1872–1930). Attorney-General 1915–18; Lord Chancellor 1919–22; Secretary of State for India 1924–8.

[4] Sir George Buchanan (1854–1924), British Ambassador to Russia 1914–18.

[5] Sir Charles des Graz (1860–1940), British Minister in Serbia.

[6] Adm. John Fisher, 1st Baron (1841–1920). Admiral of the Fleet, resigned over the Dardanelles issue in 1915.

a good thing to say. Fisher apparently is half mad with rage and age. If he didn't agree about the Dardanelles expedition he should have resigned when it was undertaken, rather than wait till it had failed.

June 8, 1915. Norton Priory

This morning I had a letter from Eddie[1] saying he was coming home tomorrow on three days leave. I am glad. So tomorrow I must go up to London and help him to have fun. I can think of nothing else which could have induced me to leave this delicious rest I am having.

June 11, 1915

In the evening I had a men's dinner party here which made all the women furious but we adored it. Only Eddie, Rothesay,[2] Michael,[3] Hugo and myself. It was the greatest fun and was followed by a glorious party at the Cavendish which was really the best of its kind. I climbed up the wall to the roof at one juncture, putting my foot through the window and cutting my ankle. Those who were left wanted to have breakfast at a cab shelter at about 5 but Cis[4] had to be got rid of first. However he sat on the bonnet of Irene's[5] motor and refused to be dislodged and Eddie eventually drove the motor, a two seater with 6 people on it down to Richmond where Cis was in camp. I didn't follow them but went to bed having dropped Marjorie, in tears incidentally, at the H. of L.

July 3, 1915

In the morning a telegram came from Diana saying that she and Edwin, Raymond and Katharine were going to Brighton for the weekend and asking me to meet them there. We dined at the Metropole [Hotel] and drank a lot. We then went and sat in their sitting room at the Grand and drank a lot more. We then, except Edwin, set out to bathe. It was about two o'clock. Going down some steps on to the beach Diana and I who were walking arm in arm took a severe fall and she sprained her ankle. She suffered agonies and had to be carried up to bed. The next morning her foot was very bad and she couldn't move.

---

[1] Capt. Eddie Grant, married Bettine Stuart-Wortley in 1917 and Laura Waugh's sister, Bridget Herbert, in 1935.

[2] Maj. Rothesay Stuart-Wortley (1892–1926).

[3] Michael Herbert (1893–1932), younger son of Sir Michael Herbert, former Ambassador in Washington and his American wife, Lelia Wilson.

[4] The Hon. Cyril 'Cis' Asquith (1890–1954), fourth son of H. H. Asquith by his first wife. Barrister and High Court judge, later Baron Asquith of Bishopstone.

[5] Irene Lawley (1889–1976), only child of 3rd Baron Wenlock; she married Colin Forbes Adam in 1920.

July 9, 1915

I went to see Diana at Arlington Street. She has broken two bones in her leg and Arthbuthnot Lane[1] is going to operate on her tomorrow in a nursing home. While I was there the motor ambulance came to take her to the home. Beautifully dressed, she was moved on to a stretcher and slowly carried downstairs, followed by a cortège consisting of the Duchess, Marjorie,[2] Irene, Nancy, myself and a few others. She looked too lovely. The Duchess, Nancy and I drove with her in the ambulance and when we arrived at the home there were Viola[3] and Iris waiting on the doorstep with bundles of flowers and baskets of fruit.

July 16, 1915

Serious news at the Foreign Office today from America. They say there is tremendous agitation being roused there in favour of stricter neutrality, i.e. forbidding the export of ammunition. Their feeling is that all the belligerents *'se moquent d'eux'* [are laughing at them]. Cotton will become a tremendous difficulty and many of the great cotton men are Germans. It is even suggested that it might be worth our while to propitiate the U.S.A. by buying all their exports of food ourselves, but as Germany would be ready to pay famine prices this seems hardly practicable.

July 20, 1915

Went to see Diana. She was very intrigued by a letter she had had from the Prime Minister[4] [Asquith]. He had been to see her the other day and they had discussed at length Venetia's marriage. Diana is quite certain that Venetia was his mistress which rather surprises me. This letter, which was rather obscurely expressed, seemed practically to be an offer to Diana to fill the vacated situation. She was in great difficulty as to how she was to answer it, partly from being uncertain as to its meaning, partly from the nature of the proposal it seemed to contain. She was anxious not to lose him but did not aspire to the position of his Egeria [i.e. counsellor], which she felt sure would entail physical duties that she couldn't or wouldn't fulfil. I advised her to concoct an answer which should be as obscure as his proposal and leave him puzzled – the old lecher.

On Monday [*July 26*] I did an odd thing. Nancy wanted me to dine with all

---

[1] Sir William Arbuthnot Lane (1856–1943), senior surgeon at Guy's Hospital.

[2] Diana's sister Marjorie (1883–1946) married Charles, 6th Marquess of Anglesey (1885–1947), in 1912. They lived at Plas Newydd on the Isle of Anglesey, Wales.

[3] Viola Tree (1884–1938), actress and singer, was the daughter of Sir Herbert Beerbohm Tree and married to Alan Parsons.

[4] Herbert Henry Asquith, 1st Earl of Oxford and Asquith (1852–1928). Liberal Prime Minister 1908–15; Prime Minister of wartime Coalition Government 1915–16; leader of the Liberal Party until 1924. Married first Helen Melland (d. 1891) and had five children, and second Margot Tennant, with whom he had two children.

of them at Kettner's, but I felt suddenly I couldn't face it. I was tired and wanted a good, peaceful dinner so I went and dined alone with a book at the Junior Carlton. I had an excellent dinner and drank Pol Roger 1904. I did enjoy myself. Afterwards I went to the Alhambra where I got tired of being alone and gave way – alas – to the need of companionship.

On Thursday [July 29] I dined at 62 Cadogan Square [home of Lord Wemyss]. We played poker after dinner and I lost £12 – oh dear oh damn. Eileen[1] was in her nurse's uniform and looked rather well. She is a strange woman. She kissed me passionately going home in the taxi almost as a matter of course. She only just misses being wonderful, but she misses it alright. She was the first unmarried woman, bar of course prostitutes, I ever kissed.

July 31, 1915

Dined with Raymond and Katharine. Katharine told me a long story about the Grand Duke Serge [of Russia]. He was at the head of the Russian ammunition department and it appears all the money that was supposed to be spent on ammunition was going to his mistress. He has been disgraced and sent to Siberia. She had it from Bluetooth Baker[2] who is likely to know, and I had noticed that we no longer got telegrams from Petrograd conveying messages from the Grand Duke to Kitchener.

August 3, 1915

Lunched at the Ritz with Edward [Horner]. It was good to see Edward leading almost a normal life again. In the afternoon I went to see Diana. The Duchess met me in the hall with the terrible news that Billy[3] had been killed. She always tells me bad news, that woman. How horrible this is. When I think of Oxford now I see nothing but ghosts.

Friday 27 August, 1915

Dined at Manchester Street alone with Diana. One of the most delicious evenings of my life. I was beautifully dressed – silk shirt and big black tie. A very hot night. Diana in a night gown only. I brought a bottle of champagne, we broke the cork, but with the help of the nurse eventually opened it. We sat side by side on the sofa and ate a cold grouse off one plate with one knife and one fork and I also ate some Camembert cheese.

After dinner Diana was divine. We went further than ever we have gone – but with such art and such distinction. She is the only person who is worth making love to, who understands the game and how to play it. She is the only

---

[1] Lady Eileen Wellesley (1887–1952), daughter of the 4th Duke of Wellington, married Capt. Cuthbert Orde in 1916.
[2] The Rt. Hon. Harold Baker (1877–1960), known as 'Bluetooth' or 'Blueie', Liberal MP for Accrington.
[3] The Hon. William 'Billy' Grenfell (1890–1915), second son of Lord Desborough.

woman with whom excessive intimacy never breeds the faintest shadow of contempt or disgust, and this is, I think, not only because we never proceed to extremes. There is a great deal to be said for the love-making that sends one away hungry, exasperating though it is. With most women, the further one goes the more one is disillusioned, but with her exactly the opposite happens. Illusion grows with knowledge. She assures me she has never abandoned herself to anyone else in this fashion. I am inclined to believe it. How I adored her.

Saturday 28 August, 1915

Lunched at Pagani's with Raymond, Alan, Ruby and Diana. Raymond told them all at lunch what we had heard at the Foreign Office as dead secret on Thursday, namely that the Grand Duke Nicholas has had his command taken from him and that he was to be succeeded by the Czar. I dined alone with Mother, Raymond dined with Diana. I felt angry and jealous though I know that not much will happen between them.

September 1, 1915

I dined with Osbert[1] on guard at St James's. I sat between him and Raymond. I thought of the days when I used to dine there with John.[2] It is an ugly business now compared to what it was, the officers being all dressed in khaki with their hideous puttees and thick service boots instead of the lovely uniforms they used to wear. The food and wine though were as good as ever.

September 3, 1915

When I first woke up my cold felt so bad that I thought I would stay in bed all day, but by about nine o'clock I felt bored so I got up and went to the Foreign Office.

Oh dear. I have just heard the terrible news that Charles[3] is dead. Blow upon blow. Poor old Rib [Lord Ribblesdale], he talked so much and so proudly of Charles the other day and he was then already dead, for it seems he died of blood poisoning a week ago.

September 6, 1915

A terrible awakening. The two front teeth which had been fixed onto one root came out. They were only put in a year ago. Luckily I had the false ones on a plate which I wore while the others were being made with me. But the shape of my mouth or something must have changed for this now fits damnably ill,

---

[1] Sir Osbert Sitwell (1892–1969), writer. Brother of Edith and Sacheverell Sitwell.

[2] Hon. John Manners (1892–1914), Duff's best friend at Oxford and, as the elder son of the 3rd Lord Manners, a distant cousin of Diana's, was killed in 1914.

[3] The Hon. Charles Lister (1887–1915), son of Lord Ribblesdale. Friend of Duff's at Oxford, he was a committed socialist. He died of wounds at Gallipoli.

is most uncomfortable and none too secure. Lunched at Arlington Street and in the afternoon went with Diana to cinematograph. How I adore being with her. She is the only companion.

On Saturday 19th September, 1915 I caught the 4 o'clock train to Belvoir. There I found only Diana, Marjorie, Violet Keppel[1] and the Duchess, and John, Mr Bouch,[2] Harry and Charlie Lindsay. We played marmora after dinner each night and I won over £50 – a great relief. In the afternoon we played tennis and in the evening before dinner Diana read to me *Guy and Pauline* [by Compton Mackenzie]. I began to think that night that I wasn't really in love with Diana at all and that she cared still less for me but the next morning as I was leaving the house at 8 o'clock she came down in her dressing gown to say goodbye and kiss, which was for her an excessive proof of solicitude and I left more puzzled than ever as to what she felt and what I felt myself.

September 23, 1915

Dined with Marjorie Trefusis at the Ritz. She was looking plain, I thought, and she isn't much fun. Odd that I should have liked her so once and that she, as she still assures me, should have loved me. I wish it had been someone else.

September 24, 1915

Sent off a telegram to Athens saying that France and England were prepared to send as many troops as Greece wanted to Salonica. All the War Dept. surprised and rather shocked at the drastic nature of this telegram.

September 28, 1915

Lunched at Arlington Street. Gerald Thorpe was there and spoke of our enormous casualties – 30,000 men, 1,400 officers he said. Dined with Nancy, Marjorie and Hugo. After dinner we all went back to the House of Lords, from which Marjorie's parents were away. My only breach of chastity in September.

September 29, 1915

Diana came back from Scotland in the morning. We went together to a cinematograph in the afternoon and I took her to Liverpool Street whence she took a train to Newmarket. She was charming. While we were waiting for the train at Liverpool Street we drank port and ate sausage rolls in the refreshment room. I don't know whether I'm in love with her or not, I fancy not, but I have far more fun with her than anyone.

---

[1] Violet Keppel (1894–1972), later Trefusis, daughter of Alice Keppel (1868–1947), the mistress of King Edward VII from 1898 until his death.
[2] Thomas Bouch (1882–1963), joint Master of Foxhounds of the Belvoir Hunt. An admirer of Diana's.

September 30, 1915

Dined with Venetia – Edwin not there. Table consisted of Venetia, Winston, Nellie, self, Lady Goonie, Bongy, Mrs Winston, Eddie Marsh. Winston terribly depressed and depressing. After the women had gone he had a tremendous argument with Bongy about conscription – he very much for it, Bongy against. Winston abused Kitchener a good deal. Said he had enlisted men and forgotten to order them rifles. Said in a few weeks time 11,000 sergeants in the army were entitled to their discharge, that they mean to demand it and that he didn't see how we would disallow it unless we had conscription. Bongy's main argument against it was financial. All very interesting.

October 1, 1915

Heard this morning at the F.O. that Tommie Robartes[1] was killed. His brother didn't come in on that account and rang up and told us. I sent a note round to Mother so she might tell Steffie who was coming up from the country. Came home and found poor little Steffie half mad with misery. She was really in love with him. It was she says the only happiness she had known since Arthur died and it is snatched away. I am so sorry for her. I heard a rumour that Eric[2] is badly wounded. I hope untrue and still more do I hope that Osbert, Bim[3] and Yvo[4] are alright, the last especially. It seems a lot to hope as they are all in the Grenadiers who I hear have suffered as usual. We had a terrible night with Steffie. She and Sibbie are both staying here. Steffie had asked Sibbie to buy her a lot of morphia[5] and Sibbie had told the chemist to give her something that looked and tasted like it but was innocuous. Steffie of course discovered this the moment she tasted it. Terrible row ensued. I was woken up. It was 1.30. Sibbie insisted on going out to try and get some real morphia from a doctor. After she had gone I heard Steffie moving about and went into her room. I found her with a fur coat on over her nightgown and a pair of shoes, on the point of going out. Tried to dissuade her without success. So thought it best to follow her, which I did having put an overcoat and a pair of trousers on. She insisted on going to Berkeley House where our flat is being altered for her. Her real reason for going was to look for some chloroform she had left there. This we eventually found and came home to bed.

---

[1] Capt. the Hon. Thomas Agar-Robartes (1880–1915) of the Coldstream Guards died of wounds received at the Battle of Loos. Eldest son of the 6th Viscount Clifton, he had been MP for St Austell and Mid-Cornwall since 1908.

[2] Eric Ednam (1894–1969), succeeded as 3rd Earl of Dudley in 1932. He married first, in 1919, Lady Rosemary Leveson Gower (d. 1930), second, in 1943, Frances Laura Long (née Charteris), divorced 1954, and third Grace Radziwill, former wife of Prince Stanislas Radziwill.

[3] Edward (Bim or Bimbo) Tennant (1897–1916), son of 1st Baron Glenconner and first cousin of Kakoo Granby, was killed in the Battle of the Somme.

[4] The Hon. Yvo Charteris (1896–1915), fourth son of the 11th Earl of Wemyss, brother of Ego and Cynthia Charteris and Mary Strickland, was killed at the Battle of Loos.

[5] In those days morphine could be bought without prescription from the chemist.

October 7, 1915

On Thursday I dined with the Montagus, Edward, Iris, Alan, Diana and after dinner Raymond and Katharine. Dinner great fun. Rather boring after dinner as we did not play cards but sat and talked. Everyone rather drunk, I only very slightly. Raymond, Katharine, Diana and I started walking home together across the park. It was very beautiful, we all loved each other so much. We dropped R & K at 10 Downing Street and then Diana and I sat down, or rather lay, on the steps that lead from Downing St. down into the Horse Guards Parade. There we remained under the shadow of the damned old Foreign Office under the very window where I work by day, locked in each other's arms for quite a time. It was odd and romantic and delightful. Then we walked very slowly and with many delicious pauses. We embraced under the lamp in the middle of the Parade, and under the dark trees of the Mall, and in St James's St. and finally we sat again on the steps of Lord Zetland's house in Arlington Street and exchanged the most wonderful kisses of all. A memorable night.

October 19, 1915

Dined with the Montagus – at least with Venetia, Edwin was at the House. The dinner was to celebrate Raymond's last night as he was to go to the war tomorrow. Poor Katharine, how sorry I feel for her. She was wonderful at dinner. I sat between her and Diana. Raymond was at his best, very cheerful and brilliantly witty. It would really be the end of everything if he were killed.

October 21, 1915

Dined at Queen Anne's Gate. Cheerful dinner. Afterwards we played bridge. I saw a letter from Cynthia to Venetia lying open on a table and starting to read it learnt suddenly that Yvo had been killed. The news apparently arrived on the 19th and most of them knew at Raymond's last dinner party. Nobody had told me because everyone thought I knew. It was a terrible shock. He was so young and so delightful. How I pity them all, especially Mary who adored him and Lord Wemyss whose favourite child he was. I slept badly and woke early and felt miserable.

October 23, 1915

Went down to Mells by the 3.30. There I found only Sir J. and Lady Horner, Lady Jekyll[1] and Lord Haldane.[2] Dear Katharine very sweet and sad and

---

[1] Agnes Jekyll (1851–1937), later Dame Agnes Jekyll, the noted cookery writer, was married to Sir Herbert Jekyll (1846–1932), a military engineer and civil servant and brother to Gertrude Jekyll, the garden designer.

[2] Lord Haldane (1856–1928), former Minister of War and Liberal Lord Chancellor. Dropped as Chancellor in May 1915 after the press accused him of pro-German sympathies.

beautiful. It poured the whole of Sunday. Talked to Haldane in the morning. He was interesting and told me all about his mission to Berlin, about the agreement with Germany on the African question which was on the point of being signed when war broke out and about his last interview with Bethmann-Hollweg[1] when the latter said that it might be that all their efforts to ensure peace between the two countries would fail, but if that were so it would not be their fault but fate – '*Es wird Schicksal sein*'. He thinks that the Emperor was with the peace party until 1913 and then the war party won him over. He says that all our failure in this war has been due to two things, the lack of public education and the lack of a General Staff. When he went to the War Office himself the first thing he did was to create a General Staff – it consisted of about 80 people which was ample for the small army then existing. He also doubled Staff College. But all this was undone by Seely[2] and partly by Asquith, who put Wolfe Murray[3] at the head of it because he was a suitable man to deal with the Ulster business though he had no qualifications at all. Kitchener finding a bad General Staff in existence, decided to do without one and do the whole work himself, which was madness. He thought that fighting against the German General Staff was the same thing as fighting against the Khalifa or the Mahdi. Haldane spoke with considerable bitterness about Kitchener and with the greatest contempt about Winston; he is intolerant of the people, whom he describes as uneducated.

November 2, 1915

Dined at Queen Anne's Gate. We played bridge afterwards. I was very drunk and after dropping Diana and Katharine at A. Street I for some insane reason tried to break into the house. I walked up to Piccadilly and there just by the Ritz climbed over the railings into the Park. I then climbed over some more railings into the garden of somebody's house, not, I think, No. 16 and then as far as I remember I realized the folly of what I was doing and got back again into the park, walked down and climbed over some more railings close to my own rooms. I can't think how I managed to get over them all in a top hat and an overcoat. The latter was considerably torn, so were my trousers. Very lucky not to have come across a policeman.

November 11, 1915

This morning came the terrible news of George Vernon's[4] death. We had heard some days ago that he was seriously ill with dysentery at Malta but lately the news had been better. I suppose there are other people who have lost as many friends as I have but it seems hardly possible. Diana telephoned the

---

[1] Theobald von Bethmann-Hollweg (1856–1921), German Chancellor 1909–17.
[2] John Seely, later 1st Baron Mottistone (1868–1947). Secretary of State for War.
[3] Gen. Sir James Wolfe Murray (1853–1919), Chief of Imperial General Staff.
[4] George, 8th Baron Vernon (1888–1915). A great admirer of Diana's.

news to me in the morning and asked me to lunch with her as she was too unhappy to face a lunch party they had asked to Arlington Street. So we went to the Hanover Restaurant and drank mulled claret which helped us to call up our last reserves of courage and gaiety to face this new blow. I went to see her again in the evening and tried to cheer her.

November 12, 1915

Diana was dining at Downing Street. She called for me at St James's St. on her way so that I could drive with her and drop her there. I think I really am in love with her and do believe that she is rather fond of me. I dined at Welbeck St. with Viola [and] Alan. Diana came in for a few minutes later with Violet and Cis Asquith and Eddie Marsh. We learnt that Winston had resigned and that Eddie is going to be Private Secretary to the Prime Minister. [*Churchill had been excluded from a small War Cabinet set up by the Prime Minister. In his disappointment he returned to the Front.*]

Saturday November 13, 1915

The beginning of my week's holiday. I went round to see Diana after leaving the Foreign Office and found her crying. She is much more unhappy about George than I thought, poor darling. It is the worst blow she has had in the war.

November 15, 1915 [Belvoir]

I thought Diana was going by the early train so I got up to go by it too and when ready to start discovered that she had arranged to go later with me and only the Duchess was going early so I wished I had stayed longer in bed. But it was a very beautiful morning, white frost and blue sky and I went for a long walk by myself and much enjoyed it. Came up to London with Diana. We could not get a carriage to ourselves which was cruel, but I enjoyed the journey. Diana very interesting. She told me how as the price of his baronetcy Joseph Beecham [father of Thomas Beecham] was made to pay £10,000. £4,000 were taken by Lady Cunard, Diana got £500 and the rest went to Edward who paid with it all his own debts, and Katharine's and his Mother's. I had never heard a word of this before. It is of course the profoundest secret.

November 21, 1915

Got up late. Went round to see Diana. Poor child, she had been crying all night. She had received a letter from the doctor who was with George when he died – such a kind well-written letter and in it enclosed a message from George himself, a farewell to Diana dictated to the doctor at the very last. At the bottom of it George had written in his own hand with the doctor said 'an almost superhuman effort'. He had made the capital 'G' and then wanting, I fancy, to write something more meaningful than his mere name in the last moment of life he had written quite distinctly the one word 'love'. It was too sad. I sobbed and she cried again.

November 27, 1915

Lunch with Sibbie at the Carlton Grill. She says that Steffie is becoming a regular *morphineuse*. I caught the 4 o'clock to Belvoir. Diana had a breakdown of tears just before dinner and had been doped with sal volatile and brandy to get her to the table. She is strange and wonderful in the way she takes her sorrow, treating it like an illness which must be got over as soon as possible, doing all she can to be cheerful, laughing and talking till the tears come like a sudden seizure and she has to give way. She tells me that when she cannot stop crying she reminds herself that in a comparatively few days she will have ceased to wish to. I think this is a new way of treating grief and perhaps the best. After dinner the Duke, Venetia, Edwin and I played bridge. The Duke in excellent form, loving Venetia and quite liking Edwin, which was a great relief as he had never met them before and was prejudiced against them. I went to bed rather drunk and slept till half past five when I awoke and crept into Diana's room, and lay with her for all too brief but quite divine a time.

December 12, 1915

Dined at Cavendish Square [with Nancy Cunard]. Everybody got rather drunk but I very, and unfortunately Lady Cunard came back after dinner. We all went on to a party arranged at the last moment in Mrs Marten's house. The latchkey broke in the door so I tried to climb in at the window which created a good deal of excitement and alarm.

December 13, 1915

Oh the agony of getting up at 7.15 every morning when one goes to bed so late. I felt a complete wreck this morning. Horrified to hear that Lady Cunard had noticed my drunkenness last night and spoken about it to Nancy. Had a Turkish bath at the Automobile [now the Royal Automobile Club] which I have just joined. Revived by this I went to Venetia's to see Diana. I found them both cooking in the kitchen. Diana looking divinely beautiful very smartly dressed with a little helmet hat and a waving plume, and a white apron over her dress. She very much concerned at my news of last night and by her advice I wrote an abject letter of apology and remorse to Lady Cunard.

December 14, 1915

My letter to Lady Cunard a great success. She came round to the F.O. this afternoon and more than forgave me. In fact I have never been on such good terms with her before.

December 21, 1915

Edward and Diana came to see me – We three dined with Viola at Welbeck Street. Diana brought dinner from the Ritz. Good dinner but not much of it, nor enough wine and the room cold. After dinner I quarrelled with Diana. She said I had been rude to Viola and so was rude to me. I left the house and came home to bed.

December 22, 1915

This morning a beautiful letter of apology from Diana. She writes 'Duff my darling – I am so haunted and wretched about what I seemed to you and what I seem to myself – as to what you seem to me, if you remember that is so much that to see you imperfect for a space or even faintly impolite makes me see red – it's natural enough as to feel critical of *you* is as maddening and absorbing as to feel critical of myself and more and worse since your metal is finer than mine and such minute blemishes stare. But Duff forgive me for I know exactly what I do – so am in more need than men – D.'

December 23, 1915

Dined at Kettner's with Diana, Edward, Viola and Alan. We had finished dinner at about half past ten and there were three glasses of brandy on the table when I suddenly noticed Diana snatch one away as though to hide it and looking up I saw an inspector and an ordinary policeman bearing down on us. They asked us what was in the glasses and we told them. They then took the names and addresses of us three men as we explained that the three glasses belonged to us.

December 24, 1915

Alan rang me up in the morning to say that he had communicated with Sir Edward Henry's [Assistant Commissioner of the Metropolitan Police] private secretary and made sure that there would be no sort of trouble about last night's incident.

December 30, 1915

Went to see Diana in the afternoon – she was going to dine with George Moore and General French. I dined at Queen Anne's Gate – Edwin, Venetia, Mrs Asquith and Masterman-Smith.[1] Edwin and Masterman-Smith had an interesting very confidential conversation after dinner which I was almost surprised they let me listen to. Edwin had been working all day at keeping the Government together, in which he said he now had a little more hope of

---

[1] Sir James Masterman-Smith (1878–1938), served in the office of First Lord of the Admiralty 1911–17.

succeeding. Apparently Edward Grey[1] has been threatening resignation.
Edwin said that he had written to Edward Grey in terms that he wouldn't use
to his footman and had spoken to him hardly less strongly, which Grey had
taken very well and thanked him for his frankness. Masterman-Smith said
that Arthur Balfour's point of view was that whatever a man's personal feelings
might be, it was his duty now not to resign. It appears that Runciman[2] and
McKenna stand or fall together. Edwin said that his great argument with them
was that they could not resign for a reason that they could not name, for the
real reason of their resignation is not any question of principle or even the
fact of compulsion but simply on the number of men who are to be taken, i.e.
the size of the army. Apparently in the summer Kitchener committed us to
the French to produce seventy divisions. Masterman-Smith said that Balfour
asked why McKenna did not resign then as he knew then what Kitchener had
pledged us to. Edwin said that at the Cabinet tomorrow the Prime Minister
will suggest that the General Staff and the Treasury shall consult together as
to what the size of the army shall be and Edwin is sure that if the Cabinet
agree to this the General Staff and the Treasury will come to an agreement.
But the danger of course is that the Cabinet will not consent to this. They will
say that a question of such importance is clearly a question for the Cabinet to
decide, not for an interdepartmental committee. Curzon[3] is especially to be
feared as they say that Curzon wants to smash the Government. One thing is
certain – Simon[4] is gone – gone beyond recall. Incidentally they mentioned
that Gallipoli is to be evacuated.

*By the end of 1915 it was clear that compulsory conscription could not be avoided.
Four Liberal ministers, Simon, McKenna, Runciman and Grey, submitted their
resignations. In the event, only Simon resigned. The bill introducing conscription
was passed in May 1916.*

I make only one resolve for the coming year, i.e. to get rid of my reputation
for drunkenness. In future I will keep a list at the end of this book in which I
will put down every evening whether I could possibly have been thought
drunk or no, for the rumour is becoming a nuisance.

---

[1] Sir Edward Grey, later Viscount Grey of Fallodon (1862–1933). Foreign Secretary 1905–16.
[2] Walter Runciman, 1st Viscount Runciman of Doxford (1870–1949). President of the Board of
   Trade 1914–16.
[3] George Nathaniel Curzon (1859–1925), later Marquess Curzon of Kedleston. Viceroy of India
   1898–1905; Lord Privy Seal 1915–16; Foreign Secretary 1919–24.
[4] Sir John Simon (1873–1954), 1st Viscount Simon. Home Secretary May 1915, resigned Jan.
   1916; Foreign Secretary in MacDonald's National Government 1931–5; Home Secretary under
   Baldwin 1935–7; Chancellor of the Exchequer under Chamberlain 1937–40; Lord Chancellor
   1940–5.

1916

January 1, 1916

New Year's Eve was a wild night. We had two tables at the Carlton and three boxes at the Gaiety. Dinner rather fun with crackers and plenty of wine. After the theatre I went round to Queen Anne's Gate where we drank in the New Year in punch with the Montagus, the Raymonds, Sidney[1] and Sybil and the Prime Minister who was looking happy, the political crisis having been successfully warded off this morning.

January 9, 1916

Diana in bed all day – she and Katharine took morphia last night. I hope she won't become a *morphineuse*. It would spoil her looks. Dined at Downing Street. The news had just arrived of the successful evacuation of Helles [a port on the Gallipoli peninsula] which all the military authorities had said was impossible. This made everyone cheerful. After dinner the Prime [Minister] and Edwin had an almost whispered conversation about Viceroys which I tried but failed to overhear.

January 16, 1916

This morning I was suddenly informed that I had to go to the Contraband Department. I received the news with mixed feelings. I was glad of a change and glad to do rather more important work than the farce of the Parliamentary Department and I shall be glad not to have to get up early in the morning in future, but I shall miss terribly my delicious afternoons with Diana. One never gets away from the Contraband Dept till about 8 o'clock. This is a cruel blow.

February 12, 1916

Lunched at Arlington Street with Alan and Diana. Alan tells me that McKenna's behaviour is very mysterious just now. That he writes long letters with his own hand to Northcliffe[2] and often disappears for an hour without saying where he is going to. Alan thinks he is preparing a great attack on Lloyd George. I wondered whether in view of his dealings with Northcliffe it might not be that they were all in a conspiracy to get rid of the P.M.

---

[1] Sidney Herbert (1890–1939), eldest son of Sir Michael Herbert, former Ambassador to Washington. Brother of Michael Herbert, both being among Duff's greatest friends. Sybil, Duff's sister, fell in love with Sidney in 1914.

[2] Alfred Harmsworth, 1st Viscount Northcliffe (1865–1922). Newspaper magnate, proprietor of *The Times, Daily Mail* and *Daily Mirror*.

February 18, 1916

At 4 Diana came to the Foreign Office to pick me up and we went together to the Pavilion Cinema. I loved her more than ever. I dined with Katharine at the Hanover. She was looking very pretty. Went to Hawtrey's[1] play and thence to a musical party at Lady Cunard's where Diana persuaded K. to go home and spent the night with her in order to take morphia together. An odd world I live in.

February 19, 1916

Diana in bed and very ill as the result of her experiments. I went there in the evening and sat and read to her, loving her very much in her abandonment to sleep and headache.

February 22, 1916

My 26th birthday. Lunched with Mother at the Carlton Grill. Had a delightful afternoon with Diana at the Pavilion Cinema. I really do believe now that she loves me. It appears that Patrick[2] is bothering her to death by his importunities, imploring her all the time to marry him.

February 23, 1916

Lunched with Diana at Scott's. We are both taking steps to get thin and lunch every day off nothing but beef steak without any vegetables or any drink except a cup of coffee afterwards. I do love her. She came for me to the F.O. at 4 o'clock and we went to the cinema. Diana made me swear to rejoin her at Arlington St. in half an hour as she was having interviews with both Patrick and Michael, who is just back from France, and wanted me to cut the tail off one and the head off the other. The way she deceives those boys is astounding!

February 25, 1916

We dined at the Ritz with the Aga Khan.[3] I enjoyed dinner. Diana was looking more beautiful than I have ever seen her, or indeed any woman look. Everybody thought so. Afterwards we went to the Empire. There is a new revue there and they bring into it an imitation of Diana which I think damned impudence and I was rather glad we arrived too late for it. Afterwards we went to a party. At the end of the evening Diana who had been promising all the time that she was going to drive home with me and had kept me there on

---

[1] Sir Charles Hawtrey (1858–1923), actor and producer.

[2] Patrick Shaw-Stewart (1888–1917). Contemporary of Duff's. One of the most brilliant young men of his generation at Oxford, he was made the youngest-ever director of Barings Bank in 1913.

[3] The Aga Khan, Aga Sultan Sir Mohammed Shah (1877–1957), 48th head of the Ismaili sect of the Shia Moslem community.

those grounds when I wanted to go to bed, said she had got to drive with Michael because he insisted and said he was going back to the war. I thereupon made a scene and said I would never forgive her. She said it was vile of me to take it in that way and not to trust her but since I insisted she wouldn't go with him. Eventually she and I drove home with Viola and Alan, dropping her first, she furious with me and not saying good-night. I realized how much I loved her by the remorse I felt and the next morning I sent round a letter apologizing. At one o'clock she came to the F.O. and I drove with her in the motor. She said she hadn't meant to come, that she hadn't really forgiven me and still thought I had behaved abominably. She was hard and unloving and left me to go to a lunch party and I then sent her a present and a note that I thought would touch her.

March 3, 1916

[I] went to a matinée at the Gaiety organized by Lady Essex. The point of it was a little play at the end written for the occasion by Knoblock[1] – a scene at a dressmaker's shop with real mannequins and real ladies. Diana and Cynthia both had speaking parts and both did them pretty badly, but looked very beautiful – Nancy, Hazel [Lavery], Mrs Lindsay and several others were also on the stage. Hazel I didn't think looked as well as the others – perhaps she was badly painted. It was rather a painful performance as it hadn't been properly rehearsed. Viola was quite funny and Lady Tree did her best.

March 6, 1916

A holiday. At about half past eleven Diana came for me. We sat and talked for a little and then went to St Paul's Cathedral, which I had never been inside before. From there we went on the top of a bus to Westminster Abbey where we saw the waxen effigies which I had never seen. Diana also showed me lots of things in the Abbey I hadn't noticed before. It was one of the most delightful mornings I have ever spent. The pleasure of doing that sort of thing with Diana is indescribable.

March 11, 1916

I stayed at the F.O. till 3 o'clock and then went straight to Paddington, where I met Diana and Patrick and we all travelled down to Mells together. Patrick is very much in love with Diana and has no idea that I am, let alone that she is in love with me which indeed nobody suspects. On arriving at Mells Patrick got a telephone message from the War Office to say that he had been appointed a liaison officer with the Mediterranean force and was to sail on Wednesday. Only Katharine was at Mells. The whole house was in confusion as they were putting hot water pipes into it. Diana and Katharine shared a large bedroom –

---

[1] Edward Knoblock (1874–1945), American playwright and novelist, who spent most of his professional life in Britain.

Patrick and I each had one, and there was one other room in which we sat and ate, otherwise all the carpets were up and the furniture covered with sheets. The first evening was very delightful. After dinner we read aloud from the Bible. Then K. and Diana went to bed, and we went to their room and all had an injection of morphia. I had a very light dose, only $\frac{1}{6}$ of a grain. Diana injected it. We lay on the bed and said poetry in turn until about 3 o'clock.

March 12, 1916

I woke up late feeling extraordinarily well. Patrick on the other hand felt very ill. He had more morphia than I.

March 26, 1916. Sunday [Walmer Castle]

A lovely morning. After lunch we motored over to Dover to see the P.M. off to France. Lloyd George, Grey and Kitchener met him there. They looked an odd lot. The P.M. wearing a very light brown leather overcoat, the collar turned up, his long white hair sticking out behind and his red face, was rather a striking, cheerful figure. Grey looked ominous with white face and black spectacles, LG looked untidy and common and ordinary. Kitchener looked like an officer who has got mixed up with a lot of strolling players and is trying to pretend he doesn't know them. We saw the boat off and then motored back to tea.

March 31, 1916

We had arranged for Diana to come and dine alone with me in my rooms. I got some cold beef, lobster, plovers' eggs and strawberries. At half past eight she telephoned to say that the Duchess had heard from French that the Zeppelins were coming and had made her promise not to go out as she wanted to know where she was in order to telephone to her. A cruel disappointment. I immediately had all the dinner and two bottles of champagne packed into a basket which I took to Arlington St. There we dined in Diana's room, she wearing only her yellow dressing gown. It was all very beautiful and remembrance worthy.

Sunday April 2, 1916

The loveliest day there has ever been. Bright dazzling sunshine, not one cloud. It was marvellous coming suddenly after a month of vile weather. Diana came for me at 1 o'clock and we walked together very slowly across the Park to Queen Anne's Gate. There we had rather a bad lunch with Edwin and Venetia. After lunch Diana had to go back to Arlington Street. I walked alone across the Park and down Piccadilly feeling half drunk with Burgundy and the beauty of the day. I thought what an infinite capacity I had for enjoyment.

April 14, 1916

A year today since I began my diary. I went to a party at the Grafton Galleries. Marjorie Trefusis was there looking very pretty. She asked me whether I ever thought of a year ago and if it made me sad. I said it did but it doesn't. For now I love Diana more than ever I loved her and Diana is worth a thousand of her and Diana, wonderfully, loves me.

April 24, 1916

Glad to be back in the Parliamentary Dept. During the morning they brought over a telegram which Birrell[1] had received from Ireland and which he hadn't been able to decypher because his secretary was away and no one else knew where the cypher was! We decyphered it and it sounded rather exciting. It said that the man arrested at Tralee had made a full confession. That he had landed with Casement,[2] that the rising was to have begun that day and that there was to have been an attack that day on Dublin Castle.

April 28, 1916

Weather still beautiful. Lunched with Alan at Bellomo's. He tells me Edwin says the Govt. must resign – that Nathan[3] had always warned them of the state of Ireland but that Birrell had refused to listen. There was a tremendous attack on Lloyd George last Sunday in the *Daily News* by the editor, Gardner. Alan tells me that the day before it appeared Gardner had a long interview with McKenna.

Sunday April 30, 1916 [The Wharf, Sutton]

A beautiful warm day. Sat in the garden in the morning while Mrs Asquith read us selections from her diary – the characters of Rosebery and Arthur Balfour very well done I thought. Gilbert Murray[4] came to lunch. He wanted to talk to the P.M. about conscientious objectors which he did after lunch. In the afternoon I managed to slip off with Diana in a canoe. We went up Paradise Marshes and then got out and lay in the long grass, she bending above me and kissing my eyes while I said the *Ode to Psyche*. After tea I was dragged indoors to play bridge with Mrs Asquith. Apparently it is settled that Birrell is to go, though McKenna was for keeping him. [*Birrell resigned on 1 May.*] McKenna is also against hanging Casement. I like McKenna, he is so

---

[1] Augustine Birrell (1850–1933), essayist and lawyer. He was Quain Professor of Law at London University 1896–9 and Chief Secretary for Ireland 1907–16.

[2] Sir Roger Casement (1864–1916), British traitor and Irish Nationalist hero. Hanged in mid-1916 for working with Germany and the Irish Nationalists in planning the Dublin Easter Rising of 1916.

[3] Sir Matthew Nathan (1862–1939), soldier and civil servant. Under-Secretary for Ireland 1914–19.

[4] Gilbert Murray (1866–1957), scholar and Regius Professor of Greek at Oxford.

genial and frankly common. I went to Diana's room at about half past two. She was very frightened tonight and would hardly let me stay. There was a dying fire in her room and I could see her body, white against the sheets.

May 3, 1916

Diana came for me at 4. She had been lunching at Downing Street. The P.M. had told her that they were having great difficulty in finding a successor for Birrell. The post had been offered to Edwin but he refused it. I suppose this was wise of him but rather unenterprising. We dined with Viola, Alan and Osbert. Diana had had a letter from Lord Wimborne.[1] He seemed to think it had all gone off very luckily and said if only the rebels had cut their telephonic communication it would have been impossible to get any troops from the Curragh in time. After dinner we read a lot of Shakespeare – Diana and I reading and taking parts – Romeo and Juliet, Antony and Cleopatra, Othello and Desdemona. Driving home she told me she had never loved me so much and I don't think I ever loved her more than this evening.

May 5, 1916

I went to a poets' party at the Bonham Carters. I sat by W. H. Davies and thought him delightful. He read some of his poems, as did also Walter de la Mare and Ralph Hodgson.[2] Lord Crewe[3] also repeated a poem by himself and Robert Ross[4] read some comic poems.

May 12, 1916

Lunched at Junior Carlton. Very little work to do in the Contraband Dept. At about 4 o'clock Campbell[5] came and told me I was to be in the Commercial Dept. in future. On the whole I am glad of this. I shan't get my afternoons but I don't think they are very busy and I shall, I hope, be there permanently and have some sensible work to do. Campbell suggested my beginning at once so I said goodbye to the Contraband and went to see Gerry Villiers.[6] I settled with him that I would begin tomorrow morning and slipped away to the matinée at the Gaiety where I found Diana.

---

[1] Ivor Guest, 1st Viscount Wimborne (1873–1939). Lord Lieutenant of Ireland 1915–18. An ardent admirer of Diana's.

[2] W. H. Davies (1871–1940), Ralph Hodgson (1871–1962), Walter de la Mare (1873–1956).

[3] Robert Crewe-Milnes, 1st Marquess of Crewe (1858–1945). Secretary of State for India, 1910–15; Ambassador to Paris 1922–8; Minister for War for a few months before the 1931 general election.

[4] Robert Ross (1869–1918), close friend of Oscar Wilde and publisher of his *Collected Works*.

[5] Sir Ronald Hugh Campbell (1883–1953), Private Secretary to the Permanent Under-Secretary at the FO 1913–19; Ambassador to Paris 1939–40 and to Portugal 1940–5.

[6] The Hon. Gerald Hyde Villiers (1882–1953), diplomat.

June 3, 1916. Saturday

Diana came to me very beautiful in the morning. I was most passionate. She drove me to the Foreign Office. Went down by the 5.15 to Sutton – where were Norah Lindsay, Diana, Letty, Edward and Mike [Michael Herbert]. We played a little tennis and then Diana, Edward and I bathed. It was very cold. Diana looked very beautiful walking back through the long grass in the sunset with her gold hair down. I kissed her face – it was as cold as marble. After dinner was dull. Diana went out with Michael. He had to motor up to London late and return to the war on Monday morning. He was very sad with a terrible premonition that he would be killed.

June 4, 1916. Sutton

Alas, a grey, wet, cold morning. Diana and I went on the river and met the Parsonses [Alan and Viola] who were staying at the Wharf. The Ian Hamiltons[1] came to lunch. He seems quite cheerful. I read aloud from Bernard Shaw's new preface. I am so sorry for poor Letty – she is going through agonies of anxiety about Ego. They have no news of him and fear the worst. She is so brave and tries so hard to be cheerful.

June 6, 1916

At half past twelve Katharine's baby was christened in St Paul's Cathedral. Diana and I, godmother and godfather, went there together – on arriving we learnt from Mrs Asquith the news of Lord Kitchener's death. [*Lord Kitchener was drowned on his way to Russia when his ship struck a mine.*] All over London the flags are flying half mast. He died at the top of his wave.

June 14, 1916

Diana came to me in the morning. She was still nervous about my love for her, and I rather wantonly played on her fears. We dined with Edward and the Parsonses. Afterwards we went to *Hamlet* at Her Majesty's. We started to walk home but in Pall Mall we met a four-wheeler and Diana and I got in. Between our kisses she said that she had been so frightened all day that I did not love her and I confessed that I had played with her whereupon she turned on me in rage and hit me in the face, jumped out of the four-wheeler and began to run home. She telephoned when she got home to say she was sorry but that I must not play with such important things.

June 15, 1916

Dined early at the Carlton. A boring dinner, I thought. Diana had arranged for everyone to go to the opera which I was determined not to do. I came

---

[1] Gen. Sir Ian Hamilton (1853–1947), CIC Mediterranean Expeditionary Force in the disastrous Dardanelles campaign in 1915. He became the scapegoat for the failure of the operation.

home alone at 9.45 (broad daylight still) although I knew she wanted me to go. I seem to love to cross her. Do I love her? I think I do.

June 18, 1916

Went round to Baroness d'Erlanger's[1] at 12 and she, her little girl, Hugo [Rumbold] and I motored down to Reigate Priory which has been taken by Mrs Gordon. We had a most excellent lunch. It was a beautiful, sunny afternoon. We played tennis and had tea under the trees. Dinner was as good as lunch – Heidsieck 1906 – afterwards Lady Kathleen [Hastings] told our fortunes by cards. Osbert, the Baroness and I motored back to London. I made love to the Baroness holding both her hands all the way. It is so difficult not to make love when motoring at night after a good dinner and sitting close to a woman. We all got out at 139 Piccadilly and the Baroness said she wanted to show us her cat which was sleeping in the kitchen, so she and I went down to get it and I kissed her. I rather wish I hadn't.

June 20, 1916

Lunched at the Cecil with Baroness d'Erlanger. This absurd flirtation with a woman old enough to be my mother is most ridiculous. I wish I could get out of it. She seems to take it for granted that I'm in love with her. I was so nervous before she arrived at the Cecil that I drank two cocktails to give me confidence. She said she didn't think we ought to see too much of each other and talked a lot of nonsense on those lines – Oh Lord!

June 22, 1916

The Baroness telephoned in the morning, said I had not been nice to her [at dinner] last night and that when we were sitting together she had felt angry eyes glaring at her – meaning I suppose Diana's. If she only knew how little cause Diana has to be jealous of her and how well Diana knows it. In the evening I had some sandwiches at the Automobile Club and went to the opera. It was *The Critic* [by Sheridan] very well staged and dressed by Hugo. He was there with the Baroness. Diana was in the dress circle as her eyes were made up preparatory to doing the tableaux again. I joined her and we went away together before the end and we drove back to Arlington Street in an open taxi through beautiful blue twilight. At Arlington Street she dressed for the tableau of the Allies in which she is Russia. She wore a huge gold Russian headdress and a lot of pearls round her neck. At my prayer she lowered her dress to the waist for a moment and stood there – the loveliest sight I have ever seen.

[1] Marie-Rose Catherine d'Aqueria de Rochegude (d. 1959) married Baron Emile d'Erlanger, senior partner of the firm of Erlangers, in 1895. They lived in London at 139 Piccadilly.

June 23, 1916

In the evening I had to dine with the Baroness. We dined at Romano's. I didn't mind dinner but afterwards when I suggested going to a cinema she said it was such a beautiful evening that we ought to go for a drive. So we drove to Regent's Park and round the outer circle. I had to kiss her and hold her in my arms and I hated it. We went back to 139 Piccadilly where I sat with her for a little while and wondered whether Byron when he lived in that house was as bored with his wife as I was with the Baroness.

June 29, 1916

Met Diana at the Cavendish and we went together to the Cecil where we lunched. She was rather depressed. We both dined with Edwin and Venetia and after dinner we went to an entertainment which consisted chiefly of Lady Constance Stewart-Richardson dancing with very few clothes on. It was quite attractive. Unfortunately in the middle of it I lost my temper with Diana and said cold and unpardonable things to her. She didn't speak to me again.

June 30, 1916

On waking I found a miserable and angry letter from Diana, written overnight. I wrote imploring pardon which was duly granted with less difficulty than I expected. Dined at Queen Anne's Gate. We had a very amusing dinner. Birrell delightful. They discussed Shakespeare afterwards, the Prime Minister saying the Sonnets were impersonal – old fool, Birrell disagreeing. I think there is a crisis in the air. The Prime [Minister] asked Mrs Long[1] to lunch next week and added 'interesting things may happen before then – too interesting'. Edwin and McKenna are by way of going to Paris on Monday to see [Peter] Bark, the Russian Minister of Finance, but they talk of putting it off.

July 1, 1916

Lunched at Arlington Street with Diana, Viola and Alan. After lunch came a letter from Louis Mallet[2] saying that he had heard from the Red Crescent that Ego was dead. This is too terribly sad. They encourage Letty to go on hoping but I'm afraid it is hopeless.

July 3, 1916

I met Diana here at a quarter to one. She had had such a sad time with poor Letty. She lay in my arms and sobbed. She looks so pretty when she cries – the only woman that I ever met whom tears embellish. I nearly cried too. This

---

[1] Sibell Vanden-Bempde-Johnson, married Brig.-Gen. Walter Long in 1910. He was killed in 1917.

[2] Sir Louis Mallet (1864–1948), British Ambassador to Turkey 1913–14.

evening the news about Ego was confirmed. There had still been a glimmer of hope before. I couldn't enjoy myself for thinking of Letty and Diana.

July 11, 1916

Met Diana in Arlington Street at twenty to eleven and we walked together to Cavendish Square. We found Nancy not yet dressed, looking rather squalid having been very drunk the night before. Diana was disgusted and saddened. Nancy's *dégringolade* is so complete that I find it rather romantic.

Dined at 10 Downing Street – a small party consisting of the Prime Minister, Mrs Asquith, Elizabeth, Lord Crewe and Lord Robert Cecil.[1] We drank some 1892 champagne, which the Prime Minister only produces for small parties as he has very little left. I thought it too old. When Mrs Asquith and Elizabeth left the room rather an interesting conversation took place. At first I felt very uncomfortable, alone with three Cabinet Ministers who I feared would say things that I should not hear. But they seemed quite unaware of my presence. They talked about the campaign in Mesopotamia. The mismanagement they said was all due to the Government of India, especially to Sir Beauchamp Duff.[2] Lord Curzon has always maintained against Lord Kitchener that it was a mistake to combine the two military offices in India, and experience had proved Lord Curzon right. The decision to attempt the capture of Baghdad was entirely due to the military experts. Kitchener said that we might take it but couldn't hold it. Even so he thought it worth doing from a political point of view. Curzon said 'Don't take it unless you can hold it'. The Prime Minister said that he had only once seen Kitchener really rattled and that was when it had been decided to evacuate Gallipoli. Kitchener came to him one morning and said he hadn't slept for two nights, thinking of the terrible casualties we were bound to suffer. He estimated them at 50,000, while other military experts put it at twice that figure. The P.M. likes quoting these instances of miscalculations of military experts. He said that Kitchener originally proposed Rundle[3] as commander of the Gallipoli expedition but afterwards he wouldn't consent to the recall of Ian Hamilton when everyone else wished it. Crewe said and the P.M. agreed that the failure of the Dardanelles expedition was entirely the failure of one man – Ian Hamilton. They all agreed in praising Archibald Hunter,[4] whom the P.M. described as the most sensible soldier he had ever met. He said that Hunter won the battle of Omdurman in spite of Kitchener and defended Ladysmith in spite of White. But he has fits of insanity.

The most dramatic story the P.M. told was about the debate in the House

[1] Lord Robert Cecil, 1st Viscount Chelwood (1864–1958). Minister of Blockade, 1916–18.
[2] Gen. Sir Beauchamp Duff (1855–1918), CIC Indian Army 1914–16.
[3] Gen. Sir Leslie Rundle (1856–1934), Governor and CIC Malta 1909–15, then succeeded Sir Ian Hamilton as CIC, Central Force, organized for home defence, until 1916.
[4] Gen. Sir Archibald Hunter (1856–1936), as CO at Aldershot, was responsible for organizing the training of Britain's New Army, 1914–18.

of Commons on the reduction of Kitchener's salary. The P.M. made a speech defending and praising Kitchener and when he sat down Bonar Law[1] said to him – 'That was a very good speech, it will make it harder than ever to get rid of him'. Four days afterwards he was dead. 'Nobody will ever know that' the P.M. added. Apparently all the Cabinet were determined to get rid of him at the time of his death.

July 31, 1916

After dinner we went to Raymond Hitchcock's[2] party at the Grafton Galleries. Diana was there though she ought not to have been as it was chiefly composed of the lowest kind of actresses and chorus girls. She was probably the only virgin in the room. The Duchess, like the old fool she is, brought her. I argued with Diana about it. She said she wanted to prove that she could do these unconventional things without losing caste. She quoted Lady Ripon[3] as having done the same. I said that Lady Ripon married first to which Diana answered that she must surpass Lady Ripon by doing as she pleased before she was married. One must not imitate the best but improve on it. She won the argument. Her mother drove her home to Montagu Square where she is still staying with Letty. I followed, found her waiting on the doorstep and we went together for the loveliest drive that perhaps we have ever had. We had the taxi open. The stars were very bright. Her hair blew in the wind and I held it back from her face and eyes.

August 1, 1916

Still hot and sunny. I went to Diana at 7 and found her in her small bedroom at the top of the house. All the first floor of Arlington Street is being made into a hospital. She told me how unhappy Wimborne is. Yesterday he thought himself Viceroy and went down to the House of Commons to hear the Prime Minister's speech.[4] To his surprise he heard the office of Viceroy ridiculed, so he came home to write a letter resigning the post, but while he was writing it he received one from the Prime Minister kicking him out. Diana was going to dine this evening at Wimborne House and the Prime Minister was going to be there. Diana telephoned to me at one [a.m.]. In her small room at

---

[1] Andrew Bonar Law (1858–1923), Secretary of State for the Colonies under Asquith 1915–16; Chancellor of the Exchequer under Lloyd George 1916–18; Leader of the House 1916–21; Conservative Prime Minister 1922–3.

[2] Raymond Hitchcock (1871–1928), American comedian and actor.

[3] Lady Constance Herbert (d. 1917), married first St George Lowther, 4th Earl of Lonsdale (1855–82) and second, in 1885, the 2nd Marquess of Ripon. A celebrated Edwardian beauty and hostess and the mother of Lady Juliet Duff.

[4] Asquith had said, 'I do not think it is urgently necessary at the moment to nominate any particular person to the post [of Lord Lieutenant of Ireland]. It is not the most desirable post in the world.'

Arlington Street she has a private telephone which unlike the one in the other room cannot be tapped by Her Grace – a great convenience.

August 12, 1916

The weather though not perfect was fine, very warm and sometimes sunny. Diana came to me soon after eleven. She was beautifully dressed and looking lovely. We drank a glass of port, selected a few books to read and started off in the excellent motor I had hired for the day. After a very delicious drive we stopped soon after one at an inn at Horsham where Diana went to the kitchen and with the help of the kitchenmaid made some delicious sandwiches with little rolls, filling them with beef, ham, cheese and salad. I bought a bottle of sparkling Moselle and we drove on to a place which I think was called Den Park. There we wandered about until we found a little hill with a wide view where we sat down under some pine trees and lunched. Diana wanted exercise so she ran round the pine trees which stood in a circle and I sat in the centre eating and drinking and watching her. She looked strange and romantic in her smart London clothes transplanted to this lonely rural scene. Then I lay with my head in her lap and she read to me *Atalanta in Calydon* [Swinburne].

August 22, 1916

Diana came for me in the evening and we went together to Queen Anne's Gate to dine with Edwin. Only the Prime Minister, the Parsonses and Bongy were there. It was not a very amusing evening. I don't share Diana's enthusiasm for the P.M. This evening I thought him particularly unattractive. He is neither witty himself nor the cause of wit in others. Wine never makes his conversation wild or whimsical but only more matter of fact and platitude. After dinner he must have his bridge which he plays badly for low points. He is oblivious of young men and lecherous of young women.

August 23, 1916

Poor Basil Hallam has been killed. It is very sad and saddens Diana. There seems to be rather a mess in the Balkans. Roumania signed the conventions pledging her to come in last Friday. She was to come in 10 days after the beginning of our *offensif affirmé* from Salonica. Now our offensive seems to have been delayed by an unexpected Bulgarian offensive and the later news from Athens is that King Tino's[1] private correspondence has been got hold of and proves that he is in collusion with the Bulgars and invited them to attack. No one knows what will happen but I hope that Roumania has gone too far to go back.

---

[1] King Constantine I of Greece 'Tino' (1868–1923) reigned from 1913 to 1917, when he abdicated. He returned to the throne following a plebiscite from 1920–3, when he was again ousted.

August 25, 1916

At 12 (midnight) Diana telephoned in great misery. She had been reading the book about Julian and Billy [Grenfell] which had made her terribly unhappy. She was sobbing as though her heart would break poor darling. She said she felt so lonely and almost got up and came to me.

August 30, 1916

Lunched at the Carlton. Diana called for me soon after 8 and we went together to 22 Mulberry Walk. Viola and Alan had the Prime Minister and Edwin to dinner besides us. They were very nervous about the success of the evening and had taken great pains bless their hearts. They had a special waiter, special food and special wine but at first Alan could only grunt with shyness and Viola only moan. However, contrary to all expectation it proved a brilliant success. The food was excellent, the conversation never flagged and the P.M. was as happy as a sandboy. After dinner Edwin read one of G. K. Chesterton's Father Brown stories aloud and then I read Max Beerbohm's essay on Switzerland, and then the P.M. read a sonnet of Keats, so badly that it was hard not to laugh and Diana said *The Ballad of Mary Hamilton*. We four guests drove away in the P.M.'s motor. We dropped Edwin first at Queen Anne's Gate and then the P.M. asked me where I lived and I saw he was determined to be left with Diana. I said I would walk from there and ran all the way across the park and up St James's Street so that I reached Arlington Street almost at the same time as the motor car. Diana was waiting. She knew I would come. I kissed her and left her and was as happy as could be.

September 11, 1916

I dined at Queen Anne's Gate. As soon as I could get away I went to the Ritz where I had settled to meet Diana, Katharine and Edward. I arrived just as Diana was leaving in a rage, having quarrelled fiercely with Edward. He had attacked her for tolerating Wimborne and Moore. I don't know what he had said exactly. I walked down Arlington Street with her. She was very bitter and said that she felt her lip curled in scorn against the whole world. Her lovely face was pale and proud but I knew that behind its white disdain a torrent of tears was waiting and being with difficulty withheld. Katharine and Edward followed us but Diana shut the door and would not come out. We came back to my rooms and discussed it all and I could not help agreeing with Edward's view of it. After they had gone Diana telephoned. She had been crying as I knew she would and she broke down again while she was talking to me and sobbed like a child. It was terrible to hear her crying without being able to hold and comfort her and terrible not to be able to tell her that I had agreed with Edward.

September 18, 1916

[*Duff is starting a holiday in Scotland; his travel arrangements have gone wrong.*]
I felt depressed and was still more so on arriving at Glasgow after nine to find
that it was too late to get anything to drink. I had an indifferent dinner at the
Great Central Hotel and afterwards looking at the news telegrams in the hall
I suddenly saw 'Prime Minister's Eldest Son Killed in Action'. It was the worst
shock I have ever had. I shall never forget that awful moment or that horrible
place. What an end to what a day! I wished I were with Diana to comfort her.
She will be very miserable and all alone. I had telegraphed to her from Appin
telling her of my misfortunes and asking her to telegraph a word of comfort
to me at Glasgow. Just after I had seen the news I got a telegram from her
'What comfort can I give you my darling now that Raymond is killed. I have
no energy or hope left until I think of you.' I went to bed – the first day of my
holiday – more miserable than I had been for a long time.

September 27, 1916

On arriving [back] in London I went home and had a bath and breakfast. I then
went to Arlington Street where I learnt that Mark Tennant and Bimbo[1] have
both been killed. One grows callous. After Raymond's death these seem of no
account though I was really fond of both Mark and Bimbo. They were young
and rich and had everything to make them happy. Diana was looking very white
and tired. She has been working too hard in the hospital and crying too much.
She has been to Mells to see Katharine once and went again today. She cried in
my arms. I travelled with her as far as Reading and came straight back.

October 14, 1916

Had a very short lunch with Diana at Rumpelmayer. She was looking pale
and ill and my love for her felt cool but she was astonishingly funny and we
laughed immoderately.

October 16, 1916

I gave Gerry Villiers and Alan dinner at the Carlton Grill. We came back here
afterwards and Alan soon went. Then I had a long conversation with Gerry
and at last realized to my astonishment that he was making love to me. I
didn't want a row with him as he is head of my Department and I particularly
want to get leave in Christmas week to go to Panshanger. So I parried his
advances as best I could and got rid of him but as I was opening the front
door to let him out he caught hold of me and kissed me which was very
unpleasant. It is years since anything of this kind has happened to me.

[1] Mark Tennant (1892–1916) and Bimbo (Edward) Tennant (1897–1916), eldest son of the 1st
Lord Glenconner, were first cousins. Mark was the brother of Kakoo Granby, later Duchess of
Rutland.

October 22, 1916

Sunday in London – a pleasure I haven't had for a long time. I slept till 11. After lunch Diana and I came back here. It was a very cold day. We pushed the sofa in front of the fire and lay side by side. At first we read the *Queen's Quain* and then we slept in each other's arms, beautifully. She went soon after 5 and Alan and I played billiards at the Bachelors'. I then had a Turkish bath after which Diana and I went to dine at Mulberry Walk. We had a very pleasant dinner and read a little *Pickwick* afterwards. Alan played the piano and Viola sang and Diana sat on the floor at my feet with her head on my knees and once when I thought she was laughing I found she was crying. I never loved her more.

October 24, 1916

I went to a supper party at 16 Charles Street, Knightsbridge.[1] I was asked in the afternoon on the telephone and couldn't hear whose party it was so I went out of curiosity. I found there Eileen and her husband, Orde, her brother George Wellesley, another man and five chorus girls. The house was the abode of one of these – Babs Walter. It was a very odd party, very odd to see Eileen in this demi-monde. I rather enjoyed it. When I went Babs as hostess came down to see me off and emboldened by wine I made advances, which she received extremely well. We kissed passionately and she made me promise to dine with her, seeming to hint that there would be more to follow.

October 31, 1916

Dined at Romano's with Babs Walter. When I saw her again I didn't think her so pretty as I expected. She was quite good company and apparently has recently married a rich man who is now in France. She talked a lot about her country house and her motors. At last we went home to her town house – a small louche one in Charles Street, Knightsbridge – which she told me had been hers before she married as I was quite willing to believe. There I rapidly had her which was very agreeable. I promised to dine with her again but I doubt if I do. She doesn't really attract me.

Sunday November 5, 1916

A horrible stormy day. I got up late – went to pick up Diana at 50 Portland Place and drove her to Queen Anne's Gate where we lunched with Edwin, Edward, Alan and Viola. We went up to Venetia's bedroom afterwards and Edwin read aloud. Later I telephoned to Diana and found her very upset as the Duchess has been getting anonymous letters saying that Diana comes here. The Duchess has not said anything to Diana about it but told Claud

---

[1] A puzzle. There is no Charles Street in Knightsbridge, only in Mayfair.

Russell[1] who repeated it. I wish I could find out the author of the letters. I suspect the servants here. I went to see Diana on my way to dinner. She was looking very beautiful in her yellow gown but so wretched. If only we had some money and could marry. I dined alone at the Bachelors' feeling very dejected.

November 11, 1916

Dined at 16 Lower Berkeley Street. After dinner, the conversation turning on sodomy, Blueie [Harold Baker] told us of a case where a man was accused of having committed it in No Man's Land, i.e. between the trenches during an attack, taking advantage of a shell hole. This story was shouted to Sir John [Horner] who heard it unmoved and only grunted 'He must have been a handy fellow'.

November 15, 1916

Nancy's wedding [to Sydney Fairbairn]. Great fun. She looked beautiful in a gold dress. Edward, Diana and I dined with the Parsonses. We had quite a happy dinner, sang afterwards and then read aloud at which Edward left. Then I drove Diana home. We had a terrible quarrel, entirely my fault. I behaved outrageously, trying at one moment to throw myself out of the taxi and saying cruel things to her. I can never forgive myself.

November 16, 1916

This morning I had a letter from her which made me terribly unhappy. I transcribe it. 'Duff dear. I cannot bear it at all. You will no longer help me with my moods, or be patient with my tired ways. You will not even let me lie quietly without raging at the little I sometimes needs must deny you. There is so rarely a night spent together that we do not make hideous with our complaints of one another. Tonight was a climax – tho' I kept calm long enough to remind you not to rate me it did not check your ill temper but augmented it, and you ridiculed me till my heart shrank from myself and then you stopped it beating by trying to step out of a fast taxi and then you ground it to atoms by telling me I caused you all possible pain. So we will rest from each other for a little and if possible return together restored to peacefulness. Diana.' I wrote her an abject and passionate apology, and sent her another letter at lunch time.

November 17, 1916

It is still freezing cold. All yesterday and today I continued to bombard Diana with letters but without success. She means to keep it up, I think, over Sunday.

---

[1] Sir Claud Russell (1871–1959), Minister to Abyssinia 1920–5, and Switzerland 1928–31; Ambassador to Portugal 1931–5.

November 18, 1916

This morning while I was having breakfast Diana telephoned and asked me to lunch with her. So that is alright again – bless her. I lunched with her very happily and loved her more than ever for this quarrel.

November 20, 1916

Lunched with Mother at her flat having first seen Diana and Edward [Horner] for a few minutes at the Bath Club. Poor E. was in very low spirits as he has failed in his Staff College exam and there is a terrible row because he had Lady Cunard's parlourmaid in the larder. The maid who was quite willing has since told Lady Cunard, I don't know why, and she told the Duchess. They are both horrified and say that Edward may never come into their houses again.

November 21, 1916

A foggy day, which I love. Dined alone at the Junior Carlton. Drank a bottle of Mouton Rothschild followed by some capital sherry which I discovered – reading *Pride and Prejudice* the while – early to bed – a pleasant evening.

Sunday December 3, 1916

I managed, by shamefully deceiving Alan, to dine alone with Diana at her bedside. Afterwards I read to her – poetry – and loved her. I went on to 24 Queen Anne's Gate. On arriving I was almost shown into the dining room where Edwin, the Prime Minister and [Lord] Reading were waiting for Crewe. I stopped the servant in time and went up to the drawing room where I found sitting on cushions round the fire Venetia, Barbara [Jekyll],[1] Lady Wimborne and Lady Goonie. They were all looking very pretty and were beautifully dressed. I liked the scene – lovely women warming themselves at the fire this bitter night while under their feet the fate of the Empire was being decided. In the next room Margot with a face as long as a book was playing bridge. At last Edwin, Reading and the Prime Minister came up – the two first rather white and careworn but the P.M. happier, less concerned and I must say more drunk than I have ever seen him. We played bridge – Venetia and I against the P.M. and Lady Goonie. He was so drunk that one felt uncomfortable. No one could have been unaware of it. He talked continually and foolishly – made false declarations which we pretended not to notice. It was an extraordinary scene. After they had gone we gathered from Edwin that the resignations of all the Cabinet are to be asked for tomorrow as happened at the forming of the Coalition. Edwin seemed happy – I expect he is safe.

[1] Barbara Jekyll (1887–1973), daughter of Sir Herbert Jekyll, married Francis McLaren, son of the 1st Baron Aberconway, in 1911. He died in 1917 and in 1922 she married Gen. Bernard Freyberg V. C., 1st Baron Freyberg (1889–1963).

December 4, 1916

Colder than ever. Alan told me before supper that Lloyd George's scheme is himself [L.G.] at the Foreign Office, [Edward] Carson at the War Office and Bonar Law at the Admiralty. He also told me that he had heard from Edwin that both Bonar Law and LG have refused to try to form a Govt. of their own.

December 5, 1916

I lunched with Diana at Bellomo's. I saw Venetia before lunch and Alan after. It seems that the P.M. at first consented to Lloyd George's small War Council of which the P.M. himself was not really to be a member but that later on the advice of his liberal colleagues, especially McKenna and Runciman, he refused it. I gathered from the rather bitter way in which Venetia spoke of him that even his loyalest adherents are rather irritated at this last lamentable lack of decision. Alan has been packing up for McKenna at the Treasury all the morning. The report now is that Lloyd George has resigned. If I were the P.M. I should accept the resignation, make Jellicoe[1] and Robertson[2] peers and First Lord and Secretary of State for War respectively. I really believe that he might then carry on and make Hardinge[3] or even Curzon Foreign Secretary. I wonder if it has occurred to him. Curzon of course wouldn't do with Hardinge as Under Secretary.

December 6, 1916

The Prime Minister resigned last night. I dined at the Carlton with Mike, Alan, Viola and Diana. After dinner we went to a party at Lady Northland's house in Bryanston Square. At supper I sat between Clare[4] and Diana. Clare was looking quite beautiful. We talked about spiritualism *à propos* of Oliver Lodge's new book.[5] Clare knows the Lodges, has been to seances and has had many messages from Bim. She firmly believes in it. Bim it appears is perfectly happy, but Yvo, from whom also she has heard, is not. He is discontented. One of the messages he is said to have transmitted was 'I question duty daily'. She has also heard from Ego. She was very interesting about it and quite charming.

After supper I was quite sober – Diana was not. I had a remarkable con-

[1] John Jellicoe, 1st Earl Jellicoe (1859–1935). Admiral of the Fleet; First Sea Lord Nov. 1916–end 1917. In Jan. 1918 he was raised to the peerage.

[2] Gen. Sir William Robertson (1860–1933), Chief of Imperial General Staff Dec. 1915–18.

[3] Charles Hardinge, 1st Baron Hardinge of Penshurst (1858–1944). Permanent Under-Secretary of State for Foreign Affairs. Later Ambassador in Paris and Viceroy of India, as Lord Hardinge of Penshurst.

[4] Clare Bethel, née Tennant (1896–1960). She married the Hon. Lionel Tennyson in 1918. Divorced 1928, when she married James Beck, an American.

[5] Sir Oliver Lodge (1851–1946), leading physicist and a dedicated believer in survival after death. The book was *Raymond or Life and Death*, published in 1916 after his son Raymond was killed in battle.

versation with her in which she was very communicative. She told me she had always loved Raymond more than me and had permitted him as much – but not more. That last night at Brighton he had lain with her, though he was not there when I went to her room in the early morning and couldn't get in. I was much moved and amazed and curiously it made me like Raymond more than ever – though were he still alive I don't know how I should feel. She assured me that she loved me best of the living, particularly lately – but I reminded her that she had often said as much while Raymond was alive and why should I believe her. It was a thrilling revelation.

December 7, 1916

I went to see Diana for a minute before lunch. She was very affectionate and did not refer to what she had said last night. She had heard from Venetia in the deepest confidence that Lloyd George had offered Edwin to be Chancellor of the Exchequer and Edwin had refused. Iris [Tree] is engaged to be married to an American [Curtis Moffat].

December 8, 1916

Dined with Diana, Edwin and Venetia at 24 Queen Anne's Gate. Edwin was in the depths of depression and could talk of nothing but the political situation. He is miserable that he had to resign and thinks he might have avoided it. I don't think he could have. He is very fond of Lloyd George and hates all the other Liberals. He was especially bitter about McKenna. He says that all might have been well if it hadn't been for McKenna and Margot on the one side dragging Asquith away from Lloyd George and Harmsworth [Lord Northcliffe] and Headley Le Bas on the other dragging Lloyd George away from Asquith.

December 17, 1916

Diana has given me the key of Arlington Street. I went there after dinner and waited. At last she came and we had a very happy drive together. It was exciting waiting for her in the dark archway. I went into the house first but it was lit up and there were people moving about in the hospital so I thought it safer to wait in the courtyard. When she came in I was standing in the corner and said nothing because I was afraid of startling her but she called for me at once because she felt I was there though she could not see me.

December 21, 1916

In the evening I was sitting here writing my diary when in walked Winston and insisted on taking me off to the Automobile to a Turkish bath. After the bath we dined in our towels lying on couches like Romans – a good dinner with champagne. He was interesting about himself. Talked of the Antwerp expedition and the Dardanelles, said he thought the coming report of the Commission of Enquiry would be on the whole favourable to him and bewailed

his inactivity. He would, he said, take any job offered him at the present time.
He is a strange creature.

December 24, 1916

Rose late – went to see Edward who has been ill. Diana and Katharine came.
It was the first time I had seen the latter since Raymond's death. She did not
seem much changed. Still very lovely and so charming and sweet, laughing
and appearing cheerful but looking utterly miserable and hopeless at
moments. The children came in after lunch. One imagined a look of Raymond
in the little baby's face. I thought it all poignantly and acutely sad. Haldane
was at lunch and in capital form. How far nicer fallen ministers always are
than reigning ones.

December 25, 1916

I went to the Foreign Office in the morning. Lunched with Steffie at Berkeley
House. We had an excellent lunch – perfect turkey and champagne, the same
as I had drunk last night. It was all very *en famille* and correct. I enjoyed it. I
went to see Diana afterwards whom I found depressed. I dined at 16 Lower
Berkeley Street [Sir John and Lady Horner]. Haldane was capital. He told us
of the various people who he had taken to see George Meredith.[1] Apparently
Meredith once asked him to bring a General and Haldane asked French who
confessed that he had never heard of Meredith and the two had a row over
some obscure point in military history. On one occasion he took [the Earl of]
Rosebery but he said that Meredith and Rosebery took a violent dislike to each
other at sight and he had to get Rosebery away as quickly as possible. A quiet
pleasant evening – and on the whole a very happy if not a merry Christmas.

December 26, 1916

I went to pick up Diana before dinner. She has sent away her maid, Adelina,
which is a pity as she knew all her secrets. We dined with Claude Lowther.[2]
We had a good dinner and a lot to drink. Claude was as intolerable as ever
and Diana abused me afterwards for having been rude to him. Alas, we
quarrelled as usual and parted in anger after a long drive in a taxi with a man
walking in front of it carrying a light on account of the fog.

December 27, 1916 [Panshanger, Hertfordshire, house belonging to the Desboroughs]

On arriving at Cole Green I met Bridget,[3] Violet de Trafford and her youngest
brother Raymond.[4] We all drove to the house together. Staying in the house

---

[1] George Meredith (1828–1909), novelist and poet.

[2] Lt.-Col. Claude Lowther bought Herstmonceux Castle, Sussex, in 1911 and worked on its
    restoration until his death in 1929.

[3] The Hon. Bridget Colebrooke, daughter of 1st Baron Colebrooke, married Lord Victor Paget in
    1922. They were divorced in 1935.

[4] Raymond de Trafford (1900–71), youngest son of Sir Humphrey de Trafford, 3rd Bt.

are four friends of Ivo's [Grenfell], all aged about 18 and they make me feel terribly old and ill at ease, Rosemary Leveson-Gower[1] and, of course, Lord and Lady Desborough.[2] Lady Rosemary is most disquietingly attractive. Sat between Violet de T. and Lady Desborough at dinner; the latter is still a miracle though I seem to feel sometimes the heroic effort she makes to be the same as she was, to bear up the weight of her sorrow and the weight of her party and to make everything a success. I thought it particularly after dinner when we played the old little games and nobody was really any good at them except myself. Lady Rosemary however helped a lot. I thought, perhaps wrongly, that Lady Desborough must be comparing Ivo's nice, quiet, gentlemanly almost speechless young friends with the noisy, drunken, ill mannered, audacious crew that Billy and Julian collected.

December 29, 1916 [Panshanger]

In the morning we played tennis. It was fun. Little games after tea. I have just finished reading Charles's [Lister] letters, which made me feel very discontented with my life. I think I am too easily pleased, too tolerant, too lazy. Looking back over the past year I can remember very few days when I was not happy but there is nothing in the whole of it which stands out as worth remembering, and I shrink at the prospect of another which will be exactly the same. The same days at the Foreign Office doing the same work, the same nights spent with the same people. I may make resolutions to live differently but I shan't keep them. I envy Charles and the adventures that he had, still more I envy Patrick who had as many and is still living. This is a phase, a mood and it will pass but I wish it wouldn't.

December 30, 1916. Panshanger

The day before yesterday I wrote to Diana saying I hoped she hadn't taken our quarrel seriously, telling her about the party [at Panshanger] and confessing that I was enjoying it. This evening after tea I had a telegram from her saying 'It is useless trying to smooth all over with feigned forgetfulness – I wonder you dare write in such a strain – I am distractedly wretched.'

I appear to have been wrong in the view I took of our quarrel – it must have been more serious than I thought. This telegram upset me a good deal. I cannot bear to make her unhappy and I have been conscious all these days of infidelity to her in my thoughts of Lady Rosemary. It is all too troubling. I have written again and telegraphed and done all that I can; but I do wonder if she is really unhappy and pray that she isn't.

---

[1] Lady Rosemary Leveson-Gower, daughter of the 4th Duke of Sutherland. She married Duff's friend, Eric Ednam, later 3rd Earl of Dudley, in 1919 and died in a plane crash in 1930.

[2] Lady Desborough (d. 1952) née Ethel Fane, married William, 1st Baron Desborough, in 1887. Always known as Ettie, she was a great beauty and famous hostess. Her sons Julian and Billy Grenfell were killed in battle in 1915; her youngest son Ivo died in a car accident in 1926.

1917

January 1, 1917

I was miserable to leave Panshanger this morning and felt strongly the old feeling of going back to school. I lunched alone at the Junior Carlton having written Diana another letter of apology. She telephoned to me to go to her before dinner. I found her meaning still to be angry with me but I won her round. She was looking tired but very lovely. In her presence I wondered about Rosemary and knew not what I thought. A great deal of discount must be allowed for novelty. She questioned me closely and suspiciously about Panshanger. I admitted that I had been attracted by Rosemary but denied absolutely that I was the least in love with her.

Lord Morley is reported to have said of Lloyd George 'For veracity, Ananias, for friendship, Brutus, for his other qualities I refer you to Signor Marconi'.

January 3, 1917

Dined at Mulberry Walk with Diana, Viola and Alan. I am not in love with Diana and I am tired of Viola and Alan. This is a terrible thing and is probably only a phase but there it is. Alan has been ill and has a swollen gland and looks so ugly and dirty. Viola ditto except for the illness and the gland. They rather revolted me and their house was looking squalid. We had a beastly dinner except for the champagne which I provided and enjoyed, not having tasted it for a week as we had none at Panshanger.

January 4, 1917

We have had at the Foreign Office such thrilling telegrams about the murder of Rasputin.[1] It appears to have been done by Felix Elston[2] whom I used to know intimately at Oxford. It took place at a supper party in his palace. The telegrams read like pages from Italian renaissance history.

January 5, 1917

I wrote to Rosemary after dinner, congratulating her on having been mentioned by Sir D. Haig[3] for 'devotion to duty'. I met Diana at 10 [p.m.] and we went together to a cinema, then for a drive to Victoria Road then back to Arlington Street where I read to her *Tristram Shandy* until Katharine who was

---

[1] Grigori Rasputin (1872–1916), the 'Mad Monk', who had considerable influence over Tsar Nicholas II and his wife Alexandra. He was assassinated by a group of Russian noblemen on 31 Dec. 1916 in an attempt to rid the court of his influence.

[2] Prince Felix Yousoupoff (1887–1967), the murderer of Rasputin, was known as Count Felix Elston when studying at Oxford.

[3] Field Marshal Sir Douglas Haig, later Earl Haig (1861–1928), had succeeded Field Marshal French as CIC of the British Expeditionary Force. Duff was later to write Haig's biography.

staying there the night came in. Diana accused me this evening of not loving her so much lately. She notices the slightest shades of feeling.

January 8, 1917

I lunched at the Garrick with Hugh Walpole[1] and Eddie Marsh. The former an old friend whom I never see. I had to conceal from him all through lunch that I hadn't read his last novel *The Dark Forest*. I like the Garrick Club. After lunch I had to go to a conference at the Ministry of Munitions about Portuguese labour. I represented the Foreign Office. It was the first conference I have ever attended. I was very busy all the rest of the afternoon.

January 14, 1917. Sunday

In the afternoon I went and had a seance with a spiritualist – a medium, Mrs Fernie. I had never done such a thing before. I was most disappointed. She said as soon as she went into the trance that there was a spirit of a young man standing by me and after one wrong shot said his name was John. This was remarkable though it can be explained by telepathy. She told me nothing definite about his past life – everything vague. Then he was supposed to be speaking to me himself and everything he said and every word he used were so utterly unlike him that with the best will in the world I could not believe. Then she mentioned other names but they were all wrong except George but the description of him did not answer. I came away very sceptical of the whole business.

January 19, 1917

Diana went to Belvoir yesterday. This morning Patrick arrived on leave from Salonica. I was delighted to see him and lunched with him and Alan. I think he is determined to marry Diana and wonder if he will succeed. He is going to Panshanger for the weekend but insisted on going to Belvoir for the night although they were none too anxious to have him. John [Granby] is there and loathes him like poison. Diana knows what is in store for her. I got this telegram from her this afternoon 'Pray God with me for courage to face this great ordeal and to let me triumph – stand by me Monday night' sent I suppose before she knew he was going there today.

I dined at Claridge's with Monty,[2] Lionel Pilcher, Lady Rosslyn,[3] Bridget and Rosemary. I sat between the two last. I was wildly happy yesterday afternoon when Bridget telephoned to me about this and had been looking forward to it ever since but the result was complete failure. I couldn't speak

---

[1] Sir Hugh Walpole (1888–1941), successful novelist, man of letters, bibliophile and patron of the arts.

[2] Montagu Bertie, 8th Earl of Abingdon and 13th Earl of Lindsey (1887–1963). Capt. Grenadier Guards. He married Bettine Grant (née Stuart-Wortley), widow of Eddie Grant, in 1928.

[3] Vera 'Tommy' Rosslyn (d. 1975), married 5th Earl of Rosslyn (1869–1939) in 1908.

to Rosemary at all. I drank a good deal to try to get courage but it was of no use. I came home afterwards and put the crown on my ineptitude by writing her a silly letter and posting it, though I knew that had I slept on it I should not have done so. Damn.

January 23, 1917

This morning I was delighted to get a letter from Rosemary – rather abrupt, like her conversation, but satisfactory. Lunched at Bellomo's with Diana. She said she had kept Patrick well in control and was only 'in a state' owing to a series of rows with the Duchess who appears to receive anonymous letters informing her of every single thing Diana does. I dined at 7 Carlton House Terrace. To my surprise and delight Rosemary was there. I didn't do very well with her – but slightly better. She hadn't liked the letter I wrote her when drunk – and no wonder. What a fool I was. She is going back to France on Monday which is damnable. I persuaded her to dine on Friday.

January 26, 1917

Dined with Edward, Patrick, Diana Wyndham, Laura[1] and Rosemary at 5 Adelphi Terrace. Rosemary was looking lovelier than ever and I was less than ever able to do any good. The other two were also charming and it was a very pleasant dinner. Edward and I both got pretty drunk. We three went on afterwards to a dance. Edward wisely didn't go in. I did and I am told my drunkenness was apparently a terrible thing. I quarrelled terribly with Diana and made her utterly miserable – fool and brute that I am.

January 27, 1917

Dined at the Café Royal in a private room with Burns, William Rawle and a man called Mundy – a professional bridge player. Afterwards we came back here and sat down to serious bridge. Mundy lost every rubber and was £113 down at 12 o'clock. I lost and won alternately and was then £9 up. Patrick and Edward arrived. We then played very high poker. Mundy won consistently – Edward and Patrick both lost about a hundred and I lost a bit – I'm not sure how much. At about 3 o'clock Patrick stopped and then I regret to say at my own suggestion we started chemin de fer. Edward got quits on this – I played wildly and ended by losing £170.

January 28, 1917

Went to see Diana before lunch. Edward was there. I find she has taken Friday evening more seriously even than I thought. She is not going to quarrel with me

---

[1] Diana Lister, daughter of Lord Ribblesdale, married Percy Wyndham in 1913; he was killed in 1914. She then married Arthur 'Boy' Capel, who died in a car accident in 1919 and finally in 1923, the 14th Earl of Westmorland. Her sister, Laura Lovat, married Maj.-Gen. Simon Fraser, 14th Lord Lovat (1871–1933), in 1910.

but her line is that it is final, that our relationship can never be the same again. I have broken my promise too. [*Duff had promised not to gamble.*] She will be sweet and kind to me and we will be friends, but not lovers any more. This is terrible – all my love for her has come back and I could not bear to lose her.

February 10, 1917

Met Diana at 4.30 and went to a cinema. As we drove away Diana suddenly melted into my arms and let me kiss her. Never had she been so heavenly. All was forgiven. I was deliriously happy. I know now that she must love me and I love her more than ever before. I don't believe we shall quarrel again and I loathe myself for my temporary infidelity and vileness.

February 17, 1917

As we were dropping Diana in Arlington Street we met Ruby. [She] persuaded Diana and me to go to the Carlton where we went up to the sitting room of two Americans and played that silly card game with three cards. I think marmora is the right name. I like a fool and being rather drunk lost £180. I went on from there to the Curzon Hotel and played chemin de fer and lost another £200. It is perfectly hellish – I shall have to sell out some more capital. Damn.

February 22, 1917

My birthday. I lunched very happily with Diana at the Cheshire Cheese. I dined alone with Mother at her flat. She gave me £100 War Loan. She little knew bless her that I am just selling out £500 capital to pay gambling debts.

February 27, 1917

Holbrook, my servant, left me today – to join the army – a mortal blow at my comfort. However Mother managed to procure me another.

March 13, 1917

In the afternoon we heard that there is revolution in Russia. Real revolution on a large scale and the army has gone over. If it is successful and does not lead to civil war it may be the best thing that could happen. The country was in a hopeless state.

March 14, 1917

The revolution seems to be doing well. The revolutionaries seem to have the game in their hands, they have caught most of the members of the Govt and possibly the Czar whom they propose to force to abdicate in favour of his son under the guardianship of the Grand Duke Michael[1] and with a representative coalition Government.

---

[1] Grand Duke Michael (1878–1918), younger brother of Tsar Nicholas II. Nominated Tsar 28 March 1917, renounced it the next day. Murdered at Perm.

March 15, 1917

Heard before leaving the Foreign Office that the Czar had abdicated.

March 24, 1917

I was hardly dressed in time to be picked up by Diana to dine with the Montagus. Eventually we drove home. They dropped me at 88 St James St. and went on. I followed, caught a taxi opposite White's, found Diana waiting at the door in Arlington St. and off we went. A drive to dream of – utterly divine. We went east in the hope of fun in Limehouse – Chinamen, opium etc. We found nothing. Long after Limehouse we got out at a coffee stall, Diana putting on my overcoat and twining my scarf round her head. We ate sausages and drank coffee, and felt like Antony and Cleopatra. A wonderful drive back, first passionate then peaceful.

March 25, 1917

Diana and I finished up at Queen Anne's Gate for lunch. Edwin was interesting after lunch, telling Alan and me how lonely Lloyd George is, how he feels having no party and no one to talk to, and full of the idea of a new, young Conservative party.

March 29, 1917

Lunched with Diana at Scott's. She was looking quite lovely, maddeningly so, today but rather tired and worn, very unlike a *jeune fille*. I then went on to Patrick's flat. Alan and Marjorie Trefusis were there and Diana came. I drove Diana home and then discovered that I had left this book behind so I returned to get it. I then had to drive Marjorie home and had just dropped her at the House of Lords when I discovered or thought I discovered that this book was missing. I felt sure she had taken it and would read it. I dashed back, got past the policemen muttering something about her having dropped a brooch to which they replied that if l wanted to get in I could do so by the back door which always remained open. I got in and ran up the back stairs until I was quite lost. Then I saw through a glass door Marjorie turning off the lights. I went through and caught her in the dark, frightening her terribly. She wouldn't believe the story of the diary, thinking that it was she herself that I had come for and eventually gave me the slip. I was quite alone in the dark house and utterly lost. I ran up and down stairs, terrified lest I should suddenly be set upon as a burglar and laughing at the odd locality for such an adventure. I couldn't find the back door again so at last went boldly out at the front. I found this book at the back of the taxi after all. I hear that at breakfast the next morning Lady Margaret Graham [Marjorie's mother] said that she had heard a terrible noise last night and that in future no one was to be allowed out of the house after ten. The same day I saw in the evening paper that it had been decided that the house hitherto occupied by the Clerk of the Parliaments was to be residence of the Lord Chancellor. I fear it may never witness such strange scenes again.

March 31, 1917

Diana was rather cross with me when I told her I had settled to dine with Goonie on Wednesday as I had promised to dine with her and Patrick that night. I drove her to the station. She was going to stay at Blenheim for the weekend and as Wimborne was going had armed herself with a revolver.

April 3, 1917

Complete reconciliation with Diana after our shadow of a quarrel last night. We lunched together at Pagani's – as happy as possible. She told me all about Blenheim. Wimborne did come to her room on Sunday night and she pointed the revolver which scared him. He said he had only come to talk to her which was all he attempted to do.

April 12, 1917 [Duff and Diana are staying in a house party in Scotland]

We spent the morning in Diana's room reading *The Egoist* [Meredith]. It was delightful – while Patrick and I enjoyed the contemplation of Diana – but he watched both our faces all the time. He had a cryptic telegram this morning to say his orders had arrived and he will probably have to go back to London tomorrow and to France on Monday. I am so sorry. I am very fond of him. I do hope that his luck will not desert him. His death now would matter to me more than anyone's and would be a terrible blow to our small diminished society.

April 14, 1917

Diana and Venetia went into Inverness to see the others off. Hot water is so hard to come by here that I was obliged yesterday and today to have a hip-bath which I had in front of Diana's fire as there is none in my room. Her diary was there and I took it away and read every word of it – it opens to my key. It was rather vile of me but I don't think she would mind so long as she didn't know or know that I knew she knew. There was really very little in it that was new to me. A few things she had kept from me with regard to her relations with Wimborne and a different account of the scene at Blenheim. The evening she telephoned to me at Olga's party she had telephoned first to Wimborne and had had a scene with him in the gateway – but she adds to her account of it that she had not dared tell me because she was ashamed. I never realized how much she loved Raymond. How right she was and how fatuous of me never to have guessed it. There is no reference to me in the diary that I could quarrel with but I do not think she loves me. We are, funnily enough, profoundly different. Without loving me she likes me more than I could like anyone. The most remarkable, or one of the most remarkable things about her is the strength of her 'likes'. I am cold hearted except where I love – her friendships are more passionate than others' loves. I rose from the perusal of this intimate diary which I had no right to read, loving, liking and admiring her more than before.

Dinner went off well enough. On my way upstairs I went into Diana's room. She was looking beautiful, asleep. I went and undressed and then returned to her. She was not angry with me as I feared but allowed me to lie with her for about an hour in quiet talk and love. More she would not allow but promised for tomorrow.

April 16, 1917

Snowing hard most of the day. Scatters[1] went out fishing and we had a peaceful day at home reading *The Egoist* and a lot of poetry. After dinner Venetia and Scatters went upstairs to see relations of Venetia's who are staying here. I sat very happily with Diana telling her how much I loved her and even reading her some pages of this book. Diana said to me aside that I must not come to her room till late, 3 o'clock, as she thought Scatters meant to try to come and she was going to lock the door and would open it when I knocked. I asked Scatters whether he would play piquet as we have done every other evening but he said not tonight. After I had undressed I looked out into the passage and found it all dark. I stole down to Diana's room and listened outside the door. I heard whispering voices and sounds of the bed shaking. I listened in agony – such emotion as I have seldom known. At last I heard Diana say in her slightly mocking voice 'Good night, duckie' – I had been there perhaps ten minutes. I went back to my room and saw Scatters leave. He was fully dressed. I lay down and wondered what I should do – perplexed in the extreme. At last having made up my mind to do nothing but anxious to see what Diana would say to me, I went to her. She was asleep already. When she woke she said at once that Scatters had been, that he had sat by the fire for a little telling her his love and that finally she had a short tussle with him but not a serious one. He had come, she said, before she was undressed or had had time to lock her door. What I had heard had not sounded like a tussle but there was nothing she said I could disprove. I told her I had been listening at the door all the time and a scene followed. She cried and reproached me bitterly with not trusting and spying on her. I felt in the wrong and implored forgiveness which only after long pleading she granted. Then we had a night of the most wild and perfect joy. The best perhaps we have ever had.

April 17, 1917

We left Beauly after lunch and went on to London by the 3.30. At Perth we had dinner. Afterwards I sat with Diana in one berth for half an hour. I told Diana that I loved her too much and that it made me unhappy which indeed

---

[1] Lt.-Col. Sir Mathew Wilson, 4th Bt. (1875–1958), generally known as 'Scatters'. He retired from the Army in 1912 but returned to serve in Egypt and win the DSO. Unionist MP 1914–22.

it does. I suffer hells of jealousy. I cannot bear to think of her being touched by men like Scatters and Wimborne or indeed by anyone. She asked me if it did not make me happier to be assured that she loved me far the best which indeed was true. Perhaps she does but I am sure it is happier not to love her too much. She was very sweet to me.

April 25, 1917

Dined at Queen Anne's Gate. Diana wouldn't pick me up as she was driving there with Scatters. Angry at this I wouldn't even look at her when she arrived or catch her eye all through dinner. Alan and Edwin and Scatters went down to the House. They returned later with F. E. Smith. I had one rubber with him, Mr Asquith and Lady Goonie and the party melted away. Diana and I remained. Diana was looking very beautiful but she was in a rather excited and unnatural state. I asked her to come home but she refused and I saw that she meant to wait for Scatters. I walked home in a black rage not only of jealousy and anger but also of sorrow that she should sink to such depths as Scatters and should *afficher* herself to him under the eyes of men of the stamp of F.E. I could not sleep for thinking of it and had a miserable night.

April 26, 1917

Early in the morning she telephoned. Although I had been thinking of it all night I hadn't decided on what line to take. At first I was cold and uncompromising, but later I gave way. She said she felt in the wrong, that she had behaved badly, that she was sorry, that she had been made angry by Goonie looking so beautiful and by fear that I loved her. I told her all I have written above and said that I thought she must be deteriorating if she could tolerate old, common, coarse men like Scatters, Wimborne and F.E. This reduced her to tears. I went to see her before going to the Foreign Office. She was looking lovely and I caressed and comforted her. I lunched with Lady Goonie at the Berkeley. We had a delightful lunch. I am certainly very near to being in love with her. She is so charming and so unexpected. At 7 I went to McEvoy's[1] studio to pick up Diana. I found Diana still depressed. My accusation of deterioration rankles. We drove for a little together before dinner. She was on the point of tears. I felt so sorry but I felt too that I was beginning one of my little periodical infidelities. I loved her less. I don't think it will last but there it is.

April 28, 1917

Dined with Diana at the Rendezvous. We had an excellent dinner and I drank a great quantity of champagne. Afterwards I wanted her to come back here and bribed her with the promise that she should read my diary. She came and

---

[1] Ambrose McEvoy (1878–1927), fashionable portrait painter. He painted several portraits of Diana.

I read her all the last month. I was drunk and had forgotten, when I started, the incident of reading hers. I had to go through with it. She took it well and assured me that she didn't mind. I regretted bitterly having done it.

April 29, 1917. Sunday

She came round this morning before I was up in order to assure me again that it all made no difference. I can hardly believe her. It was damned stupid. 'I loved her less' was what she minded most.

May 17, 1917

The government want more men for the army and we in the Foreign Office are all to be medically examined and I think they will have to let some of us go. If anyone is allowed to go I shall be as I am the youngest of the permanent staff, unmarried and I should think perfectly fit. The thought fills me with exhilaration. I don't own to it as people would believe it was bluff and I dare say too that I shall very soon heartily wish myself back. But I am eager for change. I always wished to go to the war though less now than I did at first. I envy the experience and adventure that everyone else has had. I am not afraid of death though I love life and should hate to lose it. I don't think I should make a good officer. The only drawback is the terrible blow it would be to Mother. I don't know how I should dare to tell her. I think Diana too would mind.

May 19, 1917

Was medically examined for the army and passed A. Went down to Sutton with Diana by the 5.15. I had two pretty moments with Diana in the garden. She told me I must not come to her room as it was next to Lady Horner's but said that she would come to mine and I gave her my watch so that she should know the time. I had the top attic room which on my first visit three years ago I shared with John [Manners]. I woke at four. It was already getting light so in spite of instructions I crept to Diana's room, a long and creaky journey. It was very beautiful when I arrived and we lay together until it was quite light and all the birds were singing, including a very monotonous and damnable cuckoo.

Tonight [May 20] the same took place as last night. Diana said she would come to me but at half past three I gave up hope and went to her. It was perhaps the loveliest of all nights. We lay quietly for a long time and talked. I confessed to her that I was really glad to join the army which made her cry – she was so white and darling and pathetic. I explained to her that it was no nonsense about dying for my country or beating the Germans that made me glad to join, but simply the feeling I have had for so long that I am missing something, the vague regret that one feels when not invited to a ball even though it be a ball that one hardly would have hoped to enjoy.

May 21, 1917

Felt terribly tired this morning having hardly slept at all. To support me I ate a large breakfast which I never do as a rule. After lunch I went to see Ralph Cavendish at Wellington Barracks. He is Regimental Adjutant of the Grenadiers. I don't know him very well and felt shy. Told him that I wanted to join the regiment if released from the Foreign Office. He was very nice and took me in to see Streatfeild,[1] the Colonel. He also was most charming, said he would put down my name and consider my request. After I had left Ralph came after me and said I might consider it as practically settled.

May 31, 1917

In the afternoon Mother telephoned. She has found out about my prospects of joining the army. She is naturally much upset – it is most awkward.

June 18, 1917

Today I heard to my delight that I am to be allowed to join the army.

June 22, 1917

Today I left the Foreign Office without a single regret. I went there in the morning but did not return after lunch. I love to think of the dreary files of papers that I shall not see again. Even if I survive the war I doubt whether I shall go back to the Foreign Office. I should hate to face that monotonous routine again.

June 25, 1917

Diana came for me before dinner looking lovely. We dined at Queen Anne's Gate. Dinner was pleasant and after the ladies had left I had a delightful conversation with Birrell. He talked about Browning and Tennyson both of whom of course he knew intimately. He said that Tennyson had once abused Swinburne to him for writing indecently. Tennyson's point was that it was so easy to do and to prove it he thereupon poured forth a torrent of the foulest and most excellent verse. He said that Tennyson had no objection to bawdy but hated blasphemy whereas Jowett delighted in blasphemy but loathed bawdy so that one wondered what they talked about when they were together. Browning to meet was a mixture between a diplomat and a banker. His manner was almost too effusive. He never invited anyone to break bread in his house. While Birrell was telling me all this Smuts[2] was holding forth about the war but I preferred to listen to Birrell.

---

[1] Col. Sir Henry Streatfeild (1866–1950), Col. commanding Grenadier Guards 1914–19.

[2] Field Marshal Jan Christian Smuts (1870–1950), South African statesman. In 1916, with the rank of Lt.-Gen., he took command of all imperial troops in South Africa and joined the British War Cabinet in 1917. From 1919–29 he was Prime Minister of South Africa. In 1941 he became a British Field Marshal. He had a long and close friendship with Winston Churchill.

July 5, 1917

After lunching with Lady Essex I hired a motor and came down to Bushey arriving soon after four. The first person I saw was Peter Adderley[1] who has been here a month and who gave me a pretty gloomy account. The men here are not only men who are applying for commissions in the Guards as I thought but for all regiments – and a great many, indeed the majority of them, have risen from the ranks. I was first taken into a large room with about 80 others where we had to fill up papers about ourselves. I was then shown my sleeping quarters at which my heart sank. A room with 11 beds in it. Plain iron bedsteads – a mattress in three parts piled on top of one another – and four blankets on the top of that – a wooden box at the foot of each bed, a plain wooden floor and not another stick of furniture in the room. Tea followed, reminding me of my private school and how miserable I was there. Then our kit was distributed – a common private's uniform with terrible boots – our cadet's uniform has to be made. With some difficulty I found a man willing to black my boots and brighten my buttons for me. Dinner only increased my depression. Then we had an informal lecture from the Captain, who seemed a good fellow called Clutterbuck, and then bed. There were others in the room with me – nearly all men risen from the ranks. They smoke sickening cigarettes and some of them slept in their shirts. I had a bed in the bay of the window with my head almost out of it which I was glad of. It was a warm night and a bright moon.

July 6, 1917

The washing arrangements here are not bad once one has reached them which entails a long walk down stone passages. I had a very hot bath this morning followed by a cold plunge in a small swimming bath. Then breakfast consisting of porridge which I always like and horrible looking cold ham which I didn't touch. Then parades and drills, filling up papers and drawing pay.

This morning I had a telegram from Diana saying 'Be brave darling, already I feel derelict'. I had indeed need of her exhortation. Never have I felt so miserable as this morning. I had not yet appreciated the good points of my companions mentioned above. They seemed to me just common and inhuman and it seemed unthinkable that I should have to share a room with them for four months. There were really moments when I could have cried. The strangeness, roughness and degradation of it all appalled me. I wrote to Diana and told her how unhappy I was. The worst of all was to think that these lovely summer months which I ought to be spending with her are being wasted.

---

[1] Capt. Peter Broughton Adderley, MC (1891–1918), Scots Guards.

July 7, 1917

This morning we had 'Breakfast Roll Call' at seven. I had arranged the night before to have a motor here at 12.30. I said I was going to motor straight to Tadworth as the one thing they object to here is one's going to or even passing through London. Once in the car however and within three quarters of an hour from St James's Street I could not resist the temptation. My delight to find myself once more in London was quite childish and I honestly felt as though I have been away for years. That I was here the day before yesterday seemed utterly incredible. I went to my flat, changed my shameful uniform for comfortable clothes, telephoned to Diana who had alas left for Rowsley[1] and caught the 3.12 from Charing Cross for Tadworth. I felt as happy all the time as an escaped prisoner.

July 8, 1917

I arrived in London at about 5 and went to my flat which seemed very desolate with everything put away. It was still raining hard. I telephoned to everyone I knew but not a soul was in London. Then a great cloud of depression came upon me and I felt even more miserable than I had been at Bushey and without hope. I went to the Junior Carlton, drank a pint of champagne and some sherry with a small dinner and read *Through the Looking Glass*. As if by enchantment my melancholy left me and I knew that I should not be unhappy again. Courage came back to me which I had lost, and I despised myself for having done so. I went back to my flat, changed into my uniform, spoke to the Montagus who had just returned and motored down to Bushey feeling perfectly happy.

July 9, 1917

I slept badly last night as the beds are really intolerable but I was and remain happy. I have already had three letters from Diana, almost in the form of a diary like Swift's to Stella, telling me all she has done since I left, and all full of love, wit and strangely enough wisdom, most beautiful documents which even at this distance increase my adoration of her.

July 12, 1917

This was really my first normal day here and as the others will probably be similar I will describe it. I got up at a quarter to six, before reveille and before anyone else in my room. Had a cold plunge, washed, shaved and dressed. Breakfast roll call parade at five minutes to seven. Then breakfast and time after it to enjoy a swift cigar and a glance at *The Times*. Parade at 8.30 – physical training which is very exhausting. Then a lecture, then more drill and musketry instruction. Lunch at 12.30. It amuses me at about 11 o'clock

---

[1] Stanton Woodhouse, Rowsley, a house in Derbyshire which the Rutlands took for the summer.

when the day seems half over to remember myself a little while ago sauntering down to the Foreign Office at this hour to begin my work – but it saddens me in the evening at about 8.30 when my beastly dinner is finished and there is nothing more to do, to think how at this hour in London I should be setting forth upon an evening's pleasure.

To go on with my day – lunch at 12.30, a cup of coffee in the canteen afterwards to take away the taste of lunch. Then at 1.45 the most exhausting and unpleasant parade of the day under the broiling sun – company drill. Then lectures taking one till tea time at about five. The relation between cadets and officers when out of uniform is supposed to be perfectly *sans gêne* and equal but is of course really rather strained. Just time after tennis to write to Diana before the post goes and to have a hot bath before dinner. The evenings are the times I feel depressed and long for good food and wine and pleasure and beautiful women. From nine to ten we are supposed to read our military text books. At ten to bed and lights out at 10.30. This evening at eleven just as we were getting to sleep, there was a practice fire alarm and down we all had to dash on to parade. After this day I slept perfectly in my rough blankets and was only awakened by the reveille.

July 15, 1917 [London]

Oh the joy of waking in soft sheets and turning over to sleep again. At 9.30 I was called with tea and toast, at 10 a man came to cut my hair and shave me after which I returned to bed and book. These details, once the regular routine of my life, now seem rich luxuries and noteworthy. I got up slowly and had finished by half past 12 very soon after which Diana came to me, fresh and lovely as the morning which just before her arrival had been freshened and cleaned by a short, sharp storm with thunder. We walked to the Piccadilly Hotel where we lunched. We could not have chosen better. The ostentatious luxury of the place was exactly what my mood craved. We were early and so had the full attention of a galaxy of waiters. Hors d'oeuvre followed by exceptionally cool and delicious langouste, cotelette de veau viennoise, a pêche melba and a petit suisse, all accompanied by a sparkling Moselle. We dined at Bellomo's or at least I did and she sat with me. It was a good end to a perfect day – one of the most perfect in my memory.

August 10, 1917

Today there were some forty new arrivals which necessitated a shuffling of rooms and I, to my great satisfaction, was moved from the one I have been in hitherto and of the other occupants of which I was heartily sick. There are only three others in my present room – Brassey[1] who is an attractive boy, of whom I am quite fond and who is fond of me. He is fresh from Eton and

---

[1] Gerald Charles Brassey (1898–1918), Lt. in the Grenadier Guards. Killed in action in France on 27 August 1918.

fresh in every way, clever in a way and open minded but quite without any intellectual interests. Archibald Browne – a man of 36 – a partner in a bank, well off, kind and comfortable, quite amusing with an enormous repertoire of indecent stories. He is a good fellow and cheery, always ready to stand or be stood a drink. He has taken a house in the neighbourhood where his wife lives. I get on very well with him and he amuses me. Boyle – a tiresome boy. He has been at Marlborough and then for two terms at Balliol of which he is inordinately proud and can talk of nothing else. We snub him and try to keep him in his place. It is a great relief to have got away from the other lot with whom it was really quite impossible to bridge the gulf. It is so much pleasanter to sleep with people who wash regularly and speak English.

August 18, 1917

Today at 12.30 I left Bushey in a taxi rejoicing. I arrived in London, met Diana by chance in St James's Street and went straight to the Savoy. I had an excellent lunch, in the middle of which Sybil came in with Augustus John;[1] they both looked dirty, drunken and decadent beyond words. I was ashamed of her. After lunch Alan and I went to Katharine's house where we were joined by Diana. She and I went on to a cinema and then to have ices first at Gunter's in Berkeley Square and then at Gunter's in Bond Street. I went home with her for a minute and saw the Duchess and then went to the Berkeley where Sybil is staying under the auspices of Sidney [Herbert] who is home on leave. I found her there in a sitting room with John and an atmosphere of smoke and brandy quite sickening. John who was looking very drunk went soon. Diana called for me at St James's Street looking most beautiful. It was a great joy to be there with her once more. Sidney and I had ordered dinner and I never tasted a better. Smoked salmon and caviare, lobster thermidor, grouse à la crème; and plenty of Perrier Jouet 1907. I enjoyed every mouthful of it. We went back to the Berkeley for a few minutes afterwards and then a terribly short but very happy drive with Diana. I never loved her more. I was in bed by 12 feeling utterly replete and happy and I slept soundly in my own soft bed until nearly 10.

September 3, 1917

A typical day of my life here as I now live it. Up at ten minutes to six. Shave, wash and cold shower – I have given up the plunge as the water in it is none too clean and the shower is more refreshing. Breakfast. Drill. Bayonet fighting and lectures till lunch. Lunch lasts 10 minutes after which Brassey and I run to the Golf Club for bread and cheese, coffee and liqueurs. More drill and lectures from 1.45 to 4.30, then a hot bath after which Brassey and I having changed come up to the Golf Club and have a good tea with hot buttered toast. Then I write and read for half an hour or so. Before dinner a small company

---

[1] Augustus John (1878–1961), painter.

of some six or seven of us collect and stand each other drinks. We have to go off to dinner at 8 and normally assemble again between quarter and twenty past when we remain until five minutes to nine, at which hour we have to rush back for the farce of private study, which in my case consists of lying on my bed for half an hour before getting into it.

September 16, 1917 [Staying with Lady Essex at Cassiobury]

I had a charming suite of rooms to myself, bedroom, sitting room and bathroom and enjoyed the comfort of it. I spent Sunday morning writing letters and was overcome by a feeling of depression, due to various causes – the sunless autumn morning, the tragedy of the beautiful house which has belonged to the Essexes for three hundred years and in which they now can't afford to live and only hope to sell, the prospect of six more long weeks at Bushey, and worst of all the immediate prospect of a week in camp. However, after a good lunch I revived considerably. After tea [Lady Essex] took me down to the cellars to choose my own champagne for dinner. We both deplored that the children[1] who couldn't appreciate it had to be given the same but there was no alternative. I chose Pommery 1900 of which there were only two bottles – a royal drink. Afterwards I regretted that I had allowed any of it to be wasted on uncultivated palates.

September 17, 1917

We paraded at 8 in full marching order – packs, water bottles etc. and marched off to Gorhambury to camp. It was a long march but except for a sore heel I was none the worse for it. We got there at about 12 o'clock and began by pitching our tents. We slept 8 in a tent. We managed to get a tent of quite nice fellows. We hadn't much to do all the afternoon but drank a good deal. The food given out to us was filthy. Most of the time was spent in the canteen, a long marquee, lit by two or three oil lamps with no furniture except the bar at one end. The scene inside was rather wild and picturesque – groups of men sprawling about the floor, some playing cards by the light of a candle stuck on a bayonet. I slept well on a waterproof sheet with three blankets on top of me. It started raining in the night and was still raining when we got up in the morning. Getting up was a dismal business with no possibility of getting hot water and no room to move. However it cleared up later and we spent the morning shooting on the range. After lunch we had a hard afternoon's drill from which I returned feeling utterly wretched but was revived by finding two letters from Diana. I stole off with them to the old ruin of the house where Francis Bacon lived and there enjoyed them. Before dinner a few of us as a great favour were allowed to go into Lord Verulam's house hard by and have a bath. This proved no pleasure as there were only two baths among twenty so that it was all most uncomfortable and one had to put on the same dirty

---

[1] A group of slightly younger people who were staying at the house.

clothes afterwards. When we came back it was dark and had begun to rain again. I stumbled to the canteen, drank a lot of whiskey, ate some cake and went to bed at about nine. It rained all night and the water began to come through the tent. One of the marquees was blown down, as also was the canteen.

October 30, 1917

The examination. I have no idea whether I did well or badly and am still anxious. At one moment I think that I must pass, at the next that I must fail.

November 1, 1917

I got up early feeling nervous and depressed. It was a cold misty morning. After breakfast we were told to parade in the ante-room at 8. We went trembling, prepared to hear our fate. But it was only Clutterbuck who talked to us about the examination. He said we hadn't done as well as he expected and warned us that a great many had failed. We were then dismissed till nine o'clock feeling far more depressed than before. At nine we assembled again and waited three sickening quarters of an hour before the Commandant arrived. At last he came and proceeded to read out very slowly and deliberately and in no order the names of those whom he would recommend for commissions. It was a slow and agonizing torture. Twenty-seven names were read out and then came mine. The relief and delight were unspeakable. There were fourteen failures – none of my friends amongst them. The rest of the day was spent in handing in our kit and equipment – a pleasant duty. Oh the relief that Bushey is over. If I wake up for a moment in the night I remember it and go to sleep smiling. I wonder how I could ever have borne it.

November 14, 1917 [Wellington Barracks]

My first day on the square. It wasn't as bad as I expected. It was only a half day being Wednesday and we got off at eleven. Edward [Horner] has suddenly been recalled to France. He had leave till Saturday but has to go back at once.

November 22, 1917

Today I was gazetted and so am at last a full blown Officer in the Grenadiers, which seems strange and improbable.

November 23, 1917

In the afternoon I went home with Sydney [Fairbairn] to Montagu Square where we played bridge. We had just finished two rubbers, and we had settled down to a game of skip when Sybil came in and said she wanted to speak to me for a minute. I left the room feeling rather annoyed at her mysterious ways. On the landing she said 'Edward has been killed and Diana is waiting for you outside'. I went down and found Diana standing by the area railings crying. We got into a taxi and drove away. I haven't cried so much since John was killed nor have I felt anything so deeply. After we had driven for some time we went back to her room in Arlington Street where we sat by the firelight talking a little and crying a lot. Edward meant so much in our lives. I loved no man better. His high courage and fine independence had so splendidly resisted the effects of the war that already he had begun to seem a glorious relic of the glorious past. By his death our little society loses one of the last assets that gave it distinction. And I think we have paid more than our share. To look back on our Venice party now, only four years ago, is to recall only the dead. The original four who motored out there together were Denny [Anson], Billy, George and Edward of whom not one remains. The most precious guests, in fact the only ones that I can remember while I was there were Raymond and Charles [Lister]. Both dead. Rottingdean, another high water mark of our happiness at Easter 1913 was practically the same except that we had Ego instead of Charles. Only Patrick and I remain. We can make no new friends worthy of the old ones. When one like Yvo Charteris appears promising he is immediately struck down. I had looked forward to years of happiness with Edward. He was the only companion with whom I was perfectly happy and whom I could always amuse. Patrick is more reliable in company and in every way but I never have such fun alone with Patrick as I had with Edward. I begin to feel that the dance is already over and that it is time to go.

I dined alone at the Junior Carlton. I drank the best champagne – Pommery 1906 – because I felt that Edward would have wished it and would have done so had I been killed the first. After dinner I wrote to Lady Horner and Katharine as well as I could. I was to have dined with Olga but had to throw her over. This I did from no silly kind of cant, nor because I thought it wrong to be gay that night, but simply because I was afraid that I might cry in the middle of dinner.

December 2, 1917

After 10 hours' sound sleep I woke refreshed to a very cold but very bright day. I travelled down to Taplow. At Taplow we found besides the Grenfell family most of the Horners – i.e. Francis, who has got the M.C., Lady Manners and the twins. There were also Miss Lutyens[1] and Rosemary. Lady Desborough was wonderful. Rosemary was looking most beautiful. I went for a short walk with her before tea. We talked about Edward and everything she said I agreed with. We talked about a future life and she said that more and more she was coming to believe in complete annihilation, which is also the case with me. Our rather gloomy hopeless views seemed to coincide with one another and

---

[1] Barbara 'Barbie' Lutyens (1898–1981), daughter of Sir Edwin Lutyens, married Capt. the Rt. Hon. (David) Euan Wallace (1892–1941) in 1920. He became Minister of Transport in 1939. After his death she married Herbert Agar, an American writer who won the Pulitzer Prize in 1935.

to match the evening which was very cold and bleak, harshly illuminated by an angry red sunset which we saw through the leafless branches of the avenue we were walking in. If I could love anybody besides Diana I think it would be her.

December 6, 1917

Succeeded in getting leave to go away from Friday to Sunday. Dined with Norah Lindsay in a house she had taken in Upper Berkeley Street. Eventually Bertie Stopford drove me home. He is a notorious bugger and was very attentive to me, saying I looked younger than when he last saw me which was in Venice before the war. He has been in Russia for some time and talked to me about the murder of Rasputin. After Rasputin was dead, Felix Elston fell on the body and beat it. Felix told Stopford this himself. He suspects that there had been some relationship between Felix and Rasputin. The great charm of the latter for women was that when he had them he never came and so could go on forever. Also he had three large warts on his cock.

I have forgotten to mention that at five o'clock this morning there was an air raid. I was woken by the booming of the guns. I got up and looked out of the window. It was a very bright moonlight morning. It was strange to see the so familiar streets, Pall Mall and St James's utterly deserted – no sign of life at all – and to hear the occasional explosion of a bomb, the continual thudding of the guns, and the moan of shells which seemed to whiz over one's head. It was difficult to realize that this was war going on in London. It was very cold so I soon got back to bed and the guns were still firing when I fell asleep again. This was the first air raid I have been in. Hitherto I have always just missed them.

December 12, 1917

After lunch I went to 33 Eccleston Square, where I found Goonie and Winston. His drawing room which is a library is a most charming room. He went soon but Goonie and I stayed there talking for some time. She told me what she had just heard from Winston, that there are rows going on in the Cabinet. America will be useless until the spring of 1919. Meanwhile it is imperative for us to comb out more men but Lloyd George won't do it. He daren't face the House or the country. I gathered that Winston thought that Lloyd George would have to go.

December 26, 1917

Spent the afternoon and evening with Diana. She said she would certainly marry me if we had enough money. There seems alas little prospect of that ever being the case. She goes to Belvoir tomorrow. I shall miss her – I am happy only with her. I dined with a large party at Venetia's and lost £125 at chemin de fer.

December 29, 1917

Caught the 3.20 to Reading to stay at Calcot, a house taken by the Rosslyns. I went at Rosemary's invitation. We were only four, the others being Michael, Rosemary and Lady Rosslyn. We had a good dinner and a pleasant evening. Michael, Rosemary and I sat up till one playing Truth by firelight. I found myself falling in love with her again and feeling jealous of Michael who sat by her. A very comfortable night's sleep and a very comfortable breakfast in bed, contemplating a cold, wet, morning. Michael left after lunch and we three who remained went out for a walk accompanied by five dogs and a goat. After tea I had a long talk with Rosemary and told her I loved her. She said I mustn't – that she was very fond of me but could not be in love with me. I felt terribly false to Diana, to whom I write daily and who writes beautifully to me.

So ends 1917 – which has been I think the least happy year that I have lived. Funnily enough I am thinking of Rosemary now as I was this time last year although I have hardly thought of her at all in the interval. But I know that she will really never mean anything to me – and that the one thing which is important in my life and which becomes increasingly so is my love for Diana and hers for me.

1918

January 1, 1918

I get a letter from Diana every day and write to her. It is my chief occupation.

January 3, 1918

Had to get up at 5.45 to report at Breakfast Parade – a punishment for being a minute late on parade the other day. I dined at the Ritz in Lionel's[1] sitting room. It was a bachelor party. I arrived first, then Michael. We had to wait some time for William Rawle who was the fourth. He came at last and said 'I'm sorry I'm late. Patrick Shaw-Stewart has been killed.' I felt stunned. This is the last blow. Lionel, Michael and William were all sad but none of them could have felt what I did. I courted forgetfulness in champagne but didn't get much comfort.

January 4, 1918

The line running in my head all day has been – 'There is nothing left remarkable beneath the visiting moon'. I telegraphed the news to Diana. Michael came in the afternoon. We were going to Taplow but wondered whether to

---

[1] Lionel Tennyson, 3rd Baron Tennyson (1889–1951), close friend of Duff's who married Clare Bethel, née Tennant, in 1918.

and whether Lady Desborough would have heard the news. Audrey [Ark-wright] and Phyllis[1] came. Phyllis very white but quiet and sweet. I telephoned to Katharine. We decided to go. When we arrived we found that Lady Desborough was in her room, and had already heard. She adored Patrick and was perhaps the chief person in his life. I went to see her after tea. She was sitting by the fire, almost in the dark. She has been ill. She kissed me and I couldn't help crying a little. We sat and talked about Patrick till dinner. She is the most wonderful woman in the world and the bravest. She didn't come to dinner that evening. After dinner Rosemary made me read some chapters of *South Wind* [by Norman Douglas] aloud which rather shocked Lord Desborough.

January 6, 1918

John's [Manners] birthday. I felt more and more depressed as the day went on. I had enjoyed my visit and had felt happier in my misery than I thought possible. I had been like one with a bad wound in a hospital and I felt that I was leaving the hospital before the wound was healed. I was indeed treated like an invalid these days – given the best of everything, sat in the best places, everyone being very kind to me.

January 7, 1918

I met Diana at King's Cross in the evening and we dined together at the Rendezvous. She doesn't feel Patrick's death as I do. We had a passionate drive after dinner. She gives me her caresses as a nurse gives sweets to a child – most when I am most unhappy which is not really when I want them most.

January 8, 1918

I spent the morning in the West London Police Court, watching the trial of a private soldier in the Regiment. I love police courts. I dined at the Criterion with Venetia and had to return to barracks afterwards as I was supernumerary picket officer. I think at times that I am going to be ill. The extraordinary lethargy and lack of interest that I feel all the time may be due to some physical causes besides the cloud of sadness that darkens all my days. I have felt more keenly wretched but never more unutterably sad.

January 27, 1918. Sunday

I caught the 11 o'clock train to Taplow. I have never known such a beautiful day in January – not one cloud in the sky and the temperature of the Riviera. Lunch was particularly successful, Mr Balfour being most charming and Ettie whipping in the conversation with unflagging zest. Mr Balfour played tennis after lunch and better than any of us. With the evening came back my cloud

---

[1] Phyllis Boyd (1894–1943), a lifelong friend of Diana's, married Comte Henri de Janzé in 1922.

of depression heavier than ever. Dinner hardly dissipated it, nor did a long and comfortless journey to London.

January 28, 1918

At 8 o'clock this evening I set out to dine with Mother. I was still in St James's Street when I heard loud explosions. The taxi driver stopped, said it was an air raid and advised me to take cover. I persuaded or rather bribed him to go on and reached Portland Court in safety, passing droves of terror-stricken people bolting to the Tubes for safety. Dined well with Mother and Mione – came home at eleven altho' the all clear signals had not yet gone and went to bed and slept soundly until the all clear signals woke me at between one and two. At about the same time Diana telephoned to know if I was alive.

January 29, 1918

Lunched very happily with Diana at the Piccadilly and we went together to the Coliseum. We dined at Katharine's house. She herself was out and as we only arranged it at the last moment we took with us from the Ritz a delicious little dinner. We sat comfortably in front of the fire and I have seldom enjoyed a meal more. At about ten Katharine came in and almost at the same moment we heard the guns beginning. I was on air raid duty so had to go at once to barracks. Luckily I found a taxi at Marble Arch. I had to wait about a long time in barracks. At last the all clear signal came at about one thirty and I dashed back to Oxford Square just in time to catch Diana who was on the point of leaving. We had a most exquisite drive home. I adored literally the soles of her feet.

February 18, 1918

Back to Chelsea. After my holiday [*in Bournemouth with Diana and Viola Tree*] I face it better than I did before and have I think shaken off most of my depression. An air raid started at 9.30 and I being on duty had to go into barracks. We sat there till 12 when the all clear went. We were excused early parade the next morning. When I got home Diana, bless her, telephoned to know whether I had been killed.

February 27, 1918

I went to a small party in Teddie Gerard's[1] flat. It was most amusing – everybody there being slightly drunk but nobody too much, everybody also being rather amorous to one another quite promiscuously and nobody being jealous. Teddie and Hilda Moore[2] were the most devoted couple and there was a boy whom they seem to share. The Baroness [Catherine d'Erlanger] seemed the presiding genius, sitting bolt upright in her most *grande dame*

---

[1] Teddie Gerard (1892–1942), an Argentinian-born actress and singer.
[2] Hilda Moore (1886–1919), British-born character actress.

manner, smiling benignly on everybody's love-making, and holding and pressing anybody's hand who sat down within reach. Constance [Stewart Richardson] was there and seemed to be occupying herself with Charles de Noailles.[1] Ivor Novello[2] played the piano, Constance danced and Delysia[3] sang. I was slightly attracted by Delysia but Cochran who keeps her presently arrived with Seymour Hicks.[4] There was plenty of champagne and I quite enjoyed it.

March 1, 1918

I forgot to mention that on Wednesday Francis Scott, our Commanding Officer, sent for me. He said that he had heard that I was one of a set of officers who had been gambling very high – that I had lost a large sum of money and I had paid up like a gentleman of which he was glad – at the same time other people had lost and had not paid – at least Hugo hadn't. He warned me that gambling was against King's Regulations and generally gave me a short lecture on the subject. He was extremely nice about it all, could not have been nicer and said that he was only speaking privately but that it must cease. I said it should. Tony Mildmay[5] who is acting adjutant and who has often played with us and loves the game was sitting there all the time, looking as good as gold.

March 2, 1918

When I came back to my rooms this morning I found my horrible old brass bed had disappeared and a beautiful old 18th century wooden bed had taken its place. This was the work and the gift of Diana who presently appeared. Together we went out to lunch and had the happiest meal at Bellomo's.

March 22, 1918

Lunched with Goonie at the Café Royal. I had settled to meet Diana at 2.30 but I thought the arrangement was only vague and weakly allowed myself to linger with Goonie till past three. Then Diana had left Arlington Street and it was not till four that I found her at my flat. She was angry with me and justly so. It was the most beautiful afternoon imaginable – as warm as summer. She had thought that we would go somewhere away from London and in her vexation and disappointment she cried like a child. I was terribly touched and torn with remorse. However I comforted her at last and off we went in a taxi with a volume of Keats, first to buy cakes and preserved pears and then to the

---

[1] Vicomte Charles de Noailles (1891–1981) and his wife Marie-Laure (1902–70) were noted patrons of the avant-garde in literature, art and music in France in the 1920s and 30s.
[2] Ivor Novello (1893–1951), Welsh actor, composer, songwriter and dramatist.
[3] Alice Delysia (1889–1979), French actress and singer. One of C. B. Cochran's stars.
[4] Charles Blake (C. B.) Cochran (1872–1951), the famous impresario. Sir Seymour Hicks (1871–1949), actor-manager and early film star.
[5] Capt. Sir Anthony St. John Mildmay (1894–1947), M C, Grenadier Guards.

Serpentine. There we hired a boat and went for a row. I had never been in a boat on the Serpentine before in my life. It was all most lovely and the weather incredibly delightful. After we had gone a little way we let the boat drift and sitting side by side in the stern we read *Isabella* [Keats] verse by verse – a most memorable afternoon.

March 26, 1918

I begin a new volume of my diary – I wonder if I shall finish it. I am glad to have done with the last one. It was an ugly book and it recorded my four bad months at Bushey followed by the deaths of Edward and Patrick. I hope that this may be a luckier volume. It will probably deal with France. I began my first volume here at Norton Priory where I am now beginning the fourth.

March 28, 1918

This morning we finished the musketry course at Rainham. When we reported in the Orderly Room having done so, I half expected to be warned for France at once as a large number of officers are being sent out, including some who haven't been with the regiment as long as I have. However nothing was said and I managed to get leave over Easter.

April 6, 1918

Met Diana in the afternoon. She has bought two rabbits – she is going to breed them and can talk and think of nothing else. We went back to Arlington Street to look at them. On being put together they immediately fought which didn't seem to augur well for their progeny. We dined at Claridge's. Afterwards I went for a little drive with Diana. We were going round St James's Park and were ecstatically happy when we passed a body of men marching down the Mall. Diana saw that they were Grenadiers and were going to France. Immediately she burst into such a passion of tears and sobs as I have never heard from her. She cried that she could not bear me to go. I felt so sad and so proud. The moment was most beautiful and most dramatic. I had known there was a draft to parade at Chelsea at midnight but had forgotten it. Odd that we should meet them. When she left me she told me to read the sonnet beginning '*Thy bosom is endeared with all hearts*' before I went to sleep. I did so and saw her meaning.

April 9, 1918

Began a Lewis Gun Course. Dined at Queen Anne's Gate. Wimborne came in after dinner when he and Winston had a very heated discussion about the application of Home Rule to Ireland – Wimborne saying it was madness. Diana Wyndham came to see me in the afternoon and we sat in my flat from three till five talking and I making a little love to her, half serious half in fun. She was looking very attractive and I enjoyed it.

April 20, 1918

I had to attend Adjutant's memoranda at 8 this morning and went there trembling, afraid that I had done something wrong. I was however encouraged on arriving to see several other officers standing there. We were told that we were the next to go to France and that as draft leave was now forbidden we were going to be given a few days leave before being warned for draft. This suits me admirably.

I met Diana afterwards. Together we caught the 5.20 for Beaconsfield to stay at Wilton with Mrs Astor. We found staying there – Lady Cunard, Lord Ribblesdale, Sir Edwin Lutyens,[1] Vansittart,[2] Knoblock,[3] Wolkoff.[4] It was really one of the pleasantest Saturday to Monday parties I have been to. Everybody seemed in their right place. Everybody seemed rather to like everyone else. Conversation was general and unusually amusing. Lady Cunard was not so silly as usual nor so anxious to monopolize the talk. Ribblesdale was as delightful as ever and I found Lutyens most attractive and an addition to any party. Knoblock also was amusing. There was no bridge and it snowed or rained the whole of Sunday and yet the time did not hang heavy. The house was beautifully warm, the food and wine were faultless. On Sunday I played a game of chess with Lutyens and defeated him. On both nights I went to Diana's room and was there as happy as man can ever hope to be. If this was destined to be my last country visit it was very far from being the worst.

April 25, 1918

Spent most of the morning with Mother and we lunched together with Sibbie at the Café Royal. Afterwards I went to say goodbye to the Foreign Office. I found them having tea as usual in Gerry's room. The whole place and everyone in it seemed so unchanged and dreary that I was thankful to be there no more.

April 26, 1918

My servant came at 8.30 with the news that we were certainly not to go today. I had to go into barracks and see the Commanding Officer. I learnt that we should probably go tomorrow night. Came home and made my will leaving everything to Diana. I hope Mother won't mind. I lunched with Mother at her

---

[1] Sir Edwin Lutyens (1869–1944), architect who designed a series of romantic country houses. His most famous works include the Viceroy's House in New Delhi, the British Embassy in Washington, the Cenotaph in Whitehall and designs for Liverpool's RC Cathedral.

[2] Sir Robert Vansittart, later Baron Vansittart (1881–1957). Joint Head of the Contraband Department at the FO 1914–18; Private Secretary to the Secretary of State 1920–4, and Private Secretary first to Baldwin and then to Ramsay MacDonald 1928–9; Permanent Under-Secretary in the FO, 1930–7.

[3] Edward Knoblock (1874–1945), playwright (*Kismet*) and screenwriter (*Chu Chin Chow*).

[4] Count Gabriel Wolkoff [Volkov] was attached to the Russian Embassy in London.

flat. She was unduly distressed to learn that I might go on Saturday. We dined at Queen Anne's Gate, Venetia, Viola, Cardie[1] and Ivo [Grenfell]. Fred Cripps[2] came in after dinner and Hugo and Blueie. We had a very pleasant evening and I drank a good deal. There was an air raid warning in the middle but no raid followed – I played bridge and the others went down to the kitchen and cooked supper which they brought up to us later. I won £50 and ended the evening by driving with Diana. It was in every way a worthy last night in London. I was not in bed till five.

April 27, 1918

I met Mother. We lunched at the Berkeley and it was a trying meal. Poor darling Mother could hardly speak. She said she didn't want me to go and see her in the evening – this was in fact to be our last meeting. As we left the restaurant she said to me very quickly that she wouldn't come out of the cloakroom till I had gone. She was looking very white and was on the verge of breaking down and so she left me.

I then met Diana and we went to a play called *Nothing But the Truth* which made us laugh a good deal. We had a box and there were tears between the acts. Even I shed a few at one moment holding her in my arms and feeling her body shaken with sobs. But it was all beautiful. Then we went and bought strawberries and she got sugar and cream from Arlington Street and we took them to St James's Street and ate them. We read some Browning and kissed a lot and cried a little and parted to dress – she for dinner and I for travelling. She came back to pick me up as usual and drove me to Blueie's where we were dining. She was looking very lovely but fighting all the time with tears. At dinner we were – Blueie, Diana, myself, Hugo, Sybil (who came late because I had forgotten to ask her), Michael and Venetia. The atmosphere was a little strained at first but under the influence of wine it all went well enough, I thought. I found that I had left my coat behind – Sybil volunteered to go and get it in a taxi – she returned with the wrong one. Diana and I then went for it and this made me late so that our last drive together was marred by my worrying about the time. She dropped me at Chelsea. It was very dark on the square. The draft was already formed up. Teddie, the Adjutant, was there and only laughed at my being late. Monty Bertie who is in charge of the draft had arrived but was too drunk to march to Waterloo and so had gone away again and was coming on by taxi. Teddie thought that I should probably be in the same state but I explained to him that I wasn't. I took charge and marched off the men, leading them with the drums in front. The band played nearly all the way from Chelsea to Waterloo and I felt proud, romantic and exalted.

---

[1] Lionel 'Cardie' Montagu (1883–1948), Edwin Montagu's brother.
[2] Col. Frederick (Fred) Cripps (1885–1977), later 3rd Baron Parmoor. He became Col. of the Royal Bucks Hussars in 1917.

April 28, 1918

Arrived at Boulogne, we were told we were to go on at once to Etaples. Before leaving we had an excellent omelette, fried potatoes, good white bread and plenty of butter at the Officers' Club. A dreary journey to Etaples where we arrived after 8. A miserable march in rain and darkness to the camp. I felt for the first time a little depressed and could not but remember how at that time a week ago I was sitting down to dinner at Wilton by the side of Diana. After we had got rid of the men, Monty and I set out in search of food and drink but after a long and very tiring walk we returned hungry and thirsty having found that everything was shut as it was past 10. We shared a wretched tent with a sandy floor. However I made myself fairly comfortable in my sleeping bag and slept well.

May 6, 1918 [Guards Depot, Havre]

I had to attend a Court Martial today and was there from 10 till 5 – with an hour's interval for lunch. It was a dull case with a lot of French witnesses whose evidence had to be translated. Two letters from Diana this morning and two from Mother. I dined in camp and had an extraordinarily good dinner. I always drink a pint of champagne – but the champagne they have here – called Dry Royal – is not good. Played bridge after dinner.

May 18, 1918 [St Amand]

The same lovely weather. We had a lecture from the Adjutant after breakfast – and one from the Commanding Officer after lunch. I was picket officer. We had a dull dinner with no champagne. I came early to bed and finished reading *Barchester Towers*. My great grief is that I don't know when my letters will come. I can't bear to think of Diana writing every day and my receiving nothing. I expect it will be weeks before I get anything owing to all this muddle.

May 21, 1918. St Amand

We left after tea on horseback [*to go to the front line*]. It was a pleasant ride and a beautiful evening. We went a little further than where I had ridden the other day. Then we dismounted and walked on a few hundred yards to a bank where were Battalion Headquarters. We went down a very deep dugout and found Harry Lascelles[1] who is 2nd in Command of this Battalion. He was looking very spruce and clean and unwarlike. I felt quite ashamed to be dusty and sweaty and dressed in my camouflage uniform. We left [2nd Lt. Madox] Gunther here as he was going to No. 2 company but [2nd Lt.] Inglis-Jones and I went on with a guide – he to No. 2 company and I to No. 3. We walked over

---

[1] Capt. Viscount Henry Lascelles (1882–1947), succeeded as 6th Earl of Harewood in 1929. In 1922 he married HRH Princess Mary, the Princess Royal, only daughter of George V.

green fields while the sun set beautifully and except for many shell holes the country looked peaceful enough. At last I reached my destination and in a dugout I found [Lt. George] Godman my Company Commander. He is a quiet fellow but I got later to like him very much indeed. We immediately had dinner. I was rather agreeably surprised with the food – on this evening we had soup, hot fish – the genus of which I never discovered – they were rather larger than sardines and smaller than herrings – cold beef with potatoes, peas and pickles, prunes and 'shape' and cheese. I drank whiskey and soda and port. Immediately afterwards I had to go on to relieve Clifton Brown[1] who was in the front line slits waiting for dinner. He went back and left me there feeling astonished to find myself at last in charge of a portion of the front line with nothing between myself and the German army. I was there for about two hours and then I was relieved as the whole company was moving back into support.

Altogether I was a fortnight in the line – alternating between the front line, support, reserve and rest. And I didn't write in this book during that time and cannot now give an exact account of it. We had a good deal of excitement at night and were often severely shelled. I was glad to find that I was no more frightened than other people and I really think rather less so – especially, I must confess – after dinner. The weather was wonderful, we only had one really wet day.

On May 24 when we were back in rest my letters began to arrive and after that they came frequently in large instalments. Diana has not failed to write every single day since I left – all long and most delightful letters.

We were heavily shelled one day in rest and Inglis-Jones whose company was next to ours was wounded. It was not a severe wound and I couldn't help envying him his return to England. I went up to the front again. Later when we were in reserve we had an unpleasant moment when they started sending over gas shells in the early morning. I was asleep at the time and woke with a start and immediately smelt the gas. I had some difficulty in finding my gas mask which I had imprudently taken off to sleep. We had a sergeant killed that morning.

On the whole the line was not as bad as I expected – the dirt is the chief inconvenience and the difficulty of washing. I saw it of course under favourable circumstances and it was fine all the time.

June 11, 1918

I went over to dine with Peter Adderley. We had a very pleasant dinner although the food was not so good as what we have. They are a much happier family than we are, there is less ceremony and altogether a far pleasanter

---

[1] Maj. Douglas Clifton Brown, Viscount Ruffside (1879–1958). MP 1918–52; Speaker of the House of Commons Mar. 1943–Oct. 51.

atmosphere. Dudley Coats[1] turned up after dinner and we played that absurd game Marmora. I like a fool lost £220. I had a quite extraordinarily bad lunch. We got rather drunk towards the end of the evening. I am a fool – a fool.

June 14, 1918

I am getting very bored here. The life is monotonous – the company unentertaining. There is a possibility that I may soon get 3 days leave – 'Boulogne leave' – I should try to go and see Katharine and Rosemary at St Omer [*where they were working in a hospital*]. My one joy now is Diana's letters which continue to come regularly – 44 I have already had.

June 16, 1918. Sunday

After Church Parade we had to do revolver practice. A peaceful afternoon and a very good dinner as Pilcher [Lt.-Col. W. S. Pilcher] who commands the fourth battalion came to dinner. It consisted of caviare, soup, salmon mayonnaise (tinned), excellent beef with potatoes and peas, asparagus, a sweet, sardines on toast, strawberries and cream – not a bad menu for within a few miles of the front line. I sat next to Lascelles whom I found a pleasanter companion than anyone else in the mess. He is quite cultivated – we talked about wine, books, pedigrees and houses. He has bought Chesterfield House in London.

July 1, 1918

A peaceful morning with the company doing bayonet fighting and drill. We were bombed a lot by aeroplanes at night but I slept through most of it – although they blew up an ammunition dump quite close.

July 4, 1918

Three letters from Diana today and a long one from Alan. He tells me in precious words how much Diana loves me – how she thinks of me all the time and talks of me and how at her happiest moments her face saddens and she wishes I was there. All this is meat and drink to me. He urges me to marry her and will not admit impediments. Himself he married on £400 worth of debts. Spurred by this I wrote her a long letter urging marriage. I wonder what she will say. Played poker after dinner and lost 230 francs.

July 11, 1918

I had to act as Prisoner's Friend in a Court Martial this morning. The prisoner who was accused of conveying information in a letter in a green envelope had confessed his guilt to his Company Commander and the Commanding Officer. I took the line that he hadn't written the letter, objected successfully as to all evidence as regards his confession, didn't allow him to give evidence

---

[1] Muir Dudley Coats (1897–1927), served in the Scots Guards in WWI.

himself and got him acquitted. Nobody more surprised than the prisoner. After the war I shall go to the Bar.

July 17, 1918

Warned to go up the line the next day. Carroll Carstairs[1] discovered a place in the village where one can get champagne. He and I went there before dinner and had two bottles and returned after dinner and had two more. It was very pleasant, sitting in a garden, talking about poetry and women and getting drunk.

July 18, 1918

We left at 9.30 and reached our destination about 12. We relieved Peter Adderley whom we found in a very deep fly-pestered dugout with nothing to drink. Slept from 12.30 to 3 – though we were disturbed soon after one by two Scots Guards Officers coming in trembling with fright having had a few shells dropped rather close to them. We fortified them with whiskey.

July 19, 1918

Stood to from 3 to 4.30. I wandered about between the various posts. The company is very scattered. There was a good deal of shelling. The nearest dropped about 30 yards behind us where we had been 10 seconds before.

July 20, 1918

There was a lot of shelling all night and this morning the whole place smelt of gas and explosives and corpses. There are a lot of graves all round us which haven't been dug deep enough.

We left about midnight for the front line. I was glad to leave. I very nearly lost my way going up with my platoon. We relieved No. 2 company. We are holding a very extended line. We have each section in a separate post and four or five hundred yards between some of the posts. It takes nearly two hours and a half to walk round. I slept from 12.30 to 3 a.m.

July 21, 1918

Stand to 3 a.m. to 4.15 – then breakfast. I was then on duty from 5–8 and then went round the posts. There is one which when visiting by day one is in full sight of the enemy but they don't seem very pugnacious. It was a wet morning at first but cleared up and was very pleasant – the air smelling fresh and sweet after the rain. When I got back to Company H.Q. I found that two bottles of port had arrived for me – a very welcome and well timed arrival. I could only get a cup of water to wash and shave in – after doing which I sat and drank port and wrote letters and felt cheerful. There was intermittent shelling all the

---

[1] Lt. Carroll Carstairs, an American soldier serving with the Grenadier Guards, who became an art dealer in New York after the war. He wrote a book of war memoirs called *A Generation Missing*.

time. I was on duty again from 11 to 1 and should have done another hour after lunch but Gibbon took it for me. I was glad as I was very tired. Two letters from Diana arrived at luncheon. I went to bed afterwards and slept till nearly dinner. I was on duty all night until stand to and got very tired wandering round. To bed after breakfast at about 4.30 – on duty again from 8 to 11 – another lovely morning. Slept after lunch and came on duty again at 4.30. Felt rather ill at dinner and couldn't eat anything. We were relieved by No. 4 at 11 and got back to our new position in support by 11.30. Here we are in the finest dugout that I have yet seen. It is really spacious and comfortable. Didn't feel very well and couldn't sleep much.

July 23, 1918

Stood to till nearly five. I took a digging party up to the aerodrome at 9. We worked for an hour then the rain became so heavy we had to take shelter – and at 11 as the weather looked hopeless I brought them home. We are lucky not to be in the trenches today.

Three American officers came to be attached to us for 24 hours. They made us very crowded and as they brought no rations or drink with them our supplies ran rather short. They were not bad fellows – very interested in the war and eager for information. We each took charge of one of them. We were up half the night – one of the brightest moonlight nights I ever saw.

July 24, 1918

Stood to at dawn – slept till 8 – spent the morning up at the aerodrome. After dinner we went off back to reserve. We found our kits waiting for us – our sleeping bags laid out on stretchers. I never got into bed with greater pleasure and slept as though in heaven until 10 the next morning.

August 5, 1918

I am not sleeping in the dugout this time but by myself in a bank a few hundred yards in front. It is pleasanter – more airy – but there are a lot of rats.

August 8, 1918

Spent the day reading *The Corsican* – an interesting collection of Napoleon's writings arranged into an autobiography. It has stirred up in me a little more enthusiasm for my present profession which is a good thing.

I am going out on patrol tonight and feel elated and excited – and perhaps a little bit frightened – but I'm not sure. I should be very disappointed if I were told now that I was not to go.

It didn't after all prove very exciting. I went out with the Headquarters patrol men – none of whom I knew and I had to allow myself more or less to be guided by them. We went out to Observation Trench when I went on with two men to within about 40 yards of a German machine gun post. We came in about 3.

August 10, 1918

I had a good sleep all the morning and was on duty most of the afternoon. I went out on patrol at night with 2 sections. We wandered about a good deal and at one moment I had no idea where we were. But it was a starlight night and by marching north we found ourselves in our own lines sooner than we expected. We came in rather early as there was a raid to take place at 3.15. [Lt.] De Geijer was to raid the machine gun post in front of Observation Trench. When he got there he found neither gun nor Germans. They had all got out. I met him coming back.

August 11, 1918

This afternoon I crawled out to Observation Trench to get de Geijer's respirator which he had dropped there. I found it and crawled into the Sunken Road where I found a skeleton stretching a gloved hand out of the earth. I went on to No. 10 post which I got into without being seen by the sentry. It was rather a foolish thing to do but it showed how insecure No. 10 post is.

August 20, 1918

At 9 a.m. the Commanding Officer gave us the last instructions about the battle. It seems to me a hazardous enterprise but I feel quite confident. I spent the rest of the morning superintending the men's baths. I wrote to Diana and tried to say how much I love her but failed, failed.

We had a sort of high tea before we started. We got into motor lorries at about eight and drove to somewhere near Hendecourt. There tea and biscuits were awaiting us. There was bright moonlight but before we marched off a thick mist suddenly came down. We went on to the Red Line where we were to spend the night. We reached there at about midnight. I stayed on duty till 2 – walking up and down the line. The men seemed very cheerful. At 2 I went and had something to eat and drink at Company H.Q. The barrage was to come down at five and we were to start off 20 minutes after. I got into position with my platoon some time before. The barrage was terrific – I had never heard anything to touch it. We started off at the right time. The mist was so thick that you could only see about 20 yards. My platoon was on the left – but we never succeeded in getting into touch with the rest of the Company. The first people we met were the Headquarters of the 1st Batt. Scots Guards. I saw Dudley Coats and [Col. Sir] Victor Mackenzie, their Commanding Officer. They directed me to our own front line, which we crossed and set out in what I hoped was the right direction. We met an officer in the Coldstream with a platoon. He said the Scots Guards had failed to get their objective – that everyone was lost and that the trench we were then in was full of Germans. He had two prisoners with him. I said I would work down the trench, which

I thought was Moyblain, our first objective, and clear it of the enemy. He went on and presently I met [Lt. the Hon.] Alec Robartes and [Major E. R. M.] Fryer. The latter was commanding No. 1 Coy. which should have been in support to our Coy. No. 3 but which had, although I did not know it at the time, already got in advance of it. After this I pressed on alone with my platoon, guiding myself roughly by the sound of our guns behind us. We were occasionally held up by machine-gun fire and we met one or two stray parties of Scots Guards without officers. Finally we met a fairly large party of the Shropshires who I knew should be on our right. The officer with them did not know where he was but we agreed to go on together. We ran into a small party of the enemy of whom we shot six and took two prisoners including an officer. We then learnt that we were on the outskirts of Courcelles. We had gone a great deal too far to the right. I tried to get back by going up a road to the left but could not get on owing to a machine gun firing straight down the road. There were several dead men lying about this road, one particularly unpleasant one with his face shot away. These were the first sights of the kind that I had seen and I was glad to find that they did not affect me at all. I had often feared that they might have some physical effect on me as in ordinary life I hate and always avoid disgusting sights. I went back to the beginning of the road where I found a tank which like everyone else had lost its way in the mist. It consented to go up the road in front of us and we were not troubled further by the machine gun. I got on to another road which led straight up to the Halte on the Arras to Albert railway. This was to the right of the final objective of my Company. There was a ruined building there from which a few shots were fired. We lay down and returned the fire with rifles and Lewis guns. Six Germans ran out with their hands up. We took them prisoner. Almost at the same time a party of the Shropshires came round on the left of the building. There was a steep bank on the edge of the railway along which I told the men to dig themselves fire positions. So we obtained our objective. Not only were we the first to do so but we were the only platoon in the Company who succeeded in doing so at all. I sent a report to the Commanding Officer and later in the day I got his reply – only two words 'Well Done'.

It was then 9 a.m. Not long afterwards I saw No. 1 Company coming over the hill behind us. [Major E. R. M.] Fryer came on to see me. We heard that No. 2 Coy. – which had come through No. 4 as No. 1 had through No. 3 – was on our left but there was a considerable gap between. Fryer and I started walking down the edge of the railway towards No. 2. Suddenly we noticed an enemy machine gun shooting through the hedge in front of us. We had almost walked into it. We hurried back and on the way were fired at by machine guns from the other side of the railway. Fryer told me to take a Lewis gun and a couple of sections and capture or knock out the machine gun. It was rather an alarming thing to be told to do. However I got my Lewis gun up to within about 80 yards of it creeping along the hedge. The Lewis gun fired away. When it stopped I rushed forward. Looking back I saw that I was not being followed. I learnt afterwards that the first two men behind me had been wounded and the third killed. The rest had not come on. One or two machine guns from the other side of the railway were firing at us. I dropped a few yards away from the gun I was going for and crawled up to it. At first I saw no one there. Looking down I saw one man running away up the other side of the cutting. I had a shot at him with my revolver. Presently I saw two men moving cautiously below me. I called to them in what German I could at the moment remember to surrender and throw up their hands. They did so immediately. They obviously did not realize that I was alone. They came up the cutting with their hands up – followed to my surprise by others. There were 18 or 19 in all. If they had rushed me they would have been perfectly safe for I can never hit a haystack with a revolver and my own men were 80 yards away. However they came back with me like lambs – I crawling most of the way to avoid fire from the other side of the railway. Two of them who were Red Cross men proceeded to bind up my wounded. Fryer then sent in two platoons under Delacombe [2nd Lt. 3rd Battalion] and [2nd Lt. Eric] Clough Taylor to fill up the gap.

I hardly ate anything all this day except an orange and a few biscuits. I lived chiefly on whiskey and water. The mist had cleared off at about 10 o'clock and been followed by brilliant sunshine. In the afternoon I went to a dugout about 400 or 500 yards back where Frig had his headquarters and had about an hour and a half's sleep. That evening at stand to, the Commanding Officer came along the line of the railway. He said to me 'The Major General and the Brigadier are extremely pleased with the work of your platoon and asked me to tell you so. You've done most awfully well.' After stand down I took my platoon back to the rest of the Company. They were in a steep bank some way back. It seemed almost like returning to safety although it afterwards proved to be anything but safe. There I went and lay down in a place about as long as a child's grave where I could not stretch my legs but managed to get an hour or two's sleep.

August 22, 1918

I went on duty again at 2 a.m. Another lovely moonlight night and no mist this morning. Soon after four the enemy started a bombardment. Tuffy[1] said it was the worst he had ever been in. It went on for nearly an hour and a half. We were expecting a counter attack all the time. Apparently one was started but never reached our line owing to our retaliatory barrage. We had several casualties. Two men were killed close to me and a small piece of shrapnel from the shell that killed one of them hit me in the face drawing a little blood and remaining in my cheek. At last it stopped and we had breakfast. There were some eggs which they cooked for us and very glad we were of them.

All that day, which was a very hot one, we sat in a shallow bank – and from

---

[1] Maj. Neville C. Tufnell (1887–1951), commanding No. 3 Co., 3rd Battalion, Grenadier Guards.

4.30 till 7 we were shelled continuously. We expected to be relieved that evening – had been told we were to be and lived on the hope. As the day went on the rumour changed but it was not until nearly midnight that we learnt we had to make another attack at 4 a.m. the next morning. The Commanding Officer came up and a terrible crowd there was in the small dugout which had been No. 1 Coy. Headquarters. To add to the confusion a mail was distributed. Three beautiful letters for me from Diana. I had to try to read these, to get something to eat, to understand my instructions all in a few minutes in the crowded ill-lit dugout. It was a miracle that we got the Company into position in time. They had been having casualties from shell fire all the evening and when I went to my platoon a shell fell which knocked out five more. When we were eventually formed up for the attack I had only 10 men and the climax was reached when I discovered that my platoon Sergt, Sergeant Blundy, who had been excellent all the day before, was so drunk as to be useless. He started the attack with us but we never saw him again until the next day.

The attack itself was beautiful and thrilling – one of the most memorable moments of my life. The barrage came down at 4 a.m. A creeping barrage – we advanced behind it. We kept direction by means of a star and a huge full moon shone on our right. I felt wild with excitement and glory and knew no fear. When we reached our objective, the enemy's trench, I could hardly believe it so quickly had the time passed it seemed like one moment. We found a lot of Germans dead there. The living surrendered.

Later at about 9.30 Tuffy told me to go with a few men as far down on our right as possible to try to get in touch with someone and to try to deal with 2 machine guns which were firing at us both from in front and behind. I never liked an order less. Courage is half a matter of health and energy and I was feeling worn out and not at all brave. The trench had been so knocked about by our barrage that in many places even crouching one was visible to the enemy machine guns. However I went off and although the incident was not one for which I felt I got any particular credit it was the one for which I gave myself most.

We went down the trench pretty slowly with frequent halts which were necessary as we had to run and jump and crawl half the way. At 11 o'clock we had reached the furthest point we had set out for when suddenly our guns behind put down a barrage not very far in front of us. Soon afterwards we saw our own men pouring over the ridge behind. It was a fine sight to see them come on in perfect formation as on a field day. Our only fear was lest they should mistake us for the enemy. We waited until they were close and then all stood up together and waved our hats and cheered. When they were in line with us we advanced with them for a few hundred yards. Germans were giving themselves up on all sides. We took about 80 prisoners who we brought back with us. The rest of the day was uneventful and we were relieved by the Scots Guards at nightfall – a blessed relief. We marched back to Agette. I don't think I was ever so thirsty or so tired as when we arrived there. I drank gallons of hot cocoa and certainly never enjoyed a drink so much. We spent the night in a cellar where I had only boards to lie on but I managed to sleep pretty well.

August 24, 1918

We were able to wash and shave this morning – a great pleasure. Our appearance was beginning to be too revolting. All the morning troops were passing through Agette – cavalry and artillery. It was exhilarating to see them passing in perfect security through a village that had been in German hands two days before. In the afternoon we heard we were to go further back – to a spot between Ronsart and Adinfer. We had to halt on the road as our guide was not there. While we were halted the Commanding Officer rode by with the Brigadier and I heard the Commanding Officer [Lt. Col. Andrew Thorne] say 'That's Duff'. The Brigadier stopped and congratulated me in words that made me thrill with pride, blush with pleasure and perspire with shyness.

It was glorious to get back to our new quarters. Very peaceful they seemed. Not a gun to be heard. Our kits met us there – and the final joy was to get off one's clothes, put on one's pyjamas and creep into one's sleeping bag.

August 25, 1918

A late rise, a glorious morning, a delicious breakfast out of doors, a tremendous feeling of well being. After lunch the brigadier turned up and talked to me again very flatteringly. I went down to Ronsart before tea and had a bath. After tea we all listened to the band. Champagne for dinner after which I went up to No. 1 company where we all sat round drinking port and talking about the battle.

August 28, 1918 [Berles au Bois]

Life here is a complete rest. There are no duties whatever. Today I saw the Commanding Officer's account of the battle. He ends it by a summary of the outstanding features of which he mentions as No. 1, splendid leading of No. 10 Platoon by Lt. Duff Cooper. I have really won more praise than I deserve for I was very lucky.

August 29, 1918

I heard today that Gerald Brassey has been killed.

September 1, 1918

Our Commanding Officer left us today. Everyone is sorry and so am I. He was a fine soldier and inspired confidence. He had few interests outside his profession but I had grown to like and admire him and I had recently won his approval. Lascelles now commands. I prefer him as a man but as a soldier there is the difference between the professional and the amateur.

There was a row in the garret of the house where we live tonight. Sydney and I went up and found two drunken Sergeants, one of them lying on the floor covered with blood.

September 9, 1918

This morning news came that we were all to move at once and to join the Battalion. We drove up in motor lorries – a long drive. We found the Battalion just behind Lagnicourt. Peter Adderley came to see me in the afternoon. He is just back from leave. Mother sent me a copy of a letter she had had from Streatfeild 'I want to write you a few lines to tell you that your son in our 3rd Batt. has very greatly distinguished himself in the recent severe fighting. His name has been especially mentioned to me by Col. Thorne, his commanding officer for his gallantry and leadership. You will be very proud of him as we all are here.'

September 14, 1918 [Lagnicourt]

Bombing in the morning. A glorious dinner with Nos 1 & 2 Companies in the evening. There were six of us. The menu was – caviare, turtle soup, lobster rissoles, roast chicken, chocolate pudding, foie gras. There was also plenty to drink and we had a very cheery evening. We thought we were going into the line the next day but during the evening this was cancelled – and we learnt that we were to be battalion in reserve.

September 18, 1918

We learnt this morning that our Company are to do an attack on the 24th.

September 23, 1918

We played some final dominoes in the afternoon. We marched off at 7.15, a long and very tiring marching. I slept a good deal in the night.

September 25, 1918

A terrific enemy bombardment began at about 9 a.m. I had to go up to the front line in the midst of it. My runner was wounded on the way. I found out that at one post we had had three men, including a Sergeant killed. They were terribly knocked about. Stayed on duty till 1.30 when I came back and had a good lunch – wrote to Mother and Diana, from both of whom I heard last night. We hear the attack will not be until the day after tomorrow which is a bore. The sooner the better. On duty from 8–11.30. Came back and found two bottles of port had arrived – most opportune. Drank some and slept well.

September 26, 1918

Stood to 5.30–6.30. On duty 7–10.30 – a fine sunny morning. Came back and was resting when I was called out by the Commanding Officer and there was the Major General, whom I had never seen before. I had to explain to him our plan of attack. [Capt.] Claud Sykes was with him.

I was on duty from 5 to 8.30 and put up notices at the various places in the trench where the different parties were to form up for the attack. Jaggers [de Geijer] relieved me. It took me some time to get back to the dugout as the trenches were full of troops moving up. I had dinner with Madox Gunther who is in charge of the platoon of No. 4 Coy. which is attached to us for the attack. I felt unexpectedly calm, cheerful and confident although during the last week I had several times felt fear. The nearer we came to battle the less uneasy I felt. After dinner I lay down meaning only to rest, but I slept soundly until past 3.

September 27, 1918

We had some breakfast before we started and I drank some port and had a mouthful of rum. It had been raining hard in the night but had stopped when we left the dugout at about 4. It was very dark. Zero was at 5.20 and we went over the top simultaneously with the beginning of the barrage. I was just scrambling up the parapet when two of our own trench mortars fell almost among us, wounding two men. The rest scrambled back into the trench. I waited half a minute and then went on again. We were well up to our own barrage but had no further casualties from it. We attacked in three parties. I was leading the centre platoon, [2nd Lt.] Gibbon was on the right, Madox on the left. I got too much to the left but met Jaggers who put me right. Nearly all the enemy we came in contact with surrendered at once. I soon got right down to the Canal du Nord. Here I was very nearly hit by a bomb which a small party of Germans threw before running away. It landed just behind me and hit my runner. It was light by now and a beautiful morning. We were soon in touch with the Coy. who were attacking on our left. The Germans tried to counter-attack on the left and three times they advanced over the ridge but there was no heart in it and a little Lewis gun fire sent them back each time. Machine guns continued to fire in front for some time but before midday all was quiet and the battle had rolled away from us. We lunched in a German dugout and spent the afternoon watching from the slag heap the distant battle and the large batches of German prisoners coming in. In the evening we were relieved and marched back to near Dorgnies. We found a good hot meal awaiting us and although we were very crowded we made ourselves pretty comfortable and had a good night's sleep. Our kits came up in time for us to sleep in our sleeping bags. On the whole it was a good battle.

September 29, 1918

On the way to Church parade I met Fitz [Lt. Edward Fitzgerald] who told me he had sent my name in for Paris leave. I am by way of going on the 9th. The prospect seems almost too good to be true. I am terrified lest something should occur meanwhile to interfere with it. A bath in the afternoon.

October 1, 1918

We had some partridges for lunch which Mother sent me. They were over-cooked but very good.

October 2, 1918

This morning as I was having breakfast Carroll [Carstairs] came in and told me I had got the D.S.O. Great joy and pride I felt. I knew I had been recommended for it but thought it might be reduced to a Military Cross.

Duff goes on leave to Paris.

I have had no time to write my diary for ten days and during the ten days a good deal has happened. There were five very uneventful ones at Details where we worked a little in the morning, played a little chess and a little cards and lived very badly. We had hardly anything to eat or drink. The water was so over-chlorinated that it could not be mixed with anything and all the food that was cooked with it tasted of it.

October 5, 1918

Two bottles of port arrived for me from England. I drank too much at dinner and lost too much to Carroll at cards afterwards. That night our leave passes arrived and we [Duff and Carroll Carstairs] set out early the next morning.

October 7, 1918

It was a great joy to get up this morning in Paris. A hot bath of water clearer than we have been accustomed to drink, a delicious saunter through the sunny streets, two letters from Diana at the Ritz and an excellent lunch there completed my delight.

In the afternoon I went to 18 Rue Pasquier – an establishment I knew before the war and which apparently has if anything improved since. There I was satisfied by a tall fair thin girl – rather like Nancy but better looking. Later I met Healy [a fellow officer] at Ciro's which seemed amusing – full of tarts accompanied and unaccompanied. I dined with Healy and Carroll at the Ambassadeurs. We saw there another Grenadier – Drummond in the 2nd Battalion and asked him to join us which he did.

October 8, 1918

We all meet every morning before lunch for cocktails at the Crillon bar. Drummond and I lunched at the Ritz. There I found Diana Capel[1] whom I most wanted to see. I arranged to go and see her in the evening.

---

[1] Diana Wyndham, later Countess of Westmoreland, had married 'Boy' Capel in 1917. He was a successful English businessman and keen polo player who lived in Paris. He had had an affair with Coco Chanel, and financed her first fashion boutique in 1910.

We have now got rooms at the Ritz and during the afternoon I moved my things thither from the Mirabeau. I had some tea with the others at the Ambassadeurs and then went to see Diana in her apartment at 88 Avenue du Bois.

I dined with Drummond whom I like very much, at Maxim's and we went to a revue – called *Plus Cela Change* at the Michel. Diana was there with Capel whom I don't like the look of. Afterwards we went to an establishment in the Rue de Hambourg where he was suited but I was not. I came home to bed – tired and pure.

October 10, 1918

I had arranged to go down to Versailles with Diana and lunch there. I hired a motor from the Ritz and went to her about midday. She met me with the news that Capel forbade our lunching at Versailles on account of the number of officers who would see her lunching there. It seemed silly but we lunched at Voisin where the food was beyond reproach. We went to Versailles afterwards and most beautiful it was. I longed so for my own very darling Diana to be there with me. Only she could have enjoyed it as I did. I made Diana walk from the Château to the Trianons and all round Le Hameau until she could hardly stand. She is a delightful companion. How beautiful was Versailles with its native melancholy enhanced by the yellowing branches and fallen leaves.

October 11, 1918

Diana came to the Ritz for me after lunch and we drove together. I made her take me to Lucille's because I had heard that there was a most beautiful mannequin there. This proved to be the case. A more beautiful woman I have never seen anywhere. Her beauty moved me strangely – I hardly felt desire but rather gratitude and tears. It would perhaps be a pity to know her and yet Carroll and I adopted what means we could – and that the lowest – in order to do so. We employed a waiter at Maxim's to make friends with the doorkeeper at Lucille's – but all to no effect.

October 12, 1918

We were a party of ten – all men – at the Café de Paris. There was a woman there who very much took my fancy. She gave no encouragement by look or gesture but when she left the restaurant I flushed with wine boldly followed her – drove her to her flat and then back to the Folies Bergère where we had taken two boxes for the performance of *Zig Zag*. Afterwards I went off with my new friend to an establishment where one could dance and drink – a pleasant place more like a private house. We drank a little and danced a little and then went to her flat where I lay with her quite happily till 7.30 a.m.

October 13, 1918

A fine morning. I bought some butter for breakfast on my way home. When I got back I had a bath. While I was lying in it, Carroll walked in and said 'The war is over'. It really seems as though it might be so.

October 20, 1918

Carroll and I set off early [*to return to their battalion*] and had an interesting morning. We drove through Cambrai and right on about another 15 miles or more to St Vaast where we found the Battalion. Cambrai itself is a good deal damaged but the villages beyond it are untouched. It is extraordinarily enheartening to be living again in a land where there are houses and furnished houses. The Germans appear to have taken very little. We find everything we want.

October 21, 1918

We are living in a fairly good house but the windows are all broken so it is rather draughty. I sleep in the cellar.

October 22, 1918

After lunch the Battalion moved back to Boussières. It was a tiresome march owing to the number of troops going up and the muddiness of the road. It was dark when we arrived. I got a note from Oliver Lyttelton[1] asking me to dine. He has lately become our Brigade Major. I sat between him and Claud Sykes and we had a pleasant dinner and played bridge afterwards. I bet Claud Sykes £100 to £25 that there would not be peace before Christmas.

I forgot to say that the first news which greeted me on my return to the Battalion was that Peter Adderley had just died of wounds. It does really seem that all my friends are marked out for death. A succession of calamities has left me callous – I was really fond of Peter and yet I felt that I could not *feel* his death.

October 28, 1918

This afternoon I suddenly heard that I was to go on leave on the 1st. It sounded too good to be true.

---

[1] Oliver Lyttelton DSO, MC, later 1st Viscount Chandos (1893–1972). Banker, businessman and politician. He became an MP (1940–54) and in Oct. 1940 was made President of the Board of Trade. In 1941 he joined the War Cabinet as Minister of State in Cairo, and in 1942 became Minister of Production. In 1951 he became Colonial Secretary. He married Lady Moira Osborne in 1920.

October 31, 1918

A wet morning. Left Boulogne in a very fast motor about 10. They refused at
first to let me on the boat but on my mentioning the D.A.Q.M.G. [Deputy
Assistant Quartermaster General] all went well. We had a smooth crossing
and managed to get seats in the Pullman at Folkestone. We had lunch on the
train. Somewhat to my surprise I was met at Victoria by Mother, Sibbie and
Sidney. Mother was very excited but not too overcome. She drove back with
me to 88 St James's St. where I found the flat all prepared and looking
delightful. A fire burning and the room full of flowers. As I walked into it the
telephone rang. It was Diana. I arranged for her to come when Mother had
gone. Mother and I sat and talked for some time and then I went out to the
hairdresser. I came back to the flat and waited for Diana, walking up and
down the room and wondering whether it were all true. She came – and all
that I had hoped of happiness for the last six months came true. We had so
much to say and were so happy.

November 9, 1918 [Breccles, Norfolk, country house of the Montagus]

The most perfect frosty sunny morning imaginable. Edwin and I started out
shooting at 10. The country was looking most beautiful and I contrasted it
with the stricken fields of France that I had left. We had capital sport but I
shot badly. I was glad to get back to the warm fire. They greeted us with the
news of the Kaiser's abdication. I never felt so tired. I had a bath and a sleep
before dinner. The relations of Edwin and Venetia are very distressing. She
seems hardly to be able to bear him – she cannot help showing it and he
cannot help seeing it. This night Diana and I were as happy as the night before
but more peaceful and slept deeply in each other's arms.

November 11, 1918

We left by train at about 11. Two Flying Corps officers got in at Cambridge
and said that they had received an official wireless to say that the armistice
had been signed. As we got nearer London we saw flags flying and in some
places cheering crowds. We had a motor to meet us at Liverpool Street. All
London was in uproar – singing, cheering, waving flags. In spite of real delight
I couldn't resist a feeling of profound melancholy, looking at the crowds of
silly cheering people and thinking of the dead. I went to St James's Street.
Although I felt ill I thought I must go out this night. I dined at the Ritz. I sat
between Diana and Olga. There was an enormous crowd, the intervals between
the courses were interminable and the food when it came was cold and nasty.
I could not enjoy myself and as soon as possible Diana and I slipped away
and came back to St James's Street. The streets were full of wild enthusiasm.
Diana shared the melancholy with which these filled me – and once she broke
down and sobbed.

November 12, 1918

I still felt ill. I went back to bed after my bath and remained there for a week. I had influenza but was never bad with it. My temperature only reached 102 once. Mother came to see me often and Diana twice a day. Diana read to me – we started reading *Bleak House*.

Sunday 17 November, 1918

Viola broke to the Duchess that Diana and I wanted to marry. Terrible scenes appear to have taken place at Arlington Street – the Duchess in a great state. Matters have been rather precipitated but it is a good thing to have got it out.

November 27, 1918 [The Victory Ball]

As soon as we arrived at the ball people came up and congratulated me on my engagement and asked if it were true. The ball was a beautiful sight and brought back to one all the fun of the old days before the war. As I was acknowledging the engagement to anyone who asked me I thought that the sooner I had it out with the Duchess the better and I decided to do so at once. I boldly bearded her and we withdrew to a fairly quiet sofa on the upper corridor. I found her more unreasonable and more hopelessly obstinate even than I had expected. I talked to her with great eloquence and marvellous command of temper. She was insulting, illogical, and quite impossible to keep to any point. First it was the question of money but when I began to deal with this point she said she knew nothing about money and cared less. Then it was my character, my drunkenness, my bad friends – she didn't spare the dead and abused even Raymond saying that his only pleasure was to make young girls drunk. She then said that the whole thing was a plot engineered by Olga and Alan about both of whom she was most bitter. She imagines Olga to be my greatest friend and it is useless to tell her that anything she imagines isn't true. Finally she was certain that Diana didn't love me – as a proof she gave that Diana had gone to parties last week when I was ill. She also added that it was cruel of me to talk to her on the subject as I knew it was torturing her. I left having accomplished nothing. I still wonder how I kept my temper. I have no pity for her now. I had before.

November 29, 1918

At 12 o'clock I went to see the Duke. There was something grotesquely old fashioned about the solemn interview with the heavy father. He received me very civilly, listened to all I had to say, complimented me on the way I had said it, added that he had always liked me and concluded by saying that he could not possibly allow the marriage and preferred not to discuss it. I asked him if he could give me any reason for his attitude and he refused to. I asked was it money – he practically said it was not. I asked whether he had heard anything against me. He said he had heard nothing. I tried to make him see the silly unreasonableness of his attitude and hinted that it could only drive one to take the law into one's own hands but he would say nothing except 'I am sorry I can say no more'. We were both very polite and parted with every civility. The old fool.

November 30, 1918

Eddie and I went to the War Office in the morning as my extension of leave is up. I went to the Ritz afterwards where I saw Billakin [Lt. S. Cornish, Grenadier Guards]. He is home on leave. He told me of the last battle we were in. Poor Madox Gunther was killed for which I was truly sorry. He was one of the nicest and most interesting men I had met either at Bushey, Chelsea or in France. Carroll was badly wounded in the stomach but is going to recover.

I met Diana just as I was leaving the Ritz. She had had a terrible morning with her mother and was still tearful. The Duchess says that she had rather Diana had had cancer than was married to me, or that John had been killed in the war.

December 1, 1918

Diana came in the morning. We read *Bleak House* and watched the troops lining Pall Mall and St James's St. I lunched at the Ritz and we came back to my rooms afterwards to watch the procession. Foch [Marshal of France] and the Duke of Connaught in the first carriage, Clemenceau [French Prime Minister] and Lloyd George in the second – Bonar Law, Orlando [Italian Prime Minister] and Sonnino [Italian Foreign Minister] in the third. They had a fine reception and we had a beautiful view.

December 2, 1918

I went to the War Office. They gave me a further week's extension of leave pending the arrival of definite instructions.

December 3, 1918

We dined late with the Montagus. After dinner we went to the Hyde Park Hotel to see Beaverbrook.[1] I had heard so much about him and was prepared for the worst. I was agreeably impressed. His face is hideous but I didn't think it unattractive. He is extraordinarily animated and full of life. He talks incessantly and amusingly. He has a Scots Canadian accent but has nothing of the colonial about him. He reminds one a little of Winston. A man called

---

[1] Maxwell (Max) Aitken, 1st Lord Beaverbrook (1879–1964). Conservative politician and press lord. Owner of the *Daily Express*. Minister of Aircraft Production 1940 and Minister of Supply 1941, under Churchill.

Hulton[1] was there – a large newspaper owner. They two and Rothermere[2] had just been dining with Lloyd George, who is apparently getting nervous about his General Election and is therefore calling in the help of what Beaverbrook called the 'Press Gang'.

December 6, 1918

Most disquieting news about Steffie. She has got pneumonia after influenza and is very bad. I went back to Berkeley House after lunch but there was no better news.

December 7, 1918

I spent the morning at Berkeley House. They have little hope of Steffie living. Poor Mother – poor Tolly [Wingfield – Steffie's husband]. I lunched with Diana at the Bachelors' – and went back to Berkeley House again. I had some difficulty in making up my mind whether to go down to Leatherhead or no [to stay with Beaverbrook]. But as Steffie was slightly better in the evening and I could do no earthly good by staying I went. I travelled down with Diana. There Beaverbrook greeted us and then it was time to dress for dinner. There were two other men staying in the house – Sir Edward Kemp, Prime Minister of Canada, and Colonel Bruce, a celebrated American surgeon. The house is large, ugly and comfortable. The evening was not particularly amusing but after the ladies had gone to bed Beaverbrook told us stories of his childhood which were interesting. He was one of ten children of a poor Minister in a little Canadian town called Newcastle.

My room was a long way from Diana's but I found my way there and we were very happy.

December 8, 1918

A beautiful breakfast was brought me in bed and I got up very late. What was left of the morning I spent in reading to Diana who was still in bed and who did not get up till lunch time. We read the end of the Idylls of the King [Tennyson].

There were quite a lot of people at lunch – Venetia and Scatters came together, Rothermere with his surviving son and the Prime Minister [Lloyd George] with his daughter Megan. I had never met him before beyond once shaking hands with him in a box at the theatre. There is something very remarkable about him. He creates the impression of a great man and he does it without seeming theatrical and without seeming insincere. We sat for some

---

[1] Sir Edward Hulton (1869–1925), newspaper proprietor and publisher of the Daily Sketch and Evening Standard.
[2] Harold Sidney Harmsworth, 1st Viscount Rothermere (1868–1940). Newspaper proprietor and brother of Lord Northcliffe. On Northcliffe's death in 1922 he took control of Associated Newspapers.

time over lunch after the women had gone and he could talk of nothing but the election – of what cries went down with the electorate and what did not – and speculate as to what the results would be. He is a great contrast to Mr Asquith who prefers to talk of nothing nearer home than Thucydides. At one moment he was eloquent saying how the English people had long memories, how they remembered the fires of Smithfield and the hungry forties, and that one should never rouse these memories because it was a dreadful thing to fight against ghosts.

Monday December 9, 1918

I travelled up in the morning with Diana and we arrived in London about midday. I went straight to Berkeley House. In Dover Street I met Neil Arnott [the doctor] who told me that Steffie had died not many minutes ago. Her temperature had gone down last night and she had seemed better, but they now knew that her lungs were full of poison and that the case was hopeless.

I went upstairs and found Mother in the drawing room. Mother was standing in the window looking out. We didn't speak for a long time. Tolly and Mother were both calm. Mother wanted to let people know – Sibbie, Richard and others. I said I would see to that and left them. These last four years have so inured me to death that I can no longer feel it very deeply. I was very fond of Steffie and never quarrelled with her in my life. Our relations with one another were ideal. We were always very glad to see each other and never went out of our way to do so. I had never any irksome feeling of duty towards her. For months at a time we didn't meet and I always knew that if I ever went to see her or proposed myself at the Priory she would be delighted to see me and wouldn't ask why I hadn't been before. She was content with her own life and I think she had been very happy the last year or two. She was not clever but she was the only member of the family except myself with any sound sense. I wonder what will become of her children. I went in to see Steffie. She was looking very pretty. I kissed her cold forehead and I cried. I drove Mother home – poor Mother – as soon as one anxiety and trouble leaves her another comes.

December 10, 1918

I spent the morning between Wellington Barracks and the War Office – where at last I was told that my return to France was cancelled and that they would send me orders to report to the Foreign Office.

December 12, 1918

Steffie's funeral was this morning. I went to fetch Mother and brought her to the church, St George's, where she was first married and where Arthur's [Levita] funeral too took place. I believe that that was the last time I was in it. The service was moving – especially the sight of the two little orphans in tears.

I drove to Brompton Cemetery in a motor with Tolly. The coffin was laid in the place reserved for it by the side of Arthur.

In the afternoon I went to see Lord Revelstoke[1] in the city. I found the pomp of Barings very impressive – more so than Rothschilds. He was extremely charming, said what a friend he had been of Father's and promised to do his best for me. I wonder if anything will come of it. I then went to see Campbell – Hardinge's private secretary – having received my orders this morning to report to the Foreign Office. He said he would let me know in a few days what they were going to do with me.

December 16, 1918

This morning Diana brought me a letter she had had from George Moore offering to give her, on our marriage, £6000 a year and to rent Arlington Street for her to live in. One's first feeling of course is that one can't accept it – but the more I think about it the more I like it – I mean the money – and the sillier seem the arguments against it. We don't want Arlington Street but as for the rest we do want it badly. It would make all the difference. I can hardly believe that it is a genuine offer or that he has it to spare. We talked it over and eventually Diana wrote a letter in which she refused it – but rather, I gather, in the manner in which Caesar refused the crown.

December 20, 1918

Diana and I dined with Beaverbrook. We talked of the new Sunday paper [*Sunday Express*] he is bringing out and the prices which various authors fetch. Diana asked him how much he would pay her. He said £200 for four articles. She said 'done'. And he then and there wrote her a cheque for the whole sum. She had promised to go and see Moore after dinner. She went there late and I left her half an hour there and then called for her. Meanwhile I racked my brain to find subjects for the four articles which I shall have to write. Moore still clings to his offer. I wonder what will come of it.

December 23, 1918

This morning I went back to the Foreign Office. It is eighteen months since I left it. Gerald Wellesley[2] and Collier[3] are my colleagues. My particular job is Austro-Hungary, which means principally the Czechoslovaks and the Yugoslavs.

December 29, 1918

I spent the morning writing the article for next week's *Sunday Express*. It looks quite well in print this morning but strikes me as rather dull.

[1] John Baring, 2nd Lord Revelstoke (1863–1929). Senior partner of Barings Bank.
[2] Lord Gerald Wellesley, later 7th Duke of Wellington (1885–1972), architect.
[3] Sir Laurence Collier (1890–1976), Ambassador to Norway 1942–50.

1919

January 4, 1919

This morning I was woken up by Diana's hand on my face – a lovely awakening. She had come up from Belvoir at an unearthly hour on the excuse of wishing to see the ceremony of the Guards going off to France. See it we did nor was it much of a show – and when they arrived at the station they had to come back again owing to the mutiny at Folkestone.[1]

Diana and I dined with Beaverbrook at the Savoy. We all went afterwards to the offices of the *Express* where we saw the Sunday morning paper being printed. It was interesting and fired me with journalistic ambitions. Beaverbrook was in high spirits as the circulation had gone up a lot since last week.

January 6, 1919

This morning there appeared in *The Times*: 'We are requested to state that there is no truth in the report that Lady Diana Manners is engaged to be married'. I was furious. The Duchess of course had put it in – but when taxed with it by Diana she denied it.

January 7, 1919

Today I had a letter from the Duke in which he says that if we will wait a year he will agree to the marriage and do all he can to help it, but that meanwhile there must be no engagement.

January 13, 1919

A dense fog – fit atmosphere for this unhappy day [*Diana had gone to the South of France*]. On arriving at the Foreign Office I learnt that I had been transferred to the Commercial Department – an additional blow. I am to take Alec Cadogan's[2] place as he becomes Cecil Harmsworth's[3] private secretary.

---

[1] At the end of the war, mutinies broke out in a number of army camps, including Folkstone, where on 3 Jan. 2,000 troops refused to sail for France, instead leading a protest of 10,000 soldiers through the town, demanding to be demobilized.

[2] Sir Alexander Cadogan (1884–1968), head of the League of Nations section of the FO 1921–33; Permanent Under-Secretary of State 1938–45. First UK Ambassador to the UN in New York 1945–50.

[3] Cecil Harmsworth (1849–1948), later created 1st Baron Harmsworth. Younger brother of 1st Viscount Northcliffe and 1st Viscount Rothermere. Under-Secretary of State for Foreign Affairs 1919–22.

January 14, 1919

Lunched with Mother at the Bachelors' – saw Sidney before dinner. He has got a job as Assistant Private Secretary to Winston.

January 16, 1919

I lunched alone at the Junior Carlton and had my nails done after lunch. The great advantage of the Commercial Department is that one can lunch at what time one likes and need not hurry.

January 18, 1919

I caught the 6.35 to Taplow. There I found the Desboroughs, Monica and Imogen [Grenfell], Rosemary and Eric Ednam. It was a pleasant little party and I enjoyed it. After dinner we played games and acted – going out and coming in as two people. Lord and Lady Desborough did the Duke and Duchess of Rutland discussing our engagement. He was extraordinarily like the Duke. I think Rosemary may be going to marry Eric.

January 22, 1919

Had a very busy day at the Office – not a moment to spare. Dined with Sydney Fairbairn at the Junior Carlton. We drank two bottles of champagne and he told me all his sorrows. Nancy won't live with him – he still loves her and believes her faithful. Husbands are incredible. I expect I shall be as gullible as the best.

January 23, 1919

Dined with the Ronald Grahams[1] in Queen Street. They had a party of 12. Margot [Asquith] was very friendly to me – told me I ought to help Diana more with her articles and make them better! I cited her own articles – the worst ever written – as examples, and talked nonsense on every subject. Lady Drogheda[2] invited Diana and me to honeymoon on Lord Furness's[3] yacht and gave me an account of her conversation about me with the Duchess. We played bridge afterwards. I held the best hand I've ever held in my life: Spades – Ace, King Queen, 10 & another, Hearts – Ace King and another, Diamonds – Ace, King, Queen, Clubs – Ace King & another. My partner had the knaves of Spades and Diamonds and I made grand slam.

---

[1] Sir Ronald and Lady Graham, the parents of Marjorie Trefusis. He was a diplomat.

[2] Kathleen Pelham Burn married Henry Moore, 10th Earl of Drogheda (1884–1957) in 1909. They were divorced in 1922.

[3] Marmaduke Furness, Viscount Furness (1883–1940). Chairman of Furness Shipping Co. His second wife, Thelma Morgan (1906–70), whom he married in 1926 (and divorced in 1933), was an American. She preceded Wallis Simpson as mistress of the Prince of Wales.

January 30, 1919

Alec Cadogan has got flu – so I was suddenly told today that I had to run the Enemy Exports Committee – an extremely complicated job which nobody in the office except Cadogan understands so there is no one to explain it to me. For lunch Diana and I had foie gras and biscuits at 88.

January 31, 1919

The Committee is giving me a hard life. I got to the office before 10 this morning and left after 7.30. I lunched at Queen Anne's Gate with Diana and Venetia who is just back from Paris. We had the best foie gras that I have eaten since the war – or ever.

February 12, 1919

Dinner at Wimborne House. Diana was wearing a Vermeer dress for the Three Arts Ball. We went afterwards, Diana and I, to Londonderry House en route for the Albert Hall. Diana was the only person who had dared to go there in fancy dress – an error of courage which I think she regretted. They had a regular old-fashioned pre-war ball – and I rather liked it.

Then we went on to the Albert Hall. The ball there was excellent – the best I can remember. There was a real spirit of gaiety abroad – everyone seemed to be enjoying it. It was a very cold night and some of the fog had got into the building but had been driven to the roof which was lost in a yellow haze beneath which hung a cloud of coloured air balloons. One of these occasionally descended and there were wild struggles to capture it. Our rendezvous was Lord Furness's box where there was excellent supper and champagne in plenty. There also I found Joan Belleville whom I knew years ago as Joan Lyon. She married a man who was killed in the war and then she married Frank Belleville. She has lost some of her beauty but not all. I danced with her and made love to her. She is living close to me in St James's Street, No. 73 over Rumpelmayer's. Her husband was away and I persuaded her that I might go there after the ball. I drove Diana home – came back, undressed, put on my fur coat and went to her. It was great pleasure – the first ordinary pleasure that I have had since Paris, for Diana maintains her maidenhood. I left Joan at 5. I pondered telling Diana but dared not.

February 13, 1919

Today by an odd chance Diana and I lunched at Rumpelmayer's in the very building where I betrayed her last night.

February 16, 1919

I spent my morning writing up this diary. Thank God we have finished the articles – eight of these have I written for £400.

February 25, 1919

Sybil has decided to go back to Richard. When I came back from the Foreign Office this evening I found her and Sidney in my rooms looking very miserable. I dressed and went out leaving them still there. I dined at White's and played bridge afterwards. They came and told me I was wanted on the telephone. It was Sidney. He said that Sybil had been trying to commit suicide. He had been dining with the Salisburys and she had rung him up in the middle of dinner to tell him she was doing so. She was in my rooms. He had gone round and found her in a wild state brandishing a small jack knife with which she had scratched herself slightly on the breast. He believed she had taken some drug and had called a doctor. I finished the rubber and then went back. I found her lying unconscious on the sofa. The doctor, a grotesque man who insisted on making terrible little jokes, had given her an injection to make her sick. She had drunk the best part of a bottle of brandy but nothing else. The doctor thought she could not be moved that night. But Sidney and I decided to wait and see. I went and lay down and he remained in the sitting room. At about half past one he woke me and said she had practically recovered. I went and talked to her, trying to induce her to see some sort of reason. If she couldn't face going back to Richard let her decide on a separation. Only let her decide on something and stick to it. But it was hopeless to argue with her. With great difficulty we at last persuaded her to leave the flat and Sidney took her back to the hotel where she was staying.

February 26, 1919

I went round to her hotel in the morning. She was feeling very ill but seemed prepared to go back to Richard which it had been arranged for her to do today. I tried to encourage and strengthen her resolve. I went back later and took her out to lunch at the Berkeley – a dreadful meal – she never spoke. In the afternoon she went with Richard down to the country where he is living with his family.

March 1, 1919

I dined with William Rawle. He is to be married on Monday. It was his farewell party. He had the private room at the Ritz. We sat down 32 at one long table, on which there were no decorations at all but a bottle of champagne in front of each guest. It was a fine old-fashioned sight. The food was excellent. After dinner the table was rapidly removed and gave way to several small ones and one long narrow one where William and Cardie [Montagu] proceeded to take a bank at roulette. I began playing there and rapidly lost some £40 or £50. Then Lionel and I and a few others started a game of chemin de fer at one of the six tables. I was very lucky and was at one time winning over £500. The party broke up about 3 – I won £155 on the evening.

March 2, 1919. Sunday

Diana came in the morning and reproached me for my naughtiness in gambling, but eventually forgave me. Then we went out for a walk. It was a lovely morning, spring in the air which was soft and balmy. The sun shining – the first spring day. We walked down the Strand and to Lincoln's Inn Fields where we think we should like to live. There are some charming houses there.

March 11, 1919

George Moore has deposited at a bank £500 in Diana's name and guaranteed any overdraft. He says he is prepared for her to spend that amount a month, but she thinks she will only draw on it for the rent of any house we take. That is to say we shall live where we like rent free. His generosity is princely with no hope of rewards – at least he denies any.

March 25, 1919

This evening the Rutlands had a dinner and a dance. The Queen of Roumania[1] and the Prince of Wales dined with them. A great joy for the Duchess. Diana went to Covent Garden at daybreak to buy flowers. I went with her. We started about 7.30. It was very cold and not enjoyable. We came back and had breakfast together. The dance I heard afterwards was a great success. The Prince asked Diana if she was engaged and she said she was. He said he knew that I was in his regiment and he wished he knew me.

March 27, 1919

Today I was invested with my D.S.O. I went with Mother to the Palace at 10.30. I got a ticket for her and one for Diana. Mother got a very bad seat. Diana who came late got one in the front row. I rather enjoyed the ceremony. The King asked me the usual questions – what battalion was I in, when did I get the medal, glad to give it me in return for splendid services. I think he does his job well, never showing the boredom he must feel.

After I had got mine I watched the rest of the show with Diana. We were in the front row and the man who handed the King the medals pointed us out to him. We could see they were speaking of us, the King could hardly take his eyes off us and when he finally went out bowed markedly to Diana. He is no doubt thankful she is engaged to me and thinks it a peril less in the paths of the Princes.

---

[1] Queen Marie of Romania (1875–1938), daughter of Prince Alfred, second son of Queen Victoria, and Marie, daughter of Tsar Alexander II of Russia. She married Prince Ferdinand, the heir to the Romanian throne, in 1893. He was crowned king in 1922 and died in 1927.

April 2, 1919

I lunched with Sybil at the Carlton Grill. She seemed ever so much better I thought – far more reasonable and brighter.

Diana and I dined at Lady Essex's who is at Cannes. Lady Alistair Kerr was chaperone. We went on to a ball at Lady Ancaster's.[1] They have a house at Rutland Gate with what must, I think, be the largest ballroom in London. Lady Ancaster took Diana aside on arrival and asked her not to dance certain steps for fear of shocking Princess Mary. Diana was furious and refused to dance the whole evening – except once with the Prince of Wales. When we arrived Sidney Herbert was sitting with Princess Arthur of Connaught.[2] He pointed us out and said 'That's Diana Manners' on which her comment was 'My hat' and 'That's your cousin Duff Cooper' – reply 'they say he's me in trousers'. She's a plain girl and the ugliest clumsiest dancer I ever saw. I didn't enjoy the evening as I lost Diana and had to stay too late until I found her – got stranded with Lady Dudley who was boring beyond even her wont, my best moments being in conversation with Lady Desborough on the subject of unnatural vice.

April 10, 1919

I found Diana in the evening very nervous – on the brink of tears. She had been working herself up all day to face her mother this evening on the subject of her marriage. She was dreading the struggle dreadfully.

We dined with the Horners, Katharine was there and Eddie [Marsh] and E. F. Benson[3] and Mrs Belloc Lowndes.[4] After dinner Diana had an injection of morphia to help her in the fight. I left her poor darling at the great dark door of Arlington St., brave and terrified.

April 11, 1919

I went in my luncheon time to see Carroll Carstairs. He has only just got back from France and has had a terrible time. He is still in bed and will be very lame permanently. He was looking quite well and I was delighted to see him.

Diana's interview with the Duchess was very much as might have been expected. The same old arguments and tears – a plea for delay till Letty comes back – finally a promise to approach the Duke.

---

[1] Eloise Breese, an American, married Gilbert Heathcote-Drummond-Willoughby, 2nd Earl of Ancaster (1867–1951) in 1905. They lived at Grimsthorpe Castle, Lincolnshire.

[2] Princess Arthur of Connaught (1891–1959) married Alexander Duff, 1st Duke of Fife (1862–1933), in 1913. He was Duff's mother's brother.

[3] E. F. Benson (1867–1940), novelist best-known for his 'Lucia' novels.

[4] Marie Adelaide Lowndes, née Belloc (1868–1947), novelist and sister of Hilaire Belloc. Her best-known novel was *The Lodger* about Jack the Ripper.

April 15, 1919

Diana and I dined at a new restaurant called The Ivy. We discussed our future at length. It seems to me that in many ways it would be wiser to wait but I don't like to press this view on her. She is so anxious to be married in the spring. And I have myself an uneasy consciousness of the dangers of postponement. I think of *The Statue and the Bust* [a poem by Robert Browning] and of the tide in the affairs of men which must be taken at the flood.

We went to see Katharine after dinner whom we found with Conrad.[1] Diana wanted morphia as she had to battle with her mother again, who had promised to speak to the Duke today. But when she got in she found her mother had gone to bed with a headache and had shirked taking any action at all.

April 21, 1919 [Breccles]

Another doubtful day so far as weather was concerned. I find I am wrong in supposing Venetia and Edwin happy. He confessed this evening to Diana that he had never been more miserable. Alas, I no longer like and cannot pity him. Ever since my engagement to Diana has been mooted I have felt him hostile. He has not shown it except in subtle ways, such as frequently declaring his affection for the Duchess. He is a man incapable of inspiring trust, confidence or lasting love. He has no friends or followers either in politics or in private life. He has great qualities of charm and intellect but they are all warped by something which I believe to be a mixture of cowardice, jealousy and suspicion. I was very sad to leave Breccles. These four days have been among the happiest – the furthest withdrawn from care and trouble and have made me half in love with country life.

April 24, 1919

We lunched at Rumpelmayer's. We have decided now to give in to the wretched Rutlands about their paltry months, of which there are only five more to run.

We had plovers' eggs and champagne in my rooms and then went to Miss Keane's[2] production of *Romeo and Juliet*, infamously acted by her and her husband in the principal parts but well by Ellen Terry[3] as the Nurse and most beautifully by Leon Quartermaine[4] as Mercutio. We had a quarrel afterwards because Diana wished for morphia which I refused. Perhaps I am too prejudiced against it – but I was firm.

[1] Conrad Russell (1878–1947), brother of Claud and Gilbert Russell and fourth son of Lord Arthur Russell. A very cultivated man, his life was spent farming his land at Mells and writing long and entertaining letters to his friends. A regular correspondent of Diana's until his death.
[2] Doris Keane (1881–1945), the American actress, played Juliet. Her husband, Basil Sydney, played Romeo.
[3] Ellen Terry (1848–1928) was briefly married to the painter G. F. Watts. She became Britain's leading Shakespearean actress from 1878 to 1898.
[4] Leon Quartermaine (1876–1967), actor.

April 29, 1919

I lunched with Mother – Diana lunched with hers. She and the Duke had just come back from the country. She said that Diana had quite misunderstood her. Diana had written her a letter while she was away giving in completely to the six months delay. The letter half loving, half reproachful (I didn't see it) appears to have done the trick. The Duchess now advises her to go to the Duke and thinks he will give in – which of course means that she has told him to. We dined together at the Carlton Grill Room discussing our plan of campaign.

April 30, 1919

In the evening Diana had her interview with her father. I met her afterwards at the Ritz. They have given in completely and are willing for us to be married as soon as we wish. It seems too wonderful and hard to realize. The Duke, she says, was perfect – and gave away the whole case by saying to her after the interview which only lasted about 10 minutes – 'Don't go upstairs for a little as I don't want your Mother to think I gave in at once'. I felt wonderfully happy and elated.

We dined at the Hyde Park Hotel with Beaverbrook and the Montagus. A very pleasant dinner – an animated argument on the League of Nations – Diana and Beaverbrook being pro, Edwin and I anti. Beaverbrook however gave away his entire case on the question of the admission of the Japanese into Canada, rather than permit which he was ready to let the whole League of Nations go to hell.

We had a box for the Russian Ballet which has just started again at the Alhambra. We saw *Papillons* and *The Good Humoured Ladies* which were as delightful as ever. Then to a small dance at Wimborne House which I left early in order to come home and compose a letter to the Duchess – a difficult task, which I think I performed adequately.

Friday May 2, 1919

The *Daily Express* and the *Daily Sketch* came out with the announcement of our engagement. The whole front page of the latter was taken up with pictures of Diana. Ever since, events have moved so fast and the days have been so full that I cannot hope to chronicle them. The evening papers were full of our engagement – especially the *Evening Standard.* I went to see Mother before dinner. She is delighted. I had a letter from the Duchess – a silly letter – still protesting that all her opposition had been because she doubted Diana's love for me – and that Diana never tried to convince her.

May 8, 1919

My first meeting with the Duchess – a great ordeal – lunch at Arlington Street. I went with Mike having first imbibed cocktails at White's to induce courage. It went off well enough.

A small dinner at 24 Queen Anne's Gate. Edwin gloomier than ever. Phyllis left before dinner was over at the summons of Wimborne – this infuriated Edwin. Diana and I joined her afterwards at Wimborne House where she gave me details of her latest illegal operation. We were all very cheerful and full of plans for Florence.

May 9, 1919

Another lunch at Arlington St. rather better than the first one. An old Greek called Saharoff,[1] or something like it was there – the Vickers of the Balkans. He gave Diana, whom he has seen twice, £250 as a wedding present.

Diana, Venetia, Scatters and I caught the 4.50 train for Bournemouth. We had the greatest fun from start to finish. We went of course to the Branksome Tower Hotel where Diana and I were last year. How different were our prospects then – disaster all around and probable death in front. Our present circumstances still seem too good to be true.

May 15, 1919

We dined at the Ritz with a new rich American called Mrs Cooper-Hewitt.[2] I sat next to her and found her terrible. She looks like a tart and is full of pseudo-intellectual nonsense and crude snobbery. Diana has been offered 75,000 dollars to go to America for 3 months and act cinema. The Americans at dinner swore she could get four or five times that amount. I doubt it. For a huge sum it would be worth doing – but not for a small one.

May 16, 1919

I lunched with Mother and told her about the cinema. She was horrified at the thought of Diana doing it until I mentioned figures and then she was horrified at the thought of her not doing it.

May 24, 1919

A lovely day – as every day this month. When I came home at 1 o'clock I found Diana had prepared a lovely box full of lunch – there were sandwiches, lobster, strawberries and cream, iced cream in a thermos flask, Moselle cup in a bottle. We could not find a taxi. I walked up St James's Street to look for one. When I came back I saw a little figure kneeling almost in the gutter over a waste of spilt and broken things. She had found a taxi and while the boy was carrying the box to put it in it the bottom of the box had fallen out and all our lunch was on the pavement. Everything was broken that could break. It was too pathetic. I could have cried for her disappointment and my own. Sadly we

---

[1] Sir Basil Zaharoff (1850–1936), international arms dealer and financier, reputedly one of the richest men in the world.

[2] Mrs Cooper-Hewitt, a wealthy American collector. Benefactress of the Metropolitan Museum, New York. She was involved in several American relief committees for France during WWI.

collected the pieces and carried them up to the flat again. We ate the straw-berries and the sandwiches slightly damped from the broken bottle of cup. We had a last hope that the ice-cream would be safe but the interior of the thermos flask was broken and rattled ominously – the top was bent and we couldn't open it.

May 25, 1919. Sunday

We dined at the Savoy – a large dinner in a private room for the Russian Ballet. They were all there. I was disappointed by the appearance of Tchernicheva.[1] I sat between Massine[2] and Mrs Holden.[3] I talked a little to the former in French but did not find him very forthcoming.

The following week was one of breathless hurry, crowded days, happy evenings, a stream of presents, great delight. In addition to all the labours connected with the wedding and the journey to Italy I had to do all my ordinary Foreign Office work – so that I had literally not a moment to myself.

Diana and I used to get up early so as to get some shopping done before I went to the Foreign Office. I used to go to Arlington Street to fetch her and see whatever new presents had arrived. One morning we had to get our passports *visé* at the French and Italian Consulates. It was a tiresome business and I getting cross and hot spoke at one moment roughly to Diana. Never shall I forget how her face which had been all smiles and laughter turned suddenly to tears. It was so beautiful that I could hardly regret it – and it taught me how gentle I must be. I wrote her a sonnet about it as follows:

You, like a child played in the sunshine, wild
With spring and holiday joy, laughter and play,
Until I found it in my heart to say
Hard words and frown when most I should have smiled.
Oh your reproachful tears, your day defiled,
Oh my despair while I for pardon pray,
Till with one hand you wipe your tears away,
And sudden laugh again, most like a child.
Your beauty was the first fine April day,
Your falling tears the shortest April shower,
Though I shall ever curse the cruel hour,
And loathe myself for my ungentle way.
I shall remember still that golden day,
And never cease to bless that silver shower.

Golden days they were, with faultless weather from first to last. Many of

---

[1] Lubov Tchernicheva (1890–1976), the Russian ballerina and wife of Diaghilev's Ballet Russes *régisseur*, Sergei Grigoriev.

[2] Léonide Massine (1895–1979), one of Diaghilev's most famous dancers and choreographers.

[3] Norman Holden and Marion Munro, close friends of Duff and Diana. He was a stockbroker.

the details I have forgotten. I forgot to mention that an additional claim on my time all this week was having to sit to John Lavery for my portrait. This I did from Tuesday to Friday for an hour or two before dinner – it is his wedding present to Diana and he succeeded, I thought, in making an extremely good picture and very like. Diana meanwhile was sitting to Shannon[1] and McEvoy – with neither of whose efforts was I very pleased.

May 30, 1919

We drove early in the morning to the Parsonses to get their wedding present which consisted of a charming, huge folio, early 19th century Shakespeare in about a dozen volumes.

May 31, 1919

I took Mother to see Trower[2] in the morning and we signed the marriage settlements – rather a restless lunch with Mother, Sibbie, Diana and Phyllis at Rumpelmayer's. Back to the Foreign Office afterwards and for the last time – then on to a 'seeing the presents' party at Arlington Street which was not as bad as I had feared it would be.

At 8.15 I gave my bachelor dinner party at the Savoy. I had the Pinafore room – it looked charming – all the windows open on to the river – the table covered with red roses – a gardenia buttonhole in everyone's place. It was a pleasant dinner – the food was good and great quantities of wine were drunk. Afterwards we had card tables brought. I sat down to bridge. We played 2/- points and we played till past three when I rose a winner of £180 – a sad way to treat one's guests but I couldn't but be pleased with the money.

June 1, 1919

I had a bad headache most of the day. I spent the morning arranging things in my flat – which I have let from the day after I leave for three months. I lunched at the Hyde Park Hotel with Diana and Katharine. I told them about my party. How much I missed the dead at it. How Edward would have loved it. How easily could I have replaced the eleven living with eleven dead all of whom – or at least eight out of the eleven – I should have loved better.

June 2, 1919

Today I was married.

I got up and had my bath before 10. At 10 the barber came to shave me. I could not dress because my clothes had not arrived. They had been delayed by the tailors' strike and those I had meant to go away in could not be finished. The actual wedding garment however arrived soon after 11 – so did Sidney –

---

[1] Sir James Jebusa Shannon (1862–1923), the fashionable portrait painter, was a friend of the Rutlands and painted several pictures of Diana.

[2] Thomas Trower, the Coopers' solicitor.

my best man arrayed in his old Eton v. Harrow suit – and Hugo. The latter drank what port and sherry I had left and then we all went to Buck's – the new club to which Sidney and I belong – where we put down one or two cocktails. Thence to the Bank where I cashed a cheque. We two lunched together at the Savoy – a light lunch and a bottle of champagne. As we walked out the band in compliment to me struck up the wedding march which made me feel self-conscious and absurd.

There was a great crowd outside St Margaret's – an incredible crowd. I felt no tinge of nervousness. I felt only pride and love. I held Diana's hand through most of the service and we whispered to one another now and then. I was conscious of all the love I feel for her. I was very happy and I enjoyed every moment of the ceremony – even the vestry where the presence of the Duke of Connaught, his daughter and relations from both sides did not contribute to ease or comfort.

On leaving the church we were greeted by many small lightly clad grand-children of Sir Herbert Tree who scattered rose leaves before us – also by a thousand cameras and cinematographs. The enthusiasm of the crowd was most remarkable. It was not for me but I enjoyed it thoroughly. When we reached Arlington Street we found a further crowd assembled there.

The reception seemed to pass very quickly and was not unpleasant. My only sorrow and shame was the appearance of Mione [Duff's sister, Hermione] who looked like a mad tart of the year 2000 AD. There were fortunately no tears shed by either mother and all went as merry as possible.

About five we started off in a motor. It had been an uncertain day and remained so to the last. There was a tremendous crowd waiting in Arlington Street to see us off, who positively clambered on the car. Diana's popularity with the mob is only comparable to that of Kitchener.

We had a pleasant drive down to Philip's[1] house at Lympne. The country was looking beautiful but it was not a pretty day as I should have wished – no sun – or at least no sunset.

Philip's house we found charming – almost ideal for a honeymoon. The situation is perfect with a wide view over Romney Marsh and the sea. The house and decorations are ultra modern – might not perhaps do to live with but perfect to stay in. The luxury and comfort are beyond reproach. There were a host of servants grouped to greet us. Holbrook had gone on before – Wade, Diana's maid, came with us. Fountains were playing outside the house and in. We bathed and dressed and enjoyed a faultless dinner – food excellent – champagne, port and brandy all beyond reproach. We walked very roman-tically in the garden and then sat for a little and read Donne's *Epithalamia* aloud.

---

[1] Sir Philip Sassoon, Bt. (1888–1939). Politician and connoisseur, he was a lavish host, enter-taining artists and statesmen at his houses in Park Lane, at Trent Park, High Barnet and at Port Lympne in Kent.

Our night, like so many of the main incidents in our love story was very old fashioned and conventional. There were tears, cries, bloodshed and great joy. The only unintended and slightly farcical incident was when I, meaning to turn on the light, rang by mistake the bell and Miss Wade came swiftly but most unwelcome to the assistance of her poor little mistress. We sent her away swearing we hadn't rung. There must have been a story and a laugh in the servants' hall.

June 3, 1919

A peaceful day. We rose late – strolled in the garden, lunched sumptuously – drove to Folkestone to see about our tickets for France – had a further little drive along the coast, came back to a sleepy evening and a large dinner, wrote letters and went to bed.

It sounds a dull day but it was a very happy one. So happy that before sleeping – we decided almost to stay another day, which resolution however I dissuaded Diana from when we woke up. It was a happy day. The great joy of waking up in bed together unashamed – although as a matter of fact we were a little ashamed in front of Wade. The fun of breakfasting there and reading together the papers which seemed to contain nothing but accounts and pictures of us. A happy day.

June 4, 1919

We were very sorry to leave. At about 10 we motored in to Folkestone – taking Wade and leaving Holbrook. We were installed in our cabin on the boat before the London train arrived. We were treated like Royalty. The landing officer or whatever he called himself came into our cabin, saluted, stood at attention and asked to be allowed to congratulate us. He then, which was more to the point, did all that was necessary about our passports, secured us best seats on the Paris train, saw that we were first to leave the boat and had all our small baggage carried straight to the train by his men without allowing it to pass through the *douane*. We met the Aga Khan on the boat who, although he was going to the Peace Conference on the business of the Empire, had not our advantages.

June 7, 1919

We had a hearty lunch at the Café de Paris and left Paris by the 2.30 express for Pisa. It was a very hot and dirty journey but we had a comfortable compartment and rather enjoyed it. We slept wonderfully well although I did not climb to my upper berth but shared Diana's.

June 8, 1919

A lovely morning. We enjoyed the beauty of the Bay of Genoa. We arrived at Pisa after lunch and had a couple of hours to spend there. This is just time to see what is worth seeing, all of which is very conveniently gathered together in one corner. We liked the Campo Santo best and were also delighted with the Baptistery and pleased with the Cathedral. We climbed to the top of the Leaning Tower – Diana insisted on walking round the top where there is no railing. I dared not accompany her and I felt sick with terror to see her. It is of course perfectly safe – but I am a coward about high places and get worse as I grow older. I am quite ashamed of it.

We had a hot journey from Pisa to Florence. Ivor Wimborne met us at the station and drove us to the villa he has taken – Berenson's[1] villa. It is quite beautiful. We got out of the carriage at the bottom of the hill and approached the villa through a long avenue of cypresses at the top of which Phyllis appeared in evening dress, waving a fan, looking what she herself would have called 'very Alfred de Musset'. She and the Duke of Marlborough are the only other inhabitants of the villa.

Diana and I have a delightful little suite to ourselves – two bedrooms, sitting room and bath. The whole house could not be more comfortable, cleaner, or in better taste. It is full of flowers inside and out – and there is a delightful library. The food is excellent and there is plenty of champagne imported by Ivor. After dinner Ivor, the Duke and Phyllis went out to a party leaving Diana and me alone. We wandered in the garden which was more beautiful than words can say. I had never seen fireflies before, the garden was full of them, they seemed to me a miracle, the scent of the flowers was intoxicating, the moon was full. We seemed to have reached almost the limit of beauty.

June 10, 1919

Another quiet and happy day. We did the Pitti gallery in the afternoon – we liked especially the Raphael picture of his mistress, and the Mantegna.

They all went out after dinner and we had a happy evening together, except when talking about the dead as we so often do. I suggested that we should imagine one or two of them sitting in the empty chairs around us. This was too much for Diana and made her cry. We were sitting on the terrace – it was a lovely night and after I had made this unhappy suggestion the unoccupied chairs looked terribly empty.

June 11, 1919

This morning we got up a little earlier and went to bathe in the pool below Vincigliata. It is a charming spot. I went there ten years ago. We wore nothing – Diana's white body dazzled in the sunlight and glistened in the shade. Too lovely she looked in this strange setting – reminiscent of some old Italian allegorical picture. But the water was not clear enough – dead leaves, sticks, flies, tadpoles and a thousand foreign bodies spoilt the bathe for me.

---

[1] Bernard Berenson (1865–1959), American critic and connoisseur of Italian art.

June 21, 1919 [Staying in Lord Grimthorpe's villa at Ravello]

We spent the morning wandering through the garden and reading the *Symposium* aloud – in Jowett's translation. In the evening we found our way with some difficulty down to the sea. We discovered a beautiful secluded spot between rocks which went sheer into the water and here we bathed without dresses and without towels. It was a lovely bathe – we were terribly hot and the water was clear as crystal. There are two dogs in the house which I love. We took them with us on our walk. They were most disturbed when we went into the sea and stood howling on the rocks. The climb up the hill again was very severe – it took us about an hour to do and it took Diana several days to recover. She became more and more stiff and at one time could hardly walk.

After dinner we walked again in the garden and again Diana took off her dress. It happened that her pearls fell with it. We did not discover the loss until next morning when we had a terrible moment of doubt, anxiety and suspicion. Eventually we looked for them in the garden and by a miracle found them where they had fallen.

June 24, 1919

We are reading now Frank Harris's *Life of Oscar Wilde* which we found here. We spent most of the morning at it. This morning for the first time we lost sight of the sun – great clouds were rolling about in a mysterious and enchanting manner. At one moment we were lost in one of them, at the next we were surrounded by them but bathed in sunlight.

At last I have been able to catch up time in my diary. I am writing this on the day I write of. For the last two months I have been in arrears – sometimes as much as a month. It is a great relief like having finished a task. I wish I had never got so far behind for I have been forced to write hurriedly and have done no justice to these golden days which are doubtless the happiest that I shall ever know.

We felt sad at our last dinner. Afterwards we walked in the garden. Diana cried because we were going away and at the thought that we might never be so happy again. Blissfully happy we have been here and it is sad to go, but we can't put it off as we have engaged and paid for our berths on the ship from Naples to Marseilles.

June 28, 1919 (Marseilles)

It was a long while before we could get off the ship. When we succeeded in doing so we drove to Cooks who informed us that we couldn't get a sleeping berth to Paris for several days and who refused to cash a cheque. This necessitated a visit to the Consul-General who of course made everything alright. I got very cross and irritable with these vexations. I am bad at keeping cheerful when things go wrong. Diana is wonderful.

After lunch we went to a cinema and while we were there news arrived that peace was signed. The whole town immediately became *en fête*.

Duff and Diana returned to England at the beginning of July – staying in borrowed houses until their own in Gower Street was ready.

July 18, 1919

We have been much excited in these days over our new motor car which Beaverbrook gave us. Diana drives it. Today she drove it into a milk cart in Stafford Street, upset the cart and flooded the street. The owners of the dog shop dashed out with all their dogs on leashes and immediately set them to drink in the gutter. She also slightly damaged one of the doors of the car.

July 19, 1919

We walked across the Park to Carlton House Terrace where we were to see the procession from Lady Herbert's house [*a procession and firework display in Hyde Park to celebrate the peace*]. We had some difficulty in crossing the route but eventually succeeded, Diana shouting shamelessly to the police that she had to go to Clarence House [*London residence of the Duke of Connaught*].

We saw the procession well enough and enjoyed it very much. Foch was by far the most impressive figure. The massed colours were beautiful. We started out about 8.30 to dine with Marion Holden. It took us nearly an hour to get there – tube to Piccadilly Circus, thence to Oxford Circus where there was such a crowd that we gave it up and walked. Diana is perfect in those circumstances, loves the crowd, never cross. She was looking lovely. I told her I had never seen her look so pretty. She was eager as a child for the fireworks.

It was past nine when we arrived at 6 Green Street. Viola and Alan were there. They had almost finished dinner but there were plenty of good cold things to eat. We ate hastily and before we had finished there was a rumour that the fireworks had begun. They all dashed upstairs – Diana of course went first – I lingering over a glass of port came last. We climbed to the top floor whence there were steps up to the roof. I was at the bottom of these – just about to go up. I heard suddenly a crash of breaking glass – then after what seemed minutes the terrible thud of a falling body. At my left hand there was a door like the door of a cupboard. It led into a narrow little box room lit by a skylight about thirty feet from the floor. Through this Diana had fallen. I found her lying on the ground. It was a ghastly moment. She said at once that she was alright then added that she thought she had broken her leg. She was in a good deal of pain but was brave beyond belief. I knelt by her, holding her in my arms until the doctor came who saw at once that she had broken her leg above the knee. With the help of chloroform and two men with a stretcher we moved her from the floor on to a bed in a housemaid's room on the same floor. The first two doctors who arrived were called Whalteck and Wharry – they with the help of Diana's old Doctor Hood who gave the chloroform set her leg on a rough sort of splint. Doctor Furber came later and finally Arbuthnot Lane.

Viola went to break the news to the Duchess. It was a terrible night. Furber succeeded in finding Sister Manley – a very nice Irish nurse who used to be in the Rutland Hospital. I sat by Diana's side most of the night and slept a little on a sofa. As the result of chloroform and morphine she didn't suffer much this night. I left her in the morning to return to Little College Street and wash and change. I had to walk nearly all the way. It was raining hard. All the bunting flags and decorations in the streets looked sad and bedraggled. There was no sign of life except in Piccadilly where I was passed by four or five large motor lorries quite full of German prisoners – in spite of the rain they looked cheerful. I suppose they were going home.

I spent the rest of the day with Diana and henceforth I spent all my leisure with her. My life now became quite regular and uneventful. Every morning I go to see her before going to the Office. I lunch quickly at a Club, get to her again by a quarter to two and stay an hour with her – go straight back to her on leaving the Office and dine in her room, stay with her until about eleven and then to bed. That first night I slept in Mrs Holden's room as she was away, the next I slept for the last time at Little College Street, then for a week at Mother's flat as she was away, finally I moved into Katharine's house 17 Oxford Square, where I am very happy and comfortable.

My only amusement these days has been driving our motor. I had never driven one before. Holbrook instructed me. I learnt in two or three days.

I have been a good deal troubled all this time by a rash on my legs which I thought was eczema and treated accordingly with drugs and lotions and careful dieting which excluded alcohol – a severe privation. At last Doctor Pritchard whom I was consulting took me to a skin specialist who diagnosed it as tinia. [*It was in fact psoriasis.*]

September 2, 1919

The Holdens went away leaving us alone in the house. We have no servants here except Marjorie's kitchen maid to cook for us and an old male retainer of the Holdens who occasionally opens the front door. For food we rely very largely on presents of game. At the moment we have eighteen birds in the house. Next week we are to move to Arlington Street. The chief trouble at present is to cure Diana of taking morphia. She has been having it ever since her accident and now cannot do without it. Every evening there is a scene until she gets it.

September 3, 1919

On Tuesday evening first Beaverbrook and then Edwin came to see Diana. The first is very full of his attacks in the *Daily Express* on Winston. We discussed with Edwin the cause of these and he believes it to be an argument which Max and Winston had one night in Paris when Winston coined the phrase 'the press is easier squashed than squared'. Edwin thinks Max never forgave this – an absurdly trivial cause for such a procedure. Max himself told us that he had received a very strong letter from Bonar Law on the subject of these attacks. He had merely replied that he did not control the articles in the *Express* and that he had forwarded the letter to Blumenfeld.[1]

Edwin after I had left confided to Diana all his schemes and difficulties. He is no longer working harmoniously with Chelmsford and longs to get rid of him.[2] He would like to replace him with himself and change the whole Government of India. He has written to Lloyd George proposing this but hasn't sent the letter. Alternatively he proposes to make a figurehead like Arthur of Connaught Viceroy and act himself as Grand Vizier.

September 11, 1919

A wonderfully hot day. I met Felix Elston at lunch with Diana. I hadn't seen him for years. He seemed in no way altered by having murdered Rasputin – but rather sillier. He says that Russia can only be saved by the Cross – only Good can defeat Evil. Attributes all the trouble to Jews and Germans and believes the latter will restore the monarchy.

When I got back to Green Street this evening I found Diana with her leg down flat on the bed. All this while it has been held up in a sling by the means of an erection like a gallows on the bed. It was so delightful to see it normal again.

September 23, 1919 [Arlington Street]

Sidney and Venetia dined with us. Diana sat up in a chair to dinner. It was our first dinner party and a very pleasant one. We had a long narrow table. Venetia and Diana at each end, Sidney and I in the middle on the same side. Behind the table stood two little fruit trees which Venetia had given, laden the one with apples, the other with plums. On the table stood one of our beautiful white Bow china horses. We ate oyster scallops beautifully cooked, roast duck, roly poly treacle pudding and Stilton cheese. We drank Roederer 1911 and port. Venetia and Sidney are very much together now. Edwin is away at Breccles whither Venetia returns tomorrow.

September 24, 1919

Gerry Villiers has gone away to be circumcised – after the performance of which rite he intends to take a holiday. So I am left in charge of the Department for six weeks. I shall have a lot to do. This morning – a bright bitter cold winter morning – I arrived before 10 which will in future have to be my hour.

---

[1] Ralph Blumenfeld (RDB) (1864–1948), an American; edited the *Daily Express* for twenty-eight years from 1904.

[2] Edwin Montagu became Secretary of State for India in 1917. Lord Chelmsford was the Viceroy.

September 27, 1919

Today the railway strike began. It was a beautiful cold autumn morning and there was rather a pleasant scent of excitement and revolution in the air. I noticed on my way back to the Foreign Office that St James's Street was full of policemen and the Horse Guards Parade was full of sailors and motor lorries. Lawford [Raymond Lawford, F.O. colleague] had seen H. G. Wells lunching at the Reform. He said that this was the beginning of revolution – that all revolutions had begun so. [*The strike was settled on 5 October.*]

October 13, 1919

We had a little dinner party at Arlington Street of Iris and her husband,[1] Katharine and Alan. Neither Moffat nor Alan had dressed for dinner which annoyed me and spoilt the *mise en scène.* Iris dresses more pronouncedly Café Royal than ever. Moffat on the whole is an agreeable surprise. He is nice looking, quiet in manner, very little accent. He wouldn't drink much until it came to the brandy of which he had his full share, but without, I thought, appreciating the quality. Then he sent round to his house for some new wonderful drug which was supposed to produce a thousand queer effects. He, Iris and Diana all tried it. On the girls it produced no effect at all, nor on him until suddenly he went green, left the room in a hurry and was sick on the stairs.

October 17, 1919

Arbuthnot Lane telephoned to say that Diana was not to get up. Her leg had been photographed again and it appears that the results are not altogether satisfactory. This was rather a blow to us. She cried a little but was very brave. Diana and I dined at Arlington Street but afterwards I went out as she had Rubinstein[2] and other musicians coming to play and people to hear them. [*Duff was tone deaf.*]

October 20, 1919

On my way to the Foreign Office this morning I met Doctor Hood. He evidently blames Lane very much for the mismanagement of Diana's leg. She will not be quite well he thinks until a year from the date of the accident. Meanwhile he says she mustn't think of going abroad. This is very depressing.

I lunched and dined at Arlington Street. Diana had the doctors there and was rather unhappy about the splint they said she must wear. The Duchess came up today but mercifully went out to lunch. Diana had better news about her leg and will only have to wear a very small splint.

---

[1] Curtis Moffat (1887–1949), an American photographer, married Iris Tree in 1919.
[2] Artur Rubinstein (1887–1982), one of the great pianists of the twentieth century.

October 23, 1919

Eddie and Marjorie came to dinner with us. It was Eddie's last night in London; he and Albany were to leave the next morning and don't intend to return until the summer of 1921. Before leaving he had for the purposes of his divorce from Bettine[1] to commit adultery. He had left this to the last minute and was going after dinner to a flat he had taken at the Savoy where he was to meet a woman he had never seen and spend the night with her. He had arranged for a detective to be there and for evidence to be duly collected. He had tried it the night before but the whole thing had broken down as the lady had failed to turn up. This formed our chief subject of conversation at dinner. It was suggested that Marjorie should take the place of the lady or that I should in disguise. Eventually soon after dinner Eddie went off alone to his tryst.

October 24, 1919

I went to see him off at the station this morning. I only got there a few minutes before the train left so I didn't hear much of what happened last night. I gathered however that after a great deal of champagne he had contrived to commit the necessary crime in very deed – he said 'One might as well be hung for a sheep as a lamb – but there is an age limit'. The lady apparently was like an old sheep. I rather envied him and Barry, setting out on their adventures.

October 29, 1919

We dined at the Ritz with the Montagus. When we arrived there we found they had just got Diana Capel. I didn't know she was in London and I was delighted to see her. She was looking most lovely. She has had her hair cut short but is letting it grow again. Dinner was not very successful. The two Dianas never harmonize – I don't know why it is.

The conversation fell on reading other people's letters. Edwin told how he had once found in a book addressed to Venetia the most compromising letter he had ever read. He had written her thereupon a severe reproof, warning, remonstrance, but then had changed his mind, thought his own letter too pompous and had destroyed both. He had never mentioned it till this moment. Venetia was somewhat taken aback – but faced it well – said she remembered the book and the letter and had often wondered whether he had found it. I thought Edwin had handled the matter rather prettily. It all passed with a laugh.

We went back and sat at Arlington Street afterwards and talked disjointedly. Then it rained and they couldn't get a taxi. I started walking Diana [Capel]

---

[1] Bettine Stuart-Wortley and Eddie Grant married in 1917. She later married Montagu Bertie and he married Bridget Herbert.

home. In Piccadilly we got a taxi and I drove with her to Curzon Street. I made
love to her and kissed her and promised to meet her next day. I felt rather
guilty when I got home.

October 31, 1919

This day last year I arrived in London on leave from France. It seems much
more than one year.

Lunched at the Ritz with Diana, Marjorie and the Duke. We were talking to
[J. M.] Barrie[1] in the hall when up came Marjorie with the Queen of Spain[2]
and introduced us. I was quite unprepared for the honour and the sudden
change in posture – from looking down at the minute Barrie to looking up at
the immense Queen was most disconcerting. She is a fine looking woman.

November 1, 1919

I thought Diana was going to *Elijah* at the Albert Hall in the afternoon so I
arranged – secretly – to lunch with Diana Capel. At the last moment she
decided not to go but I couldn't alter my plan. I had to lie terribly. We lunched
at Sherry's and it was very agreeable. She was looking charming. Intrigue of
this sort has a fatal fascination. I don't care for her one thousandth part as
much as I care for my own Diana, and when I got back to the latter and found
her very low with a headache having been alone all day and wretched that I
hadn't lunched with her but believing all my lies, I felt a monster of wickedness
and cruelty.

November 4, 1919

This evening we had a memorable dinner party – Winston, Beaverbrook,
Nellie Romilly and the Montagus. For the last six months Beaverbrook has
been bitterly and mercilessly attacking Winston in the *Daily Express* and this
evening was their first meeting. From the point of view of the dinner party it
was a tremendous success. Winston arrived first, then Nellie, then Max. The
two shook hands. They were both obviously nervous – Max more so than
Winston. Then the Montagus arrived. We had dinner in the bedroom as usual.
The table is very narrow which I think promotes conversation. The food was
excellent, the champagne circulated freely and the conversation never flagged.
It started on general topics such as the Douglas Pennant[3] enquiry on which
everyone was agreed but gradually veered round to politics and Russia.

---

[1] Sir James Matthew Barrie (1860–1937), playwright and novelist. Author of *Peter Pan*.
[2] Queen Victoria Eugenia (Ena) of Spain (1887–1969), daughter of Prince Henry of Battenberg
   and Princess Beatrice, a daughter of Queen Victoria. She married Alfonso XIII of Spain
   (1886–1941) in 1906.
[3] The Hon. Violet Douglas-Pennant (1869–1945) became Commandant of the newly formed
   Women's Royal Air Force (WRAF) in June 1918. She was summarily dismissed in August
   1918. Public protests led to a Select Committee Inquiry in the House of Lords 1918–19. Her
   dismissal was upheld.

Winston was at his very best, witty, courteous, eloquent. I never liked him so much. Max showed up badly. He was violent and rather rude. I several times feared disaster but it was always avoided. Edwin took a fairly neutral middle line and acted rather as arbitrator. They ended perfectly good friends and both said they had enjoyed themselves tremendously. I think they had. Max said the *Daily Express* is now going to start a campaign against [Field Marshal] French. Diana begged him not to.

November 5, 1919

I took Diana to the Opera, wheeled her into the Royal Box and then went off and dined with the other Diana. I said I was going there but concealed the fact that we dined alone. We had a pleasant evening, sitting by the fire and making love. She doesn't care at all for me and I not really very much for her but it amuses us.

I dashed off at eleven to retrieve Diana – travelled by tube to Covent Garden and arrived there only to find that the Opera had been over nearly half an hour. She had gone on to the Savoy and left a note for me. I found her there with Hutchinson[1] trying to get supper.

November 11, 1919. Armistice Day

I went to the cenotaph at 11 o'clock for two minutes silence. Poincaré drove up to lay wreaths. The silence was impressive.

This evening was the Victory Ball. Lord Furness lent us one of his cars for the night. We contrived to lift Diana's chair and all into the motor and we had a very successful evening. She wore an eighteenth-century Russian dress with a very pretty high cap and looked lovely. I wore a beard during the earlier part of the evening but took it off later. Otherwise I was in ordinary evening clothes. We dined with Beaverbrook at the Hyde Park Hotel. The ball was great fun. I sat in the box most of the time eagerly scanning the crowd for Diana Capel. I found her at last and we went and sat on the same seat where at the Victory Ball last year I sat with the Duchess. Diana C. was looking very well in gold trousers. When I got back to the box I found Beaverbrook pouring his heart out to Diana – saying how devoted he was to her and for her sake devoted also to me – how there was nothing in the world he wouldn't do for us and how he was the best friend we had. He was very drunk.

December 4, 1919

We dined at Queen Anne's Gate. Edwin wasn't there as he is too busy with his India Bill in the House. We all were to go on to the ball at Covent Garden. Diana and Venetia dressed after dinner in wonderful 18th century dresses, wigs two feet high and panniers sticking out a yard each side. Mrs Reggie

---

[1] John (Hutchy) Hutchinson KC (1884–1942), barrister and Liberal politician.

Fellowes[1] I hadn't met before. She is the notorious Princesse de Broglie, the destroyer of many a happy home – I expected to find her attractive and I wasn't disappointed. I got on well with her especially when we reached the subject of pornography. I found her well versed in the subject from Casanova to Pierre Louÿs, and she had even read Aubrey Beardsley's *Venus and Tannhäuser*. I made no impression on her however and couldn't get her to dance with me at the ball.

The ball was pretty but I didn't enjoy it very much. Diana looked lovely. We didn't get home till 3 – drove home in Ivor's car. Diana once in couldn't get out again owing to the height of her headdress. They had to open the top of the car to deliver her.

December 16, 1919

Phyllis lunched with us in Arlington Street and we went afterwards to the studio where we saw Diana on the film – driving in the motor to Battersea Park and walking there. I thought she looked lovely.

We dined with Katharine – read some of *Henry IV Pt. 1* after dinner and then a most beautiful new poem by [J. C.] Squire called *The Moon*. There was a good deal of fog and when we telephoned for a taxi they refused to come for less than 15/-. Diana then settled to stay the night with Katharine. I was rather annoyed but determined not to be or not to show it. I soon picked up a taxi myself but felt lonely going to bed alone. First thing next morning I went out to Boucheron and bought a Christmas present for Diana Capel.

December 17, 1919

Diana came back to Arlington Street in the morning and went to bed. Manley telephoned to me that she wasn't very well and wouldn't lunch. I lunched at the Junior Carlton and went to see her for a minute afterwards. The Duke was there. I thought she was looking very bad, obviously suffering from a debauch of morphia.

When we got to bed I charged Diana with her naughtiness. She at first denied but eventually confessed. I told her how ugly it had made her look. Fear of ugliness is I think the best preventive.

December 23, 1919

This morning just as I was going out to lunch Diana Capel telephoned. I had no idea she was in London and was delighted to hear her. She had come over from Paris the day before. Capel had meanwhile started for the South of

[1] Daisy Fellowes (1887–1962), married the Hon. Reginald Fellowes (1884–1953) in 1919. She was born Daisy Decazes, daughter of the Duc Decazes and the sewing-machine heiress Isabelle Singer, and had previously been married to the Prince de Broglie. She was considered one of the best-dressed women in the world.

France where she was to join him in a fortnight. She had settled to lunch with Lady Rosslyn and asked me to lunch there too.

We drove together to Westbourne Terrace where we lunched with Lady Rosslyn, whom I like very much. After lunch I drove off with Diana to Bains to get some books, she having settled to meet Lady Rosslyn again at 3 – at Asprey's. We had a long and very pleasant drive, long because of the blocks in the traffic, pleasant because I kissed her – and it was long past three when we got back to Asprey's. She jumped out and I was driving off to the Foreign Office when I noticed that she had left in the taxi the book she had just bought. I turned back to the shop and found her with Lady Rosslyn still on the pavement in front of it. I put the book into Diana's hands and at the same time noticed an expression of horror on the face of Lady Rosslyn who was standing behind her. But I thought no more of it and drove away.

December 24, 1919

The first thing I saw in the *Daily Express* this morning was the death of Boy Capel, Diana's husband, who was killed in a motor accident in the South of France on Monday. I was very shocked.

December 31, 1919

I felt wakeful [after dinner] so went on to the Albert Hall where there was a fancy dress ball. I managed to get in without a ticket by a subterfuge and with the help of Godfrey Wentworth whom I met at the door. He took me up to the Duke of Manchester's box where were all the lesser lights of the stage and a great quantity of champagne. Just as I was going I met Iris who introduced me to Cathleen Nesbitt.[1] The latter I immediately drove home, making instantaneous and frantic love to her the while. I found her charming and so she found me. I told her how I had loved her as Jessica, Perdita and the Duchess of Malfi. I expressed a wish to kiss her feet having admired them when bare in the part of Perdita. She obligingly removed her stocking. We talked a lot of poetry, said we would arrange no further meeting lest we should spoil the romance, we would leave it to the fates. It was half past five when I got to bed and I was drunk.

---

[1] Cathleen Nesbitt (1888–1982), the actress, was one of the great beauties of her day and continued acting into her nineties. She had been engaged to Rupert Brooke.

PART TWO

1920–1939

Between the Wars

1920

January 5, 1920 (London)

We dined with the Montagus. Edwin maintained that Margot had ruined Asquith – Birrell and most of us said she had made extraordinarily little difference to him. I made Edwin angry by saying that Winston was the first politician who had dared say we ought to trade with Germany.

January 14, 1920

We went to *Julius Caesar* excellently produced and enjoyed it enormously. Diana and I went on to a dance. It was a small but decorated dance as Prince Albert [Duke of York, future King George VI] was there. I didn't enjoy it much – sat with Kakoo.[1] At the end we went off together with Kakoo and Guy and Frances Charteris. Miss June Chaplin said that we might take her car. We found one standing at the door which we thought was it and off we went.

January 15, 1920

After we had finished lunch at Arlington St. in came Kakoo with the news that we had last night taken Prince Albert's car – just as he was going – that he had been kept waiting three quarters of an hour – that he had been told that Diana had taken it and was much surprised. It is a shame that all the blame should fall on her as it was no more her fault than anyone else's. She has written him a letter of abject apology.

We dined with the Holdens. Very late – about half past two, Diana and I went to the 'Pan Ball' at Covent Garden. I met Cathleen Nesbitt there. We retired to a dark corner and embraced. After a little however she said that after all she didn't love me. She had thought she did but she didn't. I was too civil to assure her that her lack of feeling was reciprocated.

January 16, 1920

I met Diana [after lunch]. She had lunched alone at the Ivy. She had had a civil letter from Prince Albert about the motor incident. We dined together at Arlington Street and went to the Philharmonic Hall to hear Shackleton's[2] adventures. Shackleton himself wasn't there, but his second in command, Wild, told the story very adequately. It was a quite thrilling entertainment and we thoroughly enjoyed it. On the way back we bought some peptonised cocoa and cooked it in our room before going to bed.

---

[1] Kathleen 'Kakoo' Granby, née Tennant (1894–1989), married Diana's brother John, later 9th Duke of Rutland, in 1916.

[2] Sir Ernest Shackleton (1874–1922), the Antarctic explorer. His fellow explorer, Frank Wild (1874–1939), went on five major Antarctic journeys including Shackleton's.

January 21, 1920

After dinner I had a long talk with Lady Rosslyn whom I found charming. She told me how terrible it had been for her breaking the news that day to Diana [Capel]. How Diana had arrived full of spirits and tried to drag her into Asprey's to choose a Christmas present for me, how she had to restrain her and get her away and tell her. It must have been ghastly. She told me also how impossible Diana's relations with Capel were becoming, how he had entirely ceased to live with her and hardly ever spoke to her. That he confessed she had got on his nerves and he could hardly bear her presence.

January 23, 1920

We dined at Wimborne House. Ivor left the room with the ladies which gave the conversation a chance. It turned on survival of personality. Winston said the older he grew the more disillusioned and discontented he became and above all the more weary of and disgusted with his own personality. If he had the choice between immortality and being blown out like a candle he would choose the latter. Birrell cordially agreed. I didn't and don't. I could con- template an unending series of existences with equanimity. It is a question of appetite. Then we talked politics and continued to after we joined the ladies. Winston was splendidly reactionary – and shocked even Birrell who although he has always been a liberal is full of Tory prejudices and principles. Winston said that he was all out now to fight labour, it was his one object in politics. He said he was a monarchist, swore we would have all the Kings back on their thrones, even the Hohenzollerns – he attributed the calamitous state of Central Europe to the incompetence and corruption of the new republics. He compared the Peace Treaty with the Treaty of Vienna much to the advantage of the latter. He thanked God he was in no way responsible for the Peace Treaty which he would have been ashamed to put his name to. I was delighted with everything he said.

January 24, 1920

Katharine had a little dinner with us and we went to see Masefield's *Pompey the Great* acted by F. R. Benson.[1] A miserable play, I thought it. We had supper at Queen Anne's Gate. I drank a good deal and demurred at going when Diana wanted to with the result that she and Katharine left without me and went home together. I was furious but did nothing, thinking it wiser to let my wrath evaporate with the fumes of wine. She came back early next morning – at nine o'clock – I was cross for a little and she cried but all ended happily. She and Katharine had had morphia and talked all night.

---

[1] Sir Frank Benson (1858–1939), British actor-manager, whose touring company and acting school greatly influenced contemporary theatre.

February 2, 1920 [Paris]

Another lovely morning. I was looking forward all day to Diana's arrival. I miss her most in amusing surroundings as she is the only person who perfectly shares my amusement. My infidelities are entirely of the flesh. Long habit of promiscuity asserts itself. I feel guilty of no faithlessness, only of filthiness.

February 3, 1920

We [went] to a play at the Porte Saint Martin, *Béranger* written by Sacha Guitry,[1] acted by him in the title role and by his father in the part of Talleyrand. I have seldom if ever enjoyed a play more – beautifully acted by all, including Yvonne Printemps[2] in the part of Lisette. It was all particularly interesting to me, who thinks one day to write a book on Talleyrand.

February 5, 1920

We wandered around Les Halles purchasing *pâtés de foie gras* and then went to Molyneux[3] the dressmaker. There we saw Hébé the beautiful model. She is the one I saw at Lucile's when I was here in October 1918. She is I think the most beautiful woman I ever saw.

February 7, 1920

We set off for London this morning with about eight separate packages including two *pâtés de foie gras* packed separately, one of which Diana carried in each hand, and a plaster bust of a woman whose wrappings did not conceal its character and which I had to carry in both arms.

February 13, 1920

We lunched with Letty in Montagu Square. Mrs Dudley Ward[4] was there and very pretty she looked. She is really very nice too and quite amusing. On my way back to the Office I fell in with Bland[5] who is now Lord Hardinge's private

---

[1] Sacha Guitry (1885–1957), French playwright, director and actor. His father was the actor Lucien Guitry.

[2] Yvonne Printemps (1895–1977), French singer and actress. Married Sacha Guitry in 1919, later divorced him and married Pierre Fresnay, the French film star.

[3] Edward Molyneux (1891–1974), an Irish couturier who worked in Paris between the wars. He escaped to London in 1940 but returned in 1944 and reopened a Paris salon in addition to one in London.

[4] Winifred (Freda) Dudley Ward, née Winifred May Birkin (1894–1983), an Anglo-American textile heiress. She married first William Dudley Ward (1877–1946), a Liberal MP (divorced 1931), and second Pedro, Marquès de Casa Maury (c.1895–1968), the Spanish-Cuban racing driver. Mistress of Edward, Prince of Wales for many years after they first met in 1918.

[5] Sir Nevile Bland (1886–1972), Ambassador to the Netherlands 1942–8; Private Secretary to the Permanent Under-Secretary at the Foreign Office.

secretary and protested to him about being sent to the D.O.T. He implied that it was inevitable.

I haven't written a word in my diary for over two months. This is the longest I have let it go for the last five years. The conversation with Bland recorded above resulted in my being sent to the Egyptian Department temporarily. I worked very hard there which was one of the reasons why I had no time to write in this book. I get on well with Murray[1] – the other member of it. After about six weeks of it I was transferred to the Central Europe Dept where I deal with the Balkans. I like this better than Egypt and much better than the Commercial. I have kept notes of events which I have now time to transcribe.

March 2, 1920

We went to see the pictures by Augustus John. I have to write an article for Diana as editress of *Femina*.[2] We thought they might provide subject matter.

In March 1920 the Coopers moved into No. 90 Gower Street, Bloomsbury, which they had acquired on a fifty-year lease for £90 a year. They had also rented the first-floor flat at No. 92, knocked down the wall between and so acquired their master bedroom and a large bathroom. A few years later they extended further, taking over the first-floor flat at No. 94, making a library and bath/dressing room for Duff.

March 15, 1920

The housemaid and cook who have now moved into Gower Street thought there were burglars in the house in the middle of the night. Mad with fright they climbed out on to the roof and thence to the roof of the next house where their screams were heard by the police. They were helped down and a large body of police then forced their way into the house, where there was no sign of burglars nor of anything having been touched. The maids however refused to go back into the house and turned up at Arlington Street at 3 a.m. dressed in their nightgowns and covered in soot.

March 17, 1920

We dined with the Cranbornes.[3] We had a very pleasant dinner and played poker afterwards. I find Lady Cranborne more and more unexpectedly attractive.

---

[1] John Murray (1883–1937), head of the Egyptian Department in the FO. He had spent fourteen years in the Egyptian Civil Service and came to the FO in 1919. Died young while serving as Minister in Mexico.

[2] 'I had agreed to be editor of a paper called *Femina* that was short-lived but I was only a figurehead and had no hand in its death.' Diana Cooper, *Autobiography*. The articles written by Duff but signed by Diana helped to give them additional income.

[3] Robert 'Bobbety' Cecil, Viscount Cranborne, later 5th Marquess of Salisbury (1893–1972). He married Elizabeth 'Betty' Cavendish, daughter of Lord Richard Cavendish, in 1915.

March 20, 1920. Saturday

A great event today. We moved into Gower Street. It is rather uncomfortable and bare at present, but Diana's bedroom in which we live is practically finished and very charming.

April 10, 1920

My last day in the Egypt Department. I am to go on Monday to the Central Europe Department and am rather glad of the change. I lunched at White's and travelled down to Rugby in the afternoon to stay at Ashby.[1] I found the Montagus there, Birrell, the Reggie Felloweses and Claude Lowther.[2] It was quite a pleasant party and I found Mrs Fellowes more attractive than ever.

April 19, 1920

An extremely unpleasant dinner at the Hyde Park Hotel under the auspices of Beaverbrook. I like him less the more I know him. He was rude to me and I to him – but I thought I scored. We went on to Drury Lane theatre to see Pavlova[3] dance.

May 4, 1920

We dined with the Tennysons. At the end of dinner Dr Furber telephoned to say that Mione had been to him to ask for poison in order to kill herself. He had of course refused to give her any and she had gone away vowing self-destruction. We telephoned to her hotel but she wasn't in so we could do nothing. However we stopped there on our way home and found her comfortably in bed. We argued with her a little and she promised not to kill herself in the immediate future.

May 12, 1920

We dined with Felix Elston in his little flat. Mrs Hwfa[4] was there, Serge Obolensky and his wife and half a dozen nondescript Russian refugees. The food was excellent and the wine though erratic in appearance, beginning with port and ending with champagne, was good in quality and sufficient in quantity. They sang Russian songs and drank Russian toasts and it was all rather charming. I sat between Mrs Hwfa who couldn't hear what I said and a Russian who couldn't understand it. I left Diana to enjoy the music after dinner and went off to Lady Rosslyn by appointment. We went for a brief

---

[1] Ashby St Ledgers, Northamptonshire, the country house restored and altered by Lutyens for Lord Wimborne.

[2] Claude Lowther, poet, wit and dandy. Friend of the Duchess of Rutland.

[3] Anna Pavlova (1881–1931), the renowned Russian ballerina, brought to Paris by Diaghilev in 1909. In 1910 she formed her own company, which performed throughout the world for the next fifteen years.

[4] Mrs Hwfa Williams, a great friend of King Edward VII.

moment to the cinema and then back to her house where my love-making progressed. It did not go beyond a certain very definite point and it was all very delightful. I am still young enough, thank God, to love love-making for its own sake.

May 14, 1920

In the evening just as we were going out to dinner Sybil appeared at Gower Street – hopelessly drunk. We were at a loss as to what to do with her and were already late for dinner but succeeded in getting her into a taxi to whom we gave instructions to drive to Bexley [*where she lived*]. Apparently however she went to the Moffats instead. I had a pitifully penitential letter from her some days later, explaining and attributing her state to cocktails following on long abstinence and great fatigue.

May 21, 1920 [Breccles]

I have been reading Ronald Knox's[1] book about Patrick [Shaw-Stewart]. He never consulted me before publishing nor asked either me or Diana for letters. This irritates me. The book as it stands is bad and dull. I have written a letter of protest to Knox but don't think I shall send it. I have an idea of writing a book myself about all the dead – but I have no time.

May 23, 1920

The most beautiful day we have yet had – not one cloud in the sky. Very hot with a faint breeze. An amusing lunch, Winston entertaining us with stories of Christian Science which seemed to impress him. In the afternoon we sat under the trees while he painted the group of us.

At dinner Winston and Oliver [Lyttelton] became boring on the subject of the war. Winston prefers military conversation to all other. It has become an obsession with him. At dinner he produced a telegram which had just reached him describing violent fighting between Turks and French in Asia Minor. Apparently he and Edwin had both always foretold that this would be the result of the Turkish Treaty.[2]

May 25, 1920

Another perfect day. Diana and others went into Norwich in the afternoon. I stayed behind and played chess with Winston. He has just taken to it with all the tremendous enthusiasm with which he is inspired by anything new. We

---

[1] Ronald Knox (1888–1957), Roman Catholic priest and translator of the Bible. Scholar at Balliol at the same time as Duff was at Oxford.

[2] The Treaty of Sèvres, 1920, split up most of the old Turkish Empire between France and Britain, though the area of Turkey-in-Europe around Constantinople was given to Greece. In 1922 Mustafa Kemal drove the Greeks out and by the Treaty of Lausanne in 1923, Turkey regained this territory.

played game after game until we were late for dinner. More chess with Winston after dinner. His enthusiasm is so attractive. I think him the most delightful of men.

May 26, 1920

The weather broke this morning. It was raining hard when we left Breccles in our car at 10 o'clock. We had hardly gone a quarter of a mile when looking down to arrange our belongings Diana forgot to steer and before we knew what had happened the car was on its side in a ditch. Miraculously we were neither of us in the least hurt nor was the car damaged, not a pane of glass broken. With some difficulty we climbed out of the window and returned on foot to Breccles where we got the aid of seven men who pulled the car out of the ditch and set it on its legs again. It seemed none the worse and at 12 o'clock we started off again. We stopped at Newmarket and bought some food in the town for our lunch. Halfway up the hill out of Newmarket the motor stopped and refused to start again. By the luckiest of chances we were exactly opposite a motor shop whence we got help. While two men buried their heads in the entrails of the car we sat on a seat by the roadside and ate our lunch – cold veal and ham pie, sandwiches and cake, ginger beer and port. We always take with us the charming little 18th century picnic box which Marjorie gave me for a wedding present. We must have looked odd sitting by the wayside eating with gilt knives and forks and drinking ginger beer out of a golden cup.

May 29, 1920

I lunched with Lady Rosslyn at the Savoy having told Diana I was lunching on guard. We had a delightful lunch. She was most entertaining. After lunch we went to a cinema and I didn't get home till half past four having said I would be back about three. I found Diana in a dreadful state. She had persuaded herself that I was dead – had been frantically telephoning all over London and was quite beside herself. I felt extremely guilty – but lied successfully and everything was soon alright.

May 31, 1920

The end of my short holiday. I returned to the Foreign Office, the Egyptian Dept. and Murray. Since I have been away the Egyptian nationalists have been persuaded to negotiate and some of them are now in London and Milner is dealing with them.

During the war a British protectorate was set up in Egypt as a war measure. After the Armistice, Sa'ad Zaghlul Pasha,[1] leader of the nationalist movement, demanded Egyptian independence and asked to go with his delegation to England to talk to the

---

[1] Sa'ad Zaghlul (1857–1927). Egyptian statesman and patriot, leader of the Wafd party and nationalist movement of 1918–19. Egyptian Prime Minister Jan.–Nov. 1924.

British Government. The Foreign Office refused. A similar request was put forward by the moderate Prime Minister of Egypt, Rushdi Pasha, and his colleague, Adly (Adli) Pasha Yakan. Though supported by the High Commissioner, this too was turned down by the Foreign Office. Rushdi and Adly resigned, Zaghlul incited unrest. Order was restored by British forces in Egypt and Zaghlul was arrested and deported. In March 1919 Lord Allenby was appointed High Commissioner and insisted on the release of Zaghlul. The British Government sent out Lord Milner as head of a Mission of Inquiry which was in Egypt from December 1919 to February 1920. In June 1920 Zaghlul agreed to meet Milner in London.

June 1, 1920

Sa'ad Zaghlul and the rest of the Egyptian nationalists are coming over at the end of the week.

June 2, 1920

Our Wedding Day. Derby Day. A day of most wonderful weather. We lunched in Kensington Gardens. It was great fun. [Later I saw] Scatters [who] told me some new rhymes about the Royal Family supposed to be composed by the young princes.

'A stands for Arthur, a prince of some grit
He *thinks* he's a hero, we *know* he's a shit'

and

'W stands for Windsor – a high sounding name
It does for the public but we're Huns all the same'

June 4, 1920

We went to Lady Ribblesdale's ball. I had a long supper there with Lady Cranborne whom I find entrancing. Lovely to look at, beautiful to hear, delightful to talk to, flatteringly appreciative, understanding and inspiring. I like no one better.

June 9, 1920

I lunched clandestinely at the Savoy with Lady Rosslyn. She is good company and had a pleasant lunch but she takes things too seriously – told me that she was thinking too much of me, getting too fond. This is a pity as I am only the very least bit attracted by her. So she becomes a complication which I fear I must drop especially as I find myself falling almost into love in another direction. Lady Cranborne I like more every time I see her and she seems to like me. I spent most of the ball at Victoria Bullock's[1] this evening with her

---

[1] Lady Victoria, née Stanley (1892–1927), widow of Neil Primrose (1882–1917), had married Capt. Sir Malcolm Bullock (1890–1966) in 1919.

and thought her adorable. Daisy Fellowes was there and many other beauties but I had eyes for none of them. She pressed my hand when we parted and said in her low shy voice how much she had enjoyed herself. I fear she flirts but she appears so heavenly sincere.

June 10, 1920

We dined at Hurlingham with Ivor. Diana and I came back early. I had to finish her article for next month's *Femina*. We did it together in the Library. We had quite a love scene. She said she had never loved me more or been so happy.

June 13, 1920 [The Manor House, Sutton Courtenay]

Poor Norah [Lindsay] is very unhappy because Harry insists on selling the place and she will have nowhere to live. It was looking lovely today. Diana and I managed to get a bit alone together on the river. Margot came over from the Wharf bringing Mrs Keppel[1] and Dean Inge[2] – an odd couple. In the middle of the afternoon, to the surprise of everyone except Norah who hadn't warned us, the King of Portugal arrived. He played tennis with great energy and skill. Lord De La Warr[3] came over from Oxford, also [Prince] Paul of Serbia whom I found much nicer than I had ever thought him. I was still feeling ill and thinking too much of Lady Cranborne – a great mistake to think so much of someone seen so little – building too high on too slight foundation. It must be many days before I see her again. Perhaps I shan't love her, perhaps she doesn't in the least like me but was only thankful for a partner as all women are at balls.

June 16, 1920

Diana came up from Blenheim this morning where she went yesterday for the night and persuaded me to go back there with her this evening and return tomorrow morning. I had never seen Blenheim before and was much impressed with its beauty and magnificence. The Duke [of Marlborough] keeps high state – wears his Garter for dinner and has a host of powdered footmen. The dining room is beautiful and so is the bridge over the lake. There was a party of about 20 people. We had the most magnificent bedroom – the best in the house – I don't know why.

---

[1] Alice Keppel, wife of Col. the Hon. George Keppel, was the long-standing mistress of (Albert) Edward, Prince of Wales, later King Edward VII.

[2] William Ralph Inge, Dean of St Paul's (1860–1954). He wrote weekly articles in the *Evening Standard* and was nicknamed 'the gloomy dean'.

[3] Herbrand (Buck) Sackville, 9th Earl de la Warr (1900–76). Chairman National Labour Party 1931–43; Under-Secretary of State for the Colonies 1936–7; Lord Privy Seal May 1937–Oct. 1938; President of Board of Education 1938–40.

June 22, 1920

We dined with the McKennas – a large party. When we got home we found Katharine and Belloc[1] at Gower Street. Belloc read French poetry aloud but quite unintelligibly. He and I argued about the construction of Shakespeare's sonnets. While we were dressing for dinner came a telephone message from the Cranbornes asking us to dine on July 14th which gave me a thrill of happiness. [*The Coopers later had to refuse this invitation.*] I think of her absurdly much and pray that I shall see her tomorrow.

July 2, 1920

A contretemps has arisen with regard to the Zaghlul negotiations. Some days ago we had a telegram from Allenby[2] saying he had evidence to convict a certain Abdul Rahman Fahmi of responsibility for bomb outrages etc. The man is the secretary of Zaghlul's organization in Cairo though the two are said to have quarrelled over this policy of assassination. Allenby asked whether he should proceed. Murray suggested that he should be instructed to proceed but that meanwhile Lord Milner should explain to Zaghlul what was happening. Curzon said it was quite unnecessary to inform Zaghlul and he scratched Milner's name off the paper, Murray marked it for Milner to see. A telegram then went off to Allenby telling him to carry on. The next morning Milner who had seen a copy of the telegram intervened and the telegram of last night was cancelled. The man had however already been arrested. Now Zaghlul as Murray foresaw hears for the first time from his own people in Egypt that his secretary has been arrested – he is of course furious and threatens to break off negotiations.

Mrs Dudley Ward came to dinner and we went to the Russian ballet. Mrs D.W. is charming, as pretty as can be and such a good sense of humour. Her rather high, childish voice makes her sound silly but she isn't. Dinner was a success, the ballet was charming and we went on to a supper party. I sat next to Mrs Dudley Ward and talked to her all the time with great pleasure. I had never got on with her before.

July 14, 1920

Diana is obsessed by a groundless fear. Because she imagines a little hardness in her right breast she thinks she has cancer. Dr Furber whom she saw this morning assured her there is nothing in it. But she cannot get it out of her mind and this evening before dinner she was almost hysterical. We dined at Wimborne House – a party of about 40 people to meet the King and Queen of Spain. The party was a great success. The King and Queen stayed till

---

[1] Hilaire Belloc (1870–1953), poet and author.
[2] Field Marshal Edmund Allenby, 1st Viscount Allenby (1861–1936). High Commissioner for Egypt 1919–25.

after two. I had an interesting talk with Lady Curzon – she was delightfully indiscreet – told me that d'Abernon[1] to Berlin was Curzon's very own appointment, that [Sir] George Grahame is going as Ambassador to Brussels and Hardinge most probably to Paris. I got on very well with her which I never have before. I danced with Mrs Fellowes who was looking very attractive. But I missed the person whom I most wished to see.

July 15, 1920

After lunch Diana told me her fears were much worse today. I found she was really in a terrible state. I insisted on taking her straight to Dr Hood. Furber had reassured her insufficiently. Hood was extremely nice and pooh-poohed the whole thing utterly – told her it was pure imagination. This did have some effect but she was by then in such a state of nerves that it couldn't calm her. She said she must have morphia after we had left Hood so we went again to Furber who refused morphia but gave an injection of 'omnipon' after which I took her back to Gower Street, telephoned to the Foreign Office to say I couldn't come back that afternoon and then we lay on the sofa and I read to her till dinner. By then she was much better.

July 17, 1920

This morning Diana was worse than ever. She was possessed with terror. I took [her] once more to Hood who once more reassured her. He did her some good and gave her a soothing medicine which also helped her. We then started off in the car to stay with Juliet[2] in Kent. I hoped that driving the car would occupy Diana's mind to the exclusion of other things. At New Cross we had a puncture and waited there nearly two hours while they were mending it. It was a quarter to nine when we eventually arrived at Juliet's. She has a very pretty old house constructed out of six cottages. There was no one there except Keith Trevor and the American boy 'Chips' Channon[3] whom we met at Norah's.

July 19, 1920

This morning Diana was worse than ever. We decided that I had better take my holiday at once so as not to leave her during these days and that we must try to go away to the country although we have engagements in London every night this week. I went to the Foreign Office to propose going on leave which

---

[1] Sir Edgar Vincent, 1st Viscount d'Abernon (1857–1941). Financier and diplomat. Ambassador to Berlin 1920–6.

[2] Lady Juliet Lowther (1881–1965), daughter of the 4th Earl of Lonsdale, married Sir Robin Duff in 1903. He was killed in action in 1914 and in 1919 she married Major Keith Trevor (divorced 1926).

[3] Sir Henry 'Chips' Channon (1897–1958). An American by birth, he became a British subject and in 1935 a Conservative MP. He married Lady Honor Guinness (1909–76) in 1933 (divorced 1945). His diaries, published in 1967, are celebrated for their mix of the social and the political.

pleased everyone as it is most convenient to them and I acquired merit for adaptability. I then rejoined Diana at Gower Street. She had arranged to see Arbuthnot Lane at once. She was in a worse state than she had been yet. I went with her to Lane who utterly scouted her fears, laughing at them more successfully and convincingly and at the same time more kindly and sympathetically than either Hood or Furber. I hope that this has finally cured her but she is worn out after the week's agony.

July 21, 1920 Norton Priory [recently bought by Marion and Norman Holden]

Terrible weather – steady rain from morning till tea time. I have persuaded Diana that she would like to go to Clovelly and today I wrote to Diana Capel and Tommy Rosslyn proposing ourselves. After tea we motored over to Bognor to see the Duchess's cottage.[1] It is still unfinished, but rather charming, so very near the sea. I was pleasantly surprised with it and hope that it will be left to Diana in the fullness of time. She gets wonderfully better every day and although all her fears are not yet gone she is herself again.

August 4, 1920

We left Norton Priory at about half past ten and caught a train at Chichester. The weather was getting worse all the time and we accomplished the drive from Bideford to Clovelly in pouring rain. Diana Capel and Tommy Rosslyn met us on the doorstep. They are alone here with their children. We had quite a good dinner with champagne and conversation was maintained, but I felt nervous and constrained. All the responsibility of this party is on me. Diana only came to please me. She is not really intimate with either of our hostesses, to both of whom I have recently made love. The situation is an uncomfortable one and of my own creating. This place, Clovelly, is where I have been happiest in my life. Twelve years ago I came here first, a boy of eighteen devoured by shyness. There was a house party of some twenty people not one of whom I knew except John Manners (as whose friend I came). My present hostess, now twice a widow, was then a child with her hair down her back. Laura [Wyndham], her elder sister, though only sixteen, was the principal charmer of the party with whom Eileen Wellesley competed for our love. I loved Laura and wrote sonnets to her until two years later when she married Lovat. For the next five years Clovelly was always an annual landmark. It seemed different from every other place and the days spent there were different from the rest of the year. It was an enchanted fairyland of innocent love-making and poetry. Midnight bathing, strictly prohibited by the elders, was one of the main delights and long clandestine meetings after we were all supposed to be in bed. To revisit such a place with such associations must necessarily be sad.

---

[1] A small pebble-dash Georgian house at Aldwick, its garden giving directly on to the beach. Much loved by Duff and Diana, it was their only summer and weekend retreat until they acquired the Château de St Firmin at Chantilly after the war.

Diana in spite of the fears which she has not yet left behind her coped marvellously with the situation. She stayed in bed most of the morning and then we would all walk down to the village before lunch. I walked one evening with Diana to Gallantry Bower, the loveliest spot of all, where I have so often in the past lain long hours with John pondering on the future.

The evenings passed fairly successfully with conversation and occasionally a little reading or a little game. I was hardly ever alone with either of our hostesses and when I was felt shy with Tommy to whom I have no longer any wish to make love, much as I like her, but happy with Diana C. of whom I am as fond as ever. The weather was very kind to us and improved daily. The visit was not a complete failure. I may have been morbidly self-conscious about it as one is apt to be about one's own work, but I am afraid that everyone was a little glad when it came to an end.

August 9, 1920 (London)

I lunched with Diana at the Ritz. We did some shopping afterwards, buying the things we thought we should want for Deauville. I left her to go to the London Library and when I rejoined her found that her old fears which had been growing all day had reached a crisis. I persuaded her to go again to see Sir Arbuthnot Lane and we went there together on our way to dinner and the train. After Lane had examined her and said the usual cheering things he asked to speak to me alone which I knew was exactly what she has always dreaded happening. However all that he wished to say was that he thought it would do her more good than anything to have a child and even apart from that the fact of living together was good for her. He hoped we did not use preventives. I hurried him back to her for I knew that all this while she was in an agony of suspense. We effectively reassured her and she came away really happy. We caught the night train for Southampton.

We had a successful journey. The sea was rough but not excessively. Diana and I slept in our little bunk and did not fail to carry out the Doctor's orders.

The villa belongs to Baroness d'Erlanger and is pretty and very comfortable. We had the best rooms. The food was excellent. I got up first and went out to look for a barber. I arrived at the Potinière at the most favourable midday moment and fell in love with Deauville at once. Nothing can be gayer than the appearance of the Potinière at noon. Then the Paris papers have just arrived and are being shouted by their vendors. People buy them but seldom bother to open them as the news of the absurd outside busy world seems of no importance at Deauville. It is as much as one can do to read the headlines and to learn without the faintest interest that Poland who had lost the war with Russia yesterday has won it today. One strolls about in a divine *dolce far niente*, greeting friends with one of the inevitable Deauville questions. Did they win last night, have they bathed this morning, are they going to the races, will they have a drink. The last question inevitably answered in the affirmative, leads one to Ciro's where the cocktails are flowing and are deliciously assisted by potato chips and shrimps.

In the afternoon are the races which are not like English races but are a joy for all – or at least for me. I never betted on them to any extent that could cause anxiety and so enjoyed them thoroughly, watching the contest from the box of Mr Hennessy's mistress with the bland and beautiful Peggy Kurton [a musical comedy star], who was always glad to share half a bottle of champagne between each to celebrate a victory or console for a defeat. Thence to Ciro's again or else to the Casino to have a little gamble before dinner.

Ivor [Wimborne] always insisted on dining in the villa which we thought a little dull but it made a pleasant contrast to the casino, where we always went afterwards to gamble until supper which we usually had soon after 12. Supper was fun, watching the dancing and drinking incredible quantities of champagne. We usually returned to the rooms after supper and gambled a little more. Three was a reasonable hour to go to bed – sometimes we were as late as five.

Chemin de fer has always been my passion but I have never played it under ideal conditions before. I brought £50 to gamble with, determined to make it last me my stay. On the first evening I changed my English notes one by one until I reached the last – with this I won back all that I had lost and more. For a day or two I won steadily and was several thousand francs to the good but at the end of the week I started losing and on Sunday night Diana and I both lost every franc. The next morning I went down to Ciro's without even the price of a drink in my pocket feeling a little depressed, but after several cocktails at other people's expense and having borrowed 1000 francs from Ralph [Peto] I found my spirits revive rapidly. I lost all that however and had to borrow two more thousand from Fred [Cripps] and one from Cardie. Diana borrowed 1000 from Ivor. With these I won back everything, paid all debts and all expenses and came away about £100 to the good – a great performance.[1]

During the first week we were there Diana's spirits were wonderful and her fears seemed to be a thing of the past. But gradually as the novelty of the place and the amusements wore off her spirits began to fall and the fears returned.

Monday August 23, 1920 [London]

The Times this morning published a more or less correct account of the result of Milner's conversations with Zaghlul. The situation is still very unsatisfactory as nobody, neither the Egyptians nor ourselves, are in any way bound by the agreement. The Cabinet have never considered it. Before telegraphing the terms to Egypt they were shown to Curzon and Bonar Law, to both of whom they came as a shock. I wonder that Milner didn't get some measure of Cabinet concurrence before going so far.

---

[1] The exchange rate was then about 50 francs to the pound.

August 24, 1920

Diana's fears have all returned and today they were worse than ever. I persuaded her to see another Doctor – a Portuguese quack called Gomes in whom many people have great faith. He came about half past six, stayed some time and did her a lot of good. Gomes told me that Diana has intestinal sepsis and a slightly defective thyroid which are the causes of all her trouble. Her fears and anxieties are symptoms of this. There is not the faintest suspicion of cancer.

August 29, 1920

Diana's birthday. I gave her a kitten – the daughter of the one she had lost. I had it brought in when we were called in the morning. It was a great surprise and she was delighted. Diana has been offered £12,000 to do a cinema. We hardly know yet whether to believe it. We discussed tonight the possibility, if it comes true, of my leaving the Foreign Office and going into politics. It is what I should love above everything but fear I shall lack the energy ever to take the plunge.

September 1, 1920

I met Diana at her hairdresser's at 1.30 and she drove me home to lunch. I am nervous driving with her and nervous to think of her driving by herself. Holbrook informed me with delight this evening that he had seen a motor accident near our house today. A man on a motor bicycle with his wife in a side car had collided with a taxi and been thrown head foremost down the area. 'His brains', Holbrook said, 'were all over the place.'

September 3, 1920

Ralph [Peto] who has just returned from Deauville came to lunch with us. We mentioned to him our ideas about my leaving the Foreign Office and going into politics. He was all in favour of the plan, said that once in Parliament it was easy to make money by getting directorships etc. How far his enthusiasm and encouragement were real and how far the fruit of an excellent bottle of Burgundy I can't say. I grow more and more impatient with the dull routine of the Office. Political ambition and love of pleasure both point in the same direction.

September 6, 1920

In the afternoon Diana went to her first film rehearsal and appears to have been very successful. [*The film was* The Glorious Adventure, *a Restoration melodrama, directed by John Stuart Blackton.*]

September 9, 1920

After lunch Diana and I went to the New Theatre to see about our tickets for tonight. Some working girls who were passing recognized her and followed her to ask for her autograph. She had to sign about a dozen. She is wonderfully popular. When we walked into the theatre in the evening there was loud applause from the pit.

Sunday September 12, 1920 [Belvoir]

The most beautiful summer's day of the whole year. This morning the terrace bathed in sunshine was a wonder. I spent some time trying to translate Sacha Guitry's *L'Illusioniste*. After tea I sat on the terrace till the sunset, finishing the *Last Chronicle of Barset*. It was a wonderful evening. Conversation the whole evening about country matters, hunting and clergymen might have come straight out of Trollope.

October 4, 1920

Murray has come back. There was some excitement on Saturday as Curzon suddenly required a statement of the Department's views on the Milner-Zaghlul agreement. [*The Milner plan was that the Protectorate should be replaced by a treaty which would recognize Egyptian independence while retaining some British control over administration. The Cabinet was divided on the issue.*]

October 20, 1920

We dined with Blueie. Alan and Viola were there, also Phyllis, Keynes[1] and Mrs McKenna. We had a pleasant evening and very spirited, almost heated, conversation. I argued with Mrs McKenna, who maddens me. She admires everything I hate. Sinn Fein, Bolshevism, violence, bad manners. There is something especially repulsive in such ideas being harboured by the smug little wife of an enormously rich banker. McKenna himself came in later. He is almost equally irritating in his patronizing cocksure self-confidence. Madame Roland must have been such a woman as her. I hope their heads will fall when the revolution comes. Keynes is a dull dog.

October 23, 1920

I left the Foreign Office at 4.30 and we caught the 5.15 for Didcot to stay at the Wharf [country home of H. H. and Margot Asquith]. It was a long time since I had been there and as usual we both decided never to go again though in some ways it was less bad than usual. Our bedroom at the Wharf was the best in it – one that I never knew existed.

On both evenings there was nothing whatever for Diana to do. She was

---

[1] John Maynard Keynes, Baron Keynes (1883–1946), economist. Author of *The Economic Consequences of the Peace* (1919).

given Margot's beastly book[1] and told to sit and read it. It is incredible to take so much trouble to get people to your house and then take no trouble whatever to entertain them. We have been asked to go there nearly every Sunday this summer, have accepted and chucked twice and yet they go on asking us. We shall never go again.

November 4, 1920

We dined with the Winstons. The Montagus and the Laverys were there, Jack and Goonie and Michael [Herbert]. Winston was in his best form, ragging Edwin about Gandhi who he said ought to be lain bound hand and foot at the gates of Delhi and then trampled on by an enormous elephant with the new Viceroy seated on its back. He believes firmly that there is a world wide movement of reaction in progress at the present time, and he is optimistic of the future. Edwin of course is pessimistic and mutters of the revolution that is to come. He tells me that in the Cabinet Winston is the chief opponent of Milner's Egyptian schemes which they were discussing this morning. There was a debate on the subject in the Lords this afternoon where the opposition Salisbury and Selborne was satisfactorily disposed of by Curzon and Milner.

November 6, 1920 [Pixton Park, Somerset, home of Aubrey and Mary Herbert[2]]

One of the most delightful days of my life. We woke to a bright morning of sunshine and frost. Not a cloud in the sky. The autumn tints were beautiful beyond belief and when we started out to shoot at about ten the smell of autumn in the fresh morning air was intoxicating. It is the loveliest shooting in the world. The country is so hilly that every pheasant is a high one. There is a good deal of walking and a continual change of view and always the sound of running water. There are three rivers and one of them is always at the bottom of the valley. I was shooting better than I have been. The bag was about 80 pheasants. The ladies came out to lunch which we had sitting in a field with no idea of putting on coats or feeling cold. The only fault I had to find with the day was that we stopped shooting too early and had a long walk home.

I sat next to Lady Cranborne at dinner and opened by saying I had been waiting for her to apologize for cutting my dance when I saw her last. She defended herself and counter-attacked, and was as provocating, as subtly flattering, as mysteriously charming as ever.

---

[1] The first volume of Margot Asquith's *Autobiography*, based on her diaries, was published in 1920, the second in 1922.

[2] The Hon. Aubrey Herbert (1880–1923), a Conservative MP from 1911 and champion of Albanian independence. He married Mary de Vesci in 1910.

November 7, 1920

The weather broke today. In the afternoon I stayed in and began writing Diana's next article for *Femina* in the form of a reply to Arnold Bennett's[1] book on women. Aubrey interrupted me a good deal and made me help him carry wood for the fire from the kitchen to all the other rooms in the house. I love Aubrey. He is so sincerely eccentric. He has an unfailing sense of humour, a deep interest in interesting things and a wild enthusiasm for justice and mercy, tempered with a sweet reasonableness.

November 10, 1920

We went to a dance at the Pembrokes[2] where the King of Spain was. I didn't enjoy it. I left before Diana. She had an adventure with the King of Spain. He began his attack by trying to put a hand up her dress and when repulsed asked for an appointment making his intentions crudely clear. She warned him there would be nothing doing whereat he put back his pocket book in which he had been about to write her address. He left her saying that men always won in the end. I think he was drunk.

November 11, 1920. Armistice Day

I had a good view of the unveiling of the cenotaph and was impressed. The Unknown Warrior moved me to verse. I wrote –

He did not see the tears a nation shed,
He did not know a King stood at his bier,
Nor feel the welcome of the mighty dead,
Whose high companionship he came to share.
His was a simpler homelier joy than these.
When the plain wood struck English earth there passed
A tremor through that dust, those bones knew peace
To lie in their dear native land at last.

We dined with Lady Herbert. A huge dinner party. The Duke of York there – the Prince of Wales after dinner. Danced with Diana C. and Monica Grenfell [daughter of Lord and Lady Desborough] after dinner and then had supper with my own Diana. While we were at it having rather fun talking to Winston the Cranbornes arrived. Then Diana wanted to go and I wanted to stay. We argued a little in the hall and I said that when she wanted to stay longer than I did I never minded going alone and leaving her. At this she flounced out of

---

[1] Arnold Bennett (1867–1931), novelist, playwright and man of letters. His essay *Our Women: Chapters on Sex-Discord* was published in 1920.

[2] Reginald Herbert, 15th Earl of Pembroke (1880–1960), and his wife, Lady Beatrice Paget (1883–1973), daughter of the 6th Marquess of Anglesey.

the house in rage. Out of the house and into the fog before they had even got us a taxi, leaving me standing in the hall without my hat and coat, looking ridiculous before a host of menservants. I put on my hat and coat and followed her, furious – caught her up near the Crimean Memorial and was really angry with her, using hard, bitter words. She burst into a torrent of tears, said I had looked at her as though I hated her. It was a terrible scene. I tried to make amends and stop her crying but couldn't. We drove home still crying and arguing. The tears went on until we were in bed. She blurted out in the middle of her sobs that it was all due to her jealousy of Diana C., and that she hated herself for being jealous which she had sworn she would never be. It was far the worst quarrel we have ever had.

November 12, 1920

Diana still suffering from the effects of last night's storm. Eyes and head aching. She didn't get up till the evening. I lunched by her bed. She had to dine at Wimborne House. I dined clandestinely with Diana C. at the Carlton Grill. We went on to the Alhambra and after leaving her I went to White's. Diana had a party at Gower St. but as it was mainly musical I was in no hurry to go. Her performers were Rubinstein the pianist, Olga [Lynn], Bruce[1] and Ruth Draper.[2] I was in time to hear the last and very excellent she was.

November 14, 1920 [Taplow Court]

After lunch Mr Balfour [Arthur Balfour] read aloud a very absurd eulogium of Diana from one of the Sunday papers. In revenge I gave her a passage from a review of a life of him in the *Observer* which she read out and which was even more absurd than the bit about her. He didn't like it at all.

November 15, 1920

In the evening Diana had to dine with Ruby – a musical party with Rubinstein. I wasn't asked and so arranged to dine with Diana Capel and confessed as much. Diana was much perturbed and frankly jealous. She took the line of ragging me and treating it as a joke but I could see she was annoyed. We dined at the Carlton Grill Room and went to *The White Headed Boy*[3] – an amusing Irish play. Driving home I made more love to Diana than I have ever done and she resisted less. I thought she seemed to love me rather. Diana didn't come back from her party until 12.30. I wish she wasn't jealous – but I suppose if she wasn't she wouldn't love me – and that if I thought she loved anyone more than me I should be jealous of her. I wonder. I do love her so infinitely more than the other Diana, but I love also romance and intrigue and cannot live without them.

---

[1] Bruce Ottley (1890–1945), composer. Chairman of the Royal Opera House in the 1930s.
[2] Ruth Draper (1884–1956), a brilliant monologuist renowned for her vivid character sketches.
[3] A play by Lennox Robinson (1886–1958), Irish writer and director.

November 16, 1920

The chief news today was the fall of Venizelos[1] – a small thunderbolt in Foreign Affairs. We dined with the Ancasters to meet the King and Queen of Spain. After dinner I had a delightfully long time with Lady Cranborne. I am not sure that I love her but I do like her very much. When I came down I met Diana C. who had just arrived. We danced a little and then went up to the sitting room which nobody else seemed to know of. I sat with her a long time and loved her very much. But all this part of my evening was spoilt by not having relieved nature after dinner so that I was in an agony. However I put this right when Diana [C] left and then had a very agreeable supper with Violet Keppel.[2] Having thus had an innings with all my loves I left with my belovedest well pleased at 2 a.m.

November 17, 1920

We lunched today with the Laverys. Only Freda and the Prince of Wales were there. I had never been introduced to him before, and found him quite wonderfully charming. Of course there is a leaven of snobbery, or I should prefer to call it loyalty, which magnifies the emotion one feels about him. But judged by any standards he has exceptional charm. He has shy but most beautiful manners. Hazel was very nervous. John I thought quite unmoved. Diana too was singularly self-possessed, considering how nervous some things make her. Freda of course was quite at home. She seemed only to want him to appear at his best. Her manner towards and about him is perfect. Luncheon was really very successful. Conversation never flagged and was amusing.

December 1, 1920

We dined at the Hyde Park Hotel with Beaverbrook, the Montagus and Rothermere. The last named is I think one of the most repulsive men I ever met. He looks like a pig and when not speaking snores quietly to himself. He is rude, pompous, extremely stupid, common beyond any other member of his family and beyond belief, utterly devoid of the slightest streak of humour or dash of originality. In spite of him or perhaps because of him we had rather a pleasant dinner. It was fun ragging him as nothing in the world could make him perceive that he was being ragged.

December 12, 1920. Sunday

A dark foggy day, snow lying thick on the ground, freezing hard. We lay late in bed reading the papers and *Martin Chuzzlewit*.

---

[1] Eleutherios Venizelos (1864–1936), the Greek Prime Minister, was defeated in the elections of November 1920.

[2] Violet de Trafford (1893–1968) married the Hon. Rupert Keppel (1886–1964) in 1919, divorced 1921.

[After dinner] we went to a very small party at Juliet's – not more than twenty couples including the Prince of Wales. The Prince hardly left Freda's side. They say he loves her terribly and that either she must give in to him or break off altogether as he can bear it no longer. He refused apparently to shake hands with Michael [Herbert] because he is jealous of him.

December 31, 1920

I made many New Year's resolutions – above all to read more and to resist the temptation of every lighted candle.

1921

January 7, 1921

Returned to the Foreign Office. I found that a good deal had happened in my absence. The Cabinet had decided to publish the report of the Milner Mission but to reserve their own decision until it had been submitted to the Imperial Cabinet. Meanwhile the Sultan is to be asked to send over delegates in the spring.

January 11, 1921

We lunched with Barbara Wallace[1] and her husband in Upper Brook Street. I hadn't met him before and liked him very much. The Richard Nortons[2] were there, both of whom I like. After lunch we three men talked politics and discussed the prospects of getting seats. Richard was very encouraging to me – said I ought to get someone to pay my expenses. He is in touch with the Unionist party machinery and promised to mention my name to Malcolm Ramsay. All the afternoon I had visions of the House of Commons.

January 13, 1921

This morning we had a long telegram from Allenby, pointing out that no delegation worth the name could be collected to go to England except on the understanding that they are to negotiate on the basis of the so-called Milner-Zaghlul agreement as published in August. The people of Egypt consider that we are pledged to that. On the other hand Allenby is afraid of giving Egypt the right to diplomatic representatives abroad and of withdrawing the garrison.

---

[1] Barbara 'Barbie' Wallace, the daughter of Sir Edwin Lutyens, was married to the Rt. Hon. Euan Wallace MP (1892–1941). They became great friends of the Coopers.

[2] The Hon. Richard Norton, later 6th Lord Grantley (1892–1954). He married Jean Kinloch in 1919. She became the mistress of Lord Beaverbrook.

January 20, 1921

The Times in a leading article this morning on Winston's new post [Colonial Secretary] assumes that he is taking over Egypt as well as the mandated territories. This is not the case but we hear that he wishes it were and is doing his best to work it. Nothing could possibly have a worse effect on Egypt at the present time. A telegram this evening from Allenby proposing to set off on his Sudan trip and postpone everything until he comes back at about the time of the opening of Parliament. We fear the Cabinet will agree to this proposal which will prolong the period of suspense and uncertainty and can only do harm.

January 21, 1921

We sent off several telegrams to Egypt today and Curzon sent for Murray and explained his policy. He does not intend to be hurried. The Milner Report will be published when Parliament meets. It will doubtless be strongly criticized. H.M.G. will then state their intention of substituting a treaty for the existing Protectorate. On this basis it is to be assumed that a suitable delegation will come from Egypt, who will realize from speeches in Parliament and articles in the press what the attitude of England is.

January 28, 1921

The Holdens came to dinner and we had an agreeable evening with them. There was talk of my leaving the Foreign Office and going into business. I don't want to go into business but I do want to go into the House of Commons which I could not afford to do at present without the £600 a year of my salary.

February 15, 1921

My last day at the Foreign Office prior to a month's holiday. It was a delight to leave it. I dined with Lady Randolph. I played bridge afterwards with Birkenhead, Lady Randolph and Mrs Beckett.[1] F.E. has given up drink for a year with the result that he is very cross and gloomy – a warning against temperance.

February 25, 1921 [Cap Ferrat]

We had a short but excellent dinner at Lapérouse before catching the train for the South. We had a lit-salon which was excellently comfortable and we passed a most agreeable night sleeping pretty soundly until we reached Avignon. When we got to the Côte d'Azur Diana was surprised and delighted with the scenery. She has never been here before. I haven't been since 1908 when Father died at Mentone.

---

[1] Muriel Paget (1878–1941), daughter of Lord Berkeley Paget, married the Hon. Rupert Beckett (1870–1955) in 1896.

March 1, 1921

In the evening we dined at the hotel. It was a 'gala' dinner with toys and fireworks and although the food was filthy and the wine was worse, was rather amusing. The company was strangely mixed, consisting partly of very respectable English families and partly of the most flaming French tarts who are apparently being kept here by men who are staying in the vicinity.

March 3, 1921

We went to Cannes where we had arranged to stay the night at the Carlton Hotel. We went into the rooms before dinner and won a thousand francs. Dinner was at the Casino. It was a great gala dinner, excellent food and everything very prettily done under the auspices of Poiret.[1] Everything was green and yellow – tables, flowers, favours, toys etc.

March 12, 1921

A lovely morning. I sat most of the morning by the sea writing Diana's article for next month. [After dinner] we went to Monte Carlo, taking only 1500 francs as we were determined not to lose more on our last night. It happened that we did very well and came away with three more thousand. We have won roughly 10,000 francs in all – about £200.

March 14, 1921 (Paris)

We went to the Ritz Hotel where we had a slight altercation as Diana on learning that we could not have a room for less than 100 francs a day wanted to put our luggage on the taxi again and go elsewhere. I refused and she gave in. We had a charming little room, the Rue Cambon end, looking out on the gardens. Afterwards we joined a party of Ivor Novello, Gladys Cooper,[2] Bobbie Andrews[3] and Olga at Rizzi's where Fischer and others sing sentimental songs which are rather dull and indecent ones which are difficult to follow. Ivor Novello and Gladys Cooper are madly in love with each other. They flew over from England and were sick all the way.

March 15, 1921

It was a heavenly morning. We strolled up the Champs-Elysées. There was a most beautiful magnolia tree there in full flower. We lunched with Nancy [Cunard]. She appears to have quite recovered. She has charming rooms at the very top of the hotel with a wonderful view over the whole of Paris. The Sacré Coeur glittered in the sun. In the afternoon I was left to myself and bought a lot of books – Sainte-Beuve's *Causeries de Lundi*, Lenôtre's works,

---

[1] Paul Poiret (1879–1944), pioneering French fashion designer.
[2] Dame Gladys Cooper (1888–1971), actress.
[3] Robert (Bobbie) Andrews (1895–1981), friend and lover of Ivor Novello for thirty-five years.

Rovigo's Memoirs [A. J. M. Savany, Napoleon's chief of police whom he made Duke of Rovigo.] We dined with Charles Mendl[1] who had a large dull party. There was music afterwards so of course I was bored. We went on afterwards to Ciro's where we met Molyneux, the dressmaker, who has offered to give Diana as many dresses as she likes for nothing as an advertisement.

March 18, 1921

I telephoned to Violet Keppel who is staying with Ralph Lambton and asked her to come with me to Maison Lafittes. She consented, picked me up with a car of Ralph Lambton's and off we went. It was great fun – a lovely afternoon – we lost on every race except the last on which we won back all we had lost and more. She told me that the marriage of Violet Trefusis[2] has been annulled and it is rumoured that before they were married Denys Trefusis signed an agreement that they would never live together. The general feeling seems to be that she has behaved badly and it appears that she is now living in Sapphic sin with Vita Nicolson.

March 19, 1921

We travelled to London by the midday train. The sea was very rough and Diana was sick just as we reached Dover. We went straight to Arlington Street. The Duke told me I had been blackballed for the Turf. Lord Wemyss had put me up and Drogheda[3] had seconded me. It upset me very much – more than I should have allowed it to. I couldn't get it off my mind for days. We were also met with the news that Diana's contract with *Femina* is concluded, which was another blow. Combined with the natural regret at the holidays being over, all this tended to depress us considerably. We dined sadly at home and went to bed.

March 22, 1921

We dined with the Ribblesdales. Dinner was well enough. Afterwards I expected we should play bridge but it was never suggested. I sat in a corner with Cynthia for about an hour and a half. Much as I like her and much as I have to say to her I was exhausted long before the time was up – and so I think was she. I don't understand how people who don't play cards can bear dinner parties.

---

[1] Charles Mendl (1871–1958), appointed Paris representative of the FO News Department in 1920. He was knighted in 1924 and was Press Attaché at the British Embassy in Paris 1926–40. He married Elsie de Wolfe, a very successful interior decorator, in 1926.

[2] Violet Keppel reluctantly married Denys Trefusis in 1919 at a period when she was having a passionate lesbian affair with Vita Sackville-West, which lasted until 1920.

[3] Hugo Charteris, 11th Earl of Wemyss (1857–1937), and Henry Moore, 10th Earl of Drogheda (1884–1957).

March 29, 1921

Dinner at Gower Street. The Parsonses came and we all went to the first night of *Bulldog Drummond*,[1] a capital crook play produced by Gerald du Maurier.[2] There was one of the worst breakdowns by one of the actors that I have ever seen on the stage. He couldn't remember one word of his part. In spite of this the play was a great success. We went round to see Gerald afterwards and were driven home together with the Charles Hawtreys.

April 3, 1921 [Belvoir]

A most beautiful morning. Diana and I walked in the Spring Garden before lunch. It was a mass of flowers and blossom. We sat there and I read to her *Love o'Women* [short story by Kipling] which she had never read. It was delightfully warm and sunny, birds singing, everything perfect. In the afternoon we finished reading *Love o'Women* on the terrace. The end of it, which I have read a hundred times, made us both cry.

April 7, 1921

I went to see Diana Capel before dinner. She was very charming. I have hopes. We dined with Lady Colefax.[3] It was a large party. Afterwards there was dancing. Later I was sitting talking to Denys Trefusis when the Harold Nicolsons[4] arrived. 'Good God', he said, 'there's Vita Nicolson, I must go', which he immediately did. She was looking very handsome.

April 8, 1921

The strike news is bad. Everyone discusses revolution. Diana is terrified of it. She was to have gone to Paris tomorrow in order to try on some dresses. I had arranged to go to Breccles where Diana Capel is. Owing to the rumours of revolution Diana hesitated about Paris and I advised her to go. Before dinner this evening she learnt for the first time that Diana Capel was going to be at Breccles. She immediately telegraphed to Ivor Wimborne to meet her in Paris. We dined at home together and read Lytton Strachey's *Queen Victoria* after dinner. We went to bed early but not happily. Diana cried, said I didn't want

---

[1] Bulldog Drummond was an adventure hero created by 'Sapper', pseudonym of H. C. McNeile (1888–1937). He was the most popular fictional character until the arrival of Ian Fleming's James Bond.

[2] Gerald du Maurier played Capt. Hugh ('Bulldog') Drummond. The play was revived in December 1922 at Wyndham's Theatre.

[3] Sibyl Colefax (1874–1950), American wife of Sir Arthur Colefax. She was a prominent society hostess and the co-founder of the interior design firm Colefax & Fowler.

[4] Sir Harold Nicolson (1886–1968), diplomat and writer, married Vita Sackville-West in 1913. He was National Labour MP 1935–45 and Parliamentary Secretary to the Ministry of Information under Duff Cooper 1940–1.

her to come to Breccles – exaggerated and misconstrued everything. It was all very sad.

April 9, 1921

This morning Diana had still not settled whether to go to Paris or not but when I got back for lunch she was packed for Breccles, all quarrels and sadness were forgotten and everything was well. We had a very happy lunch together and then went off to Liverpool Street. We travelled down with Edwin who came straight from the Cabinet which he had left sitting. He thought the strike would be averted. He talked almost without a pause till Cambridge and was intensely interesting. He told us everything that had been happening in the Cabinet during the last few days and what everyone had said. Edwin said that the real struggle during the last few days had not been between the Government and the miners but between the moderates and the extremists inside the unions. If the strike came off it would be the work of the revolutionaries and there would be bloodshed.

April 15, 1921

In the evening we went with the Duchess to see Sarah Bernhardt[1] in *Daniel* – rather a terrible sight I thought. Collapse of the strike.

May 3, 1921

Dined with the Horners. Had a long argument with Winston afterwards about Egypt – he pointing triumphantly to the apparent failure of our policy. He was very bad at details but good in general. His great line was that you could only make concessions to people you had beaten. He instanced the success of South Africa.

May 6, 1921

We dined at home – Hutchinson came. He told us that Mendl of Paris is saying terrible things of us both – that I am drunk from morning till night and that Diana longs to sleep with every man she meets and is only restrained by fear of my mad jealousy.

May 23, 1921

There have been considerable disturbances in Egypt both at the end of last week and again today, when there was a very serious outbreak at Alexandria. With the help of the military it was easily suppressed, but not before a considerable number of Europeans, but no British subjects, had been killed. The riot was not anti-British but anti-Greek and Italian. The Italians especially seem to have brought it partly on themselves. The whole thing has considerably

---

[1] Sarah Bernhardt (1845–1923), the distinguished French actress, made her debut in 1862 and continued acting until 1922. *Daniel* was a play by Louis Verneuil.

strengthened our hands by showing how little they are fit for complete independence and how incapable they are of keeping themselves in order without assistance.

May 28, 1921

Lunched at home with Diana and we caught the 3 o'clock for Badminton to stay at Lyegrove with Diana Capel. I hadn't been there since the beginning of 1918. So much has happened to us all since then. I never had one moment alone with Diana C. In our bedroom there was a book that I gave her last year with an inscription in it. I knew that Diana would want to read it as it was *The Three Clerks* by Trollope so I had hastily to purloin it and tear out the offending page.

June 1, 1921. Derby Day

I hadn't made up my mind in the morning what to back. I went to White's to get my hair cut and the barber advised Humorist. I backed it £10 each way, a large bet for me, and it won at 6 to 1.

The Duchess and Mrs Ansell [an Australian friend of the Duchess] came to lunch with us. There were long discussions as to what action Diana should take with regard to Mr Blackton,[1] her film producer who has failed to produce the money. He was to have begun the film on April 1st and finished it by the end of May, but owing to his financial supporters having let him down he hasn't yet been able to start. He has already paid Diana a thousand pounds and she is anxious now to have no more to do with the whole business. Mrs Ansell who is hoping for a commission from Blackton urges Diana to give him more time.

We dined at Wimborne House. They had a party of about forty people. It was a fine display and a beautiful bevy of women. Afterwards we danced. Lady Curzon was very nice to me and said that His Lordship had that very day praised my work to her. It was à propos of my draft Treaty with Egypt which I got back from him today.

We left about one and as it was our wedding day I gave Diana a little shagreen box which I had bought for her in Paris. She had taken me to see it there and I had pretended not to think it worth the money. Afterwards I went back to the shop and bought it for her. She cried with pleasure when I gave it her. She had got for me the first edition of Trollope's *Three Clerks* and also of his Autobiography. We were both so happy. I love her far more than I did two years ago.

---

[1] J. Stuart Blackton (1875–1941), an American film director and producer of the silent film era. Founder of Vitagraph Studios, which he sold to Warner Brothers in 1925.

June 2, 1921

At the Foreign Office today Murray and Lindsay[1] were somewhat rattled by the evidence of Boyle, who has just returned from Egypt and who says that all Milnerism and all reforms must be abandoned – that we must go back to Cromerism and increase the garrison. This seems to be the view of most people who return from Egypt now.

We dined with the Carnarvons – a large dull party of people who didn't know each other. When I came to bed I found the room in darkness, when I turned on the light I discovered Diana standing in a corner, wearing her wedding dress.

Sunday June 5, 1921

Diana and I went for a drive in our car. We went to the Hall, Bushey, which I hadn't seen since the blessed day when I left it in November 1917. It is now a hotel. I remembered very vividly how wretched I had been there. I looked at the dingy golf club which had then seemed Paradise and thought of Peter Adderley and Gerald Brassey, my two friends there who are both dead.

June 7, 1921

Diana came to the Foreign Office for me in another car she is thinking of buying – a Standard which I liked best of those I have so far seen. We dined with Beaverbrook in his new little house by Hurlingham. It is very charming. He has made a real tennis court there. The Montagus and Scatters formed the party. Max is very full of his attack on the Govt. over their alleged intention to assist Greece against the nationalist Turks. Edwin of course sympathizes with him and talks of resignation. They are very angry with Winston who has gone over to the Prime Minister and turned anti-Turk.

June 22, 1921

The [Lansdowne] ball was amusing – especially the marshalling of the Royal supper party by Wolkoff and me. We had to tell them all whom they were to take in. When I told the Prince of Wales on his arrival that he had to take Lady Pembroke into supper he said 'Good God, is it that sort of show – I must go somewhere and put on my Garter'. He had got it sticking out of his trouser pocket. Lord Curzon took the wrong partner in with the result that Princess Alice[2] who ought to have gone with him was left alone. Luckily Charlie

---

[1] Sir Ronald Lindsay (1877–1945), diplomat. Assistant Under-Secretary of State in charge of Near Eastern Affairs 1921–4. In 1925 he became Ambassador to Turkey. His last post was Ambassador to the US 1930–9.

[2] Princess Alice of Albany, Countess of Athlone (1883–1981), daughter of Prince Albert, 1st Duke of Albany, Queen Victoria's youngest son. She married Prince Alexander of Teck (1874–1957) in 1904. In 1917 he abandoned his German title, adopted the family name of Cambridge and was created Earl of Athlone.

Anglesey also failed to find his partner so I sent them in together. After this preliminary canter the ball was dull and I left about one.

June 25, 1921. Saturday

We have got a new dog – a present. It is a Dalmatian called Adam, 9 months old and arrived this morning. Its chief characteristic is fear. It began by lying on the floor and relieving nature out of sheer terror until I thought it would never stop. However it gradually became more at home and we like it though I fear it is a silly dog.

June 29, 1921

The Hutchinsons and Lytton Strachey[1] came to dinner. Desmond MacCarthy[2] was to have come but never turned up. I don't care for Lytton Strachey; his absurd eunuch's voice makes me shy.

July 6, 1921

Diana went to Knole today to do her film there. I lunched at Arlington Street – a singularly trying affair. I sat between the American Ambassadress [Mrs George Harvey] and Mrs Corrigan.[3] The former is a nice old thing with very little to say for herself. The latter I thought atrocious. As Diana was not likely to be back in time for dinner I dined without her with the Ednams at 17 Oxford Square. It seemed a pleasant enough party when I arrived there. When they said 'We are waiting for Lady Cranborne' my joy was complete. I sat beside her and I talked to her most of the time and we both had plenty to say. It was an excellently arranged party – eight for bridge. And all the time I was thinking ahead and scheming for the drive home. Luck that loves a lover befriended me. Rosemary, Edwin and I started a rubber of skip. This was a danger I shouldn't have risked as it might have hampered my freedom and kept me chained. My hopes however were still so faint. Then Lady Cranborne asked for a taxi. All seemed lost when suddenly I won the rubber of skip in the third hand. Then of course the Montagus offered to drop me. I said I was going to White's, an unlikely lie, but I had it ready. Evelyn [Fitzgerald], Lady Cranborne and I in the hall together, only one taxi, an argument as to who shall drop whom. Evelyn mercifully bound for a ball in Wimpole Street seems, I suggest, the nearest. We drive him there, leave him and are alone. I felt as shy as a boy of seventeen with his first love, talked about Evelyn without knowing what I said while the taxi flew towards Charles Street. Then we struck a fortunate

---

[1] Lytton Strachey (1880–1932), critic and biographer, and a prominent member of the Bloomsbury group. His book *Eminent Victorians* was published in 1918.

[2] Sir Desmond MacCarthy (1877–1952), literary and dramatic critic. Member of the Bloomsbury group, Literary Editor of the *New Statesman* 1920–7, and from 1928 senior literary critic on the *Sunday Times*. One of the best conversationalists of his time.

[3] Mrs Laura Corrigan (c. 1863–1948), a wealthy and snobbish American and a leading London hostess.

vein of conversation – wished we were in Paris where there would be amusing places to go to and dance – there is nowhere in London – is there nowhere? – such a pity to go in on such a lovely night. At this moment the taxi mistaking the number of the house drew up by a coincidence most truly comic before Diana Capel's. Desperately I said 'Let us go to Hampstead and breathe in the fresh air on the heath'. She didn't dissent, murmuring only that she mustn't be too late. The driver muttered about a tyre that would need blowing up so I changed the direction to the Inner Circle. She suggested opening the car which I did quickly.[1] It was more romantic though less Lotharian. Still I had difficulty in speaking – telling her at first only how happy I was. Then I told her how I loved her, how I adored her – how long I had done so, how I went to balls only in the hope of seeing her. She doubted me and I showed her the only letter she had ever written me which I had still in my pocket book. I said I would never trouble her with my love, that I adored Diana and was supremely happy. I only wanted her to know I loved her and should do so always. She was pleased I think. I held her hand and kissed it. It was a heavy summer night with a faint breeze that blew back her soft hair. I gently touched her hair and longed to kiss her. Suddenly heavy rain drops fell as though it were the beginning of a storm. But they stopped as suddenly which added to the strangeness and the wonder of the scene. Then a policeman stopped us because you are not allowed to drive round the Inner Circle unless you are going to a house there. We turned back. When we came to Charles Street I drew her towards me to kiss her, but she asked me gently not to and I gave way. I went home almost laughing with happiness. It will be one of my loveliest memories. All the while I harbour a small doubt in my heart as to whether she may not after all be only a silly little flirt with a singularly enchanting manner of her own.

July 7, 1921

We had a hard day at the Foreign Office. I didn't leave till 8.20. The explanation was that Curzon in the Cabinet was taunted by Massey,[2] the Prime Minister of New Zealand, with not knowing his own mind, whereupon he replied that not only did he know it but that he had ready in the Foreign Office two alternative draft treaties which he could circulate to the Cabinet. He then came across to the Office and told us to prepare the treaties forthwith.

In the evening we went to the State Ball. I had never been to one before – nor ever worn my full dress uniform. I enjoyed it, I enjoyed dressing up, and the pomp and pageantry but most I enjoyed seeing Betty again. We settled last night on the exchange of Christian names in the traditional romantic manner. I found her wonderfully soon considering the crowd and stayed with her delightfully long. We sat in a large room where no one else came and we

---

[1] At that date London taxis were convertible.
[2] William Ferguson Massey (1856–1925), Prime Minister of New Zealand 1912–25.

talked so much more easily than ever before. She told me that she had long
been teased by her family about her liking for me and that they had returned
to it this evening at dinner and she had blushed. This was another very happy
evening for me.

July 9, 1921

This morning Letty was married to Guy [Benson]. I thought there was rather
too much show and jolliness for a second wedding and that Letty was dressed
rather too like a virgin bride. The Duchess sobbed at what she felt Lady
Wemyss must be feeling but Lady Wemyss appeared unmoved.

In the afternoon as I was sitting in the Office about four thinking of going,
the telephone rang and Crowe[1] asked for Murray, who was at Lords and had
so far as I was aware no intention of returning. Crowe said that Curzon
particularly wanted to talk about Egypt. While I was still speaking to Crowe,
Murray to my intense delight reappeared. Then we had a most hectic afternoon. Murray and Crowe came out from Curzon at five with a treaty in scraps
and fragments which with the aid of the last typist in the Office I had to
present in a respectable form by a quarter to six. They took it across to Carlton
House Terrace and I went home, but couldn't leave London till I heard the
result in case my services were further needed. Not until eight did Murray
telephone to say I could go.

Then off we started in the car for Monkey Island.[2] It was a heavenly evening
after a grilling day. The drive was delightful and all went well. We arrived
there soon after 9.30 and found everything ready for us. It was still broad
daylight. We had dinner of cold salmon and duck in our little temple and two
bottles of champagne. It was as beautiful and as romantic as could be. Mr
Tinker, the proprietor, was very genial and rather drunk, his daughter waited
on us admirably. We went to bed soon after dinner and slept well.

July 11, 1921

Another day of boiling heat. We circulated to the Cabinet this morning the
final draft of the Egypt Treaty chiefly written by Curzon himself. The delegation arrive this evening.

July 12, 1921

This afternoon Adly[3] had his first interview with Lord Curzon. They were
alone and got on fairly well. Curzon asked him what the Delegation wanted.
Adly replied the Milner report plus the Zaghlul reservations. Curzon

---

[1] Sir Eyre Crowe (1864–1925), Permanent Under-Secretary of State for Foreign Affairs, 1920–5.
[2] An island in the Thames near Bray in Berkshire. A fishing lodge and fishing temple were built
   by the 3rd Duke of Marlborough soon after 1723; in 1840 they became a riverside inn.
[3] Adli (Adly) Pasha Yakan, Egyptian statesman; Liberal Constituionalist Prime Minister, Mar.
   1921–Mar. 1922, June 1926–Apr. 1927, Oct. 1929–Jan. 1930.

apparently was surprised at this and said it was deplorable. But of course Adly must ask for the maximum to start with.

July 13, 1921

I had to leave [lunch] hurriedly in order to get back to the Foreign Office for the first meeting with the Egyptian Delegation which took place at 3. There were seven of them. We were five – Lord Curzon, Vansittart, Lindsay, Murray and I. We had to write hard all the time taking notes of what occurred. We were in there from 3 to 6 and then I had to dictate the minutes which took me till half past eight. I didn't think Curzon was good as a negotiator. He was too much the parliamentarian, too argumentative and anxious to score. I thought Adly was good. They, the Egyptians, seemed on the whole fairly reasonable.

July 15, 1921

My minutes of the last two meetings passed Lord Curzon with hardly any corrections.

Then on to a ball at Crewe House which is the best house in the world for that purpose. I found Betty at once and after one dance secured her. We had a long altogether delightful supper. She was charming beyond words. She flatters me and I don't know whether to believe her. Nor does she know whether to believe me. It was a wonderfully successful party – everybody enjoyed it. The secret of success is to have plenty of champagne and no stairs. It was nearly three before we got home. I have never had a harder week, both of work and play – and I feel perfectly well at the end of it which is due I think to the beautiful hot, dry weather. I ought to live in a hot climate.

July 21, 1921

We had Felix Yousoupoff and Curtis Moffat to dinner. Felix came with his pockets full of diamonds and pearls which he wants to sell. He is confident that he will be back in Russia under a Czar within a year. He has great charm.

July 22, 1921

A hurried dinner at Gower Street after which I went with Diana to see some parts of her film. I thought it beautiful and her performance exquisite. She looked so lovely and her gestures were replete with dignity and breeding, which of course one never sees in film actresses and which consequently are the more striking.

July 27, 1921

We dined with Lady Ridley at a flat in Mount St. Juliet and Winston were there. I tried to impress Winston about Egypt. I explained that either there would be a treaty or not – if not negotiations would break down either over the military question or over some other. If it broke down over the military question we should be justified in the eyes of the world – if it broke down over anything else we should not be so justified. So long as the troops remained in Egypt nothing else really mattered. Winston seemed inclined to agree but said he had understood that Curzon was prepared to withdraw the troops from Cairo.

August 21, 1921 [Deauville]

It was a damp and gloomy day. We motored out to Guillaume le Conquérant with Max [Beaverbrook] for lunch. I like him much better than I used to – and he me. We dined with him at Ciro's and had a very pleasant dinner. I left him there with Diana and went off determined to improve our fortunes. I cashed a larger cheque than I had yet done – for 5,000 francs thinking it would be lucky, which for a time it was. I had won at one moment nearly 3,000 francs but it all went finally, together with the 5,000. Our losses are really getting serious, close on £400. Diana takes them bravely – says her £500 bonus on account of the postponement of the film will pay for them. She is loving Max and he her.

August 24, 1921

I sat next Daisy Fellowes [at supper] and afterwards drove her home. I took her in my arms and kissed her most passionately and intimately to which she offered no objection at all. I was surprised as she had never encouraged me. Back to the Casino where in spite of my luck in love I won more money. Altogether the best evening we have had in Deauville.

August 26, 1921

[After lunch] Diana and Ivor went for a drive and I slipped off to join Daisy at her villa. She was awaiting me. We went for a drive in her car – a beautiful Hispano Suiza. It was a pretty drive; I held and kissed her hands which are the loveliest ever seen. We came to Cabourg, a bright little place by the sea where we drank chocolate. I got on wonderfully well with her although she is strangely different from anyone I have ever known.

I got back late and Diana was cross because she had been waiting for me. I had to lie which I hate doing to her. We dined at the Casino – Diana, Ivor, Max and Bonar Law [who had resigned from the Government on the grounds of ill health]. It was rather a dull dinner. Bonar Law was gloomy and rather aggressive. He cares only for talking about politics. The only thing of interest he said so far as I can remember was that when he was in the Government nothing was ever submitted to the Cabinet until he and Lloyd George were agreed upon it.

August 27, 1921

I awoke early and anxious, remembering that I had rashly asked Daisy to write to me and foreseeing now that the letter would probably be brought to me in

Diana's presence and would not admit of explanation. However all went well. Diana was still half asleep when the letter came and I successfully concealed it.

A large dinner at the Casino. Afterwards in the rooms I found Daisy and said that if we could arrange a supper we would have it together. This we eventually did and very pleasant it was. We talked about books and I found she had read a good many although she was alas under the impression that *La Chartreuse de Parme* was by Flaubert.[1] I walked with her to her villa where we sat in a summer house in the garden. A sea mist had risen which added to the romance of the scene. I kissed and caressed and did all that I could to make her happy. She resisted at first, then less, but everything she wouldn't permit. I left her at her own entreaty sitting there a speck of white with dark head and great bright eyes surrounded by the mist.

When I got back to the Casino I found Diana in a fearful state. Because she hadn't seen me for an hour she had of course leapt to the conclusion that I had been assassinated. She had been back to the hotel to look for me and was employing Lois[2] and Dudley Ward in the search. I was terribly sorry for her poor darling – I took her and the other two back to supper where a bottle of champagne helped to restore equanimity. Then back to the rooms where suddenly I found my luck. I couldn't lose and cleared about 10,000 francs which made up for all our losses and left something substantial to the good. I came away at about 5 with some 21,000 francs which went far to restore Diana's humour. But I fear she will never forgive Daisy and will regard her with suspicion henceforth.

August 30, 1921 (London)

Edwin came to dinner. [He] gave us a very graphic account of Winston's agony over the death of his little girl who died last week[3] and of how Lloyd George had taken advantage of it to make up all his differences with Winston. He also gave us a very amusing account of a row he is having with Curzon. Edwin wants to publish a lot of anti-Bolshevist evidence showing that they are spending huge sums on sending bombs etc. into India while at the same time asking charity from the world in their famine.

September 5, 1921

There was a telegram today from Scott in Cairo saying that he and Sarwat, the acting Prime Minister, were very anxious that certain members of Parliament whom Zaghlul has invited to visit Egypt should be prevented from going. This is a difficult proposition. In the first place we don't know who they are.

---

[1] *La Chartreuse de Parme*, published in 1839, is by Stendhal, the pseudonym of Marie-Henri Beyle (1783–1842).

[2] Lois Sturt (1903–37), youngest daughter of 2nd Baron Alington (1859–1919). She married Evan Morgan, later 2nd Viscount Tredegar, in 1928.

[3] Marigold Churchill died from a diphtheria-like illness on 23 August 1921, aged just under four.

I joined Diana later at an exhibition of her film.[1] She looks wonderfully beautiful in it. Gerald Lawrence, her film lover, drove us home.

September 10, 1921

Curzon much annoyed about the M.P.s – says the whole case has been mismanaged. We had a wail from him this morning but no instructions. Lindsay has decided to act on his own responsibility and let them go with a warning. I am sure he is right.

September 14, 1921

Alan and [St John] Hutchinson came together with Viola to dinner. Alan has got a new game of guessing quotations which Diana adores. A peaceful day at the Office. I went to White's before dinner where I saw Lionel [Tennyson]. He had made 78 that afternoon playing for the rest of England against the champion county. Pretty good considering he went to bed drunk at 4 o'clock this morning and had done the same for the last three nights.

September 29, 1921

A very important telegram arrived from Egypt today. Zaghlul and his M.P.s are going too far. The Government want to forbid them under martial law to continue their journeys about the country. It would be a very serious step to take and might lead to having to deport them. I wrote a minute which I thought rather good and sent it in to Crowe. [*Murray was away on holiday.*]

October 2, 1921

Allenby arrived at the Foreign Office very opportunely this morning, Crowe having just said he wanted to see him this afternoon. I was present at the interview between Crowe and Allenby when a telegram was drafted authorizing Scott to take any steps he might consider necessary even to arrest and deport Zaghlul and the M.P.s. Copies of the draft telegram were sent to Curzon at Kedleston and the Prime Minister at Gairloch for their approval.

Sunday [at Ashby] was a beautiful day and passed agreeably. We went to Althorp which I had never seen. The pictures are wonderful but the house itself I thought gloomy. Lord Spencer[2] was there and showed us over. As he kept pointing to Gainsboroughs and Reynolds and saying 'That's my aunt, that's my uncle' I thought he must be gaga. But he was quite right. His father was born in 1798.

---

[1] *The Glorious Adventure* produced by J. Stuart Blackton. Diana played Lady Beatrice Fair.
[2] 6th Earl Spencer (1857–1922).

October 5, 1921 [London]

I dined at Buck's as Diana went to Chaliapin's[1] concert. We went on to Claridge's where we had a supper party. Supper was not very much fun, but afterwards having dropped the older members and with the addition of Rubinstein, Olga, Fred, Ralph, Ruby and others we went back to Gower Street where Chaliapin sang and Rubinstein played. I wandered about the house and garden with Tommy [Rosslyn] and made a good deal of love to her, which she received almost too well. I was sorry afterwards because I don't really love her and I do really like her. My Diana was equally engaged with Chaliapin and he with her. It was all rather fun and went on till four.

October 7, 1921

We lunched with Philip Sassoon. Lloyd George however was there, his secretary Davies[2] and Orpen[3] – also Mrs Gubbay.[4] Lloyd George was full of life and conversation. We discussed Chaliapin whom Diana is anxious to make meet the Prime Minister.

October 11, 1921

We dined with Philip. It was a successful party. Lloyd George interrogated Chaliapin about conditions in Russia – Maurice[5] acting as interpreter. After dinner Chaliapin sang.

October 20, 1921

There was a Cabinet on Egypt today. We don't know by whom it was called. Curzon saw Allenby who insists on retaining troops in Cairo and having them on the Canal too. Curzon apparently agrees. He was rude to Lindsay today. Told him the question of troops was not his business.

October 21, 1921

The Prime Minister says it is time to put his foot down somewhere and he has chosen Egypt for the operation. A sub-committee of the Cabinet has been formed and Allenby's return to Egypt which was fixed for tomorrow has, much to his rage, been put off.

---

[1] Feodor Chaliapin (1873–1938), the Russian bass, was considered the greatest singer of his day. His most famous role was Boris in *Boris Godunov*. As exuberant in life as on the stage, he was a great admirer of Diana, as was she of him. In 1922 he went into self-imposed exile from Russia and died in Paris sixteen years later.

[2] J. T. Davies was Lloyd George's personal secretary.

[3] Sir William Orpen (1878–1931), successful Irish artist and portrait painter.

[4] Hannah Gubbay, née Ezra, widow of David Gubbay, was a first cousin of Philip Sassoon. She was very close to him and frequently acted as his hostess.

[5] Maurice Baring (1874–1945), poet, journalist and author.

October 31, 1921

Today I lunched with Daisy. It was the happiest and most successful luncheon we have had – and at the end of it I loved her more than I had done before. Murray I found had written a memo on the possibility of annexing Egypt which as a logical alternative to agreement he was inclined to favour. I convinced him that it was utterly impracticable, principally by the argument that having recognized Egyptian nationalism as far as we already have it is impossible to deny it all hope, which annexation would imply.

November 4, 1921

Apparently the Prime Minister refused to make any concessions whatever to the Egyptians beyond what the Cabinet agreed to originally before the Delegation arrived. Even Allenby thinks this is disastrous. It is largely his fault for not having spoken up to the Cabinet in favour of concessions. A Cabinet has been called for 5 this afternoon and Allenby told to attend. If they put off his journey again it will be the limit.

November 5, 1921

Diana and I went down to Breccles after lunch. We had to change at Ely and wait there half an hour. We walked to the cathedral which was looking most beautiful. It stands so well and the surroundings are all lovely. There was a service going on and the interior was very dim. Outside it was a perfect autumn evening – the trees all russet brown and frost in the air. I enjoyed fully 'this little moment mercifully given'. Love has robbed me of no immortal things so far as I'm aware but given many more mortal ones than I deserve.

At Breccles they were letting off fireworks when we arrived. The party was rather gloomy but was enlivened after dinner by the arrival of Winston. We had a tremendous Egyptian argument, Edwin supporting me warmly. They were only agreed in their contempt for Allenby who had apparently been very weak in the Cabinet. Winston said that if he had charge of Egypt the first thing he would do would be to get rid of Allenby and Zaghlul. Edwin said that if Winston had charge he would come to an agreement with Adly in three months, giving him more than anybody had yet proposed to do. The only reason why Winston is taking such an intransigent line with regard to Egypt is that he hopes by so doing to make the Irish settlement more palatable to the Tories. He says the chances of an agreement in Ireland are 7 to 2 on. We drank a lot and argued heatedly. Winston doesn't get drunk but takes a great deal.

November 28, 1921

A very thick fog. I had arranged to lunch with Daisy at the Hanover where I waited for her a long time and then telephoned. She couldn't face the fog and asked me to come to her flat. Her flat is charming, looking out over the gardens of Devonshire House. She was at her prettiest and most seductive.

She told me that George Moore had written a sonnet in French on her hands, which irritated me so I wrote one too and sent it her.

Two lily hands are all of my desire
They hold my hope, my pleasure, my despair,
As calm as marble and as light as air,
Gentle as snow and pitiless as fire.
White hands that I would bind about my head
To chase its trouble with cold finger tips –
Kind hands that I would press against my lips
Until my hunger and my thirst were dead.
Frail heirs of beauty that can never die,
Fair fragile cups that hold immortal wine,
That still inspires but cannot satisfy
Patient, imperious desires of mine.
Rest on my lids, shutting out earth and sky
Making a night where only her eyes shine.

November 30, 1921

Mr Percy Hill, the man who did up our house sent in his bill this morning for the first time – £1900 – a terrible blow.

I left the Foreign Office at six to meet Daisy at an afternoon party at Maud Cunard's. She was looking very pretty. She dropped me at White's – she would only let me kiss her hand once and then held it closed. I wrote her another sonnet –

You left me with shut palm that I had kissed,
You left me, and you never turned your head,
You left me with a thousand words unsaid,
With still-born hopes, and golden chances missed.
And when you looked into your opening hand
Did you a ruby or my heart behold?
Was it a fairy tale too often told
Or a new story of true fairyland?
Love made the story mine, but love may lie,
Love is a flying bird, but love may fall,
Love lives in me like fire, but love may die,
Love is the best of life, but is not all.
Love is the one star in a cloudy sky.
Love me, my love, e'er love flies past recall.

Considering what a long time it is since I wrote any verse I am surprised at how easily I do it. Neither of these sonnets took 20 minutes to write – and they really are not bad. This last one I made up in the taxi going from White's to Gower Street and finished in the taxi from Gower St. to Green St.

December 6, 1921

A long telegram from Allenby today suggesting that we should at once put into force the terms of the treaty which Egypt rejected, i.e. abolish the protectorate, grant them control of foreign affairs etc. It seems to me a foolish suggestion. Why give, for nothing whatever in return, all that the Cabinet were persuaded with great difficulty to offer in the hope of settling the Egyptian question? We have put up a minute to this effect.

December 23, 1921

Zaghlul has been arrested and sent off to Suez whence he is to be deported either to Ceylon or the Seychelles. There has been serious rioting in Cairo.

December 31, 1921

The usual New Year resolutions were made but postponed for the present as I have a week in Paris before me.

1922

January 13, 1922

A dreadful day of fog and cold. We were met this morning at the Foreign Office by a batch of telegrams from Allenby. Sarwat[1] is prepared to form a Government and can do so on certain conditions which Allenby wishes to offer him and for which he wants H.M.G.'s approval. The situation looks really hopeful and a possible solution of the Egyptian question seems in sight. It is unlucky that Curzon should be at Cannes at the moment. Briand[2] resigned yesterday – a blow to the Entente.

January 16, 1922

We lunched at home and played dominoes. Diana excited about the first night of her film. There was a wonderful crowd at Covent Garden and the film was quite a success. Diana looks lovely in it. I don't think much of the production.

January 18, 1922

There was a Cabinet on Egypt today when they failed miserably to come to

---

[1] Abdel Khalek Sarwat (d. 1928), Egyptian politician. Prime Minister Mar. 1922–Nov. 1922, Apr. 1927–Mar. 1928.
[2] Aristide Briand (1862–1932), French Prime Minister 1921–2, had negotiated a security pact with Lloyd George at Cannes but resigned when he failed to obtain its ratification. Foreign Minister 1925–32.

any decision and have merely telegraphed to Allenby to send someone home to give them further information.

January 21, 1922

A reply from Allenby – unless his advice is accepted he will resign. Allenby knows that Curzon is supporting him – the question is will Curzon, if Allenby's resignation is accepted, resign too? He clearly ought to. Or on the other hand will Winston and the rest of the Cabinet give way? I believe they will. Murray doesn't.

I went to Buck's before lunch where I met Edwin for a moment and informed him of Allenby's threatened resignation. He was much interested. He said he himself hadn't supported Curzon because he thought we were giving away everything and gaining nothing. He said that, as a result of our dinner with Winston last year, whenever Curzon says that he has the support of the Foreign Office Winston replies that he knows all about that and that the support is only that of a few young Bolshevists. When he said this in the Cabinet, Curzon said that he had no right as Colonial Secretary to say such a thing, whereupon Winston replied that he might not have the right as Colonial Secretary but that in certain eventualities he soon would have the right to say it as member for Dundee.

January 22, 1922

A thick fog. We lunched with the Laverys. We went there in the tube and could hardly grope our way from the station to them. Hazel had had Winston and Michael Collins[1] to dinner the night before and was very full of them and their delight with themselves at having come to an agreement with Craig.[2]

I had to go to the Foreign Office in the afternoon to get out some papers which the Prime Minister wanted and then I had to go to Victoria to meet Selby[3] as he may have to appear before the Cabinet tomorrow and nobody knows his address. I missed him in the crowd and fog so I accosted another with Cairo labelled luggage and asked him if he knew Selby. By great luck he did and knew that he had been on the train and thought he was staying at the Station Hotel. I then tried the Grosvenor where I found him. He insisted on telling me all the woes of Egypt at once. He feels very strongly. Is prepared to resign himself if Allenby does which is silly. He showed me a telegram he had got from Allenby at Marseilles saying all the advisers would resign too.

---

[1] Michael Collins (1890–1922), the legendary Irish patriot and CIC Irish Free State Army. Hazel Lavery was a supporter of Sinn Fein and had developed a romantic attachment to Collins. He frequently visited her when he was in London in 1921 as one of the Irish delegates attempting to negotiate a truce with the British. In August 1922 Collins was assassinated in Ireland.

[2] James Craig, 1st Viscount Craigavon (1871–1940) and Ulster MP, became in 1921 the first Prime Minister of Northern Ireland and sat in its Parliament.

[3] Sir Walford Selby (1881–1965), diplomat. First Secretary and Head of Chancery at Cairo, working with Allenby, 1919–22; British Minister in Vienna 1933–7.

I then called at Van's [Vansittart] to tell him I had caught Selby. He has a charming house in Catherine Street. His wife, who was looking very pretty, made us cocktails. He had been talking to Curzon all the afternoon about Egypt. I didn't gather from him that Curzon would resign.

January 23, 1922

Selby came to the Office in the morning. He is in a state almost of frenzy. He spent two hours with Lord Curzon who wisely did not bring him before the Cabinet. Edwin lunched with Diana and me and we discussed the Egyptian question the whole time, Edwin's great point being that if you give away the Protectorate without getting a treaty in return you have no legal justification for remaining in Egypt at all. He went to see Curzon after lunch who no doubt intended to appeal for his help. The Cabinet decided that a Cabinet Committee should on the following day endeavour to draw up a draft which should provide an acceptable compromise.

January 24, 1922

The Cabinet Committee produced a telegram to Allenby asking him not to resign and offering to ask Parliament to say that when agreement had been reached on certain other points the Protectorate should be abolished. This is quite useless. It amounts to saying that if a treaty is ever arrived at we promise to carry out one side of it.

In the evening Bland sent for me and asked whether I would take on the job of private secretary to [Cecil] Harmsworth, the Parliamentary Under-Secretary. It means an additional £150 a year and less work. It is a job I have always coveted. In some ways I regret giving up Egypt in which I had got really interested, but nevertheless I am very pleased.

January 26, 1922

I had an interview with Mr Hill [the builder] with regard to his bill. I offered him £1300. He said it was impossible but agreed to go away and think about it and see me again on Saturday. I saw Edwin. Winston now wants to send George Lloyd[1] to Egypt. Edwin said the latter would very likely agree with Allenby.

January 29, 1922. Sunday

Lunched at home and motored to Harrow in the afternoon. We dined with

---

[1] George Lloyd, 1st Baron Lloyd (1879–1941). Politician and colonial administrator. Governor of Bombay 1918–24; High Commissioner for Egypt 1925–9. He opposed Chamberlain's foreign policy and became Secretary of State for the Colonies under Churchill in 1940.

the Carl Meyers[1] – not a soul there we knew. Diana sat between Sargent[2] and Alfred Mond.[3] I had never met Sargent and liked him. You would never think he was an American or a painter.

February 2, 1922

Today Diana's cold bad again. She went to bed in the evening instead of coming to dinner with Goonie. I went. Edwin and Winston were there. Winston said at the beginning of dinner that we mustn't discuss Egypt or Kenya and we didn't. It was really a very pleasant evening, slightly spoilt for me by the fact that the smaller of my crown teeth split and came off – but my moustache now effectively conceals such things. Winston was strong on the merits of monarchy and I cordially agreed.

February 3, 1922

Allenby left Cairo today and appears to have had a great send-off from all parties and nationalities. Northcliffe has been staying with him and has obviously espoused his cause, seeing in it no doubt a good weapon to attack the Government with – *tant mieux*.

February 4, 1922

I spent my last morning in the Egyptian Department. The two years I have passed there have been extraordinarily interesting and instructive and I have enjoyed them. If only the Government would give way there seems every prospect of a satisfactory settlement.

In February 1922 Allenby's proposals were accepted and the British Protectorate in Egypt abolished.

February 8, 1922

A terribly busy day – a shower of Parliamentary Questions. Harmsworth was nervous about the matters that might be raised so asked me to come back after dinner. This was a bore as I was dining with the Jowitts[4] preparatory to the fancy dress ball at the Albert Hall. I went straight from the House to dinner without dressing and straight back to the House. I stayed till 11 – then

[1] Sir Carl Meyer, 1st Bt. (1851–1922), Director of the National Bank of Egypt and Vice-Chairman of De Beers, married Adele Levis in 1883. She and her children were painted by John Singer Sargent in 1896.
[2] John Singer Sargent (1856–1925), American painter.
[3] Alfred Mond, 1st Baron Melchett (1868–1930). Industrialist, financier and politician, co-founder of the great chemical giant of Brunner, Mond & Co., later ICI.
[4] William Jowitt, Earl Jowitt (1885–1957), married Lesley McIntyre in 1913. Though a Liberal MP from 1922, in 1929 he changed parties and became Labour Attorney-General under Ramsay MacDonald. In 1940–5 he served in Churchill's Coalition Government and from 1945–51 was Lord Chancellor under Attlee.

back to the Jowitts where Diana made me up with whiskers and a frock coat 1880 to match herself. The ball when we got there I couldn't enjoy – I felt tired and cross. Drink only made me tireder.

February 15, 1922

Edward Cunard [nephew of Lady Cunard] has been had up for accosting private soldiers in the Park. He pleaded guilty and was fined £5. He now of course says that he was innocent and that his solicitors told him to plead guilty in order to prevent it getting into the papers. But it has appeared in the papers all the same. Nobody talks of anything else.

February 18, 1922

I have got a fortnight behind with my diary. My new job which I thought was going to be easy is far more strenuous than anything I have done before. I have literally not a moment to myself all day and am continually dashing about from one place to another.

February 28, 1922

Princess Mary's wedding.[1] Diana went to the Abbey to write an account of it for the *Daily Mail*. I had great difficulty in getting to the Office. Had to spend luncheon time writing Diana's article.

We went to a party at Katharine's. Alan says that Edwin is going out of office. The Conservatives have made it a condition of their adherence to Lloyd George. Edwin himself is quite cheerful about it. Alan will be out of a job too. The party, a farewell to Chaliapin, was rather grim.

March 9, 1922

This morning there appeared in the press a statement from the Government of India to the effect that it was essential from the point of view of Moslem feeling in India to restore to Turkey Constantinople, Thrace, Smyrna and the Holy Places. Edwin had apparently authorized this publication without consulting the Cabinet. In the afternoon Austen Chamberlain[2] announced in the House of Commons Edwin's resignation. What possessed Edwin to do it nobody seems able to explain. Whether it was because he knew he would have to go anyhow and thought this a good way of doing it, or whether it was pure loss of head, or whether a mixture of both I can't say. His resignation was received with cheers in the House.

---

[1] Princess Mary, Countess of Harewood (1897–1965), only daughter of King George V and Queen Mary, married Henry Lascelles, Viscount Lascelles (1882–1947) in 1922. He succeeded his father as 6th Earl of Harewood in 1929. In 1932 Princess Mary was created Princess Royal.

[2] Sir Austen Chamberlain (1863–1937), Conservative politician. Half-brother of Neville Chamberlain. Chancellor of the Exchequer 1919–21; Lord Privy Seal and Leader of the House 1921–2 in Lloyd George's Coalition Government. Foreign Secretary under Baldwin 1924–9.

March 10, 1922

Edwin is very sad about his resignation. He can't speak of it without crying.

March 17, 1922

We dined with the Holdens. Max Beaverbrook was there. He told us his views of the Montagu incident. Edwin he is sure had no idea of the seriousness of what he did. He was horrified when Max suggested to him that he would be asked to resign. Max says he made a mistake in doing so. He ought to have refused to resign then and promised to do so in a few weeks' time in his own way. Before going to see Austen he promised Max that he would not resign and then did so. Max thinks there is no future for him in politics.

April 13, 1922

We were called at 7.30. Diana felt ill and depressed. She doesn't like leaving her mother at this juncture. [*The Duchess was about to have a major operation.*] To give her heart I made her have a strong whiskey and soda before leaving and had one myself. This had a marvellous effect upon our health and spirits and we drove to the station in true holiday mood talking incessantly. We arrived late for 9 o'clock dinner at the Fellowes's at 29 Rue Galilée. I hadn't seen Daisy's house before. It is very magnificent and in perfect taste.

April 14, 1922 (Paris)

A heavenly morning as warm as summer found us in indifferent health. No sleepers to be had for anywhere. We were at a loss what to do. Diana showing marvellous energy made enquiries about hiring a motor. 3 francs a kilometre seemed a lot. Eventually after much hesitation we decided to start in one and after a hurried lunch at the Ritz left about half past one. It was a fairly pleasant afternoon. We made for Auxerre – stopped at Sens, visited the Cathedral where we saw the robes of Thomas à Becket. Arrived at Auxerre about six and were delighted with it. The Touring Hotel quite excellent, far beyond our hopes. We were given a very nice room, with a bathroom, looking out over the charming red roofs of this delightful town. We walked about in it before dinner and visited the Cathedral and the other strangely similar church both of which are beautiful. We made arrangements to hire another motor for the following day at 1.30 a kilometre.

April 18, 1922, (Hyères)

Hyères was the first place I ever came to in the South of France, some 17 years ago when Father and Mother spent one Easter at Costebelle.

We got up early and walked in the town which was full of sun and colour and bustle. Diana was determined to have a picnic so she bought a large basket and filled it with galantine, a loaf of bread, a pat of butter, a piece of cheese, two eclairs, preserved fruits and a bottle of red wine. Then we hired a motor at one franc 75 per kilometre and set out for Le Lavandou – a little fishing village by the sea. It was a pretty drive through the forest and when we got there the sun was hot and we found a suitable spot on the beach where we spread our cloth and ate our lunch most delectably. Afterwards we read a little of *Richard Peverel* [*The Ordeal of Richard Peverel* by George Meredith] and then slept in the sun. We then drove on some way along the coast. We particularly like Cavalière – a pretty beach with pine trees almost to the water's edge. There was some rain in the afternoon but it cleared in the evening and the drive back was delicious through the fragrant woods. We dined in the hotel – not too badly – and had quite a good bottle of wine. Afterwards Diana insisted on visiting the local Casino, an imposing building with preparations for every form of dissipation, dancing, baccarat, boule, chemin de fer. There was a band playing and about a dozen croupiers waiting but unfortunately the only other visitors besides ourselves were two old English governesses who were sadly reading back numbers of *The Times*. We did the same for a little and then retired to bed.

April 21, 1922 (St Raphael)

We bought in the market the ingredients of a picnic, motored to a delicious sandy cove, bathed there, then lunched and slept in the sun. It was a heavenly afternoon. In the evening I wanted to go quietly to bed but Diana insisted on going to Cannes to get our money back [*they had lost 7,000 francs the previous night*]. We missed the night train and only arrived there at 11 o'clock. I had wonderful luck playing low and when it was time for us to catch the train I had won 2,500 francs. I was content with this but Diana wasn't. She insisted on missing the train, hiring a motor and staying on with the result that at 3 o'clock I had lost the 2,000 and 2,500 more. We then had a long gloomy drive home.

April 26, 1922 (London)

I lunched at Buck's, went home afterwards to have my nails done and then returned to the Foreign Office where I stayed until about half past six. Then home where I found Diana, Alan and Hutchinson eating crabs and caviare. Diana never seems to weary of that couple. I do. She dined with her father, I with Diana Capel at the Embassy. When I got home I found Diana once more with 'the boys' as she calls Alan and Hutchy.

April 30, 1922 [Breccles]

A fine sunny day, but not warm. In the afternoon we motored over to Houghton which I had never seen. I had heard so much about it and seen pictures of it that I was a little disappointed. But it is certainly a beautiful house. The square hall, the dining room and Walpole's library are quite perfect. The

Rocksavages[1] were alone and seem strangely out of place there – not at all at home – although they are in their different ways a beautiful couple and should match the house.

May 6, 1922

A fine day at last. Diana and I lunched alone together at Arlington Street. In the afternoon we set out in the car. Something went wrong with it near Hounslow. We never discovered what it was but after one unsuccessful attempt we got it satisfactorily repaired and it went beautifully for the rest of the day. I am very impressed by the friendliness, good nature and lack of avarice that one encounters among the ordinary English people as one motors about the country. This hot Saturday afternoon at Hounslow a man spent half an hour working hard at our car and then said 'I'm not going to charge you anything because I can't be sure if I've fixed it right but next time you're passing here call in and let me know'. We gave him a shilling for which he was most grateful. At the first place where we stopped they were equally good natured though less competent. It is the same everywhere in England. Taxi-drivers are wonderfully civil and sensible and so very different to the same class in France. Perhaps it is because they understand their own countrymen better, but I doubt it. The railway porters at Dover and those at Calais seem to belong to two different civilizations.

We got to Cherkley, Beaverbrook's place, about 8 o'clock and found there a dull little party. Max had a bottle of his best claret, Margaux 1888, put in front of me for my own consumption, so I enjoyed the evening.

May 7, 1922

Diana wanted to take some blossom home with us. She broke off several branches and we hid them under a tree near the drive. Bonar Law and others came to lunch. He said that the only way Lloyd George could now get out of Genoa[2] with credit would be if he were to come back and say 'The thing was worth trying – it was a great chance – I tried and I failed'. After luncheon Diana and I left. When we came to the place where we had hidden the blossom we found Max sitting with Sir Campbell Stuart[3] in earnest conversation almost on top of it. Regretfully we had to leave it there to wither.

---

[1] Sybil Sassoon (1894–1989), Sir Philip Sassoon's sister, had married George (Rock), Earl of Rocksavage (1883–1968). He succeeded as the 5th Marquess of Cholmondeley in 1923. They lived at Houghton Hall in Norfolk. She was a passionate patron of the arts.

[2] The Conference of Genoa, Apr.–May 1922, was convened to discuss the economic reconstruction of Central and Eastern Europe. Negotiations foundered when France and Belgium insisted on Soviet Russia repaying pre-war loans and returning confiscated foreign-owned property.

[3] Sir Campbell Stuart (1885–1972), a Canadian; he was a protégé of Lord Northcliffe and managing editor of the *Daily Mail* from 1921–3.

May 11, 1922

I lunched with Daisy at her flat. She was as attractive as ever. She has the loveliest hands, but only uses them to keep me at a distance. Very different to Deauville days. I spent most of the afternoon writing an article for Diana for tomorrow's *Daily Mail*. 1,000 words on the length of skirt, £50.

May 15, 1922

We left the Priory at 7.30. It was a heavenly morning – the country at its most beautiful. The drive would have been pure joy save for two mishaps. The first was missing the way near Haslemere. Trying to turn round at the top of a steep hill Diana let the engines down and as the self starter wasn't working we couldn't start it again. We got out and tried to start it down the hill – finally with terrific exertions got it rolling straight whereupon the engines started again. After this we ran out of petrol at Kingston with the result that I didn't get to the office until 11.15. We dined with Max at the Vineyard [Lord Beaverbrook's house at Hurlingham]. After dinner we were shown the best film I have ever seen called *The Cabinet of Dr Caligari*.[1] It is a German film and is not allowed to be shown in England.

May 22, 1922

Diana was sad because Dr Aarons told her today he was not very sanguine of her chances of having a baby. I really don't mind – except for her sake.

May 25, 1922

When I came back to lunch today Diana told me she had seen Bonney, the surgeon who operated on her mother. He said she had a fibroid in the womb and ought to be operated on. She has settled to have it done after Whitsun. She is very upset and nervous about it, poor darling.

May 27, 1922

Diana was in a very bad state this morning. I haven't seen her like it since the days of the cancer scare in 1920. I went to see Bonney before luncheon. I wasn't very impressed by him – thought him rather a bounder. Diana was better at luncheon time having had several cocktails. She said she must rely upon the stimulus of alcohol until the operation.

May 30, 1922

Diana saw another doctor this morning – Playfair, a great accoucheur. He said it was quite unnecessary for her to have the operation – and as she was

---

[1] *The Cabinet of Dr Caligari* (1919), a German film starring Conrad Veidt, was directed by Robert Wiene. One of the first horror films.

frightened about it advised her not to. So she is not going to have it after all –
an immense relief.

June 13, 1922

Lunched at home. Dined with Max at the Vineyard. The Montagus were there
and the Aga Khan. Max said he had heard that Lord Northcliffe has gone
mad.[1] Rothermere sent a doctor to me today for assistance in getting a passport
quickly to go out to Northcliffe in Switzerland. So it is probably true.

June 14, 1922

It is quite true about Northcliffe.

June 22, 1922

At about four Harmsworth came back from the House which had adjourned
owing to the terrible news of Sir Henry Wilson's murder.[2] I went to White's
where nobody was talking of anything else.

June 26, 1922

I watched the funeral procession of Sir Henry Wilson go past my window
across the Horse Guards parade this morning. It was a very impressive and
moving sight. It moved me to verse with the following result:

> He nobly lived and did not die in vain,
> Who with unfaltering faith, unfailing zeal
> Fell facing with drawn sword and high disdain
> The reptile foe that was not worth his steel.
> Weep not for him but for the luckless land
> That mourns a leader of her noblest few
> And lies the victim, of a craven band
> Whose folly and whose treachery he knew.

July 5, 1922

In the evening I dined with the Taylors. We played a rubber [of bridge]
afterwards and I won £25 – then [we played] chemin de fer. I started by
winning £50 and then lost steadily – was at one time £2250 down – and ended
up minus £148. We went on playing until a quarter to six. When I got home
Diana was in a terrible state. She had known where I was but not the telephone
number so couldn't get hold of me and thought I was dead. I never felt more
guilty and remorseful. I made a thousand serious resolves to behave better

---

[1] Lord Northcliffe was becoming increasingly erratic, a condition caused by a blood infection
which invaded the brain and damaged his heart. He died on 14 August 1922.

[2] Field Marshal Sir Henry Wilson (1864–1922), an Ulsterman, Unionist and Conservative
Member for North Down. He was shot by two members of Sinn Fein on the doorstep of his
London house.

and never to cause unhappiness again to her whom I love so much more than all the world.

July 6, 1922

I began to implement my good resolutions by chucking Daisy with whom I was lunching and lunching at home instead.

July 19, 1922

We dined with the Hutchinsons in Hammersmith. [Ambrose] McEvoy and Walter Sickert[1] were there. I had not met him before and thought him an attractive old boy. My father operated on him in 1865. He said 'If it hadn't been for your father I shouldn't be here now'. I said 'No more should I'. It was a cheerful evening but we stayed too late.

July 25, 1922

Diana's cold pretty bad so she stayed in bed all day but got up in the evening when we motored down to Bexley to dine with the Hart-Davises. We went in the Duchess's closed car. At dinner besides Sybil, Richard and the two children were Dick Twining and his wife and a Miss Mellor who we were told was a great spiritualist. We had a good dinner and after the children had gone to bed we were told a series of most incredible events which were said to have taken place in that house during the last few days. Miss Mellor, a fat, comfortable-looking, complacent woman, explained that the garden was haunted by evil spirits who were endeavouring to get into the house. Several queer things had happened. Two nights before when Dick and his wife were in bed he says that something happened like an explosion near his head. He swears he was awake at the time. Immediately afterwards strange coloured lights began flashing about the room, playing particularly round a picture of the Virgin Mary. He woke up his wife and they both sat up in bed for some time watching the lights. When they turned on the light they could see nothing. At last, they could bear it no longer so he went to Miss Mellor who came and proceeded to exorcize the spirits with signs and prayers. When all seemed quiet she left them, but the lights began again and she had to come back a second time. On the following night she, Richard and Dick were sitting at the dining table finishing their port after dinner when something took place which precipitated Dick from the chair on which he was sitting to another and left Richard like a man suffering from shell shock. Miss Mellor again came to the rescue and eventually restored him. Her explanation was that he was temporarily possessed by a devil. The whole thing is too incredible but there is no doubt at all that they all firmly believe it. What is most strange is that Sybil, who one would expect to be the centre of anything of that sort, has less to do with it than any of them and is apparently not much interested.

---

[1] Walter Sickert (1860–1942), artist, member of the Camden Town Group of painters.

Richard informed Diana afterwards in the strictest confidence that he knew who the medium was – that it must be Sybil – that she was always wandering in the garden at night and that the spirits all came from the garden – that at times he saw other people look out of her eyes and that a dog which she has recently acquired – a large black Borzoi – was also in league with the evil things. When I heard this I wondered whether Richard was losing his sanity – and I still do wonder. The whole atmosphere of the place was very strange and uncanny. Miss Mellor took Diana and me out to the edge of the wood to see whether we could see anything but we saw nothing. We motored back to London afterwards – a strange evening.

July 26, 1922

Venetia and Edwin came to lunch. He had just been to see his successor at the India Office – Lord Peel. Venetia is going at last to have a baby which may prevent Edwin going to India this winter. I hope for his own sake it will, as nothing more ill judged than his visit could possibly be imagined. Lord Reading has actually asked him not to go and yet he persists in his intention.

August 1, 1922

We went out to buy a luncheon basket for our forthcoming motor tour. Diana was so sweet and excited about it – sitting on the floor in the shop and playing with it like a child. We dined together and went to *The Second Mrs Tanqueray* [by Arthur Wing Pinero] – remarkably well acted by Gladys Cooper. Diana was in such floods of tears at the end that we had to leave hurriedly. She went on sobbing in the taxi. We joined Iris and Curtis at the Eiffel Tower, where we had a bottle of champagne. There was a terrible young man there called Ronald Firbank who writes novels.

August 24, 1922 [Deauville]

We lunched on Henri de Rothschild's yacht – a good but very boring meal. Some excellent Mouton Rothschild which he owns. We all dined at the Casino. The dinner was so rich one couldn't eat it. The first course was hot caviare between pancakes soaked in butter and covered in cream. I greedily ate it but felt so sick afterwards that I couldn't eat any more.

August 28, 1922 [Venice]

Soon after eleven we set forth for the Lido. On the launch from Danieli's we met Ralph [Peto], who seemed in a very queer state. He said that they had accused him of being drunk yesterday and that he was prepared to kill anybody who repeated the accusation. He abused everybody especially Ruby and said that the people here were all buggers or sapphists – all this in front of his little daughter Rosemary who was sitting on his knee. At the Lido we found a host of friends – Daisy amongst them. After lunch when I was sitting with Daisy they brought her a note and when I asked her what it was she said that Ralph kept writing her mad notes – all this convinces me that they have a liaison.

August 29, 1922 [Venice]

Diana's birthday. I gave her the Kodak last night. She was very pleased with it. Another perfect day. Alan and Lois [Sturt] arrived in time for lunch. Lois was in subdued form having cried all night because her dog had jumped out of the train and she didn't know what had become of it. A restless night owing to mosquitoes.

Meeting Ozzie [Dickinson] reminded me of when I first met him here in Venice nine years ago. Of the others who formed our party then not one remains. George Vernon, Edward Horner, Denis Anson, Raymond Asquith, Patrick Shaw-Stewart, Charles Lister, Billy Grenfell – all, all dead.

September 2, 1922 [Venice]

Diana spent the afternoon making preparations for our party. She got an arc light which she had hung outside the window of the big room. It illuminated the whole thing beautifully. In the dining room she hung festoons of fruit under the silver candelabra. The effect was charming. A host of people came to the party and it was really a great success. I enjoyed it very much. About 4 o'clock when nearly everyone had gone Lois started doing stunts, turning somersaults, *danses d'apaches* etc.

September 4, 1922

Weather still bad. The Mosleys[1] came to lunch with us. In the afternoon we went to see the Palazzo Labbia[2] and Diana formed the plan of taking part of it on long lease for 15,000 lire a year.[3] It could be made beautiful but needs a lot of doing up.

September 7, 1922 [Venice]

This was the evening of the Mosleys' fancy dress barge party. I wore a Longhi cape, mask and hat with knee breeches. Diana looked lovely in her Longhi dress brought from London. She made Alan up as a Venetian Jew and he looked very well. The Mosleys came to dinner with us first – at least Lady Cynthia didn't arrive until we had finished. We set out for the barges about 10 o'clock. It was not a very nice night but the barges – there were three of them – were moored together in a sheltered place on the lagoon and it wasn't

---

[1] Sir Oswald 'Tom' Mosley (1896–1980), a Conservative MP, married Lady Cynthia Curzon in 1920. In 1931 he launched the New Party and in 1932 founded the British Union of Fascists. Cynthia Mosley died in 1933 and in 1936 he married Diana Guinness, formerly Mitford, sister to Nancy, Pamela, Unity, Jessica and Deborah. Hitler was present at the marriage.

[2] One of the most sumptuous palaces in Venice, its main room completely frescoed by Tiepolo.

[3] About £150.

cold. The general effect was really extraordinarily pretty. The barges were hung with Chinese lanterns – most of the people were in fancy dress – there was a piano on one of the barges – Olga and other people sang and there was dancing. There was quite a good cold supper and plenty of good champagne. Daisy with white hair looked beautiful. I sat with her most of the time. At about 2 we all went to the Hotel Britannia, where Elsa Maxwell[1] gave us coffee and eggs, and then went on dancing there. At 4.30 I insisted on coming home as I was tired out. Some of them stayed up till dawn. Elsa Maxwell's conduct was strange. She had promised to help the party in every way, to play the piano for them and to provide the late supper. At 1 o'clock however she had not appeared and it was then stated that she had gone once round the barges in her gondola and then home to bed. Tom Mosley then went to her hotel where he found her in bed and where no orders about the supper had been given. She said she had been unable to find the barges on the lagoon and she had come home in despair. This was plainly not true. However she then got up and did everything possible. She is a strange woman and she hates anybody giving a party except herself. Tom Mosley made a declaration of love to Diana this evening. She told him not to be silly. He said he had adored her all this summer – that he had never felt anything like it in his life before.

September 14, 1922 (Venice)

Our sad last day in Venice and the first fine one for so long. We met Foa [an antique dealer] and two other men at Palazzo Labbia to make definite arrangements about decorating it. But we had hardly begun when the present occupier who had previously agreed to let it to us for £150 a year came forward and said he would also want £200 premium. He had never mentioned such a thing before and we were so angry that we decided to give it up altogether. It was a cruel disappointment to Diana and a slight one to me. It was also a slight relief as I think it would have been rather a foolish extravagance.

September 19, 1922 (London)

I went with Diana and Hutchy to the National Gallery, where the pictures seem so much better than those in Italy. The fact is that there are no bad pictures in the National Gallery and they are all so admirably hung.

September 20, 1922

Curzon's first conversation with Poincaré [French Prime Minister] today was fairly satisfactory. They have agreed on the necessity of a conference. Meanwhile instructions have been sent to the naval Commander-in-Chief in the Mediterranean to take any action that may be necessary to prevent Kemal's[2]

---

[1] Elsa Maxwell (1883–1963), international party-giver and socialite.
[2] Mustafa Kemal Atatürk (1881–1938), founder and first President of the new Republic of Turkey, created in 1923, following the Treaty of Lausanne.

forces crossing the Straits. This might lead to an incident like Navarino or Copenhagen.

September 22, 1922

Latest reports from Constantinople say that Kemal is determined to advance on Constantinople and Chanak. This will mean war. There is an amusing telegram from Curzon this morning recounting interviews with the Serbians and Roumanians in Paris. Curzon is a master of the art of modesty, giving himself the *beau rôle* in conversations. The 2nd Battalion of the Grenadiers and one Coldstream battalion are going out.

September 24, 1922

Curzon has agreed with Poincaré and Sforza [Italian Minister for Foreign Affairs] on the terms of the invitation to be addressed to Kemal. It did not look as though he would be able to do so and it is a great triumph for him to have succeeded. It looks now as though all will be well. I think we have been very rash and are lucky to have got so well out of it. I disagree with most people in that I think the French were right to withdraw from Chanak. The troops there were serving no practicable purpose and were a provocation to Kemal's victorious army, especially after our bellicose declaration of Sept. 16. Had Kemal attacked and annihilated them, which it appears he might easily have done, we should have been irrevocably committed to a long, costly and unnecessary war. I think England and Lloyd George have lost prestige while France and Curzon have gained it. There was an extraordinary scene at the interview on Friday when Poincaré lost all control and stormed at Curzon to such an extent that he left the room in protest. Poincaré had to come out after him and apologize in order to get him back.

September 25, 1922

We dined with Jack and Goonie Churchill. The Laverys and the Claud Russells were there. Hazel is still mourning Michael Collins and thinks it necessary to go about with the expression of a widow. She was with him the night before he was shot. Jack says that Winston made a lot of use of her as an intermediary between himself and Collins. We had a good dinner.

October 9, 1922

In the afternoon at the Foreign Office Bland sent for me and said that Curzon's first action on returning in glory from Paris and settling the fate of nations was to ring up Crowe and say he thought I was having too much leave. I told Bland what leave I had had and by slightly diminishing the Easter and Whitsun episodes found that I had had less than my due. I also told him that I was intending to go away that day for three days' shooting at Belvoir. Crowe then sent a minute in to Curzon saying what leave I had had, that he understood I was intending to go away for three days and that he saw no reason for preventing me.

October 12, 1922 [Belvoir]

This was the last day's shooting. Diana was to have come out to lunch but the others appeared without her and said she had been suddenly summoned to London in connection with the new film[1] which is starting next week. It appears that this afternoon Mrs Blackton, the film producer's wife, was most insulting to Diana, lost her temper, raved at her like a fishwife. I have written a strong letter to Blackton on the subject.

October 13, 1922

This morning Bland showed me Curzon's minute on the statement Crowe sent him about my leave. 'It is not so much his ordinary leave to which I object as his ability while performing his duties to enjoy an amount of social relaxation unclaimed by his fellow workers.' Such utterly meaningless drivel I never read. I said so and Bland agreed. He told me that Crowe's comment had been that this was just the kind of incident which made it impossible to have any respect for the Secretary of State.

October 14, 1922

We lunched at the Embassy and immediately after lunch left in the car for Beaulieu where Diana has got to do her film and where we have taken a small house called Hilltop. We had a beautiful drive – the sun being almost too bright as it was in our eyes most of the way. We had a puncture within a few miles of our destination and successfully changed the wheel ourselves. The house is not too bad. The maids whom we sent on in advance had taken the best bedrooms, refusing to sleep in attics. We had dinner, played dominoes and went to bed.

October 15, 1922 (Beaulieu)

This morning we motored over to Crichel – a most, most beautiful drive – the loveliest autumn weather imaginable. On the way back we passed the chapel at Thorney Hill near Avon where is the memorial to John [Manners]. The chapel was locked but by climbing up and looking in the windows we could see the memorial, and very beautiful I thought it and very like. It is where he would have liked to lie, on that lonely windswept hill, looking over the wide expanse of the New Forest that he loved.

October 16, 1922 (London)

Harmsworth told me this afternoon that he didn't mean to stand again for Parliament. He is afraid of dying like Northcliffe [his brother] from overwork!

---

[1] *The Virgin Queen*, also directed by J. Stuart Blackton. Diana played Queen Elizabeth I.

I told him of my incident with Lord Curzon. He was outraged, said it was infernal cheek on Curzon's part, swore he would 'put it right'. I don't know what he will do. It seems certain now that there will be a general election. I dined at the Embassy with Diana Capel – she went home early and I went to White's where I played bridge at shilling points and lost £119 – Fool! fool! fool!

October 19, 1922

This is a day of great events. [Austen] Chamberlain was defeated at the Carlton Club in the morning.[1] The Prime Minister [Lloyd George] resigned in the afternoon. As I write this I am awaiting the return of Harmsworth who has gone over to No. 10. He found the Prime Minister extremely cheerful, but wondering what he was going to say at Leeds on Saturday.

October 29, 1922

After lunch we all went to see as much of Diana's film as has been done. She looks beautiful in it and acts much better than she did in the other, I thought.

November 1, 1922

My new master is appointed, Ronald McNeill.[2] I wonder how I shall like him.

November 3, 1922

I lunched with Sydney Fairbairn at Buck's. Maud Cunard had asked me to see him with a view to inducing him to come to some satisfactory arrangement with Nancy. They want him to be divorced. I think he would be willing so long as it doesn't cost him anything. We discussed all this over a bottle of claret followed by a great many glasses of port.

November 9, 1922

In the afternoon I received my first communication from McNeill – very civil, saying he hoped I might continue to be his private secretary etc. I motored down with Maurice, Scatters, Diana C. and Barbara to Bethnal Green to a political meeting. On the way down Scatters asked me to speak. I have of course no right to do so, but there seemed little chance of its ever being heard of so I said I would. It was a very noisy meeting, full of communists who hardly allowed one to get a hearing, but I managed to speak for some time, a thing I haven't done since I left Oxford, and I thoroughly enjoyed it.

---

[1] Austen Chamberlain wanted to continue as Conservative leader of a coalition government, but Conservative MPs voted for independent Conservative action at the next general election. Bonar Law became leader in his place and won a large majority in the November 1922 general election.

[2] Ronald McNeill, Lord Cushendun (1861–1936). Conservative MP 1911–27; Parliamentary Under-Secretary for Foreign Affairs 1922–4 under Bonar Law.

November 16, 1922

An anxious day for me awaiting news of Sidney's election[1] on which I had a bet of £200 to £250. Poor Edwin badly beat for Cambridgeshire and Winston beat at Dundee. At last about six o'clock at White's I got the news. Sidney was in. Immense relief.

November 20, 1922

McNeill arrived at the Office soon after midday and showed a most depressing reluctance to go out to lunch. At a quarter to two I left him and went to the Garrick.

November 28, 1922

All these days our minds, Diana's and mine, have been absorbingly occupied with one subject – which we call 'the plan'. Briefly it is that we should go to America in order that she may in a few years make a large fortune on the film. It involves my giving up the Foreign Office. The idea is that when we come back I should stand for Parliament. To many it may appear that I have decided to give up working and live on my wife. I shall have therefore to work very hard and endeavour to write my book about Talleyrand. It is the only way in which I can ever get into Parliament, the only way in which either of us can ever travel which we both long to do. I feel sure it is right though I naturally hesitate to give up a profession at which I have worked for nearly ten years and which I like. It will be a great adventure and infinitely better than sinking into a secure rut.

December 31, 1922

This has been a very happy year for me. Diana and I agreed last night that if we never have a worse one we shan't do badly. My New Year resolutions are to get up earlier, to grow thinner and not to gamble.

1923

January 13, 1923 [Paris]

[In the afternoon] I went to the Travellers' where I found various friends and whence I went on with Ali Mackintosh[2] to a most astonishing brothel in the Rue de la Poissonière – where every form of vice takes place in public – one walks at will from room to room and watches whatever happens to be going on – if one lingers one is pounced on but can easily avoid unwelcome attentions.

---

[1] The Conservatives had a comfortable majority in the November election.
[2] Capt. Alastair Mackintosh (1889–1919), author of *No Alibi*.

January 16, 1923 [St Moritz]

In the afternoon we made our first attempt at skiing. We took an instructor with us and went to what is called the nursery. It seemed terribly difficult and we made very little progress. During the last few minutes however it seemed to me that things were going better and I was not without hope.

January 17, 1923

Diana's foot hurt her so much this morning that she went to a doctor who gave her something to put on it which did a lot of good. I practised skiing all the morning but made very little progress. I am such a coward about it. We lunched at the Carlton – more skiing in the afternoon which left us both in great pain – Diana with a knee, I with an ankle. Jack Wilson gave a huge dinner this evening in a room at the Palace. I sat between Lady Curzon and a Miss Emery – an American girl to whom Ali Mackintosh is said to be engaged. Lady Curzon was very genial and pleasant. She had just been speaking to her husband on the telephone. He had once more good hopes of the Lausanne Conference. She had told him we were here, at which news she said 'he was much thrilled'. I suggested that he would probably complain about my having too much leave which rather irritated her. 'You don't seem to know George' she said 'there is nothing petty about him.' She told me that Rumbold[1] would probably replace d'Abernon at Berlin – and she also told me as a deadly secret that they were thinking of offering Washington to Mr Asquith, who according to Crewe would accept it. She said that Curzon was very pleased with Harold Nicolson, who would probably replace Vansittart.

January 23, 1923

I saw Lady Curzon who told me she had bad news from Lausanne. The French had ratted altogether and were prepared to give way to the Turks on every point. 'George' was much distressed.

February 6, 1923 (London)

Luncheon at home. Hutchy came and afterwards we all went to Marlborough St. Police Court – Diana having been summonsed for leaving her motor car in a side street. We fought the case, Hutchy defending, but she was fined 10/-. This afternoon Venetia's baby was born – a girl. Edwin came in and described the birth, Venetia's great courage and her endeavours to conceal from him that it was going to take place today etc.

---

[1] Sir Horace Rumbold, 9th Bt. (1869–1941). High Commissioner and Ambassador at Constantinople 1920–3; deputy to Lord Curzon at the first Lausanne Conference Nov. 1922–Feb. 1923, and chief British delegate at the second Lausanne Conference, finally signing the Peace Treaty with Turkey in July 1923. From 1928–33 he was British Ambassador in Berlin.

February 13, 1923

Opening of Parliament. Went to the House – heard Ramsay MacDonald[1] who was good, moderate, rather statesmanlike, Asquith who was bad, boring, gaga, Bonar Law who was good but dull.

February 19, 1923

It was an interesting night in the House. Lloyd George made a very eloquent, clever, disingenuous speech. The best I have ever heard him make – but I haven't heard him often. Simon also was good. The Prime Minister [Bonar Law] without any eloquence but by sheer logic and good sense quite annihilated them – or so it seemed to me. It is wonderful how he listens and replies without even making or using a single note. Every minute I spend in that House makes me long more passionately to be a member of it. The Prime Minster seems very tired.

February 22, 1923

My thirty-third birthday. Diana forgot about it in the morning but remembered later. She gave me a very nice Sir Thomas Browne. Sibbie gave me the works of F. Jammes[2]. Mother sent me £12.

April 4, 1923

A real warm spring day. I went out early and the weather went to my head. I bought new clothes, gloves, shoes, wine and sauntered down Bond Street in the sun and across the Park to the Foreign Office.

April 23, 1923

Lunched at Buck's. Winston was there, looking wonderfully younger and thinner. In the afternoon I went to the General Meeting of the Garrick Club where certain proposals with regard to architectural alterations were put forward. I, greatly daring, spoke against the resolutions which were defeated. Several people congratulated me on my speech.

April 26, 1923

The Royal Wedding.[3] We had very good seats in the Abbey. The Mosleys were next us and the Dudley Wards immediately behind. I enjoyed it. We skipped out by the North Door as soon as it was over and so had an excellent view of

---

[1] Ramsay MacDonald (1866–1937), Labour Prime Minister and Foreign Minister 1924; Prime Minister 1929–31; Prime Minister in the National Government Oct. 1931–June 1935.

[2] Francis Jammes (1868–1938), French poet.

[3] Albert, Duke of York, later King George VI (1895–1952), married Lady Elizabeth Bowes-Lyon (1900–2002), youngest daughter of the 14th Earl of Strathmore.

them driving away. We picked Jasper Ridley[1] up in the crowd going away and drove him home. In an outburst of confidence he told us that he had for long been in love with Elizabeth Lyon and that he was miserable about her marriage. He had never believed she would do it and it had been a very sudden *volte face* on her part as she had refused the Duke of York several times. We hurried home, lunched quickly, and then I had to write Diana's article on the wedding for the American press. She is getting £150 for it.

May 11, 1923

I lunched with Sybil. She has become a Roman Catholic and is learning Hebrew as she doesn't like reading the Bible in translation.

May 15, 1923

Diana has received an offer to go and appear in *The Miracle* in New York next autumn.

The Miracle had been a great success in London when produced by C. B. Cochran at Olympia before the war, starring the Italian actress Maria Carmi. Loosely based on a medieval miracle play, it was the story of a wonder-working statue of the Virgin in a great cathedral, which came to life and took the place of a beautiful young nun to enable her to go out and experience the world. The great Austrian director Max Reinhardt (1873–1940) was now planning a new and still more extravagant production for New York.

May 29, 1923

The two chief events while we were away were the change of Prime Minister [*Bonar Law had resigned owing to throat cancer and been replaced by Baldwin*] and the engagement of Diana Capel to Burghy.[2] They are to be married on Thursday week. I spoke to her on the telephone yesterday. She sounded wonderfully happy.

June 12, 1923

I lunched at Buck's and in the afternoon I went to see Duse[3] in *Ghosts* [by Ibsen]. I had taken two seats and got Kakoo to go with me. It occurred to me afterwards that she was hardly the right person to take to *Ghosts*. However she was very sweet and I explained the story to her as best I could. Our seats were in row W and it was almost impossible to hear. The effort of listening quite

---

[1] The Hon. (Sir) Jasper Ridley (1887–1951), later Chairman of Coutts & Co. and the National Provincial Bank. Married Countess Nathalie Benckendorff, daughter of the Russian Ambassador, in 1911.

[2] Vere (Burghy) Fane, 14th Earl of Westmorland (1893–1948). Lt.-Cdr. Royal Navy 1914–19, gentleman rider and trainer.

[3] Eleonora Duse (1858–1924), legendary Italian actress.

spoilt the whole thing for me and I can't say I enjoyed it or was able at all to appreciate Duse.

June 18, 1923

We went to a party given by Freda which I enjoyed. I danced with Poppy Baring[1] who is a very attractive girl. The Prince of Wales was there and was rather in wine. He was staying at Windsor for Ascot and had come up clandestinely with Prince George [Duke of Kent] after the rest of the party had gone to bed. He gave an amusing account of poker in the royal circle. Daisy and Fred [Cripps] left soon to go on to Rectors but later I got a message from Daisy to go and pick her up at her house. It was about half past three. I went trembling with hope. As I turned the corner into Stratton Street I saw Reggie who had very shortly before left the party with Lois getting out of a taxi at the corner. As it is a cul de sac there was no escape so I drove on to the end, rang the bell, the door was opened by Daisy. I explained to her quickly what had happened and bolted into the cellars where I remained until all was quiet above when I slipped out.

July 5, 1923

Went home and found Diana arranging our house for the party. It looked lovely. We dined with Maurice [Baring]. It was an excellent dinner, a great deal was drunk and it was great fun. Diana and I went off to receive our guests. The garden looked too lovely – illuminated with lime-light – and the party was I think a great success. First Rubinstein played and then there was supper which most people had in the garden. I sat in the dining room with Betty looking out on the garden which looked fantastically lovely. Diana had a lot of rose leaves to throw. Maurice and Viola danced a comic orgiastic dance. At the bottom of the garden we had a Russian orchestra. Then Chaliapin sang. Afterwards there was more supper and Viola did what I thought very boring stunts.

August 3, 1923

I went to the Foreign Office in the morning and took leave of McNeill, who was busy inditing a letter to *The Times* on the subject of the Bulgarian outlet on the Aegean. We dined in the Savoy Grill room, or at least I dined there while Diana wrestled with Mr Morris Gest[2] upstairs about the terms of her autumn engagement. She had been told to stand out for 2000 dollars a week but he beat her down to 1500.

---

[1] Poppy Baring (1901–79), daughter of Sir Godfrey Baring. She married Peter Thursby in 1928.
[2] Morris Gest, Reinhardt's business manager.

August 8, 1923 [Salzburg]

We arrived at Salzburg at 4 o'clock. We were met at the station by a short, entirely bald man with a round face, carrying a stick but wearing no hat. This was Mr Kommer,[1] half colleague, half toady of Reinhardt. He spoke excellent English. We drove off with him to the Schloss Leopoldskron. On arrival we were enchanted with its beauty – a large baroque building of the 17th century perfectly situated on a lake. We were shown to our suite of rooms which were on a palatial scale, bare and beautiful. After having a bath and changing we went down to tea on the terrace where we met Reinhardt. He speaks no English but understands it pretty well. I was favourably impressed by him. After tea we went with Kommer for a walk round the lake. Dinner was a disappointment as regards both food and drink – the latter consisting of beer until halfway through and then white wine. After dinner there was music in the great hall, a magnificent room, lit by candlelight, four musicians sitting in the middle. Berners[2] and the two Sitwells who are staying in Salzburg came. I got bored with the music in spite of the beauty of the scene and slipped off to bed.

August 9, 1923

When I came back from my bath this morning I found Diana reading this book. She had turned to last year's Venice where of course she found a good deal about Daisy. I was so angry that I gave her no chance to be. We lunched at a place called Hellbrunn with Berners, the Sitwells and a little creature called Walton[3] who writes music – a very bad lunch. We saw the waterworks afterwards. Diana had an interview with Reinhardt in the evening. He described her part to her and she says that he did it so beautifully that it made her cry. The tears seem to have made a great impression on him. Dinner this evening was even worse than the night before. It consists of only three courses, a nasty egg, a pasta dish, hot meat, cake. The beer is drinkable, the wine is not. There were no women except Diana.

August 10, 1923

We did some shopping in Salzburg and lunched at the Europa. When we got home in the evening I found the following telegram from Richard: 'Have received telegram from Frankfurt signed Hadow Munster stating Mione's mental condition very serious suggesting I should go immediately, have not informed your Mother and cannot go myself; Sibbie is still in Paris so cannot

---

[1] Dr Rudolf Kommer (d. 1943), 'Kaetchen', Max Reinhardt's right-hand man, who was to become Diana's close friend and guardian angel throughout her years with *The Miracle*.

[2] Gerald Berners, 14th Baron (1883–1950). Composer, author, painter and eccentric, he was the model for Lord Merlin in Nancy Mitford's *The Pursuit of Love* (1945).

[3] Sir William Walton (1902–83), composer. Sacheverell and Osbert Sitwell were his patrons (he lived with them from 1919–34), as were Lord Berners and the poet Siegfried Sassoon.

consult her and therefore leave it to you to decide what should be done – do not know Mione's address but presumably Sissy Hadow or Muriel Munster do – dare not ask your Mother'. I replied that I could not possibly go and that I could only suggest requesting the Consul-General at Frankfurt to do anything possible. Diana is not very well. I could neither leave her here nor take her – so that settles it so far as I'm concerned. I really don't think it's my duty to go as I don't see of what help I can be. And if it is my duty I am not going to do it – Mione is much safer under restraint than she ever has been.

August 21, 1923 (Venice)

I had a miserable letter from Mother who has gone to Frankfurt to see Mione. She found her quite mad. She is in a home. Before going there she owed £69 to another nursing home – a surgical one – which poor Mother can't pay and I must. Diana, Olga and I dined with the Cole Porters[1] at the Palazzo Barbaro. I enjoyed the evening very much. It is a beautiful palace in its way and the food was best Parisian – a wonderful change after worst Venetian which is all we have had hitherto. The champagne was Pommery 1911 – the first real wine I have drunk since leaving Paris. I sat next Mrs Cole Porter. She is very beautiful. The rooms are full of Sargents, who used to stay there a lot with Mrs Curtis. Also there is a volume of Browning there, annotated by Mrs Curtis. 'Mr B. read this' on such and such a date, and against a Toccata of Galuppi's 'R.B. read this often'. Olga sang after dinner. It was all very beautiful – especially seen from the balcony with the alternative view of a large moon shining on the Grand Canal.

August 26, 1923

A perfect day. I met Paul Munster[2] whom I hadn't seen for ten years. He had just come from Frankfurt and told me a lot about Mione's condition. It was all brought on by drink and drugs. She will probably never be quite the same. I foresee that poor Mother will be tied to her for life. I had a more cheerful letter from Mother this morning. In the afternoon we went with the Cole Porters to San Francesco del Deserto. As women are not allowed to visit the garden Diana dressed up in a suit of mine. The disguise was very ineffective but it enabled her to get into the garden which wasn't worth seeing. As soon as she was in the monks spotted her and she had to come out again.

We dined with the Cole Porters. After dinner they had singers come on the Canal under the window. Wonderful moonlight. It was all too beautiful. When we got home Diana complained that I didn't love her enough, or that at any rate I didn't love her romantically. I explained that happiness and romance don't go together. Romance cannot survive without difficulties and dangers.

---

[1] Cole Porter (1893–1964), American songwriter and composer and his wife Linda.

[2] Count Paul Munster (d. 1968) was a German who settled in London after the First World War. His wife, Peggy Ward (1905–82), was English.

Duff in 1913, aged 23

Diana and her father, at about the time of her engagement

Second Lieutenant A.D.
Cooper, Grenadier Guards

Duff and Diana,
date unknown

my wedding 1919

The Wedding - 2 June 1919

Campaigning at Oldham, 1924

David Low on the St. George's by-election

Cartoon by David Low, probably 1930 (John Julius is still a baby). Easily identifiable - apart from Duff and Diana - are Stanley Baldwin, Lloyd George, Lord Beaverbrook, Sir John Simon, Winston Churchill, Mahatma Gandhi, Ramsay MacDonald, James Maxton and Sir Oswald Mosley

RESTORING THE AMIABILITY OF OUR PUBLIC LIFE.

After the recent frictions in various political quarters, Low is taking advantage of the fine weather to give the poor dears a day on the river. Politeness is requested.

A DAY OFF.

Above left Diana, Max Beaverbrook and Duff at Deauville, date unknown; *Above right* Duff and John Julius, Bognor, 1932

Arriving at 10 Downing Street to hear Chamberlain's report on his meeting with Hitler, 1938

The Secretary of State for War leaves
o Gower Street, 1935

THE GREAT FLOWER SHOW:
OR, GARDENERS' GRIEF.

MR. DUFF COOPER. "I WISH I COULD GET MINE TO LOOK LIKE SOME OF THE
FOREIGN EXHIBITS."

artoon by Ernest Shepard,
unch, 1936

Edward VIII and Helen Fitzgerald on the *Nahlin*, summer 1936 (The subject of the jigsaw puzzle is not without interest)

Diana reading aloud to a fascinated Duff

She was suffering really from the same thing that I have been feeling here. These perfect moonlight nights in Venice are incomplete without some love affair.

August 29, 1923 [Diana's birthday]

Woke with violent pain – owing no doubt to poison in last night's scampi. Went out early before Diana woke to buy her present – a crucifix that she had admired. Stayed in all the morning – suffering. In the afternoon Diana and I went in a gondola to the Armenian monastery. We read the last canto of *Childe Harold* on the way. We enjoyed it so much – the happiest afternoon I have had this year in Venice. We dined at the Grand Hotel. On my left I had a Marchesa di Medici, née Soranzo. She told me that her grandfather who is still alive is nearly a hundred and that his father was here in Venice when the Republic was abolished in 1797, that he was one of the few who wished to resist Napoleon, for which he was banished. He swore he would not have a child until he returned to Venice, which he did after 1815. We went on the Piazza after dinner and were just too late to witness a scene in which a young American girl who is staying on the Lido was hissed and hooted and finally almost driven off the Piazza for being in ordinary decolleté evening dress. A rather hostile crowd gathered round our party too, but they were soon moved off by the police.

September 1, 1923

After bathing, I went to the bar [at the Lido] and lunched there. I went back with Berners to the palace and arrived in the middle of a first-rate row between Viola and Olga. The people upstairs from whom we rent the apartment had seized Viola's boxes because she hasn't paid the rent. It is taken in her name. Viola had said it was all Olga's fault and they were shrieking with rage at each other when we arrived. Later Berners and I went up to see the man, who proved perfectly reasonable and quite nice. Viola's vagueness and reluctance to pay had frightened him.

September 7, 1923

We spent the morning visiting the beauties of Ravenna. I was rather dis-appointed, knowing nothing of Byzantine things and therefore rather failing properly to appreciate them. Raymond [de Trafford] was frankly Philistine and most amusing – his one question being always how much money one could get for the object in question. We started after lunch for Rimini, visiting the church outside Ravenna on the way, which is the best of the lot. Arrived at Rimini we saw Sigismondo Malatesta's church which I liked better than anything. It is a marvellous document of the early renaissance. I was thrilled by it and wanted to stay there longer.

September 10, 1923 [en route to the South of France]

At Ventimiglia we had only a minute to catch the connection. Diana went for the tickets while I saw to the luggage. When I joined her at the ticket office I found her expostulating to the man behind the *guichet* who refused to sell the tickets on the grounds that the train had already gone. Finally he imitated her bad Italian and excited gestures to her face in the most insolent way. I was furious and spat at him. We went off to make a desperate effort to catch the train which really had gone by now. The man from the ticket office however pursued us, assisted by a gendarme. I was arrested and led off to a small room where a nice little man was sitting whose precise functions I never fathomed. There we were left while the accuser went off to prepare his *procès-verbal*. Presently Diana went after him and suggested that he should accept an apology. But he very rudely refused to do anything of the kind. Then our little man went to the head of the station, who said the whole thing was nonsense, that there was no need for me to apologize and that we could go at once. So all ended well although we had some further difficulty about getting the tickets, which had to be done through a third party.

September 19, 1923 (London)

I am really glad to be back. I cannot bear to be long away from London. I love it and never loved it more than this time. I found all well at the Foreign Office and nothing whatever for me to do, McNeill still away.

September 23, 1923 (Belvoir)

Between tea and dinner I read aloud to Diana and the Duchess a detective story called *The Mysterious Affair at Styles* [by Agatha Christie]. I went on with it in our bedroom at 11 o'clock – we being in bed and the Duchess sitting by the fire. I read straight on till past two and finished the book.

September 26, 1923

This morning came the sad, sad news of Aubrey Herbert's death. In a way it is perhaps better so as he was rapidly going blind. I shall miss him. He was different to other people and better – a great gentleman. Poor Mary.

I went to Buck's at teatime – Sidney, Mike and Rothesay [Stuart-Wortley] were there. The appearance of Rothesay is miraculous. He was nearly dead of diabetes a few months ago and there were no hopes of his recovery. Now owing to the new 'insulin' treatment he looks better than he ever did in his life and he is able to eat and drink practically what he likes.

October 12, 1923

I went to see Daisy before dinner and dined with her at the Carlton. She is writing a novel and can talk of nothing else which is rather a bore, but she was looking very beautiful. Eventually I drove her home to her flat where she was alone. I went in and the desires of over two years were at last gratified.

October 25, 1923

Buffles[1] gave a dinner party at Buck's. There were about ten of us. Maurice as usual balanced glasses on his head and everybody threw things at them. This suddenly developed into a wild orgy of breakage – every glass, cup and plate in the room being smashed and McEwen, the steward, who happened to come in in the middle received a glass in the face which cut his forehead. I think I was the only person who threw nothing yet nobody was drunk except Buffles. The Slav came out in Serge Obolensky who was very wild.

October 26, 1923

Diana had her hair cut today. I think it's a pity – but when she asked me to mention any woman I admired who still had long hair I couldn't think of one. Saw Daisy before dinner and was nearly caught *flagrante delicto* by the housemaid. Her charm for me is waning rapidly – in pace with her concessions.

October 27, 1923

Daisy telephoned this morning and seemed anxious to see me before luncheon. I went about a quarter to one and found her with nothing on but a dressing gown – in fact cleared for action, which was rather exhausting at that hour. Having kept me at arms length for two years she now seems unable to have too much of me.

October 31, 1923 [At Plas Newydd, home of the Angleseys where the Prince of Wales was staying]

Dinner was full dress, one or two people coming in from outside. I hadn't brought my medals. After dinner I played bridge. The Prince played poker which he apparently does very badly.

November 1, 1923

A grey day but fine except for one heavy shower in the afternoon. The Prince left the house early to take part in a series of functions at Bangor and elsewhere. No guests this evening – short coats and black ties, so my medals were no longer missing. Diana sat next the Prince and got on very well with him. He complained of his life. He hasn't had a day to himself for weeks but was looking forward to one day's hunting next Monday which he has now to give up in order to attend Bonar Law's funeral. He described the gloom of Buckingham Palace, how he himself and all of them 'freeze up' the moment they get inside it. How bad-tempered his father is. How the Duchess of York

---

[1] Sir John Milbanke (1902–47).

is the one bright spot there, they all love her and the King is in a good temper whenever she is there. More cards after dinner. The Prince lost £40 at poker which, however, he can well afford. It was a pleasant visit and I enjoyed it. Marjorie was an admirable hostess, not being made at all nervous by the presence of royalty and making everything go easily and without any stiff formality. Charlie was very nice too, so unfailingly good natured, always smiling and calm and tired.

November 13, 1923

Went to the House of Commons in the afternoon. I had never seen it so crowded. Baldwin's[1] speech on Bonar Law [*who had died on 30 October*] was extremely moving and very much better than Ramsay MacDonald's, Asquith's or Lloyd George's.

November 14, 1923

This morning I broke to McNeill my plan of going with Diana to America. He put no difficulties in the way so that now is settled and seems too good to be true.

November 23, 1923

I went to the Ritz to see Mrs Barrymore.[2] I had a rather passionate interview with her. She said she had never been unfaithful to her husband whom she loves, that she was very much attracted by me and that when I came back from America she would tell me definitely yes, or no. I rather like her, but not very much. She never stops talking and talks a lot of nonsense but is amusing with it all – and sincere.

November 24, 1923

The Angleseys, Lettie and Charlie Lindsay came to lunch, and afterwards Marjorie drove us to the station. There were several people there to see us off – Maud Cunard, John and Hazel Lavery, Goonie, Sir James Dunn,[3] bringing with him a dozen Cliquot '06 as a parting present, Chips Channon and others. We had a good send-off. Hutchy and Alan came down in the train with us. First impressions of the *Aquitania* were of tremendous size, great luxury and remarkably good taste. Our suite consisting of bedroom, sitting room and bathroom is charming – but these private rooms are rather smaller than I expected whereas the public ones are bigger. We had a very cheerful dinner

---

[1] Stanley Baldwin, 1st Earl Baldwin of Bewdley (1867–1947). Conservative Chancellor of the Exchequer under Bonar Law 1922–3; Prime Minister May 1923–Jan. 1924, and Nov. 1924–June 1929; Lord President of the Council in the National Government 1931–5; Prime Minister 1935–7.

[2] Mrs John Barrymore, née Blanche Oelrichs of New York. She was married to John (Jack) Barrymore, the American actor.

[3] Sir James Dunn (1875–1956), industrialist and financier who owned Algoma Steel.

followed by Hearts [a card game] until a late hour. We consumed 5 of Dunn's dozen.

November 26, 1923 [At sea]

A lovely day – bright sunshine and blue calm sea. It is odd that there is not a soul we know on this boat except an American called Marsh who lives at Warwick Castle. We had an uneventful day, sitting about, reading, watching the immigrants etc. The sea got rather rough in the night and Diana was frightened. Our cabin is very comfortable and we have so far enjoyed the voyage.

December 1 and we are expected to get in early tomorrow morning. It is a little rougher today and this morning we have been passing through some fog which caused us to slow down. Our chief friend on the boat has been the dispenser, who is also a masseur, who rubs Diana's arm twice a day. He is a character and a wit – a descendant of Sam Weller. On Thursday he showed us all over the ship – engines, kitchens, steerage etc. Thursday was Thanksgiving Day – an American festival which was celebrated by a gala dinner – a young American woman at the next table to ours got very drunk. There was a concert yesterday evening. A Mr Morris, formerly American 'ambassador' in Sweden, or so he says, was the chairman. He asked Diana to give a signed photograph for sale. It went for £12. The concert was in aid of some charity or other and was the worst I ever heard.

December 2, 1923

We arrived at New York early this morning. At the quarantine station where the reporters came aboard we were greeted on behalf of Mr Willey of the *New York Times* by Major Parker who said he knew me and whose face I remember from the days when I used to go to the Bachelors' Club. He was kind and nice and helpful and full of hatred of America and Americans as everyone who isn't American (and some who are) seem to be. Morris Gest came aboard as soon as we reached the dock. There were also of course innumerable reporters. Chaliapin was on the quay – Kommer and others. We drove to the Ambassador Hotel. First impressions of New York were disappointing. If it has beauty it is not the kind that leaps to the eye. The Ambassador Hotel however seemed very nice and our rooms are beautiful. We went to lunch at a restaurant called Pierre's which had been recommended to us. It was a dark and gloomy place. The food was good. I had my flask of whiskey with me and poured it openly in my Perrier which nobody seemed to mind.[1] We felt depressed.

---

[1] These were the Prohibition years, during which the sale of alcohol was banned throughout the United States.

December 3, 1923

In the morning I went with Diana to a rehearsal which interested me very much. I left her there and walked to Knoedler's, where I found Carroll [Carstairs]. He took me to the Knickerbocker Club, of which he made me a member for a week and where he gave me the key of his own locker, full of drink. Thence we went to the Racquet Club of which he also made me a member. At 5.30 I had an interview with Morris Gest, as Diana wanted me to obtain an assurance from him that she should play the part of the Madonna on the first night. The interview was friendly but he wouldn't quite give me what I wanted although he practically assured me it would be so. He said he would send me a telegram letting me know definitely after I had sailed. Diana didn't think this good enough. Later we went to the Biltmore where Diana and I left our party and joined Cole Porter. There was a good cabaret show there and we went on again to supper with a man called Irving Berlin[1] who writes music. He had a nice flat and gave us eggs and champagne. We had only been drinking whiskey out of flasks hitherto.

Without telling Diana, Gest – a publicist of genius – had re-engaged Carmi and was feeding the gossip columns with stories of the rivalry and jealousy between the two women. He was now encouraging speculation on which would play the Madonna on the first night. This ended on the morning of the première when the two publicly drew lots – Gest having secretly arranged that Diana should win. Diana nearly died of embarrassment; Carmi was so furious that she shortly afterwards refused to have anything more to do with the production.

December 4, 1923

I joined Diana at the rehearsal in the morning – left her there and went on to the Knickerbocker where I met Hugo [Rumbold] and Carroll. They all want me to put off my return until next Wednesday and sail on the *Paris*. I don't think I shall change. I don't much care for my life here. Diana is working all day and miserable as I shall be to leave her I shall be equally miserable to do so four days later. Today she was rehearsing all the afternoon till six o'clock and then again from half past eight till half past eleven. Then she dressed and we went to a ball at the Ritz given by Mr Condé Nast.[2] From a spectacular point of view it was beautiful. Supper was elaborate. Water until halfway through and then plenty of rather bad champagne.

---

[1] Irving Berlin (1888–1989), American songwriter, composer of 'White Christmas' and 'Alexander's Ragtime Band'.

[2] Condé Nast (1873–1942), the successful American magazine publisher. He bought *Vogue*, *House and Garden* and *Vanity Fair* between 1909 and 1914.

December 8, 1923

A sad awakening and a sad parting – I nearly cried. A fine morning and a smooth sea. There are several people I know on the boat. This boat is dry which means that one has to go to the Doctor with a list of the drink one thinks one will want on the voyage, he writes it out in the form of a prescription and the bottles are sent to one's cabin.

December 14, 1923

We arrived at Cherbourg at daybreak – a beautiful morning – dead calm. I felt very sad and sentimental at the thought of coming home without Diana. I made up some verses:

The hills of France grow faint behind
Our vessel's track of silver foam
As wafted by a favouring wind
She heads for home.
But what is home without thy face?
(Men fought for Helen – not for Troy)
A whited tomb – an empty place,
A broken toy.

When we reached Southampton and I stood on deck looking down at the people who had come to meet the boat I had the greatest difficulty in not crying – and only partly succeeded. We got into London at about half past six where I was met by Holbrook. I drove straight to the Foreign Office where I dealt with some letters and looked up some election results.[1] I was glad to find that Sidney had got in again.

December 19, 1923

I went to dinner at Freda's house in Portland Place. Freda asked me at luncheon time, saying that Poppy Baring wanted me to come. I was rather surprised to find when I arrived that Freda wasn't there and that our party consisted only of Poppy, Myrtle Farquharson[2] and a young man called Astaire[3] – an American actor. Poppy was looking lovely, all in white, like a dark red rose. She is what I imagine Josephine must have been when young. It was a strange and beautiful evening. After dinner we sat round the fire, talking and telling ghost stories. Then we went to the Embassy where while the others danced I talked a lot to Poppy and liked her very much. When I was

---

[1] In the general election of December 1923, the Conservatives lost their majority in the House of Commons. Baldwin remained as Prime Minister until 21 Jan. 1924, when the Government was defeated and the first Labour Government under Ramsay MacDonald took office.

[2] Myrtle Farquharson became Mrs Robin d'Erlanger in 1925.

[3] Fred Astaire (1899–1987), actor, dancer and choreographer.

alone with Poppy in the taxi to drive her home, I put my arms round her and kissed her. She clung to me passionately. We drove to Gower Street and she came in with me. She lay on the sofa looking so lovely in a dim light – a flutter of white silk from which her head emerged with the short jet black hair spread out behind it – her large dark eyes were bent on me sometimes full of grave and anxious meditation at others starlit with laughter, for even when she was saying the most sad and solemn things – such as what must I think of her – or how she had tonight broken her last resolution of never being made love to by a married man – even at such moments I could make her laugh. I felt very unrepentant of my sin.

December 21, 1923

This morning came the first news of Diana – two letters from her – a real deep joy. I caught the 9.15 to Paris. I rang up Mrs Barrymore to whom I had telegraphed asking her to dine. She insisted on my dining with her at her house – 11 Rue Leroux – at nine. I had to agree although I would much rather have dined at a restaurant and gone to a play. She had promised me in London that she would give me an answer in Paris to a very important suggestion that I had made to her. When I saw her again my heart sank for I found that she no longer attracted me and I dreaded lest the answer should be in the affirmative. Fortunately it wasn't although I believe that had I pressed my suit very strongly it might have been different. But I didn't. We had rather a gloomy dinner, sitting opposite one another in a dim light with very little to eat and less to drink. She was talking nonsense all the time and I was hating her. It was a little better after dinner when we drank crème de menthe and I repeated poems of Poe to her. I managed to get away about 11.

December 31, 1923 [London]

Seven letters from Diana – from December 14th to December 20th. They do take a long time to come. McNeill was at the Office today – the first time I had seen him since I went to America. I learnt today that I am to be promoted tomorrow to being First Secretary. This will mean a little more money and it will also mean that I shall shortly have to give up my present job which I shall regret. I think they are going to leave me at it until McNeill's successor has settled down.

This has been a wonderfully happy year for me with an amount of leave and foreign travel rare in the life of a hard-working civil servant. I can hardly hope the next one will be as good.

1924

January 1, 1924

I lunched at the Embassy. I had made a great new year's resolution to get thin and I started to put it in practice at luncheon, eating nothing but cold beef and refusing to drink. I was rather shaken however by Nellie [Romilly], who said she vastly preferred fat men to thin ones and that I was better looking now than I was when she first knew me and when I was very thin.

January 3, 1924

In the evening I had a dinner party at 90 Gower Street. Michael, Eddie, Fred and Rothesay came. I took trouble about it and it was a great success. We had caviare, turtle soup, homard newburg, perdrix aux choux, asparagus (which cost £1 a bundle), blackberry ice, mushrooms, sherry, Mumm 1911, light port, 1875 brandy. They all enjoyed it and praised the fare which certainly was damned good.

January 5, 1924 (Sussex)

A fine, still morning and not too cold. The country was looking lovely in its austerest winter garb. The birds were fairly plentiful in the morning and I never shot better – nor indeed so well. Mason[1] says he will probably give up the shoot next year. He can't afford it with a Labour Government in. This will be very sad. We had a capital lunch – Chambertin 1904 – and I was able to shoot three drives in the afternoon where there were not many birds.

January 6, 1924 (Ashby St Ledgers)

After a good night's sleep I got up to a beautiful bright winter's morning – wandered about the house and grounds, read the paper etc. until luncheon. Poppy only appeared after we had begun luncheon, as I had still had no word with her my only chance of doing so seemed to be to undertake to play golf. We had a long drive and a short game of golf as it was so miserably cold. However it gave me the opportunity I desired. Poppy is a strangely discreet and reserved little creature. In public she never allows even a look or a smile to escape her and even in private she says little. I don't think I have ever had a word of affection from her. After dinner Poppy was most anxious not to be made to play poker which she hates so I generously sacrificed myself and played instead of her. I went to her room that night at two o'clock – a very long, dangerous and difficult journey in the dark over loud creaking boards and round a dozen corners. In bed she was divine but I am terribly afraid we

---

[1] A. E. W. Mason (1865–1948), the novelist and dramatist. His most successful book was *The Four Feathers*, published in 1902. From 1906–10 he was a Liberal MP.

were very rash. She thinks she is a virgin. I don't know why she thinks so. We lay for a long time afterwards whispering and laughing. She has scruples which I have to laugh away but I feel rather ashamed of doing so. She said that in church on Christmas day she had been appalled by the thought that she had committed adultery. In the midst of all this she never says a word of love so that I was quite surprised when as I was going she begged me to stay a little longer.

January 8, 1924

In the evening I went to the Albert Hall to see what was called the Labour Victory demonstration. It was a very tame show. It struck no note of revolution but rather one of respectable middle-class nonconformity. They sang hymns between the speeches which were all about God.

January 12, 1924

I went to White's and wrote to Diana and then went home, read and rearranged her war letters to me. Reading them again I find them wonderful stuff – vivid and moving to a degree. I believe that if they are preserved they will live and I shall try to preserve them. Not the least pleasure of reading them again was the comparison which both stood so well with the ones I am getting now. I had six today by three separate posts. They are as full of love as the old ones. And how little I deserve all that expenditure of love! I dined at the Embassy and brought Poppy home with the inevitable result.

On 17 January 1924 a vote of No Confidence was carried in the House and Baldwin's government fell. Labour, who had come in second at the election, was supported by the Liberals and the Labour leader, Ramsay MacDonald became Prime Minister.

January 15, 1924

The opening of Parliament. I was there until the House adjourned after the Prime Minister's speech at 7.30. Ramsay MacDonald spoke rather well, Lloyd George rather badly, Baldwin very badly. I dined with Mrs Vansittart. Myrtle Farquharson, Chips Channon and an American diplomat called Blair were there. This was the eve of Diana's first night. I made them all send a telegram to her. I had already sent one. We went on to the Embassy where were a lot of friends. I got another telegram sent to Diana. I spent most of the following day in the House but left in time to dine with Goonie. She had Winston and Clemmie, the Spears,[1] Birrell, Juliet and a young Australian journalist called

---

[1] Brig.-Gen. Sir (Edward) Louis Spears, Bt. (1886–1974), National Liberal MP 1922–4, Conservative MP 1931–45. Churchill's representative with de Gaulle from June 1940 and First British Minister to Syria and Lebanon 1942–4.

Bracken.[1] It was a very enjoyable evening. I had some heated argument with Winston. He is very anxious to prevent at all costs a Labour Government coming into power.

January 21, 1924

I had a long journey to London [from Grimsthorpe] this morning as a railway strike broke out last night. The train took three hours and a half. There was a great rush of work at the Office and I didn't get my luncheon until three. I spent the rest of the day in the House watching the death agonies of the Government. It was a very interesting scene. Baldwin spoke well and so did Hogg.[2] The Liberals looked thoroughly ashamed of themselves.

January 22, 1924

I lunched at Buck's. In the afternoon I took a sad farewell of McNeill. I am truly sorry to lose him.

January 24, 1924

I was rather late arriving at the Office this morning and found that my new master, Arthur Ponsonby,[3] had been there some time before me. Considering his detestable principles he seems a decent enough fellow. He was in the Office twenty years ago and left after a row with Sanderson whose last words to him were 'If ever you want to come back you won't be able to'. Most of the afternoon was spent in piloting Ponsonby round the Office introducing him to people. I thought I was dining with Cole Porter at the Ritz as he had sent me a telegram saying 'Can you dine with us Ritz Thursday night nine o'clock'. I, of course, assumed that he meant the Ritz in London but apparently he meant the Ritz in Paris.

January 25, 1924

I had a very busy day with Ponsonby. They wanted him to take [Maurice] Ingram as my successor. He inspected Ingram but didn't like him – thought he seemed too old – preferred [Nevile] Butler and insisted on having him. I don't know what is to become of me. Bland said at first that I was to take Ingram's place. I pointed out that that would be a queer kind of promotion – as it would amount to going back to what I was doing four years ago.

---

[1] Brendan Bracken, 1st Viscount (1901–58). Publisher of financial journals, including the *Financial Times* and the *Economist*, and from 1929 Conservative MP. A loyal friend and supporter of Winston Churchill, he became his PPS in 1939 and Minister of Information in 1941.

[2] Douglas Hogg, 1st Viscount Hailsham (1872–1950). Conservative Attorney-General under Bonar Law and Baldwin, 1922–4 and 1924–8. Secretary of State for War 1931–5; Lord Chancellor 1935–Mar. 1938; Lord President of the Council, Mar.–Oct. 1938.

[3] Arthur Ponsonby, 1st Baron Ponsonby of Shulbrede (1871–1946). Diplomat 1894–1902; Liberal MP 1908–18. He then joined the Labour Party. In 1922 regained a seat in Parliament, as Labour MP for Sheffield, and in 1924 became Under-Secretary of State at the FO.

January 28, 1924

I had three letters from Diana this morning with accounts of her first night and press cuttings. It seems to have been a wonderful success.

January 29, 1924

For the first time I succeeded in arriving at the Office before Ponsonby – at a quarter to ten. I was kept very busy all day until 7. A telegram from C. B. Cochran this morning saying 'Wife's performance exquisitely beautiful unquestionably work of sensitive artist with many individual subtleties the result of thought and complete mastery of rare resources'.

It is amusing to watch the new administration grappling with the Foreign Office but I am glad that I am giving up my private secretarial job. It is impossible to dislike Ponsonby but the people that he sees and that are his friends and the views he holds are equally disgusting. The Prime Minister makes a lot of use of him and practically employs him as a private secretary. They go through all papers together and in the Prime Minister's absence it is Ponsonby who decides everything. But already they are getting into difficulties with their own supporters, who are impatient for the recognition of Russia and cannot understand why there should be an hour's delay. Already they say that the *Daily Herald* is getting out of hand. Already they begin to adopt the official point of view.

February 1, 1924

The Government sent off their recognition of Russia this evening.

February 7, 1924

Nevile Butler began today to take over my job, I instructing him. I still don't know where I am going. I dined at 7 with Berners and went down to Hammersmith to see the first night of *The Way of the World*.[1] It was well acted but the scenery was very modern and foreign and the dresses were hideous. Afterwards there was a party at Hutchy's. The first thing that happened was that Desmond MacCarthy fell down stairs and broke his knee cap. This threw rather a gloom over the proceedings. I soon got away and was driven back by Vita Nicolson. I have long wanted to make love to her and this evening I did so. I kissed her on the mouth. She was very surprised but not displeased.

February 13, 1924

I was told this evening that I was to become Head of the Communications Department. It is a damned fool job but slack and easy and one is one's own master so I don't mind much. It makes me more than ever determined not to

---

[1] This production of Congreve's *The Way of the World* was produced by Nigel Playfair at the Lyric Theatre, Hammersmith. Edith Evans played Mrs Millament.

stay on in the Foreign Office. Bland was very apologetic when he told me and said it would be only for a year.

February 22, 1924

My thirty-fourth birthday. At last some of the last American mail which has been held up at the docks owing to the strike since last Sunday is beginning to trickle through. I lunched at Arlington Street and talked to the Duke before luncheon about succeeding Yate [the MP for Melton Mowbray]. He is all for it but no longer takes any part in the Conservative Association of which John [Granby] is now the chairman. I am arranging to see John tomorrow.

I went to see Vita in the afternoon. I sat talking to her for half an hour feeling very shy and then walked with her to the tube. I don't think it's a very promising affair.

February 23, 1924

John [Granby] lunched with me at Buck's and was quite enthusiastic about my succeeding Yate. He is going to see Colonel Gretton about it, who is the most important person concerned.

I had several letters from Diana this morning – complaining that I am falling away from her, that I don't write often enough and in one suggesting that I am in love with Poppy. I have sent her a most indignant rejoinder and have written her a sonnet as follows:

Doubt not, sweet love, oh never dare to doubt
Lest Doubt and Calumny should breed Distrust,
Lest the pure steel of our true love show rust,
And all our hosts of joy be put to rout.
Our citadel of love is girt about
By envious armies – Weariness, Disgust,
Jealousy, Separation, Age and Lust
And still the traitor at the gate is Doubt.
Mount guard with me, beloved, you and I
Will baffle our besiegers with disdain,
The royal standard of our love flies high
As e'er it flew, and shall not dip again.
So all assaults shall only serve to prove
Our faith impregnable, our changeless love.

February 26, 1924

I lunched at Arlington Street. John came in afterwards. He had been having luncheon with Colonel Gretton who had been quite favourable to my candidature. There is only one other competitor in the field – a man called Martin. The important person to square is Sir Arthur Hazlerigg, to whom the Duke is going to write this afternoon. I dined with Vita at the Ivy Restaurant and we went to a very bad play called *The Way Things Happen*. I was shy, ill at ease and did not enjoy the evening. I don't care in the least for Vita or even admire her. What a silly flirtation to have let oneself in for.

February 28, 1924

I dined at Claridge's with Ivor Churchill[1] and Tony Rothschild[2]. They had a party of fourteen. I sat between Clare Tennyson and Lady Curzon (of Kedleston). The latter was very amusing. She complained bitterly of having her husband always at home now and thanked God he was going to Oxford tomorrow night of which she was taking advantage to give a fancy dress party. She also told me that Mosley had recently made such violent advances to her at St Moritz that she had been compelled to fight him, striking him in the face with both hands to keep him off.

February 29, 1924

[After dinner] I went to Lady Curzon's party which was I think almost without exception the best party I have ever been to. Everyone was in the highest spirits, everyone was in fancy dress and several wore one or two different ones during the course of the evening. The stately rooms of Carlton House Terrace looked more like a Montmartre restaurant, littered with confetti, masks, streamers, celluloid balls etc. I wore first a skeleton mask in which nobody recognized me and I had the greatest fun. When I finally had to take it off to drink I later put on another different one and again escaped recognition for a long time. All the women looked beautiful, or so I thought, but perhaps Kakoo in a short red wig looked the most beautiful of all. Malcolm Bullock[3] appeared as Lord Curzon himself, wearing Curzon's own collar, garter and star. Curzon would have been furious had he known and he will probably find out. There was a general spirit of gaiety, absence of restraint, looseness of conversation and wildness of behaviour that I have seldom seen equalled. The hours flew away. I hardly remember whom I danced with – I don't seem to have been very long with anyone. I sat for some time by Lady Warrender[4] and thought her perfect. It was past half past four when I got home.

March 5, 1924

I had a letter last night from the Central Office saying that Mr McNeill had mentioned my name to them and asking me to call. I also had one from the Duke enclosing one from Sir A. Hazlerigg saying he was glad that I was allowing my name to go forward.

---

[1] Lord Ivor Churchill (1898–1956), son of the 9th Duke of Marlborough and Consuelo Vanderbilt.
[2] Anthony de Rothschild (1887–1961), merchant banker, partner at N. M. Rothschild.
[3] Capt. Sir Malcolm Bullock, 1st Bt. (1890–1966). Conservative MP 1923–50.
[4] Dorothy (Dollie) Warrender, née Rawson, married Victor Warrender (1899–1993), later 1st Baron Bruntisfield, in 1920, divorced 1945.

March 10, 1924

I dined in Upper Grosvenor Street with Lady Warrender. With Lady Warrender I am in love. She is a beautiful wild creature. After dinner we went to the Embassy, from there we went to the Mayfair Club, from there we went to Gower Street and from there back to Upper Grosvenor Street. It was nearly five when I went to bed. I danced with her at all the restaurants and during all the drives our hands and sometimes our feet were clasped.

March 14, 1924

I dined with the Warrenders. We were about twenty-four people to dinner. Lord Curzon, who seemed rather out of his place in such a young party, was extraordinarily genial and pleasant. It was a very good dinner and a very cheerful party – toys, balloons, masks and all the rest of it. Dollie and I had to make several expeditions to an upper room to bring these down and at last I kissed her which I have been so longing to do. She is perfect. I danced with her a lot. The party grew very wild at the end with lancers and gallops. It was a quarter to five when I got home.

March 16, 1924 (Grimsthorpe)

Tonight there was an idea started that Dollie should go out hunting tomorrow disguised as Ivor's [Wimborne] second horseman, as strangers are not allowed out with the Cottesmore now. They sent for the man's clothes and Dollie came down dressed in them. I thought she looked lovely – but when she took the hat off and all her hair came down I was overcome. I remembered a passage in the Fairy Queen when Britomart similarly discovers her sex. There followed a violent discussion as to whether she should do it or not. The women were of course all for it, anxious to see her make a fool of herself – Victor, Colin and I were against. Ivor having committed himself dared not go back on it although he was obviously alarmed. She gave in eventually.

March 17, 1924

I met Dollie at six at a cinema where we sat and talked more intimately than we had done before. She loves me, or she thinks she does, and I love her. But had I to choose between her and Diana I should no more hesitate than a man would who had to choose between life and death. And yet I love her terribly and am frightened at the harm that we may do. If I were a good man I should see her no more. I am so amazed and so flattered at her loving me.

March 18, 1924

I dined with Dollie, my divine Dollie whom I love continually more. But why she loves me is a mystery. Her principal interest in life is horses. She despises the Foot Guards because they don't have to do riding school. She said so this evening at dinner and we argued the point. As for intellectual interests I doubt whether she can read. She certainly would never wish to. But she is quite beautiful. A small head, well set on a long neck and long body. She is taller than I am in her shoes. God knows I am not modest but why such a woman should care for me is a mystery that I cannot solve. There is insanity in her family. Perhaps that is the explanation.

March 19, 1924

John told me yesterday that Melton had gone against me. It was a disappointment but not a surprise. I am more than ever determined to get in for somewhere. Great excitement in London today over the Westminster election. On my way back after luncheon I met Betty Cranborne and Rosemary driving about in a 'Vote for Churchill' car. [*Winston Churchill was standing as an Independent Anti-Socialist candidate in the Westminster Abbey by-election.*]

March 20, 1924

At about a quarter to one the news came through on the tape 'Mr Churchill returned'. I immediately sent him off a telegram – 'Heartiest congratulations on glorious victory' and went out to luncheon. By the time I got there the news had been reversed and his defeat was confirmed. I wrote him a letter in the afternoon explaining and condoling. Next day I got a telegram from him saying 'Thank you so much dear Duff. Winston'.

March 26, 1924

Dollie picked me up at White's. We went to Ciro's together, which was foolish – and then to Gower Street, which was perhaps more foolish still. This is a wicked business – the worst perhaps that I have ever been engaged in. It is unfortunate too that I should like Victor so much and that he should like me. As regards Diana I feel now, strangely enough, less guilty than I did. Before the conquest was completed there was a glamour and romance about the matter that it made it seem too like real love and real love for another is the only crime against Diana that I could never forgive myself and that she could never forgive me. But with the flight of that illusion the wrong that I do Dollie grows greater. Having begun it is impossible to stop. She is entrancingly lovely, a delightful companion and seems really to love me which is too flattering to resist. But when I see her in her charming home, with her lovely children, her young and pleasant and adoring husband I feel ashamed.

April 7, 1924

Lots of letters and good news from Diana this morning. She suggests that I should go out to her on the *Mauretania* on May 10, and that we should come back together on the *Aquitania* on May 28 – an excellent plan.

April 15, 1924

I dined at Claridge's with the Lytteltons, Arthur Duff, Dollie and the Duke and Duchess of York. They are an attractive little couple – so very fond of each other, and she so unspoilt, unaffected and charming.

April 17, 1924

I left London by the 11 o'clock train. It was a beautiful, smooth and sunny crossing. At the Ritz in Paris I found a note waiting for me from Dollie which guided me to her room where she was herself, looking most beautiful. She came down with me to my room which was two floors below. We both had to dine with Elsa [Maxwell] who had a dinner party of about thirty people in a private room at the Ritz. We all went on to the Jardin de Ma Soeur where we stayed late. At last we got home and at last to bed – a beautiful night.

April 20, 1924 (Paris)

I got rather drunk tonight and when I got to my room was afflicted with hiccoughs. I then cut myself shaving. What with waiting for the hiccoughs to pass and stanching the blood, I was nearly an hour before calling on Dollie. This put her out and I followed it by worse for after a little I fell into a very heavy sleep. She says that I snored and that it was impossible to wake me. When I did wake she was really angry and disgusted. I had much trouble in getting her partially right.

May 5, 1924

This morning I got a letter from Diana in which she said *à propos* of £200 she has lately sent me 'I hope it will be enough, tho' I expect you to drop it on plovers' eggs and Lady Warrender before I can look round' – so she's on to that, as I thought she would be.

May 6, 1924

After luncheon I went to see Mr Stanley Tubbs and Colonel Ricardo at the Junior Carlton. They are the local pundits of the Stroud division – Tubbs having formerly been member. There is of course somebody else in the field – a man who contested it in 1910 – but it is doubtful whether his health is good enough. I thought, no doubt fatuously, that I impressed them favourably. They said they considered it almost a safe seat and that they were therefore entitled to the best available candidate – ex-Ministers etc. But still I have a slightly hopeful feeling about it.

May 7, 1924

The boat train for Southampton left Waterloo at 10 a.m. The Duchess came to see me off with eleventh hour messages and letters for Diana. Her appearance was ghastly. Her interest in public affairs and her supply of inaccurate information seem to increase rather than diminish with age. Standing on the platform at that early hour, she had to explain to me the wickedness of giving up the Russian Embassy to the Bolsheviks and to inform me that the Belgian Congo scandals of fifteen years ago were all nonsense and only a form of German propaganda.

May 12, 1924. Monday [At sea]

Tomorrow we shall be in. I sent Diana a marconigram this morning, saying 'Swift with thee tomorrow' – a few minutes afterwards I got one from her saying – 'O the wind and the rain, I'se frightened'. I suppose they are having bad weather in New York. We have had a certain amount of fog and rain today – but the sea is calm.

May 13, 1924

We got in about half past one. Diana was there. I was one of the first off the boat. She met me at the bottom of the gangway. She was looking lovely. We were a little shy at first, but not very. We got to the Colony restaurant by three o'clock and had a very good and very happy lunch there – together with an excellent bottle of claret. In the afternoon we rested. Hugo came in about 7 when Diana had to go off to the theatre. I followed her after a sandwich and saw the first and last acts, spending the second one [*during which she did not appear*] in her dressing room. Her performance was better even than I expected – most, most beautiful. When we got home she cried and said I no longer loved her. I think it was only because she was tired. After a glass of champagne she cheered up.

May 30, 1924

I lunched at the Colony with Valentine[1] and Mrs Hearst.[2] After luncheon we went to see the house the Hearsts are having prepared for them on Riverside Drive. It consists of the three top floors of a huge apartment building. It is a fantastic place – only half finished, in the hands of the workmen, but Davids, Fragonards, Greuzes, Bouchers etc. jostling each other on the walls. I then went to *The Miracle* – Diana was doing the Nun and doing it beautifully. There was a wonderful scene afterwards, the whole company collected outside the theatre to cheer Diana as she went. Morris Gest said the next day that in all his experience he had never known a star so unanimously beloved.

June 1, 1924 [At sea]

Another lovely day – passed at piquet, bezique and reading. [Diana] got a

---

[1] Valentine, Viscount Castlerosse, later 6th Earl of Kenmare (1860–1941). Social columnist and leader writer for the *Sunday Express*, he was an intimate friend of Lord Beaverbrook.

[2] Mrs William Randolph Hearst, wife of the famous publisher and newspaper owner.

telegram from the *Daily Express* after dinner offering £300 for three articles of 1500 words on America.

Most of my spare time on the rest of the trip was spent in writing these articles which I got finished on the last day. The weather got steadily worse. On Wednesday it was really very rough. Furniture was flying all over the ship. Diana got terribly frightened. Tuesday night we could hardly get any sleep at all. On Wednesday the doctor gave her a sleeping draught. I was glad to find that I felt perfectly well throughout. We led a regular life and the time passed quickly. On Wednesday Diana got a telegram asking her to do a film in Germany.

June 13, 1924

I went to call on Daisy and from her to the Warrenders. Dollie and Victor were both there. He suggested Horncastle as a constituency for me. Since my return I have been approached by Oldham and the Bosworth division of Leicestershire. The Stroud division is still going also. I have consulted Edwin who is strongly in favour of Oldham. He says a borough has many advantages besides prestige. Afterwards I changed and met Diana and we both went on to a party given at Eresby House. I first danced with Mrs Barrymore and was glad to escape from her. Then I danced with Dollie and of course the dance went on too long. It covered several dances and several suppers and was I fear conspicuous. A dance with Kakoo and one or two with Betty followed. I really love Betty far more than Dollie and much prefer her company as she is at least twice as intelligent. Leaving the house about 3.30 I managed to introduce Diana to the Warrenders and we all drove home together. But Diana didn't melt to them. She was alright that evening but the next morning she was bitter about my love for Dollie. She has spiritually so much less though materially so much more cause for jealousy than she knows.

June 19, 1924

We dined with [J. M.] Barrie in his flat in the Adelphi. Only Katharine was there. It is the most beautifully situated flat in London. The whole length of the river from the Tower to Chelsea is stretched below it. The view when we arrived in the setting sun was superlatively beautiful. St Paul's looked most wonderful and strangely near. We had a very pleasant dinner – plain but not bad food and excellent wine. Barrie was very funny ragging K. about her conversion to Catholicism. We went on the roof afterwards and talked with all the lights of London below us. We stayed till 12 – a memorable evening.

June 24, 1924

Diana dined with Cruger.[1] He had been spending the day with Dollie who

---

[1] Bertram Cruger, an American admirer of Diana's, who she had met in New York. A good-looking, wealthy man-about-town.

had taken him down to Petworth. Apparently she had been madly indiscreet to him and everything that she had said Diana wrenched from him during the evening and repeated back to me again having made me swear a great oath that it should go no further. Diana's pride was deeply hurt for Dollie had said that I loved her and that Diana made me scenes of jealousy. I made no attempt to defend Dollie and finally promised that I would break with her for good. It is a bore – but for the best.

June 25, 1924

When I got back to the Office after luncheon Dollie telephoned. According to my promise to Diana I was horrid to her, answering in monosyllables, saying I couldn't see her, refusing to give a reason. After I had done it I felt wretched. I went to Buck's later and played bridge. There I got a note from her asking me to explain and saying she wouldn't telephone again until she heard from me. I think I have behaved badly all round – so has everybody – Cruger worst of all. It is a bad business but the only thing to do now is to be firm and end it once for all.

'What seem I to myself, do you ask of me?
No hero I confess.' [from *A Light Woman* by Robert Browning]

June 26, 1924

I lunched with Edward Grigg[1] at the Oxford and Cambridge Club in order to discuss the prospects of Oldham. He didn't advise me to stand unless it could be arranged that he and I should run it together which the local people won't agree to. I shall follow his advice.

June 27, 1924

We lunched with the Asquiths – a gloomy little party. I sat next to Margot and found her as positive, as aggressive and as nonsensical as ever. The old boy on the other hand with whom I was left after luncheon was in a wonderfully genial and pleasant mood. He gave me some of his views on the present Government. He has no opinion at all of the Prime Minister and says that Graham[2] and Snowden[3] – in that order are by far their best men.

---

[1] Edward Grigg, 1st Baron Altrincham (1879–1955), married Joan Poynder, daughter of Lord and Lady Islington, in 1923. Military Secretary and Special Adviser to the Prince of Wales 1919–20; Private Secretary to Lloyd George 1920–2; Liberal MP for Oldham (which at that time returned two MPs) 1922–5; Governor of Kenya 1925–30; Conservative MP for Altrincham 1933–45; Minister Resident in the Middle East 1944–5.

[2] William Graham (1887–1932), Labour Financial Secretary to the Treasury 1924 and President of the Board of Trade 1929–31.

[3] Philip Snowden, Viscount Snowden (1864–1937). Labour Chancellor of the Exchequer 1924 and 1929–31.

June 28, 1924

This morning I got a long letter from Dollie asking me what it was all about, saying how miserable she was and how cruelly I had behaved. She begged me to ring her up and presently she rang up herself. We had a difficult conversation. I told her that I didn't hate her, that I wasn't angry with her – I said indeed that I loved her as much as ever – but that I couldn't explain and that it was better that I shouldn't see her. She said she had never in her life loved anyone as much as me. She begged me to write to her and I said I would although I had nothing to say that I hadn't said already. I could only hope that it would yet all come right.

Soon after twelve Diana and I started motoring to Mells. I told her that Dollie had telephoned. She begins to feel a little guilty about the whole business. She is reassured, I think, as to my love, and consequently less bitter about Dollie. The portrait of Leila in Maurice's 'C' has upset her because she sees in it resemblances to herself.

July 4, 1924

I went to the Central Office where I had an interview with Colonel Jackson[1] and Mr Howcroft, the president of the Oldham Conservative Association. They want me to stand for Oldham. I find it very difficult to make up my mind.

July 5, 1924

I went this morning to a new doctor for my psoriasis. He injected me in the bottom which gave me a lot of pain for about 6 hours.

July 7, 1924

We went to a ball at Lady Massereene's. Diana went first to a party at Olga's. I danced with Dollie before Diana arrived and had settled that if she hadn't come by 1.30 which was the time she said she would be there by I would go off with Dollie. I was just about to do so when Diana appeared. Fortunately I saw her in time. I wish she wasn't jealous. My feelings for Dollie are purely sensual.

July 9, 1924

In the afternoon I went to see Colonel Jackson. He was very nice – said they would pay my election expenses. He said I ought to try to get another job. I don't see how I can. Edwin thinks I might. I see that I shall have very soon to come to a decision about Oldham.

---

[1] Sir Stanley Jackson (1870–1947), cricketer, politician and administrator. Chairman of the Conservative Party 1923–7.

July 10, 1924

At six I went to see Max Beaverbrook to talk to him about my political prospects. He was extremely nice. He was most strongly in favour of my going into politics at all costs. But he discouraged the idea of Oldham, saying I ought to be able to get a much safer seat. He advised me to go all out for Stroud. He also mentioned Ashton-under-Lyme. I am more unsettled than ever. I was beginning to like the idea of Oldham.

July 15, 1924

I had Colonel Ricardo to lunch with me at White's Club. He is the President of the Stroud Association. They are going to decide upon a candidate tomorrow and I am going down there to appear before the Committee. They have two other men up for it and I fear I have very little chance of being selected. We are not to make speeches to the Committee but only to answer questions.

July 16, 1924

I appeared before the Association. There were six or seven of them there. They asked me very few questions – would I contribute £300 a year to the Association, was my health good, was I Church of England. To all of these I answered in the affirmative. My two competitors were Geoffrey Peto – a relation of Ralph's – and Sir Somebody Nelson. The latter the more formidable of the two – a very rich man from India – strongly recommended by Leslie Wilson and supported by the Central Office. I'm afraid he'll get it. I was strongly attracted by the look of the country. It seemed a beautiful place. Changed and dined and then drove out to Juliet's. [Her] party was lovely to look at. I went into the garden with Dollie. She was furious with me at first as I had cut her dance while I was with Violet. But I effectually calmed her wrath and we were very rash together in the shadows of the garden. Then Diana started calling for me. At first I didn't answer but she went on. It was most trying. When I eventually rejoined her she said they were all waiting for me to go. She was furious. I have never seen her so angry. We drove back with the de Janzés. When they left us the storm broke. My only line was complete submission and promise to have done with Dollie for good. Even this hardly sufficed. It was a terrible night.

July 17, 1924

This morning I quarrelled again with Dollie. Once more it is I who am really to blame and most unjustly I put the blame on to her. However it is better to finish it. The danger and the fear of really hurting Diana are too great. When I came home in the evening I found a letter from Colonel Ricardo saying that they had chosen Sir Frank Nelson. I was afraid they would but it is a cruel disappointment.

July 18, 1924

Today I burnt my boats and sent in my resignation. It seemed a terribly drastic step – giving up a profession I had worked at for ten years. But I am sure I'm right.

July 24, 1924

I went to the Curzons' dance. Came back home and found the Prince of Wales there – together with Freda, Mike and Eddie. At 2 a.m. we all set out on the Treasure Hunt. The Prince, Freda and Mike in one car, Diana, Venetia, Eddie and I in another. It was very exciting and very dangerous. We went badly wrong halfway through and ended nearly last. We then all went back to Gordon Place and cooked eggs and bacon in the kitchen. The Prince was charming. Mike is terribly proprietary over Freda in front of him. We didn't get to bed till 5.

July 29, 1924

I am writing this on what will presumably be my last afternoon in the Foreign Office. I have been in it for nearly eleven years but I leave it without one pang of regret.

July 30, 1924

This morning Diana, Venetia and I drove down to Winston's new place[1] in Kent for luncheon. It is a charming place with a wonderful view and Winston is ruining himself over it – so at least Clemmie says. She is really quite sad about it. Only they two were there – and their children. Winston was in wonderful form and insisted on a champagne luncheon in our honour. We played Mah Jong after luncheon.

July 31, 1924

I went to the Foreign Office in the morning for the last time. When I left it at luncheon time just as usual but knowing that I was not coming back, without having said goodbye to anyone, I had an odd sensation of doing something surreptitious and rather disgraceful.

I arrived at Manchester about half past six where I was met by Mr Howcraft, the chairman of the Conservative Association, and Mr Greenwood, the member for Stockport. With them I drove to Oldham to the house of Dr Martland with whom I was to stay the night. The household consisted of the doctor, his very aged wife and his very ugly daughter. Dinner at seven fifteen was an ordeal. I was feeling none too well, as though only champagne could revive me which the doctor's very sweet Graves was quite powerless to do. I

---

[1] Chartwell, a manor house in Kent which Churchill bought in September 1922 and owned until his death in 1965.

further found it quite impossible to join in the conversation so that they must have thought me very dull. At the meeting which followed however I acquitted myself adequately and was unanimously adopted as candidate. I felt a little nervous before speaking but was reassured by the sound of my own voice. Nothing could have been more calculated to make one nervous. They all assembled and started the meeting while I waited in another room. Then I was asked to step forward and found myself in a small room where were about 30 people seated round the wall. There was a table in the middle at which the chairman sat – and one chair by his side for me. There I sat while they all stared at me and the Chairman talked about me – and then I had to get up and give them my views. This however I succeeded in doing to their satisfaction. [*He was adopted as the Conservative candidate for Oldham.*]

August 19, 1924

At 9.30 this morning Jimmy Dunn was on the telephone with the suggestion that we should join the yacht at Cowes and sail immediately for Deauville. It was a very pretty morning of wind and sun and threatening showers. Jimmy met us at Cowes and rowed us out to the yacht. We were from the first rather appalled by the smallness of it – only 60 tons. We were shown our cabin – a very comfortable looking one on deck – and then proceeded to have lunch. The other members of the party were Lady Queensberry,[1] Miss Courtland and Jimmy's son Philip. I hadn't met any of them before. Lady Queensberry is quite pretty. She was on the stage. Luncheon went well with the assistance of a great quantity of champagne. After luncheon we decided to start although the Captain warned us that it would not be a pleasant crossing. The first hour was pleasant enough. We all sat on deck. But as soon as we got clear of the Isle of Wight we realized what we had got to face. Miss Courtland was the first to disappear below closely followed by Philip Dunn. Then Diana went to her cabin feeling very sick and very frightened. Jimmy called for more champagne and then lay at full length in the saloon apparently sleeping. It was now almost impossible even to sit upright, let alone to stand so that Lady Queensberry and I the sole survivors were continually thrown into each other's arms – a situation of which I took full advantage – meeting with no reluctance upon her part. It was a very funny scene. The sea got rougher and rougher, she and I got more and more affectionate and all the time we never said a word for fear of awaking Jimmy who lay with closed eyes at our side. Then I went to see how Diana was getting on. She had been very sick and was determined that we should turn back. She then came along and persuaded Jimmy to do so. He didn't really want much persuading. It would have been madness to go on and even had all gone well we could never have got into Deauville that night. So back we turned – Diana returned to her cabin, Jimmy

---

[1] Francis Douglas, 11th Marquess of Queensberry (1896–1954), married Irene Clarice Richards, musical comedy actress in 1917.

closed his eyes again and Lady Queensberry and I proceeded to play cards like
Cupid and Campaspe. By dinner time we were safe in Southampton Water.

In August Diana had to return to New York for the re-opening of The Miracle.
Duff and Diana sailed to New York on the Berengaria. *The Prince of Wales was
on board travelling with the Mountbattens.*

August 23, 1924

I like the *Berengaria*. We have got the best cabin we've had yet. After dinner
we three played Mah Jong with Jean Norton. The Prince came and talked to
us for some time before we went to bed. The beds on this boat are very
comfortable.

August 24, 1924

I spent most of the morning writing my diary which I hadn't done for a week –
then walked with Diana ten times round the deck. After lunch we played
bezique with Tommy [Bouch] most of the afternoon. The Prince asked us to
dinner. The Chiltons – he is our Counsellor in Washington – were there with
two little girls. After dinner we all went to his suite and played poker, bridge
and Mah Jong. It was quite a cheerful evening and went on until about one.

August 25, 1924

An uneventful day. Diana, Tommy and I played poker with the Prince and the
Mountbattens[1] all the afternoon. I won £19. Louis Mountbatten has insisted
on our all going in for a tug of war and we had our first practice this evening.
We are an absurdly light team consisting of Chilton – the only heavy one –
the Prince who weighs just over 9 stone, Arthur Duff, Tommy Lascelles,[2]
David Boyle, Tommy Bouch, Mountbatten and myself. Mountbatten says the
secret lies in doing it the right way and together.

August 26, 1924

I bathe every morning in the swimming bath and then try to read till luncheon.
We had two more tug of war practices today and seemed to have made some
progress. In the afternoon we easily pulled over a team of sailors and then
gave them three extra men and very nearly won again.

---

[1] Lord Louis Mountbatten, later Admiral of the Fleet 1st Earl Mountbatten of Burma (1900–79),
married in 1922 Edwina Cassel (1901–60), daughter of Sir Ernest Cassel (1852–1921), the
financier. He was murdered by the IRA in 1979.

[2] Sir Alan 'Tommy' Lascelles (1887–1981), Assistant Private Secretary to the Prince of Wales
1920–9, and from 1935 to George V, Edward VIII and George VI. He became Private Secretary
to the last in 1943 and retained the post until the end of the first year of Queen Elizabeth II's
reign.

August 27, 1924

Tommy Bouch is on Diana's nerves. He does become a bore. She didn't get up for lunch today in order to avoid seeing him. In the afternoon were the sports and the tug of war. We were ignominiously defeated. The Americans after seeing us pull yesterday changed their team which was entirely composed of very heavy young athletes against whom we had no chance.

August 28, 1924

We all foregathered in the Prince's cabin late at night where we had sandwiches, cold grouse and drinks. His charm is devastating and unfailing.

September 6, 1924 [New York]

I went for a drive with Diana in her new car. It is nervous work being driven by her at present as she understands neither the working of the car nor the traffic laws of New York completely.

September 20, 1924

This morning I left New York. I was miserable to leave Diana whom I have never loved more nor been so happy with. But I was glad to get away. My life in New York is utterly unprofitable and not particularly pleasant. I never have time to do anything – and yet don't have very much fun.

October 8, 1924

There was an excellent paragraph in the most conspicuous part of the *Daily Mail* (Manchester edition) this morning on the subject of Diana returning to help me at Oldham. It will do good. After an early luncheon I went down there and was shown over the Dronsfield works. Nothing bores me so much as being shown machinery – but I talked to several of the men and it may do good.

In the evening I went round and made speeches at three more clubs – Coldhurst, St Paul's and St Peters. I did best at the first and last. The last was the best meeting I've had. They all compare me to Winston and say I am better than he was when he began.

October 9, 1924

I arrived in London about half past four. Here I was met with the news that Parliament was dissolved and that the General Election was to be on October 29th. This is at least 10 days earlier than I had ever expected and leaves me very little time. I telegraphed at once to Diana, urging her to sail the day after tomorrow in the *Homeric*, a ship which we seem fated to sail in. I then went to Buck's, which this evening had all the appearance of a political club. There were so many ex-members and candidates and nobody talking of anything but the election. I was so glad to be in it and no longer an onlooker.

October 10, 1924

I went down to the Central Office in the morning in order to get them to give me one of the leaders to come and speak for me. All was pandemonium there – but very exciting. I only succeeded in getting my name put on a list which already seemed pretty long. I walked back to White's and taking my courage in my hands wrote to Lord Derby asking him to come and help me. I wrote also to Ronald McNeill and [Sir] Philip Lloyd Graeme. I caught the 5 o'clock train to Wilton where I found a telegram from Lord Derby saying he would come any day we liked – excepting one. I slept badly. I am getting too excited about this election.

Duff succeeded triumphantly at the general election on 29 October 1924, coming top of the poll with a majority of 13,000 over the Socialist.

The next morning we motored to Belvoir. The relief from work, the rest from anxiety and the feeling of success were wonderful.

November 15, 1924

This morning Edwin died. They think it was sleepy sickness. It is all very mysterious. Venetia came to see us in the afternoon. She was wonderfully composed.

November 18, 1924

We have been trying these days to get me the job of Private Secretary, Parliamentary, to Winston. Sidney first proposed it. This morning Winston sent for me to the Treasury and we had a long conversation. He said he was very flattered at my wanting the job and that he was prepared to give it me but he strongly dissuaded me from taking it. He said I ought to get on by making speeches and that having a job of that sort could only hinder me. The experience that it gave of Government offices etc. was just the experience I already had. We left it open but I am sure he is right.

December 2, 1924

I went down to the House in the morning with Frank Meyer to secure seats for the afternoon. I felt a considerable thrill of excitement on going into it as a member for the first time. It was a curious sensation and quite extraordinarily reminiscent of being a new boy at school.

December 3, 1924

This morning Diana left [*for America and further performances of* The Miracle]. Never before have I been so sad at parting with her. The house seems sad and miserable without her and it is for such a long time. Dollie telephoned asking

me to luncheon but I refused sternly. In the afternoon I took the oath and my
seat in the House of Commons.

December 15, 1924

I made my maiden speech [*on the future of Egypt*] in the House of Commons,
the success of which was extraordinary – surpassing anything I had ever
hoped for.

1925

January 9, 1925 [Belvoir]

This was a beautiful morning. Just as we were going in to luncheon they
brought me a telegram 'Lady Agnes [Duff's mother] very dangerously ill'. It
was a great shock. I decided to go to London at once and to Nice tomorrow.
Sybil announced her intention of coming with me. I had much rather have
gone alone.

January 11, 1925

We were met at Nice by Mr Edwardes and the doctor with the terribly sad
news that Mother had died that morning at 8 o'clock. I don't think she knew
that she was dying and she suffered hardly at all. It was heart failure. It was a
terrible day. I spent an awful afternoon wandering about Nice with him
looking for an undertaker. I spent a still more terrible evening and night in
great and at times uncontrollable grief. The body was moved at five o'clock in
the morning and I felt better after that.

January 14, 1925

This morning we had a Requiem Eucharist at 8 o'clock – rather a beautiful
service – and the first part of the burial service at 2.15. Then the coffin left for
Marseilles for cremation. I had, I was thankful to say, arranged for Sybil to
leave the same afternoon for London by the Blue Train with Jessie, Mother's
maid. I heaved a sigh of relief when I saw the last of her.

January 15, 1925

The cremation was at 2.30 – a grim, macabre, rather painful, rather comic
scene.

February 11, 1925

I dined in the House with a 'group' that I have joined which is presided over
by Spencer Blady. I expected to be bored but enjoyed it very much. I sat

between Colum Stuart[1] and Macmillan.[2] I got on well with the latter and liked him very much. We had a discussion afterwards about the political levy and the House of Lords. I was glad to find that a great many people agreed with me on the former subject.

February 14, 1925

In the evening I went to White's, having nothing to do, where I found Maurice who had just finished dinner and was going to *The Vortex*, a play by Noël Coward.[3] I had a sandwich and went too. I thought the play very second rate stuff.

February 17, 1925

It was a dull afternoon in the House. I stayed there until half past eight and then Sidney and I went and dined with Winston at 11 Downing Street. I had never been in the house before and thought it charming. Nobody was there but we three. We had a very good dinner and a delightful talk. Winston was in excellent form – discussing politics in general and recent events. He said that the Coalition might have remained in power if Lloyd George had met Parliament which he had urged him strongly to do. He is in favour of an Anglo-Franco-German alliance. I thoroughly enjoyed the evening.

February 19, 1925

I lunched with the Laverys. They had the Bernard Shaws. I don't find Bernard Shaw amusing.

February 24, 1925

I dined at the House with a dozen other members who are all opposed to the Political Levy Bill.[4] Feeling on the subject is running quite high. Mr Bardsley who came up from Oldham today is strongly in favour of it. We still don't know what line the Government will take. I should like to speak on the subject but I expect there will be tremendous competition.

---

[1] Lord Colum Crichton-Stuart (1886–1957), Conservative MP 1922–45.

[2] Harold Macmillan, 1st Earl of Stockton (1894–1986). Conservative MP, came into government under Churchill in May 1940. Minister Resident at Allied Forces HQ, Algiers, 1943–4; UK High Commissioner in Italy 1944–5; Prime Minister 1957–63.

[3] Sir Noël Coward (1899–1973). *The Vortex*, his play about drug addiction, written when he was twenty-five, was his first big success. He became a great friend of Diana.

[4] The Political Levy Bill was designed to ensure that trade union members gave written confirmation of their willingness that a small proportion of their subscription should go to the Labour Party.

February 25, 1925

After Questions about twenty of us went on a deputation to the Prime Minister about the Political Levy. Skelton stated our case briefly and well. Clifton Brown, Hudson, Colefax, Lloyd spoke. The Prime Minister replied that he regretted the division in the party but there it had to be faced. One side would be disappointed, and that was all he could say at present.

February 27, 1925

I went to the House in the morning – a private member's bill on Workmen's Compensation introduced by a Labour member. I thought the opposition to it was feeble and asserted my independence by voting for it although the Government were against. I dined with Malcolm Bullock previous to the Speaker's levée. I went on to the levée. Winston talked to me there and urged me to speak next Friday. I should like to but I doubt whether I shall get the chance.

I find it impossible to keep my diary these days. I haven't a minute to spare. I have hardly time to deal with my correspondence in the morning and the rest of the day is in the House. I have had two disappointments there this week. I hoped to speak on Thursday on the Geneva Protocol but there was a row about Kirkwood, the whole Labour party left the House and Ramsay MacDonald never spoke. What I particularly wished to do was to show how all his criticisms of the Treaty of Mutual Assistance applied with equal force to the Geneva Protocol. In the circumstances I didn't think it worth while speaking.[1] On Friday I wanted to speak on the Political Levy but there were so many on our side with maiden speeches that I never got in. The Prime Minister's speech on Friday had a wonderful effect on the House. It was vague and rather off the point and although I liked it myself I was afraid it wouldn't impress other people. But it did – and completely silenced all those who were most vehement for the bill.

On the 24th [March] I made my second speech in the House. I had a long wait from 3 till 10 before I got in. The subject was the Geneva Protocol.[2] The speech was a success. Several people said it was better than the first one. Winston who hadn't heard me before was most enthusiastic.

I am now writing weekly articles for the *Saturday Review* on the House of Commons. I did the first one this week; it was poor stuff.

In April Duff and Diana went on a trip to France with Ivor Wimborne. On their return Duff kept only a skeleton diary.

---

[1] The Labour Government had rejected the Treaty, and the Labour Opposition was now blaming the Conservatives for rejecting the Protocol.

[2] 'The Protocol for the Prohibition of the Use in War of Asphyxiating, Poisonous or Other Gases, and of Bacteriological Methods of Warfare'. It was signed on 17 June and entered into force on 8 Jan. 1928.

May 8, 1925

In the evening we were going out to dinner with the Aga Khan. Diana had been to see her father and had just come back with her mother to Gower Street to dress when they telephoned that the Duke had had a heart attack and they must go at once. He was dead before they got there.

August 12, 1925. Excelsior Hotel. Lido

For three months I have written nothing in this book. I was so busy during the summer in London that I had no time to write. What with the House of Commons, my correspondence, visits to the Constituency and other places to speak, in addition to writing a weekly article for the *Saturday Review*, I had hardly a moment to myself.

During the summer I read a paper on Egypt to the Institute of International Affairs, spoke on the League of Nations at East Ham, addressed an assembly of teachers, went to Walsall for a Conservative fête, went twice to Oldham and spoke twice in the House – once on the Widows' Pensions and once – only a few words – on the Oldham by-election.[1] I wanted to speak on the naval debate – against the construction of the cruisers – but I couldn't get in.

We had a heavenly Whitsuntide at the cottage at Bognor – one of the best weeks I have ever had.

I saw Daisy and Dollie once or twice but had no other affairs.

The House rose on the 7th August. Diana went to Salzburg and I came here [Venice]. I want to see once for all whether I can cure psoriasis by sun. I go to a sun cure establishment five minutes walk from here at seven every morning and lie in the sun for three hours. I do the same in the afternoon. This is only the second day of it. The usual people are here. The Cole Porters have the Palazzo Papadopoli, the Wimbornes the top floor of the Palazzo Polignac. Lady Abdy[2] is at present the principal attraction. I came back from Venice in a gondola with her the night before last. It was a beautiful bright moonlight scene and of course I had to make love to her. But I don't care for her nor she for me. On the whole I am rather bored here.

August 16, 1925

The usual day. Sun bath morning and afternoon. The Cole Porters gave a party. They had the garden of their palazzo illuminated and some Russian dancers. It was pretty but not very pretty and I didn't enjoy it. The truth of the matter is there is no man I like and no woman who attracts me here. This makes things dull – and in addition I am always tired in the evening after my

---

[1] The Oldham by-election was necessary because Duff's Liberal colleague, Sir Edward Grigg, was appointed Governor of Kenya. The seat was not contested by the Conservatives and was won by Mr Wiggins, a local Liberal with Conservative support.

[2] Iya Abdy, née DeGay (d. 1993), married Sir Robert Abdy (1896–1976) in 1923, they divorced in 1928. She was a leader of fashion in the 1920s.

sun baths. Gladys [Cooper] and Olga left today for Salzburg. I should have liked to go with them but it would be madness to break my cure just when it is beginning to do good.

August 17, 1925

I dined this evening with Elsa Maxwell – a ghastly party. We didn't sit down to dinner until a quarter past ten. Nearly all foreigners except the Mosleys – who are worse than foreigners. Dancing between the courses – bread and fruit thrown – deadly boring. I slipped away about midnight.

In the summer of 1925 Max Reinhardt took his production of The Miracle *to the Salzburg Festival.*

August 29, 1925 [Salzburg]

Diana's birthday. The whole party went out to luncheon at Hellbrunn. I loathe above everything moving about in hordes and this was consequently a very trying day. We went to a pantomime or ballet in the afternoon at which I found it impossible to keep awake and in the evening I went to *The Miracle* which is not nearly so well done as in New York, but Diana is better than she used to be – or certainly seems so. Afterwards there was a very large and very dull dinner party at Leopoldskron. We sat down at half past eleven. I was glad to get to bed about 2.

September 7, 1925 (London)

We went to the *Daily Express* offices where Max had a supper party consisting of ourselves and Tallulah Bankhead,[1] her sister and brother in law. It went rather well and I liked Tallulah for the first time.

September 26, 1925 (Midland Hotel, Manchester)

I spent the morning in my room reading and preparing a speech, and after a fortifying luncheon I proceeded in the train and the rain to Oldham where I stood on the steps of the Town Hall while 2,500 boy scouts filed past. Thence I went to the Blue Coat School and then to a terrible tea which lasted from five to seven in Greenacres Hall. Then I had to make my speech to this enormous audience of small boys. I hadn't realized what it would be and had prepared quite the wrong sort of speech. It was a failure but I doubt it could have been a success. I knew that I wasn't holding their attention – a terrible feeling which I have never had before. Afterwards I attended a small meeting of the chief members of my executive committee, whom I found very dissatisfied and critical of the Government. Their main grounds of criticism are: 1. The failure to deal with the political levy. 2. The settlement of the French debt. 3. The subsidy to the miners. 4. The alleged weakness in dealing with

---

[1] Tallulah Bankhead (1902–68), American actress, film star and wit.

the Reds. I did my best to pacify them. The Hall Porter this morning told me to back Seredella for the Newbury Cup. I had £5 each way and it won at 10 to 1. This almost but not quite pays my losses at Gosford and Drummond.[1]

October 12, 1925

I had a busy morning tidying up at Gower Street which we have let for three months [*while Diana was in America*]. I went to see Daisy where things passed off as usual. I dined with her and Fred [Cripps] at the Embassy. She had expected to spend the rest of the evening with Fred which accounted for my afternoon visit but they had a slight quarrel which resulted in my finding myself in bed with her, waiting while she smoked opium and then being indulged in every fancy. It was pleasant at the time but I had a reaction of disgust afterwards. There is no pleasing one.

October 19, 1925. Midland Hotel, Manchester

I had a rush in London as I had to go and see my doctor – have a violet ray treatment [*for his psoriasis*] and a blood test. I travelled up to Manchester and thence to Oldham where I made three speeches at the St James's, Waterhead and Clarksfield Clubs. I didn't speak badly and did it without any stimulant as the doctor had advised me not to drink anything for some hours after the violet rays.

October 30, 1925

This morning I flew to Paris – a new and unpleasant experience. I felt rather sick and very frightened. Saved very little time and got no luncheon – never again.

November 9, 1925

All these days my mind is obsessed with thoughts of the Under Secretaryship of Foreign Affairs which Ronald McNeill has left to go to the Treasury. The *Manchester Guardian* has said that I was the obvious person to go there and several people have asked me whether I am going. I fear that there is really little hope. Sidney knows nothing. I can't think of anything else.

November 13, 1925

I heard from Sidney that the Prime Minister has settled about the Foreign Office and it is not to be me.

November 15, 1925. Sunday

I lunched today at the Café Royal. This is the first day of teetotalism and not drinking at meals.

---

[1] Gosford House, home of the Wemyss family, in East Lothian; Drummond Castle, Perthshire, home of the Ancasters. Duff had been staying at both.

November 18, 1925

This morning when I saw the amendments on the Locarno debate I decided to speak – and spent the morning preparing. Austen Chamberlain opened the debate and spoke for an hour – then Ramsay MacDonald, then Lloyd George. Then to my surprise, and somewhat to my horror, nobody got up but myself. I started badly, striking the wrong note in abuse of Ll. G. but I recovered, spoke for 20 minutes and was well cheered when I sat down. I received a great many congratulations afterwards.

Once more I have neglected my diary for six weeks. While the House is sitting I have so much to do that I find no time for anything. I had a very pleasant Christmas at Wilton and ended the year by going to a fancy dress ball at the Albert Hall with Sidney and Mike – all wearing the same disguise and amusing ourselves enormously.

1926

Duff had given up keeping a diary at this time, apart from a few entries at the beginning of the year, presumably because of his increasingly busy political career; but he did keep one during the General Strike of 1926.[1]

Monday May 3, 1926

This morning we drove up from Breccles. We wondered whether we should have any difficulty in getting petrol but at Barton Mills they gave us as much as we wanted. After luncheon I drove down to the House of Commons. Questions went quickly and nothing of interest occurred until the Prime Minister [Baldwin] came in, when the Conservatives stood up cheering and waving their order papers. This seemed to irritate the Opposition who felt obliged to do the same thing rather aggressively, both for Thomas[2] and Ramsay MacDonald. He said that he did not propose to vote against the address on the declaration of a state of emergency. But his party took no notice of this and all voted against it, he weakly voting with them.

The Prime Minister spoke for about an hour – an excellent speech which was well received. Thomas followed him and also spoke well and with moderation. He is a better orator than the Prime Minister. Lloyd George then

---

[1] The General Strike was called by the Trades Union Congress over the issue of threatened wage cuts. It involved certain key industrial sectors: docks, electricity, gas, railways. Well-organized government measures and lack of real public support led to its collapse after nine days. The miners continued to strike but returned to work in August.

[2] J. H. Thomas (1874–1949), trade unionist and politician. Secretary of State for the Dominions 1931–5.

delivered a miserable speech, blaming the Government for withdrawing the subsidy which he had originally blamed them for granting. He also attempted to distinguish between two different kinds of general strike, arguing that a strike to compel Parliament to legislate was obviously wrong and unconstitutional, but that a general strike over a mere wages dispute might be justifiable. As Winston pointed out afterwards no such distinction exists and the present strike is in fact an attempt to compel Parliament to legislate, i.e. to prolong the subsidy which was the only way of averting the strike. I never heard Lloyd George worse – every fact, every figure, every date was wrong. Sir Robert Horne followed him and spoke well. Then Ramsay MacDonald who looked ill and made a rather muddled speech but not a bad one. Winston replied for the Government. He spoke with great eloquence and great firmness. His speech sounded at times provocative, but having read it since I can find nothing in it to criticize. This was supposed to conclude the debate. But when he sat down Kenworthy[1] got up. The House could hardly have emptied more rapidly if there had been a fire. Many members had been sitting there, as I had, for five solid hours. The dining-rooms filled up as rapidly as the House emptied and it was impossible for some time to get a table. The Whips wouldn't let us go because they thought the debate might collapse at any minute and then in the natural course of business we should have had to proceed with the Budget resolutions. It was not until past nine that Sidney and I found a table in the Strangers' dining-room. I strolled back into the House soon after ten. My namesake Couper,[2] who was sitting next to me, asked me whether I was going to speak. I said no, having never thought of doing so, but I then began to think of it and when Headlam[3] sat down I got up. The Speaker put on an incoherent Labour Member. When he had finished I got up again and was called. I spoke for only nine minutes. I tried to distinguish between the issues, i.e. the dispute in the coal trade and the general strike. There was only one other speaker after me, and the House rose at eleven. There was a huge crowd in the square outside – sightseers – but no sight to see. I went to the Café de Paris to pick up Diana, who had been dining with Ivor Wimborne. She was in very good spirits, having had her anxiety about her mother's health removed. We went home – waited for a little for Max to ring us up with the latest news – but as he didn't we went to bed.

Tuesday May 4, 1926

We received *The Times* newspaper this morning – only slightly smaller than usual. Maurice [Baring] came to lunch feeling ill and very depressed. Diana also was depressed and anxious. I drove down to the House in a taxi. There

---

[1] Lt.-Cdr. the Hon. Joseph Kenworthy, RN, MP, later 10th Baron Strabolgi (1886–1953).
[2] James Couper (d. 1946), MP for Glasgow, Maryhill, elected 1924.
[3] Sir Cuthbert Headlam (1876–1964), Conservative MP, Parliamentary and Financial Secretary to the Admiralty 1926–9.

were as many as ever of these today and a few buses. Questions were got through quickly as there were hardly any order papers, so that nobody except the asker of each question knew what was being asked. On the Budget resolutions Snowden explained that the Labour Party must vote against them but would not debate. Lloyd George said the same, so we then spent the afternoon trooping through the division lobbies. There were nine divisions. At half-past five there was a meeting of Conservative members in a committee room. The Prime Minister took the chair and Steel-Maitland made a speech on the facts of the situation and corrected various misstatements which Thomas and Ramsay MacDonald had made yesterday. The Prime Minister said that some members for industrial constituencies might be well advised to visit them but asked them not to do so without consulting the Whips, as it was important to keep a large majority in the House.

Subsequently we had a meeting of Lancashire and Cheshire members where everybody talked about themselves and no useful purpose was served. I walked home about seven o'clock. In Trafalgar Square I met Winston. He looked young and carefree. I showed him the evening paper I had just bought – a single leaf, the size of a half-sheet of writing paper. Except that there were more motor cars than usual about with more people in them, there was nothing unusual in the appearance of the streets.

Maurice came to dinner. He was much more cheerful than in the morning, because he has got a job – A.D.C. to Trenchard[1] – and he had been working all the afternoon. But Diana was as unhappy as ever. She insisted on ringing up Clemmie Churchill after dinner in search of news. She learnt that the Government were issuing a newspaper from the office of the *Morning Post* – and that Winston was at work at it then. Hilary [Belloc] came round later, in the highest possible spirits, and cheered us all up.

Wednesday May 5, 1926

A wet morning and so dark that at midday it was impossible to see to read without electric light. The electric light was faint and yellow. I went to White's, where there were a lot of people discussing absurd rumours – one was that Winston had been assassinated. There were some half dozen in full policemen's uniform. Buffles Milbanke very smart as a sergeant. I went on to Buck's where everybody was asking what they could do. Tommy Bouch had been sent off yesterday to feed starving horses – but when he got to them couldn't persuade them to eat. Diana asked me this morning how soon we could with honour leave the country. I said not till the massacres begin. We lunched in Avenue Road with John and Kakoo. John is a special constable and works every night from six to nine. Diana drove me down to the House and I got her a seat in the Speaker's Gallery. There were a lot of questions about the new newspaper, the *British Gazette*, which

---

[1] Marshal of the RAF (Hugh), 1st Viscount Trenchard (1873–1956). Creator of the RAF.

contained an attack on the Trade Unions. The debate was on the regulations which the Government is bringing into force. Joynson Hicks[1] made a good quite moderate speech. Henderson[2] followed. Later Hugh Cecil[3] spoke and then Thomas, who said that the Government and the T.U.C. had reached an agreement on Sunday night, and the latter were still trying to persuade the miners to accept it when the Government broke off negotiations on account of the strike in the *Daily Mail* offices.

It seemed to me and to many in our Party that this statement was rather damaging to the Government's position. We had some heated arguments in the lobbies. I talked to Winston, who said that Thomas's statement to which the Prime Minister had agreed was untrue. Maurice, Hutchy, Diana and I all dined in the House and went back to the debate after dinner. On the adjournment the Prime Minister made a further statement which put rather a different light on the matter, but I still think the Government were over-hasty in breaking off negotiations. Thomas replied and made a poor show. He can't speak the truth.

Thursday May 6, 1926

The weather still very cold. I went to Buck's before luncheon. The streets are much emptier today owing to the taxis having come out. We went down to the House. Diana went to the Ladies' Gallery. It was a dull and trying afternoon. The more violent of the Labour Members spoke and made such ridiculous and tiresome speeches that it made me feel physically ill to listen to them. I went to a meeting of the Westminster branch of the Primrose League in the Caxton Hall. I had thought there would be nobody there so had hardly bothered to prepare a speech. I found a very enthusiastic audience, of about two hundred people – and I spoke for about half an hour quite well. I then went to the Eiffel Tower to get some dinner. Then I returned to the House. At eleven o'clock [Sir John] Simon made a most important and impressive speech, in which he condemned the strike uncompromisingly and laid special stress upon its illegality. The Labour Party left the Chamber before he began, but all the Liberal Party were there with the exception of Lloyd George and they were solidly behind him. That speech may prove the way to his supplanting Lloyd George as their leader. The latter has missed another chance.

Afterwards about a dozen or more of us went to Printing House Square, as last night they had great difficulty in sending *The Times* off; those who were engaged in doing so had a severe fight with the picket. We found drinks and sandwiches prepared for us in the board room, where we had a long wait.

---

[1] William Joynson Hicks, 1st Viscount Brentford (1865–1932). Conservative MP; Home Secretary 1924–9.

[2] Arthur Henderson (1863–1935), Labour Home Secretary 1924; Chief Whip 1925–7; Foreign Secretary 1929–31.

[3] Lord Hugh Cecil, later Lord Quickswood (1869–1956). MP for Oxford University 1910–37; Provost of Eton 1936–44.

When the moment came and we sallied forth to fight we found there was practically no opposition at all. It was really a waste of time, but rather amusing. I walked all the way home and arrived about three o'clock.

Friday May 7, 1926

The House met at eleven o'clock. Diana drove me down there, and we arrived shortly after eleven. A few little bills of minor importance were dealt with. I left shortly before one, seeing that there was going to be no division. I was sorry afterwards, as there was a heated discussion on the adjournment. Diana and I went to a play called *The Ringer* [by Edgar Wallace] in the evening which we enjoyed. Afterwards we drove people home to Dalston and Hackney – and other foot passengers back to the Tottenham Court Road. We finally had a little supper at the Eiffel Tower – Clifford Sharp[1] was there and proudly presented us with a copy of the *New Statesman* almost up to pre-strike strength. It was full of lies but had an article by Hilary which made up for them. The news with regard to the strike is on the whole reassuring.

Saturday May 8, 1926

I have nothing to do. I passed the morning pleasantly enough in reading a French book called *La Mort et la Résurrection* by M. de la Piverdière – one of a series of famous crimes. I went to Buck's before dinner and played a game of bridge with Tommy, Eddie and others. Eddie is a special constable. Everybody at Buck's is doing something. I only am idle. Tommy, Hilary and Maurice came to dinner. It was not a very successful evening. Hilary hates talking about the strike and nobody can talk of anything else. He holds such peculiar and impossible views about politics that to argue with him on that subject is like talking to a brilliant Hottentot. We made him read some of his own poetry to us before he left – and he read it most beautifully.

Sunday May 9, 1926

An uneventful day. Diana drove down to Binfield in the morning to see Iris and distributed copies of the *Sunday Express* on her way. I lunched at White's. Lionel Tennyson was there, dressed as a full police inspector. Afterwards I joined Hilary, who was lunching at Buck's, where he and Maurice and I sat round the table till nearly five o'clock. We dined with Christabel McLaren[2] – the Jowitts, the Holdens and Maurice were there. It was quite pleasant. We played bridge afterwards and I won £17.

---

[1] Clifford Sharp (1883–1935), editor of the *New Statesman* 1913–17 and 1919–30.
[2] Christabel Melville (1890–1970) married Henry McLaren, later 2nd Baron Aberconway (1879–1953), in 1910. He was an industrialist and Liberal MP 1910–32. They created a famous garden at Bodnant, North Wales.

Monday May 10, 1926

I went to Buck's in the morning. Nobody had any news. They are all becoming special constables. Tom Trower [Duff's solicitor] was in the highest spirits, having become a whole-time constable and thus escaped from his office.

The Home Office vote was down for discussion in the House – and the debate beginning on the *British Gazette* and Special Constables wandered far and wide. I got up to speak once but I was glad afterwards that I hadn't. There were some violent and some mild speeches. It all fizzled out about eight o'clock.

Maurice, Hilary and Diana dined with me in the House. Afterwards we joined Venetia and went with her to the Eiffel Tower. She had been in a railway accident on her way from Breccles at Bishop's Stortford – one man was killed.

Tuesday May 11, 1926

Venetia, Diana and I lunched at home. Ivor Wimborne came in afterwards in a high state of excitement. He had been with J. H. Thomas all the morning and with Lord Reading and he asserted that they were coming to terms with the Government. I don't know whether there can be anything in it. The House opened calmly. I went to the library to write an article for the *Saturday Review* and strolling back into the Chamber about six o'clock found Simon delivering a very important speech. In the course of it he produced a formula for agreement. Opinion differed as to its value. Both sides are so suspicious. The House was adjourned at seven. I went to Buck's and then had to return to the House as I had promised to dine with Lady Astor[1] who has just discovered Will Rogers.[2] We were in a party of twelve – all men, except her, in a private room, and Will Rogers was, I must say, most amusing. But he went on too long. Thence I went to pick up Diana at the Holdens' and she later drove me down to *The Times*, where I worked, counting papers, till nearly four. David Margesson[3] was very optimistic. He had seen Ramsay MacDonald, who was angry at Simon's attempt to butt in – but otherwise hopeful. Diana came and worked at *The Times* office too – against my instructions.

Wednesday May 12, 1926

Ivor Wimborne telephoned early this morning and said that the T.U.C. had decided last night to call off the strike, and that they were going to Downing

---

[1] Nancy Langhorne (1879–1964) married Waldorf, later 2nd Viscount, Astor in 1906. In 1919 she was elected as a Conservative member and became the first woman to sit in Parliament. A prominent and influential hostess, she supported the policy of appeasement in the 1930s.

[2] Will Rogers (1879–1935), a Cherokee Indian whose cowboy skills were legendary. A star of Broadway and Hollywood, he travelled the world and became a national figure.

[3] David Margesson, 1st Viscount (1890–1965). Conservative politician. From 1931–40 Government Chief Whip.

Street this morning to settle it. I confess that I didn't believe him. I went to the offices of the *Saturday Review* about twelve to give them my article and then strolled to Buck's. There I saw on the tape that the T.U.C. leaders really were at Downing Street, and then while I was having a drink with Tom Trower the news came through that the strike was definitely off. The relief was tremendous. I never hoped for so sudden and so entirely satisfactory an end. I came home to lunch. Tommy Bouch, Venetia and Diana Westmorland were there. We were all in the highest spirits. Tommy drove me down to the House. The Prime Minister had a tremendous reception. He only said a few words – and Ramsay MacDonald said equally few.

Thursday May 13, 1926

This morning, thinking that all was over, Diana and Venetia left for Paris. When I went to Buck's, however, I found everybody in consternation. The triumph of yesterday had given way to panic. All the strikers were said to be still out and there were rumours of worse riots last night than on any previous one. The same feeling prevailed in the House of Commons. It was rumoured that employers were refusing to take people back except at reduced wages. More moderate Labour Members who were supposed to have been against the strike before were said to think that it was justified now. We were promised a statement by the Prime Minister at 6.30. The House at that hour was more crowded than ever. Ramsay MacDonald spoke first and was rather feeble but very moderate. The Prime Minister then delivered an admirable speech. He took the firmest possible stand against any attempt to reduce wages or to lengthen hours. Ever since the strike began until yesterday morning I have had a sensation of sick anxiety. This afternoon it returned but the Prime Minister's speech dispelled it for good. Thomas followed with a few misrepresentations. He contrasted the Prime Minister's statement of yesterday about no victimization with certain notices issued by the Admiralty and War Office, concealing the fact, until forced by a question to reveal it, that the notices had been issued several days before, while the strike was still on. Lloyd George made a short speech which for once was not mischievous and the House broke up feeling that everything was once more well. I came home and dressed for dinner for the first time since the trouble began. I dined at Buck's with Sidney, who had to go off afterwards, as the Prime Minister was meeting the miners.

Friday May 14, 1926

At four o'clock the Prime Minister made a statement to the effect that the railways had just arrived at an agreement, that negotiations with the dockers were going on satisfactorily and that he had prepared himself proposals for settling the mines dispute which he was going to submit to both parties. Ramsay MacDonald and Lloyd George had nothing to say except to express the hope that Baldwin himself would take part in the negotiations between the mine owners and the miners. It was the final culminating scene in the greatest personal and public triumph that any Prime Minister has ever had.

Sunday May 16, 1926

We lunched with Juliet. Maurice and Lord Birkenhead were there. The latter is of course anxious to claim all the credit for everything. Sidney tells me that he really has been extremely useful and sensible throughout. He told us at luncheon that he had written Baldwin's final message after the strike.

We dined with Max – rather a picnic dinner in the office of the *Daily Express*. He has just come to terms with his strikers. Jean [Norton] and Edwina [Mountbatten] who have been working the telephone switchboard in the *Daily Express* ever since the strike began were both at dinner in their overalls looking extraordinarily pretty. It was a pleasant evening. Max told us the story of the strike from his point of view, and of the bitter quarrel that he had with Winston.

Apart from a travel diary of a trip to Canada in August and September 1930, Duff does not keep a diary until the start of January 1933, though this is abandoned by the end of May. In early 1928 Baldwin had appointed him to the War Office as Financial Secretary, where his main job was to help prepare the Army Estimates. In the general election of May 1929, Duff lost Oldham to Labour. John Julius, his and Diana's only child, was born in September. In 1931 Duff was re-elected at the St George's division of Westminster by-election and became Under-Secretary at the War Office under Lord Crewe in Ramsay MacDonald's National Government. He also completed his book Talleyrand *which was published in 1932.*

1933

After it closed in New York, Diana – who frequently played the Nun instead of the Madonna – had toured America in The Miracle. *In the summer of 1927 came a tour of Central Europe. The production then went to London, where it opened at the Lyceum in April 1932; and from July of that year until January 1933 it played in Manchester, Birmingham, Glasgow, Edinburgh, Southampton, Liverpool and Cardiff.*

January 1, 1933

The year 1932 has been for me an uneventful one, in contrast to 1931 which was crowded with events – our visit to Sweden, the St George's by-election, my illness, the political crisis, the National Government and the General Election. During 1932 I have continued quietly to function at the War Office and have only made two speeches in the House of Commons, one introducing estimates and the other on the subject of Waterloo Bridge.

For me the chief event of the year has been the publication of my *Talleyrand* which I had been contemplating for fourteen years and actually writing for three. It came out on October 3rd and has had a greater success than I had dared to expect. The publisher tells me that over 5,000 copies have sold already, which at the present state of the trade is remarkable for a 12/6 book.

I am beginning once more to keep a diary, and once more I am starting a new year with new resolves. The diary is to be a weekly instead of a daily one. The latter becomes a burden and a bore. The intention is to review every Sunday morning the events of the week and the progress that I have made with my resolutions.

There is every reason to think that this year will be for me as uneventful politically as last. I have no grounds to hope for promotion. For this reason I am anxious to make full use of the comparative leisure I shall enjoy in getting on with the next book that I mean to write – a history of Venice. I ought to be able to devote at least two hours work to it every morning and, when the House is not sitting, at least as many more in the afternoon. This is the main resolution. Subsidiary ones are to reduce my weight – I weigh nearly 12 stone – and to give up drinking all forms of spirits. Every Sunday success or failure in these three departments will be recorded.

This first instalment is being written at Cranborne. Diana and I arrived here yesterday from Southampton where she is acting *The Miracle* and where we have just spent together two rather miserable days. We think that we are suffering from the after effects of suppressed influenza. I also am suffering from psoriasis – my chronic ailment, which has hardly ever been worse.

January 7, 1933 (Crichel, Lord Alington's house)

I am writing this second instalment on Saturday evening because tomorrow we are to make an early start. Diana is joining me here from Southampton tonight and tomorrow we motor to Lyegrove to stay with Diana Westmorland. It is on the road to Cardiff, where *The Miracle* opens on Monday.

This has not been a good week for keeping my main resolution. I haven't done one minute's work at my book nor even read a line that will help me with it. The excuse is twofold. In the first place I have not, until yesterday, been feeling well. Still recovering from the flu I never had. In the second place this week can count as the end of the holidays. Three days of it have been spent shooting and another one in the country. Shooting is the only sport I indulge in – and these three days will probably be the last of the season.

As far as my other resolutions are concerned I have kept the 'no spirits' one religiously. I weighed myself on Wednesday. 11 stone 10½ – exactly what I weighed last July and two pounds more than this time last year.

January 15, 1933. 90 Gower Street

January is half over and not the slightest effort has been made to keep my great resolution. I think resolutions are a mistake for they are no sooner made than circumstances arise which seem determined to thwart them.

On Saturday morning [15 January] I did some work at the War Office, lunched with Fred [Cripps] at the Ritz and wasted the rest of the day at White's. I had been in bed and asleep for an hour or two when the telephone rang. It was Iris to tell me that Alan was dead. I had heard that morning that he was ill but did not realize it was serious. Diana arrived from Cardiff at 3.30 and I had to break the news to her.

January 22, 1933 (90 Gower Street)

Diana found Viola wonderfully calm and serene. She has a firm and comfortable faith in a future life and doesn't mind death. Iris [Moffat] came to luncheon. She was in high spirits. She never liked Alan much.

I have done some work this week – but very little. I fail to reduce any weight although I eat no bread, nor butter nor potatoes. I have adhered religiously to the resolution not to drink spirits.

January 29, 1933 (90 Gower Street)

A week of influenza. My temperature never went above 100 and I never felt really bad. I read Bruce Lockhart's *Memoirs of a British Agent* – a most entertaining book – also the new Wells novel *The Bulpington of Blup* – a failure – *I'll Tell You Everything* by Priestley and Bullett – very slight and not unamusing, a new shocker called *Stamboul Train* [Graham Greene] and Fielding's *Voyage to Lisbon*, of which I recently bought a first edition for £3.10, and reread the *Jungle Book* of which I also bought first editions – £3.30 for the two. The only serious reading I did was Arnold Toynbee's account of 1931, which he calls *Annus Terribilis*.

February 2, 1933 (90 Gower Street)

I want to prevent this diary from becoming a mere record of luncheons and dinners – a fate which has overtaken all my diaries in the past. Meals are the pegs, the landmarks in life and it is difficult to avoid recording them.

[*February 7*] I dined at the American Embassy. I hadn't been there before and was astounded by the beauty of Mr Mellon's[1] pictures. Every one a gem. The two best Goyas I've ever seen, the best Raeburn, excellent Rembrandts, El Grecos and Sir Joshuas galore. I think it very fine of the old man to have brought them all the way from America for his short sojourn here. The food

---

[1] Andrew Mellon (1855–1937), banker and art collector, was Ambassador to London Feb. 1932–Mar. 1933. In 1937 his pictures were donated to the National Gallery of Art in Washington.

and wine were super excellent. We went on afterwards to a private show of the film of *Cavalcade* which was worth seeing. I had to leave before the end to join Diana at a small party at Londonderry House. I didn't get there till twelve by which time the Prime Minister and most of the Cabinet had left. It was an exceptionally delightful party. Young and old admirably mixed. I spent most of the time with Mrs Horstmann,[1] who is strangely attractive although really very plain. She was enormously impressed by the elegance of the entertainment and its character. It is of course true that nowhere else in the world nowadays, and not often in England, are there parties where statesmen, ambassadors and debutantes meet. We didn't get home till past three.

The following day [*February 8*] the House met. I was very nearly late for my questions owing to sitting too long at luncheon at Sybil Cholmondeley's[2] – Kensington Palace Gardens, the back of beyond. It had been amusing there. Philip [Sassoon], who had just come back from Berlin, had found it more military than before the war.

[*February 11*] I went up to Golders Green in the afternoon. John Julius was being taken to see *The Miracle* for the first time. I thought it would frighten him but but he took it quite calmly and enjoyed it enormously.

February 19, 1933 (90 Gower Street)

Last night we were dining at White's – three or four of us – and were expecting Simon Lovat[3] who had said he would dine there too and play bridge. An empty place was kept for him next to me. This morning in the paper I see that he fell dead at a race meeting yesterday afternoon. It is a curious sensation to have sat next an empty place that was waiting for a dead man.

None of my New Year resolutions have been kept except the one not to drink spirits. That has only once been broken, when I spoke at Lewes and had a whiskey and soda before the meeting. This week however I have begun to have Italian lessons. Bassani is the name of my teacher – he is a Professor at the London University. I can understand him perfectly and the danger is that he will talk all the time.

February 26, 1933 (90 Gower Street)

Pybus[4] has been kicked out of the Ministry of Transport and Oliver[5] has

---

[1] Lali Horstmann (d. 1954), wife of Frederick (Freddie) Horstmann (d. 1947), former German Minister in Lisbon. He retired from the diplomatic service when Hitler came to power. She later wrote a memoir, *Nothing but Tears*.

[2] Sybil Rocksavage became Marchioness of Cholmondeley in 1923, when her husband succeeded as 5th Marquess.

[3] Simon Fraser, 14th Lord Lovat (1871–1933). Under-Secretary of State for the Dominions 1926–8.

[4] Sir John Pybus, 1st Bt. (d. 1935). Minister of Transport 1931–3.

[5] Oliver Stanley (1896–1950), Conservative MP; Minister of Transport 1933–4; Minister of Labour 1934–5; President of the Board of Education 1935–7; President of the Board of Trade 1937–40; Colonial Secretary 1942–5.

got his job. Douglas Hacking[1] has got Oliver's. Some people think I am disappointed but I am not. I never hoped for the M. of Transport and shouldn't have liked it. Although I was a Minister before Oliver was he has had more opportunities to distinguish himself both in the last House and in this and he has taken full advantage of them. When the Government was formed I should have liked another post better than the one I have – Foreign, Home, Colonial or India Office – in that order – but so far as Oliver is concerned I certainly don't feel and am not entitled to a shadow of jealousy.

I attended a debate between Tom Mosley and Maxton[2] on Fascism v. Socialism, in which I thought that Mosley got the best of it.

March 12, 1933. Queen's Hotel Southsea [where Diana was acting in The Miracle]

It is a great relief to have got the Estimates speech over and to have finished my article for the *Quarterly*. The first four days of last week were complicated by the double task and rendered still more tiresome by not feeling well owing to my cough. The speech passed off satisfactorily. I spoke altogether five times during the debate and everybody was complimentary about it. Diana who had been worried about my health rang up Euan [Wallace] during that afternoon to ask how I was and he tactlessly said he thought I looked very ill. She immediately motored up to London from Southsea after her performance and arrived about one to find me in the best of spirits.

March 26, 1933. 90 Gower Street

On Thursday morning I was told that General Fisher, Director of Recruiting, wished to speak to me. I imagined it was some small matter of routine. He seemed nervous and began by telling me he was one of Lord Haig's executors. I thought it was to do with the long dispute that has been going on about his equestrian statue. He then told me that he wanted me to write Haig's life. I was astonished and immediately thought of all my disqualifications – not being a soldier, not being interested really in military matters, having read very little on such subjects and comparatively little about the war – and not having known the man. I mentioned them. He said that he and his co-executors had thought of them all. They had offered the job first to John Buchan[3] who had accepted but Lady Haig, who is now very undependable, had taken strong exception and had written him an insulting letter. The matter was dropped for the time and George Trevelyan [the historian] was approached. He had at first liked the idea but had finally

---

[1] Sir Douglas Hacking, 1st Lord Hacking (1884–1950). Conservative MP. Under-Secretary of State, Home Office 1933–4; War Office 1934–5; Dominions Office 1935–6. Party Chairman, 1936–42.

[2] James Maxton (1885–1946), leader of the Glasgow-based Independent Labour Party.

[3] John Buchan, 1st Baron Tweedsmuir (1875–1940). Barrister and author of many books, including *The Thirty-Nine Steps* and *Greenmantle*. From 1935 until his death he was Governor-General of Canada.

refused on the ground that he had done nothing of the kind before and that it would interfere with his other work. Then, having calmed Lady Haig, they had gone back to Buchan but he refused to reconsider it.

I was and have been in great perplexity. It is a great opportunity. The material is wonderful. Many volumes of Haig's diary most carefully kept have never seen the light. The book, whoever wrote it, would be of the greatest importance. It would take me a long time but Fisher assures me there is no hurry – he mentioned three or even four years. I might and probably should be criticized for undertaking such heavy work while a Minister. I don't mind that, but supposing I were promoted to higher office I might really have no time at all except during the summer holidays.

On the whole I have practically decided to accept but I shall insist on being given a completely free hand to put in or leave out what I like and to make the book whatever length I please. I envisage one volume rather than two. [*It turned out to be two.*]

April 30, 1933

All is now settled with regard to the life of Haig. The great difficulty that was expected to arise in connection with Lady Haig has been overcome. It was thought that she would not agree to my writing it. She is hardly sane and impossible to deal with. She insulted John Buchan when it was suggested that he should do it and has wanted General Maurice[1] to do it, to which they would not agree. She has also suggested Spears. The only person who has any influence with her is Doria Scott[2] with whom, I think, the idea that I should write the book originated. Lady Haig lives alone in a flat in Edinburgh and will see nobody. Doria has been up there this last week and has succeeded beyond her own or anyone else's expectations. Lady Haig made very little objection and has signed a letter which will commit her.

It will mean a tremendous amount of work for me – and of a new kind. I am very ignorant of the history of the war. I had a pleasant Easter holiday, chiefly at Plas Newydd. There I led a peaceful life, reading most of the morning and playing golf in the afternoon. I got through the first volume of the *Official History of the War* – John Charteris's *Life of Haig* – French's *1914* and Esher's *Tragedy of Lord Kitchener*. So I have made a beginning. Now at the start of a new month I am determined to renew that resolution about working which has been so ill kept since January. It should be easier now as my task is a more definite one and I will set down here every week how far I have been successful.

---

[1] Sir Frederick Maurice (1871–1951). As a serving Maj.-Gen. in 1918, he publicly criticized Lloyd George's conduct of the war and had to resign his commission.

[2] Lady Victoria (Doria) Scott (1908–93), Haig's daughter who was married to Col. Andrew Montagu-Douglas-Scott (1906–71).

May 9, 1933

The announcement that I am to write Haig's life appeared in *The Times* on Wednesday with the request that people would send me important letters or documents in their possession. The result has been that every morning I have had nearly an hour's work answering letters and have received nothing of any value.

May 15, 1933

I have finished *Foch* by Liddell Hart and have read a quarter of *Sir Douglas Haig's Command* which strikes me as a pretty good book. It is very difficult to work in London at this time of year. There are continual distractions. We went to Breccles for the weekend. Just before luncheon the butler blew his brains out which was rather distressing. We came back to London in the afternoon.

Duff's diary breaks off at the end of May 1933. He does not return to it until January 1936, when he calls it 'A Diary of the New Reign'. Meanwhile he had been made Financial Secretary to the Treasury (Neville Chamberlain was the Chancellor) and, in late 1935, Secretary of State for War and a member of the Cabinet in Baldwin's Government.

1936
A Diary of the New Reign

January 17, 1936

I was talking about claret and burgundy to Mr Berry in his wine shop at the bottom of St James's Street on Friday afternoon, January 17, when he suddenly pointed to the street and exclaimed 'I don't like that'. It was a poster with the words 'The King – A Cold'. I had been shooting the day before with the Prince of Wales at Windsor, where I had caught a cold myself. It was a filthy day, dark and snowing – but we had quite a cheerful morning.

We lunched at the Fort [Fort Belvedere, home of the Prince of Wales]. I had to hurry off immediately afterwards as there was a meeting of the Defence Requirements Committee at 3.30. The Prince came out in the snow to see me off. He was in the highest spirits and hadn't heard a word then of his father's illness. Owing to the fog and the snow the drive from the Fort to White's, which should take 45 minutes, took about an hour and a quarter. It was 22 minutes past three when I arrived at White's where I had arranged for my change of clothes to be waiting and I managed to get to Downing Street before the meeting had started. I am terribly overworked these days – what with the War Office, the D.R.C. and correcting the proofs of the second volume of *Haig*, I have time for nothing. Also I have a bad cough and cold. I was glad therefore to spend the weekend in London. The death of Kipling, the illness of the King and the weather threw a gloom over everything. I had seen Kipling only the week before at a meeting of the War Graves Commission when he seemed quite well and cheerful.

On Saturday Liddell Hart[1] came to luncheon with me. When I became S. of S. for War I thought it well to make friends with him, although his name stinks at the War Office and although he had written two most unkind and damaging reviews of my *Haig Vol. 1* in *The Times* and the *Literary Supplement*. But he is very intelligent and devotes his whole mind to questions of defence – so it is silly to treat him as an enemy, to be irritated by his criticism and not to listen to his advice. We sat talking until four o'clock. I can't like him.

Monday January 20, 1936

I didn't leave the house until after luncheon when I went to the War Office. On arriving there I got a message to say that the Prime Minister [Baldwin] wanted to see me at once. I went along to Downing Street, supposing, naturally, that he wanted to talk to me about the D.R.C. I found him in the Cabinet room and to my surprise he said 'I don't want to talk to you about the D.R.C. but about the Prince of Wales.' The Prince had come up to see him from Sandringham the previous afternoon and they had had a long conversation. I gathered that the King's life was despaired of and that it was only a matter of hours. The P.M. is very much disturbed about the Prince's relations with Mrs Simpson.[2] He thinks that if it becomes generally known the country won't stand it. 'If she were what I call a respectable whore' he said, he wouldn't mind, by which he meant somebody whom the Prince occasionally saw in secret but didn't spend his whole time with. I think the Prince's staff are very much against him – especially Halsey.[3]

Why the P.M. had sent for me I don't know. He said that he knew I was a friend of the Prince's but he didn't suggest that I should take any action. I think he may have had it in his mind that I might advise Wallis Simpson to clear out – for a bit at any rate – because he said that that would be the best thing that could happen. I shall certainly do nothing of the kind. She would tell the Prince who would never forgive me. We talked until the D.R.C. met at 3.30. The P.M. left in the middle to prepare his broadcast on the King's death.

I dined that night at the Army & Navy Club – a dinner given by Sir Frederick Maurice for German ex-service men – a delegation of whom had just arrived in London. I sat between two German generals, one of whom could speak

---

[1] Sir Basil Liddell Hart (1895–1970), influential military historian and strategist. Military correspondent of the *Daily Telegraph* 1925–35 and defence adviser to *The Times* 1935–9.

[2] Bessie Wallis Warfield (1896–1986), an American, was married first to Lt. Earl Winfield Spencer and second, in 1928, to Ernest Simpson, a British-American businessman, living in London (divorced in 1936). She met the Prince of Wales at a house party in 1931 and they became lovers some years later.

[3] Adm. Sir Lionel Halsey (1872–1949), equerry to the Prince of Wales.

nothing but his own tongue. My German is shamefully rusty and although I can understand fairly well it tires me terribly to listen and still more to try to talk. So I didn't enjoy myself. When the time came to drink the King's health Maurice stood up and read the latest message from Sandringham. 'The King's life is drawing peacefully to its close.' There was something extraordinarily moving about these words and I was profoundly affected. The presence of the Germans increased perhaps the poignancy. This completed the gloom in which the party had started and I slipped away as soon as I could. I picked up Diana. We went to bed without knowing whether the King was dead. He died, in fact, a few minutes before midnight.

Hilary Belloc and Katharine Asquith came to luncheon with us next day. I was glad to find that they both shared the universal sorrow. Hilary's anarchical mind is apt to go against the stream and to deride what others are feeling. But of the King he said 'He was a good man. He will go to heaven.'

I had to attend the Privy Council in the afternoon and was considerably rushed as I had been in negotiation to buy a second hand Privy Councillor's uniform and had never even tried it on. I hurried round to Moss Bros. in the morning and found that it fortunately fitted almost perfectly. I had to put it on after luncheon and go down to St James's Palace. The ceremony was rather impressive but not as much so as it might have been. I thought that Edward VIII looked very young and very lonely. I had to dash back afterwards, change my clothes and return to the House of Commons to swear the oath.

Diana wrote a letter of sympathy to the King to which she had the following reply:

21.1.36 Dear Diana – Your letter was most kind and human. I do thank you for it and for the mention of the word confidence. As you know I shall do my utmost to see that it is not misplaced. Wallis to whom you gave your note is and will always be the most wonderful friend and help to me. She gives me the courage to carry on. Yours sincerely Edward RI

I didn't go to hear the proclamation read out the next morning although we had tickets for the roof of St James's Palace. I thought it would make my cold worse. I gave my ticket to Liz[1] Paget who went with Diana. They saw the King at a window with Wallis and Ernest Simpson, Helen Fitzgerald and Hugh Sefton.[2] This is just the kind of thing that I hope so much he won't do. It causes so much criticism and does so much harm. Already people are beginning to talk about her and to criticize him.

---

[1] Lady Elizabeth Paget daughter of Diana's sister, Marjorie Anglesey, married Raimund von Hofmannsthal in 1939. He was the son of Hugo von Hofmannsthal, the Austrian poet and librettist of operas by Richard Strauss.

[2] Hugh Sefton, 7th Earl of Sefton (1898–1972), a close friend of the Prince of Wales, as was Helen Fitzgerald, née Dunn (sister of Lady Beaverbrook), m. 1928 Hon. Evelyn Fitzgerald (1879–1946).

On Tuesday the 23rd the House met to pass a resolution on the King's death. The Prime Minister's speech was excellent – very much better, I thought, than the one he had broadcast two nights before.

On the 25th I lunched with the Athlones. They had invited me before the King's death and I thought the luncheon would be put off, but telephoned to make sure and found that it wasn't. The point of it was to meet the Duke of Coburg, her brother[1]. It was a gloomy little party – so like a small German bourgeois household. It reminded me of the days when I was learning German in Hanover. I was tactfully left alone with the Duke of Coburg after luncheon in order that he might explain to me the present situation in Germany and assure me of Hitler's[2] pacific intentions. In the middle of our conversation his Duchess reappeared carrying some hideous samples of ribbon in order to consult him as to how the wreath that they were sending to the funeral should be tied. He dismissed her with a volley of muttered German curses and was afterwards unable to pick up the thread of his argument.

On Monday morning, January 27th, I went with other representatives of the Privy Council to present our address to the King. We stood in a semi-circle while the Prime Minister read it out. The King stood in the middle of the room looking very embarrassed and ill at ease. But when it came to his turn he did it very well. He first read the formal reply and then added a few informal words of his own – to the effect that so many familiar faces robbed the occasion of much of its formality etc. This went extremely well and the Privy Councillors were delighted. He then walked twice round the little group – first shaking hands and then having a word with nearly everyone. To me he talked about our day's shooting at Windsor and said that he knew then that his father was ill.

We dined with Freddie Lonsdale[3] that evening at the Garrick Club. He had quite a large party. I sat next to Wallis. She talked to me a great deal about the King. I told her how well his informal little speech had gone with the Privy Council whereupon she repeated it word for word. Apparently he had spent a very long time composing it – walking up and down the room and dictating it to her. But it had been his own idea. She talked very sensibly – said she had not allowed him to come to her flat since his father's death, had insisted on his using the large Daimler type of motor car in which people could see him – and even suggested that it would be better if she were to go away altogether. I think she is a nice woman and a sensible woman – but she is as hard as nails and she doesn't love him.

This section of diary ends as above, but continues in November 1936 giving Duff's account of the abdication of the King.

---

[1] Prince Charles Edward, 2nd Duke of Albany (1884–1954), Duke of Saxe-Coburg and Gotha, married Princess Viktoria Adelheid of Schleswig-Holstein (1885–1970). He became President of the German Red Cross in 1933 and a member of the Nazi party in 1935.

[2] Adolf Hitler (1889–1945) became Chancellor of Germany in 1933 and President in 1934.

[3] Frederick Lonsdale (1881–1954), the successful playwright, author of *The Last of Mrs Cheyney*.

I think it well to set down the facts as they are known to me regarding the King's abdication while they are still fresh in my memory.

On November 16 (1936) as I was going down to dinner in the House of Commons I ran into the Prime Minister, who said I was the very person he was looking for and asked me to come to his room. There he informed me that the King had told him that day that he intended to marry Mrs Simpson and to abdicate. The Prime Minister had naturally sought to dissuade him from such a course but had not succeeded. I asked him at once whether the King had said anything about time. When did he propose to take any action? How soon? About this the Prime Minister knew nothing. He was not intending to tell the Cabinet at present, but the King had said he would like to discuss the matter with me and Sam Hoare,[1] the two members of the Cabinet whom he knew best. The Prime Minister said 'Of course you and Sam are his contemporaries', which was a little surprising as Sam is 10 years older than I. He had no objection to our seeing the King and I should probably be sent for next day. As we separated he said that he was not at all sure that the Yorks would not prove the best solution. The King had many good qualities but not those which best fitted him for his post, whereas the Duke of York would be just like his father.

The next morning Alec Hardinge[2] rang me up to say that the King would like to see me at half past three. I explained that I had to answer questions in the House of Commons but that I would get to the Palace as near that time as possible. I got to the Palace soon after 3.30. Hardinge whom I saw first said he supposed I knew why I had been sent for. He could guess but couldn't know as the King had never mentioned the matter to any of his staff. He spoke with some bitterness of the King.

I hadn't seen the King to speak to, except for one moment before the Armistice Day ceremony, since I left the yacht at Athens towards the end of August. [*Duff and Diana had joined the King and Mrs Simpson the previous August for a Mediterranean cruise on the King's chartered yacht, the* Nahlin.] He made a brief enquiry about what I had been doing since and then came straight to the point. He told me that he meant to marry Wallis and that if he couldn't do so and remain King he must abdicate. If he was obliged to do so he wanted to do it in the most dignified way which would cause the minimum of inconvenience to the country. He said that his father's position and popularity had largely depended on his happy married life, and that since he had become King he had realized that it was a task which could not be properly carried out except by a married man. As Prince of Wales he had been able to go about a good deal and do many things which he couldn't do as King. The life was an impossibly lonely one for a single man.

---

[1] Samuel Hoare, 1st Viscount Templewood (1880–1959). Conservative politician. Foreign Secretary 1935; First Lord of the Admiralty 1936–7; Home Secretary 1937–9.

[2] Alexander Hardinge, 2nd Baron Hardinge of Penshurst (1894–1960). Assistant Private

I said that I supposed he had already heard all the arguments that could possibly be used to dissuade him from such an intention, and that I did not therefore wish to waste his time or mine by repeating them. There was one however which I wished to emphasize, and that was that the whole blame for the catastrophe if it occurred would be placed upon Wallis both now and in history. He seemed a little shaken by this and said that it would be very unfair. I agreed, but repeated that it would be so.

I also asked him if he had considered what sort of a life his would be. I had always thought that the life of an ex-monarch was the most miserable that a man could lead. Minor royalties could fall into the position of private citizens but those who had once been rulers could never find a normal place in society. I quoted the case of the King of Spain. 'Oh I shan't be like Alfonso' he exclaimed – 'He was kicked out. I shall go of my own accord.' 'But how will you spend your time?' I asked. 'Oh you know me, Duff. I'm always busy. I shall find plenty to do.'

I had my doubts but I once more asked him whether it was quite useless to attempt to dissuade him. He assured me that it was. He said he considered himself a very lucky man because Wallis was willing to marry him. The Prime Minister had told him that while the country would never accept such a marriage they would not object so strongly to his having a mistress. That, he thought, was the height of hypocrisy. That had been Edward VII's principle. Everybody could do what they liked so long as they kept up appearances. If couples wanted to come to court they must come together, no matter how unfaithful they were to one another. The late King had left society alone so that nobody knew where they were. 'Society' he said 'is suspended in midair, like this chair' taking up a chair. 'Nobody knows what is right.'

I didn't want to get into a discussion on the relative merits of the old European and the modern American system, so I said that if he was absolutely determined to do this thing it was the duty of his friends and advisers to consider how best it could be done. Personally I thought that, given time, while it would be very difficult it might not prove impossible. I thought that his face brightened up at this. He told me that he had seen Sam Hoare that morning who had said quite definitely that if he married he would have to go. The night before he had told his mother who 'had been very nice about it – had said she hoped I would be happy, but had obviously not thought it possible that I could stay'.

I repeated that it was a question of time. If he had thought of getting married before the coronation he must dismiss the thought. That was plainly impossible. The coronation itself would be the occasion of ugly scenes. What I would suggest was that he should consent to wait a year. That he should go through with the coronation and afterwards go to India for the Durbar. That

---

Secretary to George V, Private Secretary to Edward VIII and to George VI. Succeeded his father, who had been Permanent Under-Secretary at the FO, as Lord Hardinge of Penshurst.

during that period he should ostentatiously separate himself from Wallis. That she should go to America or in any case leave the country. At the end of a year his own position would be immensely strengthened. People would have seen that he had done his best to get on without her but had found it impossible. There would be far greater sympathy with him than he could expect today.

He was not responsive to the idea. He said he would not like to go through a solemn ceremony like the coronation without being perfectly frank with the country beforehand. He would not like to be keeping something up his sleeve. 'Mind you' he said 'if I can stay and marry Wallis she is going to be Queen or nothing.' If he had then thought of a morganatic marriage he had evidently dismissed it from his mind. And he felt strongly that some statement must be made soon. The English press had behaved very well. 'You may be surprised' he said 'in view of certain conversations we have had in the past, to know that old Max Beaverbrook has been of great help to me in this matter.' I didn't express surprise as I was already fully aware of the fact, Max having told everything to Diana. He complained bitterly of the American press. I said I thought it would be difficult to find a formula for any announcement. Although there had been a great deal of gossip the average man in the street still knew nothing and, frankly, it would come to him as a tremendous shock to learn that the King of England intended to marry an American lady who had been twice married already. He winced at the word twice and said that the first marriage hadn't really counted. What, if anything, he meant by that I didn't enquire.

I was with him for nearly an hour. He was very quiet and reasonable and we parted on the best of terms, he suggesting that we might meet again the following week. I gave Alec Hardinge an outline of what I had said before I left the palace. The King had said to me about him 'I'm afraid Alec has not been playing quite straight with me'.

Simon [the Home Secretary] came into my room in the House of Commons later that afternoon, and I told him most of what had passed between me and the King. He characteristically expressed no views but thought that the Prime Minister was inclined to underrate the difficulties and dangers of the situation.

These days were very busy. On the 19th I dined at the Artillery Mess at Woolwich. It was the first time that I had been there and I enjoyed it. There were no speeches. I drove there and back with Victor Warrender and on our return we went into the Channons where Diana was dining. They had a big dinner party, the King, the Kents, Prince Paul and Princess Olga,[1] Wallis, and a dozen others. The King was in the highest spirits. He talked to me about recruiting, about the Artillery Mess and about the B.B.C. I explained to him the measure of its independence. 'I'll change that' he said 'it will be the last

---

[1] Prince Paul of Yugoslavia (1893–1976) married Princess Olga of Greece (1903–97). He acted as Regent for his cousin King Peter II from 1934–41.

thing I do before I go.' He said this quite loud and with a laugh, as though he were looking forward to going.

After he had left I took Wallis aside. She had of course been told about my interview. I tried to impress on her the importance of her leaving the country. She said he wouldn't hear of it and that if she went he would follow. I believe on the other hand that she could persuade him to anything, even to a year's separation. But I don't believe she would face the risk of losing him during the interval. I tried to convince her that separation now was the only alternative to abdication which would be disastrous. I doubt if I produced any effect.

On Tuesday while I was dressing Esmond Harmsworth[1] telephoned to say he particularly wanted to see me that night. Diana had gone out that evening so I had the house to myself. Esmond arrived soon after eleven and, as I expected, he had come to talk about the King. He had been seeing a great deal of him during these days I gathered, and was close in his counsels. It was at the King's suggestion that he had come to see me and to ask me what I thought about the latest plan, which he proceeded to tell me. It was proposed now that the King should confer upon Wallis some ducal title and that he should marry her but that she should not become Queen. She would be his wife and live in his house but would not appear upon great occasions of state such as the opening of Parliament or the Coronation. The King was going to see the Prime Minister again tomorrow and put this proposal before him. It would of course require legislation.

I said that I saw great difficulties in it, but that there was no course which did not present great difficulties. I did not think that this plan was impossible, but it could only be carried out after a delay. The divorce proceedings would not be over until the end of April, the Coronation was fixed for the 12th of May. It was unthinkable that the marriage could take place between the two. I therefore again pressed strongly the case for a year's separation. Without that I was convinced the public could never be brought to accept the idea. With it I believed they might.

Esmond quite agreed with me. He said that he would see Wallis the next morning and put it to her. He thought as I did that she could persuade the King to accept it, that she could in fact persuade him to accept anything. 'After all' he said 'we are trying to help them. They must do something to help us.'

There was a Cabinet the next morning and fortunately it finished early so that I was able to have a talk with the Prime Minister afterwards. He took me up to his private sitting room. I said that I thought it right to tell him what had passed between Esmond and myself, and to give him my views. I also

---

[1] Esmond Cecil Harmsworth, 2nd Viscount Rothermere (1898–1978). Newspaper proprietor. Conservative MP 1922–9. In 1932 he became Chairman of Associated Newspapers. He was a friend of the Prince of Wales and Mrs Simpson, and played an important part in keeping the press silent about their friendship.

thought he ought to know what the King was going to propose to him that evening.

The idea was not new to him and he was strongly opposed to it. He didn't believe that such legislation would get through the House of Commons. He was convinced that the Dominions wouldn't look at it. He said that feeling in the Dominions was already very violent, particularly in Australia. He told me the story which had made a great impression on him of the rough Anzac who had said that he didn't mind the King keeping a mistress but had added 'It was a bit thick though, his taking that woman to visit the graves at Gallipoli.'

The Prime Minister was disturbed at the part that was being played by Esmond Harmsworth, of whom he spoke with great hostility. Nothing could be worse than that there should be a Rothermere and Beaverbrook press campaign on the subject. He didn't think that my idea of a year's separation would work. It was too late. I told him of my talk with Winston and of Winston's views, suggesting that such views so strongly expressed might influence the King. I left him feeling for the first time that it really would come to abdication.

The next evening I was to have left for Plas Newydd. I was going with the Wallaces by the Irish mail and dining with them in Hill Street at 7.30. When I arrived there I found a message from my secretary to the effect that a special Cabinet had been called for Friday morning and that Ministers who had left London were being asked to return. No agenda was being issued. I saw Esmond Harmsworth later that evening at White's and had a long talk with him. He was still seeing a lot of the King and of Wallis and still harping on the possibility of the morganatic marriage. He said it would have a good press. The *News Chronicle* and the *Daily Herald* would support it as well as his own papers and Beaverbrook's.

The Cabinet met at 11.30 on November 27th in the Prime Minister's room in the House of Commons. Everybody was present except Halifax.[1] The Prime Minister first emphasized the special secrecy of our proceedings. It would be given out that Spanish affairs were the cause of our meeting. He then proceeded to relate the facts in a manner not unlike that which he subsequently employed when speaking in the House of Commons. It is curious that writing now, a month after the event, I cannot recall what reason he gave for the suddenness and urgency of his action in summoning the Cabinet. Was it that the Press were beginning to get out of hand? He said that a paper called *Cavalcade* had had a poster 'the King goes his own way' and that a Labour member had recently remarked 'Are you going to have a fascist monarchy?' He spoke with great con-

---

[1] Edward Wood, 1st Earl of Halifax (1881–1959). Governor-General and Viceroy of India 1926–31; Lord Privy Seal and Leader of the House of Lords 1935–7; Lord President of the Council under Chamberlain 1937; Foreign Secretary after Eden's resignation in Feb. 1938 until end 1940; Ambassador in Washington 1941–6.

tempt of Harmsworth. He had consulted Attlee[1] who had said definitely that he and his party wouldn't look at the morganatic solution. When he told Attlee that according to Harmsworth, Elias,[2] the owner of the *Daily Herald*, was prepared to support it, Attlee had answered 'the policy of the *Daily Herald* is decided by the T.U.C.' The Cabinet lasted only an hour and a quarter. There was very little discussion after the Prime Minister had spoken. There seemed to be general agreement that the morganatic proposal was unthinkable. They said there was no precedent. I referred them to the one of the Archduke Franz Ferdinand.[3] But I didn't support the proposal. I only urged the desirability of gaining time. I said that in private life when the wrong people wanted to marry one another the best expedient was usually to persuade them to wait a year. I told them how when I had seen the King he had said Wallis was to be Queen or nothing. He had already abandoned that position. It was an advance. Nobody knew how the situation might alter in a year. The Prime Minister said he thought the situation had gone too far to permit of postponement. I think that everyone agreed with him. It was decided the opinions of the Dominion Prime Ministers should be obtained as soon as possible.

On Friday afternoon, November 30th Winston caught me in the lobby and said he wanted to speak to me, wished to let me know the direction in which his mind was working. We went into the room behind the Speaker's chair where he delivered himself of an oration. What crime, he asked, had the King committed? Had we not sworn allegiance to him? Were we not bound to that oath? Was he to be condemned unheard? Was he seeking to do anything that was not permitted to the meanest of his subjects? For his own part he would need satisfaction on a great many points before he could consider himself absolved from his oath of allegiance.

I said that I was sorry to hear that Max had returned from America and had gone straight to the Fort. Winston was annoyed at my saying that. Thought it a very small point and implied that it was only because I personally disliked Max that I feared his influence. We didn't pursue the subject – and that evening when we met at dinner at Venetia's – a dinner given for Winston's birthday – no further reference was made to it.

December 1, 1936

I left early for Leeds where I had to attend a recruiting luncheon. I caught a train back and bought two local evening newspapers at the station. They both contained an account of a speech delivered by the Bishop of Bradford in

---

[1] Clement Attlee, Earl Attlee (1883–1967), Leader of the Labour Party from 1935; Deputy Prime Minister 1942–5; Labour Prime Minister 1945–51.

[2] Julius Elias, Viscount Southwood (1873–1946), a printer and newspaper proprietor, acquired the *Daily Herald* in 1929.

[3] Archduke Franz Ferdinand (1863–1914) married Sophie Chotek von Chotkova in 1900. As she was not of royal descent, the marriage took place only after Ferdinand agreed to renounce all rights of succession for his children.

which, referring to the coronation and its religious significance, he said something to the effect that many people regretted that the King did not give more evidence that he himself realized what that religious significance meant. I suppose it was the first time in the century that the sovereign of Great Britain had been openly rebuked.

[December 2, 1936]

There was a Cabinet meeting, an important one for me because at last my memorandum on recruiting, most of which I had written in September, came up for discussion. The Chancellor fought every point and of course the only decision come to was to refer it to a Cabinet Committee. This I had expected but it might have been done six weeks before.

After that and other matters had been settled the Prime Minister said he was to see the King again and proposed to tell him that the Cabinet was not prepared to introduce the necessary bill to legalize the morganatic marriage. I made my last plea for delay. Kingsley Wood[1] said 'But if he agreed to the separation and delay of a year would you promise to introduce the legislation at the end of that period if he still wanted it?' I said no, that we should only undertake to reconsider the whole question. Nobody supported me. After the Cabinet had broken up, the Prime Minister said to me in the hall – 'I'm sorry Duff, that I can't agree with you on this matter.' I said that he was probably right but that I was so anxious to avoid abdication and I could see no other way than the one I proposed.

I had a curious luncheon that day at the Cholmondeleys. He wanted to give a demonstration of the Margaret Morris system of physical training.[2] We were a luncheon party of some twenty people and afterwards he made a speech explaining the system and when he had finished six enormous naked men charged into the luxuriously furnished drawing room and went through a series of violent exercises until they became extremely hot, which was not very pleasant for the spectators.

The next morning (Thursday December 3rd) the hunt was up. In every morning newspaper 'the King and Mrs Simpson' was front page news. Only the *News Chronicle* openly supported the morganatic marriage.

On the morning of Friday December 4th there was a meeting of the Cabinet in the Prime Minister's room at the House of Commons at 10.30. The first matter discussed was the King's desire to broadcast a message to the nation. We had the text of the broadcast read out to us. The main points were that he was the type of man who could never make a marriage of convenience; he had long hoped that he would find the woman whom he could love; he had found

---

[1] Sir Kingsley Wood (1881–1943), Conservative MP 1918–43; Minister of Health 1935–8; Air Minister 1938–40; Chancellor of the Exchequer 1940–3.

[2] Margaret Morris (1891–1980), a physiotherapist and dancer, pioneered a form of co-ordinated exercise and dance which survives as Margaret Morris Movement or MMM.

her now and he wanted to marry her; neither he nor she had ever proposed that she should be Queen; it could be arranged differently; finally he proposed to go away for a little now and leave the country to think over it. What exactly this last proposal meant I never understood.

There was no doubt, I think, in the mind of any member of the Cabinet that this broadcast could not be allowed. So long as the King is King every utterance that he makes must be on the advice of Ministers who must take full responsibility for every word. If therefore we could not advise him to make this speech we could not allow him to.

Our main concern at this meeting was what if any statement we could make before the weekend. It seemed at first that there was nothing to be said on that day and that we should have to ask the House to sit again on Saturday. Gradually however the view emerged from discussion that we might now inform the House that the Cabinet had definitely turned down the possibility of a morganatic marriage. It was strongly felt that it would be of great value to get this proposal out of the way so that during the weekend the situation should present itself out of two alternatives – renunciation or abdication. It was therefore decided that such an announcement should be made before the House rose at 4 o'clock.

I lunched with Emerald [Cunard] who was in a very excited state. She hasn't, of course, the faintest idea of what the British constitution is all about. I forget who was there but I remember that Ivor Churchill and I were the only ones with moderate views. Everyone else was violently on the side of the King. It was curious how everybody who had sought the views of taxi-drivers, hairdressers, hospital nurses, clerks or servants had heard exactly what they wanted to hear, that is to say their own opinion.

I went back to the House in the afternoon. A private member's bill was under discussion. A division took place about 3.40. We did not want a discussion on the statement so the tellers were instructed not to hurry. Winston noticed the delay and realized the cause of it. He talked loudly to those around him of the twisting crooked tricks of the Government. But after the statement there were seven minutes to go and neither he nor anyone else found anything to say. David Margesson who had had luncheon with Winston said he was in a highly emotional state, on the edge of tears all the time.

It was impossible during these days to attend to any other work.

1938

Stanley Baldwin had resigned on 31 May 1937 and was succeeded as Prime Minister by Neville Chamberlain. Duff, at this time Secretary of State for War, had never got on with Chamberlain, and had fully expected to be dismissed. Instead he had been offered the post of First Lord of the Admiralty.

Sunday January 9, 1938

At the beginning of most years I make resolutions, and more than once I have set them down on paper and begun to keep some record of how they fare and of my life in general. I suppose that upon each of such occasions these resolutions have appeared more important than their predecessor and more likely to prove enduring.

The past year has not been for me particularly successful. I began it under a cloud which was the result of the King's abdication. I was thought to blame for having gone with him on the yachting cruise and I was suspected, not unnaturally but quite unjustly, of having been aware of what he intended to do and of having encouraged him to do it. There was a whispering campaign against me. Some said I ought to resign, others that I should certainly be turned out when the Government was reformed. So firmly was this believed that Mike Wardell[1] came and offered me a position on the *Evening Standard*. It was to be something in the nature of political adviser and the pay was to be princely. The knowledge that this was waiting for me helped me to await events with a fair measure of equanimity.

I suppose that I shall never know who was really behind this campaign. From two or three separate sources I learnt that it was Anthony Eden.[2] It seemed to me improbable because I have never, so far as I am aware, crossed his path. On the contrary I have often supported him in Cabinet and sometimes been his only supporter.

At the same time I had incurred more than once the wrath of Neville Chamberlain.[3] I had felt that he, as Chancellor, was unnecessarily delaying the reforms I wanted to introduce into the Army in order to encourage recruiting. I had unwisely attacked him in Cabinet. Further I had made speeches that were considered indiscreet. I had attacked the Bishop of Birmingham and other clerics for their pacifist utterances, and I had said that we ought not to employ Communists in positions of trust, which seems a fairly self-evident proposition, but which was one not strictly in accord with Government policy.

Looking back on it now, I believe that I was much nearer being dropped than I thought at the time. I was quite astonished when the Prime Minister offered the Admiralty. I had thought that I should either go or remain where I was. At the time I had rather have remained where I was, but now I am very glad that I was moved. However to be moved from an office after having held

---

[1] Michael Wardell, Manager of the *Evening Standard*.

[2] Sir Anthony Eden, 1st Earl of Avon (1897–1977). Foreign Secretary 1935–8, 1940–5 and 1951–5; Prime Minister 1955–7.

[3] Neville Chamberlain (1869–1940), Chancellor of the Exchequer 1923–4; Minister of Health 1924–9 under Baldwin; Chancellor of the Exchequer in the National Government under MacDonald 1931–5 and again under Baldwin 1935–7; Prime Minister National Government May 1937–May 1940.

it for 18 months must imply some measure of failure, an impression which I have got somehow to wipe out in my new position.

I don't think that at present I have succeeded in doing so. I know myself that I did not do badly at the War Office and that that was also the opinion of the Army. But it takes some time for the opinion of a service to reach the public, and many of those who were my advisers and supporters have been dismissed.

Whether I shall do well at the Admiralty remains to be seen. I doubt whether I have any particular gift for administration, and during recent weeks I have been suffering from a certain lack of self-confidence which is new to me and depressing. It was intensified by a row with the Prime Minister over a speech I made to a few constituents at Pimlico [in December 1937]. I criticized Attlee for his visit to Spain and I was reported as having said that we should accept the Japanese apology for the incident at Wuhu.[1] The Prime Minister wrote me a letter in terms which almost seemed to demand my resignation. I was handed it as I was getting into the train to Blenheim where I was going to shoot. Owing to the worry of it I lost 5 lbs in the next 36 hours. I at first wrote a letter of resignation but didn't send it. I had to return to London the next afternoon, Saturday, owing to the illness of Diana's mother. On Sunday I sent him an explanation and a humble apology. When I met him on Monday morning he could not possibly have been nicer. I was forgiven but remained rattled.

I ought not really to mind or to worry because I really believe I should be happier out of office. My political ambitions have dwindled. I always wanted to be Prime Minister. I want to be no longer. I have got near enough to see the position without its glamour. I see more plainly the endless, thankless work, the worry and responsibility and the abuse. F. S. Oliver says that the great statesman must have a passion for power. I don't think that I have any desire for it. I have a growing dislike for public speaking and for publicity.

I love leisure and I should never relapse into idleness for there are books that I want to write and I really enjoy writing. On the other hand I like my present job better than any I could be offered. I came to it completely ignorant but I am learning rapidly and I feel that it is one I can grasp. I like being in Admiralty House, I love the Admiralty yacht *Enchantress*. So I am determined to make a success if I can, and then if I care to retire from politics I shall be hardly over fifty so I shall still have time for other activities.

I know that one of the main criticisms of me has been that I am too social, that I give too much time to parties and pleasure. Kakoo told me the other day that the Queen, who is my friend, had said that I couldn't be a successful Minister if I burnt the candle at both ends. There is something in it and I am determined that there shan't be. I ought not to be seen having supper at

---

[1] On 5 Dec. 1937, Japanese troops advancing on Nanking in China bombed Wuhu on the Yangtse river, damaging HMS *Ladybird* and two British-owned river steamers.

restaurants. I ought not to go to parties. I seldom do and don't enjoy them. I ought not to drink too much.

The only excuse for restaurants or parties at my age [47] is, in my opinion, love. Now at present so far as I can be said to be in love with anybody I suppose I am in love with Caroline[1] but it is as vague, as shadowy and as one-sided an affair as Dante's love for Beatrice. It consists solely of an occasional luncheon in Soho. Perhaps the number of them had better be diminished.

With regard to drink I have decided to adopt a system based on the division of days with five categories – as follows.

A = No drink until dinner, then only one sort
B = Either only one sort at luncheon or dinner or nothing until dinner then more sorts than one
C = More sorts both at luncheon and dinner but nothing between
D = No restrictions but no excess
E = Excess

I spent last Lent on the A regime and lost a good deal of weight.

I began this year here at Plas Newydd where I am happier than at any other place. Everything is charming, including the company – for while I love Caroline best, Liz is a good second. Diana and I travelled up on the night of the 30th having, except Diana, spent the day attending her mother's funeral at Belvoir. The Duchess died on the Wednesday before Christmas, Christmas being on Saturday, but John decided to conceal the fact in order not to have to cancel all Christmas arrangements. It was a bold and I think a wise decision. It worked admirably. The announcement was made on Monday evening. Diana has been very sad and curiously enough, although of course she knew the truth, she kept her spirits up wonderfully until the announcement was made.

The matter which is most engaging my attention at the Admiralty at present is the future of the Fleet Air Arm. I think I shall be largely judged by my success or failure in dealing with this question. The problems are many and it is at least doubtful whether the Air Ministry are anxious to help. Swinton[2] was very angry when the Fleet Air Arm was taken away from the Air Ministry. He said and wrote things to Tom Inskip,[3] so the latter told me, which he thought at the time would make it impossible for them to speak to one another

---

[1] Caroline Paget (1913–76), Diana's niece. Eldest daughter of the Marquess and Marchioness of Anglesey. She married Michael Duff in 1949.

[2] Philip Cunliffe-Lister, 1st Earl of Swinton (1884–1972). Born Philip Lloyd-Graeme, he changed his name in 1924. Conservative MP 1918–35; President of the Board of Trade 1921–31; Colonial Secretary 1932–5; Minister for Air 1935–8; Resident Minister in West Africa 1942–4.

[3] Thomas Inskip, 1st Viscount Caldecote (1876–1947). Lawyer and statesman. Attorney-General 1928–9 and 1932–44; Minister for the Co-ordination of Defence 1936–8. In Sept. 1939 he was briefly Lord Chancellor and from 1940 to 1946 Lord Chief Justice.

except officially again. Having so much resented the change he may be determined to make it a failure.

January 16, 1938

I went for a walk with Liz on Sunday afternoon. We discussed her future. I think she would marry Raimund [von Hofmannsthal] if he were free and had a little money, and I think she would be foolish to do so. She is so accustomed to living surrounded by great wealth that she has no idea how much she would miss it. She is very beautiful, and good and wise with a lovely sense of humour and ready laughter. I believe hers is a nicer nature than Caroline's, and much simpler. Caroline rang me up when I got to London to say she couldn't lunch with me the next day as had been arranged. I gave her a sonnet to take away with her – not a very good one and of a valedictory character. I am determined to take no further pains with her. It is only disturbing, wrong and ridiculous.

All these days I receive sad letters from Diana at Mégève [*where she was on a skiing holiday with John Julius*]. She doesn't easily get over her mother's death.

February 6, 1938. Admiralty House

Good news this week has been the consent of the Treasury to our subsidizing two of the armour plate firms for the erection of new plant to enable them to extend their production. With regard to our construction programme I have written to the Chancellor saying that I cannot produce what he asks for, 'a very much smaller programme', without a Cabinet decision. To reduce and slow down our preparations at this time seems to me indefensible.

At the end of the week came news of sensational events at Berlin.[1] The news is bad in so far as it represents a victory for the Nazis against the Army, for the extremists against the moderates, for the hotheads against the cool. It is good in so far as it shows the weakness of the regime and must further weaken it. I had nearly written that it is good in that it removes Ribbentrop[2] from London, but is really bad because it puts him in a more important position, and he may be succeeded here by a more attractive personality who will be more successful in the task of deceiving the English.

February 13, 1938. Admiralty House

A good summing-up of the results of the German crisis was quoted by Anthony to the Cabinet on Wednesday, 'Germany is now more menacing but less formidable.'

---

[1] On 4 Feb. Hitler became Supreme Commander of the Wehrmacht (German Armed Forces).

[2] Joachim von Ribbentrop (1893–1946). German politician, joined the Nazi Party in 1932 and in 1933 became foreign policy adviser to Hitler. From 1936–8 he was German Ambassador in England, returned to Germany as Foreign Minister and negotiated the Soviet–German Non-Aggression Pact of 1939. He was captured after the war, tried at Nuremberg in 1946, found guilty and executed.

I have agreed with the Chancellor on a figure for my estimates, leaving for the time being the construction programme out of the question. We both gave away more than we wanted to, and I had some difficulty in persuading Chatfield[1] to accept the final settlement because it did mean the delay of certain preparations for war which are necessary. Inskip has produced a memorandum which so far as I can understand it means fixing a global sum for all rearmament and leaving the three services to squabble over its distribution. Both that and my construction programme will come before the Cabinet on Wednesday. Thinking it important to secure an ally I went to see Sam Hoare [Home Secretary] on Friday afternoon. He seemed most willing and keen to help. I think he likes the prospect of attacking Simon [Chancellor of the Exchequer] and doesn't mind differing from Inskip. The prospect of the battle has revived my interest in and sharpened my appetite for politics.

Venetia had a dinner party on Tuesday, where I had some fairly heated arguments with Winston on the subject of recognition of Italy's conquest of Abyssinia. He said we should never recognize, that it would be the depth of humiliation. I found him foolish and irritating.

February 20, 1938. Admiralty House

The past week has been a busy one, full of events. The full significance of Hitler's summons to Schuschnigg [the Austrian Chancellor] appeared gradually. It was nothing less than the end of Austria's independence. A portentous development in European history about which nobody in England seems to give a damn. At the Cabinet on Wednesday full information was not yet to hand and comparatively little time was spent on Foreign Affairs.

The main subject of discussion was a report which Inskip has produced on the future of rearmament. The demands of the three services over the next four years amount to something in the nature of £2,000,000,000, and the Treasury say £1,650,000,000 is all the money that can be made available. Inskip's simple solution of the problem is to divide that sum in certain proportions to be decided upon between the three services. My advisers tell me that according to their calculations the Admiralty would be reduced to annual construction programmes, the total cost of each of which would be reduced to about £12,000,000. The one that we had already put forward for this year was £70,000,000 and last year's was very little less. It would mean that we could not possibly complete even the modest plan to which we are committed, let alone the New Standard which has not yet been approved but which all the experts consider is the minimum consistent with security. I told the Cabinet this and pointed out that if we were at war, which I thought we soon might be, we shouldn't dream of accepting an arbitrary figure given us

---

[1] Alfred Chatfield, 1st Baron Chatfield (1873–1967). Admiral of the Fleet 1935; First Sea Lord 1933–Aug. 1938; Minister for Co-ordination of Defence 1939–40.

by the Treasury. However the Cabinet eventually adopted the Inskip report and postponed consideration of my reconstruction programme as being affected by the report.

I protested that consideration of the report would take months, that the programme must be settled before the defence debate at the beginning of March and that it was unfair to make the report apply to the 1938 programme of one of the services and not of the others. It was however eventually settled that I should discuss the question with the Chancellor and the Minister for Co-ordination.

On Friday morning we were suddenly informed that the Cabinet was to meet on Saturday afternoon – a very unusual procedure. The Prime Minister in opening proceedings spoke for nearly an hour covering the recent history of our relations with Italy and the urgent need of reaching an agreement. He then revealed that his views were not shared by the Foreign Secretary. The issue between them was that the Prime Minister was anxious to open conversations at once and to announce publicly that we were doing so. The Foreign Secretary thought that we must obtain some further assurances from Mussolini,[1] especially with regard to Spain, before starting conversations. I believe that *au fond* Anthony doesn't want to start conversations at all, or to be friends with Italy ever. He did not, or so it seemed to me, state his case very well, and I felt that anyone who had not already made up his mind must have been convinced by the Prime Minister.

Anthony had said that he believed there was some secret agreement between Hitler and Mussolini and that the latter had received some *quid pro quo* for his acquiescence in the assault on Austria. Grandi[2] had denied that this was so. The Prime Minister had believed Grandi was speaking the truth but Anthony hadn't. I said that this did not seem to me of very great importance. What was it that Mussolini had received? The most obvious guess was that it was an assurance that Hitler would come to his assistance if we attacked him. Such an assurance was of little importance so far as we were concerned as we had no intention of attacking anyone.

At the end of the discussion Anthony made it plain that he meant to resign. There was a silence of consternation, for many, it seems, had not expected that this was coming. Everybody realized what a tremendous blow it would be for the Government. It might even bring about the Government's fall.

At the meeting at 3 the Prime Minister opened by saying that efforts to find a solution had failed, and that indeed it was not merely on the steps to be taken in this instance that he differed with the Foreign Secretary but that

---

[1] Benito Mussolini (1883–1945) ruled Italy as a Fascist dictator 1922–43. He was deposed in July 1943, arrested, rescued by the Germans and set up a Fascist state in northern Italy. On 27 April 1945 he and his mistress, Clara Petacci, were captured by Italian partisans and executed the next day.

[2] Count Dino Grandi (1895–1988). Italian Foreign Minister 1929–32; Italian Ambassador to London 1932–8.

there was a deeper difference of outlook which made it difficult for them to work together. Anthony agreed with this.

We know not what will happen. My own belief is that he means to go, because he doesn't want to make terms with Italy and he feels that he will never be allowed to pursue his own policy with the P.M. at his shoulder. If he goes it will certainly be a body blow for the National Government. There were crowds in Downing Street last night and tonight and when he drove off there were loud cheers. This I am afraid will stiffen his attitude because he will feel that he has popular opinion behind him – which indeed he has. [*Anthony Eden resigned later that evening.*]

February 27, 1938. Admiralty House

'Thank heaven the danger,
The crisis is past'

At the Cabinet on Wednesday we discussed my Construction Programme. I put forward three – my original one [70 million], a 36 million one, and a half-way house to the tune of 48 million. I spoke strongly in favour of the first but I knew I shouldn't get it. Simon wanted 4 more million off the 48 and Inskip wanted even further reductions. Sam Hoare and Halifax [Foreign Secretary] spoke up for me but the P.M. eventually said that we – Simon, Inskip and I – must discuss it further and come back to the Cabinet if we couldn't agree.

March 6, 1938. Admiralty House

Last Sunday was the first spring day. I lunched at the Angleseys, sat between Caroline and Liz. The sun poured in at the windows and I felt perfectly happy – one of those rare moments.

February has seen the maintenance of my resolutions – twenty-one A days out of 28 – one E day – the first of the year – my birthday eve. Also I have increased my interest in my work and my confidence in my own ability to do it.

Henderson[1] had his first interview with Hitler on Thursday which was not at all encouraging. Delbos[2] told Phipps[3] this week that if Hitler attacked Czechoslovakia France would certainly fight. They would then be fighting for their lives and we should be obliged sooner or later to come to their assistance. This is what I have always feared would happen.

---

[1] Sir Nevile Henderson (1882–1942), diplomat. Ambassador to Berlin 1937–9. Supporter of Chamberlain's policy of appeasement.
[2] Yvon Delbos (1885–1956), French Foreign Minister 1936–8.
[3] Sir Eric Phipps (1875–1945), Ambassador to Berlin 1933–7 and to Paris 1937–9.

On Friday evening we had the Rothschilds,[1] George Gage[2] and Liz to dinner. It was a mildly pleasant evening and I thought I had successfully drowned in champagne a cold which I had caught from Diana and had been fighting for two or three days. But on Saturday morning I woke up with a temperature of 101. I felt pretty wretched all the morning but got better as the day went on.

March 17, 1938. Admiralty House

I thought when I wrote the above on March 6 that I was cured, for all that Sunday I felt wonderful. Early in the morning however I woke up feeling worse and when my temperature was taken it was over 102. The result is that I am still in bed. I have missed four Cabinet meetings and today I should have introduced the Navy Estimates which were introduced instead by Geoffrey Shakespeare.[3]

Last Saturday there was an emergency Cabinet in the morning over the Austrian *coup d'état*.[4] I sent the Prime Minister a letter beforehand suggesting that a suitable reaction on our part would be an increase in our already published naval construction programme. He read my letter to the Cabinet but said that he would prefer an increase in the Air Force.

There was another Cabinet on Monday and before it I wrote the P.M. another letter pointing out that more air construction wasn't going to impress anybody, that we probably shouldn't get delivery even if we gave the orders and that if we did we shouldn't have the pilots. The increased naval construction on the other hand was easily practicable and had in fact been contemplated and it would be a direct reply to the aggressive policies of both Germany and Japan. He read it to the Cabinet but said that it didn't alter his views.

March 27, 1938. Beechwood, Lavington [home of Euan and Barbie Wallace]

I learnt there was to be a special Cabinet meeting [on March 22] and I determined to go to it. The agenda arrived after I had gone back to bed. There were two documents – drafted apparently by Halifax – a note to the French Govt. and a parliamentary statement. The note was a cold refusal to give any support to France if she went to war on account of Czechoslovakia and the parliamentary statement read like a declaration of isolation. When the night nurse came she found that my temperature had gone up again. I told her it was due to the documents I had been reading and that in any case I meant to

---

[1] Victor Rothschild, 3rd Baron (1910–90), zoologist. From 1939–45 he served in MI5 as head of counter-sabotage and became a bomb disposal expert. In 1933 he married Barbara Hutchinson. They were divorced in 1945 and the following year he married Tess Mayor.

[2] Henry Rainald 'George' Gage, 6th Viscount Gage (1895–1982), married first, in 1931, Hon. Imogen 'Mogs' Grenfell (d. 1969), second, in 1971, Diana Campbell-Gray (d. 1992).

[3] Sir Geoffrey Shakespeare (1893–1980), Liberal National politician. Parliamentary and Financial Secretary to the Admiralty 1937–40.

[4] On 12 March 1938, German troops marched into Austria and on 13 March Hitler announced the legislation on the *Anschluss* (annexation) of Austria into the German Reich.

go to the Cabinet next day. I fought hard at the Cabinet not quite in favour of giving the guarantee to Czechoslovakia but for making a more friendly gesture to France. I insisted that when France fought Germany we should have to fight too whether we liked it or not, so that we might as well say so. It was decided that the two statements should be redrafted but that the policy should remain.

I felt ill and depressed.

On Wednesday afternoon [22 March] Diana and I drove down to Beechwood. The next day the weather was perfect and I spent most of it lying out of doors in the sunshine. Hilary came over to luncheon. He was fairly cheerful. He said that the Prime Minister had written a poem that went:

Dear Czechoslovakia
I don't think they'll attack yer
But I'm not going to back yer.

The Prime Minister's speech in the House on Thursday [23 March] was a great success. It was very different in tone and emphasis from the draft the Cabinet were asked to consider last Tuesday. Without saying so definitely, he quite clearly implied that if France went to war we should go too. This was all that I wanted.

April 3, 1938. Pulteney Street, Bath

The end of March and of the first quarter of the year 1938. The main public events have been the resignation of Anthony Eden and the absorption of Austria. Both are to be deplored. The former has materially weakened the Government. It has both diminished our popularity in the country and diminished our efficiency. Anthony, although I disagreed with him about Italy, was a good Foreign Secretary. His whole heart and mind was in his work and he knew Europe. I am afraid Halifax will be a bad Foreign Secretary. He knows very little about Europe, very little about foreigners, very little about men. He is a great friend of Geoffrey Dawson[1] whose influence is pernicious, and I think he is also a friend of Lothian's[2] who is always wrong. Nancy Astor is to give a reception for him which it is very foolish of him to allow her to do as she and her friends are justly suspected of being pro-German.

So far as my private life is concerned these have been very uneventful months. My distaste for politics and the life that they impose doesn't decrease. Lately, especially having been in the country during such lovely weather, I have longed to live there. Whether I should be happy doing so I cannot say. I should of course write which would keep me busy, but I should have some

---

[1] Geoffrey Dawson [previously Robinson] (1874–1944), editor of *The Times* 1912–19 and 1923–41.

[2] Philip Henry Kerr, 11th Marquess of Lothian (1882–1940). Ambassador to Washington 1939–40.

leisure and be able to travel. A Cabinet Minister in the House of Commons is a slave. However I have now the job I like the best and I must do it as well as I can and keep it as long as I can which in any case cannot be very long.

April 22, 1938. Plas Newydd

Here I am once more and I continue to write the diary which I began here when the year was new. Nearly a third of it has passed and from my personal point of view its passage has been satisfactory.

I was unlucky to miss the introduction of the Navy Estimates [*when he was ill*]. It is the only opportunity that I get in the year of making any impression on the House of Commons and when I was at the War Office I always made a success of it. So far as the Admiralty is concerned four matters have principally occupied my attention. The first has been the future of the Fleet Air Arm. The difficulties do not diminish. It is unfortunate that the transference of the F.A.A. from the Air Ministry to the Admiralty should have coincided with a great expansion of the Air Force. The result is that the Air Ministry have some justification for saying that they have too much on their hands already to have either the time or the resources with which to help us.

The second matter that has been a source of difficulty has been our 1938 construction programme and the whole question of our future naval standard. I tried to persuade the Chancellor to agree to a flotilla of destroyers being added to the former, but he wouldn't. With regard to the latter the Cabinet are further from a decision than ever. I produced a paper at the last meeting urging that certain measures for the protection of oil reserves, merchant vessels etc. from air attack should be undertaken at once and not included in the absurd financial 'ration' to which it is sought to limit each Department, but nothing came of it. I don't get on well with the Prime Minister. I irritate him. At this same Cabinet meeting there was discussion about informing the French of our military plans. These have now been so far reduced that it is proposed to tell the French that the prospect of our sending a force to the continent in the event of war is too remote to be worth discussing.

So far as the Navy is concerned the Government will have to make up their mind sooner or later whether they intend to have a fleet capable of fighting Germany and Japan at the same time or not. That is all it amounts to.

We are just completing a very successful holiday. It began on the 13th with a visit to Windsor Castle. There was no party there – only the Household and a couple of Guards Officers with their wives to dinner. So Diana and I sat on the right of the King and Queen. I got on with her better than ever and found her more than ever charming. There is nobody to whom I enjoy talking so much. It was not until we were eating the ice that she said 'Oh dear, I'm afraid I must talk on the other side now' and after dinner I sat with her from the moment we joined the ladies until she went to bed. In the interval I had a good talk with the King who seemed much healthier, happier and more sure of himself than when we last stayed there just a year ago.

We left Windsor on Thursday morning and travelled to Paris by the 2 o'clock train. I found that all the French Ministers with whom I talked were very sceptical about the value of our agreement with Italy.[1] Daladier[2] went so far as to say that it had saved Mussolini from disaster. They all take the view that Italy's word is not worth having, that she will always betray her allies as she did in the last war. I argued that Italy will certainly pursue her own interests – who doesn't? – but that her interests lie with ours.

On the day of our arrival we wrote our names on the Duke and Duchess of Windsor[3] but we heard no more of them and so inferred that we were not in favour.

Every afternoon while I was there except two I paid a visit to a brothel. On one of the days excepted I had tea with Nadège de Ganay[4] which from one point of view amounted to the same thing although combined with a good deal of political gossip. She is an intimate friend of Sarraut,[5] who is once more Minister of the Interior and who tells her everything.

May 1, 1938. On board H.M.S. Enchantress. At sea

I have had a busy week preparing a paper for the Cabinet on the future of the Navy. In it I suggest that we should abandon the absurd new system of rationing the defence departments. I suggest that the sensible plan must be to ascertain your needs for defence first and then enquire as to your means of meeting them. If it is really the case that they cannot be met, then there must be some fundamental change of policy either foreign, imperial or domestic. I sent advance copies of my paper to the P.M., the Chancellor and Inskip on Thursday. There is however a danger that he and the P.M. may decide to withhold it.

April has been a bad month for good resolutions – only 7 A days and 9 D days. But this has been due to convalescence, holidays and Paris.

May 8, 1938. On board H.M.S. Enchantress – St Peter Port, Guernsey

As I feared, Simon prevented my memorandum from being circulated to the Cabinet. I had a talk with him about it on Thursday which was, as I knew it would be, pure waste of time. Simon had no suggestion to make except that I should at least put forward some proposal, as Hore-Belisha[6] had done, whereby the money could be saved. My answer is that before the Admiralty

---

[1] On 16 April 1938 the Anglo-Italian Pact had been signed, by which the British Government recognized Italian sovereignty over Ethiopia and Italy promised to withdraw her troops from Spain at the end of the Civil War.

[2] Edouard Daladier (1884–1970), French Prime Minister 1933 and 1934 and 1938–40.

[3] When in foreign countries it was customary to sign the visitors' book of embassies or royalty.

[4] Comtesse de Ganay, née Fontenay, was married to Comte Elie de Ganay.

[5] Albert Sarraut (1872–1962), French radical socialist politician. Minister of the Interior 1936 and 1938–40.

[6] Leslie Hore-Belisha, Baron Hore-Belisha (1893–1957). Minister for War 1936–40.

can be asked to sketch an imaginary Fleet they must be told for what purpose it is to be used. If we are told it is to fight Germany and Japan and that the Treasury figure is the limit we can only answer 'it can't be done for the money'. Either their demands must be smaller or their figure must be higher.

May 15, 1938. Mottisfont Abbey

My meeting with the P.M., Simon and Inskip on Monday resulted in a long and profitless argument which at moments became on the Prime Minister's side rather acrimonious. I cannot help irritating him. The upshot of it was that the Chancellor wrote me a letter asking for certain definite figures which we are preparing for him. I am inclined to believe now that the best plan may be to avoid taking any decision on policy as a whole and to rely upon the Treasury being obliged to agree to what we want from time to time as we want it.

I had an amusing but rather trying incident with Dollie Warrender this week. She is an old love whom I see from time to time but whom I hadn't seen this year. One afternoon we went to Gower Street whence all the furniture has been removed. I bolted the front door but shortly after our arrival there came a hammering upon it and a ringing of the bell. It could not have been more inconvenient. Finally I went down and found some people who had been given the key and told to come and see over the house with a view to buying. I was in some difficulty as to what I should say to them but finally told them to come back later. They must have suspected the worst – and they were right.

May 22, 1938. Manor House, Cranborne

We learnt of the changes in the Cabinet on Monday afternoon. I was pleased with them for I shall get on better with Kingsley Wood[1] than I did with Swinton. And I am very glad that Edward[2] [Stanley] has got into the Cabinet at last. He and Portia are over the moon with delight. Barbie is very disappointed that Euan isn't there too, but he himself is quite happy with his promotion to Financial Secretary to the Treasury – a pleasant job which almost invariably leads farther.

But if one compares the calibre of those who have entered the Cabinet last year with that of those who have left it the result cannot be called encouraging.

Baldwin	Winterton[3]
Ramsay MacDonald	De La Warr

---

[1] Sir Kingsley Wood had become Secretary of State for Air.

[2] Edward Stanley, Lord Stanley (1894–1938), elder son of the 17th Earl of Derby and brother of Oliver Stanley, married the Hon. Sibyl (Portia) Cadogan (1893–69) in 1917. He was made Dominions Secretary by Chamberlain in May 1938 but died the following September.

[3] Edward Turnour, 6th Earl Winterton (1883–1962). Chancellor of the Duchy of Lancaster, 1937–9.

Runciman	Burgin[1]
Eden	Maugham[2]
Swinton	Stanley
Ormsby Gore[3]	Colville[4]

Arranged like that in two columns one is bound to admit that the left hand column wins on the test of ability in every case.

À propos of what Brendan told me last week a paragraph appeared on Monday in the 'Londoner's Log' of the *Evening Standard*, which Randolph Churchill[5] writes, to the effect that the Prime Minister was having trouble with the Admiralty over expenditure, and contrasting the unaccommodating spirit shown by the Admiralty with the more reasonable attitude of the War Office. I charged Brendan with having supplied the information to Randolph which he strenuously denied and he suggested that it was Sam Hoare who had told Max. He says that Sam is very thick with Max and I conclude that it must be Sam he meant by 'one of my colleagues who is not one of my friends'.

Another old friend turned up this week – Daisy Fellowes – a mistress of fifteen years standing and my own age. She still attracts me and I dined with her Monday and Wednesday, returning to Claridge's to our mutual satisfaction.

On Friday afternoon we drove down to Cranborne. With the evening papers came the news that two Sudeten-Deutsch[6] farmers had been shot in Czechoslovakia – and then a message from the Resident Clerk at the Admiralty to say there was to be a meeting of Ministers at 5 o'clock the following day. It was a very beautiful evening. This place was looking as like an earthly paradise as it is possible to conceive. Betty has given all her time to the garden of recent years and made it more beautiful than ever. The folly and horror of war seemed ten times more foolish and horrible in such surroundings. And I feel that war is very near. I couldn't help remembering another beautiful Sunday twenty-four years ago when I was staying at Stanway and when I was recalled to the Foreign Office, where I was then working in the Cypher Department.

May 29, 1938. West House, Aldwick

After a very pleasant luncheon we motored up to London through the country looking its most beautiful in perfect weather and did it in two hours and twenty minutes which was much too fast. The Cabinet met at 5. We only sat for an hour as there was very little to say. The general feeling of the Cabinet seemed to be that great, brutal Czechoslovakia was bullying poor, peaceful

---

[1] The Rt. Hon. Edward Burgin (1887–1945), Minister of Transport 1937–9.

[2] Frederic Maugham, 1st Viscount Maugham (1866–1958). Lord Chancellor 1938–Sept. 1939.

[3] William Ormsby-Gore, 4th Baron Harlech (1885–1964), Colonial Secretary 1936–38.

[4] John Colville, 1st Lord Clydesmuir (1894–1954). Secretary of State for Scotland May 1938–40.

[5] Randolph Churchill (1911–68), son of Winston Churchill.

[6] Encouraged by Hitler, the Sudetens, the German minority in Czechoslovakia, were demanding self-determination.

little Germany. Such at least was the opinion of the Lord Chancellor, whom I find a most undesirable addition to the Cabinet. It was decided to send off a telegram to tell the French to go carefully and not to rely too much on us, and another to urge the Czechs to make large concessions.

The result was better than everybody could have foreseen and quite different. The crisis passed over, the Germans decided to do nothing and everybody believes it was entirely due to the firmness of the British Government. I consider this a complete misapprehension – but so is history written. Even well informed people like Winston with no desire to give credit to the Government believe that it is so. And Belloc who came to dinner here on Friday night was under the impression that we had said to the Germans that if they crossed the Czechoslovak frontier we should go to war. Of course we never said anything of the kind.

We lunched with the new German Ambassador[1] that day. He seems a decent, dull sort of Hun. She is rather a nice old girl but can hardly speak English. We conversed principally in German and mine is very bad. The night before we went to a big dinner party at the Italian Embassy. Grandi pretends to think that the new Anglo-Italian accord was the cause why the crisis passed off so satisfactorily. It had, of course, nothing to do with it.

June 6, 1938. West House

On Wednesday (June 1st) there was a ball at Buckingham Palace. It was different from any ball there had ever been there before. There was very little ceremony. Those who were told to follow in the supper procession were not told whom to take in as used to be the case but simply to take a lady. It was a sit down supper for everybody which is also a change – and Ambrose's band, with a crooner, and smoking allowed everywhere. I think everybody must have enjoyed it, I did. Caroline was looking very beautiful in a red satin dress that I had given her for the occasion. She is plainly in love with Rex Whistler[2] now. He has no money and a lot of hungry relations. He is however a charming man and would be delightful to live with.

June 19, 1939. West House

On Tuesday morning we had a meeting of four or five Ministers to discuss the terms of the statement the Prime Minister was to make in the afternoon on the subject of the bombing of British ships in Spanish ports. The Prime Minister had changed his mind on the subject and come round to the view which I expressed at the last Cabinet meeting and which he was then unwilling to accept, namely that we are under no obligation to protect these ships once they are in Spanish harbours any more than we are to protect British subjects

---

[1] Dr Theodor Kordt (1893–1962), lawyer and career diplomat. Ambassador to London 1938–9.
[2] Rex Whistler (1905–44), mural painter and book illustrator. His most impressive mural is at Plas Newydd, Anglesey; in his youth he also painted the murals in the Tate Gallery restaurant.

who go into Spain in order to take part in the war.[1] The statement when made went pretty well.

June 26, 1938. West House

This has been a pleasant week. On Monday afternoon I travelled down to Weymouth in the special train with the King and we went on board the *Victoria and Albert*. My cabin in the yacht was most luxurious. We had a dinner party on board each night. I don't find the King easy to talk to but I like him. He is simple and without guile.

July 10, 1938. West House

The main subject of discussion at the Cabinet on Wednesday was whether we should now give financial assistance to China. The sum was £20,000,000 and it was said that that would enable them to continue the war [against Japan] for another year. Halifax was in favour of doing it. Simon stated the objections but sat on the fence. I said that my continual obsession was the possibility of having to fight a war simultaneously against Germany, Italy and Japan. I was not sure that we should win that war. The suggested loan to China would be direct intervention in the Far Eastern War. Was this the moment to do it, when the Czechoslovak question was still unsettled, when our relations with Italy were passing through a period of deterioration and when the new Government in Japan was definitely more moderate than its predecessor and was endeavouring to improve Anglo-Japanese relations? It had been said that our prestige would suffer if the Japs won. But it would suffer much more if we had definitely backed the Chinese and yet the Japs won. Could anybody believe that £20,000,000 was going to make the difference between victory or defeat? The Prime Minister was inclined to take my view. No decision was reached and we are to discuss it again next week.

July 23, 1938

On Wednesday the Prime Minister informed us of Captain Wiedemann's [Hitler's aide] visit, which it had been intended to keep dead secret but which had got out to the Press. He had come direct from Hitler; Ribbentrop had not been informed. The main motive of his mission was to suggest that Anglo-German conversations should be continued – that every possible subject of dissention should be discussed and settled and that Goering[2] should come here to negotiate. The reply of Halifax had been non-committal. It was obvi-

---

[1] The Spanish Civil War, 1936–9, was fought between General Franco's Nationalist troops and the Republican government. Fascist troops supported Franco, the International Brigades aided the Republicans.

[2] Reichsmarschall Hermann Goering (1893–1946), joined the Nazi Party in 1922. In 1933 he became Prussian Minister of the Interior, CIC of the Prussian police and Gestapo and Commissioner for Aviation. In 1935 he was made CIC of the Air Force. After the war he was sentenced to death at Nuremberg, but committed suicide two days later.

ously no good sending an emissary until some approach to agreement had been reached. I pointed out to the Cabinet that it would be very dangerous to let Goering come here as owing to his being such a well-known personality his appearance would probably provoke a violent demonstration of hostility which would certainly do more harm than good. Halifax was going to inform the French Government this week of everything that had taken place.

On the face of it Wiedemann's mission is a good sign. It seems to show that Hitler does not despair of an agreement with England and really wants peace. On the other hand all the information which reaches us from secret and other sources is most alarming. Rumours are rife of all leave being stopped in the German Army, of expert airmen being recalled from Spain, and of many other developments all pointing to the fact that Germany is contemplating war in September. At the same time the Czechoslovak situation shows no sign of improvement. The Czechs are being slow, obstinate and most unhelpful. It may well be that the Wiedemann mission is designed either to throw dust in our eyes or else to improve German propaganda at the outbreak of war as showing how Germany to the last moment was anxious for peace and how it was only the failure of any response from England to these well intended overtures that precipitated the catastrophe.

July 31, 1938. Firle Place [home of Viscount Gage]

My interview with the Chancellor on Monday was satisfactory. I expected he would try to beat me down to accepting a round sum of £400 million for the next three years. My people thought they could just do with 405m but I succeeded in getting 410. The Controller and the others were very pleased.

In August 1938 Duff and Diana made an official cruise in the Baltic on the Admiralty yacht Enchantress. *Liz Paget and Brendan Bracken were also on board.*

August 5, 1938

I woke soon after 5 a.m. and saw the pilot coming on board from the Elbe lightship. Went back to bed for an hour and a half and got up again in time to see the firing of the salute to Germany. Breakfast about 8 – and soon afterwards we entered the Kiel Canal. The passage through the Canal, which took about seven hours, was very pleasant and different from what I had expected. Pretty green fields on each side and cattle feeding right down to the banks. It all looked very fertile and prosperous.

August 6, 1938

We left the ship a little before ten and drove in the motor cars to the house of Admiral [Conrad] Albrecht. There a lot of introductions took place and we went on board his yacht and sailed out to Laboe, where stands the naval war memorial. It was ugly but impressive. I was provided with an enormous wreath which two sailors carried in front of me. The admiral walked on one side of me and another official on the other. Dead marches were played the while. Diana said that I looked exactly as though I were going to execution. On our voyage back we visited the *Grille*, Hitler's new yacht. She is a fine boat – the interior decorations are simple and in rather good modern taste. He makes hardly any use of her but is due to pay her a visit on August 22.

We enjoyed a little peace until dinner. We had a discussion beforehand about toasts. They had had none at luncheon but I thought we had better do so and I drank *auf den Führer und Reichskanzler* – Admiral Albrecht gave the King. I think they enjoyed the evening and with the aid of plenty of champagne it passed off pleasantly enough.

August 7, 1938

The superficial impression produced by such a short visit to Germany was one of a prosperous and contented country. The standard of living may be low, but there are no signs of poverty. All the sailors we saw looked well-fed, smart and happy. They never failed to salute, but there seemed little trace of that old inhuman Prussian discipline which according to all accounts exists no longer. It is a sad and fearful thought that we may have to fight again these admirable people. Admirable but for me not likeable – for I never find them sympathetic.

August 8, 1938. Gdynia

At 8.15 we all went out to dine with Colonel Beck.[1] I sat between the wife of his *Chef de Cabinet* and the wife of the liaison officer – a pretty Dutch woman. The dinner was good and there was plenty to drink. I think Beck had more than his share for during an interminable conversation that I had with him afterwards I found him difficult to follow, tedious and very repetitive. The gist of what he said was that the Baltic States were as one – that all they desired was to be left alone, that he believed that their policy coincided with that of England and that he was most anxious that I should convey all this important information to my colleagues.

August 10, 1938

We sailed at 8 and anchored soon after 9 outside Danzig. I went ashore in the barge and called first on Greiser,[2] the President of the Senate, and then on Burckhardt,[3] the High Commissioner. The two visits provided a striking contrast. At Greiser's – he was the man who cocked a snook at the League of

---

[1] Colonel Josef Beck (1894–1944), Prime Minister of Poland 1932–9.

[2] Arthur Greiser (1897–1946), Nazi President of the Senate in Danzig, later Governor of Warthegau, Poland. He was responsible for the murder of 100,000 Jews and in 1946 was sentenced to death and executed.

[3] Carl Burckhardt (1891–1974), League of Nations High Commissioner 1937–9, historian, biographer and essayist. He was Swiss Minister to France after the war.

Nations – I was received with much clicking of heels and Nazi salutes. Conversation took place at a long table where four or five sat in order of rank and a photographer walked round. We talked German and had nothing to say. Burckhardt on the other hand met me himself in the hall, so that I thought he was the secretary. We sat in a small sitting room and I found his conversation so interesting that I was sorry to leave him when my time was up. Since he has been at Danzig he has become more optimistic for the future than he was at Geneva. He believes that the German regime may gradually grow more reasonable, that the worst elements and personalities may disappear. He told me a great deal about Hitler that was extremely interesting. He speaks beautiful French – not Hitler but Burckhardt – and takes a great deal of trouble about what he says.

August 11, 1938

At half past four George [Gage] and I went out with Greiser and Burckhardt to duck shoot. It was very amusing. The first thing we did on arrival at the rendezvous was to sit down at a prepared table and eat and drink. There were cocktails and whiskey and soda, seven or eight men in uniform to wait on us and an army of keepers. We then drove out in a buggy to our various butts. The scene was a broad marsh – very thick rushes – a lovely evening. We shot for about three-quarters of an hour – I got three duck and a snipe but I'm not sure that any of the duck were gathered. The total bag was eight duck and the snipe. We then went back to the table and resumed eating and drinking. Then the game was all laid out, and the keepers, more numerous considerably than the bag, stood over it and played a tune on their horns. Greiser then made them a short speech, thanking them for their services and telling them what a distinguished guest – *Hohe Gast* – they had had the privilege of entertaining. I bowed and smirked. We then returned to the table and had another drink all round.

August 15, 1938 [Helsingfors, Finland]

We had a dinner party on board and Diana and I thought it the stickiest and heaviest of all the parties we have had or attended. The Prime Minister and his wife impose an intolerable burden and cast an impenetrable gloom. He speaks, when he does, from behind a moustache which entirely conceals his face and he makes no more effort than his wife does to maintain conversation. Diana was quite exhausted at the end of it, but I dare say the Finns enjoyed it in their melancholy way.

August 23, 1938 (Copenhagen)

In the afternoon I had an audience with the King, which was not very exciting. He said he was glad I had come here as they see too much of the Germans and not enough of the English. He seemed fully alive to the German menace. I was with him for only about twenty minutes.

August 28, 1938 (Langeland)

Just before we were going ashore [Lt.-Cdr] Tommy [Thompson][1] brought me a telegram to say that a meeting of Ministers was to take place at Downing Street on Tuesday morning. Hasty calculations showed that we could just get back in time if we went by the Kiel Canal as we had not intended to do, and if there were no delays due to other causes.

August 30, 1938

I woke up on Tuesday morning to find the ship at anchor in the Thames – and learnt that we were nine miles short of Gravesend and that we were held up by fog. I was afraid that after all I should miss the Cabinet meeting. But the fog soon lifted and we arrived in plenty of time.

The emergency Cabinet had been called by Chamberlain following reports that German troops were massing on the Czech frontier. This marked the beginning of the Munich crisis and underlined the disagreements between Duff and Chamberlain. Duff wanted it made clear to Hitler that there would be a European war if he attacked Czechoslovakia, Chamberlain did not want to make any threats that he believed could not be put into action – and he had public opinion behind him.

Halifax described the situation. He spoke for over half an hour. He said that there were two alternative suppositions. Either Hitler was determined on war, in which case there was nothing to be done except to prepare for it, or else he had not yet made up his mind. If this were the case we could either tell him now that if he invaded Czechoslovakia we should declare war, or else we could continue to keep him guessing. Halifax himself was in favour of the latter policy and made out a very good case for it.

I said that in my opinion the great danger was that Hitler might think he could get away with a lightning attack which would give him the Sudeten territories before France or England had had time to move. He would then stop – declare for peace and give good terms to the Czechs. I said that if such a policy were to come off it would be disastrous from the point of view of the future of Europe. All the smaller Powers would give up hope and would immediately make the best terms they could with Germany. England would be humiliated and the Government would be very hard hit. However I did not believe that that policy would succeed because I thought the French would come in as soon as the Germans crossed the Czech frontier. That would mean a European war. I said that confusion often arose owing to the fact that people argued whether we should or should not fight for Czechoslovakia. Nobody wanted to fight for Czechoslovakia. But that was not the issue. The issue was

---

[1] Lt.-Cdr. C. R. (Tommy) Thompson was a Flag Lieutenant on the *Enchantress*. He later joined Winston Churchill's staff and was responsible for arranging the Prime Minister's journeys at home and abroad.

could we or could we not keep out of a European war in which France was engaged? I was convinced that we could not. I didn't think that we ought to tell Hitler that if he crossed the frontier we should declare war. That would be too crude a method of procedure. We had no mandate to make such a statement and a direct threat to a man of his temperament might have the opposite effect to that intended. I therefore agreed to the policy of keeping him guessing, but I thought we should do everything in our power to make sure that he guessed right, by which I meant that he should come to the conclusion that Great Britain would come in if there were war. I suggested that we might take some action to show which way our minds were moving such as bringing the crews of our ships up to full complement which would amount to semi-mobilization. The Prime Minister was against such action. He described it as a policy of pinpricking which would not really serve any useful purpose and was only likely to irritate. There was a good deal of support for my views from Buck De la Warr, Walter Elliot,[1] Oliver Stanley and Eddie Winterton. Nevile Henderson attended the Cabinet. What he had to say was not – I thought – at all impressive.

August 31, 1938

We had a meeting of Service Ministers with their principal advisers under the chairmanship of Tom Inskip this morning. We discussed our preparations for war and whether there was anything more we could do. So far as the Navy was concerned we decided to hurry up the return of the *Repulse* and to send the *Hood* to Gibraltar instead of the Eastern Mediterranean as had previously been arranged. There is nothing more that we can do short of bringing the crews up to full complement which would be a form of semi mobilization and would of course attract a great deal of attention.

September 2, 1938

The question that has been principally occupying Backhouse[2] and me is the potential threat to our fleet caused by the German naval manoeuvres in the North Sea – and as the result of it we have determined to send the Fleet up to the north by the westerly rather than the easterly route. I completed today a paper depicting the present naval situation, which is as bad as it could be, five of our fifteen capital ships being out of action. I go on to describe the action which we have already taken to increase our preparedness, action which was limited by the Cabinet's decision that we were to do nothing which would attract public attention, and I conclude by saying what further steps could be taken:

1) Equipping 7th Destroyer Flotilla.

---

[1] Walter Elliot (1888–1958), Minister of Health 1938–40.
[2] Adm. Sir Roger Backhouse (1878–1939), Third Sea Lord and Controller of the Navy 1928–32; CIC Home Fleet 1935–Apr. 1938; First Sea Lord and Chief of Naval Staff, 1938–9.

2) Bringing crews of minesweepers up to full strength.

3) Ditto minelayers.

4) Ditto the whole fleet.

5) General mobilization.

On Sunday night Euan and I travelled up to Drumlanrig – and there I stayed for three days – grouse driving every day. I enjoyed it enormously. I am nowhere quite so happy as on the hill. I shot badly but not too badly.

September 9, 1938

Backhouse came into my room just before luncheon to tell me that he had just learnt that the latest secret service reports indicated that the Germans were definitely moving troops in the direction of Czechoslovakia. This was serious news but there seemed to be no action that we could take upon it. It was indeed to have been expected that such a move would have been made earlier.

Markham[1] telephoned from the Admiralty to say that just after I had gone [to Plas Newydd] the Prime Minister had wanted to see me and had seen instead the First Sea Lord and it had been decided to take steps 2 and 3 referred to above and to give them full publicity. I was annoyed not to have been there and don't understand why step No. 1 was not taken too.

September 11, 1938. Plas Newydd

I went for a walk with Marjorie in the afternoon and discussed poor Liz's problems. Marjorie, who is so brilliantly clever, is curiously stupid and inhuman about it. She is afraid to discuss it with Liz, and Liz is equally horrified at the idea of discussing it with her. And Liz feels, I think, that the whole world is against her and Raimund. Even Caroline and Rex now share my view that it would be a great mistake for them to marry. And so Liz feels that Raimund has given up everything for her and I'm afraid that she may run off and marry him as soon as his divorce is through, which I am told may be in a fortnight. I urged Marjorie to take a kinder line towards Liz and agree to her seeing as much of Raimund as she liked provided she would give a definite promise that she wouldn't marry him for a year. I don't think that my advice made much impression.

September 12, 1938. London

There were a lot of Foreign Office telegrams to read, including one admirable one instructing Henderson to make it quite plain to the German Government where we should stand in the event of war. In reply to this there was a series of messages from Henderson which seemed to me to be almost hysterical, imploring the Government not to insist upon his carrying out these instruc-

---

[1] Sir Henry Markham (1897–1946), Duff's Private Secretary at the Admiralty.

tions which he was sure would have the opposite effect to that desired. And the Government had given way. By the Government now is meant the P.M., Simon, Halifax and Sam Hoare.

The Cabinet met at 11. Halifax gave us a resumé of events. I spoke up and said that on all sides we had been advised to do the same thing – to make plain to Germany that we should fight. This advice came from the press, almost unanimous on Sunday, from the Opposition, from Winston, from the French Government, from the US Government and even from the Vatican – this advice, supported by such an overwhelming weight of opinion, we were rejecting on the counter-advice of one man, the hysterical Henderson. The P.M., who hates any opposition, replied rather tartly that it wasn't one man but the result of one man's contacts with many others. He was on the spot and must know more about it than the Vatican. Besides it was not a question of never taking the action suggested but only of not taking it now when Hitler's speech was still in the making, and when it might produce the opposite effect of that desired and drive him to making a violent speech instead of a conciliatory one. I said that I expected he would make a conciliatory one as, according to all our information his plans for war will not be ripe for at least ten days, but that I did hope that after the conciliatory speech, if he made it, we should reconsider the desirability of taking some action on the lines suggested. Oliver, Buck and Eddie Winterton put in rather feeble oars on the same side.

At 6.30 Winston came to see me and I got Backhouse in to meet him. We had an interesting talk on naval preparations. Winston was in excellent form, but very critical of the Government for not pursuing the policy which I have been urging.

I dined with Oliver at Buck's. Anthony Winn[1] came in after we had finished dinner. He is working on *The Times*. He told us that *The Times* are starting tomorrow morning a correspondence on the desirability of the Czechs handing over the whole of the Sudeten territory to Germany. Nothing more mischievous at the moment could be imagined. Oliver and I took so serious a view of it that we rang up Downing Street, and told the Private Secretary what we had heard. He rang me back after about 20 minutes and told me that Edward Halifax had taken the same view of it as we had, that he had immediately got on to Geoffrey Dawson and had spoken to him very strongly. But it was too late to stop the edition and Dawson had promised to do his best to 'bottle up' the correspondence whatever that may mean.

---

[1] The Hon. Anthony Winn, the *Times* lobby correspondent during the Munich crisis. He resigned his position when his story on Duff's resignation was suppressed by his editor. Killed in action 1940.

September 13, 1938

Hitler's speech[1] last night committed him to nothing, but was violent in tone and calculated to give trouble. I came to the conclusion today that it would be a wise move to mobilize the Fleet. The time I felt was past for messages or words. The sands were running out. Facts were needed to convince both Hitler and the German people of our intention to fight if war was inevitable. From secret service sources we learnt this morning that all German embassies and legations had been informed that Hitler intended to invade Czecho-slovakia on September 25th.

At 6 o'clock there was a meeting of Service Ministers and Chiefs of Staff at 10 Downing Street. We had each prepared statements of the further steps that could be taken to increase our war readiness. When the Prime Minister asked me to introduce the Admiralty statement I began by saying that while I realized that the meeting was not qualified to give authority for such action I felt bound to propose that the Fleet should be mobilized. I said that while this step could be justified on grounds of national security, it was not on those grounds primarily that I put it forward, but because I believed that it would have an effect, which nothing else now could produce, upon the mind and imagination of Hitler and of Germany.

I thought at the time that both the Prime Minister and Halifax were rather impressed. Neither of them said a word against it. Only Hore-Belisha said he thought it would have the opposite effect to that intended – that it would exasperate Hitler and drive him to extremities. The Prime Minister said we could discuss it at the Cabinet on the following day. I asked Halifax whether we could afford to wait so long – whether the situation was not so critical as to justify calling the Cabinet together the same night. Halifax hesitated long before replying to my question – and finally said that he thought we could wait.

September 14, 1938. Cabinet at 11 a.m.

The Prime Minister opened proceedings and spoke for 50 minutes, gradually revealing to us his intention of paying a personal visit to Hitler. We were being told, not consulted, for the telegrams had already gone off. Approval was unanimous and enthusiastic. I said that the danger I foresaw was that we might strengthen the case of the Germans, if they accepted the plan that we proposed and the Czechs didn't, and we might be represented as having betrayed and deserted the Czechs. Eddie Winterton made a foolish and very rhetorical intervention to the effect that we ought to realize that we were being driven to this policy by our own shameful neglect of our defences and our fear of the German Air Force. I said that that was nonsense – that we were adopting this policy owing to our determination to avoid war at almost any

---

[1] Hitler had demanded self-determination for the Sudetens and promised them assistance.

price. That so far from having unduly neglected our defences, I personally was quite confident that if it came to war we should win the war. It was on the whole a singularly unanimous Cabinet.

Diana telephoned from Geneva. She had been sitting next to De Valera[1] when Euan who had been host at the dinner – a British Empire dinner – had made the announcement. De Valera had been the first to break the silence that followed – and he had said 'this [*Chamberlain's proposed visit to Hitler at Berchtesgaden*] is the greatest thing that has ever been done'.

September 17, 1938

A beautiful misty autumn morning. I had plenty of time to read telegrams and papers at the Admiralty before going to Cabinet at 11.00. The Prime Minister told us the story of his visit to Berchtesgaden. Looking back upon what he said, the curious thing seems to me now to have been that he recounted his experiences with some satisfaction.[2] Although he said that at first sight Hitler struck him as 'the commonest looking little dog' he had ever seen without one sign of distinction, nevertheless he was obviously pleased at the reports he had subsequently received of the good impression that he had made. He told us with obvious satisfaction how Hitler had said to someone that he had felt that he – Chamberlain – was 'a man'. But the bare facts of the interview were frightful. None of the elaborate schemes that we had discussed in Cabinet and which the Prime Minister had intended to put forward had ever been mentioned. He had felt that the atmosphere did not allow of it. After ranting and raving at him, Hitler had talked about self-determination and asked the P.M. whether he accepted the principle. The P.M. had replied that he must consult his colleagues. From beginning to end Hitler had shown not the slightest sign of yielding on a single point. The P.M. seemed to expect us all to accept that principle without further discussion because the time was getting on. The French, we heard, were getting restive. Not a word had yet been said to them since the P.M. left England, and one of the dangers against which I had warned the Cabinet seemed to be materializing – namely trouble with the French. I said and others agreed with me that we must have further time for discussion, and that it would be better to take no decision until discussions with the French had taken place, lest they should be in a position to say that we had sold the pass without even consulting them.

We met again at 3. The Lord Chancellor opened the ball and was, as I expected him to be, deplorable. He said that according to the principles of Canning and Disraeli, Great Britain should never intervene unless her own

---

[1] Eamon de Valera (1882–1975), Irish politician and statesman. Prime Minister of the Republic of Ireland 1921–48, 1951–4, and 1957–9. In 1938 he was President of the Assembly of the League of Nations.

[2] Chamberlain had accepted in principle that the Sudetens should have self-determination and that non-Czech areas be seceded. Hitler agreed not to use force.

interests were directly affected, and unless she could do so with overwhelming force.

I followed him and said that the main interest of this country had always been to prevent any one power from obtaining undue predominance in Europe. That we were now faced with probably the most formidable power that had ever dominated Europe and resistance to that Power was quite obviously a British interest. As for 'overwhelming force' it was quite true that we hadn't got it but it was also true that we had no means of acquiring it. So if we held to the Lord Chancellor's doctrine of defeatism it meant that we could never intervene again – that we were, in fact, finished. I said that if I thought surrender would bring lasting peace I should be in favour of surrender but that I did not believe there would ever be peace in Europe so long as Nazism ruled in Germany. The next act of aggression might be one that it would be far harder for us to resist. Supposing it were an attack on one of our colonies. We shouldn't have a friend in Europe to assist us, nor even the sympathy of the United States which was ours today. We certainly shouldn't catch up the Germans in rearmament. On the contrary they would increase their lead. However, despite all the arguments in favour of taking a strong stand now which would almost certainly lead to war, I was so impressed by the fearful responsibility of incurring a war that might possibly be avoided that I thought it worth while to postpone it, in the very faint hope that some internal event might bring about the fall of the Nazi regime. But there were limits to the humiliation I was prepared to accept. If Hitler was willing to agree to a plebiscite being carried out under fair conditions with international control I thought we could agree to it and insist upon the Czechs accepting it. At present we had no indication that Hitler was prepared to go so far.

No conclusion was recorded and we separated at about 5.40.

September 19, 1938

Some of the papers this morning contained statements as to the terms which the French and British Ministers in consultation yesterday decided should be offered to the Czechs. They amount in substance to the cession of the Sudeten territories in return for a guarantee by England and France of the remainder [of Czechoslovakia's borders].

The Cabinet met at 11 and we learnt that the reports which had reached the press from the French were substantially correct. The Prime Minister described at length the negotiations of the previous day which had lasted until midnight. The Lord Chancellor [Lord Maugham], who is my *bête noire* in the Cabinet, dithered at the thought of the guarantee, and Hailsham,[1] who is just as great a coward, supported him. Hore-Belisha was also violently against it on rather different lines. He said that by giving away the frontier as suggested

---

[1] Douglas Hogg (see footnote for 1 Jan. 1924) had been made Lord Hailsham in 1928; Lord President of the Council Mar.–Oct. 1938.

we left Czechoslovakia indefensible, which is doubtless true. I said that we couldn't possibly go back now upon what had been agreed yesterday. The French Ministers were at that very moment urging these proposals on their colleagues and we could imagine what their feelings would be if they were now told that these proposals no longer held the field. Oliver said that he accepted them with great reluctance and that he would have preferred to have adopted a different line from the first. The Prime Minister challenged Oliver to say what the policy was that he would have preferred, which put him in rather a difficult position. I said that I thought the difference was one of emphasis rather than of opinion. Some of us were thinking most about the preservation of peace, others of us were thinking more of how far we could go in the direction of humiliating surrender – but we were all agreed in wanting to avoid war and avoid humiliation.

September 20, 1938

Every morning one wakes with a feeling of sickening anxiety which gradually gives way to the excitements of the day. In the afternoon I went round to the Stanleys. Oliver and I feel strongly that there ought to be another Cabinet meeting before the Prime Minister goes back to Germany. He must insist when he sees Hitler on some minimum concessions – such as an international commission, demobilization etc.

September 21, 1938

There was a Cabinet at 3 o'clock this afternoon. On the questions of the Polish and Hungarian minorities [in Czechoslovakia] the Prime Minister reminded us that Hitler had said at their first interview that he was not interested in them; that his sole concern was with the Germans. If at their next interview Hitler took a different line, the P.M. said quite firmly that he would refuse to discuss the question but would say that he must return to consult his colleagues. There was a good deal of talk about the guarantee – who should be parties to it and whether it should be joint or several. Then came the question of *modus operandi*. The Prime Minister said he thought that Hitler would want to march his troops in at once in order to occupy the districts where there was an overwhelming German majority. Oliver said that there must be a decent interval in order to enable those who wanted to leave to do so. He couldn't abandon the Czechs and still more the German Social Democrats etc. to the tender mercies of the Nazis. I said that I had no doubt that if once we agreed to German troops marching in before the frontier had been fixed they would not stop until they had overrun the whole of Czechoslovakia. They would very easily find an excuse to do so, as they would always be having trouble on the outskirts of the occupied territory. I then said that in my opinion we had reached the limit. Not a shadow of a concession nor a word of good will had we received in return. I hoped that when the Prime Minister saw Hitler tomorrow he would say to him that he had done all and more than he had undertaken, that he was bringing him Czechoslovakia's head on a charger – that he had incurred in order to do this charges of surrender, betrayal and cowardice. Further he could not go. He would prefer, if it were necessary, to go to war. He would do so with the country solid behind him – and with all the sympathy and probably later with the assistance of the United States.

I think that what I said produced an effect. Nobody controverted it. Sam Hoare, to my great surprise, whispered to me that he had said just the same to the Prime Minister this morning. And later he told me that he was convinced as I was that there was a point beyond which we couldn't go. The P.M. so he said was equally convinced. This is satisfactory.

September 22, 1938

When I got back to the Admiralty and read the Foreign Office telegrams I found one that had been sent off after yesterday's Cabinet meeting which seemed to envisage our agreeing to the early occupation of Czechoslovakia by German troops. As this was just the point that I had most strongly objected to in Cabinet, and as nobody had differed from the view I expressed, I immediately wrote to Edward Halifax saying that I thought I ought to make it plain that I could never consent to such procedure.

I lunched at home. We had hardly sat down before Markham came along with Halifax's reply to my letter. He said that he entirely agreed with me. That he had no intention of allowing German troops to enter Czechoslovakia except with the consent of the Czechoslovak Government. This so far as it went was satisfactory.

Winston came to see me in the afternoon. He was in a state of great excitement and violent in his denunciation of the Prime Minister. I explained the situation to him as I saw it and encouraged him to hope for war which was what he wanted.

September 23, 1938

I had a letter from Edward Halifax this morning explaining away last night's meeting. It appears now that the breach has occurred as was to be expected over the question of the immediate occupation of Czechoslovakia by German troops. This is one point, the other is the delimitation of the frontier. Hitler has shown the Prime Minister the line that he proposes which is, of course, in advance of what we had considered would be fair. He has offered after a certain period of months to hold a plebiscite in the more advanced doubtful districts under international control. The Prime Minister has said that he is prepared to put the question of the frontier line to the Czech Government, but that he is not prepared to consent to the German troops marching in forthwith.

At 4 I went to see John Simon at his request. Walter Elliot and Kingsley Wood were there and we were joined later by Oliver, John Colville and Hailsham. Simon seemed to me to be in a robust mood – quite prepared for the fray. He and Halifax had removed the ban on Czech mobilization in spite of a rather feeble protest from the Prime Minister at Godesberg.

During the afternoon Simon and Halifax sent a telegram to the P.M. asking for his authority to get on with all preparations including mobilization. Before dinner I took it upon myself to authorize the recalling of men from leave, the bringing of all crews up to full complement, the dispatch of 1900 men to the Mediterranean to bring that fleet up to establishment and to man the Suez Canal defences – and also one or two minor measures.

September 24, 1938

The Prime Minister left Godesberg early and was due in London about noon. The text of the German ultimatum to Czechoslovakia has arrived. It is couched in the most violent terms and the conditions are such as could only be imposed on a people defeated after a long war.

At 5.30 the Cabinet met. The Prime Minister looked none the worse for his experiences. He spoke for over an hour. What he said amounted to the fact that Hitler had adopted a certain position from the start and had refused to budge an inch from it. Many of the most important points seem hardly to have arisen during their discussion – notably the international guarantee. Having said that he had informed Hitler that he was creating an impossible situation, having said that he 'snorted' with indignation when he read the German terms, the Prime Minister concluded to my astonishment, by saying that he considered that we should accept those terms and that we should advise the Czechs to do so.

It then appeared that the terms had not been circulated to all the members of the Cabinet, and it was therefore suggested that the Cabinet should adjourn in order to give members time to read them and sleep on them and that we should meet again the following morning. I protested against this. I said that from what the Prime Minister had told us it appeared to me that the Germans were still convinced that under no circumstances would we fight, that there still existed one method and one method only of persuading them to the contrary and that was by instantly declaring full mobilization. I said that I was sure popular opinion would eventually compel us to go to the assistance of the Czechs. That hitherto we had been faced with the unpleasant alternatives of peace with dishonour or war. I now saw a third possibility, namely war with dishonour, by which I meant being kicked into war by the boot of public opinion, when those for whom we were fighting had already been defeated.

Hore-Belisha spoke in favour of mobilization and Eddie Winterton did the same. Oliver supported me as also did Buck and Walter. What was more interesting was that nobody else committed himself. Neither Simon nor Sam Hoare said a word. I pointed out that the Chiefs of Staff had reported yesterday that immediate mobilization was of urgent and vital importance, and I suggested that we might some day have to explain why we had disregarded their advice. This angered the Prime Minister. He said that I had omitted to mention that this advice was given only on the assumption that there was a danger of war with Germany within the next few days. I said I thought it would be difficult to deny that any such danger existed.

I finally suggested that we should approach the Egyptian Government with a view to putting into force the precautionary period with regard to the protection of the Suez Canal. I said that I didn't think anybody could have any objection to the preliminary steps being taken to protect one of the most vital and vulnerable points in the Empire. The P.M., who was now in a thoroughly bad temper so far as I was concerned, said that he did object very strongly – and that he saw no reason why we should take such a step at present.

Personally I believe that Hitler has cast a spell over Neville. After all Hitler's achievement is not due to his intellectual attainments nor to his oratorical powers but to the extraordinary influence which he seems able to exercise over his fellow creatures. I believe that Neville is under that influence at the present time. 'It all depends' he said 'on whether we can trust Hitler.' 'Trust him for what?' I asked. 'He has got everything he wants for the present and he has given no promises for the future.' Neville also said that he had been told and he believed it that he had made a very favourable impression himself on Hitler and that he believed he might be able to exercise a useful influence over him.

A bad night.

Sunday September 25, 1938

The Cabinet met at 10.30. One of the first points that I raised was that of the guarantee, but we didn't get very far with it – and then each member of the Cabinet in turn proceeded to state his views. Halifax spoke first – in a low voice and with great emotion. He said that hitherto his views had been entirely in accordance with those of the Prime Minister, but that now he was afraid there was some divergence between them. Then after explaining how in the watches of the night he had gradually come to change his mind, he stated that he thought we could not advise the Czechs to accept the ultimatum and that if France went to their help he thought that we should go to the help of France. This came as a great surprise to those who think as I do. Our next unexpected ally was Hailsham. He produced an article which he had cut from the *Daily Telegraph* and which expounded with chapter and verse the numerous previous occasions on which Hitler had made firm promises which he had always broken. Therefore Hailsham came reluctantly to the conclusion that we must stand by the Czechs and the French.

A message was brought in that Masaryk[1] wished to see the Prime Minister this afternoon. I said there was one question that obviously he would ask – 'If

---

[1] Jan Masaryk (1886–1948), Czech Ambassador to London 1924–39. In 1941 he became Foreign Minister in the Czech Provisional Government in London and after 1945 in Czechoslovakia. He was found dead in 1948 after the Communist takeover, having either committed suicide or been killed by the Communists.

we reject Hitler's ultimatum, will England support us?' and that we ought to make up our mind what the answer was to be to that question before we left the room. I said that I had consented to the Berchtesgaden terms, because I thought it might postpone war, but that that argument no longer influenced me in face of the Godesberg terms because I thought that if we accepted them we should be swept out of office and that the country would go to war under worse leaders. I said that the issue now was not self-determination nor the manner in which it should be carried, but so far as we were concerned it was the honour and soul of England that was at stake. Those who were in favour of accepting the ultimatum, besides the Prime Minister and Stanhope, were the Lord Chancellor, Kingsley Wood, Tom Inskip, Zetland, Simon, Burgin, Morrison and Ernie Brown.[1]

When everybody had spoken Neville summed up – said that while there were differences of opinion between us we must try not to exaggerate them, that it would be a great mistake to show weakness at the centre at the present time. He was going to see the Czech Minister that afternoon and the two French Ministers would be received by him and some of his colleagues later. By 'some of his colleagues' he means the Big Four – himself, Sam [Hoare], Simon and Halifax. I said that this arrangement was very unsatisfactory. The discussion had lasted for over five hours and had disclosed deep division of opinion. The section that thought as I did was not represented at all on the body that was to interview the French Ministers, and we were not satisfied that the views which we held were fairly stated on these occasions. We had reached no conclusion on the important issue to which I had referred before, namely what was to be said to the French. The Prime Minister had said that we must not show weakness at the centre – but it was better to show it than to be paralysed by it which was what was now happening. I therefore felt that it was better that I should go because my continual presence in the Cabinet was only a source of delay and annoyance to those who thought differently from me. The Prime Minister said he had been expecting me to suggest doing so but he must ask me not to take any precipitate action. I agreed not to. Oliver suggested that the Big Four should have two interviews with the French and that the Cabinet should meet between those interviews. To this the Prime Minister agreed.

At 11.30 we were sent for to go back to Downing Street. We were told that the French had been very evasive, but according to his [the PM's] own account they hadn't been nearly so evasive as he had. I practically said as much and made myself pretty offensive. The French had at least said that if Czecho-slovakia were attacked they would 'fulfil their obligations', but they had not

---

[1] Earl Stanhope (1880–1967), President of the Board of Education; Lawrence Dundas, 2nd Marquess of Zetland (1876–1961), Secretary of State for India; William (Shakespeare or 'Shakes') Morrison (1893–1961), Minister of Agriculture (later 1st Viscount Dunrossil), and Ernest Brown (1881–1962), Minister of Labour.

apparently said in so many words that they would go to war, nor could I discover that they had been pressed to do so. However at the end the Prime Minister said that he proposed to make a final effort. He was sending Horace Wilson[1] to Hitler tomorrow with a personal letter appealing to him to allow the details of the transfer of territory to be settled by an international body of Germans, Czechs and English. If he refused this appeal, Horace Wilson was to tell him that France would fight for Czechoslovakia and that we should fight on the same side. The Prime Minister made this announcement almost casually and I could hardly believe my ears. It was after all a complete reversal of what [he] himself had advised us to do the day before. And it was a reversal of the policy which a majority of the Cabinet had supported. I had to ask him to repeat it for I thought I had misunderstood it. None of the 'yes men' who had supported his policy all day said a word in criticism of its reversal. Oliver observed rather acidly that apparently we were to tell the Germans that the French would fight, although we had just heard that the French themselves refused to say as much. However, there it was. The Prime Minister looked, for the first time, absolutely worn out, and I felt very sorry for him.

September 26, 1938

We had a Cabinet meeting at 12 this morning. The French Ministers were just leaving and I had a word with Daladier [French Prime Minister]. I asked him if he was satisfied and he said yes, that everything was very satisfactory. The P.M. told us that the French had been quite definite this morning that they would fight, and that we had quite definitely assured them that we would support them. It was odd to notice that not a murmur of protest came from any of those who had yesterday advocated a different policy. I felt it incumbent upon me in view of what I had said yesterday about resigning to state that I was in entire agreement with the policy now adopted. I added that if in our recent meetings I had expressed my opinions too frequently and too forcibly and had thereby added to the Prime Minister's heavy burden, I was very sorry.

September 27, 1938

When I got back from luncheon there was a telegram from Henderson, saying that he had seen Goering the previous evening. Goering had been 'absolutely confident'. It had been quite obvious from his conversation and from one that he had had with General Bodenschatz 'that the die is cast, that British mediation is at an end and that if delegates do not arrive at Berlin with full authority to make the best terms they can on their own with the Germans before 2 p.m.,

---

[1] Sir Horace Wilson (1882–1972), an influential senior civil servant, was an *éminence grise* to Chamberlain, who relied greatly on his advice; but he knew little about defence or foreign affairs. In 1939 he was made Permanent Under-Secretary to the Treasury and Head of the Civil Service.

tomorrow general mobilization will be ordered at that hour and occupation of Sudeten territory will begin immediately'.

Henderson's own incredible comment on this is 'If His Majesty's Government do not at this eleventh hour advise the Czechs in the name of humanity and of the Czechs themselves ... to make the best terms they can with Berlin we shall be exposing Czechoslovakia to the same fate as Abyssinia'.

Having read this telegram I sent a message to the Prime Minister saying that in my opinion we should mobilize immediately – that I could see no justification for delay. Later I heard that the Chiefs of Staff were with the Prime Minister and later still I learnt from Backhouse that it had at last been decided to mobilize the Fleet. The Prime Minister would announce it this evening in his broadcast speech; meanwhile he wished no action to be taken which would give it publicity. This at least is satisfactory.

At 8 p.m. we listened in to the Prime Minister's broadcast. It was a most depressing utterance. There was no mention of France in it nor a word of sympathy for Czechoslovakia. The only sympathy expressed was for Hitler whose feeling about the Sudetens the Prime Minister said that he could well understand. And he never said a word about the mobilization of the Fleet. I was furious.

I then got a message to say there was a Cabinet at 9.30. The meeting was opened by the Prime Minister who recounted to us a series of gloomy reports. Horace Wilson told us of his mission to Germany. He had not delivered the important part of his message, namely that to the effect that England and France would fight, at his first interview with Hitler. When he had delivered it on the following day it was so tied up with conditional clauses that it had lost half its force. It was significant that even after he had told Hitler this the latter remarked that he couldn't believe that we should fall out. In Horace Wilson's opinion the only thing to do now was to advise the Czechs to evacuate the territory. He had drawn up a draft telegram containing this advice.

I spoke at once. I thought it important to get my oar in before the Big Four, as once they had spoken I knew that the yes men who are the majority of the Cabinet would agree with them. I said that we had listened to a recital by the Prime Minister of all the gloomiest facts he could collect. Not a word had been said about the brighter side – about President Roosevelt's[1] telegram, and one from the President of Brazil. Not a word about the much better reports that were now coming from France about the hardening of opinion and the temper of the people. Not a word about the similar tendency of world opinion regarding Hitler's ultimatum and his last speech. Our Military Attaché in Berlin was no doubt much under the influence of his Ambassador, who had shown himself a defeatist from the first. As for the Dominions, could we expect that they would ever be all united on the prospect of coming into a

---

[1] Franklin D. Roosevelt (1882–1945), President of the United States 1932–45. Roosevelt wanted to strengthen nations threatened or attacked while preserving American neutrality.

European War? They were not necessary to us for the conduct of a war. We began the last one with S. Africa in a state of revolution. If we now were to desert the Czechs, or even advise them to surrender, we should be guilty of one of the basest betrayals in history. I was bound to say that I had been disappointed that the P.M. in his broadcast had been unable to give them a word of praise or encouragement, and had reserved all his sympathy for Hitler. If we gave way now, I was going to say that it would be the end of England and of democracy – but I didn't really believe that – what I did believe was that it would be the end of this Government and certainly of my connection with it.

Halifax then produced another plan which the Cabinet hadn't seen but which he had sent to Henderson with instructions to submit it to Hitler. Oliver protested strongly against this very important step having been taken without consultation with the Cabinet. John Simon then eagerly denied any responsibility for Horace Wilson's draft telegram and declared that he hadn't even read it. The Prime Minister then also more or less denied responsibility. He said that as this did seem the last chance he had thought it shouldn't be thrown away without the Cabinet having an opportunity of discussing it. That I had expressed my dissent from it very eloquently and that as the Foreign Secretary agreed with me and nobody seemed in favour of it there was no more to be said. So the Cabinet broke up. As I left I said to the P.M. that I apologized for having criticized his speech – but that I had to say what I thought. I added that I had understood that he was going to announce the mobilization of the Fleet in his broadcast. He said he had meant to originally but that later he had decided not to. I said, casually, that there was, I supposed no point in keeping it secret. He agreed. I felt that if I had asked whether I could make a press announcement he might have hesitated; as it was I hurried home, got on to the Press Section in the Admiralty and told them to give it without delay to all the morning papers.

September 28, 1938

Privy Council at 10.30 for the Order-in-Council authorizing mobilization. The King kept me behind after the others had gone and we had half an hour's talk. He was very nice and very cheerful, envisaging the war with great equanimity.

I lunched at Buck's with Diana and the Cranbornes. They are of course boiling with anti-government indignation. I drove down to the House with them. Then there came the Prime Minister's speech. I listened to it in considerable gloom until he came to the end when he announced his latest *démarche* [*the proposal for a four-power conference at Munich*] and its unexpected success. The telegram announcing Hitler's agreement was only handed to him while he was speaking. The scene was remarkable, all Government supporters rising and cheering while the Opposition sat glum and silent. And then, when Attlee gave the plan his blessing our side, all rose again and cheered him – cheers with which the opposition had to join, though looking a little foolish.

Now I believe for the first time that there will not be a war. It seems hardly credible that four men meeting together cannot agree upon the method of handing over certain territories the cession of which has already been decided. I believe also that the mobilization of the Fleet has had something to do with it, because by that action we eventually succeeded in persuading Hitler that we were prepared to fight.

September 29, 1938

I thought I should sleep well last night but I didn't. I woke at 6 and got up at 6.30. We drove down to Heston to see the P.M. off. It was John Simon's idea that the whole Cabinet should turn up as a pleasant surprise for him. It was certainly a surprise. There is a slight sense of anticlimax. We are going on with all our war preparations.

I dined at the Other Club. They already had news to the effect that agreement had been reached at Munich and that the occupation was to begin on the 1st and to be completed on the 10th.[1] I was extremely depressed. It seemed to me that we might as well have accepted the Godesberg ultimatum and have had done with it. It was a fiery dinner. I insulted Prof. Lindemann[2] – Bob Boothby[3] and I insulted Garvin[4] so that he left in a rage. Then everybody insulted everybody else and Winston ended by saying that at the next General Election he would speak on every socialist platform in the country against the Government.

September 30, 1938

The full terms of the Munich agreement are in the paper this morning. At first sight, I felt that I couldn't agree to them. The principle of invasion remains. The German troops are to march in tomorrow and the Czechs are to leave all their installations intact. This means that they will have to hand over all their fortifications, guns etc. upon which they have spent millions, and they will receive no compensation for them. The International Commission will enjoy increased powers, but our representative on it is to be Nevile Henderson who in my opinion has played a sorry part in the whole business and who is violently anti-Czech and pro-German. While I was dressing this morning I decided that I must resign.

---

[1] The agreement stipulated that the Czechs were to evacuate specified areas; an international commission would decide the new frontiers; an international force would occupy the areas under dispute; and England, France, Italy and Germany would guarantee Czechoslovakia's independence.

[2] Frederick Lindemann, 1st Viscount Cherwell (1886–1957). An Oxford physicist, known as 'the Prof', he was Churchill's closest scientific adviser throughout the war.

[3] Robert 'Bob' Boothby (1900–86), knighted 1953 and created a peer as Lord Boothby 1958. Conservative MP 1924–58. Member of pre-war anti-appeasement group in the Commons. After the war one of the leading supporters of a United Europe.

[4] James Garvin (1868–1947), editor of the *Observer* 1908–42.

I motored down with Diana and Rex to lunch with Marjorie and Caroline. It was a beautiful autumn day – and I was in high spirits at the prospect of my new liberty though with many regrets at the thought of what I must forfeit – my work at the Admiralty, Admiralty House, the *Enchantress* etc.

When I got back to the Admiralty I learnt that there was to be a Cabinet at 7. Buck De La Warr came to see me about 6.30. He talked a lot of nonsense. He thinks this is a thoroughly evil Government but believes that we can thwart its intentions more successfully by remaining in it than by going out. I think it's a very good Government and I don't want to thwart it. It is merely a question of how much one can swallow. We went to the Cabinet together and had the greatest difficulty in getting into Downing Street owing to the enormous crowds of cheering people. The Prime Minister arrived at about 20 minutes past 7 amid scenes of indescribable enthusiasm. He spoke to the mob from the window. I felt very lonely in the midst of so much happiness that I could not share.

The Cabinet meeting lasted little more than half an hour. The Prime Minister explained the differences between the Munich and the Godesberg terms – and they are really considerably greater than I had understood. Nevertheless after a few questions had been asked and many congratulations had been offered I felt it my duty to offer my resignation.

I said that not only were the terms not good enough but also that I was alarmed about the future. We must all admit that we should not have gone so far to meet Germany's demands if our defences had been stronger. It had more than once been said in Cabinet that after having turned this corner we must get on more rapidly with rearmament. But how could we do so when the Prime Minister had just informed the crowd that we had peace 'for our time' – and we had entered into an agreement never to go to war with Germany?

The Prime Minister smiled at me in a quite friendly way and said that it was a matter to be settled between him and me. Oliver then made an appeal to me to reconsider my decision. He had agreed with me, he said, throughout but he now felt quite able to support and defend this policy. Leslie Hore-Belisha spoke in the same sense – and so I think did Eddie Winterton, but I cannot be sure. How soon one forgets! Then Sam Hoare intervened rather crossly. He said it was most improper and quite without precedent to discuss personal matters of this sort in Cabinet, and he hoped the discussion would not be prolonged. It was odd that he should have said this considering that last February we spent two days discussing whether Anthony should go or not. I think he said it because he hates me, is anxious to get rid of me and feared that further discussion might lead to my staying on.

Leslie drove me back to Admiralty House and came in. He urged me strongly not to go. I dined alone with Diana and went early to bed – but slept badly.

Duff's resignation to the Prime Minister was published in the evening papers on 1
October. His resignation speech in the House of Commons was on 3 October.

1939

Though Hitler had agreed to join in an international guarantee of Czechoslovakia
he had no intention of doing so. On 15 March 1939 German forces entered Prague,
and Bohemia and Moravia became German protectorates. The German annexation
of Czechoslovakia was followed by the Italian occupation of Albania. On 30 March,
Chamberlain offered to guarantee Poland against attack. This led, in August, to a
formal military alliance. Hitler invaded Poland on 1 September and on 3 September
Chamberlain declared war on Germany.

August 23, 1939

The crisis began on Tuesday, August 22. We had slept the night before in a
caravan at Mells, having gone over there to see the Clovelly Players perform
the *Merchant of Venice.* Everything had been spoilt by a thunderstorm which
put out all the electric light and drenched the open air theatre. It was still
raining when we woke next morning. We decided to drive back to Bognor,
which we had left the day before in cloudless sunshine, as quickly as possible.
We stopped at Conrad's house and he told us that the morning papers contained the news of the German–Soviet [non-aggression] pact. There was hardly
any comment on it in the press, as the news appeared to have arrived too late
for comment to appear in the country editions of the London papers.

We got home in time for luncheon and found the weather there still fine. I
had written an article which was to appear on that day, in which I urged
that the agreement with Russia should be expedited. The *Evening Standard*
telephoned to say that it was now out of date and could I either alter it or write
them another. I spent most of the afternoon writing one in which I criticized
and condemned the failure of the Government.

On Thursday [24 August] the House of Commons met. I went with Anthony
[Eden] to the Savoy where we had luncheon in a private room with Winston,
Archie Sinclair[1] and Duncan Sandys.[2] We were all very gloomy. Archie had

---

[1] Sir Archibald Sinclair, 1st Viscount Thurso (1890–1970). Private Secretary to Churchill at the
War Office and Colonial Office 1919–22. Elected Liberal Member of Parliament 1922. In
1935 became leader of the Opposition Liberals, and was against Chamberlain, Munich and
appeasement. He became Secretary of State for Air under Churchill in 1940.

[2] Duncan Sandys, later Lord Duncan-Sandys (1908–87). He married Churchill's eldest daughter
Diana in 1935 (d. 1960) and the same year was elected a Conservative MP. From 1941 held
various ministerial posts and was a leading proponent of European unity after the war. He
was made a peer in 1974 and became Chairman of Lonrho Ltd.

seen the Prime Minister whom he had found angry – angry with everybody, particularly with Hitler – and also surprised.

Hilary came to luncheon and dinner on Sunday [27 August]. He did not believe there would be war. I wrote an article on the two breeds of Bolshevism, to the effect that there is nothing to choose between the philosophies of Moscow and Berlin.

On Monday [28 August] came the news that the House was to meet on Tuesday and that we were closing the Mediterranean to British shipping. This Monday was the most beautiful day we have had all the summer.

On Tuesday [29 August] I travelled up to London. Diana and Venetia came too. I lunched at Monseigneur with Caroline, Liz and Raimund. We had a gay luncheon. Then to the House of Commons. The Prime Minister's speech lasted only twenty minutes. He told us nothing and one wondered why the House had been summoned. Greenwood[1] urged immediate evacuation. Archie was shorter than either of them. I sat on the terrace with Brendan afterwards. He was just back from America where he had stayed only twenty minutes. We went to his house where Winston was. He seemed gloomy. We travelled back to Bognor by the 5.30. We read Kipling aloud after dinner.

August 31, 1939

Barbie rang up to say she had heard from Euan that evacuation would begin on Saturday. Apparently it was announced on the wireless in the course of the morning. It seems that yesterday's wave of optimism has receded – but there is, in my opinion, no more cause for its recession than there was for its advance. I don't believe that Hitler can get out of this crisis without a war, unless he is let out by the weakness of our Government and the French. I believe that it would be better to have a war now than to let him out and have a war later, when he may have organized and prepared and persuaded Russia to fight for him.

September 3, 1939

It seems already quite a long time since I wrote what is written above. On Friday morning – September 1 – I played golf at Goodwood. I never played worse. I couldn't concentrate because I was thinking of what had happened the night before. We had listened in to the 11 o'clock news and had heard the German 16 points to Poland given out without commentary. I was horrified. And I was the more horrified because Diana hearing them said that they did not seem to her unreasonable. I tried to explain how they meant the end of Poland, but I felt that the reactions of millions of people might well be the

---

[1] Arthur Greenwood (1880–1954), Labour MP, elected Deputy Leader in 1935.

same as those of Diana. I rang up Winston – who said that he felt exactly as I did, but that he had already spoken to the *Daily Mail* who were inclined to take a favourable view of the German proposals. I then got on to Camrose[1] who also agreed with me. He was awaiting some guidance from the Foreign Office as to what the Press was to say, but had received none hitherto. I urged that the *Daily Telegraph* should come out with a strong leading article condemning the terms.

When we finished our round of golf we went into the club house for a drink. Two men sitting at the bar were discussing future race meetings. One of the two, the club secretary, I knew slightly. As we left he said to me 'Hitler started on Poland this morning'. I asked him what he meant. He said that the Germans had invaded Poland and bombed several cities. He took it quite calmly. That was how I heard that the war had started. The news came to me as a relief. When we got back there was a message to say that the House of Commons was meeting at 6 o'clock. We had an excellent luncheon of lobster and cold grouse – Montrachet 1924 and Château Yquem 1921. I think we were all in pretty good spirits except Diana, who, poor darling, cannot face the war at all. I went to the House of Commons. I thought the Prime Minister's speech was unimpressive and I thought that neither Greenwood nor Archie rose to the occasion.

Diana and I dined with Winston, George Lloyd and Diana and Duncan Sandys at the Savoy Grill. Winston confided to Diana that he had been asked to join the War Cabinet, and told her to tell me to wait patiently as he would not fail me. Winston left at 9.30 to go and see the Prime Minister. After he had gone George Lloyd told me that Winston had also assured him that he meant to get me in. But I'm not at all sure that I want to go in under the present Prime Minister.

When we went out into the streets we found them quite dark and no taxi available. Bendor [2nd Duke of Westminster] came along in a Rolls Royce and gave us a lift to Victoria. As we went he inveighed against the Jews, rejoiced to think we were not at war yet and said that after all Hitler knew that we were his best friends. I said that I hoped he would soon find out that we were his most implacable and remorseless enemies.

I had plenty to do the next morning [September 2] – dealing with correspondence and completing an article that I had partly written coming up in the train. I went to White's before lunch. Tommy MacDougal [an old friend of Duff's] who was there said 'I can't understand why the Duke of Westminster says that the war is caused by the Jews and Duff Cooper'.

We lunched at Monseigneur with Liz and Raimund. What took place in the House of Commons that afternoon is history. The feeling when the Prime Minister made his statement was astonishing. Anthony was sitting between

[1] William Berry, 1st Viscount Camrose (1879–1951). Newspaper proprietor and owner of the *Daily Telegraph*.

Amery[1] and me. Many of those sitting in front of us turned round and urged him to speak. Old Wardlaw-Milne who was sitting on the other side of me was feeling as strongly as anybody. He is a very loyal supporter of the Government. I thought it would be much better if he spoke than if any of us did – and I urged him to do so. He did and it carried great weight. The whole thing was over in half an hour. I have never felt so moved.

I went back to pick up Diana at Chapel St.[2] and we went to the Savoy Grill. I felt that I could eat nothing – but dealt very successfully with a cold grouse. Euan left a message for me to say that I must keep my hair on – that the announcement had taken the whole Cabinet by surprise and that they had insisted on holding another Cabinet meeting that night.

At about 10.30 I went round to Winston's flat, which he had asked me to do. Clemmie was there when I arrived, but she did not stay throughout the meeting which went on until past two o'clock. She was more violent in her denunciation of the Prime Minister even than Winston. He considered that he had been very ill-treated as he had agreed the night before to join the Cabinet, but throughout the day he had not heard a word from the Prime Minister. He had wished to speak that night in the House, but feeling himself already almost a member of the Government had refrained from doing so.

There were present at his flat that evening Anthony, Bob Boothby, Brendan and Duncan Sandys. We were all in a state of bewildered rage. Bob was very convinced that Chamberlain had lost the Conservative Party forever and that it was in Winston's power to go to the House of Commons tomorrow and break him and take his place. He felt very strongly that in no circumstances now should Winston consent to serve under him. On the other hand if Winston now backed Chamberlain he could save him. Was it better to split the country at such a moment or bolster up Chamberlain? That seemed at one time the decision that Winston had to take. He himself, very undecided, said that he had no wish to be Prime Minister, doubted his fitness for the position. Anthony was also in a state of great perplexity. He was not to be a member of the War Cabinet but only Dominions Secretary. He did not relish the prospect. The War Cabinet as then composed was to consist of the P.M., Halifax, Simon, Chatfield, Hankey[3] and Winston. Winston showed me a letter he had written to the P.M. that morning, beginning 'Haven't we rather an old team?' He went on to add up their ages and work out the average which came to just under 65, so, as he put it, they very nearly qualified for the old age pension. We all urged that he should refuse to serve unless Anthony was

---

[1] Leopold (Leo) Amery (1873–1955), journalist and statesman. First Lord of the Admiralty 1922–4; Colonial Secretary 1924–9; Secretary of State for India under Churchill 1940–5.

[2] No. 34 Chapel Street, Belgravia, which Diana had inherited from her mother and to which they had moved on leaving Admiralty House.

[3] Sir Maurice Hankey, 1st Lord Hankey (1877–1963). Joined the War Cabinet in 1938 as Minister without Portfolio. Under Churchill he was Chancellor of the Duchy of Lancaster and then Paymaster-General.

included in the War Cabinet, as otherwise he would be in a minority of one. Brendan pressed that he should also insist on my inclusion and that of Bobbety [Cranborne] – 'the other Ministers' as he put it 'who had resigned for conscience's sake'. Winston left us for a bit and went to draft a letter to the P.M. saying that the events of the day had created a new situation, and that he hoped he would make no announcement of his inclusion in the War Cabinet at present. It was to have been announced on that Saturday morning.

Later Winston succeeded in getting through to someone whom he described as 'a friend', who would be able to tell him what had taken place at the Cabinet. Unfortunately his secretary gave the show away by coming in and saying 'Mr Hore-Belisha is on the telephone'. He came back with the information that after a very stormy Cabinet – stormy in every sense for it was attended by a terrific thunderstorm – it had been decided that the Prime Minister should announce when the House met at 12 the next morning that a final ultimatum had been delivered to Germany and that we should be at war that afternoon. This altered the whole situation. Our heated discussion cooled down.

The next morning [September 3] I went out early as I hadn't a razor in London and I had to get shaved. I went to White's where I found that the barber never came on Sunday. I met Juby Lancaster[1] who said that he had heard there was to be an important announcement on the radio at 10. There was no radio at White's but the announcement came up on the tape. It was that we should be at war with Germany at noon.

I went from there to Ronnie Tree's[2] house at Queen Anne's Gate where there was a meeting of our group. For the first time we had invited Winston and his friends. He didn't come himself as he was preparing his speech and awaiting a possible reply from the Prime Minister. Nor did Brendan, but Bob and Duncan Sandys were there.

Most of the talking was done by Anthony and Leo Amery and the principal subject of discussion was whether Anthony should join the Government, which he professed great reluctance to do. At 11 we listened to the P.M. broadcasting and we all thought he did it very well. Then the meeting broke up.

As we left the house we heard strange sounds and said laughing that it sounded like an air raid warning – which indeed it proved to be. We walked on towards the House of Commons – Anthony, Derrick Gunston[3] and I. Derrick said 'We're walking pretty fast, aren't we?' which we were. When we arrived there we were directed to a room opposite the downstairs smoking room which was full of an odd mixture of people – servants, typists and the Speaker. We didn't stay there long but wandered out on to the terrace where

---

[1] Col. Claude (Juby) Lancaster (1899–1977), MP 1939–50. Married Nancy Tree, née Perkins, a niece of Nancy Astor and former wife of Ronald Tree (see below) in 1948. She was a well-known interior decorator.
[2] Ronald Tree (1897–1976), Conservative MP 1933–45. Owner of Ditchley Park in Oxfordshire.
[3] Maj. Sir Derrick Gunston MC (1891–1985), Conservative MP 1924–45.

we watched the balloons go up, which they did with great speed. It was a beautiful morning. The House met at 12 as arranged and the All Clear signal went during prayers. I did not think the Prime Minister so good as he had been on the radio, nor did I think any of the speeches reached a very high level.

This was a week of absolutely perfect weather which all seemed wasted and thrown away. Diana was all the time in a state of almost suicidal depression and terrified lest she should indeed commit suicide, which she thinks she might do if I were obliged to leave. I also was depressed at feeling useless and out of it – but I somewhat recovered towards the end of the week, as I found myself coming to the conclusion that perhaps the best war work I could do was propaganda in America. I had already arranged a lecture tour which was to have opened at the beginning of December. I thought I might perhaps advance the date of this. In this way also I could get Diana out of the country; she, however much the sea passage alarmed her, would be all right once we were there. In the meantime my work would be attending the House of Commons, writing my articles and preparing my lectures.

This morning – September 11 – I received a telegram from the agent who was arranging my lecture tour in America, hoping that I was still coming and suggesting that I should come earlier.

September 13, 1939

Winston came up to me in the smoking room this afternoon and said that he was afraid that he had not given his mind sufficiently to the question of my going to America when I had asked him about it at the Other Club. He was still against it owing to the uncertainty of the future and impermanence of the Government. He wished there was some job he could give me under the Admiralty – but he simply couldn't think of one – nor could I. I told him I had nothing whatever to do at present as my contract with the *Evening Standard* comes to an end in three weeks and they did not wish to renew it. He suggested that I should take over the contract he had been obliged to break with the *Daily Mirror* and promised to communicate with them about it. I told him that I had no wish to get into the present Government or serve under Chamberlain again – but that I looked forward to the time when he [Winston] would become Prime Minister.

September 15, 1939

John Julius's tenth birthday. He has become such a very nice little boy lately. I think he improves.

[Sunday 17 September, 1939]

Just before luncheon came the news that Russia had invaded Poland. Everybody seems very surprised – Euan more than anybody. But what did they expect? It seems to me quite natural that Stalin should want to make sure of getting his share of the booty. It will shorten the Polish resistance by a few weeks but will not affect the final issue. It may strengthen the peace offensive when it comes.

[September 21, 1939]

In the afternoon I had an interview with the Prime Minister as I wanted to get his approval of my going to America. I had thought that he would have said one word of regret at not having been able to offer me a post in the Government and perhaps would have suggested that he might be able to later. It would not have meant anything but would have been civil. He said nothing of the kind but merely suggested that in six weeks time when 'things would be getting pretty hot here' a man of my age might be criticized for leaving the country. I said that that was my own responsibility and was a question that I could settle for myself. After some humming and hawing he said that it would be a good thing for me to go – and so I left him. I wasn't with him for more than ten minutes and I left with a feeling of intensified dislike.

PART THREE

1944–1951

Algiers, Paris and Retirement

Soon after the outbreak of war in 1939 Duff and Diana embarked on the lecture tour to the USA, to put Britain's case to neutral America and to try to counter the isolationist views then being propagated by Col. Charles A. Lindbergh.[1] They returned early in 1940, and when Churchill became Prime Minister in May 1940 he made Duff his Minister of Information. The appointment was not a success. Duff was responsible for arranging – against the advice of the Foreign Office – for General de Gaulle to make his famous broadcast to the French nation after the fall of France, but the press, terrified of censorship, mounted a virulent campaign against him. He was also criticized for allowing Diana to have John Julius evacuated to America.

It was with some relief, therefore, that in July 1941 he agreed to go on a special mission to the Far East – where the Japanese were causing serious concern – to report on the situation there with particular regard to defence. It was, however, far too late: in December the Japanese bombed Pearl Harbor and a month later he was ordered home. Back in England, as Chancellor of the Duchy of Lancaster, he headed the Security Executive; still feeling underemployed, however, he wrote a life of the biblical King David. Then in September 1943 Churchill and Eden suggested that he should go to Algiers as British representative to the newly-formed French Committee of National Liberation (CFNL), with the prospect of being Ambassador in Paris when the time came.

The CFNL represented all the French resistance groups opposed to the Nazis and the Vichy regime, with General de Gaulle as its President. Duff's brief was to build it up as an effective body with which the Allies could deal, while doing his best to gain the confidence of General de Gaulle (despite Churchill's deep mistrust of him). In early January 1944 he and Diana left for Algiers. Winston Churchill was at that time in Marrakesh, convalescing from pneumonia.

1944

Monday January 3, 1944

We left the aerodrome at one o'clock and arrived at Algiers at 11 the same morning after a very smooth and comfortable journey. We were taken to the house which we were to inhabit and which is at present in a very bad state of

---

[1] Charles Lindbergh (1902–74) made the first solo non-stop flight across the Atlantic in May 1927 and became an international hero. In 1941 he was the leading spokesman for the America First Committee which opposed voluntary American entry into World War II.

repair with no hot water, towels or cooking facilities. Mr and Mrs Rooker[1] are sharing with us and we are to mess with Harold Macmillan.[2] We lunched at his house; he having to attend some official function was not present, but he came in afterwards and I spent the afternoon discussing the situation with him.

It was a day of crisis, such days being frequent here, the immediate difficulty having to do with the acceptance by de Gaulle[3] of the Prime Minister's invitation to visit him. De Gaulle suspected that he was being summoned to the Prime Minister's presence in a way which might injure his dignity and he wished to know what particular subject the Prime Minister intended to discuss. He said that if it was merely to be a general conversation it was very likely to end in a quarrel, which would do more harm than good. On the other hand, if the Prime Minister had suspected that there was any reluctance on the part of de Gaulle to accept his invitation he would certainly have it withdrawn. Therefore Macmillan's difficult task was to try to bring them together, and arrangements were made for the Prime Minister to see de Gaulle on Friday. We then telephoned to the Prime Minister, and I spoke to him. Diana and I are to go down there on Sunday after de Gaulle's visit.

We also had tea that day with Dr Beneš,[4] who came attended by two assistants. He talked as volubly as ever and at great length. He was well satisfied with his visit to Russia and we understood him to say that Russia not only recognized but guaranteed the future frontiers of Czechoslovakia. He was very clear about the future both of France and Germany. He considered that a strong France in the west was just as important to Czechoslovakia as a strong Russia in the east. He said that at present there was no alternative leader to de Gaulle and that we should give him such support as we could. There was no danger, in his opinion, of de Gaulle becoming a dictator. The French people could be relied upon to see that this did not happen. He was in favour of the partition of Germany. When I suggested to him that such a partition would probably be against the will of the whole German people, and therefore if not accepted would be merely a façade which might encourage other nations to disregard the future German menace and allow the different German states secretly to work together and to prepare for revenge, he agreed that there was a great deal to be said for that view, but, even so, he thought that partition would be useful combined with close surveillance.

Diana was in an overwrought state, suffering from a reaction to the pills she had taken to calm herself for the journey. A good many cocktails and

---

[1] Kingsley Rooker (1887–1951), Counsellor at the Embassy.

[2] Harold Macmillan was British Resident at Allied Forces HQ in Algiers Jan. 1943–Jan. 1944, when he became British Resident on the Advisory Council for Italy.

[3] Gen. Charles de Gaulle (1890–1970), leader of the Free French 1940–3; Co-President with General Giraud of the CFNL 1943; President of the Provisional Government 1944, and head of the French Government 1945–6; President of the French Republic 1958–69.

[4] Eduard Beneš (1884–1948), President of Czechoslovakia 1935–9 and 1945–8.

Algerian wine did not improve the situation. She got in a state of exaggerated depression about the ugliness of the villa and the impossibility of improving it owing to the complete absence of all commodities in Algiers. I am more concerned about the lack of comfort – especially of hot water. This however can be put right while the other can't. We had therefore a pretty bad night in wet sheets.

January 4, 1944

At 7 I went to see Massigli,[1] who was extremely affable. He asked me whether I had brought any letter from the Foreign Office officially stating that I had been appointed. I had already been warned that I was likely be asked this question as it had been previously put to Vanier,[2] the Canadian Representative, and he had been told that the Russian and American Ambassadors had each brought something of the kind. When Massigli raised the question, therefore, I said that it was probably my fault for not having asked for such a letter and I felt sure that the Secretary of State would write one were I to tell him about it. Massigli was quite satisfied and said that he himself attached no importance to the matter, but that the General thought it important.

We dined at the Macmillan villa. Harold was not feeling very well and had gone to bed, but I went up and had a long talk with him after dinner. He said that he thought de Gaulle's resentment against the Prime Minister was not unnatural. The Prime Minister had arrived here in a British man-of-war, had made no sign to any official representative of the Committee, i.e. the Government of the country, but had sent for General Georges,[3] who was in open opposition to the Committee. He had later settled near Tunis without asking to see the Governor-General of Tunisia, and had then moved to Marrakesh, again not asking to see the Governor-General, and had finally sent an invitation to de Gaulle to visit him as though he were in his own country and not in de Gaulle's country. It is to be hoped that the visit will pass off successfully.

January 5, 1944

There is still no hot water in the villa and there seems little prospect of getting any. Admiral Sir John Cunningham,[4] Commander-in-Chief, Mediterranean, came to see me this morning. I think he felt a little embarrassed by the fact that the last time we met, when I was First Lord of the Admiralty, I had told

[1] René Massigli (1888–1988), Minister for Foreign Affairs in the CFNL, and French Ambassador to London 1944–55.

[2] Maj.-Gen. Georges Vanier (1888–1967), Canadian representative to the CFNL and Canadian Ambassador to France 1944–53; Governor-General of Canada 1959–67.

[3] Gen. Joseph Georges was considered one of those responsible for the military defeat of France. He was critical of de Gaulle and the FCNL. He was in Algiers as a guest of General Giraud.

[4] Adm. Sir John Cunningham (1885–1962). In 1937 he was Assistant Chief of Naval Staff (Air), becoming Fifth Sea Lord in 1938. He became Allied CIC Mediterranean in 1943.

him that I had decided that he should relinquish the job he was then doing, viz., that of Fifth Sea Lord in charge of the Fleet Air Arm, of which he was not making a success. I had not a very high opinion of his qualities. Admiral Cunningham said that there was no, either official or domestic, accommodation to be obtained and this I know to be quite true. Some of his post Captains were conducting their office work seated on bidets.

De Gaulle has arranged to entertain the Resident-General of Morocco when he goes to see the Prime Minister on Friday. He will lunch with the P.M. and then give a party in the evening at the Residency-General. This, he says, will make an excuse for his visit and will act as cover for the Prime Minister's presence there, as if he were to go there without any excuse it might attract attention and arouse suspicions. I think he has got out of his difficulty rather cleverly – for he thus preserves his own dignity under the cloak of solicitude for the Prime Minister's safety.

In the afternoon I saw General Vanier, who was as charming as ever. He raised one point about future military policy. He understood that the French force accompanying the invasion of Northern France was to be merely a token force, whereas greater strength would be used in the attack from the Mediterranean [*Operation Anvil, the plan for an amphibious landing in the South of France*]. He thought this was a pity, as it might be invidious for the French to be represented only by a token force in the major and more important part of the invasion.

We went in the evening to the reception which Harold was giving in his villa. There was a very large crowd and all the more important people in Algiers were there with the exception of de Gaulle and Giraud.[1] Giraud sent his representative, who came and apologized to me for his absence. I was glad to see General Catroux[2] again who was very friendly, and equally glad to see General de Lattre de Tassigny,[3] whom I had met in London a few weeks before. Massigli was also there. I identified Madame de Lesseps[4] and managed to be introduced to her. She is very pretty. I talked to her husband for some time and got on well with him. We have mutual friends. She is English.

---

[1] Gen. Henri Giraud (1879–1949), CIC French Forces in North Africa 1942–4; Co-President with de Gaulle of the CFNL until July 1943, then CIC French Forces until Apr. 1944.

[2] Gen. Georges Catroux (1877–1969). As Governor-General of Indo-China, he had refused Pétain's order to return to France in July 1940 and had joined General de Gaulle in London. In 1943 he was appointed CIC Free French Forces in the Middle East and in June 1944 Governor-General of Algeria.

[3] Gen. Jean de Lattre de Tassigny (1889–1952), Commander of Vichy Forces 1941–2, but resisted German occupation of southern zone and was imprisoned. Escaped to Algiers in 1943, became Commander of French 1st Army and fought with American troops in France and Germany.

[4] Diana de Lesseps, wife of Comte Victor (Totor) de Lesseps, a descendant of Ferdinand de Lesseps, builder of the Suez and Panama canals.

January 6, 1944

I lunched at the Hurlevent – a small crowded restaurant – with the Duprees[1] and John Wyndham.[2] It was a meatless day, but the food was not bad. In the afternoon I attended a meeting of the *Assemblée*. The vote of the Ministry of Information [M. Bonnet[3]] was under consideration. I heard one or two short speeches and the Minister wind up. His speech reminded me very much of ones I had made myself on similar occasions. The usual apology for the censorship, and the usual explanation that mistakes were bound to happen occasionally and that there was no intention of interfering with the freedom of opinion but only of protecting the security of the forces. Also the usual defence of the broadcasting services and the usual regrets that shortage of technical apparatus rendered them less efficient than they might be. Randolph[4] arrived here this afternoon. I went round to see him at the Macmillan villa and took him up to ours. He was, as ever, full of life and talk and pugnacity, and generally in good form. He is about to go into Yugoslavia with Fitzroy Maclean[5] on a mission to Tito. It had all been settled satisfactorily according to Randolph, when the Foreign Office quite unnecessarily intervened and suggested making terms with Tito and insisting on his recognition of the King. This has caused delay and confusion.

We dined with Admiral Cunningham. Alexander[6] was there, and we had a pleasant evening. He did not seem optimistic about the Italian campaign and did not expect to be in Rome for months. We had arranged to meet Randolph at the Macmillan villa after dinner but when we got there at about eleven he had not returned so we went to bed. I heard later that he had got home at 1.30 and had had to be carried up to bed.

January 7, 1944

I spoke to the Prime Minister, who said that he could now see de Gaulle on Sunday, which de Gaulle had originally suggested. I hope it will be possible to arrange this. He said that in that case I could come on Monday. I told him that I thought I was entitled to a better villa than the one I had here, as I shall

---

[1] Tom and Anne Dupree. He was Press Attaché on Duff's staff in Algiers.

[2] John Wyndham, 1st Lord Egremont and 6th Lord Leconfield (1920–72). Harold Macmillan's Private Secretary 1940–5, 1955–6 and 1957–63.

[3] Henri Bonnet (1888–1976), French diplomat who represented the Free French in the US 1940–3; Minister of Information for the CFNL 1943–4; French Ambassador to the US 1944–5.

[4] During World War II, Randolph Churchill served in Intelligence at GHQ Middle East. In January 1944 he was parachuted into Yugoslavia as a member of Fitzroy Maclean's mission to support General Tito.

[5] Sir Fitzroy Maclean (1911–96), diplomat 1933–41, Conservative MP 1941–74, and soldier in the 1st SAS regiment 1941–5. Head of Military Mission to Yugoslavia 1943–5.

[6] Field Marshal Sir Harold Alexander, 1st Earl Alexander of Tunis (1891–1969). CIC in North Africa 1942–3 and Supreme Allied Commander in Sicily and Italy 1944–5.

be here continuously whereas the Generals and Air Marshals have been here very little in the past and will be here less often in the future. I also wanted some batmen as servants, as I could not continue to rely on Italian prisoners. He said he quite agreed with me and would mention the matter to Maitland Wilson,[1] who was with him at the time. I hope something will come of this.

January 8, 1944

We lunched with General and Madame Catroux – a party of about fourteen. General Giraud was there. The women were all old and ugly, except Madame Catroux's daughter-in-law, who was only ugly. I had a talk with Catroux after lunch. He was very affable and frank. He said that the situation in Syria and the Lebanon had greatly improved, but that, of course, Spears was a continual stumbling-block to a better understanding. He also talked about Giraud and admitted that he was too old-fashioned a soldier for the present war.

From 1941 Syria and Lebanon, former French mandates, had been jointly occupied by British and Free French forces with an agreement they should become independent after the war. General Spears, as British Minister, had to implement this promise but de Gaulle and Catroux, who wanted to keep French influence and power in the region, suspected his motives. Duff Cooper, supported by Eden, felt that Spears's presence in the Levant was poisoning Anglo-French relations. In December 1944 Churchill forced Spears to resign.

I spoke to the Prime Minister before dinner. [He] said he had discussed our difficulties with the Generals. Alexander told him that he himself was waited on by Italian prisoners. I said that his case was quite different from mine, as he was fighting the war and nobody expected him to entertain foreigners. I also said that Macmillan had always been waited on by soldiers. The Prime Minister said that if they were fit they ought to be fighting and not acting as batmen.

January 9, 1944

A day even more beautiful that the one before. Palewski[2] called before dinner. He told me that if de Gaulle's visit to the Prime Minister resulted merely in formal and ceremonious conversations more harm than good would have been done. There were three matters which he thought demanded discussion. First, he wanted to *panser la blessure* [dress the wound] of the Syrian business, and wanted to obtain an assurance from the Prime Minister of assistance in concluding the treaty. Secondly, he wanted to come to some agreement about

---

[1] Gen. Sir Henry Maitland (Jumbo) Wilson, 1st Lord Wilson (1881–1964). GOC-in-C British troops in Egypt 1939–41; GOC British Forces in Palestine and Transjordan 1941; CIC Middle East 1943; Supreme Commander Mediterranean 1944–5. Head of Joint Staff Mission in Washington 1945–7.

[2] Gaston Palewski (1901–84), General de Gaulle's *Chef de Cabinet* and most trusted adviser.

the administration of France after the invasion; thirdly he wanted to obtain the Prime Minister's agreement to the one French division which was to take part in the northern invasion being under the command of General Leclerc,[1] who is said to be the most popular man in France after de Gaulle.

I said I thought it would be a good thing if de Gaulle would mention this third matter first, for the Prime Minister would be favourably impressed if he thought de Gaulle was more interested in winning the war than in anything else. With regard to Syria, he could hardly expect the Prime Minister to give any very definite undertaking, but the P.M.'s policy was, and always had been, to maintain the French in the Levant, and I was sure that he would give some general assurance to that effect. The most difficult of the three items was that of administration. This was a complicated subject which Mr Eden was dealing with in London and Lord Halifax in Washington. The Prime Minister would probably not be fully informed of the most recent developments, and I should be inclined to discourage going into it too deeply, as it might lead to mis-understanding. On the other hand, there would be no harm in mentioning it.

We dined this evening in the Macmillan villa. Randolph turned up again; also Bloggs.[2] Late in the evening Mr Velacott, former headmaster of Harrow, came in. We then made our escape. Randolph was pretty drunk by then and I felt sure he would say something to shock the headmaster. He had already, in front of Bloggs, referred to 'that bloody old fool Baldwin'.

January 10, 1944

I went down to the office early this morning, and at ten I went to see General Maitland Wilson about my house etc. He called in General Gale.[3] They both seemed genuinely shocked when I told them I couldn't get a hot bath in my villa and that I had neither a butler nor a cook. Gale undertook to see to all these matters at once.

I then drove with Rooker down to the aerodrome where Winston's private York was awaiting us. It is a most luxurious machine, and as soon as we went on board the steward offered us champagne cocktails which were not refused. It was really a delightful journey. Perfect weather, an excellent lunch on board, and wonderful views of the Mediterranean and the Atlas Mountains. It took us about $3\frac{3}{4}$ hours.

Clemmie and Sarah[4] met us and took us straight to the villa where they are

[1] General Leclerc (1902–47) was the French Resistance alias of Philippe de Hauteclocque. He was Commander of the French Second Armoured Division which had fought with the British Eighth Army in Tunisia, took part in D-Day and were the first troops to reach Paris on 25 Aug. 1944. He was killed in an aeroplane crash in 1947.
[2] Windham ('Bloggs') Baldwin (1904–76), son of the Prime Minister, succeeded his brother as 3rd Earl Baldwin of Bewdley. He served in the RAF 1940–5.
[3] Lt.-Gen. Humfrey Gale (1890–1971), Deputy COS and Chief Administrative Officer to General Eisenhower 1942–5.
[4] Sarah Churchill (1914–82), Winston's daughter, married first, in 1936, Vic Oliver (d. 1964),

all living – a beautiful place belonging to a rich American woman. There we found Winston in his siren suit and his enormous Californian hat. When it got cooler he completed this get-up with a silk dressing gown. He was very pleased to see us. I had a long talk with him before dinner.

He has a huge staff here, including half-a-dozen cypher girls and a map-room, with a naval officer permanently on duty. He took me there and showed me how important the Russian advance was. He thought it was far better than Stalin had expected when he was in Teheran. He is still very sticky about de Gaulle, and I'm afraid their interview on Wednesday is not likely to be suc-cessful. He keeps harping on General Georges and wants to get him back into the Committee. He also feels personally responsible for the future of Boisson and Peyrouton, and favourably inclined towards Flandin.[1] He admits that Giraud is no use, but wants him to remain as a kind of figurehead – 'a sort of Duke of Cambridge' as he put it – 'with a Wolseley in the shape of de Lattre doing the work'.

We were fourteen at dinner. Max Beaverbrook is here and Lord Moran[2] and his son. The rest are staff. The food was excellent and we sat talking after dinner until after one. I have never known Winston in better form or more cheerful. Max on the other hand was very silent. He is never quite at his ease except in his own house.

January 11, 1944

They had chosen a pleasant place for the picnic. There were large supplies of food and drink – two servants to wait as well as the staff, and a host of American military police standing around to protect. He (Churchill) sat there for more than an hour after lunch reading the *Memoirs of Captain Gronow*.[3] This was the seventh picnic they had had during the fourteen days they have been here. It seemed to me a curious form of entertainment. I drove back with Clemmie, Diana going with Winston. Clemmie said she had given Winston a candle curtain lecture this morning on the importance of not quarrelling with de Gaulle. He had grumbled at the time, but she thought it would bear fruit.

I sat between Winston and Colville at dinner, and all went well until, just as we were leaving, a message came from Algiers to say that General de Lattre de Tassigny, whom Winston had invited for later in the week, had reported

actor, divorced 1945; second, in 1949, Anthony Beauchamp (d. 1957); and third, in 1962, the 23rd Baron Audley.

[1] Marcel Peyrouton, Pierre Boisson and Pierre Etienne Flandin were three senior French ex-Vichy officials. Peyrouton and Boisson were ex-Governor-Generals of Algeria and French West Africa respectively. Flandin was an old political friend of Churchill's. De Gaulle had arrested all three and threatened prosecution on the grounds of collaboration.

[2] Charles Wilson, 1st Baron Moran (1882–1977). Doctor and Dean of St Mary's Medical School; President, Royal College of Physicians 1941–50. Personal physician and confidant to Sir Winston Churchill.

[3] R. H. Gronow (1794–1865) wrote four volumes of memoirs, *Reminiscences of Regency and Victorian Life 1810–60*.

that de Gaulle, whose permission to come he had asked, had answered that it would be most inopportune for him to do so at the present time. This produced an explosion. Winston wanted to send a message at once to tell de Gaulle not to come. Max, of course, encouraged this folly. I did my best to calm him, and he decided to do nothing.

January 12, 1944

I was woken by the telephone ringing at 8.15. 'Colonel Warden'[1] wishes 'to speak to me'. He said he had been thinking things over. The matter was not so simple – would I go over and see him – he might want me to stay longer. All arrangements had been made for us to fly this morning. He was in bed, and had apparently worked himself up again about de Gaulle. He suggested sending him a note to the airfield to say he was sorry he had been troubled to come so far but that he would not be able to see him after all. I strongly dissuaded him from this course, pointing out that we knew nothing of the reason which had caused de Gaulle to prevent de Lattre from coming here. He might have perfectly good reasons for having done so. De Lattre had not yet received an official appointment and de Gaulle might wish to consult the P.M. as to what was to be done with him. Alternatively, he might have thought that Giraud would be annoyed at a junior officer receiving such an invitation when he was not invited.

This worked, but Winston then said he would receive de Gaulle on a purely social basis, would talk about the weather and the beauty of the place and then say 'good-bye'. This was better, but I suggested that Palewski would probably ask me whether there were going to be serious conversations after lunch – what was I to say? He said he didn't mind having a talk if de Gaulle asked for it, but that he would not take the initiative. Nor would he see him alone. If he did, de Gaulle would misrepresent what he had said. I must be present and Max too, and de Gaulle could bring whom he liked. I should have to alter my plans and stay over till tomorrow. I had no objection.

All passed off well. Winston was in a bad mood when de Gaulle arrived and was not very welcoming. He had just read of the shooting of Ciano, Bono,[2] etc. which had rather shocked him. As lunch proceeded, however, Winston thawed. He had Diana on one side and Palewski on the other. De Gaulle sat opposite, next to Clemmie. When the ladies left, Winston invited de Gaulle to sit next to him, but things were still sticky. We then moved out into the garden – Winston, Max, the British Consul and me on the one side – de Gaulle and Palewski on the other. The conversation lasted about two hours. Winston was admirable, I thought, and de Gaulle very difficult and unhelpful.

---

[1] During the war, Churchill travelled under the assumed name of Colonel Warden.
[2] Count Galeazzo Ciano (1903–44), Italian Foreign Minister and Mussolini's son-in-law, and Marshal Emilio de Bono were shot by the Fascists on 11 Jan. 1944 in revenge for their role in toppling Mussolini in July 1943.

He talked as though he were Stalin and Roosevelt combined. Winston dealt first with the prisoners question – talked about Georges – about Syria – and almost every subject in his abominable French – always on the line 'Why should we quarrel? Why can't we be friends?' De Gaulle did very little towards meeting him half way, but they parted friends and the Prime Minister agreed to attend the review on the following day.

January 13, 1944

The review was a great success. We had to get up early as it took place at 9 o'clock. Winston was in the uniform of an Air Commodore. I could see that he was very much moved by the loud cries of '*Vive Churchill*' which predominated even over the cries of '*Vive de Gaulle*'. I couldn't help thinking, as I watched them standing together taking the salute, of the incident 24 hours earlier when Winston had said that he would not receive de Gaulle at all. After Winston had left, de Gaulle made a short speech in appreciation of the privilege they had enjoyed in having the *premier ministre britannique* at their review and extolling the alliance.

There followed a picnic which involved a two hours' drive to the foothills. It took place at a very beautiful spot and everyone enjoyed it. Winston was in a heavenly mood – very funny and very happy.

January 14, 1944

We went round to the villa in the morning. I had a short walk and talk with the P.M. He is angry with Harold [Macmillan], whom he thinks turned against Giraud. This is hardly just. The difference, he explained, between us and the U.S.A. was that Vichy had betrayed us but had not betrayed the Americans. They had continued on friendly terms up to the invasion of North Africa, and even then Roosevelt had prepared a proclamation praising Pétain[1] up to the skies as the grand old man of Vichy. 'Crikey, I said, don't do that, we all think he's one of the biggest stinkers unhung.'

January 15, 1944 (Algiers)

Since I have been away we have been supplied with two soldier servants, one of whom was formerly footman to Murray Graham and seems very efficient. The engineers have been working but have not yet succeeded in producing any hot water.

---

[1] Marshal Henri Philippe Pétain (1856–1951). After a distinguished army career, Pétain, aged eighty-three, agreed to head the Vichy Government in occupied France. In 1945 he was arrested, found guilty of treason and sentenced to death. The sentence was later commuted to life imprisonment.

January 16, 1944

Michael Duff,[1] who is working here, came in before dinner. We dined at the Murphy villa which is now inhabited by Mr Chapin,[2] who is Counsellor to the American Ambassador. Chapin told me at dinner that he thought that the President's attitude towards France[3] was affected by memories of the Civil War, and he would like the Vichyites to be treated no worse than the defeated southern leaders were after victory.

January 17, 1944

We lunched with Harold Macmillan. He had the Russian Ambassador, Monsieur Bogomolov,[4] and his wife there, and also Vyshinsky[5] who is his opposite number. He is also the man who acted as prosecutor in most of the famous purge trials in Russia. I did not care much for the Ambassador, but his wife was a nice bright young woman. Vyshinsky was very friendly and smiling, but speaks hardly a word of either French or English.

January 18, 1944

The great event of this morning was the advent of the hot water. My own bath was tepid and rather dirty, but later, I am told, it came through hot and clean. This, while it makes the villa more habitable, does not in any way get over the main difficulties. The greatest difficulty of all is Mrs Rooker, with whom it is quite impossible to share a house.

January 19, 1944

Mr [Gerald] Norman, the *Times* correspondent, came to see me at 10.15. He had just returned from Syria and the Lebanon and was very interesting on the subject. He said that he believes that the incidents there were all enormously exaggerated by Spears, who is universally disliked except by his own entourage. Relations between the French and British armies have always been, and still remain, completely satisfactory, but the feelings of the French against Spears, and of him against them, are of the most intense and violent hatred. It is most unfortunate that Spears should be there, and there will be no peace so long as he remains.

---

[1] Sir Michael Duff, Bt. (1907–80) later married Lady Caroline Paget, Diana's niece.

[2] Selden Chapin (1899–1963), American diplomat 1925–60. He was Counsellor, American Diplomatic Mission Algiers in 1943, becoming Chargé d'Affaires, Algiers and Paris 1944–5.

[3] The United States Government had recognized Vichy in 1940. Roosevelt favoured Giraud over de Gaulle as French leader.

[4] Alexander Bogomolov, ex-Professor of Marxism and formerly Russian Ambassador to Vichy. Soviet Ambassador in Algiers and Paris.

[5] Andrei Vyshinsky (1883–1954), Soviet diplomat and jurist. Chief Prosecutor in Stalin's Great Purge trials of 1934–8. Deputy Commissar for Foreign Affairs 1940–9 and Soviet representative on Allied Commissions for the Mediterranean and Italy. In 1949 he became Soviet Foreign Minister and in 1953 Permanent Soviet Representative at the UN.

January 22, 1944

We dined with General de Gaulle. I sat between Madame de Gaulle and Madame Catroux. Madame de Gaulle is rather a pathetic little woman who I should think has a hard life. She is obviously forbidden to put on any make-up. She hates Algiers, and, I think, hates everything that has to do with public life. Diana got on pretty well with de Gaulle, and I had a conversation with him after dinner.

He said that he tries, every day for a short time, to imagine himself looking down on events without prejudice, and from the point of view of the future historian. It then seems to him that of all things the most ridiculous is that the British and French should not be on the best of terms. I did not suggest to him, although I thought of doing so, that he himself was as responsible as anybody for misunderstandings, but I did say that he must understand that, for us, the most important of all things was to retain the friendship of the United States, and that they approached these problems from a different angle to ours. Vichy had betrayed France and had betrayed England, but they had not betrayed the United States, who had – rightly or wrongly – remained for a long time on amicable terms with them.

I then raised again the question of the three accused, and asked whether they were still in prison. He laughed, and said he supposed he would have to take the finest château in North Africa and put them in it surrounded by every luxury, and when asked why, he would have to explain that it was because they were friends of President Roosevelt and Mr Churchill. He said that the English and Americans could not understand the bitterness felt by the French against those whom they considered had betrayed them and subsequently persecuted them. I said that I perfectly understood that, but the Prime Minister saw things from a personal angle. He had had lunch with Boisson and Peyrouton and had told them to count on him. Therefore he felt a measure of responsibility. De Gaulle's only reply was that he never ought to have met them, still less have had lunch with them. I saw that it was useless to argue. He spoke well of de Lattre, but in rather a patronizing way, said that he had, of course, served Vichy as other soldiers, including General Juin,[1] had done, but that he was a good General and would command the expeditionary force that would invade from the south. I think he was trying to be as agreeable as possible, but it does not come easily to him.

---

[1] Gen. Alphonse Juin (1888–1967), a long-standing friend of de Gaulle. In 1941, under the Vichy Government, he commanded all French troops in Morocco. In 1942 he joined the Allies, and took command of French forces fighting Germany in Tunisia. In 1943 he commanded the Free French forces in Italy.

January 23, 1944

An exceptionally beautiful day – we drove out to Tipaza to lunch and were much impressed by the beauty of the place. We walked, after lunch, by the sea among the ruins. Diana was in delightfully high spirits and we both felt very happy.

January 25, 1944

I went to see Monsieur Massigli at his request. He said that General Spears had been stirring up fresh trouble in the Levant. To his certain knowledge the General had been interviewed recently by a number of journalists at Damascus, and had told them that so long as their own troops were under French control they had not got the real essence of independence. The result has been a violent press campaign, and also agitation in the Syrian chamber in favour of handing over the troops to the local Governments.

I replied that I could not, of course, accept this statement that His Majesty's Minister was taking any part in mischievous intrigues against French interests in the Levant, as I was sure that His Majesty's Government desired nothing but peace and quietness to prevail there, and continued to recognize, as they always had, the preponderant position that France held in Syria and the Lebanon. I said, however, that I would report the matter to the Foreign Office.

I then raised again the matter of the three accused politicians, and asked him how it now stood. He said he had made enquiries himself that afternoon, and had learned that a suitable residence for these men had not yet been found, but that the search continued. I asked him what were the prospects of the preliminary enquiry into their cases taking place. He said he doubted very much whether there would be any enquiry at all pending the return to France. They were proceeding with the case of Pucheu,[1] and that was quite enough for the present.

January 26, 1944

At a quarter to five Madame Flandin arrived, and stayed over an hour, during which she did most of the talking. It is difficult to argue with an unfortunate woman whose husband is in prison charged with treason, and who is naturally very anxious to know what is to become of him. One has to remember that all the time, in order to make the necessary allowances. I think she is a hard woman, and I doubt whether she is really very unhappy. She betrayed herself once or twice by falling into praises of Pétain and denunciations of de Gaulle, describing the regime here as purely Nazi and therefore opposed to her husband, who had always been the great exponent of democracy. She said he

---

[1] Pierre Pucheu, former Vichy Minister of the Interior. In May 1943 he arrived in North Africa, having been promised a safe-conduct by Giraud. He was arrested by the CFNL in August 1943, and in March 1944 put on trial for his life.

had a miserable cell and no opportunities for exercise, although apparently she can see him whenever she wishes and he has no complaint with regard to his food. I said that I had missed no opportunity of urging his case, and that I hoped to be able to obtain a great improvement in his conditions.

January 27, 1944

This morning I received a letter from General Gale saying that he had received instructions from the Commander-in-Chief to put the Villa Bel-Air at my disposal, and also his country villa at the disposal of my Counsellor. In return for this, they asked me to hand over the villa we are now in. This is a great step forward, and I shall accept the offer with gratitude. The only difficulty now is that Diana would prefer to stay on at our present villa, because she is so interested in her scheme for putting the garden at the disposal of the civil servants.

January 30, 1944

They brought up a telegram to the villa this morning from the Prime Minister about the accused politicians, complaining that nothing had been done about finding them a suitable residence and saying that unless I could give him some hope that something would be done in the near future he would stir up the President, who would take further action.

February 3, 1944

Chapin came to see me this morning. He showed me, in confidence, a long letter from the President to Mr Wilson [the American representative to Algiers] which contained his instructions on coming here. It was also a considered defence of the American policy towards Vichy, both before and after America came into the war. So far as the past was concerned it was a good statement, but it went on to deal with the Committee, to attack de Gaulle, and to give reasons why the Committee should not be recognized as the Government of France. The President said that the Committee could not be considered to be properly representative of the French Government entitled to govern France after the liberation.

The answer is, first, that it is much more representative than many of the Governments, such as those of Yugoslavia, Greece and Poland, which the United States have already recognized, and secondly, it has always stated that it will resign its functions as soon as any representative French Assembly comes into being. What the President fails to understand is that there must be some provisional authority to deal with the situation which will exist in the interval which must occur between the partial or total liberation of France and the setting up of a properly constituted representative Government.

February 5, 1944

We had the Catroux to lunch today. Before lunch the General, without my having referred to the matter, told me that, in his opinion, there was no truth in the report that Spears had been responsible for the agitation in the Levant concerning the control of the active troops. He said that, on the contrary, during his recent visit, he had found Spears most helpful and friendly. I felt obliged to telegraph this information to London.

February 11, 1944

We had the weekly office meeting in the afternoon. Gridley [Economic Adviser] told us that the Americans seem to have changed their view with regard to economic control and are now all for handing everything over to the French. It is very curious. They have so much reduced their staff here that they are hardly able to deal with these matters, and he says that with the French their stock is falling all the time, while ours is rising. Before he went away, Macmillan said rather the same to me; he felt that the Americans were pulling out of here altogether, and doubted very much whether Murphy[1] would come back.

February 16, 1944

This morning we had a meeting in the office of the people engaged in the Special Services:– [including] Dodds-Parker,[2] Rooker, Reilly,[3] and Muggeridge.[4] I am glad to think that although there is a good deal of bickering between our various branches we are very much ahead of the French in this respect. All their people seem to be at one another's throats. I was impressed by Muggeridge, who struck me as very intelligent.

February 17, 1944

Lady Spears[5] arrived in time for a luncheon party which we had arranged previously for all the elements of the extreme Right:– [including] Generals Giraud and Georges. I think it went well. Giraud was in great form and very charming. He had just heard that his youngest daughter, aged 16, had escaped from France although she was living under surveillance, and had crossed the

---

[1] Robert Murphy (1894–1978), American diplomat and President Roosevelt's personal representative in French North Africa 1942–4.

[2] Col. Sir Douglas Dodds-Parker MP (b. 1909), Mission Commander Special Operations Executive (SOE) Western and Central Mediterranean, 1943–4.

[3] Sir Patrick Reilly (1909–99), First Secretary on Duff's staff in Algiers and Paris 1944–5, Minister in Paris 1953–6 and Ambassador 1965–8.

[4] Malcolm Muggeridge (1903–90), journalist and broadcaster. In MI6 1940–5. After the war he became a leader writer on the *Daily Telegraph* and, in 1952, editor of *Punch*.

[5] Mary (May) Borden (1886–1968), American wife of Sir (Edward) Louis Spears. She ran a mobile field hospital at the front in the First World War and in the Middle East in the second.

Pyrenees and arrived safely at Gibraltar. His wife and other two daughters are in prison.

Before dinner the De Lesseps brought in Médéric, who has been one of the mainsprings of the resistance movement in France and is said to have killed more Germans with his own hands than anybody; also d'Astier [Henri d'Astier de la Vigerie] who lives here and is thought to be responsible for the murder of Darlan.[1]

February 21, 1944

Le Troquer[2] telephoned in the afternoon to inform me that the three accused were now 'convenablement' housed in the villa that has been found for them. I expressed my gratitude. I think it would be a good thing to try to find out whether the villa really is suitable and is not a tumbledown barn with no roof to it.

February 22, 1944. My birthday

We dined with Chapin – a fork dinner followed by quite a good film which went on till midnight. We sat at small tables for dinner. I sat at one with Catroux and two American ladies, one of whom was called Virginia Stanley. She seemed to me extremely attractive – more so than anyone I have so far met here – which is not saying very much. Standards must adapt themselves to circumstances. She plays gin rummy.

February 25, 1944

Madame Flandin came to see me this morning, and thanked me for what I had done. She says the villa is quite comfortable, but the food is worse than it was when her husband was in prison. This, I suggested, and she was inclined to agree, might only be due to the sudden change and would get put right in time. She is now afraid that if Pucheu is shot there will be reprisals in France which will lead to further reprisals here, in which her husband might be involved. I tried to reassure her, and I really think he is in no danger, but I also think there is no hope of his being released until the end of the war. She said that it was very unjust to hold him without trying him. I agreed, but could not help pointing out to her that many other – I did not say far better men,

---

[1] Adm. Jean-François Darlan (1881–1942) was a senior figure in the Vichy Government. He was trapped in Algiers by the Allied landings in North Africa in November 1942 and assassinated in December.

[2] André Le Troquer (1888–1963), a lawyer and socialist député, who opposed the German occupation, escaped to North Africa in 1940, and was later in London and Algiers. Commissioner for War and Air on the Committee, and for the Administration of Liberated Territories 1944. President of the Municipal Council of Paris 1945–7; Minister of the Interior 1946 and of Defence 1946–8; President of the Assemblée Nationale 1956–8.

but thought it – such as Mandel[1] and Blum[2] had not only been held by Vichy for three years without trial but, at the end, had been handed over to the Germans.

March 6, 1944

At lunchtime we heard that Martha Hemingway[3] had returned, and she came up to the villa in the early afternoon. In the evening I had to speak at the American Officers' Club, where I gave them a resumé of what I had said last week about the beginning of the war. I cut it down to half-an-hour, but it was not very easy, as there was a cat in the building which never ceased to make the most terrible and comic noises throughout my performance. This was punctuated by an occasional cat hunt on the part of a member of the audience, who by trying to make things better made them worse.

March 7, 1944

We had a lunch party at the house. The point of it was for Monsieur André Gide.[4] [He] was quite different from what I had expected – a very clear-minded, active, and for his years, young looking man – not at all eccentric, dressed like an English country gentleman in tweeds and spats. I liked him. He told me he had recently finished a complete translation of *Hamlet*, which was to be published in America and possibly here.

March 8, 1944

The Pucheu trial goes better and better for the accused. The French are much worried about it. The obvious solution is to put it off until after the liberation of France. It would be a grave miscarriage of justice if they were to shoot him on the evidence as produced hitherto. I saw Palewski in the evening, who was cynical about it and obviously would like to see him shot, but I warned him it would have a disastrous effect in England and America.

March 9, 1944

We had a large dinner party in the evening. Martha talked the greater part of

---

[1] Georges Mandel (1885–1944), a French politician who was Minister of the Colonies 1938–40. A noted anti-appeaser, he fled to Morocco after the fall of France, but was arrested, imprisoned, turned over to the Gestapo and with Léon Blum sent to Buchenwald. He was returned in 1944 and was murdered by the Vichy secret police.

[2] Léon Blum (1872–1950), a Socialist politician, was Prime Minister of France 1936–7 and in 1938. He was arrested by Pétain in 1940, tried in 1942 as a traitor and held prisoner by the Germans until 1945.

[3] Martha Gellhorn (1908–98), American journalist and war correspondent. Married Ernest Hemingway in 1940; the marriage ended in 1944.

[4] André Gide (1869–1951), French writer, winner of the Nobel Prize for Literature in 1947. He was in Tunisia and Algeria 1942–5.

the evening with [Emmanuel] d'Astier.[1] It was plainly an affair and I wasn't surprised when I found she had accepted to dine with him the next night. Afterwards I had a long conversation with d'Astier, telling him that I was quite sure that if Pucheu were shot it would do harm to the cause of the Committee both in England and in America. He said that, on the other hand, if he were not shot it would be a slap in the face for the French resistance movement. Not having read the evidence, they would be quite unable to understand what had happened, and even the popularity of General de Gaulle could not survive it. As for the harm it would do in other countries, it would all be forgotten in a fortnight. He also intimated that it was not our business anyhow. Chapin later took part in the conversation, reaffirming my opinion. Afterwards, he and I thought it might be a good thing if we went together to see Massigli.

March 10, 1944

This morning it seemed to me less desirable to do as we had agreed to do last night, and I was glad to find that when I consulted Chapin he had reacted in the same way. For one thing the case is still *sub judice* and it would therefore be improper to prejudge the result, and for another thing if it got about that the English and Americans were intervening in a purely French affair it would inevitably cause resentment, which would do Pucheu more harm than good.

Before luncheon I went to see Harold Macmillan, who got back yesterday. He had seen a lot of the Prime Minister in England, and had spent two weekends at Chequers. He said that the P.M. was in a much better mood about the French and had said definitely that he was in favour of de Gaulle.

We had an office meeting at 4 p.m. The main subject of discussion was the Pucheu trial, and Gosling[2] said that both Frénay[3] and Mendès-France,[4] who were two of the more reasonable members of the Committee, were strongly in favour of his being shot, believing that his death would save the lives of large numbers of Frenchmen still in France.

---

[1] Emmanuel d'Astier de la Vigerie (1900–69), French journalist and politician [and brother of Henri, p. 296]. He refused to accept Vichy and joined Raymond Aubrac and Jean Cavilles in forming the Libération-sud resistance and edited their clandestine journal, *Libération*. He became Commissioner of the Interior under the CFNL in 1943, and was elected to the Chamber of Deputies in 1945 with Communist support.

[2] Major Gosling, Duff's banking and currency adviser.

[3] Henri Frénay (1905–88). An army officer, he became disillusioned with the Vichy Government, joined the French Resistance in 1941 and was instrumental in the formation of the *Combat* group. In November 1943 he escaped to Algiers and was appointed Commissioner for Prisoners and Refugees by de Gaulle.

[4] Pierre Mendès-France (1907–82). A member of the Radical Party in the French *Assemblée*, he was opposed to Vichy and escaped to England to join the Free French. Appointed Commissioner for National Economy by de Gaulle. Member of the *Assemblée* 1967–73.

March 11, 1944

When I got to the office I learned that Pucheu had been condemned to death this morning.

I today received a personal telegram from the Prime Minister in reply to a letter I wrote him some time ago about the future use of the Leclerc Division. He tells me that he is much in favour of the Division fighting with the main invasion forces from England, that Eisenhower[1] agrees with him, and that he is, therefore, doing all in his power to overcome the difficulties of transportation. I am glad to have this information to give de Gaulle, which ought to cheer him up. I had an interview with the General before dinner. He talked to me about the future command of any French force taking part in Anvil. The Commander-in-Chief [General Maitland Wilson] had mentioned it to me last night, saying that he thought the force must be commanded by an American, although the preponderance of the troops would be French.

General de Gaulle said that he had no objection to the Americans having command of the initial landing operations, but that subsequently, when there would be seven French divisions as against two or three American, the French must have an independent command, whether the Americans were included in it or not. I asked him as I left whether he thought it would be necessary to shoot Pucheu, and he said he was afraid it would. He spoke gravely about it, and expressed his admiration for the way in which Pucheu had conducted himself during the trial.

March 13, 1944

In the afternoon there came a long telegram from the Foreign Office about the negotiations that have been going on in Washington on the subject of the civil administration after the liberation. Apparently complete agreement was reached by all the authorities concerned on a procedure which would have satisfied the French, but, at the last moment, it was turned down by the President against the wishes of Cordell Hull,[2] the State Department, and ourselves. We are now leaving the Americans to fight it out with their President. It does seem intolerable that one obstinate old man should hold up everything in this way.

March 20, 1944

Pucheu was shot this morning. He met his death apparently with great courage, shaking hands with the firing squad and giving the order to fire himself. I am very glad that they allowed him to do this and did not bind him.

---

[1] Gen. Dwight D. Eisenhower (1890–1969), Allied CIC. Republican President of the USA, 1952–61.

[2] Cordell Hull (1871–1955), Democratic Senator who became Secretary of State [for Foreign Affairs] under President Roosevelt from 1933–44. In 1945 he received the Nobel Peace Prize for his efforts towards the establishment of the UN.

I have written a despatch to the Foreign Office, in which I tried to give an objective and unemotional account of what has happened; and I also sent a private telegram to the Prime Minister, who I fear may take a strong view about it and be unduly prejudiced against the Committee.

March 28, 1944

Harold Macmillan came round to see me before dinner. He was depressed about the general situation. He thought it quite likely that Anthony would leave the Foreign Office, as the work of the Department combined with leading the House of Commons was too much for one man at the present time. The House was becoming more and more difficult. We agreed that he would be much wiser to stick to the F.O. We also agreed that if Bobbety [Cranborne] took it over, as seems possible, the P.M. would find him much more obstinate and harder to deal with than Anthony, which we both thought would be a good thing. Harold said that he was gradually organizing himself out of existence, and that he would be glad to go home.

April 1, 1944

I went out to see Vanier in the afternoon in order to meet General Leclerc, a dapper little soldier exactly like an English officer, quiet and giving one the impression of competence. I told Leclerc and Vanier that I understood that it was almost certain that his division would go to England to take part in the invasion. He was naturally delighted to hear it.

I dined with the Dutch Minister at the Cercle [Le Cercle Inter-Alliée – a club]. The party included the Norwegian and Cuban Ministers. The Cuban Minister was very talkative and flushed before dinner, grew rapidly more silent and paler after we sat down, and when a large plate of very unappetizing macaroni was put before him he became quite green and darted from the room never to be seen again. Only Pleven[1] and I realized what had overcome him. We were both very much amused. The dinner was quite uneatable and I was glad when Pleven and Diethelm[2] rose and said that they had work to do.

April 4, 1944

In the afternoon papers there appeared a decree making de Gaulle Chief of the Forces. As this seemed to me only to put him in the same position as the Prime Minister or the President, I did not attach too much importance to it. Just before dinner I had a message from General Rooks[3] to say that some

---

[1] René Pleven (1901–93). A member of the Free French, he helped to found the Democratic and Socialist Union of the Resistance (UDSR). Finance Minister under de Gaulle.

[2] André Diethelm, a civil servant who joined de Gaulle in 1941 and was Commissioner of the Interior, responsible for political action in France.

[3] Maj. Gen. Lowell Rooks (1893–1973), US Army Commanding General 90th Division, NW Europe 1942–5.

important papers would be brought up to me. They revealed the fact that General Giraud intended to resign on account of this afternoon's decree.

April 5, 1944

I met General Maitland Wilson, General Devers[1] and General Rooks at A.F.H.Q. at 9.30. They seemed to have no very clear view of what was to be done at all – especially the Americans – but they thought it would be a great pity if Giraud went. I therefore said that I would see him this morning and try to dissuade him. When I got to the office I found that he had asked to see me, and he came at 11.30. I put forward all the arguments I could think of against his resignation, but he was very firm saying that he was sure that I should resign in similar circumstances, which was true.

I went to see Murphy at half past six. He had just arrived from the United States. Giraud was going to see him at 7. I told him briefly what the situation was. He was reticent and gave me no indication of the line he was going to take. I didn't like him, and hope he will not stay here.

April 6, 1944

It seems that Giraud saw de Gaulle yesterday, who offered him the post of Inspector-General of the Forces, which he refused. He subsequently saw Murphy, who did not advise him to withdraw his resignation, thereby failing on his first arrival to give me the cooperation which I had never failed to obtain from Chapin.

Massigli came to see me in the morning. He was inclined to pooh-pooh Giraud's resignation, taking the line that it matters little now as the Pucheu trial has killed Giraud so far as the Army was concerned.

General Juin, who returned from Italy last night on an urgent message from Giraud, came to lunch with me. He had seen Giraud and said that the whole thing now depended on the question of title. If he were left with the title of Commander-in-Chief he would stay, even without any powers, but he would not become Inspector-General. General Juin thought that de Gaulle did not want Giraud to go. I liked him very much. On the whole, he is the most impressive of the French generals whom I have met.

April 8, 1944

I was called at 5, having been awake long before owing to the noises that were going on of preparations. General Cochet[2] with two other Frenchmen came at about half past six, and we started on our long drive. We did not arrive at our objective for lunch until after one. It was a deserted spot, the sky was dark

[1] Gen. Jacob L. Devers (1887–1979). US Army, CIC US European Theatre of Operations 1943–4; Deputy Supreme Allied Commander Mediterranean 1944; CIC 6th Army Group NW Europe 1944–5.

[2] Gen. Gabriel Cochet (1888–1973), French Resistance leader who had escaped to Algiers.

and a gale was blowing, but we received wonderful hospitality – a lunch such as one could not imagine in war-time or hardly in peace – French wines: Chambertin 1921 and Roederer, six or seven courses, including two sheep roasted whole, and we were forced to partake of everything. I did not want anything more to eat for twenty-four hours. Our hosts were three charming old Arabs – Boushaghas. They had gone to great pains to prepare for us. They made me a present of a tame gazelle, and we were expecting a wonderful day of sport to follow. On leaving, at about half past four, we were met near Djelfa by a messenger to say that it was desired that I should return to Algiers as soon as possible. So Freddie[1] and I left the rest of them to go on, and turned back.

Eric Duncannon[2] had just brought Virginia[3] back from a party, so that he was able to tell me all that had happened. The Prime Minister had sent a long telegram telling me to do all that I could to prevent Giraud from resigning.

April 9, 1944 – Easter Day

At 7.30 I went to see de Gaulle. He was in plain clothes. I had never seen him out of uniform before. He agreed still to do anything he could to retain Giraud and said that he sincerely wanted to, but that he could not be allowed to play any really important part as he was incapable.

10 April, 1944

I had a talk with Gosling this morning. He tells me that the French are in some confusion with regard to currency questions. They want to be left to decide when they get into France what the rate of exchange is to be, as it must depend on the amount of paper that the Germans have printed. We are trying to force them before they go there either to raise it to 300 or to commit themselves to not doing so. We apparently have refused to print any more notes for them, and they have therefore had them printed in America and are very dissatisfied with the result, saying that the notes are too like dollars.

I dined with Freddie, Virginia and Bloggs. At the end of dinner the tame gazelle which the Boushaghas had given me arrived. He was remarkably calm after a five-hour motor journey, and we put him to bed in a passage in the yard. Later, just as we were going to bed, Teddie Phillips[4] arrived and told us all

---

[1] Freddie Fane, formerly Secretary of the Travellers' Club in Paris, had been appointed Comptroller of Duff and Diana's household in Algiers.

[2] Maj. Lord (Eric) Duncannon, later 10th Earl of Bessborough (1913–93). He joined the Foreign Service after the war and became first Duff's Private Secretary and subsequently First Secretary in Paris 1944–9.

[3] Virginia Cowles (1910–83), journalist and author. In 1944 she was war correspondent for the *Sunday Times*. She married Aidan Crawley (1908–93); Labour MP 1945–51; Conservative MP 1962–4.

[4] Teddie Phillips (b. 1907), a member of the Naval Mission to Algiers and subsequently Comptroller of the British Embassy in Paris.

that had passed after we left. They had gone on having tremendous banquets to the last, and the shooting had been very badly managed. They had, however, got about ten partridges, two gazelles, two bustards and twenty hares. He had enjoyed it enormously. I doubt whether I should have enjoyed it at the time as much as he did, but I should have liked to have had it to look back upon.

April 11, 1944

This morning I took the gazelle out on a lead and stupidly allowed him to escape. We had a tremendous hunt through the woods before he was brought back. He seems none the worse, but a little nervous. We now have added two tame partridges to the zoo, which were sent over by Catroux. I think Diana will like the gazelle and I am keeping it as a surprise for her. [*Diana had gone to England for John Julius's holidays.*]

April 13, 1944

At 5 I went to see Giraud, and talked to him at length. He seemed more determined than ever to go. He was particularly irritated because he had heard that the police had been told to keep an eye on his movements.

April 14, 1944

I received a personal telegram from the Prime Minister conveying a message from him to Giraud, urging that he should accept the posts he has been offered. It was extremely well worded and I took it immediately round to Giraud and read out to him an improvised translation. He was visibly moved, but continued to argue in the same senseless way to the effect that the Army was now being put under the command of Monsieur Diethelm.

April 15, 1944

The first thing that I read in the paper this morning was the decision of the Committee, taken yesterday afternoon, to put Giraud *en réserve de commandement,* so it is now too late. I went to see Catroux none the less, and he explained to me that Giraud's position is similar to that of a British Field Marshal, that is to say he will remain on the active list with pay and allowances and perquisites.

I spent part of the afternoon writing a telegram to the Prime Minister on the upshot of the Giraud case. I consider that it is now over, that Giraud, owing to his own folly, has lost everything and now possesses only a nuisance value which might be exploited either here or in London by those who wish to do harm to the Committee.

April 30, 1944 (Rabat)

This morning we visited some very beautiful public gardens which led down to the sea, and then attended a luncheon in a Moorish house. We were a party of about twenty, and there were three round tables. We sat on cushions and ate with our fingers. The meal began with an excellent dish of Spanish origin – pastillia. The second course consisted of three sheep roasted whole – one for each table, which was followed by three turkeys and after that four chickens, for each table; then cous-cous, and then sweets and oranges. Our host, who sat at our table, plied us with food throughout, and we all had to eat a great deal more than we needed. The quality of the food was superlative and we finished up with mint tea – three glasses each.

May 3, 1944

We had a lunch party. I had a talk with d'Astier [Baron Emmanuel] afterwards. He was interesting about de Gaulle, whom he sees, just as I do, as a difficult character suffering from a fatal inferiority complex and unaccustomed to the ways of the world. He has been terribly hurt in his *amour-propre* by the recently imposed ban on correspondence.[1] He did not mind France being treated differently from Russia and the United States, but he couldn't bear that she should be treated the same as any other second-rate or neutral power.

May 8, 1944

On my way from the office to the villa it occurred to me that it was worth considering the desirability of inviting de Gaulle to go to London now. It seemed to me that it would rob him of all his grievances if he accepted, and put him very much in the wrong if he refused, so I sent off a personal telegram to the Prime Minister and the Secretary of State suggesting it.

May 15, 1944

I went to the Assembly in the afternoon to hear the final stages of the debate on foreign affairs. Massigli wound up, and was as inaudible as ever. After he had spoken Gazier got up and proposed that in future the CFNL should take the style of the Provisional Government of the French Republic. This was carried unanimously and the President of the Chamber then called on de Gaulle to speak as Chief of the Provisional Government. De Gaulle made no reference to the resolution that had been passed, but read aloud two telegrams that he had received from Juin while all the members stood.

May 18, 1944

Roger Makins[2] came back here this morning from London. He told me that the general view there was in favour of the French Committee, but that everything was being held up by Washington. My proposal that de Gaulle should come to London had been forwarded to the President, and he was

---

[1] Regulations had been imposed by the British forbidding all communications with England, with exceptions only for Americans and Russians.
[2] Sir Roger Makins, 1st Lord Sherfield (1904–96). Harold Macmillan's diplomatic adviser in Algiers and Italy, Ambassador to Washington 1953–6.

surprised that I had not yet heard any more about it. He was afraid that the resolution about the Provisional Government produced a bad effect.

May 22, 1944

I received this morning the long-awaited reply to my telegram of May 8th, in which I suggested that de Gaulle should be invited to go to London. It was a long telegram which sent various complimentary messages to de Gaulle about the conduct of the French troops in Italy and the *Richelieu* in the Pacific, and finally said that I could tell him he was going to be invited to London at some unspecified date. I felt that such a message would hardly make a good impression, as he must now be half-expecting the invitation and this would only be a disappointment. I therefore telegraphed back asking whether I could not give him some indication of the approximate date of the visit.

May 23, 1944

In the afternoon we gave a garden party, taking advantage of the fact that the Grenadier Guards band was here. In the middle I received a telegram from London saying that they could not give a date for de Gaulle's visit, but that the invitation should be conveyed to him as soon as possible. I therefore arranged to see him at 9.30 and spent an hour with him. I found him in an easy – even genial – mood, and he accepted the invitation without any hesitation.

May 27, 1944

I went to see Massigli in the morning. He wanted an assurance about de Gaulle having full liberty of communication while he was in England. I drafted a telegram on the subject. Before I sent it off I received one from London inviting him to be the guest of H.M.G. and assuring him that he would have full liberty of communication, etc. I went to see de Gaulle to convey to him the information and assurances I had received in the morning. I had hoped he would be pleased, but he gave no indication of being so, and was as grumpy and sulky as usual, complaining bitterly about the intention of the American Government to issue their own francs when they entered France.

May 29, 1944

Of course, the statement in the press about which the Prime Minister telegraphed yesterday has had the inevitable reaction and produced a semi-official statement in *The New York Times* to the effect that the President would not send anybody to take part in the conversations in London with de Gaulle. This was so worded as to convey the impression that the United States would not be represented. At the same time, a most unfortunate message has been transmitted by Reuters, saying that Eisenhower was ready to carry on the government of France, and would work with anybody who was willing to fight for France now.

June 1, 1944

This morning I had a telegram from the P.M. telling me to ask de Gaulle to come as soon as he wished and offering to send out his own York to fetch him, but making no reference to my request for an assurance that the conversations would be tripartite. Went and told Massigli and suggested to him that I should urge de Gaulle to accept the invitation, as once he arrived in London it would really be impossible for the Americans to refuse to take part in the conversations; but if they did he could return immediately, thus putting the President completely in the wrong.

June 2, 1944

A telegram from the Prime Minister this morning, reproving me for not having given his message yesterday, saying that time was most essential, and that he was sending out two Yorks overnight for de Gaulle's party and enclosing a personal message to de Gaulle saying:

> 'Come please now with your colleagues at the earliest possible moment and in deepest secrecy. I give you my personal assurance that it is in the interests of France.'

I saw de Gaulle at 11 o'clock this morning and conveyed to him the personal and pressing appeal from the Prime Minister that he should go to London without delay. He said that it was plain that this meant that the Americans would take no part in the conversations. I replied that this was not necessarily the case, that it meant merely that the Americans had not yet consented to do so, but that I was sure that when he had arrived in London it would prove impossible for them to refuse, and if they did, he could return to Algiers. He said that that would be a definite break with the Americans which would be most harmful.

We argued for an hour. I said that if, as he thought, the President wanted to sabotage the visit, he would be playing straight into the President's hands by refusing to go, and it would be he and not the Americans who would be blamed for the failure. He said that he might go from a military standpoint only, taking General Béthouart[1] with him and visiting the French troops in England. I said that seemed to me a very good solution. He could go on in the Prime Minister's own plane, and when he got there could find out how matters stood, and if all was well his colleagues could follow him later. I could not see that he would lose anything by going, whereas he might lose everything by refusing to go. Above all, he would finally lose the regard of the Prime Minister, who would decide that he was an impossible man to deal with.

I then went to see General Wilson, having previously arranged to do so. I told

---

[1] Gen. Antoine Émile Béthouart (1889–1982), de Gaulle's COS for National Defence, later in command of troops occupying the French Zone of Austria after the war.

him that I was disturbed to think that the French were being left completely in the dark with regard to projected operations in the Mediterranean, and were perhaps being led to believe that what was only a cover plan was a real plan. He told me that General Béthouart and General de Lattre were both completely in his confidence and knew absolutely everything. They had undertaken not to convey that information to their junior officers and he was satisfied that they were both keeping their word.

I went to see de Gaulle and stayed with him until after 12. The argument which seemed to have most effect on him was that simply as a soldier it was his duty to help the battle which was about to take place. He said he might consent to go in that capacity only, in which case he would not take any of his Ministers with him. We had a very animated discussion and I spoke to him very frankly and at times rather rudely, but he took it all in very good part and said he would let me have his answer at 10 o'clock on the following morning. He asked me to give my personal word of honour that when he got to London his movements would be free and that he would have complete liberty to make use of his cyphers for telegrams, etc. I said that I had already given him this assurance, having been authorized to do so by H.M.G., but he asked me to repeat it on my own responsibility. I said I gladly would, but of course I was not a member of the Government and all I could say was that if the Government went back on their word, which I didn't think possible, I myself would resign.

June 3, 1944

I felt extremely anxious this morning and was most relieved when Palewski turned up with a letter from de Gaulle agreeing to go. We then had to make the necessary arrangements as soon as possible.

I drove off to the airfield at about 3 o'clock. The two Yorks were there and most of the party had assembled. De Gaulle himself was last to arrive and I was relieved when I saw him inside the plane. We got to Rabat in 2 hours. In view of the need for secrecy de Gaulle decided not to leave the airfield and to have dinner on the plane. Dinner was rather a sticky affair and afterwards I walked up and down the airfield with de Gaulle for about an hour talking of everything except, I was glad to say, the present situation. We finally left and had an excellent flight. I slept fairly well and we struck the ground at Northolt at exactly 6 a.m. the next morning. In view of the great secrecy that had been enjoined on us, I was rather surprised to see a large Air Force band and a Guard of Honour of at least 50 men. The band played the *Marseillaise* extremely well and I drove off with Oliver Harvey[1] to the Dorchester.

I was told we were both (de Gaulle and I) to go down to lunch with the

---

[1] Oliver Harvey, 1st Lord Harvey of Tasburgh (1893–1968). A diplomat, he was Anthony Eden's Private Secretary from 1936–8 and 1941–3. He succeeded Duff as Ambassador in Paris in 1948.

Prime Minister at his 'advance headquarters'. I did not know where we were going. It proved to be a train standing in a siding at the small station of Droyford. Here the Prime Minister had been living for the last few days. It seemed to me a perfectly absurd scheme, as he had only one telephone and would have been much better situated from every point of view if he had remained in London. His staff were all complaining bitterly of the discomfort and inconvenience. One of them said to me that he intended to lead a reformed life in future because he now knew what hell was like.

Anthony, Ernest Bevin[1] and Field Marshal Smuts were there. It had not, of course, occurred to the Prime Minister that Smuts was the most unsuitable person to have selected to meet the French, as they will never forgive him for the speech in which he said France will never be a great power again. We immediately proceeded to have a conference, at which the Prime Minister, whom I had been unable to speak to before, said just what I would have advised him not to – emphasizing the fact that he had got de Gaulle over in order that he might make a speech on the radio before the battle, and saying nothing about negotiations. Anthony tried to raise the latter question without much success and at quarter past 2 we had luncheon. Towards the end of the meal Anthony again raised the question of political talks and de Gaulle said he saw no reason for them if the Americans were not to be represented. This led to an argument with the Prime Minister, which became rather heated and certainly did not advance matters.

In the afternoon we drove off to Eisenhower's headquarters, about an hour away, where de Gaulle and the other generals were shown all the plans for the invasion[2] and informed of all the details. Eisenhower also gave de Gaulle the text of the radio speech he was going to make and asked for his suggestions and corrections. He took it away with him.

Monday June 5, 1944

At 3 I went to see Viénot,[3] who said he thought that the previous day had not been by any means a success. The important thing now is to get the General to agree to the opening of conversations, and Viénot therefore suggested that Anthony should write a letter, repeating the assurance he had already given in the House of Commons that we, the British, would not negotiate with anybody except the Committee.

---

[1] Ernest Bevin (1881–1951), trade unionist and Labour politician. Minister of Labour and National Service under Churchill 1940–5 and a member of the War Cabinet. Foreign Secretary under Attlee 1945–51.

[2] The Normandy landings of 6 June 1944, codenamed Operation Overlord.

[3] Pierre Viénot (1897–1944), French politician who escaped to London in April 1943 after being imprisoned in France by Vichy, and was appointed the CFLN's Ambassador to London. In June 1944 he accompanied de Gaulle to Bayeux, returned as Ambassador to London and died of a heart attack on 20 July 1944.

Tuesday June 6, 1944

John Julius rang me up early this morning [from Eton], I having sent him a telegram yesterday, and I promised to go down and see him on Thursday. I heard that the invasion had begun. It was to have taken place, we had been told, on the night of Sunday, but was put off on account of the weather, and we were told that while it might be on Monday night it was more likely not to be until Wednesday – so I was quite surprised at the news.

I went to the Foreign Office, where a conference was going on in Anthony's room. Apparently there had been terrible scenes the night before. The Prime Minister had been given to understand that de Gaulle had refused to broadcast and also refused to send his liaison officers to France. The first accusation was a misunderstanding. What he had said was that he would not follow on Eisenhower's broadcast. Eisenhower, having asked him to amend the text of it, had disregarded all his suggestions. Forty million copies of Eisenhower's broadcast had already been printed. They had therefore simply been wasting de Gaulle's time by asking him to amend it. The other difficulty was that de Gaulle had said that as his liaison officers were trained only for administrative duties and as no agreement had been reached with regard to civil affairs, he would not allow his officers to go to France. The Prime Minister had insulted Viénot in a most violent way during the night, telling him that he was a blackmailer, and had written a letter to de Gaulle, telling him to go back to Algiers immediately. Fortunately the letter had not been sent off.

I saw de Gaulle at 3. I pointed out to him that in his own interests he ought to agree to the officers going, as otherwise it would be said of him that he had refused to help us in the battle itself. He was in a very difficult mood as Viénot had repeated to him all the violent things that the Prime Minister had said during the night, but he eventually agreed to send at least some of his officers if not all.

Wednesday June 7, 1944

Alphand[1] came to see me at 10.15 in great distress about the financial complications. He said that if Eisenhower published a statement he had drawn up about the American-made francs which they are going to launch on France, he was afraid that de Gaulle would refuse to accept any responsibility for them. They would then have no backing and great confusion might arise.

At 5.30 I went to a meeting of the Executive Committee at my constituency. They asked me to tell them something about the French situation and they were quite astonished to learn the facts. They had no idea that the French Committee were actually governing almost the whole of the French Empire

---

[1] Hervé Alphand (1907–94), Director-General, Ministry of Foreign Affairs. French Ambassador to Washington 1956–65. His wife, Claude, was a talented guitarist and singer.

with complete success, were controlling an organized army, navy and air force and had an elected assembly working in Algiers.

I dined at the Connaught Hotel with de Gaulle, Anthony, Charles Peake,[1] Viénot and two or three other Frenchmen. We had a discussion after dinner, the main point of which was to persuade de Gaulle to enter into conversations with us although the Americans refused to take part in them. He said it was a waste of time and it would be a humiliation to both our countries to be obliged, after coming to an agreement, to go and ask the United States for their kind approval. Anthony was wonderfully patient and argued with him on the lines of 'she stoops to conquer', which we found some difficulty in translating into French. I thought it went fairly well, although on the following day Viénot said that he thought the General had been *odieux*.

June 9, 1944

At 4 I saw Viénot who had brought with him to the Foreign Office his reply to Anthony's letter. [Anthony] had to go up to York that evening and so I took over Viénot's reply to the Prime Minister. I had to listen to a long fulmination against de Gaulle, and when I got on to the question of the francs and the danger of them not being acceptable to the French people, he said that of course the French would jump at them as they had the American and British Governments behind them. I assured him that neither the American nor the British Governments were backing this money, whereupon he rang his bell and said 'Send for the Chancellor of the Exchequer'. It turned out that Anderson[2] had already left for the country – much to the Prime Minister's annoyance, although he himself was about to leave a little later – so a Mr Fraser[3] came over from the Treasury, who confirmed everything I had said. He spoke up with great firmness and courage. He said the liability for the francs was more than we could possibly undertake. The Prime Minister said 'What did it matter – every country would be bankrupt after the war.' Fraser replied that on the contrary France was very far from being bankrupt. She had vast gold reserves put away in the United States. The Prime Minister's difficulty is that if he accepts the statement which the French Government are prepared to put out to the effect that they accept responsibility for the money, he will be to a large extent recognizing them as a Government, whereas, if no such notice goes out, there will be no backing behind the notes. I was rather distressed by

[1] Sir Charles Peake (1897–1958), British representative to the FCNL in London 1942–3 and political adviser to the Supreme Commander, Allied Expeditionary Force 1943–5. Ambassador to Belgrade 1946–51 and to Greece 1951–7.

[2] John Anderson, 1st Viscount Waverley (1882–1958). Civil Service administrator and politician. Lord President of the Council and member of the War Cabinet 1940–3; Chancellor of the Exchequer 1943–5.

[3] Lionel Fraser (1895–1965), a merchant banker at Helbert Wagg & Co., Chairman 1954–62. In 1940–5 he worked at the Treasury, where his responsibilities included liaison with governments-in-exile of occupied countries.

the levity with which he seemed to treat the whole matter.

On the following morning I saw two telegrams which the Prime Minister had addressed to the President in which he put the case very clearly and well. In the interval he had seen specimens of these notes and his artistic feelings had been shocked by the clumsy workmanship, which gives the notes themselves the appearance of counterfeit money.

June 10, 1944

This morning I got a message saying de Gaulle would like to see me at 11 o'clock. When I saw him he said that he was in a hurry to get back to Algiers but he wanted to go to France first. He was in a gloomy mood and annoyed at Eisenhower's latest broadcast. He feels he is being made to appear in agreement with the British and Americans and accept their plans for imposing AMGOT [Allied Military Government for Occupied Territories] on the French.

June 12, 1944

At 10.15 I went to see Viénot, who was anxious about de Gaulle's visit to France and said it would be a mean and cruel thing if the Prime Minister, who first suggested to de Gaulle that they might go together, were to go there first. I happened to know that the Prime Minister had left that morning for France so I assured Viénot that if he did go it would not in any way be intended as a revenge on de Gaulle and I felt sure there would be no difficulty in de Gaulle going later.

June 13, 1944

At 11 I went to the Foreign Office, left at 12.30, driving straight to White's where I was met with a message from the Foreign Office that Anthony wanted to see me at once. He had had a long and difficult morning with the Prime Minister and the American Ambassador and General Marshall.[1] The two latter had been quite hopeless. Smuts had been present and had said to Winant[2] 'You have got to make up your mind sooner or later between Pétain and de Gaulle', which had somewhat irritated Winant, who declared that the United States had no intention of going back to Vichy. This, however, is what they would really like to do. Anthony said that he had never been so unhappy or so perplexed by anything as he was by the French situation at the time, and he could not see what was going to be the result.

June 15, 1944

I went down to the Foreign Office where I was rung up by Viénot, who wanted to see me. I went along to him and he told me that de Gaulle's visit to France

---

[1] Gen. George C. Marshall (1880–1959), US Army COS 1939–45.
[2] John Gilbert Winant (1889–1947), American Ambassador to London 1941–6.

yesterday had been a great success and had cheered him up a great deal. He had been very depressed before. He now wanted to get back to Algiers as soon as possible and I said that I thought I could arrange it for tomorrow night. He also wanted to know what gesture de Gaulle should make before leaving and whether I thought it desirable that he should see the Prime Minister again.

[Later] I went back to the Foreign Office and we discussed the question of the 'gesture' with Anthony and others. We thought that on the whole it would be better that de Gaulle should not see Winston again but that he might write a civil letter saying goodbye and putting himself at the Prime Minister's disposal should he wish to see him before he goes.

16 June, 1944

As I walked into the Dorchester the hall porter was speaking to the Prime Minister's Secretary who said that the P.M. wanted to see me at a quarter to six. The Prime Minister had received a farewell letter from General de Gaulle which was extremely polite, and while I sat with him he dictated a reply a good deal cooler in tone. I fear that it is impossible to get him to take a really reasonable view of the situation. He even said that Massigli had had no right to open the letter which had come into his possession addressed to me from Spears. I said that if the same thing had happened to anybody in the service of his Majesty's Government the only difference in our procedure would have been that, after reading and photographing it, we should have put it back in the envelope and sent it on to its destination with all the appearance of its never having been opened. I thought that far from behaving badly the French had been very straightforward about it.

June 18, 1944 (Algiers)

Massigli came to see me at 5.30. He said that, on the whole, the General was well pleased with his visit. He had been much impressed by the sympathy of the feeling on his side amongst the public, press and House of Commons. Massigli thought this a very good thing, as it would cure any anglophobia from which he might have suffered. He had also been impressed by the popularity of the Allies in France, and had realized that it would not do for him to quarrel with them.

June 19, 1944

Just before lunch a colonel on General Catroux's staff called on me with a letter from him, asking me to see in the afternoon a certain Colonel Dur. The latter proved to be a rather wild-looking man, much mutilated by war wounds, but obviously full of energy. He had an extraordinary story to the effect that Hitler was living disguised as a Polish Jew at No. 2, Avenue Wilson, Perpignan, that he would be leaving there on Saturday next, but that, meanwhile, it would be quite easy to bomb the house where he was. The object of his visit was both to reconnoitre the military situation and also to prepare a plan of escape should he need it later. He had the most detailed information on every point, but would not say where he had got it from. Nor was he very clear as to why he had brought the story to me rather than to the French authorities, saying vaguely that he thought they would waste time which was of vital importance.

Dodds-Parker was away, so I got hold of Brooks Richards,[1] and we decided to check up on him as best we could. Brooks Richards came up while I was at dinner to say that he had been discussing the matter with his own people and he felt that there was a question of high policy involved. The Government might not wish Hitler to be killed in this way and might be afraid of making a martyr of him, or have some other reason for hesitation. I said I was prepared to take all the responsibility involved, and that they had my authority to go ahead with their preparations.

June 20, 1944

The more I think of Colonel Dur's story the less I believe in it. It is quite incredible that Hitler could absent himself from a central position, where he could take decisions and give orders, even for a week at the present time. Brooks Richards has seen Dur again, told him that everything can be arranged and an aeroplane is waiting, but unless he will reveal his sources of information we cannot believe his story.

June 21, 1944

Brooks Richards had seen Frénay about Colonel Dur's story. He had told Colonel Dur that we should take no action unless he would disclose the source of his information. He had asked for twenty-four hours to think this over, since when no more had been heard of him. It looks as though he invented the whole story in order to revenge himself on his enemies in Perpignan.

June 22, 1944

I went to see Massigli at 5 o'clock and found him in the depths of despair. More trouble in Syria. We have apparently announced that we intend to rearm and equip the Syrian gendarmerie. This certainly looks like an attempt to go away from our definite promise that we would give the Syrian native troops no assistance – financial or material. Massigli sees in it a deliberate attempt on the part of Spears to wreck the negotiations in London; it looks rather like it.

---

[1] Sir Brooks Richards (1918–2002) served with SOE during the war, latterly as head of SOE's French section in Algiers under Lt.-Col. Douglas Dodds-Parker. He was recruited by Duff to join the staff of the Paris Embassy where he remained until 1948. Later Ambassador to Vietnam 1972–4 and Greece 1974–8.

June 23, 1944

A strange little man called the Abbé Pierre came to see me at 5. He had recently come out of the maquis; he had carried de Gaulle's crippled brother[1] from France to Geneva. He had a face like a saint painted by El Greco. He was obviously a very sincere fanatic. He had a religious faith in de Gaulle and Gaullisme, without any clear idea what he meant by the latter. He thought it a pity that de Gaulle should be surrounded by politicians, but did not seem to know what he meant by the word. He had some terrible stories of the suffering and tortures which have been endured by the people of the resistance. He talked almost uninterruptedly for about an hour. The most sensible thing he said was the importance of getting those forces of the right and of religion which would have nothing to do with the Third Republic to play their part in the Fourth Republic, and he was going to make it his special duty in North Africa, where those forces of the right were strongly represented, to persuade them as to where their duty lay. I was much impressed by him, but I fear he is the sort of man who might do de Gaulle, whom he has seen twice, more harm than good by convincing him that he has a divine mission.

June 26, 1944

Spears has produced a long telegram attempting to justify his conduct and abusing Massigli. I do not think he makes out a good case, and I sent a further telegram on the subject to the F.O.

June 29, 1944

I went to see Massigli. He said that de Gaulle had decided to go to Washington next week. The object of his visit would be to thank the President for all that America had done. He would stay a very short time as he wished to visit Canada also and to be back here by July 14. This is very satisfactory.

He added that it was very foolish of the Americans not to come to some agreement about civil affairs. They suspected de Gaulle of harbouring designs of a non-democratic nature. If he were doing so – and Massigli did not seem to dismiss the possibility – the Americans were helping him by putting difficulties in the way of Le Troquer going there and setting up a proper constitutional machine which would be under the control of the Committee.

June 30, 1944

Harold Macmillan came and had a long talk. He has an idea that the Committee ought to move into France as soon as possible, settling even in so small a place as Caen. I don't think this is a very good idea. He has just come back

---

[1] Pierre de Gaulle (1897–1995), fought in the First World War, was a resistance fighter in the second, and president of the Municipal Council of Paris, 1947–51.

from London and he had got the impression from Clemmie that the Prime Minister was rather sorry about the way he had handled de Gaulle.

July 11, 1944

I had a very interesting talk with Monsieur Blesson, who has been the French Minister at the Vatican during these years. He told me the true story of Mussolini's overthrow which was quite different from anything that has appeared in the press. It seems that Mussolini had no intention of resigning, but that the King sent for him after he had been defeated by the Cabinet and arranged to have him practically kidnapped when he left the Palace. It also appears that Ciano and Grandi, who had plotted his overthrow and were in with the King and Badoglio[1] as they thought, were really double-crossed by the latter, who was determined to get rid of all the Fascists at one blow.

July 12, 1944

I have written a long letter to Anthony about the position in the Far East. At his press conference in Washington de Gaulle indicated that France would have no intention of giving up any part of her Empire, but that in accordance with decisions taken at the Brazzaville Conference the Empire would be based upon a new principle of federation. I had already suggested to the Foreign Office that we should take this opportunity of coming to some agreement with the French about our future policy in the Middle East in order that we might have one in common, and I have now suggested that we should extend any such understanding to cover the Far East as well. It seems to me the plainest common sense that we, being the two great powers who have important interests in Arab and in Asiatic countries, should come together and should brook no interference from America or Russia, who have no similar responsibilities. The trouble is that one sends in these suggestions to the Foreign Office and nothing comes back. One doesn't even know whether they have received the slightest consideration.

July 14, 1944

Chapin, who returned with de Gaulle last night, came to see me in the afternoon, and said that everything had gone extremely well in Washington, but that as all the conversations between the General and the President had been à deux nobody knew any of the details. There was not, so far as he was aware, any immediate prospect of an American ambassador being sent out.

We went to a cocktail party given by de Gaulle. I had a short talk with him about the success of his visit to Washington. Characteristically, he refused to be enthusiastic about it, but merely said that it had gone quite well and that the general atmosphere had been quite favourable. I asked him whether the

---

[1] Pietro Badoglio (1871–1956). Appointed head of the Italian Government 25 July 1943 and signed the Italian surrender in September.

President had been in a good humour, to which he replied that he had at any rate sought to give the impression that he was in a good humour.

July 17, 1944

At 5 o'clock I went to see de Gaulle. He said he wanted to tell me about his conversations with the President. The main subjects had been (1) the present arrangements in France; (2) the future of Germany; (3) the necessity for the U.S. to retain certain strategic bases after the war. He was in a calm and friendly mood and talked to me also about Anglo-French relations, which he feared would never improve so long as we pursue our present policy in the Levant.

July 20, 1944

The plane with Randolph Churchill, Evelyn Waugh[1] and Philip Jordan[2] in it crashed in Yugoslavia. Fortunately none of them were seriously hurt.

A report came this evening that an attempt has been made to assassinate Hitler.[3]

July 25, 1944

It was a very hot day, and I drove out with Diana and Victor to Tipaza to lunch, and we then went on a little further and bathed in the sea. We got back at about half past five and found that Randolph had arrived. He has got water on both knees as a result of his accident, but is in his usual high spirits and doesn't seem to have suffered much, although ten out of the nineteen people in the aeroplane were killed. He was very lucky to be able to slip out of the plane through a hole in the floor before being burnt alive. Evelyn Waugh and Philip Jordan were with him at the right end of the plane and also got out. We are again getting rather overwhelmed by the guests. Randolph is a liability in a house.

August 3, 1944

The Prime Minister made an excellent speech yesterday, excellent especially from the point of view of France. He included France with Great Britain, the United States and Russia as the four great Powers who would settle European affairs, and he paid an unexpectedly warm tribute to General de Gaulle. At 3.30 I saw the General. He said it would be disastrous if the Leclerc Division

---

[1] Evelyn Waugh (1903–66), novelist, was a friend and admirer of Diana's, with whom he had a long correspondence. These letters were published in 1991 as *Mr Wu and Mrs Stitch*, edited by Diana's granddaughter, Artemis Cooper.

[2] Philip Jordan (1902–51), journalist and war correspondent, covered the bombing of Guernica in the Spanish Civil War and wrote for the *News Chronicle* 1939–42.

[3] On 20 July 1944, a group of army officers attempted to assassinate Hitler by activating a bomb in a briefcase at a conference he was attending. Hitler survived and the plotters were executed.

was not made use of as soon as possible. He expressed no gratitude for the Prime Minister's speech and hardly any satisfaction.

August 10, 1944

I received a telegram from the Prime Minister saying he was arriving in Algiers on the following day, that I was to keep the matter extremely secret but I could tell General de Gaulle that the Prime Minister would receive him if he wished to pay him a visit. Randolph was to have left tomorrow morning, but of course decided to stay another day.

I went to see de Gaulle at 6 o'clock and gave him this information. He said that he thought nothing would be gained by an interview with the Prime Minister at the present time. I did my best to persuade him to change his mind, reminding him of the extremely warm terms in which the Prime Minister had referred to him in the House of Commons and saying that it was only common civility to pay a call on so distinguished a traveller passing through French territory. I spent three quarters of an hour with him, but did not succeed in convincing him, though I persuaded him to send a polite letter to the P.M. saying that he did not wish to disturb the short time he was to have at Algiers between his two flights.

It occurred to me during dinner that it was worth while making one more appeal to General de Gaulle, so with the help of Totor de Lesseps I wrote him a letter after dinner, pointing out that he had promised to write a letter which was, after all, only a gesture of politeness and that as he was prepared to make such a gesture, why not go a little further and pay a call, which would have a much more useful effect. He replied that he had already written the letter, which Palewski would deliver the next morning; and I could do no more. It is incredibly stupid on his part – one of the most foolish things he has yet done.

August 11, 1944

The Prime Minister's plane arrived at 8.45. He drove with Randolph and me to the villa and sat talking for about an hour before having his bath. I had a long argument with him about Spears and found him very obstinate. He was most optimistic about the war in general and on the whole was in excellent form. We drove back to the aerodrome at about 12 o'clock, Randolph accompanying us. Unfortunately, Randolph came to my support about Spears, which only irritated his father the more. Randolph however thought I had made some impression and advised me to follow it up by a letter, which I did.

August 15, 1944

I saw Massigli. It appears that de Gaulle is now in a violent rage because the Prime Minister has gone to Corsica without warning the French authorities, and because he was not consulted before General Wilson issued his appeal and orders to the French people. I said I thought it quite absurd to make a fuss about such small matters at a moment like this. (We had heard at midday that the landings in the South of France had taken place successfully.) We were now in the middle of a battle, and the Prime Minister had a perfect right to visit any part of the battlefield he chose to. Massigli really agreed with me, but I gathered that he had found the General in so violent a mood that he had not been able to make any protest.

August 17, 1944

Chapin tells me that there have been many difficulties about de Gaulle's visit to Brittany. S.H.A.E.F. [Supreme Headquarters, Allied Expeditionary Force] wanted him to put it off for a few days, which he refused to do. They then told him that his own plane was not safe for the journey and offered to send him a Fortress. He said that he must go in a French plane, but would accept a Fortress if it bore French cockades and the whole of the crew were doubled with French substitutes. These men will, in fact, be passengers, as there are no French crews, apparently, acquainted with Fortresses.

Massigli told me this morning that he did not think de Gaulle would last a year in France, and if he continues to behave in this temperamental manner it certainly seems doubtful.

We heard this afternoon that the Americans had taken Chartres, Dreux and Orleans. It seems almost too good to be true.

August 23, 1944

Our radio has gone out of order, with the result that I did not hear the announcement of the liberation of Paris until, in the middle of lunch, Sweeney [Duff's batman] told us that he had it as a fact from the Sergeant-Major. It was naturally a day of great excitement here. I paid an official call on Monsieur Queuille, who is Acting President of the Committee, and on General Catroux in the evening to offer them my congratulations.

August 26, 1944

The news was not so good yesterday, as it appeared that the announcement of the liberation of Paris had been premature and fighting was still going on there. This morning, all seems to be well. De Gaulle is there and the situation is completely in hand, and the Germans driven out.

August 28, 1944

There was a great deal of excitement this morning about our departure. The Committee wished to leave at once in the French cruiser *Jeanne d'Arc* which will take them to Cherbourg, and I at first thought that it would be a good thing for our advance party to go with them. They, however, were not too anxious to take any British personnel on board a French ship, and foresaw difficulties about giving preference to the members of one mission rather than to those of another. Later, we got a telegram from the Foreign Office saying that our advance party should go via London and should leave as soon as possible. We arranged for them to go by air tomorrow.

August 29, 1944

The first echelon of our mission – fifteen in all – left about midday. We got a telegram this morning that I should follow them by the same route in a few days. This suits me extremely well, as I want to go to London on the way to Paris, and I had already made up my mind to leave on Saturday.

September 2, 1944

We had a smooth journey. I think the designer of the York has discovered the shape of an armchair in which it is quite impossible to be comfortable, and I found there was no way of sleeping, or even resting. If this is typical of the civil transport plane in which we are going to compete against the U.S., we are already beaten.

September 3, 1944 (London)

We drove to the Dorchester where we found a sitting room but no bedroom or bathroom vacant, so we went on to Claridge's, having left our luggage to follow us in a truck; we were kept waiting for it for four hours. An hour after our arrival at Claridge's, John Julius, who had been sleeping the night at the Dorchester – a fact of which the manager had not informed us – appeared. All this was enough to irritate one, but my satisfaction of being back in London survived all irritation. The weather was cold and grey, which was a very pleasant change from Algiers.

September 4, 1944 (London)

At 3.30 I went to see Anthony, who explained to me the present position with regard to Spears. He is going, or has gone, back with a very firm directive which he has promised to observe. He has also gone under the clear under-standing that he is there for two months only or for the duration of the German war – whichever is the shorter period. It is a poor sort of compromise, but it satisfied Winston, who said to Anthony when arguing the case 'I am committed to sending him back'. Anthony asked him to whom he was committed, and he admitted that he had said to me that he would send Spears back whatever I said to the contrary – an extraordinary example of childishness in so great a man.

On 13 September 1944 Duff, accompanied by Diana, left London to take up his post as Ambassador to France. The Allies, on the Americans' insistence, delayed formal recognition of de Gaulle's provisional government until 23 October 1944.

September 13, 1944

We drove down to Hendon where our party was already assembled. There were two planes and an escort of some forty-eight Spitfires. The plane we went in is a very comfortable Dakota. We were only six in it: ourselves, Captain Wharton,[1] Teddie Phillips, Brigadier Daly[2] and Eric Duncannon. It was a perfect morning and we enjoyed the flight. It was extremely interesting to see the traces of the war as we went along. We flew quite slowly over Paris and saw all the familiar buildings. The streets looked very empty, but I do not think they are really emptier than the London streets, and there are many more bicycles and horse carriages. We were met by the staff, Holman,[3] Reilly, etc., and also by representatives of General de Gaulle and the Ministry of Foreign Affairs. We were attended on our way from Le Bourget by French police motor cyclists, and everywhere as we passed the people seemed pleased to see us, saluting and waving. We went to the Arc de Triomphe where I had to lay a wreath on the grave of the Unknown Soldier, and then to the Berkeley Hotel, where we always used to stay, and which Freddie [Fane] has requisitioned complete for us and the staff. There we had an excellent lunch, and then went round to the Embassy. The whole of the ground floor is choc-a-bloc with the furniture of thirty-two different households who stored it there when they had to leave Paris in 1940. This is gradually being removed. The rooms are in perfect condition. There is at present a lack of electricity and no water at all. I think we shall probably get into it in a few weeks.

September 14, 1944

I went to the Quai d'Orsay, where I made the acquaintance of the new Minister for Foreign Affairs, Monsieur Bidault.[4] He seemed curiously young and somewhat overcome by his responsibilities, admitting himself that he knew nothing, and had had no experience. On the whole, I liked him, but whether he will prove a big enough man for the job I am inclined to doubt. Massigli came to see me in the afternoon. He is very glad to be going to London [as Ambassador]. He told me that his wife, whom I have never seen, had arrived suddenly, having had a wonderful journey from Switzerland, passing through the German lines. He said that he thought that the Communists had had a great setback, and were losing ground all over the country.

---

[1] Capt. Eric Wharton RN, Naval Attaché at the Paris Embassy.
[2] Brig. Denis Daly (1890–1956), Military Attaché at the Paris Embassy.
[3] Sir Adrian Holman (1895–1974), Minister in Paris 1944–6, Ambassador to Cuba 1950–4.
[4] Georges Bidault (1899–1983) joined the Resistance in 1941 and edited *Combat* where he worked with Albert Camus. In July 1943 he became President of the *Conseil National de la Résistance* (CNR). Appointed Foreign Minister in de Gaulle's Provisional Government. Prime Minister of France 1946, 1949–50 and 1958–61.

September 15, 1944

Desmond Morton[1] came to see me. He said that the Prime Minister would want to come here as soon as possible after the opening of Parliament, which would be in a fortnight to three weeks. I said that he could not possibly come until he had recognized the Government, and that we must arrange for him to receive a proper invitation from de Gaulle. Nothing could do more harm than if he came as part of S.H.A.E.F., and lived outside Paris with them at Versailles.

September 17, 1944

I went to church in the Embassy church and thought it was quite a good congregation considering. It had been re-opened only last Sunday, but everything seemed to go well. The old parson aged 82 came to see me afterwards, together with the younger one who had come from Cannes, both of whom had been interned.

We lunched with the Charles de Polignacs.[2] They seemed little changed and we had quite a good lunch. The Duchesse D'Ayen[3] was there, who was beautiful when I last met her six years ago. She had aged very much. Her husband has been a prisoner in Germany for two years – not a prisoner of war – and she has no news of him, nor of her son, who has been fighting in the maquis. Nelly de Vogüé[4] was there, and also her husband, whom I had not met before. He has been a leading light in the resistance movement, and was wearing the F.F.I.[5] armlet.

We went for a drive round the Bois after lunch. It is looking lovely – full of cheerful people, many of them rowing on the ponds. It was much nicer than when it was crowded with motor cars in the old days.

---

[1] Maj. Sir Desmond Morton (1891–1971). An army officer, he served in the Foreign Office as an intelligence officer 1919–39. He was a close friend of Churchill, who brought him to 10 Downing Street to liaise with the FO. He later became Churchill's contact with the Allied governments in London.

[2] Count and Countess Charles de Polignac were old friends of the Coopers. They had travelled to North Africa together in 1928.

[3] Solange de Labriffe married the Duc d'Ayen in 1919. He died in Belsen in April 1945, and her son was killed in action in October 1944.

[4] Nelly de Vogüé, née Marie-Henriette Jaunez, was married to Count Jean de Vogüé, a naval officer from an influential aristocratic family. He had fought in the Resistance under the name of 'Vaillant'.

[5] The FFI (Forces Françaises de l'Intérieur) were created in February 1944 by order of the CFLN. They became part of the Allied Armed Forces, assisted in the liberation of Paris and were integrated into the regular armed forces in September 1944.

September 19, 1944

Signor Nitti[1] came to see me this morning. He is in great distress because the Italians are now being treated by the French as enemies. This is partly their own fault, as the Bonomi Government has not recognized de Gaulle. He therefore suggests that he should be allowed to go to Italy to explain to them the position. His old father, who was at one time Prime Minister of Italy, has been carried off as a prisoner to Germany.

September 21, 1944

Mr Muir, the Editor of the *Continental Daily Mail*, came to see me. He is much distressed at his inability to get permission from S.H.A.E.F. for his assistants to come out from England. He has need of seventeen of them, and cannot produce his paper properly without their help. Meanwhile, the London *Daily Mail* has produced a violent attack on S.H.A.E.F. in general, stating that France is full of American businessmen dressed in uniform, while British businessmen are refused permission to come here.

Victor and Tess dined with us, and Martha [Gellhorn] and Freddie. After dinner, Johnny and Baba Lucinge[2] came round. I heard that they had not behaved too well during the war. I thought she looked old and thin and frightened, and she asked me if I could help her to get a visa for England.

September 22, 1944

We lunched at the Ritz with Monsieur and Madame Massigli. Madame Massigli is a good-looking Swiss and speaks admirable English; I should think she will do very well in London. The Ritz looked exactly as it did pre-war, with Mrs Corrigan sitting in one corner of it.

I went to see Nadège de Ganay before dinner. She protested strongly that she had always been pro-British during the war and how she was in with the resistance movement. I thought she protested rather too much. In the evening André Roy,[3] Totor de Lesseps, and Solange D'Ayen came to dinner. Solange said that the Lucinges had been quite all right during the war, which I was glad to hear, but she was not prepared to say as much for Nadège, although she had nothing definite against her.

---

[1] Federico Nitti (1903–47), a doctor and biologist whose family had left Italy for Paris in 1927 to escape Fascism. He provided medical aid to the Resistance and the FFI. In 1944 he became *chef de service* at the Institut Pasteur.

[2] Baba d'Erlanger (1901–45) was married to Prince Jean-Louis (Johnny) de Faucigny-Lucinge (1903–92). She had been arrested as a Jew in 1943.

[3] André Roy, a friend of the de Lesseps whom the Coopers had met in Algiers.

September 23, 1944

Chapin came to see me. He told me that Jefferson Caffery[1] had been definitely appointed Ambassador (or rather Representative with the rank of Ambassador), but that the French had not even been asked for their agreement. He had to announce this to Monsieur Bidault who had not concealed the fact that he was much hurt by the lack of courtesy on the part of the Americans. Chapin did not himself seem enthusiastic about Caffery, although he had to be guarded about what he said.

At 11 o'clock Luizet[2] – Prefect of Police – whom I had last seen in Algiers – came, and we set out to visit some of the torture chambers which the Germans had made use of in Paris. It was a moving and terrible experience. We were shown things that only could be believed after being seen. My own hope is that the fullest publicity will be given to these horrors in order that the English and American people may never again make the mistake they have so often repeated of believing that the Germans are normal people and that the Nazis are any different from the ordinary Germans.

September 26, 1944

We lunched with the Lucinges. M. and Madame Bourdet[3] were there. He is now in control of all the theatres. Christian Bérard,[4] a funny little man with a huge beard, who is a great producer and artist [and] Edward Molyneux [were] also there and Palewski. Charles de Beistegui[5] came in, whom I had not seen for many years. He was little changed.

We went to a cinema show at the Ministry of Information where we found Bidault and Teitgen, as well as many of our old Algiers friends. They had some extremely interesting French and German films – French ones of the liberation and German ones of the defences all along the coast, which certainly looked most formidable, and another one trying to throw discredit on the resistance movement by representing them all as gangsters.

---

[1] The Hon. Jefferson Caffery (1886–1974), an American career diplomat, Ambassador to Paris 1944–9.

[2] Charles Luizet (1903–47) joined de Gaulle after the fall of France and worked clandestinely in North Africa. He became Prefect of liberated Corsica in 1943, and Prefect of Police in Paris at the liberation.

[3] Edouard Bourdet (1887–1945), playwright, married Denise Rémond (1892–1967) in 1922. He was Administrator-General of the Comédie Française 1936–40, she was a journalist. His son, Claude, fought in the Resistance and founded *Combat*.

[4] Christian (Bébé) Bérard (1902–49), painter and designer. He worked with Balanchine, Massine, Jean-Louis Barrault and Jean Cocteau.

[5] Charles de Beistegui (1895–1970), a Mexican-American, was known for his wealth, his collections and his passion for architecture and interior decoration.

27 September, 1944

Admiral Ramsay[1] and Victor came to lunch. Ramsay was delightful – very interesting and indiscreet – especially about Monty and the preparations for Overlord. When I got back to the office, I heard from Charles Peake that the V.C.I.G.S. [Vice Chief of Imperial General Staff] had heard that the P.M. contemplates coming here next week. This will be much too soon. The Embassy is not ready, and the French authorities must be warned, both from the point of view of security and from the point of view of common civility. I immediately sent a personal telegram to Anthony pointing out the objections.

September 28, 1944

The Eire Minister, Mr Sean Murphy, called on me this morning. He had been Eire Minister to Vichy and has recently arrived here under the impression that he will be Minister to the Provisional Government. I told him that I thought he would have to be re-accredited. He was very friendly and seemed to be quite a nice man. He said he hadn't heard from his own Government for months. I didn't offer to put any of our facilities at his disposal, for I didn't see that we should go out of our way to help neutrals.

  Beck [the local MI5 man], who is going to London tomorrow, came to see me. He told me that P. G. Wodehouse[2] is living in our hotel – the Bristol [*the Coopers had moved to this hotel on 24 September*]. I knew that he was here, but not that he was in the Bristol. Beck, very wisely, was afraid that if the press got hold of the story it might cause difficulties both here and at home. If the English people were told that Wodehouse was living in luxury on the same floor of the same hotel as the British Ambassador, they would not be best pleased; and the French people might also say that if he were a Frenchman he would have been locked up long ago. I rang up Victor who said he would do what he could to have Wodehouse removed from the hotel.

October 2, 1944

Brooks Richards brought Colonel Buckmaster[3] to see me. He has been running for the last two years underground organizations all over France

---

[1] Adm. Sir Bertram Ramsay (1883–1945) was the naval officer responsible for the evacuation of Dunkirk in 1940, for planning the invasion of North Africa and Sicily in 1942 and 1943, and of Europe in 1944, working under Eisenhower and alongside General Montgomery. He died in an air crash in January 1945.

[2] Sir Pelham Grenville (Plum) Wodehouse (1881–1975), acclaimed writer of comic novels. He was captured in France in 1940, and while interned in Germany was tricked into making five humorous broadcasts to the US about his experiences. In Sept. 1943 the Wodehouses were permitted to move to Paris. After the liberation he was ostracized as a collaborator, though the MI5 investigation found no evidence of this. He spent the rest of his life in America.

[3] Col. Maurice Buckmaster (1902–92). A businessman, he joined the SOE in 1941, where he became head of the independent French section, responsible for over five hundred agents parachuted into France.

independently of the French. The Gaullist people have never been quite happy about his activities, and they naturally want to break them all up now. He is going round to thank the various people and to wind up the various organizations, many of whom are longing to go on working with us rather than with the French. He had been on a triumphal tour through Normandy and was going up to Lille tomorrow. I asked him how much he thought he could use his people for post-war work in Germany. He seemed very hopeful.

October 3, 1944

It was a beautiful morning and I walked to the Embassy through the Champs Elysées with Teddie. He and Freddie had been on a champagne-buying expedition the day before and had lunched with the Pol Rogers,[1] from whom he had bought four dozen Pol Roger 1928 at 82 francs a bottle, which seems extraordinarily cheap.

At 4 o'clock I had a meeting of the members of the Special Services. They are none of them quite certain as to what their future is going to be in Paris, but 'C'[2] is expected to come out next week. They have succeeded in moving P. G. Wodehouse to another hotel. The press had already got hold of the story that he was at the Bristol, and it appeared on Monday in the *Daily Telegraph*.

October 4, 1944

We dined with Comtesse Jean de Polignac.[3] Her house was cold but the dinner was good. The company consisted of her uncle and aunt – Stanislas de Castellane[4] and his wife, Hervé Alphand, Drian,[5] and the Comtesse Palffy.[6]

October 5, 1944

I went round to the Ritz at a quarter to seven, where I joined Coleridge Kennard[7] and Marlene Dietrich,[8] whom I hadn't seen since Hollywood at the beginning of 1940.[9] She had not changed much.

---

[1] Odette Pol Roger, née Wallace (1911–2000), was married to Jacques Pol Roger, a director of the family champagne business. She became a great friend of Churchill's after Duff introduced them at the Embassy.

[2] The pseudonym of the head of the Secret Service. At this time it was Sir Stewart Menzies.

[3] Marie-Blanche, Comtesse de Polignac (1898–1958), the widow of Comte Jean de Polignac, was the daughter of the couturier Jeanne Lanvin. An accomplished musician and singer, she surrounded herself with artists and musicians.

[4] Stanislas de Castellane (1875–1959), former Deputy and later Senator for Cantal in Auvergne.

[5] Etienne Drian (1890–1965), artist, known for his portrait drawings and decorative murals.

[6] Louise (Loulou) de Vilmorin, Countess Palffy (1902–69), novelist and poet, well-known for her wit and beauty.

[7] Sir Coleridge Kennard, 1st Bt. (1885–1948), a diplomat.

[8] Marlene Dietrich (1902–92), acclaimed German film actress and cabaret star and later naturalized American. Her films included *The Blue Angel* and *Destry Rides Again*.

[9] Duff and Diana had visited Hollywood during his lecture tour in America, Oct. 1939–Mar. 1940.

October 6, 1944

I went to see Bidault at the Quai d'Orsay this morning. He was extremely friendly and said that he had had the best of news from Massigli, who had apparently been staying at Chequers and had been delighted with the reception he had received from the Prime Minister. We had a pleasant and useful conversation, and I liked him still better on further acquaintance.

Le Troquer came to see me in the afternoon. It was just a friendly visit. As is usual in the case of Ministers who are out of office, he doubted whether this Government would last long. He did not believe that the Communists presented any danger and had great confidence in his own party – the Socialists. He said that he had asked de Gaulle not to be included in this Government, which I doubt, but admitted that de Gaulle had not wanted him in the Government, which I believe.

We dined with Philippe de Rothschild[1] – a party of twelve – among whom were Monsieur and Madame François Mauriac,[2] whom I was much interested to meet. He is a charming man – very simple, and much more gay and light in hand than I should have expected. Thierry[3] was there, whom we both knew well in London before and during the last war and had not seen since. He has been Ambassador in one of the Balkan States, and was serving for some time under Pétain – I don't know for how long and whether he has any hope of re-employment. I was also surprised to find Patenôtre[4] there. We met them when I lectured here before the war. He used to own the paper *Marianne*. I thought his reputation very bad and that he was probably hiding somewhere, but he seemed quite confident and talked of starting his paper again.

October 8, 1944

In the evening we went to the Vieux-Colombier theatre where they were playing a piece called *Huis Clos* [by Jean-Paul Sartre]. The subject was the reactions of three people who found themselves together in hell. It was some time before one realized where they were, and although it was interesting, it was not, I thought, wholly successful.

---

[1] Baron Philippe de Rothschild (1902–88), owner of the Mouton-Rothschild vineyards, and his wife Pauline (1908–76). He revolutionized wine-making in the twentieth century.
[2] François Mauriac (1885–1970), poet and novelist. He received the Nobel Prize for Literature in 1952.
[3] Adrien Thierry (1885–1961), diplomat, married Nadine de Rothschild in 1919.
[4] Raymond Patenôtre (1900–51). He was born in the US where his father was French Ambassador, but moved back to Paris and became a newspaper proprietor and left-wing politician. Economics Minister 1932–4. He was arrested on collaboration charges in Dec. 1944.

October 9, 1944

Monsieur Dautry[1] came to see me this morning. He was Minister of Munitions in the French Government up to the fall of France. He is a friend of the Prime Minister's and seems an intelligent and friendly man. He says that communism in France is an expression of discontent, and in his industrial experience he has always found that by removing the causes of discontent he could reduce communism to a minimum.

October 10, 1944

Today we moved into the Embassy and slept there for the first time. It was quite comfortable and we are very glad to be there. Charlie Beistegui came round in the morning to discuss the possibility of turning my sitting room into a library.

General Vanier [came], who had an interview with General de Gaulle yesterday, and had found him as difficult as usual. I haven't seen him since I have been here, and he is obviously avoiding an interview on purpose as a protest against non-recognition. It will be interesting to see what happens when the new American Ambassador arrives. He is due tomorrow.

October 16, 1944

My Czech colleague called this morning more or less to say goodbye, as he is being moved to another post. He asked if he could speak to me as man to man, and then proceeded to warn me against the Russian Ambassador [Bogomolov], who, he said, hated France and de Gaulle, and what was more was a really wicked man – deceitful and cruel. This was a very unexpected outburst from such a quiet and reticent man as Monsieur Czerny.

Then the United States Ambassador arrived [Hon. Jefferson Caffery]. I have heard little good of him, but found him quite pleasant at this first meeting. He is good-looking, well-dressed, seemed very formal, perhaps was rather shy as he had a slight stammer.

I [went] to see Massigli. He told me that he had himself protested to de Gaulle, saying that it was foolish of him to refuse to see me in view of the fact that he (Massigli) had been exceedingly well treated in England, had been to stay with the Prime Minister, and had been received by the King, and if it was a question of recognition why had de Gaulle received Bogomolov? To this de Gaulle replied that the Russian and English positions are different owing to the way the Prime Minister had treated him. This, of course, made no sense. Massigli, as usual, was very friendly, and was unusually cheerful with regard to the general situation.

---

[1] Raoul Dautry (1888–1951), a *polytechnicien* responsible for modernizing the French railways before the war. In 1939 he was brought in to oversee French rearmament after the Munich agreement.

Friday October 20, 1944

In the afternoon Cussen of M.I.5 came to talk to me about the P. G. Wodehouse case. I found that all the journalists thought that he ought to be sent to prison. Cussen takes somewhat the same line, but he does not think the evidence against him sufficient. More, however, may come to light when we get to Berlin.

I received a message from Caffery, asking if he could come and see me. He told me that the President had agreed to recognize the French Government. I was naturally extremely glad to hear this.

When I got back [from dinner] I found that Holman and Peake had been waiting to see me and had just left. I sent the car for Holman. He told me that Caffery had been to see Bidault before seeing me, and informed him of the President's decision. This he had obviously done in order to be first with the news, and he, of course, ought to have told me. What was still more strange was that Peake had got through to London on the telephone and had been definitely informed that the President had sent a message to the Prime Minister, saying that he was not prepared to recognize the Government until both the Zone of the Interior had been declared and the new Consultative Assembly had met. He had added that he hoped the matter would be dealt with by himself and the Prime Minister and not by the Foreign Office and the State Department.

October 21, 1944

I went to see Caffery this morning. He was extremely ill at ease. He showed me the telegram he had received from the State Department, which had not expressly authorized him to inform Bidault, but had merely announced the President's decision to recognize the Government and had said that I should be receiving similar instructions and should inform Bidault. He admitted that his action had been precipitate and was obviously somewhat ashamed at not having been frank with me last night. He asked me what he was to do now, and said he would do anything that I suggested. I told him he must await the instructions that I might receive, as there was no action that I could take until I had received them.

Mrs Gerald Barry[1] came to see me at 11. She had spent a week at Toulouse and said she had travelled up to the frontier, that there was no disquiet whatever in that part of France, and that all the stories about bandits, Spanish reds, Communists, etc. were unfounded. I don't think she really knew much about what she was describing. She is a pretty woman, but foolish and pretentious.

---

[1] Vera Poliakoff, the third wife of Sir Gerald Barry (1898–1968), editor of the *News Chronicle* 1936–47. In 1956 she married the art critic John Russell.

I saw Freddie Ayer[1] in the afternoon, who had also just returned from Toulouse and gave a picture very different from that of Mrs Barry. He said the situation had deteriorated, that the local F.F.I. were quite incapable of dealing with German forces, which are considerable and might prove a real danger. He suggested that they should be bombed. Spanish Red troops are crossing the Pyrenees in large numbers, meaning to live in the maquis until they can provoke a revolution in Spain. There are also stories that the Comte de Paris[2] and General Noguès[3] are active in the vicinity, and even that they have some understanding with General de Lattre. Altogether he was rather gloomy about the situation.

I went to a small cocktail party given by the Chapins in their new and magnificent apartment – 6, Avenue Foch. As I left Reber[4] arrived and told me that de Gaulle had gone off to the front without signing the decree defining the Zone of the Interior[5] which could not therefore be published till Tuesday. When I got home Miss McEntire [Duff's secretary] was speaking to the Secretary of the Minister of Information's *Chef de Cabinet*, who was telling her that the decree had already been sent to the French press and would appear in the newspapers tomorrow morning. Reber, on hearing that the decree was going to appear tomorrow, had gone off the deep end, said that the French had been guilty of a breach of faith, and that he would advise the President not to recognize the Government after all. He and Caffery had gone round to see Palewski with a view to getting the publication held up. It was obviously too late to do so.

Sunday October 22, 1944

Apparently, after their interview with Palewski they had sent quite a mild telegram to Washington, and had already instructions early this morning to the effect that the President was now willing to recognize the French Government, and Caffery was so to inform Bidault tomorrow evening, as the announcement would be made in Washington at midday.

I thereupon telegraphed to the Foreign Office saying that I proposed to act in the same way unless I received instructions to the contrary. I informed Vanier, who agreed to come with me to the Quai d'Orsay, and I sent Bogomolov a copy of the statement that I would hand to Bidault.

---

[1] Sir Alfred Jules (Freddie) Ayer (1910–89), philosopher. He served in SOE during the war and in 1944 was attached to the British Embassy, reporting on the liberated regions of France.
[2] A right-wing resistance group, the '*maquis blanc*', was loyal to the Comte de Paris.
[3] Gen. Charles Noguès (1876–1971), High Commissioner to Morocco under Vichy. After de Gaulle's arrival in 1943, he fled to Portugal.
[4] Samuel Reber, American diplomat, a political adviser on SHAEF.
[5] France was temporarily divided between a War Zone, under the authority of SHAEF, and an Interior Zone.

October 23, 1944

As instructed by the Foreign Office, I went round to see Bidault at 10.30 this morning and told him what he knew already, namely, that we were going to recognize the French Government in the afternoon.

At 5 o'clock we four Ambassadors met at the Ministry for Foreign Affairs, said our pieces and handed in our notes. Bidault was very friendly, and said that our *agréments* were granted forthwith. It is a great thing to have got this matter settled at last.

We dined with General de Gaulle. Beatrice Eden[1] came here first to pick us up. She was nervous at the prospect; being shy in English, she is still more shy in French. They sent a guide to lead us to the villa somewhere in the Bois where he is living; and which is obviously very difficult to find because all the other guests were late. We were a party of twelve. It was an extremely frigid and dreary party – worse even than his entertainments usually are. He made no reference when I arrived to the fact that his Government had been recognized by the three great powers that afternoon, and when I said that I hoped he was glad it was finished, he shrugged his shoulders and said it would never finish.

I sat between Madame de Gaulle – who never took her eyes off the General and hardly spoke – and Madame Bonnet, whose husband has been very seriously ill, and who seemed rather overawed by her surroundings. I had a talk with General de Gaulle after dinner, which was not very useful. The tone of it improved when Bidault joined us. We left soon after half-past ten. Beatrice Eden said that the things one dreaded were usually not so bad as one expected, but this had been even worse.

Wednesday October 25, 1944 (London)

I was wakened up this morning at 5 by a loud explosion, and did not get to sleep again. At 10 I went to Lesley and Roberts [Duff's tailor in St George Street] to try on some clothes, and was blandly informed by one of the men there that the man who had tried me on last time would probably not turn up, as they thought he must have been killed by the bomb, which fell near where he lived. However, he came in before I left and confirmed their statement that it was within a few hundred yards of his house. He had suffered no injury, though six of his friends had been killed – six being the total number of the dead.

I went to lunch at 10, Downing Street. About halfway through lunch, Winston started on de Gaulle and we had some friendly argument, Clemmie strongly supporting me. After lunch I went up with him to the Cabinet room and we talked for at least an hour. On the whole he was quite reasonable, and I felt that the conversation had been extremely useful. He talked of coming

---

[1] Beatrice Beckett (1905–57) married Anthony Eden in 1923. They were divorced in 1950.

over to stay with Eisenhower in Versailles, which I implored him not to do. He said that he must come to France, and he wasn't going to suggest himself and risk receiving another affront as he had received in Algiers. I said that I was sure that very soon de Gaulle would extend an invitation to him to come to France, and I gathered that in that case he would be willing to accept it.

I attended the meeting of my Executive Committee at Caxton Hall.[1] I explained to them the position, and the reasons why I did not expect to be standing for Parliament again. I also, when they asked me to make a suggestion for a successor, put forward the name of Harold Macmillan, which was extremely well received.

October 26, 1944

Thelma Cazalet[2] came to see me to talk about P. G. Wodehouse, whose daughter – recently dead – married Thelma's younger brother. She was quite sensible and saw the importance of Wodehouse keeping out of the public eye and out of the country for as long as possible.

October 27, 1944

I went to see Massigli. He was very much amused by my account of our dinner with de Gaulle. I forgot to say that when I was with Oliver Harvey yesterday a telegram was brought in from Holman saying that he had been privately informed that an invitation was likely to be forthcoming from de Gaulle to the Prime Minister to visit Paris in the very near future. Massigli and I agreed that the best time for this visit would be the 11th November, when there is to be a review of troops. In this way it would be unnecessary to announce the Prime Minister's visit before he appears, and at the same time, he could be certain of a big crowd. Massigli is certainly much more cheerful in London than he ever was in Algiers.

[In the evening] Kakoo came round and brought us a lot of game from Belvoir, which I hope will be all right when I get back to Paris on Sunday.

October 28, 1944

I was rung up by the Foreign Office to say that the Prime Minister wanted to see me before I left, and that he was at Chequers. This was awkward, as I had arranged to spend the day at Eton [*with John Julius*]. However, I went down to the Foreign Office and telephoned from there to the Prime Minister's Private Secretary at Chequers. I said that I would motor on there in the afternoon from Eton.

I arrived at about five. Clemmie sent me a message to say that she was sorry

---

[1] Duff remained Conservative MP for the St George's division of Westminster until the 1945 election.

[2] Thelma Cazalet-Keir (1899–1989), Conservative MP. Her brother Peter Cazalet (1907–73) married Leonora Rowley (d. 1944), stepdaughter of P. G. Wodehouse.

not to see me, but was spending the day in bed. After about half an hour I was taken up to see Winston, who was also in bed, but seemed in very good form. We discussed the forthcoming visit. He wanted Clemmie to come too, to which I said I saw no objection. I sat with him for about an hour discussing every sort of thing.

November 7, 1944 (Paris)

In the evening I went to the reception at the Russian Embassy. The traffic in the Rue de Grenelle was completely out of control; it took about half an hour to approach the house. All the members of the Embassy were in their smart uniforms, and Madame Bogomolov was in full evening dress. There were arc lights everywhere and cinema operators. Everybody was photographed as they went in and again upstairs while shaking hands with the Ambassador and Ambassadress. I was conducted by a junior member of the staff to a special room set apart for the more privileged guests, where there was any amount of vodka and caviare, the others being allowed only inferior sandwiches and hardly any drink.

Diana joined me there, and we went on to pick up Marie-Blanche de Polignac. We found the Tvedes,[1] Cecil Beaton,[2] and a Monsieur Vilmorin there. We all embarked in two cars to drive down to dine with Comtesse Palffy who was born Vilmorin and writes books under that name. It was nearly half an hour's drive and pouring with rain. It was very nice when we got there and we had a delightful dinner. We had just reached the coffee when I got a message that the Prime Minister wanted to speak to me most urgently between 10 and a quarter past. It was nearly 10 then, so I said that I couldn't possibly get back till a quarter to eleven. I left at once, leaving Diana behind and sending the car back for her. I was sorry to go. Louise Palffy took me to the door. I found myself kissing her and falling in love. She returned my kisses.

I got through to the Prime Minister, but only on an open line as the secret one was not working. He said he had merely rung up to enquire whether everything was going on all right. He had, in fact, nothing to say at all; the call was quite unnecessary.

November 8, 1944

I sent Madame Palffy some flowers and a letter excusing myself for not having returned last night. She sent me back a real love letter – rather beautifully written but too much *au grand sérieux*.

---

[1] Mogens Tvede (1895–1977), Danish painter and architect, married Princess Dolores (Dolly) Radziwill (1886–1966) in 1932. She was Nancy Mitford's best friend in Paris.
[2] Sir Cecil Beaton (1904–80), photographer and designer for stage, film, ballet and opera.

November 9, 1944

Just as I was going out to dinner the Prime Minister came through on the telephone. He said that the Cabinet were very anxious about his visit and had been alarmed by the report given by Howe of Scotland Yard, who has been out here and gone back. While he was here he seemed quite sanguine, but of course it is safer from his point of view to sound a warning. The Prime Minister said he would let me know later in the evening what was decided.

We came back about 11, and the Prime Minister came through again. I talked both to him and to Anthony. They were still undecided – I gathered that Anthony was the more undecided of the two. The suggestion was that the visit should be postponed for a few days. I pointed out that exactly the same dangers would exist whenever the visit took place. It would be impossible to prevent it being known beforehand if it were also desired that the Prime Minister should be seen by the people of Paris. Eventually the Prime Minister said 'All right, we will come', thereby making me feel that all the responsibility was mine.

Further telephone conversation with Louise Palffy today. We have fixed a rendezvous for Monday. She talks as though we were lovers but reminds me that we have only met twice – and never by daylight.

November 10, 1944

With reference to yesterday's diary, I heard subsequently that all the alarms that had nearly prevented the Prime Minister from coming to Paris were due to Max Beaverbrook who, inspired as usual with a spirit of mischief and hatred, had done his best to frighten the Prime Minister and Clemmie out of their lives and to stop the visit. He had been aided and abetted by Brendan, but, fortunately Anthony, assisted by what I had said on the telephone, was able to overcome the opposition.

I went to see Bidault early this morning to explain to him, according to what the Prime Minister said last night, that he was not to expect that there would be a serious political conference or any agreements arrived at, although I thought I had persuaded the Prime Minister that an informal talk round the table after lunch on Saturday might be useful. Bidault quite understood this, but at the same time said that if the situation remained exactly the same after the Prime Minister's visit as it had been before, the General would feel that he had made a mistake in strengthening the P.M.'s position by the tremendous reception he was bound to receive in France, and had got nothing out of it. I said I could only hope that the conversations, when they took place, might lead to something, but that they mustn't expect too much.

There is a great improvement in the weather. Tommy Thompson rang me up at 8 o'clock in the morning that it was definitely decided that the Prime Minister would come by air. I drove out with Diana and Beatrice and Eric to meet him at Orly. It was very cold, but he arrived in good time. I went into the Quai d'Orsay with them. They were very pleased with the rooms and with all the arrangements that had been made.

I had seen Caffery the day before about the invitation to the French from the three great powers to join in the E.A.C. [European Advisory Committee]. He had received instructions to go with me and our Russian colleague to inform the French Government that they were so invited. He had suggested that he should go himself and see Bidault first, which I said he should not do until I had received instructions, and that I would consult the Foreign Secretary when he arrived on the following day. I talked to Anthony about it this evening and to the Prime Minister, and they agreed that the three Ambassadors should inform the French Government as soon as possible.

Meanwhile, a new difficulty has arisen. Monsieur Coulet[1] has addressed a rather rude note to S.H.A.E.F. complaining of the way the Allied troops – which means the American troops – are behaving in France, and the way the American High Command are treating the French authorities. Eisenhower apparently suggested that the two Ambassadors should take it up with the French Government. I said to Caffery that I was sure that he agreed that we could not, of course, act on instructions from Eisenhower. Coulet should have gone through the French Ministry of Foreign Affairs and should have addressed himself to our Governments, and we should not report to our Governments what had happened. I accordingly handed over a copy of Coulet's note to the Secretary of State.

November 11, 1944

I went to the Quai d'Orsay at 9.30 where I met Bogomolov and Caffery and we went in and told Bidault what he knew already, and handed him our respective notes. I then went upstairs to the Prime Minister's rooms and hung about there until we left at about 10.25 for the Rue St Dominique [de Gaulle's residence]. The Prime Minister led in an open car, and I followed with Anthony in another open car which immediately broke down, so that we had to change into another. After a short wait, we started out again, the Prime Minister and de Gaulle in the first open car, Anthony and Bidault in the second. I followed with Palewski and Nicholas Lawford[2] in a closed car. The reception had to be seen to be believed. It was greater than anything I have ever known. There were crowds in every window, even in the top floors of the highest houses and on the roofs, and the cheering was the loudest and most spontaneous and most genuine.

---

[1] François Coulet (1906–84), Private Secretary to de Gaulle 1941–3, participated in the liberation of Corsica and became Commissioner of the Republic for Normandy with administrative authority over prefectural and municipal authorities in June 1944. He rejoined the Diplomatic Corps in 1945 and was subsequently Ambassador to Yugoslavia.

[2] V. G. (Nicholas) Lawford (1911–91), Assistant Secretary in the Private Office of the Foreign Secretary.

We walked down from the Arc de Triomphe to the tribune, whence we watched the march past, which lasted nearly an hour. Whenever there was a pause in the procession there were loud cries of 'CHURCHILL' from all over the crowd. We then proceeded to the statue of Clémenceau to lay another wreath, and thence to the tomb of Foch in the Invalides. The weather, which was quite good from the beginning, improved all the time, and by one o'clock there was bright sunlight.

After lunch we went upstairs: de Gaulle, Coulet, Massigli, Chauvel[1] and Palewski one side of the table – Winston, Anthony, Alec Cadogan and I on the other. We talked for about two hours – Winston talking most of the time in his uninhibited and fairly intelligible French. He speaks remarkably well, but understands very little. Both he and de Gaulle were in the happiest of humours. It was all very different from the interview at Marrakesh. There was not an unpleasant word said, although nearly every subject, including Syria, was covered. I was delighted with the result, and we agreed that it would be unnecessary to hold any further conversations between the Prime Minister and de Gaulle, but that the two Foreign Secretaries should meet again tomorrow morning.

November 12, 1944

I went round to the Quai d'Orsay for a meeting at half past ten. There were present Monsieur Bidault, Monsieur Chauvel, Monsieur Massigli, Monsieur Dejean,[2] and later Monsieur Meyrier on the French side and, on our side, Anthony, Alec Cadogan, and Walter Hankey. The principal subject for discussion was, first, the future of Europe (of Germany, especially of the Rhineland, etc.). On this there was practically complete agreement, and all went well. We then got on to the Levant and things did not go so well. In fact, after a lot of conversation, no progress was made at all. My sympathies are very much with the French in this matter, and I know that no progress can ever be made so long as Spears remains there. He, however, seems to have persuaded the Commander-in-Chief, who has half persuaded Anthony, that if he goes now there will be an immediate outbreak of disorder.

I lunched at the Quai d'Orsay – a party of about 40. Wonderful food and wine – too much of the former. Lunch, which didn't begin till before two, lasted till nearly 4, and at 5 we all went to the Hotel de Ville. Winston without any preparation plunged into a speech in French, and although he made the most frightful errors of grammar and genders, he somehow succeeded in getting away with it. The French were delighted with him and it was all a very great success.

At half-past seven I had a party downstairs for the staff, it being arranged

---

[1] Jean Chauvel (1897–1979), Secretary-General to Bidault, the highest-ranking permanent official at the Quai d'Orsay, later Ambassador in London.
[2] Maurice Dejean (1899–1982), Free French Commissioner, 1941–2.

that the Prime Minister should come at a quarter to eight and spend half an hour with them before going upstairs to dinner. Unfortunately he didn't arrive until nearly a quarter past eight, when he announced the sinking of the *Tirpitz*[1] as his excuse for being late, as though he had sunk it himself. I was only able to introduce him to a score of people.

We had a dinner party of seventeen: General and Madame de Gaulle, Mr and Mrs Churchill, Monsieur and Madame Bogomolov, Mr Jefferson Caffery, Mr and Mrs Eden, General and Madame Vanier, Air Chief Marshal and Lady Tedder,[2] Monsieur Bidault and Sir Alexander Cadogan. I sat between Madame de Gaulle and Madame Bogomolov. Madame de Gaulle was harder to talk to than ever, so I gave orders halfway through that we should have coffee in the next room. The P.M. was in better form than ever, and was delighted with Madame Bogomolov, whom I made sit next to him just before he left. I had to tell him at about twenty to 11 that he must leave as he had to return to the Quai d'Orsay before catching the train. I went to the station to see him off, feeling it had all been very successful.

November 15, 1944

I went to see Duroc in the afternoon, whom I used to know in Algiers. His real name is Comte de Bénouville.[3] He was dropped in France before D-Day and while escaping from the Germans had a motor accident in which he broke his leg. As he was in hiding he couldn't get it attended to for some weeks, and it had to be broken again and he has been in bed ever since, which is very hard on so eager and active a man at such a time. His wife was there, who seemed very nice. He was in the highest spirits, bubbling over with energy, and writing a book about the resistance.

November 16, 1944

I drove down to Verrières to pick up Louise. I found her with her two brothers. It is not an attractive house. I hadn't seen it before by daylight – nor is it an attractive suburb. We were nearly killed on the way back to Paris by a lorry that came out of a side road at 60 miles an hour while we were going down the main road in the Rolls Royce at 80 miles an hour. We missed death by inches. We had an excellent lunch at the Escargot and then returned to the Rue de Bellechasse [*a borrowed flat*] where we spent a delicious hour.

I came back to the Embassy. Fraser of the Treasury called with Rabino [financial adviser to the Embassy] at 5. He is part of a financial mission that has come out here with a view to concluding a financial agreement with the French. Later the Sergeant-Major asked to see me. All the servants are on the

---

[1] The *Tirpitz*, a 44,755-ton German battleship, was sunk by RAF bombers at Tromsø, Norway, on 12 Nov. 1944.

[2] Air Marshal Sir Arthur Tedder (1890–1967), CIC RAF, Middle East 1941–3; CIC Mediterranean Air Command 1943–5; Marshal of the RAF and Chief of Air Staff 1946.

[3] Gen. Pierre de Bénouville was a hero of the Resistance whose *nom de guerre* was Duroc.

point of mutiny because Freddie [Fane] is so unkind to them. It is most tiresome.

November 18, 1944

At 9.45, M. Loze, the *Chef de Protocol*, called with two Rolls Royces and I set forth with all my civilian staff to present my letters of credence. This morning's ceremony was short and formal but de Gaulle was very genial and smiling. His staff say they have never known him so nearly happy.

At 4 I motored down to Versailles and had an interview with Eisenhower. I found him friendly and nice but not impressive – nor was he optimistic about an early end to the war, in which I still believe.

Tuesday November 21, 1944

News came this evening that the French had arrested Mr and Mrs Wodehouse and were holding them in prison. I saw the Consul-General and told him that he should act in exactly the same manner as he would with regard to the arrest of any other British subject. I also sent a telegram to the Foreign Office referring to one I had sent more than a month ago suggesting that H.M.G. should make up their mind as to what policy they were going to follow with regard to Wodehouse, to which we have had no reply.

We dined with the Comte de Consan, a friend of the de Lesseps. Totor and Diana were there and his mother, a very nice woman who has played a great part in the Resistance. Diana de Lesseps told me at dinner that she had been dining last night in the company of Mrs Lithiby and Luizet, the *Préfet de Police*. Mrs Lithiby had said how she was always trying to avoid meeting the Wodehouses in the Bristol, and when Luizet asked her why she said because Wodehouse had broadcast from Berlin. It seems that the arrest of Wodehouse was due to this remark.

Our host had a beautiful collection of pictures – a lovely little portrait by Paul of Louis XVII, an interesting Lawrence of the Duchesse de Berry and one of the best Rembrandts I have ever seen. He also has a lot of interesting relics, including the original diary of the daughter of Louis XVI, written from the day they entered the Temple.

November 23, 1944

Harold Macmillan came to see me this morning. He had arrived late last night, having been forced down by the weather at Dijon and having completed the journey by road. He is on his way to London and thence to Washington. He is going to try to fix up his candidature for St George's while he is in London. We had an interesting talk about things in general. He would like to have the War Office after the war.

At one I went to the Rue Bellechasse to meet Loulou. She was more charming than ever. We had a delightful lunch at the Escargot and returned to Bellechasse. I cannot understand why she should love me, which she certainly seems to do and I love her more each time I see her – today especially. Diana met her the night before, dining with Cecil Beaton, and was quite overcome by her charm. She said she thought her the most attractive woman she had ever met. When I told Loulou this she only said 'And did it please you that she said that? Then it pleases me.'

November 24, 1944

Ashton-Gwatkin[1] came to see me, as he is leaving today, and discussed the result of his visit. He is prepared to ask the Treasury for an entertainment allowance of £17,000, which according to Freddie and Rabino will not prove sufficient, but he says that if we can show that this is so after some months of trial, they will, of course, have to reconsider it. He was very friendly and most anxious to help in every way, and I am glad he has been here.

At 5.30 I went to see Nadège de Ganay who was in bed, having had an accident to her knee. She tells one interminable stories of her resistance activities, rudeness to the Germans, and correct prophecies as regards the future of the war, most of which I believe to be much exaggerated, as she has a reputation of having collaborated pretty freely.

Lionel Fraser came to see me later, his financial negotiations having finally broken down. It is a pity, but I quite understand that the French Government could not bring themselves to hand over £50,000,000 in gold to the British at the present time. The French are very sorry for themselves, and cannot believe that anybody has suffered more than they have, and would not therefore understand the transfer of such a large sum to a country which they wrongly believe to be much more prosperous than they are.

Before lunch I went to the Travellers', where I got a half bottle of champagne which I took round to Rue Bellechasse, where Loulou and I drank it with great delight. She is enchanting.

Saturday November 25, 1944

Walter Lippmann[2] came at 12, and I had a very interesting talk with him for three-quarters of an hour. I think we are in very close agreement, except that he would like to see a western bloc which would include the Americans. I would rather make two bites at that cherry and start by a western European bloc, which would be simpler to construct and whose close friendship with the Americans would be inevitable. Minou[3] came in before dinner. She tells me that the reason why Bidault did so badly in the Assembly the other day was that he was drunk and according to her, which I doubt, after his speech

---

[1] Sir Frank Ashton-Gwatkin (1889–1976), Senior Inspector of HM Diplomatic Missions 1945–7.

[2] Walter Lippmann (1889–1974), American journalist and columnist, wrote for the *New York Herald Tribune* from 1931–61.

[3] Minou de Montgomerie, a friend from Algiers, subsequently married General Béthouart.

The First Lord inspects a guard of honour

Duff and Diana, c. 1938 (The yachting cap with White Ensign was a fixture after Admiralty days)

Above Diana, Duff and their dog Noel in the Packard,
one of her succession of cream convertibles, 1937
Right Duff, at a shoot arranged for him near Gdynia,
summer 1938 (It had not occurred to him to bring
shooting clothes) *Below* The Foreign Minister of Poland,
Colonel Beck, holds Duff enthralled, Gdynia, 1938

Duff at Ditchley, c.1942

Assessing the local talent in Algiers (A bare-chested Teddie Phillips and uniformed George FitzGeorge at left)

Duff in his study at Bognor, c.1943

Armistice Day in Paris, 1944 (Churchill and de Gaulle, with Duff and Anthony Eden behind)

he Embassy Library - created and entirely stocked by Duff

The Signing of the Treaty of Dunkirk by Georges Bidault and
Ernest Bevin, 1947 (Duff is behind Bevin)

uff and Susan Mary Patten,
aris, c.1947

ouise de Vilmorin and Duff,
hantilly, c.1952

verleaf Duff and Willow

he put his head on de Gaulle's shoulder and went to sleep. De Gaulle was so angry that he nearly refused to take him to Moscow.

Sunday November 26, 1944

Another beautiful morning and after church, I escaped work for an hour by going for a walk in the Champs Elysées. It was rather cold, but beautiful bright sunshine, and I looked in at the Travellers' and the Jockey Club and had a glass of champagne at both.

A most immediate telegram arrived this morning from London, saying that they are worried because the cruiser *Emile Bertin* is visiting Beirut, which they think may cause complications at a time when the situation in the east is strained as the result of the murder of Lord Moyne.[1] I telegraphed back to London that I could not see the connection between the murder of an English Minister in Cairo by Jewish terrorists and the visit of a French ship to Syria, and I felt that I should be given better reasons than were shown in their telegram if I were to make representations. I also sent a personal telegram to Anthony saying that I thought the whole thing looked to me like one of Spears' machinations.

November 27, 1944

We dined out at Verrières with Loulou Palffy and her two brothers. It is a funny rather attractive old house and we had dinner in what was formerly the nursery. We were a large party of about twenty. We sat at separate tables, and afterwards there was some music. The composer Poulenc[2] played some of his own songs and another man sang them. It was a delightful evening. Loulou was looking really beautiful and I'm afraid I hardly talked to anyone else. I'm afraid also that people thought it odd that my chauffeur should know so well the way to her house, which isn't very easy to find.

When we got back at about half past twelve there was a personal telegram from Anthony, in which he assured me that this particular affair had not originated with Spears, although he had supported it. He also told me that Spears is definitely resigning as from the 15th December next, and that as he (Spears) intends to inform the local Governments accordingly on the 26th it is another reason why there may be trouble there.

---

[1] Walter Guinness, 1st Lord Moyne (1880–1944), Minister Resident in the Middle East, had been assassinated in Cairo by terrorists from the Stern Gang in Palestine.

[2] Francis Poulenc (1889–1963), French composer, was a close friend of Marie-Blanche de Polignac and Louise de Vilmorin.

November 28, 1944

Jean Monnet[1] came to see me this morning and talked about his import programme. He expressed great anxiety as to the events of the next three months. According to him, all will depend on the extent to which the French public are made to understand the facts of the situation. They will necessarily suffer considerably from shortage of everything, especially of coal, during this period. If they think that it is due to bad management and bad government, there may be grave troubles. If they clearly understand that it is due to causes which are beyond anybody's control, they will have the good sense to put up with it while waiting for a better time. He was very sincere and earnest.

I afterwards sat next to him at lunch – a large luncheon given for Governor Lehman,[2] and the other representatives of U.N.R.R.A. Monnet was most indignant about the length of the menu, and said that it was feasts like this that gave people passing through Paris such an entirely false idea of the true position.

November 30, 1944

Muggeridge called for me at 7.30 and took me off to dine in a convent which has been the headquarters of 'C''s organization throughout the war. It was a dingy little house up against the great wall of the Santé lunatic asylum. It was inhabited by 12 or 14 nuns, only 4 of whom were in the secret and knew what was going on. Thousands of our soldiers passed through it during the war. It was once visited by the Gestapo but succeeded in proving its innocence. We were waited on by nuns, and, at the end the Mother Superior joined us. She seemed quite an ordinary little woman – not impressive but intelligent. She told me the whole history of how they had come to work for the Secret Service.

December 1, 1944

Peter Cazalet called in the afternoon to talk about his unfortunate father-in-law P. G. Wodehouse. We agreed that the best thing that could happen would be if the French would agree to get him moved out of Paris and allowed to live quietly somewhere in the country.

We dined with the Tvedes – a party of seven. We dined in his bedroom in order to be warm, and it was a fairly dreary evening until soon after 10 Loulou and her brother Roger came in and cheered everything up. They came back

---

[1] Jean Monnet (1888–1979) was sent in 1940 by the British Government to the US where he became an adviser to President Roosevelt. In 1943 he joined the CFLN in Algiers and was de Gaulle's Economic Planning Commissioner, 1944–9. He conceived the idea of the European Coal and Steel Community, of which he was first President, and is considered the principal architect of the European Union.

[2] Herbert H. Lehman (1878–1963), Democratic Senator and Governor of New York, 1933–42. Director-General of the United Nations Relief and Rehabilitation Administration (UNRRA).

with us to the Embassy. Loulou was at her best – scintillating. Diana finds her almost more fascinating than I do.

December 11, 1944 (London)

I lunched at 10 Downing Street with Winston, Clemmie and Mary.[1] Winston had just arrived from Chequers and talked of little but Greece. He was very indignant with the Americans, especially with Stettinius.[2] We got on to the subject of the Western Bloc, about which I found his views most unsound. He is against any European commitments and in favour of an overwhelmingly superior air force, and also inclined to put some faith in the nonsense of Dumbarton Oaks.[3]

December 22, 1944

Clemmie rang up this morning and asked John Julius and me to lunch at Downing Street. Bobbety and the Bishop of Winchester[4] were the other guests. I gathered that they had asked the Bishop to see what they thought of him as a potential Archbishop of Canterbury. I liked him very much, but Bobbety said he preferred the Bishop of London,[5] so I expect the latter will get it.

The P.M. was in excellent form and extremely cheerful. We stayed there until about half-past three, with the King of Greece and Anthony waiting upstairs from 3 onwards. In the evening Victor and I took John Julius to *Blithe Spirit* [by Noël Coward], in which Pempy Ward[6] is acting. She does it very well. I hadn't seen the play since I went to the first performance three and a half years ago with Caroline.

December 24, 1944 (Paris)

I went to church in the morning. It was very cold and my cold got gradually worse all day, so that in the evening I went to bed and remained there all the next day – Christmas Day – until dinner time when I got up. We had quite a cheerful Christmas dinner. I was much better on the following day, and able

---

[1] Mary Churchill (b. 1922), the Prime Minister's daughter, married Christopher Soames, later Lord Soames (1920–87), in 1947. He was Ambassador to Paris 1968–72.

[2] Edward Stettinius (1900–49), Under-Secretary of State under Roosevelt 1943–4 and Secretary of State 1944–5. He headed the delegations to the Dumbarton Oaks Conference and the San Francisco Conference, and was instrumental in setting up the United Nations Organization.

[3] The Dumbarton Oaks Conference (Aug.–Oct. 1944), at which delegates from China, the Soviet Union, the US and the UK discussed the charter of a new, permanent international organization and laid the foundation for the creation of the United Nations.

[4] Mervyn George Haigh (1887–1962).

[5] Geoffrey Francis Fisher, Baron Fisher of Lambeth (1887–1972). Bishop of London 1939–44; Archbishop of Canterbury 1945–61.

[6] Penelope Dudley Ward (1918–82), daughter of Freda Dudley Ward. An actress and film star, she married Carol Reed, the film director, in 1948.

to go out to lunch with Loulou at the Méditerranée – and very much I enjoyed it. We went to the Rue de Bellechasse afterwards and were able to forget how cold it was.

December 27, 1944

It was a lovely cold sunny day. We lunched with Philippe de Rothschild. They all went to a matinée with his little girl [Philippine de Rothschild] and John Julius. I walked home after lunch. We went down to dine at Verrières with Lulu Palffy and her two brothers. Palewski was there and I had some conversation with him about the visit to Moscow, about which he seemed very well satisfied. We drove Jean Cocteau[1] there and back.

1945

January 1, 1945

The New Year begins with new resolutions – more regular habits, more time for reading – earlier to bed. During the past year I have regularly dictated a diary – a dictated diary must be unreadable as I have proved to myself by casting my eye over last year's production. So this year I shall try to write one and to devote to it regularly the first effort of every morning. I should be at my table by 9.15 and should not be disturbed until 9.45.

Virginia Cowles and Venetia Montagu are staying in the house. Loulou Palffy brought the Greek Minister in at midnight when we drank champagne and sang Auld Lang Syne. Later Palewski came in with a Caraman-Chimay and it was past two before we got to bed.

This morning I heard John Julius playing the piano and later I learnt that he had got up early and been to Holy Communion. He has recently been confirmed and takes his religious duties seriously. He is such a good boy. At 10.30 we drove to the Rue St Dominique for General de Gaulle's New Year reception. We were bidden to wear tail coats. Only Adrian Holman and I had them. So I took him and the service attachés in uniform. I don't think I had worn tail coat and top hat since Randolph Churchill's wedding in the very early days of the war. More than half the diplomats were *en veston*. The General went through the ceremony with great dignity and ease although it was the first time he had done it.

It was a beautiful day of frosty sunlight. After luncheon the four of us, D., Venetia, J.J. and I with Ondi, the poodle, drove down to Le Butard, a charming folly at Vaucresson near St Germain. We have hopes that the Government may arrange it for us and let us use it. At present it is falling into decay. At

---

[1] Jean Cocteau (1889–1963) was a novelist, playwright, director, poet, set designer and actor. A great friend of Louise de Vilmorin and of Diana.

4 o'clock I had my usual weekly meeting, attended by all the principal members of the mission. We talked about the Franco-Soviet agreement and the possibility of a similar Franco-British one, of the difficulties and dangers of the three months that lie ahead, of the condemnation to death of Béraud.[1] His friends are trying to make it appear that he has been sentenced for being anti-British – and it has even been suggested that we should intervene on his behalf. I think it would be a mistake to do so.

Charles Peake came later with pretty good news of the war. The Germans had raided Brussels yesterday with 200 planes and had lost 100. John Foster[2] and the de Lesseps also came in. John stayed for an early dinner with us, after which we went to *Much Ado About Nothing* at the Marigny Theatre. A crowded audience of American and British soldiers enjoyed it enormously and so did we.

January 2, 1945

Charles Peake [came] with the sad news that Admiral Ramsay had been killed in a flying accident. This is a serious loss and adds to the list of distinguished men who have lost their lives in this way. He also told me that Generals Eisenhower and Bedell Smith[3] had decided, or practically decided, to evacuate Strasbourg. I said that this would be a terrible blow to French prestige and should not in my opinion be done unless the situation were almost desperate, which it is very far from being. He also told me that the Prime Minister is coming to Versailles tomorrow, and going on thence to see Montgomery.[4] I asked whether General de Gaulle had been informed. He told me he had not been. I said that he ought to be and asked him to tell General Eisenhower that I thought so. I then sent off a personal telegram to the Prime Minister on the subject of Strasbourg,[5] emphasizing the political importance of the decision which the soldiers are apt to overlook.

We had a dinner party. The food was excellent and the party went quite

---

[1] Henri Béraud (1888–1958), French novelist, editor and contributor to the collaborationist weekly *Gringoire*. Winner of the Goncourt Prize 1922. Tried for collaboration, convicted and sentenced to death, Dec. 1944, sentence commuted to twenty, then ten years' imprisonment 1949, released on grounds of ill health 1950.

[2] Sir John Foster (1903–82), distinguished lawyer, legal adviser to Eisenhower at SHAEF 1944–5. Conservative MP 1945–74.

[3] Gen. Walter Bedell Smith (1885–1961), US Army general, diplomat and administrator. COS European Theatre of Operations, and COS to General Eisenhower, 1942–5.

[4] Field Marshal Sir Bernard Montgomery, 1st Lord Montgomery of Alamein (1887–1976). As CIC Land Forces, he planned and directed the D-Day landings and led the invasion of France in June 1944.

[5] In December the Germans under Field Marshal von Rundstedt had launched an offensive in the Ardennes, threatening Strasbourg. Eisenhower wished temporarily to surrender the city, but a compromise was reached whereby the French divisions remained to defend it. Strasbourg was saved.

well. We heard afterwards that Marie-Laure[1] [de Noailles] had a very bad reputation for collaboration and for having had affairs with Germans. I told Palewski that the P.M. is coming tomorrow and told him he could tell de Gaulle. He was depressed about the contemplated retreat. I hope and believe that the Prime Minister will be against it.

January 3, 1944

First thing this morning came a telegram from Anthony, instructing me to inform de Gaulle of the Prime Minister's visit and suggesting a meeting between the two. I spoke to Charles [Peake] to find out when the P.M. would be arriving. He said 1 p.m., later 1.45. He also said that Eisenhower persisted in not informing de Gaulle. He said it was not his business to do so. I said I had done so myself last night and had been authorized to do so this morning. Palewski came round with a telegram de Gaulle had sent to the P.M. repeating one he had sent to the President, protesting most violently against the proposed evacuation of Alsace and Lorraine. The telegram had gone off this morning so would not have reached the P.M. before he left.

I heard during lunch that Winston had arrived safely, half an hour late. De Gaulle decided to go down to Versailles to see him. After a late lunch they spent all the afternoon in conference and I gathered vaguely that the result was fairly satisfactory.

January 4, 1944

I had a talk with Scarlett[2] in the morning about Freddie Ayer coming to the Embassy in order to have cover for whatever work he will be engaged on. I have always said that unless his work was above board as far as the French were concerned I had rather not be responsible for him, as I am sure that the Embassy should know nothing of any activities that cannot be disclosed to the French.

About 11.45 there came a message to the effect that the Prime Minister had not left owing to the weather, and that General Eisenhower hoped I would go down to Versailles for lunch. I managed to get to Versailles before one, despite a heavy snowstorm and frozen roads. Eisenhower and Alan Brooke[3] were there when I arrived, and I went up to see Winston who was working in bed. He had intended, when he found he couldn't fly today, to come in to Paris to lunch with us – but Eisenhower had forbidden it on grounds of security. He seemed pleased with the result of yesterday's conference and said that de

---

[1] Marie-Laure Bischoffsheim (1902–70) married Count Charles de Noailles in 1923. A novelist and poet, she was a collector and patron of art and artists. She had had an accident during the occupation while driving with a German officer.

[2] Sir Peter Scarlett (1905–87) was at the Embassy in Paris 1944–6. Ambassador to Norway 1955 and Minister to the Vatican, 1960–5.

[3] Field Marshal Sir Alan Brooke, 1st Viscount Alanbrooke (1883–1963). Chief of Imperial General Staff 1941–5.

Gaulle was satisfied with the compromise by which it had been agreed to leave two French divisions to fight it out at Strasbourg. He had had a quite friendly conversation with de Gaulle after the *conseil de guerre*. At luncheon there were only six of us. It was not a very cheerful meal. The food was most inferior, and according to American custom there was a large glass of iced water before each guest and nothing else was offered except tea or coffee. There had been sherry, gin etc. before lunch and Winston had been wise enough when offered it to say he would prefer a whiskey and soda which he carried into lunch with him and which was replenished in the course of the meal. I do not find Eisenhower either interesting or impressive – but nice and friendly. The main subject of conversation towards the end of lunch was when and where the Russians would attack. There was great hope that it would be soon. But surely we ought to know?

I left as soon as I could get away but arrived half an hour late for my appointment with Loulou in the Place Vendôme. She was therefore in a state of some agitation. She isn't well. She coughs a lot and she takes our love affair too seriously. She is often on the verge of tears, but she has a wonderful sense of humour and I have recently introduced her to *The Diary of a Nobody*[1] which she adores. She is very, very charming.

January 5, 1945

At 9.30 I met the American Ambassador at the Quai d'Orsay and Bidault handed us identical notes on the serious economic condition of France and the urgent need of imports. Bidault wastes no time and the interview lasted less than fifteen minutes. He is getting a bad name for drunkenness[2] I am sorry to say. It would be a great pity if he came to grief over it.

A bag came in this morning and in *The Times* of yesterday I read that it was now considered certain that Charlie Lansdowne had been killed. So George Mercer Nairne[3] who has just become my personal assistant is Lord Lansdowne. He seemed rather stunned by the news himself although he must have been expecting it. He received a letter by the same bag from his aunt. She poor woman has lost all her three sons. I said I hoped he would go on working with me. He said that he would.

At 4 I went to see General de Gaulle. I found him in quite a pleasant mood. He told me of his visit to Moscow and we discussed future Anglo-French relations and the possibility of a pact. He is not keen on one, or doesn't wish to appear so. Nor is Winston.

---

[1] *The Diary of a Nobody* by George and Weedon Grossmith, first published in 1892.
[2] Bidault became known in diplomatic circles as 'In Bido Veritas' (see Antony Beevor and Artemis Cooper, *Paris After the Liberation, 1944–1949*).
[3] George Mercer Nairne, 8th Marquess of Lansdowne (1912–99), succeeded his uncle, Charles, 7th Marquess (b. 1917), who had been killed in action in Italy, 20 Aug. 1944.

January 6, 1945

We had George Mercer Nairne to lunch. There was a wonderful dish of truffles. We dined with the Bourdets. Loulou was there. I sat between her and Madame Bourdet. I thought she made our relationship all too obvious, but perhaps others didn't notice it. She was more charming than ever, and afterwards was persuaded to read some of her poems aloud. They had a tremendous success with everyone. It was Twelfth Night and we ate *la galette* – the prize fell to me. Loulou made us paper crowns out of newspaper and I crowned Madame Bourdet queen.

January 7, 1944

I went to church this morning. It was very cold. I have never noticed how very different are the accounts of Our Lord's birth in Matthew and in Luke. Mark and John don't mention it. The head of the Church Army preached. He and two of his Paris assistants called on me afterwards. I offered them cigarettes but he said it was a Church Army rule not to smoke. So when sherry was brought in I said I supposed that was forbidden too – but he said there were exceptions and they all lapped it up gratefully.

Victor came round and we all motored down to Verrières for lunch. Loulou had written out some of her poems for me and designed a beautiful cover for them with my initials all over it. She was childishly delighted and delightful about it. After lunch Hervé Alphand, Salacrou[1] and Mai de Brissac arrived. I was rather horrified to see her, as she was notorious for collaboration and was said to have been the mistress both of Flandin and of Paul Morand.[2] But Salacrou is now her lover. He played a great part in the resistance and his innocence is supposed to cover her guilt. There was a lot of talk and argument. They were all against Mauriac, who had an article in this morning's *Figaro* appealing for charity in dealing with the collaborators.

January 8, 1945

There were a lot of people in the drawing room when I got back, including Cyril Connolly,[3] who has come to stay for a few days. We left him to dine with Venetia and J.J. and went ourselves to the Russian Embassy. I never felt more strongly what barbarians the Russians are. They seemed utterly out of place in that beautiful 18th-century house, which they have done their best to make hideous. The food was foul, we were waited on by two blowsy women dressed anyhow, for whom the ambassadress had to keep ringing a bell. The party included the American and Chinese Ambassadors and the latter's wife, Bidault, a Russian General who spoke only a little English and the Counsellor

---

[1] Armand Salacrou (1899–1989), French playwright.
[2] Paul Morand (1889–1975), French novelist and diplomat. Vichy Ambassador in Berne 1944.
[3] Cyril Connolly (1903–74), writer and critic, author of *The Unquiet Grave*.

of the Russian Embassy who spoke only Russian. We were compelled to drink a great many toasts in vodka and there was nothing pleasant about the evening.

January 9, 1945

I wrote a telegram on the subject of General de Gaulle being invited to the next meeting of the Big Three. It will probably irritate Winston but the question ought to be considered and every argument is in favour of the invitation. I repeated my telegram to Washington and Moscow.

Charles Peake came in before dinner. He said the war is not going as well as is represented in the press both here and in London. He is much distressed about the state of Anglo-American relations. There has been a great deal of writing up of Montgomery in the English press at the expense of the American generals, which they bitterly resent.

January 11, 1945

At 6.30 came General Morgan,[1] to have a talk about things in general. He was not at all optimistic. He thought the Germans would escape from the bulge – said there was now a slight shade of odds against our having to abandon Strasbourg – that if the Russians didn't attack before the end of February it would be too late, and that then the Germans could move large numbers of troops from the east to the west and we should be in a dangerous position, that they were ahead of us in jet propulsion and were, or seemed to be, saving their planes for some big offensive, that Montgomery was giving great trouble and was hated by the Americans, that we were doing exactly what it had been decided we should not do, namely attack Japan on a large scale before having defeated Germany, and that the Americans were very flat-footed and tactless with the French. It was all rather depressing.

January 13, 1945

At a quarter to twelve I went to see Bidault at the Quai d'Orsay and handed him a note on the subject of the Levant. The Foreign Office are getting impatient because the French still delay the re-equipment of the gendarmerie and the transfer of the *troupes speciales* to the native governments. We had a long talk. I found him as usual reasonable, but he has to think of his government as I have to think of mine. They are both rather foolish. When I left him we agreed that if the matter were left to us we could settle it very easily. I had half an hour before lunch, so I went to the Travellers' and made notes of our conversation and had a glass of port. It was a very cold morning – especially at the Quai d'Orsay, where Bidault and I sat in our overcoats. I picked up Loulou at the Rue Barbet de Jouy and went to the Escargot for lunch. During it we had a violent quarrel because she is so anti-American and anti-Jew. In

---

[1] Lt.-Gen. Sir Frederick Morgan (1894–1967), the original planner of Overlord, the Allied invasion of Europe. COS to Eisenhower, 1944–5, then Chief of Operations for UNRRA in Germany.

the course of it I told her she herself was half American and half German and not French at all. She cried – said she would never forgive me and that it was all over between us. However all ended happily.

January 15, 1945

They now turn off the electricity at 8.30 so that I had my bath in the dark. Our heating is also controlled by the electricity so that the house gets very cold in the course of the morning. It comes on again for an hour about lunchtime. I went at noon to pay my visit of ceremony on the Papal Nuncio[1] – a jolly, old, fat Italian priest with an atrocious accent. He had been in Turkey for a long time and looked rather like a Turk.

At 6.30 I went to the Quai d'Orsay where Bidault handed to Bogomolov, Caffery and me a memorandum setting forth the French demand to be represented at the next meeting of the Big Three. It is just as well that I sent the F.O. a warning telegram last week on this same subject.

We dined at the Véfour, an old-fashioned restaurant near the Palais Royal. I am not sure whether Cocteau or Bébé Bérard was the host. The other guests [included] Cyril Connolly, Philippe de Rothschild and Loulou. The lights all went out as we arrived so that we had to send back to the Embassy for candles which when they arrived much improved the *mise en scène*. It was a very pleasant evening. The food was good – the wine was plentiful.

January 16, 1945

We were better prepared this morning to face the dark and the cold. I had two candles in my bathroom and a good wood fire in my sitting room. After lunch I met Loulou at the Rue de Bellechasse. She was cold and hungry having lunched out and not had enough to eat. People really are suffering from hunger and cold in Paris – and difficulty of transport. I lent her my car for the rest of the afternoon.

January 19, 1945

The news from the Polish front continues to be astonishingly good but the situation round Strasbourg still gives cause for anxiety. Charles Peake, who has also returned from London, says that the meeting of the Big Three is fixed for the end of this month and is to take place in London. Holman, the third to return from London, says that Stalin and the P.M. were willing to invite de Gaulle but that Roosevelt refused. Victor came to dine alone with me. The Germans go on parachuting French *miliciens*[2] into France, most of whom seem to be successfully dealt with.

---

[1] Angelo Giuseppe Roncalli (1881–1963), appointed Papal Nuncio to France in 1944, created Cardinal and appointed Patriarch of Venice in 1953. In 1958 elected Pope, taking the name John XXIII.

[2] The Milice Française, the 5,000-strong police force of the Vichy Government.

January 20, 1945

It snowed again all last night. I went round to the Place Vendôme to pick up Loulou for lunch. The Escargot has ceased to function from want of food. The Méditerranée has been shut down for black marketing. So have many others. The only one we could find open was La Cremaillière, which was very full.

Ali Forbes[1] came [in the afternoon]. He had been in Italy, had seen Harold [Macmillan] and was entirely convinced that our policy in Greece is right. He and Cyril and Venetia dined and we had some animated discussion. I think Cyril is an ass – and a glance at the book he has just brought out called *The Unquiet Grave* strengthens my opinion. He loves literature, but can't read Dickens or Balzac and thinks Osbert Sitwell about the best of modern writers.

January 22, 1945

John Julius left today which makes us sad. George took him to the aerodrome and he got off at 2.45 having promised to ask the Foreign Office to telephone us when he arrived. Diana soon began to worry and to ring up the Foreign Office and the Dorchester, neither of whom had heard of him up to seven o'clock. She was in a fever of anxiety until we learnt that the plane had had to land at Ford and that he was in the train on the way to London.

January 25, 1945

At 4 came Admiral Burrough.[2] I discovered from him that Diana, without telling me, had written to the First Lord asking that Eric Wharton should not be taken away, which was very naughty of her.

Loulou and Palewski were coming to dinner. Loulou looked so ill that Diana insisted on taking her temperature. It was over 103. Yet she wanted to sit with us at dinner. She was obviously getting worse all the time – so at last Diana took her upstairs and put her to bed. We sent for her doctor. He had no medicaments at all but we had some M & B which he agreed to give her. Diana slept on the sofa in her room all night. I felt very anxious about her. She isn't strong and there is a lot of tuberculosis in her family.

January 27, 1945

We had a rather foolish telegram from the Foreign Office about the Levant, saying that they relied upon me and my staff to persuade the French not to be stiff-necked. I am replying that unfortunately General de Gaulle's neck is naturally stiff and that nothing has happened recently to render it more

---

[1] Alastair Forbes (1918–2005). As a marine he had been attached to the Free French; he later became a journalist and wrote regularly for the *Daily Mail*.

[2] Rear-Adm. Sir Harold Burrough (1888–1977) became Allied Naval Commander, Expeditionary Force, after the death of Admiral Ramsay.

supple. They don't seem to understand that there can be no peace in the Levant so long as the native populations believe that they have two European Powers to deal with, and that if they get into trouble with one they have only to appeal to the other.

January 28, 1945. Sunday

I sent off a protest about the visit of Harry Hopkins.[1] He has been here for several days – has seen Bidault and de Gaulle – must obviously be on a mission from the President and yet has made no sign to me although I know him personally. I have just received a letter from Alec Cadogan saying that they would have liked to invite de Gaulle to the forthcoming meeting, but that the President was strongly opposed. I suspect the latter of having sent Hopkins here to explain that it was not his fault at all but that we are to blame.

January 29, 1944

Freddie Ayer came to see me about the question of his joining my staff. He showed me his written instructions from 'C'. They seemed to me pretty straightforward. He is not to do any active S.S. work but merely to keep his eyes open for people who might be used later. I think he will be very useful.

Totor de Lesseps came at 5. I had sent for him – his Diana had given mine some days ago a list of certain of our friends which was supposed to come from the *Sûreté*, accusing them of being pederasts and collaborationists. It was very ill-informed – alleging for instance that Loulou had lived during the occupation with a German called Stuazi – the latter probably being a confusion for Esterházy to whom she is vaguely engaged, who has never left Hungary. She herself came back to France only last April. Of course Jean Cocteau and Bébé Bérard are pederasts – but what of it? Anyhow I frightened Totor – I said I must have an explanation or an apology or I should report the matter to Pellabon, the head of the *Sûreté*. I said the paper didn't read like a police report but like a gossip column. I slightly suspected that Totor might have had something to do with it himself.

January 30, 1945

The Duchesse d'Ayen and Jean Cocteau came to lunch. She is a pathetic figure. Her husband is a prisoner in Germany and her only son has recently been killed. She was so beautiful five years ago. I find Cocteau can be rather boring. They both came up to see Loulou after lunch and I found Cocteau still there when I went back to play picquet with her at 5.30. He had been talking nonsense all that time and persuaded her that he and she were a king and

---

[1] Harry Hopkins (1890–1946), President Roosevelt's intimate adviser and unofficial emissary to Churchill and Stalin as administrator of Lend-Lease. He attended most of the major Big Three war conferences.

queen, to whom no ordinary laws applied and who were above mundane affairs.

January 31, 1945

There is disquieting news from the Levant. To my mind the French are showing patience in the face of a good deal of provocation. Wadsworth,[1] the American representative who was in hand and glove with Spears, is making mischief. No time could be more inconvenient for trouble, as the natives are no doubt fully aware.

We dined with the de Lesseps. Totor seemed nervous at first and she tried to discuss the row with me at dinner. But I said firmly that I preferred not to. I suppose we shall have to let it slide, but I hope it has given Totor some sleepless nights. We had an excellent dinner. They have a very small but charming apartment. There was only just room for eight of us round the table and only just room for the table in the room.

So ends January. It has been a cruel month for the people of France, and I am glad to see the last of it. For me it has been a very busy month. I never seem to have a moment to spare. I haven't had a single day off and have hardly left the house. Two walks with John Julius is all the exercise I can remember. Yet I seem to have no time to read. I have been reading *Reconstruction* by Ferrero all the month and haven't finished it.

February 3, 1945

The warm weather seems to have spread to the east and the thaw is said to be holding up the Russian advance. Gill [British Council representative in Paris] came to see me this morning. Harold Nicolson cannot come over to give the first of a series of lectures that is being arranged, so they want me to do it. I firmly refused. An ambassador shouldn't lecture. He speaks for the country and is therefore condemned to platitudes or to risk putting his foot in it, especially at such a time as this.

I wrote another long telegram about Syria, in reply to one from the Foreign Office telling me to 'educate' the French Government on the subject. I said I did not possess the necessary qualifications any more than a newly-appointed French Ambassador in London could 'educate' the India Office about India – and I reminded them that France's connection with Syria dated from the Crusades.

February 5, 1945

At 4 I had my weekly meeting. Rabino gave us an account of his visit to London with Pleven. It had been very successful from Pleven's point of view.

---

[1] George Wadsworth (1902–79), the first US diplomat to be accredited to Syria in 1942, became Minister in October 1944 when the US Government officially recognized Syria and Lebanon as independent states.

We agreed to give the French Government full information concerning French accounts in British banks, and to wipe out the Simon–Reynaud agreement. Considering that we were recently asking for 50 million pounds in gold in consideration of it, this latter was certainly a large concession. We also agreed to furnish them with a large amount of goods, including 5,000 locomotives which according to the best information we don't possess.

February 8, 1945

We had a dinner party. We went in arm in arm, a fashion that is going out and ought to be revived. It is the most convenient as well as the most graceful way of moving a number of people from one room to another. The evening was I think a great success. When most of the guests had gone, the remainder including the Offroys[1] and the people staying in the house moved into the green drawing room, where Loulou sang to the guitar and everyone was delighted.

February 10, 1945

I did an hour's work with Loulou on the book [the French translation of Duff's book *David*]. After our work [she] went back to Verrières. She has been here over a fortnight and it has been a very happy visit for both of us. She is an adorable companion. I don't think I have ever known her equal – except Diana, who is almost as fond of her as I am. But she is not well and I am worried about her health. One feels her body is too frail for all the energy and genius it contains.

February 11, 1945

A wet and uneventful Sunday. I read the letters of Lord Cowley, who succeeded his father as ambassador in Paris after an interval of six years. He was here from 1852 to 1867. Only 80 years ago – but what a different world. They thought the Crimea 'the most gigantic expedition ever undertaken' – yet in the darkest days of it the Emperor and Empress [Napoleon III and the Empress Eugénie] paid a state visit to London which the Queen returned – state balls, fancy-dress hunting parties and everything.

February 12, 1945

Early in the morning came instructions to convey messages to de Gaulle from the Big Three – inviting France to occupy a zone in Germany and to be a member of the central controlling body. This invitation to be delivered by the three ambassadors simultaneously and not before 9 o'clock. The news was to be released at 9.30, so the implication seemed to be that the General could not be trusted with it for more than half an hour.

---

[1] Raymond Offroy and his wife were friends of the Coopers from Algiers, where he had been Assistant Secretary to the Cabinet of the Committee.

At four I paid my return call on the Turkish Ambassador. He scoffed at the idea of Syria and the Lebanon being fit for self-government and said that the Arab Union was a monster with three heads.

I had to leave in the middle [of dinner] to convey my message to de Gaulle. It was a comic scene – the three ill-assorted ambassadors sitting one side of the table – the gloomy General on the other. We each with our envelope in our hands – the grinning Bogomolov explaining in abominable French, the purpose of our visit. The General solemnly receiving the letters, beginning to read Bogo's which was couched in very exquisite Russian, whereupon Bogo extracted from his trouser pocket a very crumpled French version – then de Gaulle looked at mine – asked if they were all the same and being informed that they were said he had taken [account] of them – so good night. We were not in the room much more than five minutes.

February 13, 1945

The Lebanese Minister [came] who brought with him as a recommendation a letter from Louis Spears! He talked at considerable length about the wrongs of the Lebanon but did not seem altogether unreasonable. He said that Palestine should be an entirely Arab state. I asked him how about the Jews. He said that if the British would only close their eyes for a few minutes the Arabs would soon settle the Jewish question.

February 14, 1945

An odd thing happened today. Loulou had asked me to get her some paper clips, which she said were unprocurable in Paris. I was putting a handful into an envelope when it occurred to me that as it was St Valentine and such a lovely morning I would go out and buy a pretty box to put them in. The walk was a pleasure but I had forgotten that nearly all the shops are shut between 12 and 2. In the window of one at the corner of the Faubourg St Honoré and the Rue Royale I saw exactly what I wanted – an old silver snuff box with the faint design of a château on it. The door was open so I went in but found only a charwoman who had opened the door to sweep out the dust. Eventually I came home empty-handed and emptied the snuff out of my own snuff box and put the clips in that. I was however so pleased with the one in the window that I thought I would ask Diana to give it me for my birthday next week. In the afternoon Diana and I went for a walk. I had thought of showing her the box but forgot to. We drove down the left bank of the Seine as far as Notre Dame and walked back along the quais and through the Tuileries Gardens. We both enjoyed it and were very happy. After I had been working in my room for a little while Loulou came down and handed me the very box that I had admired this morning. This was really a remarkable coincidence. She had been to one or two shops and had found nothing when as she was walking back, having given up the search, she noticed this one in the shop window.

What makes it more interesting is that there is nothing very striking about the box.

February 15, 1945

In the afternoon I walked with Diana to the Avenue Foch, where she had something to do. It was another sunny afternoon but not so nice as yesterday. After I had left her I went on to the Rue de la Pompe, where I used to stay when I was learning French 32–33 years ago. I looked up at the balcony of what was my room at the corner of the seventh floor, whence I used to look down on Paris at night and think about my future. One can see from there the pink house that Boni de Castellane[1] built. Sometimes there were parties being given there and I used to long to be at them. I worked very hard. I spent six weeks there in June–July 1913 and did not go out in the evening once, which was something of an achievement at the age of 23. The apartment appeared to be uninhabited. The little shop below it where we used to buy our stationery was unaltered.

February 16, 1945

We went at 12 to see the Bayeux tapestry unrolled at the Louvre. It had been specially arranged for our benefit and I enjoyed it immensely. It was slowly unrolled across a long narrow table, an expert explaining as it went along. It was better than most films. Diana and I went to a tea party at Nadège's where there were a lot of old women. They say that Nadège was responsible for the death of the late Dutch Minister. She dined with him and it is alleged stayed on after the other guests had left. The exertion was too much for him. A good death.

February 19, 1945

I was nearly late for my appointment with Bidault at 3.30. I had two missions – first to ask him to expedite the French reply to the Syrian request for a statement of their terms. He promised to let me have it by Thursday. The other was a personal invitation to him from Anthony, asking him to go to London on Wednesday or Thursday to be told all about Yalta. He was most anxious to accept but doubted whether the General would let him. He had done everything he could to persuade the General to accept the President's invitation to Algiers. The General was in a very bad mood just now – suffering terribly from toothache. Bidault talked rather wildly about resigning. He means well.

February 20, 1945

Victor has lent me the MI5 – or rather the 020 – file about Alfred Kraus, the

---

[1] Boni de Castellane (1867–1932), Deputy for the Basses-Alpes, elder brother of Stanislas.

Austrian who married Daisy's daughter, Jacqueline.[1] It is a thrilling story. He is a very bad man. I spent a good deal of this morning reading it. I spoke to Diana [who was in London] on the telephone early. She told me that the Massiglis are not popular in London – she especially – and that he had said of us that we entertained only collaborationists.

February 21, 1945

This morning Gridley [Duff's Economic Counsellor] and Monnet came to see me. The more I see of Monnet the more I like him. He strikes me as the ablest Frenchman here and it will be a great pity when he returns to private life, as he is looking forward to doing in the near future. He is not altogether popular with the powers that be because he was not an early Gaullist nor even an over-enthusiastic one. He said that he was satisfied with the result of his efforts in America, and that as many supplies would shortly be sent to France as France could deal with.

February 22, 1945

My 55th birthday – *Eheu fugaces labuntur anni*. It was a beautiful day and I enjoyed my birthday. I drove down to Verrières for Loulou. She had as presents for me another silver snuff box, a pretty illustrated edition of La Fontaine's fables in two volumes, the complete works of Beaudelaire in one, *L'Esprit de Rivard* and what she thought was the first edition of the *Ballad of Reading Gaol* and for which I am sure she had paid more than it's worth. We lunched at a most delightful restaurant that she knew of called Les Plats Mijotes. It was the best I have been to yet and the most expensive, a delightful atmosphere and a charming restaurateur. We were very happy and we went afterwards to Minou's flat which was available, where we translated into French a short speech I had prepared for the opening of Paul Maze's[2] exhibition.

February 24, 1945

I had to go and see General de Gaulle at 4.30. I found him in a good humour with nothing particular to say. He was glad that Bidault was going to England and seemed rather apologetic about having refused to go to Algiers. He said that if the President had given him any indication of the subjects he wished to discuss it would have been different. This seemed to me a very poor reason for refusing but I didn't say so. The conversation was very friendly. I saw Bidault at 5.30. He handed me his note about the Levant with the intimation that I should find it satisfactory. When I got home and read it I found there was not a word in it about terms for Syria. It was simply a repetition of the

---

[1] Daisy Fellowes's daughter Jacqueline de Broglie had married an Austrian, Alfred Kraus, who was accused of betraying members of the Resistance and imprisoned in England. She herself had had her head shaved after the liberation.

[2] Paul Maze (1887–1979), French artist living in England.

French case with regard to the special troops and the gendarmerie. I was much annoyed – the more so when I found that they are making difficulties about being one of the inviting powers to San Francisco. Also they are refusing to help us by the loan of a ship, which we need for the repatriation of prisoners of war. With these accumulated grievances I demanded to see Bidault again tonight.

I spent a heated half-hour with [him]. I think the poor little man really agrees with me but he can't stand up to de Gaulle. Whenever I get him into an argumentative hole from which he can't escape he says 'Very well then, I must resign'. I am really sorry for him.

February 26, 1945 (London)

To the Foreign Office about noon. The meeting I found was not till 12.30 so I went to Wiltons and had half a dozen oysters. Only Alec Cadogan, Chauvel, Massigli and the Counsellor of the American Embassy present, Winant being ill. We agreed on a compromise about the invitation to San Francisco,[1] which it is to be hoped the American Government will accept.

Luncheon in the Annexe – Winston, Bidault, Anthony, Massigli and me. Winston was gay but tiresome. [He] not only says that the Big Three may meet again without France but intends to announce the same in his speech tomorrow. The effect of doing so will be, Massigli says, disastrous. Bidault says it will mean the end of him. Anthony is going to do his best to persuade Winston not to say it. At 6.45 I had an audience with the King at Buckingham Palace. It went better than my audiences usually do. No silences and I made him laugh. As I was leaving I met the Queen in the passage and she asked me to come to her sitting room where we mixed ourselves cocktails. It was a very long time since I had had a talk with her – four or five years – I used to get on so well with her. She ought not to have allowed herself to get so fat.

March 1, 1945 (Paris)

To welcome me I found a poem from Loulou – some sixty alexandrines – to my mind the best thing she has written – free from all surrealist influence – as clear as crystal – simple and original. I spoke to her on the telephone before I had read the poem – she seemed as delightful and as affectionate as ever.

March 6, 1945

The squabble about the terms of the invitation has finally led to the exclusion of France from being one of the inviting powers to the San Francisco conference. It has been rather a storm in a teacup – but it won't do Bidault any good.

Attlee arrived later in the morning. [He] is less impressive every time one

---

[1] The San Francisco Conference (Apr.–June 1945), the international meeting that established the United Nations.

sees him. I took him to call on de Gaulle at 7, where he was more tongue-tied than ever. De Gaulle on the other hand was positively genial.

March 7, 1945

I spent most of this morning drafting a long despatch to the Foreign Office. The occasion for it was one that I had just read from Knatchbull-Hugessen[1] in Brussels recounting the apprehension felt by the Belgians of French penetration and domination. It seems of course early days to envisage France as a menace, but the freedom of the Low Countries from French interference is one of the oldest and soundest principles of British foreign policy, and the answer to the problem now would seem to me to be the formation of a group of Western European democracies which I have been urging on the Foreign Office for the last twelve months.

Attlee looked in to say goodbye. He is overcome with shyness in a drawing room. He is really a poor specimen and I felt ashamed of the Lord President of the Council and Deputy Prime Minister.

March 12, 1945

Gill brought Professor Goddard, who has come over with 25 million units of penicillin as a gift to France. He is going to lecture at the Sorbonne about it. He tells me that it cures both forms of venereal disease and nearly all blood poisoning, but is quite useless against tuberculosis, cancer or the common cold. He is very like a child. We had several people in before dinner, including Nancy Cunard[2] whom neither of us had seen for, I suppose, about fifteen years. She was really less changed than one would have expected. She stayed and dined alone with us. She talked well of her experiences in Spain during the civil war, of her detention on Ellis Island etc. She was very thin and we wondered whether she might be really in want. I hope not. Before dinner came in also Britten,[3] the new musician, who seemed nice, simple and unaffected.

March 13, 1945

We had a cocktail party in the evening for the WVS [Women's Voluntary Service] ladies who are touring France. A cocktail party at the end of a long day is a high trial. To have to stand up for nearly two hours and look pleased is an ordeal which neither Lord Lyons [Ambassador to Paris 1867–87] nor Lord Stratford de Redcliffe [Ambassador to Constantinople 1842–58] ever had to endure.

---

[1] Sir Hughe Knatchbull-Hugessen (1886–1971), Ambassador to Belgium 1944–7.
[2] Nancy Cunard had been a journalist covering the Spanish Civil War, and had been detained on Ellis Island for her pro-black activities and writing.
[3] Benjamin Britten, later Lord Britten (1913–76), composer. The first night of his opera *Peter Grimes* was in 1945.

March 17, 1945

Diana and Bloggs went off this morning on a trip to Burgundy. John Foster and Kit Steel[1] came. John asked my opinion about 'fraternization'. I said it was quite absurd to try to stop it by imposing penalties. Troops were bound either to fraternize with the civilian population or to massacre them. Steel told me of a terrible incident. The Americans had crowded a lot of German prisoners into a railway truck where there was no air, and when they arrived at their destination 104 were dead from suffocation. It will have to come out. I went to a cocktail party at Admiral d'Argenlieu's.[2] French cocktail parties are the worst because the drinks are so bad.

March 22, 1945

I worked till dinner – reading the minutes of the Yalta conference. It is really astonishing that Stalin, when opposing France's membership of the Control Commission, should have had the impudence to say that the Commission should consist 'only of those Powers who had stood firmly against Germany from the beginning'.

March 26, 1945

There was some doubt this morning as to whether the Chancellor [Sir John Anderson] was coming or not – but he eventually arrived and was lucky to do so, for halfway across the Channel he discovered by chance that the pilot was taking him to Brussels. For dinner we had a small hastily-collected party for [him] – the Plevens, Hervé Alphand and Palewski, which with Loulou made us 8. It went quite exceptionally well. Palewski and Alphand made good links between Loulou and the Plevens, who hadn't met her. She recited some of her own poems and sang to the guitar after dinner. Old John beamed with delight and not quite understanding the words looked very sly hoping that they were improper which they were not. Pleven was quite enraptured and fell obviously in love with Loulou. Madame Pleven was less pleased.

March 27, 1945

At 12.30 John Anderson and I set out for the Ministry of Finance, where we were received with much pomp and circumstance. The signing of the Financial Agreement took place and then the press were admitted. Sir John was asked to say a few words. He was totally unprepared and he acquitted himself remarkably well. I had no idea that he had such a knowledge of French. He spoke for about five minutes without hesitating and without – so far as I could

---

[1] Sir Christopher (Kit) Steel (1903–73), British Political Officer SHAEF, 1945; Ambassador to Bonn 1957–63.
[2] Adm. Georges Thierry d'Argenlieu (1889–1964), CIC Free French Navy. A priest before the war, he returned to religious life after 1947.

detect – an error. The fact is, I suppose, that he has learnt the language thoroughly and remembers it, but has had so little practice that he cannot understand it when spoken fast.

I drove him to Le Bourget. He told me he thought Winston was very much under Max's influence. Max had done his utmost to wreck the Financial Agreement. He also told me that the President would have liked to come to Paris but that Winston had stopped it on the grounds that he must not go to Paris before going to London. This was a possibility that had never occurred to me.

March 30, 1945. Good Friday

Colonel Gielgud[1] came to see me this morning. He says there are about 8,000 undernourished British subjects in France, and he has a scheme for providing them with monthly parcels of food. He is going to London to get his scheme approved and he wanted my support, which I gladly gave. The opening of the Hertford Hospital [the British Hospital in Neuilly] is being held up owing to the refusal of the Ministry of Labour to allow the nurses required to come out from England. Gielgud said he would try to do something about this too.

March 31, 1945

I went to see Bidault. The French want to be allowed to run the Saar mines. As they have the necessary engineers and technicians who know the mines we had better let them, but we probably shan't. The Americans or the Russians will object. He was indignant about the proposal that America and Russia should have three votes each in the future world organization. He still harps on the idea of reaffirming the Anglo-French declaration of 1940.

April 5, 1945

I had an agitated morning, as Gen. de Gaulle wanted to see me at 10.30. The General was most friendly and most anxious for an Anglo-French treaty – which he said he had always wanted. He still said however that there was no hurry. I said it would be much better before San Francisco than afterwards. I felt that he was very much alive to the Russian menace, and that he had only recently become so. I dictated two long telegrams concerning our conversation, one dealing with things in general and the Rhine in particular, the other dealing with the Levant. In the military world de Gaulle is making difficulties about supplying troops to guard lines of communication. He says he won't do so until the zones of occupation have been settled, which is really quite ridiculous.

Chauvel talked to me after dinner. He said that he and Bidault had seen de

---

[1] Lt.-Col. Lewis Gielgud (1894–1953), the eldest brother of the actor Sir John Gielgud, was in the Intelligence Corps 1941–4, British Red Cross Sub-Commissioner in Paris 1945, and Co-ordinating Officer, Inter-Allied Reparation Agency in Brussels 1946–9.

Gaulle after I had left him this morning. They had found him in such a good mood, so eager to get on with the Alliance, that they were all now in favour of trying to conclude a real alliance before San Francisco. He seemed excited for so cold-blooded a creature – and talked faster than ever and was more difficult than ever to understand.

April 6, 1945

At 4 I went to see Bidault. He confirmed all that Chauvel said last night. We had half an hour's conversation. Having dawdled so long, they are now in a hurry. It is always the way. I sent as the result a 'most immediate' telegram to London proposing that Chauvel should go over early next week with drafts of 1) an exchange of letters on the subject of the Levant 2) ditto on the Rhine 3) an all-in agreement. I hope that something will come of it.

April 7, 1945

At 12 Gridley came. He hopes to be of some help to France in the matter of coal. France now needs coal desperately – her recovery depends on it – and the time will come, as he says, when our coal trade will need the French market which it would be madness to lose now. Just before lunch Diana and John Julius returned from their visit to the front. They had had a wonderful time. They had crossed the Rhine. They had collected booty from the Siegfried Line. They had seen shells falling and German prisoners coming in with their hands up. General de Lattre had been wonderfully kind to them.

April 10, 1945 (Lyon)

Near Courcelles, which is many miles from Lyon, we found M. Farge,[1] the Commissioner of the Republic, awaiting us. There was also a detachment of troops and a band that played the two national anthems. Our first stop was at Villefranche, a small place where we had a really splendid reception. There was a vast crowd and great enthusiasm and admirable organization. We shook hands with the Mayor on the steps of the Hôtel de Ville – Diana was presented with a bouquet and we drove on again. Our next stop was on the outskirts of Lyon, by a ruined house which had been the scene of a battle between the Germans and the F.F.I. We inspected a detachment of the latter, who then marched past while their rather pathetic band attempted to play the national anthems. They were little more than boys, ill-equipped and ill-attired, but they had fought bravely and were longing to be allowed to fight again. Then on to Mr Parr's [Consul-General at Lyon] house at Lyon, a splendid, most luxurious house belonging to a collaborator now in prison. It had every modern convenience, some good pictures and many valuable and beautifully bound books lying about. Mr Parr himself is a character. He was wearing a top hat, tail coat and eyeglass – he takes snuff – as I do – and is extremely old-world and

---

[1] Yves Farge (1899–1953), Regional Commissioner of the Republic for Lyon.

punctilious. But he is also a scholar and has a good sense of humour. He is highly competent and seems to be very popular with the French.

April 11, 1945

A heavy day – 9.50 call on M. Farge at the Prefecture. Received by a band and the playing of the two National Anthems. After lunch we proceeded to the Chamber of Commerce where the President read very badly a speech to which I had to reply extempore. We walked round the showrooms and Diana was presented with presents of silk. Thence to the University where I had a solemn reception in the amphitheatre and had conferred upon me a *doctorat de lettres – honoris causa*. Long speeches were read. Needless to say the national anthems were played. The hall was full of somewhat unruly undergraduates who made rude noises while the Professor of English Literature spoke – he (a Frenchman) being obviously the joke of the university. On the whole this was the most enjoyable part of the day.

When we finally left there was a guard of about 200 bearing torches lining the approach – and for the last time that day we heard the national anthem. Lyon really could not have done more had we been Their Majesties themselves instead of their unworthy representatives.

April 13, 1945 (Avignon)

We were awoken with the news of President Roosevelt's sudden death. This is something of a calamity and the Prime Minister will feel it very much. So far as France is concerned it is certainly not a disaster – but all will now depend on Truman,[1] of whom nobody knows anything.

April 20, 1945 (Paris)

Chauvel never went to London although he was invited. The reason was that de Gaulle couldn't decide upon the text of the drafts he was to take with him, and hasn't decided yet. Had I been here I might have brought a little pressure to bear.

Midsummer weather and hotter here than in the south of France. I drove down to Verrières to fetch Loulou for lunch. We were very glad to see each other again and she was very sweet. We lunched at the Escargot – very happily. I dined alone with Dollie Bruntisfield – a very faded beauty with whom I had a big affair twenty-five years ago. Her husband, Victor Warrender that was, has recently divorced her. She has not grown any wiser with the years.

---

[1] Harry S. Truman (1884–1972), Democratic Senator from Missouri 1934–44, Vice-President of the US in 1944 and President after Roosevelt's death in April 1945. Almost immediately he took the momentous decision to use the atomic bomb against Japan. He strongly supported the creation of the UN and formulated the Truman Doctrine and the Marshall Plan. Elected President in his own right in 1948, but the progress of the Korean War (1950–3) made him unpopular and he did not stand in the presidential election of 1953.

April 23, 1945

Admiral Shelley[1] came in early this morning. He is at present sharing Daisy's house with Brigadier Daly, and he is disturbed by the prospect of Daisy occupying a part of it and bringing her daughter, the wife of Kraus the spy, to live there. I told him that Daisy had never liked that particular daughter and it was therefore unlikely that she would want her to live in the house.

Soon after lunch Mr Bullitt[2] came to see me. He has a house at Chantilly which Diana is after. He says we can have it as soon as the American generals who are now in it move out. He is now a major in the French Army serving on de Lattre's staff. He told me what a tremendous success John Julius had had with all the French officers.

April 24, 1945

The Russians are now in Berlin. Palewski came round before lunch. The Germans have offered to leave prisoners where they are if we will undertake not to use them again in war. The Americans have agreed and have informed us that they take this to cover the Japanese war. We have agreed with the mental reservation that it doesn't cover the Japanese war. The French are proposing to say they will agree on the understanding that the undertaking applies only to the war against Germany – so that it is all a nice muddle.

April 27, 1945

The Czech Minister came this morning to ask whether I could help a former Mayor of Prague, who had been for six years in Buchenwald, to get to England. He was touchingly grateful when I said I would arrange for him to be flown to England as soon as he wished. George later saw the Mayor who gave him a terrible account of Buchenwald. Not a day had passed in six years without some executions. He himself had been on the list of those to be hanged ten days before the liberation, and he had hidden in a sewer until the Americans arrived.

April 29, 1945. Sunday

John Julius and I went to church this morning and I read the lesson. In the sermon game I got to the end of the alphabet by spelling choir with a Q as it is spelt in the Prayer Book – which J.J. and I thought was fair.

April 30, 1945

A bitterly cold morning. Instructions came for me in a most immediate

---

[1] Vice-Adm. Richard Shelley (1892–1968), Naval Attaché, later changed his name to Benyon.
[2] William C. Bullitt (1891–1967), Ambassador to France 1936–41, fought with the Free French under General de Lattre de Tassigny, 1944–5.

telegram to make representations about the voyage of the *Montcalm* to Beirut.[1]
I believe myself that our people in the Levant exaggerate the danger of the
situation, and it is very hard for us to argue that the French mustn't send
troops while we ourselves retain such large forces there. I lunched alone with
John Julius. He has had wonderful holidays – stayed with de Lattre, crossed
the Rhine into Germany, stopped at Lyon, Avignon, Marseilles, Nice, flown
to Algiers – motored to Tipasa, Bousaada etc. and never spent more than three
nights in the same place. I was very sorry to say goodbye to him after lunch.
He arrived safely in London.

At 3.45 I went to see General de Gaulle according to instructions. I found
him, as I expected, in a most unyielding mood. We wrangled for some time.
He said frankly that he was convinced that it was our policy to oust the French
from the Levant. It is impossible to dissuade him from this view – and there
is indeed much evidence in favour of it, such as the large number of troops
we keep there and the permanent barracks we have built for them.

I had been sent de Gaulle's box for the first night of *Antoine et Cléopatre* at
the Français. The play, uncut, ran from 7 to 11 with one short interval. Loulou
watched it like a child with eyes of wonder and horror – she hid them whenever
there was a suicide – and whenever I looked at her she smiled bravely like a
frightened child saying 'I'm not really frightened'. She is in a very emotional
state just now, and cries very easily. She says she is too much in love – but at
present it alarms her and makes her fear it may lead to great unhappiness.

May 1, 1945

The first news was the presence of Daisy in Paris. She arrived last night. She
is sharing her house with the Brigadier [Daly]. When I told Loulou on the
telephone that Daisy was here she was genuinely alarmed. I assured her that
there was no cause, that I had known Daisy for 25 years and was quite
immune. She persisted that Daisy hated her and would bring her bad luck. It
is remarkable how other women fear Daisy even now when she is 55.

May 2, 1945

While I was dressing Sweeny [Duff's valet] came to tell me that Hitler's
death was officially announced from Germany. This is great news. Hitler and
Mussolini both dead within a few days. Thank God.

May 3, 1945

The Americans have stopped issuing equipment to the French army on the
grounds that it can no longer be of any use in the war against Germany. Nor
are the French at present getting any equipment from us. Yet it is our policy
to build up a strong French army as soon as possible. All the Generals at

---

[1] The French were about to increase their garrison in Lebanon and Syria, and the British
representatives there felt that this would cause unrest.

S.H.A.E.F. are violently anti-French except Morgan. Tedder is the worst. They are much irritated by de Gaulle's refusal to move out of Strasbourg.

Loulou gave me a lovely present today – three beautiful decanters and three glasses – all fitted into a case. It was sweet and foolish of her. She has so little money.

May 4, 1945

During dinner we heard that all Germans in northwest Germany, Holland and Denmark had surrendered. There now remains Norway and Czecho-slovakia. This piecemeal method of ending the war robs it of dramatic effect and must put something of a damper on popular rejoicing.

Arthur Forbes [British Air Ministry representative to SHAEF] came to see me this morning. He told me that the most rabidly anti-French influence in London is that of Prof. Lindemann [Lord Cherwell]. He is against the French Air Mission being shown anything of importance and anticipates being at war with France shortly. The most pro-French of Ministers is Stafford Cripps.[1] Max is less enthusiastic about Russia than he used to be.

May 5, 1945

The event this morning was the arrival of telegrams from the Prime Minister and a personal message from him to de Gaulle, offering to withdraw all British troops from the Levant as soon as the French have completed a treaty with the States [of Syria and Lebanon]. I took this to the General this afternoon and found him in a much better mood than on the last occasion. Palewski, whom I saw first, told me he is now desperately anxious to conclude a treaty with England which he believes is the only thing that can prevent another war. He is obsessed by the Russian menace – and that is one of the many reasons why he is so anxious to retain a base in the Levant. He [de Gaulle] told me that Beynet[2] was returning to Syria in a few days and that he would hand over one brigade of the Special Troops to the States. I asked him to make some announcement to this effect as soon as possible. He smiled and said 'Je ferai cela pour vous, Monsieur l'Ambassadeur.' It was a friendly interview.

May 7, 1945

General Redman[3] came to see me this morning and told me that the uncon-ditional surrender of Germany had been signed in the early hours of this morning at Rheims. [He] also said that the news was not to be divulged, which

---

[1] Sir Stafford Cripps (1889–1952), Labour President of the Board of Trade 1945–7; Chancellor of the Exchequer 1947–50.
[2] Gen. Etienne Beynet (1883–1969), General Officer CIC and High Commissioner, Levant, 1944–6.
[3] Lt.-Gen. Sir Harold Redman (1899–1986), head of SHAEF Mission to the French High Command 1944–5.

I said was nonsense. Having mismanaged the war for 5 years the authorities are already beginning to mismanage the peace. The declaration of war was bungled on Sept. 2nd 1939 and the announcement of unconditional surrender is being bungled now. However it is great news. Diana broke down when I told her.

May 8, 1945. Peace Day

Wonderful weather – very hot. After lunch we listened to Winston declaring the end of the war. It was disappointing. Then the sirens sounded the all clear and the church bells rang. It was a very moving moment. My eyes were full of tears. We dined at Maxim's. We went upstairs after dinner and it was very amusing to watch the vast happy crowds. They danced downstairs.

May 9, 1945

We went at 10 a.m. to the solemn Te Deum at Notre-Dame. It was not somehow as impressive as it should have been. De Gaulle was met at the entrance by the Cardinal, who had not been allowed to be present at the last Te Deum at the time of the Liberation. At the end the ambassadors of the three great powers followed the General out, and each stood beside him in turn while the band played the three national anthems. The congregation inside the church applauded the General with shouts and clapping of hands. I have recently been reading the letters of Robert Lytton. He was surprised when at the Te Deum in the same place on September 13th 1855 the audience greeted Napoleon III in the same way. The ceremony had not been advertised and the streets were empty. I never saw Paris so dead as this morning. I suppose everybody was sleeping off the night before. Diana and I drove down to Chantilly in the afternoon to inspect Bill Bullitt's house which he said we could have as soon as the American general who was living there left it. The General had already gone and the house is perfectly charming. I hope we get it.

May 11, 1945

We dined early and went to T. S. Eliot's[1] lecture. The room was too hot and the lecture was too dull. He has an unpleasant voice in English and an abominable accent in French. I am sure he is not the great poet he is said to be. Contemporary opinions are always wrong. I have just been reading correspondence between the two Lord Lyttons, who were both consider-able writers in their way but whose opinions on their contemporaries are astonishing.

---

[1] Thomas Stearns Eliot (1888–1965), American-born poet, playwright and critic. Author of *The Waste Land*.

May 12, 1945

My only outside visitor today was Paul Reynaud.[1] He seems full of energy and quite self-confident. He is strongly in favour of the Western Bloc, which he believes is the only way of preserving Western Europe from being crushed between the giants of the east and the west. At present he says he is going to devote his time to finishing the book that he began in prison. I believe it is to be called '*Comment la France a sauvé le monde*'. I have always rather liked him. For dinner we had only Loulou and Bébé Bérard. A very pleasant quiet evening. Bébé knows a great deal about English literature and has perfect taste both in English and French. It is remarkable how little Loulou has read. This has helped perhaps to preserve her originality.

May 15, 1945

Pierre de Bénouville – he is dropping the name of Duroc at last – came with a Colonel Degliame to tell me about the difficulties the French are having in saving the lives of starving French deportees in Germany and in getting them out. I hope I may be able to help them.

May 16, 1945 (St Tropez)

At St Tropez we were received by the Mayor and *Préfet*, a guard of honour and a band which played the four national anthems and which we then followed at a very quick march through the brightly decorated streets of the little town. This brought us at last to the *mairie*, or to what is left of it, where the guard of honour all let off their guns, dating from the 1st Empire, almost in our faces. This was most unpleasant and I thought dangerous, as although there was only powder in the guns splinters or pebbles might easily get blown about. For some minutes guns were going off in every direction. We then had a *vin d'honneur* in the one habitable room of the *mairie*.

May 18, 1945 (Paris)

Kingsley Rooker came. He has persuaded S.H.A.E.F. to give priority to French deportees in Germany and to repatriate 5000 a day by air. Tommy Thompson telephoned from London to say that the Prime Minister is thinking of taking a holiday next month and might go to Bendor's [the Duke of Westminster] place in les Landes. I was to warn de Gaulle. I went to see de Gaulle before dinner. He was pleased to hear that Winston was coming to France but not effusive. He talked about the importance of Anglo-French friendship but he does nothing to help it. I didn't tell him so. I now wish I had.

Palewski asked Loulou to call at his office this morning. After a great deal

---

[1] Paul Reynaud (1878–1966), French Prime Minister 1940. Arrested by Pétain, he was tried in 1942 and imprisoned by the Germans until 1945. Re-elected to the Chamber of Deputies in 1946.

of palaver about patriotic duties etc. which only puzzled her, she gradually realized that he was asking her to act as a spy on me in return for money. He told her she would have *la vie facile*. She said that her *vie* was already quite *facile* owing to the generosity of her brothers. She said he almost produced a cheque book. She was much distressed about it and had meant not to tell me. But what a frightful fool the man must be – and how utterly unfit for any responsible position.

May 19, 1945

Diana, Venetia, Raimund and I motored down to Verrières and dined with the three brothers and Loulou. It would have been a melancholy occasion in most families, as André [de Vilmorin] is leaving tomorrow for the clinic at Chateaubriand to undergo a terrible operation. He may remain there for many months and perhaps never return. They were all more gay and amusing than usual – the house was a mass of roses – I played backgammon with André after dinner and it was an altogether delightful evening.

May 21, 1945. *Whit Monday*

I had a personal telegram from Anthony saying that Massigli had suggested to him at luncheon that I should see more of Chauvel, who was anxious to help but could not do so if he didn't know what was going on. This irritated me, because I suspect Massigli of trying to do me harm in London. I had not seen Chauvel lately, as since the fiasco of his visit to London (which he had promised to explain to me) I had heard nothing from him. When I did see him this afternoon, he said he had not asked me to come because frankly he had no explanation to offer except that the General had changed his mind. There seems to be a complete lack of liaison between the Quai d'Orsay and the Rue St Dominique. Chauvel knows nothing. He hopes that Bidault will return on Wednesday as he does have some slight influence with de Gaulle.

May 22, 1945

I had to face three cocktail parties – the first at the Russian embassy. Bogomolov was very friendly and insisted on sending for some vodka to drink with me. There was none for the common herd. I made the acquaintance of the new Dutch Ambassador and his wife. She is reputed to have been the mistress of Himmler.[1]

May 23, 1945

The Archduke Otto[2] came to see me this morning with a letter for the Prime

---

[1] Heinrich Himmler (1900–45), head of the Waffen SS under Hitler and from 1944–5 head of the German Army.
[2] Archduke Otto von Habsburg (b. 1912), pretender to the Austro-Hungarian throne, spent the war in the US. He returned to Europe in 1945, relinquished his claim to the throne in 1961 and became an MEP for Bavaria in 1979.

Minister. His grievance is that the late President had told him that no political leaders would be allowed back into Austria until steps had been taken to find out the will of the people, but that what had actually happened was that the Communists had been allowed back and had been helped to form a Government and that everybody else was still excluded. He is extremely good-looking and full of charm. It seems sad that the Habsburgs should have produced after all these centuries such an admirable litter of princes when it is too late.

May 24, 1945

I called on Herriot[1] at the Bristol. I found him in wonderful form. He has a breadth of view and a gift of expression which compare very favourably with those of the men of the Fourth Republic. Soon after 5 I went out to the airport to meet Field Marshal Montgomery. Everything passed off well. Considering that his arrival had not been announced it was astonishing how many people there were all along the route – and their enthusiasm was tremendous. We gave him tea and he sat talking until it was time to dress for dinner. I find him pleasant, simple and easy, with a frank engaging vanity that nobody could object to. We were 24 for dinner. Diana had decorated the centre drawing room, where we dined, with flags and swords and laurel wreaths. We had up the Borghese plate for the first time and the table and walls were covered with red roses – no other flowers in the room, which was lit only by candles. It looked really very beautiful. Loulou had a new white dress and so had Diana. They both looked lovely. Caffery arrived drunk and admitted as much to Diana. He got drunker as the evening wore on. A young woman with a guitar [Anna Marly] sang the songs of the Resistance extremely well. The party seemed a great success.

May 25, 1945

Soon after 12, Diana and I left with Daly for the Invalides. It was a sunny morning and the scene in the courtyard where de Gaulle decorated Monty with the Grande Croix of the Légion d'Honneur was very fine indeed. It was followed by a men's luncheon party at the Rue St Dominique. De Gaulle was in a very amiable mood and made a quite excellent speech at the end proposing Monty's health, to which the latter replied quite adequately in English.

May 26, 1945

I was called away from dinner last night by a 'most immediate' telegram *en clair* from London saying that the situation in Syria was deteriorating, and that I must see the General at once and get him to do something which would have a calming effect. As Palewski was at dinner I told him about it, and asked

---

[1] Edouard Herriot (1872–1957), French Prime Minister 1924–5. Arrested by the Vichy authorities in 1942, he was interned until 1945. President of the National Assembly 1947–54.

him to arrange for me to see de Gaulle this morning. I went to the Rue St Dominique where I had a quite unsatisfactory interview. All was going well, and he had almost agreed to conversations either here or in London and to making a statement that no more troops would be sent to the Levant meanwhile, when I mentioned that the Americans would take part in such conversations. Thereupon he flew into a rage, said that the Americans were in no way concerned, and that he would not allow France to be put into the dock before the Anglo-Americans. I argued vainly with him for some time and left him still sulky.

May 27, 1945. Sunday (Poitiers)

We left in two cars soon after 2.30. George [Lansdowne] and Penelope [Lloyd-Thomas, Diana's Social Secretary] went ahead in the Humber and we followed in the Rolls. We pursued our way in sheets of rain to Sainte Maure where we had been directed by Teddie to a very dingy-looking little inn called the Veau d'Or. They gave us a private room at the back of the garden and produced the menu of the dinner they were preparing for us. It included no less than 17 separate items. Much to their regret we struck out two of the main dishes – *Langue sauce tomates* and *Noix de veau à la broche* – so that we were left with only *Potage Parmentier, Artichauts-radis, Pâté Maison, Escargots Sainte Mauriens, Oeufs à la crème, Pommes duchesse, Asperges vinaigrette, Fromage de Sainte Maure, Crème Pompadour, Brioche maison, Fraises, Cerises, Café*. We drank *vin de Chinon* and some Armagnac. The whole meal including that of the three servants who said that they also had had more than they could eat, cost only 1300 francs, which is less than half what lunch for two costs at the Escargot in Paris. There is abundance of everything in this particular corner of France and they say they have had no shortages.

May 31, 1945 (Château de Massan, near Auch)

It was a fine morning and I woke early feeling none the worse for the many *vins d'honneur* and the deep potations of the day before. From my window I could see in the unclouded morning sky the snow-capped peaks of the Pyrenees. In my bedroom there was a splendid dressing case presented by Napoleon to the Duc de Felton, one of our host's ancestors. When I was dressed I walked out on the southern side of the house, which is the back of it, in order to have a good look at it. As I came round to the north and the front door I saw the village band collected and a small crowd of people. When I got back through the door that I had gone out by I was met by my host, who introduced me to the mayor of the village and the members of the council, about a dozen hard-handed sons of the soil. Speeches were made on both sides and a magnum of champagne was consumed. Then we went out on the steps where the village band made a gallant assault on God Save the King and a slightly more successful one on the Marseillaise. An old lady of 80, the doyenne of the village, was led up, who presented us with a basket containing strawberries on one side, cherries on the other and a handsome turkey in the middle. The progeny of our host, three of the prettiest children I ever saw, two girls and a boy, came to bid us goodbye and off we drove to the next village where the same ceremonies took place. We had four more before we reached Toulouse. M. Bertaux, the *commissaire* for Toulouse, met us some 40 kilometres outside the town. He is an attractive man with a splendid record. He is perhaps rather too conscious of both these facts, but he is much more a man of the world than any of the other *commissaires* I have met and if he sticks to politics he should go far. Here again the usual ceremonies took place, the gift consisting of a gold medal and *vin d'honneur* being confined to Byrrh – one of the most unpalatable and least refreshing of drinks in my opinion. Nancy Cunard, much to our surprise, was at lunch. I believe that Nancy, whose whole life has been spent in violent revolt against her mother, will end by becoming exactly like her. Didn't Oscar Wilde say 'all women end by becoming like their mothers; that's their tragedy'?

[*Paris*] A good deal has happened in my absence. Anthony had made a statement in the House of Commons to the effect that our Commander-in-Chief Middle East[1] (General Sir Bernard Paget) had been ordered to take charge in the Levant. This had been communicated to de Gaulle in a message from the Prime Minister which unfortunately had reached him an hour after the statement had been made in the House. It is all most regrettable, but de Gaulle has brought it upon himself by refusing to listen to any warning or to do anything that he is asked.

June 1, 1945

As the day wore on it became clear that de Gaulle did not mean to see me. First Palewski couldn't be found, then he couldn't find the General, then he promised to ring up later and didn't do so – finally at about 4.30 came the message that he was too busy to see me today. I then telephoned to Bidault and saw him at 7. He was extremely depressed. He is fully conscious of the mistakes that France has made, and of his own inability to prevent them. He finds de Gaulle a hard master but is quite convinced that de Gaulle is at present indispensable to France. I felt sorry for him.

In 1945 there was a further crisis in the Levant when the French refusal to transfer control of the local armed forces to the Syrian and Lebanese governments led to disorder, culminating in a French bombardment of Damascus and British intervention. After long negotiations, agreement was finally reached on simultaneous British and French withdrawal from the area, which was completed in 1946.

---

[1] Gen. Sir Bernard Paget (1887–1961), CIC Home Forces 1941–3 and CIC Middle East Forces 1944–6.

June 2, 1945

Our wedding day – the 26th anniversary. There was a message from Bidault asking me to call on him at 12.30. I found [him] in a state of great indignation. General Paget has issued a proclamation that seems designed to humiliate the French and which I am sure was quite unnecessary. They say it is worse than Fashoda. The General is naturally in a rage and the problem which seemed to be solving itself is complicated. I always had a poor opinion of Paget.

June 3, 1945. Sunday

Soon after dinner I had a telephone message to say a most immediate telegram had arrived, they were then decyphering it and I had better come back at once [from Chantilly]. I left as soon as I had swallowed my coffee. The news was that the French were sending the *Jeanne d'Arc* [a French naval cruiser] back from Oran to Beirut. A more idiotic gesture at this moment could hardly be imagined. I asked to see de Gaulle but he refused to see me so that I then went round to see Bidault. He knew why I had come and said at once that he considered it a *sottise*. At the same time he pointed out that we had further infuriated de Gaulle by sending British soldiers to seize the Office des Services Panificalles in Syria and imposing British censorship on the French radio. It looks to me as though Paget were losing his head. Bidault promised sadly to telephone again to de Gaulle – he said it would be the fourth time that night. He said that if we could make a conciliatory gesture it would help him enormously.

June 4, 1945

Admiral Shelley came to tell me that the *Jeanne d'Arc* had sailed, despite orders to the contrary from C.inC. Med. At 3.30 I went to see de Gaulle at his invitation. We had a stormy interview. He could not have been more stiff if he had been declaring war. He told me that French soldiers in the Levant had been ordered to stay where they were, and to fire on Syrian or British troops if force were used against them. We got into a heated argument. He is genuinely convinced that the whole incident has been arranged by the British in order to carry out their long-planned policy of driving the French out of the Levant in order to take their place. I said that if we wanted these disorders, why had we implored him not to send the ships that caused the disorders? He replied rather feebly that we should have found some other excuse. We had a very unpleasant half-hour. At 6.45 I went to see Bidault. He gave me the very welcome news that the *Jeanne d'Arc* would not go to Beirut – adding that he had been forbidden to tell me so. He said that if only the Prime Minister in his statement tomorrow could say something conciliatory it would help enormously. I promised to ask him to – and I did so by telegraph when I got back. Anthony is ill with a duodenal ulcer – so Winston is dealing with the Foreign Office. Bidault asked me whether Anthony's illness was a diplomatic one – and said he felt like having one himself. I said no. Nor did I think, as he seemed to, that there was any difference between Anthony and the P.M. on the Levant as there was between himself and the General.

June 5, 1945

[Gerald] Norman [the *Times* correspondent] came to see me this morning and we had as usual a frank and helpful talk. He himself is now inclined to take the view that it must always have been our policy to clear the French out of the Levant. This was the more interesting as just before he came I had sent off a telegram to the effect that while I would never allow de Gaulle or anyone else to assert this without contradiction I thought we ought nevertheless to bear in mind the very strong evidence that exists to support such a theory.

June 6, 1945. D-Day

We left the embassy at eight and the earth at Le Bourget at 8.30. They gave us a very comfortable aeroplane for once. Our party consisted of General Vanier, the three service attachés and George [Lansdowne]. We landed near Caen where our car met us and we immediately hurried off to the first ceremony somewhere on the beach, where we arrived just as the ceremony was over and the public was dispersing. We were met by the *préfet* and after I had laid a wreath on the American war memorial our car joined the cortège and we drove back in the direction from which we had come. It was a beautiful, breezy morning and the countryside, so like England, made me a little homesick. We arrived at Bayeux, where the Mayor was making a speech on the microphone. When the arrival of the British Ambassador was announced there were loud cheers. It was an exceptionally beautiful evening.

We went to dine with the Fitzgeorges [Commander George Fitzgeorge[1], Naval Attaché]. There was music and dancing after dinner and three French sailors who sang. Afterwards I talked to various people, perhaps a little more to Daisy [de Cabrol][2] than the others but not much. This however distressed Loulou and she suddenly dashed from the room. After a while Diana went to look for her but she was nowhere to be found. She had walked back to the Rue de Bellechasse, whither we followed her. We found her in bed, poor darling, very unhappy. We had a great many tears, but she was fairly calm before we left. It was charming, if rather odd, to see Diana trying to comfort her, assuring her that I really loved her.

---

[1] George Fitzgeorge (1892–1960), grandson of HRH The Duke of Cambridge.

[2] Marguerite (Daisy), née d'Harcourt, Baronne de Cabrol (b. 1915), wife of Hugues (Fred), Baron Cabrol de Moute. They were among the closest friends of the Duke and Duchess of Windsor.

June 8, 1945

At 12 came the Vicomte de Ramolino, the Prince Napoleon's[1] bear-leader. He wanted to discuss with me the possibility of the Prince making an English marriage – I think he probably had Princess Margaret Rose[2] in view. I gave him no encouragement in that direction – but I said there was no reason why he shouldn't marry some nice English girl.

June 10, 1945

I worked from 4 to 6 when I went to see Daisy de Cabrol. She is looking very pretty and is a sweet but not very clever girl. She is very proud of being the only one in Paris who is faithful to her husband and says she intends to remain so. I really don't mind. Stephen Spender[3] was with Diana and Loelia[4] when I got back. He seems very pleased with himself.

June 11, 1945

Daly came this morning. De Gaulle was to have decorated a number of English generals, nobody below the rank of Lieut.-Gen., on June 18. He has now announced that it will be a purely French ceremony and that the British generals are not to come – a small-minded, rude and foolish gesture. Loulou came soon after 12.30. She was looking prettier than ever this morning. When she is very tired she can look quite plain. She brought me a beautiful poem she had written for the day I went to Caen. She thinks herself that the poems she has written for me are the best she has done – and I agree. It is sad that they can hardly be published at present. This one, I think, might be. It had been a dull morning but the sun now came out and we went down to the Coq Hardi for lunch. We had a very happy luncheon, bathed in sunshine, and went afterwards to the flat of Jacques Franck.[5]

June 14, 1945

Just before lunch Caffery came round. He wanted to tell me the trouble there had been over Eisenhower's visit today. De Gaulle had said that he wouldn't receive Tedder and Freddy Morgan because they are English. [Eisenhower] had replied that he came as Head of SHAEF and wouldn't come without them. A compromise had finally been reached by which they were to take part

---

[1] Prince Louis Napoléon (1914–97), the great-great-grandson of King Jérome. He had served with great bravery in the Foreign Legion, and had been granted residence in France by de Gaulle.

[2] HRH The Princess Margaret, Countess of Snowdon (1930–2002), younger daughter of King George VI and Queen Elizabeth.

[3] Sir Stephen Spender (1909–95), poet. In 1945 he was working with the Control Commission in Germany. Literary Counsellor to UNESCO 1945–7.

[4] Loelia, Duchess of Westminster (1902–93), later Lady Lindsay of Dowhill.

[5] Jacques Franck, an interior decorator and friend of Louise de Vilmorin.

in the ceremonies but not to be invited to the dinner, which it was then to be said was not official but a private party given by de G. for Ike. This is all the more absurd as my Military Attaché, and I suppose all the allied Military Attachés, have been asked. I sometimes think de Gaulle may go mad. He looked awful today from what I could see of him at the Arc de Triomphe, where he conferred the Cross of the Liberation on Ike [Eisenhower]. The Corps Diplomatique were, as usual, very badly placed at this ceremony. It was followed by a reception at the Hôtel de Ville where there were speeches, confusion and a *vin d'honneur*. I find no coolness in the welcome of any of my French friends, and Ike, who is annoyed at the way Tedder and Morgan have been treated, went out of his way to be civil to me. When I got back I found there was some excitement, because the Prime Minister wished to speak to me on the secret telephone and all our secret telephones were abolished months ago. However some of our experts managed to fix one up in an hour and I got through to him at 8.30. All he wanted to say was that he felt he must have a holiday after all. A few days ago he had telegraphed to say it was definitely off. He now thinks he can come on July 4. I must tell de Gaulle. Not just yet, I think. I lunched and dined alone today and found it very agreeable.

June 15, 1945

De Gaulle has stopped not only the decoration of British and Canadian officers by himself, which was to have taken place on the 18th, but also the decoration of French officers by me which was to have taken place on the 20th. The French officers of all three arms are shocked. He is behaving like a fool, and proving that he is incapable of filling the great position that he occupies.

I had a dinner party of what I hoped were gay young people for the amusement of Loelia. I didn't think it went very well. I can't entertain without Diana.

June 17, 1945. Sunday

I dined at the Quai d'Orsay. The dinner was for the Sultan of Morocco. We sat down over 100 at one huge table. It was all beautifully done – the flowers were pretty, the service was quick and the food was good. After the departure of the Moroccans I had a few very friendly words with Bidault. When I said goodnight he insisted on conducting me through the spacious salons to the door. When I begged him not to he said 'I think it is a good thing that M. Palewski should see that I am accompanying you, and should see how glad I am to do it'. Palewski was making love to Madame Alphand on a sofa. This confirms the view that I was beginning to form on information from other sources, that Palewski's influence is anti-English.

June 18, 1945

The great *défilé* [*to celebrate the Peace*]. The weather was perfect. There was not a cloud in the sky and yet it was not too hot. The show was extremely well done. There were over 50,000 men on parade, and a tremendous display of motor vehicles of all sorts and aeroplanes. But one couldn't help thinking how all these and most of the equipment was of Anglo-American origin. Not a single English or American flag was shown. There was no evidence of an ounce of gratitude and one felt throughout that France was boasting very loud, having very little to boast about.

June 20, 1945

May Spears [came to see me]. She and her ambulance had taken part in the *défilé* on Monday and on each of her four jeeps she had flown a little Union Jack pennant by the side of the tricolour. I had not noticed them but Vanier who was standing by me had, and remarked on them to me. At the same time I saw de Gaulle talking over his shoulder to Diethelm. Sure enough he had spotted them, with the result that the General commanding the Division sent for the Colonel in charge of the ambulance, who told him the ambulance was to be dissolved immediately and the British members of it to be repatriated. Lady Spears is justly indignant. The ambulance has been serving on all fronts for $4\frac{1}{2}$ years and has looked after 20,000 French wounded. The folly and the pettiness of de Gaulle pass belief. I told her there was nothing I could do except mention the matter to Bidault. He was most indignant and made a note of it. *Après tout*, he said, *on ne fait pas la guerre aux femmes.*

June 26, 1945

Loulou has written a very remarkable and beautiful piece called *Le coeur de la soirée* – dealing with the history of her heart and concluding with a description of the unhappy evening at the Fitzgeorges. I call it a 'piece' because it is not an essay, nor a story, nor a poem – and I can find no other name for it. She has dedicated it to Diana, to whom she said that that evening had broken her heart and killed her love for me. They spent this morning together and Diana told her that she must go on loving me – to which she replied that she couldn't help doing so, much as it distressed her. She and I lunched together at the Méditerranée and were very happy, which was more than the *patron* was, who said he was being ruined by the new Minister of Food who was rendering the profession of *hôtelier* quite impossible.

June 28, 1945

Arthur Forbes [Air Attaché at the Embassy] came and recounted an interesting conversation he had had with Saillant,[1] in the course of which the latter had expressed the view that the Syrian question would never be satisfactorily settled so long as de Gaulle was there, but that he had gathered from a

[1] Louis Saillant, prominent trade unionist, President of the CNR (Conseil National de la Résistance).

conversation which he had recently had with de Gaulle that the latter might now be willing to go.

Palewski asked Loulou to call on him this afternoon and solemnly informed her that he was instructed by General de Gaulle to ask her to convey to me his assurance, in which Palewski joined, that they both regretted that owing to recent events their relations with the British Embassy could not be what they had been in the past but that they wished me to know that they still had nothing but the friendliest feelings towards me personally. This seems to me – I must say – the most extraordinary procedure. I am surprised that de Gaulle lends himself to it. Palewski went on, she said, to abuse the English violently, especially the Prime Minister.

July 2, 1945 (London)

I went round to the Foreign Office and saw Oliver Harvey and Ronnie Campbell.[1] The latter showed me the most recent telegrams from the Levant. It now looks to me as though the French were trying to come to terms with the Syrians independently of us, which they think would be a great score off us, but with which we should be of course delighted. It is typical of de Gaulle's mentality. I only hope it comes off.

July 7, 1945 (London)

Dr Weizmann[2] came [to see me.] He has recently returned from Palestine, where he said the great tragedy of Jewry had been brought too painfully close to him. He was very melancholy. He believes that four and a half million Jews have been massacred. Winston had promised him that he would deal with the Palestine question as soon as the German war was over – but he seemed to have changed since the murder of Moyne and he now says it can only be settled at the peace conference, and meanwhile he is refusing to see Weizmann.

July 8, 1945 [Bognor]

A perfect day – not a cloud in the sky yet not too hot. Raimund and I bathed in the sea and Caroline watched us. Afterwards we sat in the garden to dry – eating prawns and drinking vodka. I said 'this is heaven' and it was – a memorable moment of perfect contentment.

July 12, 1945 (Biarritz)

George [Lansdowne] and I left Le Bourget about 10 o'clock. We had a large Dakota to ourselves and after a smooth journey we arrived at Bordeaux about 12.30. When we reached the villa where the P.M. is living we found him

---

[1] Sir Ronald Ian Campbell (1890–1983), Assistant Under-Secretary of State 1945–6; Ambassador to Egypt 1946–50.

[2] Dr Chaim Weizmann (1874–1952), President of the World Zionist Organization 1935–46, first President of the State of Israel 1949–52.

exhausted in an armchair with a whiskey and soda. He had been compelled to watch pelota in the blazing sun and was taking a rest. Clemmie however sent him a message that he must return, which he did, taking us with him. We watched some peasant dances, at the end of which he made a speech in his bad French. It is curious that he likes making speeches in French. He admitted so to me afterwards. He knows so little that he doesn't notice nor mind his own mistakes. I hate making French speeches unprepared because I know the mistakes that I make and regret them when it is too late to correct them.

Before dinner we bathed, Winston, Mary [Churchill], Tommy Thompson, Jock Colville, George and I. It was delicious, very warm although a great thunderstorm was blowing down on us from Spain. Winston's method of bathing is to wallow like a walrus in shallow water, floating about and abandoning himself to the waves. A number of the inhabitants watched with evident amazement this extraordinary spectacle. He is adored by the population here as throughout France. We dined very late as there was great delay in producing a very inferior dinner. Winston's main subject of conversation was the election. He is by no means confident of the result but he thinks it will be all right. There is some indignation among the French that de Gaulle should have made no gesture of recognition of the Prime Minister's presence in France. Winston said to me himself 'if he had taken a holiday in Scotland I think I should have sent him a message to say I hoped he was having a good time'. The P.M. wanted to consult me as to the desirability of my approaching de Gaulle with the suggestion that they might have a conversation in Paris on Sunday if the P.M. stopped there on his way to Berlin. I was very strongly in favour of the plan. The French have now handed over the Special Troops to the Syrians, and if we could now come to an agreement for the simultaneous Anglo-French evacuation of the Levant the whole question might be settled without any of the delays or difficulties of an international conference. We argued the subject at great length before and after dinner and he changed his view more than once, but when we eventually went to bed at 2 a.m. I had convinced him and had his authority to take up the matter in Paris.

July 13, 1945

I felt that we should leave early, as there was no time to lose if I was to succeed in my mission. George and I dashed into the sea soon after 8, left the Parme aerodrome at 10 and arrived in Paris at 12.30. I was greeted at the Embassy by a message from the P.M. to say that I was to take no action whatever on the subject we had discussed last night. This was a great disappointment to me. Another chance missed!

July 16, 1945

The Prime Minister has sent a charming message to de Gaulle on leaving French territory, thanking the French Government for having allowed him to come and expressing the hope of seeing de Gaulle before long. These are coals of fire because during the time he was here de Gaulle made no sign of civility whatever.

We dined at the Quai d'Orsay – a dinner for the Bey of Tunis. Diana sat next the Bey, who speaks no word of French or English so that conversation was impossible. She had the brilliant idea of drawing pictures for him which amused him very much – and he drew too.

July 19, 1945

We went to an exhibition of pictures by English children aged 5 to 10. We met Picasso coming out. He had been much impressed. No wonder – the pictures are just as good as his.

July 23, 1945

After I had this morning sent a message to de Gaulle saying Mountbatten would be here tomorrow and had invited some generals and an admiral to meet him at dinner, they telephoned from Potsdam[1] to say that the Prime Minister was endeavouring to prevent him from coming here and that if he came he was to be sent straight on either to Potsdam or London. This all seems to me excessively stupid. There came [before dinner] a Mlle de Jonge – the heroine of the Belgian resistance. She brought her mother. Her father had been shot. She seemed to me exactly what Joan of Arc must have been. Simple, gay, radiating heroism and taking it as the most natural thing in the world.

July 25, 1945

This morning I attended 'les funérailles nationales de Paul Valéry'. It was a remarkable performance. The weather was perfect. The hour was early – 10 a.m. double summer time, which means 8 a.m. There was a touch of autumn in the air – some trees owing to the exceptional dryness of this summer are already taking on autumnal tints. The huge gold sarcophagus surrounded by laurels in the shape of Vs was impressive and the mise en scène, the Place du Trocadéro, could not have been better. The golden statues were shrouded in crepe. Of the three speeches (the Président du Collège de France, Duhamel[2] and Capitant[3]) that of Capitant was far the best – to my surprise. It proves again that eloquence has little to do with literature. The défilé of troops turning eyes right to the coffin of this old poet who had little to do with military affairs

---

[1] Churchill was attending the Potsdam Conference (17 July–2 Aug. 1945) where he, Truman and Stalin discussed post-war arrangements in Europe as well as issuing an ultimatum to Japan, offering the choice of unconditional surrender or total destruction. Attlee took Churchill's place after becoming Labour Prime Minister on 26 July.

[2] Georges Duhamel (1884–1966), French novelist and playwright, author of Vie des Martyrs (1917) and Chronique des Pasquiers (1933–45).

[3] René Capitant (1901–70), lawyer, with de Gaulle in Algiers, Minister of Education 1944–5.

was again a reminder of how very far we are removed from the French. We have only to imagine how would be greeted the suggestion that the Brigade of Guards should march past the coffin of T. S. Eliot.

July 26, 1945 (London)

The first election results[1] were already coming through and four or five Labour gains had been recorded. There was great excitement in the hall of the Dorchester and many friends. I went round to White's. The news continued to come in and the landslide became apparent. But everybody was extraordinarily cheerful, as they were at the Rothermeres' party at the Dorchester to which I returned. Two of the first results which delighted me were the defeats of Louis Spears and of Cunningham-Reid.[2] The party was really most amusing. Many defeated candidates were present, and the results which came in every few minutes were given out on a loudspeaker. I came back to the Dorchester to see Daisy about her daughter Emmeline,[3] who has been arrested for denouncing another woman of whom she is reported to have been jealous in a lesbian attachment.

July 27, 1945

I went to see Dickie Mountbatten, with whom I had an interesting talk. It was of course Winston who prevented him from coming to Paris and he was quite angry with him for having meant to. Anthony on the other hand was in favour of his coming and of his seeing de Gaulle. I hope now that I shall be able to arrange it for his return journey. There is no doubt that the removal of Winston, Cherwell and Max will make my task easier – unless I am removed myself. It seems pretty certain that Bevin will go to the Foreign Office. I have always been on good terms with him so there should be no personal reason for his wanting to get rid of me.

July 29, 1945 [Bognor] Sunday

A delectable morning delightfully spent – golf, croquet and sea bathing, prawns and vodka. We all bathed and the sea was delicious. We lunched out of doors. A few people came in the afternoon [including] Pam Churchill[4] with little Winston aged 5. When the latter was asked whether he knew anything about recent events he said that he gathered that he had a new grandpa.

---

[1] The general election of July 1945 resulted in 393 Labour MPs being elected to 197 Conservatives. Clement Attlee became Prime Minister.

[2] Maj. Alec Cunningham-Reid DFC (d. 1977), Conservative MP, married the Hon. May Ashley in 1927, divorced 1940. Later that year he was accused by MPs of visiting Doris Duke in Honolulu to evade the Blitz.

[3] Emmeline de Castéja, served five months in Fresnes prison locked up with prostitutes.

[4] Pamela Churchill, née Digby (1920–97), married Randolph Churchill in 1939, divorced 1946. They had one son, Winston. She later married Leland Hayward, the Broadway producer, and finally in 1971, Averell Harriman. In 1993 she became American Ambassador in Paris.

According to this morning's *Observer* the Labour Government are likely to get rid of Halifax [Ambassador in Washington], Rex Leeper [Ambassador to Greece] and me. I doubt it. Nor should I greatly mind. Curiously enough Diana would mind more than I should. She loves Paris now, although she was not prepared to and didn't at first. I drafted today a letter to Bevin which I considered suitable to the occasion. I said that I should not resent but I should regret it if he decided to replace me.

July 30, 1945 (Paris)

Beatrice [Eden] stayed to dine. I then walked home with her to the Grand Hotel. I think she is rather appalled at the prospect of more intimate domestic life with Anthony now that they are out of office. They have no home in London, no car, no secretary. She seems however remarkably cheerful, was dressed in the brightest colours and never refers to the fact that her eldest son has recently been killed.[1]

July 31, 1945

Palewski came here before dinner. He and de Gaulle are really alarmed at the prospect of my possible removal. He consulted Loulou as to the best steps that he could take in order to prevent it. He did not want to act through Massigli, as he thinks Massigli carries no weight in London and may shortly be withdrawn. I told Loulou that a private letter from Palewski to Cadogan would be the best way. But it seems that Palewski doesn't know Cadogan but knows Sargent[2] well, which I said would be just as good. At 9.30 p.m. I had to go to the Quai d'Orsay to hand joint notes with Bogomolov and Caffery to Bidault, giving the result of the Potsdam conference. Bogomolov asked us both back to his embassy. There were two tables – one for the three Ambassadors, one for the three secretaries – Eric, Macarthur and Ratiani. There were things to eat – caviare, eggs, sardines etc. Bogomolov proposed 15 toasts, all being drunk in vodka – Ratiani, his own secretary, was sick on the floor. I went to the Forbes's but realised it would be wiser not to go in, so sent poor Eric to collect Diana, Loulou and John Julius. They drove me home and I remember little more. Eric foolishly stayed at Forbes's party and was eventually taken home by an Air Commodore whose name he doesn't know. He couldn't stand and was very sick.

---

[1] Simon Eden, a pilot with the RAF in Burma, was reported missing in June 1945 and confirmed dead four weeks later on 20 July. Anthony and Beatrice Eden separated in 1946 and divorced in 1950.

[2] Sir Orme (Moley) Sargent (1884–1962), Deputy Under-Secretary of State at the FO 1939–46; Permanent Under-Secretary 1946–9.

August 1, 1945

Strangely enough I felt little the worse this morning after last night's orgy. Eric on the other hand was a sad mess. I went out to lunch at Maxim's. Towards the end of the meal I felt suddenly very ill and was afraid that I was going to be sick. I managed to overcome it – walked home, lay down and had a sleep. At 5.30 we three Ambassadors had again to make communications to Bidault from Potsdam. Neither Bogo nor his secretary had been available all day, giving no sign of life until 4.30. The secretary still looked awful. Caffery said he had suffered terribly and his secretary, Macarthur, was still in bed really ill. When I got back to the Embassy I began to feel worse and worse – violent pains in the stomach and nausea. I was finally very sick and felt a little better. I had particularly wanted to be at dinner because Victor [Rothschild] was here for one night – so went and sat at the table, but had soon to leave it to be sick again. All night I suffered from griping pains and got very little sleep.

August 2, 1945

I had a bad night and stayed in bed half the morning. I went on having griping pains in the stomach all day. I sent for a doctor in the evening. He said it was only colic and gave me some grains of coal to eat and also tablets to soothe the pain. I went to bed for dinner which consisted of some boiled rice without milk.

August 4, 1945

After my bad night and as I felt no better this morning we got hold of an American Army doctor – a serious young man who made a thorough examination and pronounced that I had inflammation of the lower intestine. He gave me some medicine and some pills and I seemed to get better all day. I stayed in bed.

I started reading Evelyn Waugh's *Brideshead Revisited* today. He writes so very well that it seems a pity he hasn't got something better to write about.

August 5, 1945

I felt much better this morning after a good night. I drove down to Chantilly with Diana and John Julius. It was delightful there. I slept most of the afternoon. I find people very trying when I am drinking nothing and eating practically nothing. I drove up with Loulou. She is sad that I should have been ill during the greater part of her visit. I am sad because I am no longer in love with her. Our two sorrows mingled gently together during our drive and we were both happy.

I finished *Brideshead Revisited* in bed. I liked it better in the end. I think it the best thing he has written.

I had a letter from Bevin today. He said 'As regards your own position, I will be writing to you in due course, but, for the moment, as I am sure you will understand, there is nothing definite that I can say.' This is not very satisfactory.

August 7, 1945

There is much excitement today over the atomic bomb which fills me with the gloomiest forebodings. Man now has a weapon with which he can destroy the world. As we have made it I see no reason to suppose that he will not do so.

August 10, 1945

Bill Paley[1] came to lunch, during which Victor gave us a lecture on the atomic bomb – which was quite instructive. After lunch we heard that Japan had capitulated on condition that the Mikado was not to be interfered with. The atomic bomb has done the trick.

At 3.30 I went to see Bidault and told him I was going to London and wanted to know whether his views about the alliance were still the same. He said they were and expounded them. He said also that things were going very badly between him and de Gaulle, and he didn't know how much longer he would be in office. He also told me to tell Bevin that the most important thing for Anglo-French relations was that I should not be withdrawn. It was the one point upon which he and General de Gaulle were in complete agreement. We had as usual a very friendly conversation.

August 13, 1945 [London]. 11 o'clock at the Foreign Office

A conference presided over by Ernie Bevin. Bevin's policy and sentiments towards France could not be better. The new Under-Secretary was present and made on me a good impression. The conclusions were most satisfactory. There should now be no difficulty about the Levant and little, I hope, about Germany. I had five minutes with him in private after the meeting. He was not too reassuring about my own position. He was evidently not in a position to give me any undertaking, but I felt that he himself was well disposed.

August 15, 1945 (Nice)

We were called at 6.30 and left the house at 7.15. It was a lovely morning, just as it was, so I am told, a year ago when the landings took place which today we were commemorating. The first ceremony was the inauguration of the monument at Drammont near St Raphael. This was all beautifully arranged by the Americans and the whole thing could not have been better. Thence we went on to St Maxime where another inauguration took place – thence to St Tropez where after a long delay there was luncheon.

Great indignation because little Admiral Ortoli, who was supposed to

---

[1] William S. Paley (1901–90), President of CBS Broadcasting for fifty years.

represent General de Gaulle, took precedence over everyone including not only senior Admirals like Lemonnier and John Cunningham but also the three service Ministers. There followed the inauguration of a monument at St Tropez and a *défilé* of troops. British sailors, marines and Irish Guards with a band of the Ox. and Bucks and Irish pipes looked a thousand times better than any of the other troops.

August 21, 1945 (Paris)

Called on M. Chauvel at the Quai d'Orsay at 5. I find him difficult to understand and still more difficult to like. Bidault had forgotten to tell anybody that we wanted French desiderata re Germany in writing. This confirms my suspicion that he was drunk when I saw him on Tuesday, because I impressed it on him most emphatically more than once.

September 3, 1945

I went with Diana and J.J. to the Russian Embassy, where there was a reception for the Metropolitan of Moscow. There were dozens of priests with long beards and strange clothes and huge appetites. They filled their plates with cakes and sandwiches and retired into corners to devour them. Bogomolov was very nice to John Julius and talked to him a lot in Russian. He acquitted himself pretty well I think.

The main event of today however was a telegram which I received this morning from Bevin, asking me to come to London at the end of this week and to stay there for the conference of Foreign Ministers, which he says will probably last about a fortnight. This really suits me very well except for the fact that Loulou is due to return on the 17th. I'm afraid it will be a blow to her. I shall have a fortnight in England, which won't be leave and during which I ought to learn with some certainty my future fate. John Foster tells me that somebody asked Bevin whether I was going to be recalled and the answer was 'Not for some months at any rate'. But 'some months' is not good enough for me.

September 5, 1945

Mr Shertok[1] the Zionist called this morning. They are more hopeful of the Labour Government than they were of its predecessor, and they are approaching a showdown on the question of immigration. They are uncertain about Bevin and they fear that the Foreign Office, always pro-Arab, will decide the issue, Bevin being so far stronger a personality than George Hall.[2] Eric, who lunched with French friends, reports that General de Gaulle has returned

---

[1] Moshe Shertok, later Sharett (1849–1965). A Zionist leader, he became Israel's first Foreign Minister 1948–56 and second Prime Minister 1954–5.

[2] George Hall, 1st Viscount Hall (1881–1965). Trade unionist and politician. Parliamentary Under-Secretary of State for Foreign Affairs 1943–6; First Lord of the Admiralty 1946–51.

from Washington in a bad mood so far as England is concerned. He has no intention of being hurried into a treaty and prefers to rely upon American support. This is bad news.

September 6, 1945

At 11.30 I went to see Bidault. He was hopeful about the outcome of negotiations in London. He saw difficulties with regard to the Levant. He thought Blum would help. I asked him whether de Gaulle really wanted a treaty with England. He hesitated. There were two men in de Gaulle – *l'homme d'esprit* and *l'homme d'humeur*. It was the latter which was responsible for his follies. He knew that a treaty would be a good thing – he knew that the French people wanted it – he knew that the Quai d'Orsay wanted it – yet it was hard to say that he wanted it himself.

September 7, 1945 (London)

I wrote this morning a memorandum on the conversation that I had with Bidault yesterday and on the prospects of concluding a treaty. I also wrote a fairly long letter to Winston, because Randolph said it would please him. I went to lunch at the Bon Viveur with Freda. We had a very good lunch, a partridge each, and the bill was only £2. When I got back I received a message saying that the Prime Minister would like to see me at 3.45. He received me in the Cabinet room where I have so often sat with Winston, Chamberlain and Baldwin. I was with him nearly three-quarters of an hour. He could not have been more friendly but I did most of the talking. I always feel that he is rather shy with me. I thought it wiser to make no enquiry as to my own future, and he made no suggestion that it was not assured.

September 11, 1945

At 3.30 the first session of the Ministers' Conference took place. A huge round table round which sat the five delegations – five of each. My place is one off Bevin to his left. The Russian interpreter sits between us, Ronnie Campbell and Archie Kerr[1] on Bevin's other side. We sat till seven o'clock discussing procedure and agenda. Molotov[2] gave a certain amount of trouble. We had put the situation in Roumania on the agenda. He therefore suggested that we should also discuss Greece. Bevin was firm in his rejection of the idea. Greece is an ally he said, and that settles it. On the whole it was an amicable meeting. I dined at the French Embassy. I sat next to Bidault who ate nothing at all (the food was excellent) and drank hardly anything. I suppose he was feeling ill. Considering that neither he nor Blum understand English, and neither Attlee nor Bevin understand French, the evening went fairly well. Bevin told a great

---

[1] Archibald Clark Kerr, Lord Inverchapel (1882–1951). Ambassador to Washington 1946–8.
[2] Vyacheslav M. Molotov (1890–1986), Russian Foreign Minister.

many stories, all more or less obscene, which made Attlee rather nervous and which were difficult to translate into French.

September 13, 1945

The second meeting of the deputies took place at 11. Gusev, the Russian Ambassador, was in the chair and was plainly determined to be as obstructive as possible. He was quite impossible and when I left at 12.40 nothing whatever had been decided. I had then to attend a meeting in the Foreign Office about the Levant. Shone[1] from Beirut was there, two officials and Bevin. The last is most anxious to begin talks with the French on this subject, and his views are sensible. Shone was to see Chauvel this afternoon and I hope something may come of it. I lunched late at the Beefsteak – there was no hot food left.

September 14, 1945

There were two meetings of Ministers today. They got on to the Italian treaty and some progress was made. I felt also for the first time that I was not a mere spectator. Bevin had a little conference after each meeting in his room when he asked for advice – in both of which I took some part – and I also handed him some notes during the conferences. Molotov threw a small bombshell into the proceedings by suddenly demanding Tripolitania for Russia. The American idea is that mandates should not be handed over to separate countries, but shall be under the direct control of the United Nations Organization. This will mean that the U.N.O. will have to build up its own civil service, police and military. It is the ideal solution in every sense of the word – if it will work. I went to see Massigli at 3. He said that de Gaulle would never agree to conversations in London about the Levant alone. Would we agree to the conversations being extended, in name at least, to the whole of the Middle East?

September 15, 1945

The meeting of Ministers took place at 3. Bidault was in the chair. The old wrangle about Tripolitania continued. U.S.A. and U.K. agreed on the mandate being administered internationally, France for entrusting it to Italy – Russia wanting it for herself. Molotov said that they would not administer it on communistic lines but according to the will of the people. He added, in order to be rude, that it would not be run like Greece. At 5.30 I slipped away, just as they were deciding to refer to the deputies the question about which the principals were in fundamental disagreement. This seemed to me the height of folly.

---

[1] Sir Terence Shone (1894–1965), Minister to Syria and Lebanon 1944–6.

September 16, 1945 (Bognor)

It was a damp and gloomy morning and I felt depressed. The house is far gone in dirt and decay – the garden is a wilderness. I left soon after 5 and reached Chequers at 7.30. I found the two Attlees and their quite pretty daughter [Margaret], the two Bevins, Bob Dixon[1] and a female secretary – all in evening dress. I had at the last moment, after some hesitation, decided to bring mine. It was fortunate. I retired to put it on and when I returned found the Massiglis and Bidault had arrived – also dressed. When Winston was in Paris last year I consulted Bidault as to whether we should wear dinner jackets and he told me that he hadn't got one. He has repaired the omission. We had a good dinner – champagne, port and brandy. After the ladies had left we started a serious discussion of Anglo-French relations, which went extremely well. Both Bidault and Bevin were admirable, and the conclusion was reached that conversations should be opened in Paris with a view to settling the question of the Levant. I feel most hopeful.

September 17, 1945

Meeting of Ministers at 11. Question of the Dodecanese. Everybody in agreement that they should be given to Greece, except Molotov. Dinner at St James's Palace at 8.30. A good dinner – speeches by the Prime Minister and the heads of the four delegations. Then Bevin said 'Let's 'ave a song' and started to sing 'Cockles and Mussels' in a rich baritone. An American colonel followed with a series of sentimental Irish melodies. It was all rather unseemly and rather amusing.

September 21, 1945

This morning the meeting of the conference was the most interesting that has so far taken place. Molotov began by wasting an hour on questions of procedure and the publication of communiqués. When we turned to the conclusion of peace treaties with Roumania and Bulgaria, he questioned the U.S.A. caveat that they would sign no treaty with either country until they were satisfied that they had democratic governments, representing the will of the people. Molotov said that all the United States had against the Governments of the two countries was that they were friendly to the Soviets, and he suggested that the U.S.A. were not being 'sincere'. Byrnes[2] rose splendidly to this. He denounced Molotov and all his works. He said that Molotov's statement was both 'untrue' and 'unfair'. (Bidault told me afterwards that had

---

[1] Sir Pierson (Bob) Dixon (1904–65), PPS to Eden 1940–5 and Bevin 1945–8; Ambassador to the UN, 1954–60, and to Paris 1960–5.

[2] James Byrnes (1879–1970), American Senator. As Secretary of State 1945–7, he was President Truman's closest policy adviser.

he been in Molotov's position, so accused, he would have felt bound to leave the conference.)

I went to dinner at the Chinese Embassy. At the end of dinner Bevin and Byrnes discussed the conference across the table with remarkable frankness. They agreed that it was impossible to work with Molotov, and they mentioned the possibility of concluding separate peace treaties, with e.g. Italy, leaving Russia out. They also talked of the site of the next meeting of Ministers – Byrnes favouring Moscow, to which Bevin was opposed. He drove me as far as White's and seemed to be contemplating the possibility of a show-down with the Soviets and a public disclosure of their activities. It is very interesting.

September 23, 1945

At 10.20 the F.O. telephoned to say that the S. of S. was seeing Massigli at 10.40 and would like me to be present. I then learnt the full meaning of yesterday's crisis. Moscow, realizing I suppose how badly things were going for them at the conference, had suddenly discovered that the resolution unanimously adopted by the five ministers on the first day, recognizing the right of all five to be present at all meetings, was contrary to the terms of a resolution passed at Potsdam which would exclude France from having any say in the treaties with the Balkan States and Hungary. Bevin is prepared to fight this, but the Prime Minister takes the view that in theory Moscow is right. Bevin doesn't want the conference to break down on a point of procedure but would prefer that it should do so on a large issue of policy. Massigli had come to say that for France a large issue of policy was involved. The Russians want to make France one of their satellite powers like Czechoslovakia. If France finds she can look for support nowhere else she may be forced to become so – this will mean complete Russian domination of the continent of Europe. Bevin took the point. After Massigli had gone he told me that he thought the best thing might be to take this question of procedure back to the 'big three', saying that unless the original ruling was changed the Council of Ministers couldn't function. He said that as it is, the Dominions are furious at being excluded. If he takes this line it should mollify the French. What I least want to see is the conference going on without them.

It was 2 o'clock when [Bevin] said to me with a broad smile 'Do you think it's too early for the 'air of the dog' – I naturally said no and he summoned an office keeper who produced whiskeys and soda. He had two pretty strong ones before leaving to see the Prime Minister. Thinking the moment favourable I raised with him the question of my own future. He said at once that he would undertake that I should stay in Paris for a year. I might, of course, stay several years, but he couldn't go further than that. I might stay as long as he did, but then he didn't know how long he would stay himself. I think that that is good enough. I am uneasy about his health. I think he finds the work very hard. He complained today that he had been at work since seven. He reads slowly and has very great difficulty on paper. In fact he hardly writes anything. He has injections at intervals.[1] He is very heavy and might easily have a stroke.

I came back to the Dorchester – the Foreign Office telephoned that Massigli was expected at any minute and would I go at once. I dashed off arriving simultaneously with Massigli and we both went into Bevin's room at once. He had spent the whole afternoon with Molotov and told Massigli that he had some good news for him. This proved to be only that Molotov had said his Govt. had no objection to an Anglo-French treaty, and that we need pay no attention to articles in the opposite sense appearing in the Russian press. It is all very well to say that but how can one not pay attention to articles in an entirely Government-controlled press? That was all he would tell Massigli about his conversation with Molotov. After Massigli had gone he told me that on the various questions they had discussed he had found Molotov most reasonable and he felt much happier than he had this morning, but when I asked him about the question of procedure and the Balkan treaties he was vague and implied that he did not think we should hear much more of it. Either he was concealing something from me, or else he had allowed Molotov to avoid the main issue and fob him off with a lot of vague assurances.

September 24, 1945

I had a long letter from Winston the other day thanking me for mine. He also sent me a telegram about it and this morning Clemmie rang up to say he had been so pleased with it and had sent it to her. So it seems to have made an impression.

September 25, 1945

After lunch I went to see Clemmie Churchill. She is living in a miserable flat in Westminster Gardens belonging to the Duncan Sandys.[2] Ichabod, ichabod. She was very nice, rather sad and said that Winston is really very unhappy. She blames him for having accepted the leadership of the Conservative Party. He blames himself for having relied too much on Max's advice.

September 30, 1945. Sunday

Today was the most eventful of the conference. The deputies met at 10.30 and made little progress. Gusev was in the chair and was more than usually obtuse and obstinate. The Ministers met at 3 and it was a stormy meeting. We were back on the resolution of Sept 11th which Molotov wants rescinded. He said that when one party withdraws from a resolution it ceases to be a resolution –

---

[1] Bevin was being treated for a heart condition.
[2] Duncan Sandys, Lord Duncan-Sandys (1908–87). Had lost his parliamentary seat (the Norwood division of Lambeth), at the July general election. He returned to the House of Commons in 1950 as the MP for Streatham and became Minister of Supply in 1951 when the Conservatives were returned to power and Churchill once again became Prime Minister.

to which Bevin replied that he was talking like Hitler. At this Molotov flew into a passion, said that the chairman ought not to permit such language, asked 'Have we got a chairman or haven't we' (Byrnes was the chairman) and finally said he would not stay to be insulted and began to leave the room. Bevin immediately withdrew and apologized – long speeches were made by both. Byrnes eventually suggested adjourning till 9.30 – it was then nearly 7. He said there might be a better atmosphere after dinner. I took advantage of the interval to go round and see Liz [von Hofmannsthal] for a minute. She was looking ravishingly beautiful. She is really lovelier than Caroline.

The sitting [at 9.30 p.m.] was long and animated but made no progress at all. Molotov said there would be no communiqué and no protocol. He spoke with great bitterness of Bevin. The latter does not speak well. He rambles and repeats himself. This becomes apparent when he is translated into French. The interpreter reduces the length of what he says by half. Byrnes on the other hand speaks quite well. Just as we were about to separate for good with nothing whatever decided, Dr Wang [the Chinese representative] spoke up and appealed for a final effort to reach agreement, enlarging on the disappointment that would be felt throughout the world if the Conference were a complete failure. Byrnes supported him and it was finally decided to meet again tomorrow evening at 6.

October 2, 1945

We began again this morning at 11 and went on until 1.30. As I said to Bevin it was all a complete waste of time. The policy pursued now by Bevin and Byrnes was not to argue. Everything had been said. About 4 o'clock a silence fell. Dr Wang who was in the chair then suggested half an hour's adjournment. It dragged on until 5 when Molotov, on our reassembling, said that he had a new proposition which was that we should sign those protocols which had been agreed upon today and discuss the question of calling a conference tomorrow. Byrnes replied that it was no good signing the very little that had been agreed and that there was no point in postponing the other discussion until tomorrow unless Molotov had received fresh instructions. Had he received fresh instructions? Molotov refused to say.

Byrnes was prepared to discuss the matter now but he had nothing fresh to say. He was quite prepared to go on now or to go on later tonight but he saw no point in postponing till tomorrow. Gradually it became apparent, to my immense relief, that the conference was drawing to its close. Byrnes handled the situation with great ability – making it plain that we were breaking down not on a question of procedure but on the proposal to hold a larger conference. Wang was dignified. It was on his suggestion that the conference had continued for these last two days. It was therefore fitting that he should now close the conference. Should we meet again tonight? No. Should we meet tomorrow? No. Then he would declare the conference to be at an end. Byrnes made a little speech thanking Bevin for his hospitality – and we all retired to the bar where a good deal of quick drinking was done.

October 12, 1945 (Paris)

I had to present the O.B.E. this morning to a young woman, Mlle. De Veye, who had shown great heroism tending the wounded under fire. It is remarkable how very plain heroines usually are. I suppose they have less to lose.

October 13, 1945

I spent most of the morning completing a memorandum on the Levant, in which I recommended that if we can't reach agreement with the French we should take unilateral action and evacuate, which would force the French either to follow suit or to conquer the country. We at least would no longer be responsible.

There was a lunch at the Quai d'Orsay in honour of Esmond [Rothermere]. A small party but a huge meal – which forced me to postpone the initiation of my new thinning regime. I had a word with both Bidault and Chauvel about the Levant. Their trouble is that de Gaulle won't have any agreement on this particular issue unless it is made part of a general agreement concerning the Middle East – but there is nothing else in the Middle East in dispute. Bidault said they were willing to help us with the Jews in Palestine – but in fact there is nothing that the French can do about it.

October 17, 1945

Very little work this morning. I read an interesting book by Emery Reves[1] called *The Anatomy of Peace*. He insists that the only hope of preventing another war lies in world federation. Of course he is quite right.

Work in the evening is rendered very difficult by the light continually going out for half an hour at a time. We dined with the Windsors. The electric light was out there when we arrived. The house was beautifully lit with candles but the dinner could not be brought up except by the electric lift so that we had to wait for it until the electricity came on again. I hadn't seen the Windsors since 1940. They have both got extraordinarily thin, but otherwise look very well and he seems quite as devoted as ever.

October 21, 1945

After dinner I drove back to Paris with Elizabeth[2] [de Breteuil], Jacques[3]

---

[1] Emery Reves, formerly Imre Revesz (1904–83), a Hungarian, was a close friend of Winston Churchill and was appointed his press agent in 1937. He became a naturalized American and made his fortune by negotiating the American royalties for *The Second World War*, buying the foreign-language rights himself.

[2] Elizabeth de Breteuil was married to Prince Georges Chavchavadze, pianist.

[3] Jacques Février (1900–79), an outstanding French pianist and close friend of Poulenc.

[Février] and Loulou. They came into the Embassy and we tried to get news of the election which took place today. We were told that the answer to the first question was 90% oui and 70% oui to the second. This is good for General de Gaulle. I used to have difficulty in persuading Winston that de Gaulle's leadership would survive the liberation of France. It has in fact survived that of Winston – and how!

As well as electing a Constituent Assembly, the French had been asked to vote in a referendum on the basis for a new Constitution. The question was whether the Assembly was to be given supreme powers as the Communists wanted or restricted powers as de Gaulle insisted. The final results gave the Communists 159 seats, the Socialists 146 and the MRP (Mouvement Républicain Populaire) 152.

October 28, 1945

We returned to Paris in the evening. I dined with the Windsors. I sat between Wallis and Miss Perkins[1] as she calls herself, the ex-Minister of Labour in the U.S.A. We played bridge after dinner. The Duke talked to Miss Perkins. The pathetic thing about him is that having given up public life he still hankers after it, and still feels it his duty to entertain important people. He is so anxious to do it right. When I left he followed me out into the rain to ask whether I thought he ought to write his name on General de Gaulle and Bidault.

October 31, 1945

A quiet morning – conversations with Rooker and Scarlett. The former has been suffering from severe poisoning due to a bad oyster. He says that when one puts the vinegar or the lemon on the oyster one should always notice whether it 'draws in its skirts' which shows it is alive. If it doesn't one shouldn't eat it. I don't believe him. I have never seen an oyster behave in such a way. I tested them both at lunch and dinner and produced no reaction – nor did I suffer any ill effects.

November 3, 1945

Ben-Gurion[2] came to see me this morning – a fine old Zionist who has been fighting for his cause all his life and who despite the horrors that he has witnessed retains a broad humanity and a sense of humour. He told me that Weizmann had recently been summoned to meet George Hall and Bevin, who had solemnly warned him that if there were any more Jewish acts of violence the whole Jewish people would be held responsible. He had replied that forty years ago a Russian general, the Czar's right-hand man, had sent for him and delivered exactly the same threat. The only difference was, he

---

[1] Frances Perkins (1882–1965), US Secretary of Labor 1933–45.
[2] David Ben-Gurion (1886–1973), Chairman of the World Zionist Movement 1935–48; Prime Minister of Israel and Minister of Defence 1948–53 and 1955–63.

said, that on that occasion he was not sure that he would leave the room alive, and this time he was. He also told me that Einstein had said that if his theory were proved wrong the French would say he was a German and the Germans would say he was a Jew, but that if his theory were proved right, the French would say he was a great man and the Germans would say he was a great German.

I went to see Bidault. He was very communicative – hopeful about the Levant, which was more than Palewski was yesterday – and fairly hopeful about Germany. He said that de Gaulle would not be able to go on governing in the future as he had in the past. He would have to pay more attention to public opinion and the opinion of the Assembly. He deplored the growing weakness of the Socialist party.

November 7, 1945

It is a year ago today that I dined at Verrières, was recalled to Paris by a telephone call from Winston and first made friends with Loulou. She came to lunch today and brought André Malraux[1] and Pierre Brisson.[2] She has the widest circle of really intimate friends that one can imagine. Malraux is clearly a very remarkable man. He talks very well and a great deal. I doubt if he has any sense of humour. I went to the Russian cocktail party, it being their national *fête*. Bogo magnificent in uniform with the Czechoslovakian order of the White Lion across his chest. He was very friendly and plied me with vodka, which I can't bear since our disastrous evening last summer.

November 9, 1945 (London)

At four I attended [a] meeting at the Foreign Office. Bevin, Sargent, Oliver Harvey, Bob Howe,[3] Dixon – and somebody else from the Eastern Dept. The point of it was that Bevin has persuaded the United States to have a joint Anglo-American enquiry into Palestine. He rightly considers this a great triumph and he thinks it would be greatly enhanced if he could at the same time announce that he had reached an agreement with the French about the Levant. Did I think this possible? I told him the situation was greatly complicated by the internal crisis in France and that I feared it might well be that de Gaulle and Bidault would feel that they were not justified in taking any important decision in their present positions. He said he must postpone the meeting until 7. The second interview added little to the first. He had received the O.K. from Washington. He also defined to me his position with regard to Germany which should fit in with that of the French, and said he would like to make an agreement with the French for the mutual abolition of visas.

---

[1] André Malraux (1901–76), novelist. Fought in the Resistance and Free French Forces 1940–5. Minister of Information 1945–6 and of Cultural Affairs 1960–9.

[2] Pierre Brisson, dramatic critic, editor of *Le Figaro* 1934–64.

[3] Sir Robert Howe (1893–1981), Assistant Under-Secretary of State, 1945; Governor-General, Sudan 1947–55.

November 11, 1945 (Paris)

At 3.30 Eric and I went off to Orly to meet Winston. He arrived with Mary, his valet and two detectives, and his typist. There was a contrast between his arrival this year and last which must have struck him.

November 12, 1945

Winston wanted to go to the Louvre this morning – so we got it specially opened for him. I think he enjoyed it. For lunch we had the Blums, Charles-Roux, Odette Pol Roger, George Lansdowne and Penelope and Eric. Winston was in great form after lunch and very funny with Blum, whom he urged to fight the communists rather than make an alliance with them. He was most indignant that Thorez[1] should be allowed, with his record, to play a prominent part in public life. The visit [to the Institut de France] was a great success. Bidault turned up there, which was nice of him. He assured me that they certainly would accept both drafts about the Levant as soon as the Government had been reformed, i.e. in about 10 days. His secretary had come round this morning and told Eric that Bidault had been unable to persuade de Gaulle to take any decision at present, on the grounds that the Government was *démissionaire*. He had described the General as being *'en grève'* [on strike].

November 13, 1945

Diana and I, Winston, Mary and Eric lunched with General de Gaulle. His wife and daughter, Palewski and Lieut. Guy completed the party. He was wearing a dark blue suit in which he looks much better than in uniform. I never liked him or admired him so much. He was smiling, courteous, almost charming, and on this day and almost at the hour when his whole future was at stake not only was he perfectly calm but one might have thought he was a country gentleman living far away from Paris. [*The new Constituent Assembly was to vote on whether to re-elect de Gaulle as head of government.*] There were no interruptions, no telephone calls or messages, no secretaries hurrying in and out, no sign that anything was happening, although Winston insisted on staying till 3.30 talking about the past, and the Assembly was meeting at 3. I went on there after dropping Winston at the Embassy. The vote was taken – 555 to 0 in favour of de Gaulle, a great triumph.

November 14, 1945

Winston and Mary lunched with the Windsors, so we had a quiet luncheon. When Winston came back from his lunch I showed him over the chancery – only the ground floor and the first floor, because he has difficulty in going

---

[1] Maurice Thorez (1900–64), leader of the French Communist Party, spent the war in the Soviet Union. De Gaulle allowed him to return in 1945.

upstairs now. He told me that the Duke of Windsor is now quite willing to live in the U.S.A. which is what they want him to do, but that he would like to be attached in some way to the Embassy. [At dinner] Winston was in exceptionally good form, extremely amusing. I took them to the station. There was quite a crowd assembled to see him off, and a guard of honour. A special wagon had been attached to the train with all kinds of comfort – bedrooms, sitting-rooms etc. all full of flowers. I think he has thoroughly enjoyed his visit.

November 16, 1945

Great excitement this afternoon over the announcement that de Gaulle has resigned. The Communists insist on being given either Foreign Affairs, the Interior or War. He refuses. They then say they won't serve and he replies that he can't form a government without them. So it stands and apparently so it will stand until the Assembly meets on Monday.[1]

November 19, 1945

At three I went to the Assembly. It was an interesting but not very exciting *séance*. The upshot of it all is that de Gaulle has been asked to think again. We heard later that he had invited the three leaders to meet him tomorrow morning. Everybody is agreed that he made a great mistake in broadcasting. [*On 17 November de Gaulle had broadcast a speech saying that he would not give a Communist control of the Ministry of the Interior, nor foreign policy nor the armed forces.*] Obstinacy, tactlessness, lack of political experience and bad advice have always been his drawbacks and will end by being his undoing. Gaston came in after dinner. He seemed depressed. He said everything might be over for him in two days. If de Gaulle goes he certainly won't have a very rosy future. I asked him whether it would really be very dangerous to let the Communists have the War Office for six months. He said that in that time they could prepare the army for the *coup d'état*, the seizure of power by force.

In the end a compromise was reached. Charles Tillon[2] was made Minister for Armaments, Thorez vice-president of the Council of Ministers, and the Communists received the Ministries of Industrial Production, National Economy and Labour.

November 30, 1945

Massigli, who is over here for a few days, came to see me this morning. He was less pessimistic than usual – thinks we should settle the Levant next week and hopes to get the Rhine and Ruhr settled as between England and France before the general international settlement. I went to see Bidault at 5. He

---

[1] De Gaulle encouraged the rumour that he was about to resign over this issue.
[2] Charles Tillon (1897–1993), Communist Deputy and trade union activist. He was expelled from the Party in 1952.

showed me the proposed changes in the Levant drafts, which are of no importance. He then raised a new trouble. The Anglo-American troops which took the place of the French troops in the Val d'Aosta are being withdrawn. The French fear that the Italians will take vengeance on the pro-French part of the population. De Gaulle is excited and threatens to march in French troops. I sent off a most immediate telegram to London.

We were eight for dinner – Clarissa,[1] Randolph, Eric, Martha [Gellhorn] and an American journalist called Campbell. We went to a private showing of a film showing the trial of the conspirators against Hitler. It was deeply interesting. Randolph said we were treating the prisoners at Nuremberg just as badly as these Germans had been treated. This irritated me so much that I gave him a slap on the ear – he was sitting in front of me. He was most resentful.

December 1, 1945

A reply to my telegram came last night. They have told General Morgan to delay the withdrawal of the troops, but he can't do so indefinitely. Meanwhile the French must make some arrangement with the Italians. I went round to the Quai d'Orsay to give Bidault this news, which pleased him.

December 3, 1945

We were six for lunch – André Malraux, Loulou, Norman of *The Times* and [Darsie] Gillie of the *Manchester Guardian*. Malraux, who is now Minister of Information, was most brilliant. He is a very remarkable man. He prophesied that the Communists would attempt to obtain power by force in the next twelve months and that they would fail.

December 4, 1945

The great excitement today was the arrival from Hungary of [Count] Tommy Esterházy [to whom Louise de Vilmorin was theoretically engaged]. The train was due at 6.30 a.m. Loulou went to the station to meet him and Diana got up to accompany Loulou, so that I was wakened at 6. At about 7.30 they both came back, having learnt that the train was five hours late. Loulou spent the rest of the morning going to and fro from the station until he at last arrived. She reported on the telephone that he was charming and that all was well.

The Duke of Windsor came in at 6 in order to talk to his brother the King on a secret telephone line. I gather he is having trouble because he insists that if he goes to America he shall have some official position there. He came and had a drink with us afterwards.

---

[1] Clarissa Spencer-Churchill (b. 1920), Churchill's niece. She married, as his second wife, Anthony Eden, later 1st Earl of Avon, in 1952.

December 5, 1945

I lunched with Loulou at the Escargot. She seems to be more in love than ever. I feel guilty. I have nothing to offer her, not even my whole heart, whereas Tommy Esterházy, like all the very rich, has of course lost everything but of course remains very rich all the same and will get richer. In addition he has a great name, a charming character and loves only her. It is all very difficult.

December 7, 1945

I was called this morning with a 'most immediate' telegram. It recounted how Byrnes had suggested to Molotov, without consulting Bevin, that the three of them should meet in Moscow. Bevin had at first objected, but when Byrnes threatened to go alone he had consented with the proviso that nothing that concerned France should be discussed. The announcement was to be made at 3 this afternoon and I was to inform Bidault first. I went round to see him at 10 and told him the whole story. He took it very well and asked me to thank Bevin for the line he had taken. He said that France would of course have to protest. He himself regretted it as a step backwards – a return to the Big Three method of the past which had been responsible for many of the existing difficulties.

December 10, 1945 (London)

I went to the Foreign Office this morning at Hoyer Millar's[1] request. The Labour Party has been invited to send a representative to the MRP party conference. They had, at the desire of No. 10, rung up Paris to enquire what answer should be given. Paris had been doubtful, as the MRP were now regarded in some quarters as a party of the right. I said that of course they should send a representative. MRP are committed to the CNR [Conseil National de la Résistance] which is as socialistic as anything the Labour Party stands for.

December 13, 1945

This morning Mr de Normann [later Sir Eric de Normann] of the Office of Works came to see me. They are rather disturbed about the cost of the library – but he was very nice about it. I said it will cost £3,000 – he said that they would have to face it – I fear it may cost more. I then went to the Foreign Office and was present at the signing of the Syrian agreement by Bevin and Massigli. I was very glad to be there and I do sincerely hope that this may prove to be the real end of this tiresome question, which has been poisoning

---

[1] Sir Frederick (Derrick) Hoyer Millar, 1st Lord Inchyra (1900–89). Counsellor at the FO 1944–7; Assistant Under-Secretary 1947–8; first post-war Ambassador to Bonn 1955–7; Permanent Under-Secretary at the FO 1957–61.

Anglo-French relations for so long. Bevin was very friendly but had to hurry off to the Cabinet. He said he would like to see me again before he left for Moscow tomorrow morning. The result was that I hung about White's all the afternoon waiting to be summoned and never was.

December 17, 1945

I went into Sotheby's this morning and found a book auction in progress. I bought a first edition of Paracelsus in original boards for £4.5.0 – a first edition of *Sordello* for the same price and the original parts of *Edwin Drood* (covers of one number missing) for £1. I was pleased with these buys. I did some shopping – bought a nice edition in English of Madame de Sévigné's letters as a wedding present for Robert Cecil[1], who is being married tomorrow.

December 18, 1945

We went to Robert Cecil's wedding in Westminster Abbey. Looking for my car afterwards near the Houses of Parliament I ran into poor little Leo Amery who was looking distraught with misery. He muttered something to me about his misfortunes and I, like a fool, could think of nothing to say but that I had just been to the wedding of Bobbety's son – and his son[2] is to be hanged tomorrow.

December 23, 1945. Sunday (Paris)

I was going to church this morning when Robin Hooper[3] came with telegrams that had arrived during the night. They contained instructions to see Bidault as soon as possible and to inform him of decisions taken at Moscow, subject, so far as Bevin is concerned, to the approval of the French Government. The Council of Foreign Secretaries is to continue its labours – the deputies are to meet as soon as possible. Draft treaties with the five ex-enemy countries, Italy, Finland, Hungary, Roumania and Bulgaria, are to be drawn. All five of the united nations will draft the treaty with Italy, the U.K. and the U.S.S.R. will draft that with Finland, and the U.K., U.S.S.R. and U.S.A. will draft the other three. Then there will be summoned a peace conference of all the united nations that were seriously at war. This will take place in Paris not later than May 1st, and the draft treaties will be submitted to the conference. The final form of the treaties will be drafted by the powers, as above, in the light of the observations and recommendations of the conference. I took this to Bidault at 11.45 and he received it well. He was both surprised and delighted that the conference is to be held in Paris.

---

[1] Robert Cecil, 6th Marquess of Salisbury (1916–2003). Conservative MP, married Marjorie (Mollie) Wyndham-Quin on 18 Dec. 1945.

[2] John Amery was executed as a traitor for broadcasting from Germany during the war.

[3] Sir Robin Hooper (1914–89), Second Secretary, Paris, 1944–7; later Ambassador to Tunisia, Yemen and Greece.

December 25, 1945

The church was quite full this morning and so was our gallery. Reading the first lesson I forgot to stop at the right place, and went floundering on for another half-dozen verses. A good short sermon – so short that John Julius and I only got as far as J in the sermon game. After church we paid a visit to the Hertford Hospital where we carved the turkeys. It is an admirably run institution. Everybody seems so cheerful that it is a pleasure to go there. They have an excellent matron. Thence we went on to a place called E.L.B.A., a kind of home for indigent British subjects awaiting transport to England. Here the atmosphere was very different – gloomy and sinister – but they had quite a good lunch awaiting them – oysters, turkey etc.

John Julius in his first set of evening clothes (second-hand, bought from another boy for £5) made a fine appearance. He was kept busy lighting the huge Christmas tree in the hall. The guests began to arrive at 7.30 and an hour was devoted to giving and receiving presents and drinking cocktails. Loulou gave me 1) A fine piece of Gobelins tapestry, beautifully framed, representing the visit of Louis Philippe to Queen Victoria – 2) A silver tray with her own *chiffre* on it – very large in gold – 3) A beautiful little statue – *Le Baiser* – 4) A silver paper knife – 5) An Irish blackthorn walking stick – 6) An old *portefeuille* – 7) A black velvet cape lined with scarlet – 8) A little group of figures representing characters in Balzac and the following books – 9) Life of Balzac in 2 vols by Billy – 10) *Dominique* – 11) *La Princesse de Clèves* – 12) *Adolphe* – 13) A large edition of *Les Contes de Perrault* illustrated by Doré. My presents to her were less numerous, but included a typewriter and a very pretty 1830 dressing case and a fan – the best of the three I bought in London. We were 32 to dinner, all French, and about 60 or 70 came in afterwards, mainly English – staff etc. Diana had presents for nearly all of them. I think it was a great success. There was plenty to drink. I had a conversation with Palewski. I asked him how he thought things were going. He said they could not be going worse. I asked him if he wasn't pleased that the Peace Conference should be held in Paris. He shrugged his shoulders and said that he wasn't sure it would be. He said the whole government of the country depended upon two people only, General de Gaulle and himself. I think he was slightly tight.

December 31, 1945

I had an appointment with Loulou this morning when she came to tell me all that Palewski had said to her last night. He is undoubtedly most anti-English and admits it although he claims that he likes Diana and me personally. He is also very pugnacious with regard to the future and says that he and de Gaulle would be prepared to use force rather than give up their position. I don't myself believe this.

So ends the year – a year of great events – the defeat of Italy, of Germany and of Japan – the deaths of Hitler, of Mussolini and of Roosevelt, the victory of the Labour Party and the resignation of Winston, the French general election and the confirmation of de Gaulle's position. What does the coming year hold in store and shall I still be here at the end of it? I wonder.

1946

January 1, 1946

I attended de Gaulle's reception for the diplomatic corps this morning. Gaston Palewski was looking more revolting than usual. I suppose he had had a late night. It occurred to me that de Gaulle may have selected him as being one of the few men uglier than himself.

January 3, 1946

Loulou came after lunch. We walked in the Jardin des Plantes – it was very cold. The unhappy thing is that Loulou is beginning to get slightly on my nerves. She is too *accaparante*. It is strange that so clever a woman should not understand that it is a mistake to telephone *every* morning, to want to meet twice or three times a day if possible. No friendship can stand such a strain. I came in about 4 and worked till 7.30. When I finally went upstairs there she was with Diana, and she telephoned again after dinner which we two had alone by the fire.

January 5, 1946

A certain Monsieur Boyer came to see me this morning. He is running two newspapers, *Libé-Soir* and *L'Etoile*. According to him the power of the Communists in Paris is so great that no independent paper can exist for long without their approval. Firmly established ones like *Figaro* and openly reactionary ones like *L'Epoque* form the exception. The Communists have many underhand ways of proceeding. They get at the printers to make difficulties, persuade the vendors not to sell or show the paper etc. They have openly threatened him and have also offered him money on their own conditions. His great idea, which seems to me rather crazy, is to print a Paris evening paper in the morning in London, using the machinery of a London morning paper for the purpose. He has been in communication with the *News Chronicle* on the subject and says they are prepared to agree.

January 9, 1946

[Peter] Hope of MI5 came this morning. I asked him for the latest news of

Cole,[1] the traitor, murderer, raper and torturer at whose capture he had assisted and who had shot him through the leg. He told me that owing to the extraordinary incompetence in the Anglo-American military prison he had been allowed to escape and had been at large for two months. He also told me that evidence was accumulating against Jacqueline Kraus née de Broglie – Daisy's daughter. Soon after he left me he telephoned that Cole had been shot dead last night when resisting arrest in the Rue de Grenelle.

January 15, 1946

I felt worse this morning. After I had shaved I went back to bed. Diana and John Julius arrived about 10 and very glad I was to see them. She took my temperature and found it was a little bit up. She put me immediately on M & B [an antibiotic]. A super-secret telegram arrived from Oliver Harvey saying that Bevin had heard from a private source that things were going very badly in France, that the Communists were about to make an alliance with Herriot and would overthrow de Gaulle – and also that de Gaulle was riding for a fall, that he wanted to go out now in order to come back later with increased power. These stories together with some pessimistic remarks of Bidault in London seem to have upset Bevin. I replied that Paris was full of rumours and gossip which I didn't usually report unless I thought it well founded. No attention need be paid to Bidault's gloom as he was prone to fits of despair. I thought both rumours were improbable although Emmanuel d'Astier, a near com-munist, did say at lunch yesterday that he had much sympathy with Herriot and the Communists.

January 20, 1946. Sunday

Loulou came to dine with me. She was in much better spirits. It was I who was depressed, for about 10 o'clock came the news that Palewski had handed de Gaulle's letter of resignation to Gouin[2] and that it was irrevocable. I felt that the F.O. would feel that I was very badly informed as I had scouted the idea a few days ago. Loulou was charming, and gave me a lecture on the rottenness of France and of all Frenchmen with the exception of the *famille* Vilmorin. I feel that de Gaulle trying to be clever has been very foolish, and that he will be denounced as the man who ran away just as the Labour Government were denounced in 1931.

January 22, 1946

Loulou and André Malraux came to lunch. The latter was as usual very interesting and somewhat alarming. He is convinced that France is moving

---

[1] Harold Cole, a British army sergeant and con man who had deserted in France in 1940; later joined the French Resistance, then betrayed its largest escape line.

[2] Felix Gouin (1884–1977), French Socialist politician who succeeded de Gaulle as head of the French provisional government, Jan.–June 1946.

towards a dictatorship and I don't think he regrets it. The question is whether it is to be a dictatorship of the Communists or of de Gaulle, and it will be settled by force. He says that the resignation of de Gaulle is not the end but the beginning of Gaullism, which will now become a great movement throughout France.

January 23, 1946

We went to the Assembly to hear the nomination of the new President of the Council. Gouin was finally nominated.

January 29, 1946

I don't feel very well these days. When I get up in the morning I feel that I should like to go to bed again, and if I sit in a comfortable chair I fall asleep. I don't know whether it is the remains of flu or liver, or general tiredness and need of a rest. Some fool in the House of Commons put a question about John Julius's visit to Nuremberg.[1] He was well snubbed. Loulou saw Malraux; he is plotting Caesarism based on assassination. The Gaullists are crazy.

January 31, 1946

I still feel so tired all the time and drop off to sleep. Loulou tells me that Malraux says de Gaulle is now like a sleepwalker or a convalescent. His mind hardly seems to be working and he appears incapable of taking a decision. Malraux asked her yesterday '*Est-tu pour nous, ou pour lui?*' meaning me – to which she had replied '*Franchement, pour lui*'. He said that this would make no difference to his affection and esteem for her, but I suppose it means that I shall get no more information from that source. However it is better to be frank. I went to dinner with the Windsors. It went on too long, for when the bridge was over Wallis insisted on playing a round of *chemin de fer*. I was tired, the room was too hot, and Wallis's voice after an hour or two becomes unbearable.

February 4, 1946

I had two callers this morning. The first was General Billotte.[2] He came to tell me that he together with certain other Gaullists, including Diethelm, René Mayer, Soustelle[3] etc. were forming a new political movement, a kind of centre party, mainly with a view to fighting socialism. He gave me full details and then asked me whether HMG would finance such a movement. It was an

---

[1] In Jan. 1946, the British judges in Nuremberg passed through Paris and invited John Julius to the trials, where he spent three days.

[2] Gen. Pierre Billotte (1906–92), COS to de Gaulle, 1942–3; Assistant Chief of General Staff 1944–5.

[3] René Mayer (1895–1972), radical politician, Prime Minister 1953. Jacques Soustelle (1912–90), anthropologist and politician, Minister of Information under de Gaulle.

extraordinary request and I was astonished that it should be made by an intelligent man. I wondered whether he had any ulterior motive because he can hardly have expected a favourable reply. I said I would convey what he had said to the proper quarters but warned him not to be optimistic.

February 5, 1946

This morning early Loulou left with André for Châteaubriant. I am ashamed to admit that I was not broken-hearted. The truth is that she makes the fatal mistake of being *accaparante* to a degree that becomes a burden. That must be the reason why, with all her incomparable gifts of charm, wit, genius and sweetness, she seems never to have had a really successful love affair. She took the pug puppy [*a present from Diana*], which we had come to adore, with her.

February 6, 1946

The great excitement today has been the arrival of the first consignment of my books. I have seen none of them since 1940. They will much more than fill the new library. This evening an aide-de-camp came round from General de Gaulle with a letter in which he thanks me for the personal letter I wrote him at the time of his resignation. I thought the handwriting looked very shaky. I asked the A.D.C. how the General was. He said he wasn't well. He was terribly tired and was sleeping badly.

February 15, 1945

I lunched with Ghislaine de Polignac[1] in a private room at Larue's – and enjoyed it very much. She is a girl after my own heart, good company, a formidable appetite for pleasure and no nonsense about love. She is 26 – has had four children, feels that she has done her duty and is now determined to have a good time. I have no doubt she will succeed in doing so. I shall do my best to help her.

February 25, 1946

I heard that Bidault wanted to see me. I got there at 5.30. I found him much distressed. Personally I think the Foreign Office have been flat-footed. They have informed Massigli bluntly that as a result of the U.N.O. resolution the Anglo-French agreement of Dec. 15 is cancelled. He said that the unilateral denunciation of a treaty not three months old was unheard of – I promised to do what I could. He was also distressed about Spain [*nine Republicans, including two who had fought for the French Resistance, had been executed*] and about the financial situation.

---

[1] Ghislaine Brinquant, Princesse de Polignac (b. 1918), married Prince Edmond de Polignac in 1939 from whom she was shortly to be divorced. She was a great friend of the Duchess of Windsor.

March 1, 1946

I spent a good deal of this morning drafting a long telegram on the subject of the Ruhr. It was provoked by one from Strang[1] in which he said that a decision should soon be taken. There he was right. He went on to argue the case from different viewpoints, mainly economic, and inclined on the whole to the view that it should be completely restored to Germany. The French will never consent to this if they can help it. I hope my telegram may do some good.

March 10, 1946. Sunday

Church in the morning. Ecclesiasticus and Hebrews. I don't care much for Hebrews except Chapter II. The Ashley Clarkes[2] came to lunch. The more I see of them the more I like them. There was an announcement in the *Daily Express* yesterday that I was resigning. Diana was told in London by Bloggs – who had got it from his brother – that there was nothing against me, but that she was much criticized for receiving collaborators. She thereupon boldly went to see Bob Dixon at the Foreign Office, who told her it was all nonsense and that he had never heard anything of the kind.

March 14, 1946

The Duke of Windsor came to see me this morning at his own request. I thought he wanted to consult me about something – but not at all. He sat here for nearly an hour chattering about one thing and another. I expect the truth is that he is so *désoeuvré* that Wallis, to get him out of the house, said 'why don't you go round to see Duff one morning and have an interesting talk about politics?'

March 15, 1946

We dined with the Chinese which is always an ordeal. Today it was worse than usual because the Bidaults were an hour and a quarter late. He is getting worse. What is even more surprising is that the Chinese Ambassadress's French is getting worse, which I should have thought was impossible. She is almost unintelligible. I was lucky in having Madame Chauvel's mother the other side of me. She is always good company. She has just become a great grandmother and her own mother is still alive. Five generations living simultaneously must be rare. She was also interesting about the early life of Wallis Windsor whom she knew as Mrs Spencer in Pekin – 'Always good natured – she had only one fault. You can guess what that was. She never stopped.'

---

[1] Sir William Strang, 1st Lord Strang (1893–1978). Political adviser to General Montgomery 1945–7; Head of the FO 1949–53.
[2] Sir Ashley Clarke (1903–94), Minister in Paris 1946–9; Ambassador to Rome 1953–62.

March 28, 1946

Yesterday was spring – today is summer. The trees have all burst out and it is as warm as June. I walked out to lunch at Maxim's with the Chamber of Commerce and Pleven. The last was interesting about the resignation of de Gaulle. He himself only knew about it the day before, and he was supposed to be closer to the General than any of his colleagues. I dined with Grey of the American Embassy. There was a beautiful Mexican called Gloria Rubio.[1] She has been married to a German, is divorced and is not only exceedingly pretty but intelligent and amusing. I asked her to come to dinner tomorrow.

This was the beginning of a major new love affair. Gloria was engaged to Ahmed, son of the Egyptian Minister Fakri Pasha. The affair lasted until the end of the year when she left for Kenya with Ahmed, who was by then her husband.

April 3, 1946

I was to have lunched with Ghislaine today but she telephoned to say she had had a row with her husband – not about me – and thought it wiser to behave herself for a bit – so she wouldn't lunch. When I got back this afternoon I learnt that Oliver Harvey was arriving from London to find out exactly what Gouin meant when he talked of an Anglo-French alliance last Saturday. I gathered from Oliver when he arrived about 7 that my recent despatch on the subject had borne some fruit – and that Bevin, at any rate, was now all out for an alliance. It is typical of the Foreign Office that after having delayed for two years they should now want to settle everything in twelve hours. Will anything come of it? I hope so. A lot of arrivals today. Peter Quennell[2] and Evelyn Waugh – who hate each other – have come to stay.

April 4, 1946

I left the house with Oliver Harvey in time to reach the Quai d'Orsay at 9. We found Bidault in an excitable state. He practically told us that he might resign tomorrow on the question of the Ruhr. While he had always wanted – and still did want – an Anglo-French Alliance, he would not have it supposed that it had been brought about by a surrender on the part of France with regard to the Ruhr. If tomorrow he could get agreement in the French Government on this issue he was ready to go ahead with the alliance at once. It was not a very satisfactory conversation. We went on to see Gouin. According to him the matter was not coming before the *Conseil de Ministres* until next Tuesday. We told him this would be too late and he promised he would try to have it settled

---

[1] Gloria Rubio y Altorre (1912–80), daughter of Raphael Rubio y Altorre. She married first Count Egon von Fürstenberg, second Prince Ahmed Fakri in 1946, and third Group-Capt. Loel Guinness in 1951.

[2] Sir Peter Quennell (1905–93), writer. Editor of *Cornhill Magazine* 1944–51 and *History Today* 1951–79.

tomorrow. He is quite definitely against the political severance of the Ruhr from Germany, and is all in favour of Bevin's own plan for the handing over of the industries of the Ruhr to an international consortium. There is in fact no difference of opinion between him and Bevin.

April 5, 1946

There were rumours in the early afternoon that Bidault had resigned as the result of this morning's *Conseil de Ministres*, but there soon came out an official communiqué to the effect that there was complete agreement between Ministers and that policy with regard to the Ruhr, Rhine and Saar remained unchanged. This was in fact a victory for Bidault, who told me when I went to see him at 7.15 that he had firm support from Thorez. Bidault told me that after the next Cabinet meeting on Tuesday they would announce their intention of opening forthwith negotiations with England with a view to arriving at an alliance. They had not done so today because they did not want the two questions – the alliance and the Ruhr – to be associated. This is all very satisfactory. At last the alliance seems to be in sight.

I went to see Gloria for half an hour before seeing Bidault. She tells me she is engaged to the son of Fakri Pasha, the Egyptian Minister. She denies she loves him and says she is afraid of falling in love with me. This is all very flattering, but I fear there will be difficulties when Loulou returns next week.

April 6, 1946

I did some work in the library with Diana and John Julius and then went back to my office until 6. I went to see Gloria. It was a lovely evening, having rained all day. The view from her window of the Sacré Coeur with the sunset rays on it was memorable – very memorable to me. We have three new guests – Leo Amery, his son Julian,[1] Julian Huxley[2] – so that with Peter, Auberon,[3] Evelyn and J.J. we were 8 men and 1 woman for dinner. Evelyn was in a truculent mood and was rude to Julian Huxley.

April 8, 1946

The new Icelandic Minister came to see me this morning. People who come from those distant northern places seem to have no colour. They give the impression of having lived underground or under sea – and they don't mind sitting in complete silence. Before lunch I drove out to see Gloria for a few minutes. I'm afraid I'm very much in love with her and so she seems to be with me. And Loulou comes back tomorrow. Gloria says she cannot share

---

[1] Julian Amery, Lord Amery of Lustleigh (1919–96), married Catherine, younger daughter of Harold Macmillan, in 1950. Conservative Minister under Macmillan and Heath.
[2] Sir Julian Huxley (1887–1975), zoologist.
[3] Auberon Herbert (1922–74), son of Aubrey Herbert and brother-in-law of Evelyn Waugh, fought in the Polish Army 1940–5.

with anyone, and she is naturally prejudiced against Loulou as she is a great friend of Etty [Esterházy, formerly Palffy] from whom Loulou took two husbands.

April 12, 1946

Davidson of *The Times* came this morning. He has been attending the CGT conference and is much impressed by the power, the discipline and the ability of the Communists. It looks as though the Communists are having everything their own way everywhere. They have the great advantage of knowing what they want.

After [dinner] I picked up Loulou and we went to Gloria's party. It was well done – plenty to eat and drink – an excellent band – lovely women. I was rather nervous. There was much jealousy in the air. Everyone was looking at everyone with suspicion. Like a ball in Balzac. Ghislaine with husband and lover – Gloria almost too demonstrative to me. I was determined to give Loulou no cause for complaint but when we got home, which we did at about 1.30, I had to break it to her that certain things were over between us. Much weeping.

April 13, 1946

Loulou was very sweet and sad this morning. She said that she had cried all night – and she wrote me out a speech to make at Biarritz. I picked up Gloria and we drove to the very well named little Auberge du Fruit Défendu. There we had an excellent dinner in a small room where there were three or four tables, but none of them occupied save ours. Up a few stairs there was a bedroom. For the first time Gloria gave herself to me. I don't think I have ever loved anybody physically so much or been so supremely satisfied. We drove home in bright moonlight.

April 17, 1946

Nancy Cunard came this morning because she wanted her passport renewed. She is a strange independent creature. I wonder whether she is happy. It is odd to have known somebody so well and to know them so little. There is something green about her skin that gives her a ghastly appearance. I lunched alone with Gloria in the *salon vert*. The wife of the Spanish *chargé d'affaires*, who is an American and a friend of Eric's, told him that it was well known that Gloria was a Gestapo agent in Spain during the war and that it was monstrous that I should go to her house. I asked Gloria whether it were true and she said, of course not, but seemed hardly surprised at the question. She told me the other day that her husband Count von Fürstenberg had tried to join the Nazi party to keep his estates, but they wouldn't have him as being too much connected with the old régime. She added, wasn't it lucky? I have never known anyone less interested in politics or less inquisitive.

April 19, 1946. Good Friday

It was a beautiful morning again and everything was the more lovely for the two days' rain. I slipped out of my office this morning and walked round to the Rue Royale where I bought some red and yellow roses for Gloria. In the afternoon I worked until past 5 and then went to see Gloria. We played chess and had a very good game. She does everything well. She is wonderfully intelligent and wonderfully ignorant. We tried to explain to her at dinner the principle of the compass without much success. She dined with John [de Bendern][1] and me at the Embassy and drove with us to the station. I was really sorry to say goodbye to her.

On 25 April 1946 another meeting of the Council of Ministers opened in Paris. It was followed by the full United Nations Peace Conference, from the end of July to 15 October.

April 25, 1946

Mr Bevin arrived at Orly a little before noon. I was there to meet him and drove back to the George V with him and Oliver Harvey. He is in excellent fettle; full of life and talk. He kept me there drinking whiskey and telling stories while I was longing to go and say good morning to Gloria. As it was I only got away in time to be late for lunch. Afterwards I drove out to Gloria's only to find, alas, that the bird had flown. I came back and worked until it was time to go to the opening session of the Council of Foreign Ministers. We met at 5 and sat until past 8. On the whole it went fairly well. The first difficulty that was expected to arise was in connection with the procedure. Somewhat to everyone's surprise Molotov immediately accepted the French proposals, thus giving in on the point over which he had fought so hard in London last September. Difficulties arose over the agenda. Bidault insisted on the inclusion of Germany, Byrnes on the inclusion of Austria. Bevin says both or neither, Molotov says yes to Germany no to Austria – finally the point was left to be settled tomorrow. Bevin dined with us – a party of eight. The old boy was in wonderful form – never stopped talking and after dinner sang comic songs. He drank a formidable amount and stayed until 12.30. He got on very well with Diana.

April 26, 1946

Gouin gave a lunch for the Big Four. I sat between Bidault and Thorez. I can't help liking the latter. The meeting of Ministers took place at 4.30. The preamble of the peace treaty with Italy was actually agreed to. There followed a long haggle about reparations – which it was eventually decided to refer to a committee of experts. Later Gaston, Clarissa, J.J. and I went to a party given

---

[1] Count John de Bendern, Duff's Private Secretary. He married Patricia (Pat) Douglas in 1938.

in Rufus Clarke's[1] apartment. Gloria was there and after about an hour she and I slipped away. I hope it was not very obvious. But however great the scandal it was well worth it. I never heard nightingales singing so loudly as those in the trees under her window, and was never happier.

April 27, 1946

A full morning – visits from the Argentine *chargé d'affaires* – (why are Argentine men always so well, sometimes too well dressed?), the Dutch Ambassador (worried about the Ruhr), the Czechoslovak Minister (worried about 200,000 Hungarians in his country and the right bank of the Danube opposite Bratislava). I had hardly time to telephone to Gloria. I confessed to Diana, under pressure, that I loved Gloria. She was angry that I hadn't told her before.

April 28, 1946. Sunday

We had a lunch party at Chantilly. I drove down with Henderson,[2] Bevin's Assistant Private Secretary. He is not yet a regular member of the service, but has done an examination of which he doesn't know the result. He seemed to me very intelligent. I got from him the impression that Bevin would like to keep me in Paris, but will probably not be able to resist the pressure very much longer. I shan't mind except for leaving the library, which is becoming in my opinion the most delightful room in the world.

April 30, 1946

I went this morning to the meeting of our delegation at 10 o'clock. I expressed my views with regard to the folly of giving complete independence to Libya – and the bad effect that it would have on French North Africa. [*The issue concerned the future of the former Italian colonies, including Libya.*] If we allow the Arabs to regain complete control of that country it will relapse into the condition it was in during the 18th century. What reason have we to suppose that the character of the Arabs has changed in the last century? If they have improved they are the only race in the world who has done so. I then had a word in private with Bevin on the subject of food for France – and the possibility of doing something with regard to wheat, which might help the Socialists in the coming elections. I found him fully alive to the matter and aware of its importance.

At 3 I went to the Conference where I found it harder than ever to stay awake. At one moment Bevin said 'Tell Duff I'll call him if anything happens' and added 'he's the most sensible man in the room. It's all a waste of time.' We had a dinner party. It went well. Bevin stayed late and told interminable and very poor stories. Ashley played the piano.

---

[1] Rufus Clarke, Assistant Military Attaché at the Embassy.
[2] Sir Nicholas Henderson (b. 1919), British Ambassador in Warsaw, Bonn, Paris and Washington.

May 1, 1946

A beautiful morning and a public holiday. The streets are full of the sellers of lilies of the valley – and there is spring and gaiety in the air. The Ministers' meeting took place at 11.30. It was proposed to set up an Allied Inspectorate to enforce the treaty with Italy. Everybody was in agreement except the Russians who would have none of it, although they had agreed to it in principle last September. Argument between Molotov and Byrnes was acrimonious and ended in complete disagreement. Bevin, who was in the chair this morning, concluding the meeting said 'The next item is a 'alf-'oliday which will be passed unanimously'. It was no 'alf 'oliday for me.

May 2, 1946

I attended the meeting of the delegation at the George V at 9.30. It was another beautiful morning and I went on from there to spend a few happy minutes with Gloria. We stood on the balcony in the sunlight looking over the tops of the chestnut trees to the Eiffel Tower and the Sacré Coeur. The meeting of Ministers took place at 12. Agreement was reached on one subject – the future of the Pelagosa and Pianosa islands, which contain one lighthouse and no inhabitants.

When I came to my office about 4 the telephone rang. It was Gloria speaking from the airport to say she had suddenly been summoned to start at once and was off to America this afternoon. A sad, sad blow to me. I am really fond of her.

May 3, 1946

Before 9.30 the guests began to arrive – Mr and Mrs Bevin and Diana and I received them. There were over 700. We had all the ground floor open and it was a fairly warm evening so that guests flowed into the garden. We had the three delegations and all the Quai d'Orsay, the American and the Soviet Embassies. We had food in the dining room, a band and dancing in the ballroom. It was extremely democratic and I think on the whole it was a success. Bevin danced with great enthusiasm. I danced once with Mrs Bevin. It went on until nearly two.

May 5, 1946. Sunday

This is the day of the referendum on the constitution – I have little doubt that there will be a majority of 'Ouis'. [*The referendum had effectively become a plebiscite for or against Communism. In fact the 'Nons' won, which Duff considered a real blow to the Communists. The result meant that under the Fourth Republic the Assembly would have restricted powers.*]

May 8, 1946

Usual morning reunion at the George V followed by plenary meeting at 11. Once again Mr Byrnes sprung a surprise. He suggested that the deputies should now produce a report on the work of the conference, setting down all the subjects which had been agreed and all upon which no agreement could be reached; that the Peace Conference should then be summoned to meet here on June 15 and that this report should be submitted in the hope that the combined wisdom of twenty-one nations would discover the solutions which the four had been unable to find. What a hope! Molotov plainly didn't like the proposal and obviously will have to refer it to his Government – Bevin didn't like the date. It was however decided that the report should be drawn up and that the conference should meet at 5 tomorrow.

May 9, 1946

At 3.15 we had a talk about the Ruhr. Bevin, Harvey, Hall-Patch[1] of the Treasury and Turner of the Board of Trade for our side and Bidault, Chauvel and Alphand for theirs. I thought Bidault did extremely well and all my sympathies were with him. The Treasury and B. of T. could not answer the question I put to them after the French had gone, why the Ruhr should cost us a million a year if we took it away from Germany whereas if we leave it to Germany it will be a most valuable asset and will assist German recovery.

May 11, 1946

Usual morning meeting. Bevin was very pleased with himself this morning. The conference certainly seems to have got going again yesterday afternoon. He thinks it was largely his doing. I dare say it was, but Molotov must have received fresh instructions from Moscow. A compromise about the Italian colonies and reparations now seems possible, but Trieste remains.

May 17, 1946

The Turkish Ambassador came to see me this morning and we had a long and interesting talk. He is fairly optimistic. He thinks the Soviets made their first big mistake when they failed to evacuate Persia at the beginning of March. It was an irretrievable mistake because it resulted in the Americans developing a foreign policy. They had never had one before, but once a country adopts a foreign policy, although that policy may change, the country will never revert to not having a foreign policy at all.

---

[1] Sir Edmund Hall-Patch (1896–1975), Deputy Assistant Under-Secretary and Principal Economic Adviser to Bevin 1946–8.

May 21, 1946

I worked most of the morning at the Ruhr problem. [*Duff was writing a memorandum about the future of the Ruhr in support of the French point of view.*] Loulou had sounded in despair on the telephone this morning so I drove down to Verrières after lunch. It is sad when a journey which a year ago was all pleasure becomes a heavy duty. I found her with André and her sister. She walked round the garden with me and said some hard things. They should have hurt me but they didn't, and after I had returned to Paris she telephoned full of remorse.

May 25, 1946

I had to go this morning at 10.30 to see some Belgian *anciens combattants* on their way to London. There was to be a 'lunch', but I had made it plain that I was not prepared to eat at that hour. Of course the Belgians hadn't arrived and we were told to come back again at 11.30. On our second visit, Eric was with me, we were ushered into a hall where about 200 people were about to sit down to a copious meal. 'Lunch' in French means, I thought, 'light snack' – but there were seven courses to this one. I sat for half an hour and watched them eat. It made me feel rather sick. Later I lunched with Loulou at the Escargot. We had a meal of sunshine and storm. The worst storm was when I told her frankly that I did not intend to give up seeing Gloria when she returned. It is surely best that she should know this. I can see no reason why I should do otherwise. It will be difficult. It would be much better that Loulou should go to America with her brother André. She hasn't seen her three children for ten years.

May 29, 1946

This is the last day of that bad moon which I saw first shining over Bagatelle and Gloria's home on May 2nd. It has been a wet month and an unhappy one for me. Today it rained as hard as ever and today Diana gave me a letter she had written some days ago expressing all her unhappiness about Gloria – a sweet, heart-breaking letter. She has allowed the whole affair to assume exaggerated proportions in her mind. It is partly jealousy on her own account, partly sorrow and sympathy for Loulou, partly fear lest I should do myself harm from what she considers a most unsuitable liaison. Unfortunately both Rufus Clarke [Assistant Military Attaché] and Timothy Jones [Assistant Military Attaché] now fancy themselves in love with Loulou and they repeat to her all sorts of gossip about Gloria and me, which Loulou again repeats to Diana. The result is that Diana has one of her obsessions and can think of nothing else.

May 31, 1946

The end of a bad month – the wettest May for years, and much trouble. No sign of improvement in the weather but otherwise things are better. I am on the best of terms with Diana again and Loulou seems much happier.

June 2, 1946

Shortly before one Dickie and Edwina [Mountbatten] arrived with their daughter Patricia[1]. Dickie talks of going back to the Navy as a Rear Admiral. He looks very well – so does Edwina, but shrivelled.

June 3, 1946

We all went off the Invalides to see Dickie decorated with the *Grande Croix* of the *Légion d'Honneur* by General Juin. It was a good show.

The results of the elections are surprising. All good judges were convinced of one thing only before the event, namely that the M.R.P. must lose both to the right and the left. As it happens the M.R.P. is the only party that has made substantial gains, while both the Communists and Socialists have lost – the latter heavily. Le Troquer, whom I saw at lunch, seemed slightly depressed. He thought that Bidault would demand the Presidency of the Council.

June 4, 1946

I am sad not to be with John Julius today [at Eton]. He was so eager for one of us to go for the Fourth. But he gets great advantages from our being here and must take the rough with the smooth. We left for the Hôtel de Ville at 10.55. Le Troquer made an excellent speech welcoming Dickie, to which Dickie replied in admirable French. This made a deep impression on the audience. That any Englishman should be able to speak French is surprising, but that an Admiral should do it very well is stupefying.

At 6.30 I went round by invitation to call on Ghislaine de Polignac who now has a small apartment on the 9th floor of the George V. When I knocked at her door she came to it with her finger on her lips and pointing to the one opposite told me to wait there a second. I went through it and found myself on the roof, where I had to wait for five minutes feeling rather foolish but enjoying a good view of Paris. Then having disposed of her visitor she let me in.

June 7, 1946

A dull reception at the Chamber of Commerce followed by a call on the Windsors – in a small apartment at the Ritz. Wallis was looking strikingly plain. It is sad to think that he gave up the position of King-Emperor not to live in an island of the Hesperides with the Queen of Beauty but to share an apartment on the third floor of the Ritz with this harsh-voiced ageing woman who was never even very pretty.

---

[1] Patricia Mountbatten (b. 1924), later Countess Mountbatten of Burma, married John Knatchbull, 7th Baron Brabourne (b. 1924), a film producer, in October 1946.

June 14, 1946

At 5 I went to Le Bourget to meet the Secretary of State. I went up to his room with him and drank whiskey. He was very bitter about Herbert Morrison[1] whom he suspects of stirring up criticism of the Foreign Office. He said that he was not straight and could not be trusted. I have never heard a British Cabinet Minister use such language about a colleague to one who is not an intimate. The lack of the old school tie may prove the undoing of the Labour Party and so finally of our governmental system. Bevin was very pleased, and rightly, with what he had said about the public schools and the Foreign Service. This gave me an opportunity of telling him that the press here was full of stories about my departure, and I said I should like to know how much truth there was in them. He was embarrassed. He said the matter had not been discussed and then went on to say that when it had been brought up at the Labour Party Executive he had said that he was bound to admit that he had always had a soft corner for me because I resigned at Munich. He assured me that he would not be rushed and that he would give me fair warning. It is my impression that I shan't go before Christmas and possibly not before next spring. The prospect does not distress me in the least.

June 15, 1946

Delegation meeting at the George V this morning. Some of the French papers are speculating as to whether it is Gladwyn Jebb[2] or Oliver Harvey who is to succeed me. As we sit in a row at these conferences the situation might be embarrassing but it isn't. Although I don't want to lose the job myself I don't grudge it to either of them, and they are both well up to it. Personally I think Jebb would be the better. There is more life in him, but the Foreign Office will think he is too young as he has only reached the age of Napoleon and Wellington at Waterloo.

June 22, 1946

Morning meeting at the George V. When it was over Bob Dixon came to me and said 'the Secretary of State would like to speak to you'. As I went along I felt very much like the schoolboy summoned to the headmaster's study to get the sack. He first talked to me about the story that Bidault has an understanding with Molotov, whereby in return for concessions in the international sphere the Russians will bring pressure to bear on the French communists to induce them to play in with the M.R.P. He then said 'Now I want to speak about an internal matter'. I thought the sack was coming then, but no, he only

---

[1] Herbert Morrison, Lord Morrison of Lambeth (1888–1965). Lord President of the Council 1945–7; Leader of the Commons 1947–50.

[2] Gladwyn Jebb, 1st Baron Gladwyn (1900–96). Assistant Under-Secretary of State 1946–9 and adviser to Bevin; Ambassador to France 1954–60.

wanted to know how many missions there were in France under the control of other Departments of H.M.G. We had a very friendly conversation.

Diana was in a very bad way this morning, perpetually on the cry. I took her out to lunch at Les Tilleuls. Our lunch was like the weather, alternative sunshine and rain – the latter being floods of tears. I think she needs a rest. [Later] Diana and I drove down to Chantilly where we spent the night alone. I said *Modern Love* to her which was perhaps unwise as she saw in it many allusions to our own troubles, which led to endless argument. It was not a very happy evening.

June 24, 1946

We dined at the Meurice with Mr and Mrs Byrnes. We went upstairs after dinner and the men sat in one room while the women sat in another. This is an American habit with which I have met before and which I find very inferior to our custom of the men remaining at table for a little while after the women have left. Bevin's private conversation is marred by boasting which exceeds anything one could believe. When he and Byrnes vied with one another this evening, explaining all the things they were going to do to Molotov tomorrow, it was almost embarrassing. The final arrangement was that all points still at issue were to be reviewed – that as each was brought up Byrnes, who would be in the chair, would insist upon immediate settlement or else the relegation of the subject to the peace conference. We shall see.

June 26, 1946

The conference sat from 5 to 7.45 and agreed on nothing. We dined with the Bevins. He was in wonderful form and slightly exhilarated. Somebody asked me whether I would like to return to the House of Commons, and when I said no, Bevin said 'We're going to send Duff to the 'Ouse of Lords' – when Diana protested he seemed surprised and said 'wouldn't you like him to be a Viscount?' She said she didn't want to lose this job, to which he replied – 'Oh don't worry about that'.

June 27, 1946

The conference met at four. Molotov had obviously had fresh instructions. He agreed on a number of small points – and went almost too fast for Bevin. Just as we were packing up Byrnes said half jokingly 'why not finish up a good afternoon by agreeing with regard to the Dodecanese?' 'All right, I will' replied Molotov and that was the end of the question which has been under argument since last September. Both Bevin and Byrnes were anxious to get the credit.

June 28, 1946

I was having a sleep after lunch when Rosemary [McEntire, Duff's secretary] broke in and said that Madame Rubio wanted to speak to me on the telephone. She said she was going to the masked ball tonight where I should see her.

She said also that while in Mexico she had married Ahmed by proxy. Diana seemed happier this evening so I decided to say nothing to her about Gloria's return.

July 1, 1946

Summer, brought back by Gloria, remains. I went to a delegation meeting which was followed by a meeting on Germany. Strang and General Robertson[1] were there. Strang has doubts about the wisdom of building up a great, strong Germany and I might get him on my side. To the military and to the financial mind the problem is very simple and admits of only one solution. Germany is in a mess – the Germans are very reasonable people, good soldiers and good economists – help them to get on their feet again and all will be well. It makes me mad. Bevin half-sees the truth. He said this morning that the greater decentralization of Germany we could get, the better. I saw Hall-Patch shivering with horror.

July 2, 1946

I went later to the conference. For three hours we talked about Trieste and arrived at no conclusion. Yet I feel it will come right. Molotov wants it to. He is the cleverest of the four – Bidault the most adroit – Byrnes the most talkative and muddle-headed. It now turns on whether the internationalized district is to depend ultimately on U.N.O. or the Big Four.

July 10, 1946

I went to the conference at 4. Bidault started off and spoke for an hour, then Bevin for another hour and then Molotov again. He came down definitely against the separation of the Ruhr from Germany. Everybody is therefore against France on this issue. Bidault was very bitter about it in the bar afterwards.

July 12, 1946

A delegation meeting this morning on Germany. As the result of Molotov's attitude yesterday Bevin is now prepared to take a very firm line. He is determined to develop the Ruhr to the utmost, to make it pay in order to relieve the British tax-payer. He means to stay there. 'I must be as near the Elbe as possible.' I saw Strang and Hall-Patch shudder. I had a very good talk with Bevin afterwards. I told him that in my view the British Treasury and the Bank of England ought to be in the dock at Nuremberg. He agreed. I raised also the question of the Anglo-French alliance. He was strongly in favour of

---

[1] Gen. Sir Brian Robertson, 1st Lord Robertson of Oakridge (1896–1974). Chief Administrative Officer to Field-Marshal Alexander, CIC Allied Forces Italy 1944–5; Deputy Military Governor in British Zone of Germany 1945–7; CIC and Military Governor 1947–9; UK Commissioner, Allied High Commission 1949–50.

concluding it as soon as possible. I am to talk to Bidault about it. All very satisfactory. I went back to the conference at 5. It continued until 9.15. Molotov was more tiresome than ever and it all ended on an unhappy note of frustration and ill will. I was dining with Gloria and had to keep her waiting until this ridiculous hour. She was unhappy. She said I was no longer in love with her, that I merely wanted her physically and that our relationship was impossible. She said she had never had this sort of secret, shame-faced affair and she couldn't bear it. What she meant was that I was treating her like a tart, which indeed I am. She said she loved me and that I was nicer than anybody she had ever known but that it couldn't go on like this. When we got back to where she lived she wouldn't allow me to come up with her. This was a cruel blow – but I love her the more for her pride.

July 15, 1946

I drove down to Le Bourget to meet Winston, who arrived at 4.40. Mary and Randolph were with him. He is in great form and seems in much better health than a year ago. He has what I consider very wrong ideas. He is absorbed by the Russian menace and is all for helping the Germans to recover, with a view to making use of them against the Russians.

July 26, 1946 (London)

Diana and I had both had very bad nights. She is in a bad way altogether and the Gloria affair has assumed proportions in her mind which are fantastic. I have rashly promised that after this weekend at Deauville I will see Gloria no more. It is a pity. A great storm blew up during luncheon and when I went to the Dorchester to collect my luggage Diana was there, pathetically hoping that the weather might be too bad for me to fly to Deauville. I left her feeling like a criminal. [*The Casino at Deauville, which had been taken over by the US Army, reopened for the 1946 season.*]

July 28, 1946 (Paris)

I was called at 9 [at Deauville] and felt as well as could be expected after $3\frac{1}{2}$ hours sleep. I got up and dressed and wrote to Diana. Gloria came down to say goodbye to me. I drove away at 11.30. We reached Pacy-sur-Eure and had an indifferent lunch. I sat in the sun in the little garden afterwards and felt happy. My life is so continually surrounded by people that it is a pleasure to be alone for once and I enjoyed this drive and this lunch and sitting in the sun. It occurred to me that I was probably an existentialist without knowing it. I have always denounced it and never quite understood what it stands for. Nor am I clear how it differs from hedonism. I resolved to worry less and work less but I fear I shall find it difficult to carry out my resolution in view of the peace conference. I learnt by heart a sonnet of Rimbaud during the drive.

I reached Paris about 3.40. Ashley was waiting for me. He and I drove down to Le Bourget where the Prime Minister arrived at 4.45. I drove with him to the George V. I have always found him very difficult to talk to and today was no exception to that rule. He snaps 'quite' at whatever one says and appears to be in complete agreement, but one is not quite sure that he is.

I drove down to Verrières for dinner. In the course of dinner Loulou attacked me fiercely. She said that I was the greatest liar, the coldest heart, that I disgraced my position etc. etc. I remained quite calm and let the fire burn itself out. After dinner she was quite reasonable again and even affectionate.

July 29, 1946

I went to the George V to collect the Prime Minister and take him to see Bidault. The interview was short and not easy. Each of them understands a little of the other's language and I, who have to interpret, am never quite sure how much they have understood and how much must be interpreted. There was a preliminary meeting of heads of delegations and ambassadors, and the [Peace] Conference proper opened at 4. I had not been included in the delegation and so sat in the front row of the diplomatic box, which I am always afraid of falling out of. It was very hot and difficult to keep awake. I saw that Attlee and Alexander[1] were sleeping soundly.

July 30, 1946

I went to a meeting of the delegation this morning at 10. Attlee is always a good chairman. He wasted no time and the whole thing was over in quarter of an hour. He apologized to me for having brought me down for it, which I thought was very civil. He is not a *grand seigneur* but he is a gentleman, which is perhaps a better kind of beast.

August 9, 1946

I went to Le Bourget to meet Bevin and his wife. I drove back to the George V with his doctor, who told me he had had a bad attack of angina and that he ought to rest, but that he was very difficult to control. He also said, which surprised me, that Mrs Bevin was not much help. I suppose he dominates her too much. I had a short talk with him and thought he seemed very tired.

August 11, 1946

I had a very satisfactory talk with Loulou this morning. She sees things as I do, and understands how mournful it was for me to be followed around by a weeping, reproachful ghost. I had a delightful walk with Diana while the sun was setting. Loulou and Charlie Beistegui came to dinner. I am now Loulou's confidant and *copain*. She is frightened of Diana, who disapproves so strongly

---

[1] Albert Victor (A. V.) Alexander, Earl Alexander of Hillsborough (1885–1965). First Lord of the Admiralty 1940–5 and 1945–6 (under Attlee); Minister of Defence 1947–50.

of her affair with Rufus [Clarke]. I love my new role and love Loulou more
than ever as a friend and accomplice.

August 13, 1946

Bevin and Alexander were both at the meeting this morning. Alexander had
a statement drafted, which he wanted to make at the plenary meeting. Bevin
was at first rather vague, but when he understood the issue he was firmly
opposed to making any statement at all. This was what I also had suggested.
Alexander of course is apt to see the Peace Conference like the House of
Commons. I was never more impressed with Bevin's grasp of diplomacy and
of foreign affairs, based as it is on experience and common sense.

August 14, 1946

We heard the Bulgarian this morning. He, with the support of the Ukraine,
spoke as though Bulgaria had fought on our side in the war and the Greeks
against – and even demanded compensation from Greece. The Hungarian in
the afternoon was little better. He foolishly launched a broadside attack on
Czechoslovakia. To hear the defeated enemies boldly attacking their victors
requires a good deal of patience.

August 18, 1946. Sunday

I refused to read the second lesson laid down – Philippians ch. 2, entirely
devoted to St Paul's boasting about being circumcised, so the parson found
another one for me, Luke 18, about the Pharisee and the publican, which was
a great improvement.

August 25, 1946. Sunday

I spent the afternoon arranging my own little archives – diving into the tin
boxes that I hadn't seen for years – weeding out a little and putting in a little
more – an occupation which makes time fly. Reading my old diaries I am
astonished at how much I have forgotten and equally astonished at how much
I find myself in agreement with what I wrote.

August 28, 1946

A very wet morning. The Jews have threatened, anonymously on the telephone, to blow up the Embassy, so that we are now surrounded by policemen
and detectives.

August 31, 1946

After the morning meeting Bevin asked me to come and have a talk with him.
As usual I foresaw dismissal – and as usual it was nothing of the kind. We
had a most friendly talk. He is very much of my way of thinking about France,
but is afraid of being too frank with the French Government lest everything
he says to them be conveyed by the communists to Moscow. I told him that

in my opinion the French must sooner or later face up to communist black-mail, which is at present rendering the conduct both of internal and foreign affairs impossible.

September 1, 1946

We had a scratch dinner and at 9.30 the guests began to arrive. Diana, who had been working at it all day, had made the house look lovely. We had a wooden floor put down out of doors with lamps at the four corners and although it wasn't very warm a great many people danced out of doors and more danced indoors. It was undoubtedly a great success and incomparably the best party that has been given during the peace conference. I suppose there were about 700 people – but there was no crowd, there was plenty to eat and drink and everybody seemed to enjoy it.

September 18, 1946

I lunched with Loulou at the Escargot. Unfortunately Teddie and Gloria arrived there. Gloria sent me a note *'tiens – tiens – tiens'* which distressed Loulou. Later Gloria, whom I was to have gone to see at 7, telephoned to say she wouldn't be in and didn't want to see me anyway. I reasoned with her and she eventually agreed to meet me. When I saw her she said that I did everything for Loulou and nothing for her, that I lent Loulou a car while she had to walk etc. etc. She has a good case – I admit – but I can't do otherwise. Then I went upstairs to the Windsors' suite. We had cocktails and drove to Lapérouse where we dined, eight, in a small room. We sat round the table until 12.15. It was not amusing. Otto of Habsburg was there. It reminded me of the dinner of ex-kings at Venice in *Candide*.

September 25, 1946

I went to the delegation meeting this morning. Bevin told us how he had arranged with Molotov and the others yesterday to speed up the Peace Conference. I had half an hour's talk with him afterwards. He had made a point of seeing Molotov first and then Bidault because he is afraid, I think, of being suspected by the left in England of coming too much under the influence of Byrnes and the U.S.A. He distrusts Alphand. He wants to see Bidault in greater privacy, which I promised to try to arrange. It is odd how Alphand inspires dislike and distrust in all Englishmen. I think it is because, [though] being a highly skilled civil servant and *inspecteur de finances*, he looks and behaves like an actor. No English civil servant could ever be persuaded to take Noël Coward seriously. [*Alphand was a brilliant raconteur and mimic.*]

September 28, 1946

After the meeting this morning I had a talk with Alexander. He has a fierce cold, which renders him almost speechless. We agreed that it was a mistake for Winston to come here in order to see Byrnes, but I said that I saw no reason why it should become known that this was the object of his visit. Bob Dixon telephoned later. Alexander had told him about Winston's visit, which I of course ought to have done myself yesterday. I can't think why I didn't. Bevin was much, I think too much upset about it, and was uncertain as to whether it would not be better that he should stay at the Ritz rather than at the Embassy. I was sure that the latter was better as he would at least be under control.

Churchill arrived that day and stayed at the Embassy. He saw Byrnes privately and dined at Maxim's, in spite of a dinner having been arranged at Chantilly. An extract from Duff's letter to Bob Dixon about the visit, which is pasted into the diary, ends, 'Having possibly endangered international relations and having certainly caused immense inconvenience to a large number of people, he seemed thoroughly to enjoy himself, was with difficulty induced to go to bed soon after midnight and left at 10 a.m. the next morning for London in high spirits.'

October 7, 1946

Barley Alison[1] brought Arthur Koestler[2] to dinner. I had expected not to like him and didn't.

October 8, 1946

The conference continues. Molotov is now in the chair. Bevin spoke today. It is a lamentable entertainment. Each national spokesman reads out a carefully prepared speech. No speech relates to another. There is no argument, no debate, no eloquence.

October 9, 1946

We lunched with the Belgians to meet the Regent.[3] He made a poor impression on me. I sat next Mme. Chauvel who was born Belgian. I asked her why he had never married. She said he had served in the British Navy where people got into bad habits. Diana sat between Vyshinsky and Molotov. She got on well with the former but found the latter quite impossible even with the aid of an interpreter.

October 14, 1946

The *Ouis* won but the *Nons* polled 46% of the votes and there were 30% abstentions. This was much better for the *Nons* than anyone expected. [*The vote was on the draft constitution which was then approved. De Gaulle had denounced the draft, thus making the vote for or against himself.*]

---

[1] Barley Alison worked at the British Embassy. She later became a publisher.
[2] Arthur Koestler (1905–83), author of *Darkness at Noon*. In 1946 he was an advocate of Zionism and a separate Jewish state.
[3] Prince Charles of Belgium (1903–83) became Regent when his brother King Leopold III went into exile in Switzerland in 1945.

October 15, 1946

At three took place the last meeting of the conference. The Yugoslav delegation didn't turn up but sent a letter of protest. The Russians looked surprised and annoyed. It is thought that the Yugoslavs are getting out of hand. Otherwise all was very friendly. I was thankful to hear Bidault say *'la conférence de Paris est close'*. [I] went to the break-up party of the delegation at the George V. I thought it a grim affair. The room was too large and gloomy. Alexander would go on playing songs for the people to sing when they all wanted to dance. There was only one piano. The only drink provided was a very inferior wine-cup. Bevin slipped away shortly before midnight and I did the same. I have a tiresome spot on my face. I thought it was hardly noticeable. Mrs Bevin said to me 'I've got what you've got on your face in the inside of my lip. I think it's a small ulcer.'

October 18, 1946 (En route to Venice)

We both slept well, I very well. We were woken at 5 by the Swiss police and customs on going into Switzerland and again on leaving it and then by the Italians, but we had a *laissez-passer* for each country and nobody gave us any trouble. We stopped a long time at Domodossola and had coffee in the restaurant. There is no shortage of butter or sugar in Italy. The weather gradually improved and the sun came out when we were having luncheon. The remainder of the journey seemed rather long and dull, especially after dark. I read *The Pursuit of Love* by Nancy Mitford,[1] of which I didn't think much, but it held my attention. With a bottle of red wine and a sandwich bought in Verona, the time passed not too badly and it was wonderful, soon after ten, to find ourselves in beloved Venice again. Diana cried. It is nine years since we were here.

October 19, 1946 (Venice)

After a good night's sleep we woke to a cloudless morning. Venice was at her most beautiful. It was wonderful to find everything unchanged, the same shops selling the same goods as twenty, thirty years ago. It is 36 years since I first came here. We went to Harry's Bar, where Harry [Cipriani] himself looked as he did nine years ago. We went for a long walk, up the Merceria, over the Rialto to the Frari, which we struck by chance and visited. I have got fired again with the idea which has long been in my mind, of writing something about the history of Venice.

---

[1] Nancy Mitford (1904–73), novelist and biographer, married Peter Rodd in 1933. She fell in love with Gaston Palewski in 1942 and in 1946 moved to Paris. She became a great friend of the Coopers.

October 28, 1946

We were called at 5.30 a.m. For the second time since we have been here the bath water was hot – the first time since the night of our arrival. Otherwise it has been tepid and has done much, in this cold weather, to spoil our visit. The train left punctually at 7.

We had two separate compartments and slept a good deal during the morning. They had made us a basket of food at the Taverna last night – chicken and gorgonzola. We bought some bread and wine at Verona and lunched early. We dined early on the train and went early to bed. We slept well, but my slumbers were cruelly broken by a very heavy bag containing presents which fell off the rack on to my stomach.

I forgot to mention that on our way to the restaurant car last night we discovered Christopher Soames who was returning from Rome, whither he had been to propose to Mary Churchill who has accepted. They first met for a few minutes before dinner in the Embassy during Winston's last visit. Christopher determined at once to marry her, and although I have not a very high opinion of him I must say that he has shown great energy and determination. I don't think Winston will be best pleased. He was I think thinking of a royal marriage for his favourite daughter, which was the reason for his last visit to Belgium.

November 1, 1946

Salisbury Jones[1] came to see me this morning to talk about Christopher Soames, who he says is no use. He won't work. This was very awkward for me, as I had written to Winston that although I didn't know him very well all that I did know was to his credit and I had added that if he married Mary it would be a great pleasure for us to have her in Paris and we would do all we could to help the young *ménage*. I could hardly on the top of that agree to his being sacked. Salisbury Jones quite understood the position, and said he would give him a good talking to and see if it produced any effect. I dined with the de Benderns in their nice new flat. Pat was looking as pretty and as dirty as ever. Christopher was there. We played three rubbers. I won them all. Driving home I spoke to Christopher about his idleness. He was very sensible, admitted the charge, said that Salisbury Jones had already talked to him and promised to try to do better in future.

November 3, 1946. Sunday

Marjorie [Anglesey] died during the night. It will be a terrible blow to her children – especially to Caroline, who loved her best and who has least else. When people have been ill a long time one becomes accustomed to the idea

---

[1] Gen. Sir Guy Salisbury-Jones (1896–1985), Head of British Military Mission to France 1946– 9. Christopher Soames was on his staff.

of their death and feels it less. So it is with Diana. She feels it little now because it is not a shock, but I think she will gradually feel it more and more. It was so when her mother died.

Gaston thinks there will be a financial collapse in France between January and March, which will necessitate the recall of de Gaulle.

November 7, 1946

There were two cocktail parties, one at the Russians', their 29th anniversary, and one at the Swiss Legation. Bogomolov was most friendly and asked me whether John Julius still wanted to go to Russia to learn Russian – because if so he thought it could be managed. When Diana asked him about it some time ago he said it would be impossible, *ce n'est pas la coutume du pays*. So it was interesting that he should have changed his mind. Is this part of the policy of lifting the iron curtain?[1]

November 9, 1946

I dined at Verrières – drove Christopher Soames down. [He] says that all went well in London. He was most kindly received by Winston and Clemmie and is to be married at the end of January.

November 11, 1946

The results of yesterday's elections are strange and create a very uneasy situation. The Communists have gained seats and the various forces of the right have gained votes. This is largely due to de Gaulle's interference. He has succeeded in weakening the M.R.P. and producing a chaotic situation, which is I suppose what he wanted to do. He sees chaos as the necessary prelude to his own return.

November 14, 1946

They are all getting rather worried about the threats of the Stern Gang[2] and say I must have a guard on the front of my car. How a man sitting in the front seat of a car can prevent another man from throwing a bomb at it I cannot understand.

November 16, 1946 (Nuits Saint Georges)

We left for Nuits Saint Georges, where I was made a citizen and where I spoke successfully. This was followed by an enormous dinner party in a cellar. 250 people sat down. As was inevitable in so large a party the food was filthy, and

---

[1] On 5 Mar. 1946 Churchill gave a speech in Fulton, Missouri, where he introduced the phrase 'Iron Curtain' to describe the division in Europe between the Western powers and the Soviet sphere.

[2] The Stern Gang was a fanatically anti-British Zionist terrorist organization in Palestine, founded in 1940 by Avraham Stern (1907–42).

I didn't think much of the wine. They call themselves the *Confrérie du Taste-Vin* and it's all bogus Rabelaisian and 'ye olde' nonsense. They have a lot of silly ceremonies and wear ridiculous robes. We were all made officers of the order and again I had to make a speech. This didn't happen until past midnight. It was past two before we got home and when we left the party was in full swing. It is the kind of thing which bores me most in the world. Our car couldn't be found when we came out. They had locked it up for safety and lost the key. It was raining.

November 19, 1946 (London)

I left with John [de Bendern] at noon on the Golden Arrow. There can be no more agreeable way of spending a day than on the Golden Arrow. We had a compartment for four to ourselves and a bottle of champagne with our lunch. After lunch we played backgammon until we reached Calais. We had the best cabin on the boat and another bottle of champagne, which we shared with Augustus John. He looks very old now, but very grand. We continued to play backgammon from Dover to London. At Victoria we were somewhat surprisingly met by Gloria *and* Ahmed. While we were having drinks in my sitting room Diana and Loulou, who were dining together in Paris, telephoned. Fortunately television is not yet in general use.

December 4, 1946

Gloria has gone. She left tonight for Marseilles with her children and governess. There they are to meet Ahmed and go on to Kenya. I suppose it is all for the best but I shall miss her very much. I like to have a secret and a romance in my life.

Thorez was defeated this afternoon in his bid for the premiership and Legentilhomme,[1] whom I saw at the Sorbonne, said he thought that Gouin would be elected. I still think and hope it will be Bidault. It would be rather absurd to select as First Minister a member of the party which received the most outstanding set-back at the last election.

December 6, 1946

Gabriel Pascal[2] came to see me this morning. I said I would let [him] have the film rights of *David* for 1,500,000 francs. If it is paid to me here in Paris I shan't have to pay tax on it. [He] seemed to me rather vague. Then John Dashwood[3] came with the new 'Security' expert. They want to put a barbed-wire fence across the middle of the garden to keep the Stern Gang out. I never heard such nonsense.

---

[1] Gen. Paul Legentilhomme (1884–1975), Military Governor of Paris 1945–7.

[2] Gabriel Pascal (1894–1954), producer and film director, best known for putting Shaw on film, in particular *Caesar and Cleopatra* and *Major Barbara*.

[3] Sir John Dashwood, 10th Bt. (1896–1966). Assistant Marshal Diplomatic Corps 1933–58.

December 18, 1946 (London)

[I went] to the House of Commons where I lunched with the Anglo-French group and addressed them afterwards. I got a seat in the Chamber and listened to Questions. I had no nostalgia. On the contrary I felt like an old boy who returns to his private school and despises the folly of it. The foolish questions, the silly laughter, the childish anger and quarrels.

December 24, 1946

John Julius, Diana and I left late for Verrières, where there was a large, late dinner party. We sat at small tables. It was a pleasant dinner and afterwards I played bridge. Some of the party went to mass while others prepared the Christmas tree, to which we were all summoned some time after midnight. There were presents from all for all. I had a wonderful false library of books that were really bottles from the three brothers, a little snuff box from Louise – her more important presents being reserved for tomorrow – and one or two other things. It was past half-past three when I got to bed.

At the end of 1946 the French Government fell, to be replaced by a Socialist minority administration headed by Leon Blum. After three years, Duff's efforts to forge an Anglo-French alliance were rewarded: in January 1947 Blum told Attlee that he favoured an alliance, and though the final treaty was vaguer than Duff had wished he felt it to be a first step towards a Western European Union.

December 26, 1946

I went this morning at 11 to see Monsieur Lapie,[1] whom I found installed in the Minister's Room at the Quai d'Orsay. He was most friendly and is genuinely pro-British. We had half an hour's useful conversation. At 12 I went to see Blum at the Hôtel Matignon. I first met him there ten years ago, when he was Prime Minister and I was Secretary of State for War. He seemed to me better in health than at any time since his release, and as charming as ever. We talked for an hour and covered nearly every political subject. Unlike Lapie, who thinks the present Government may stay in power indefinitely, Blum is sure that there will be no difficulty in forming a coalition government when the time comes next month. Diana arrived at 1 and we had lunch, together with Madame Blum. It was a beautiful day, the house is magnificent and the food excellent. Two years ago the Blums were prisoners, expecting daily to be put to death.

December 27, 1946

We dined with Lapie at the Quai d'Orsay. He has lost no time in beginning to

---

[1] Pierre-Olivier Lapie (1901–94), Under-Secretary of State for Foreign Affairs at the Quai d'Orsay 1946–7.

entertain. I had a long talk afterwards with Couve de Murville.[1] He said that Blum had been very much interested by my suggestion yesterday that we might conclude an Anglo-French alliance before settling the German question. I had not been authorized to make such a suggestion.

December 31, 1946

This has been a year far less eventful than the last and far less satisfactory. In spite of General de Gaulle's resignation and the liquidation of the Levant problem there has been little if any improvement in Anglo-French relations, and the German difficulty is greater than it was owing to the growth of pro-German feeling in England. U.N.O. has not distinguished itself and the five peace treaties that have taken so long to conclude are nothing to be proud of. And the Fourth Republic is still without a President. A year ago I wondered whether I should still be here today. Here, to everybody's surprise, and to the annoyance of many, I am. It is somewhat to my credit, but still more to that of the Labour Government. They are still criticized by their own left wing for keeping me, and prophecies of my imminent departure still appear in the press. They don't worry me for I shan't mind going when the time comes – although I'm not sure where I shall go to or what I shall do. In my private life the event of the year has been the advent of Gloria. She has been the source of some unhappiness but of much delight. Delight of a kind that at my age is hardly likely to come again. And even so I doubt whether I was in love with her. She was an enchanting creature whose affection for me was astonishing and intoxicating. I am very heart-whole at the moment.

1947

January 1, 1947

Having gone to bed in good time last night I began the New Year feeling better than I often have in the past. John Julius on the other hand came home at 7 a.m.

January 4, 1947

Ashley went to London by the Golden Arrow for a meeting there tomorrow in connection with the talks that are to take place here next week concerning travel facilities from Germany. The American approach and ours differ. They don't want to encourage German travel but nor do they wish to interfere with Jews. We, i.e. our people in Berlin, want to make it easier for Germans to travel but harder for Jews, lest the latter get away into Palestine.

---

[1] Maurice Couve de Murville (1907–99), French politician and diplomat. Foreign Minister under de Gaulle 1959–68 and Prime Minister 1968–9.

January 5, 1947. Sunday

Diana and I went down to Chantilly for lunch. We took our food with us and she cooked it – *oeufs brouillés aux truffes* and cold ham. It was excellent. We walked afterwards for an hour or so. It was a perfect winter's day – bright sun, very blue sky, no wind – I never saw the place looking more beautiful.

January 7, 1947

This evening we received from the Foreign Office text of correspondence that has taken place between Blum and Attlee. The former wrote on Jan. 1st insisting on the importance of coal for the salvation of France and, basing himself on his conversation with me, said he was eager to conclude an alliance and would be proud to do so during his short term of office. Attlee replied that there was absolutely nothing doing with regard to coal, but that he was all for an alliance and would be glad to see Blum if he cared to come over to England as Blum had suggested in his letter. Since then there has been it seems another letter of which we haven't received the text, urging more warmly that Blum should go. It is no good his doing so unless they really mean business. Let's hope they do. We learnt this morning that Byrnes has resigned and that General Marshall[1] has been appointed Secretary of State. I liked Byrnes personally but I am glad of the change. I don't know Marshall but I have never heard anything but good of him. Byrnes was an Irishman and a politician. Marshall is neither.

January 9, 1947

This has been a day of some excitement. In the morning there arrived from London a draft memorandum for the Cabinet, suggesting the opening of negotiations for concluding a Customs Union with France. My views were wanted before the submission of the paper to the Cabinet. In a covering letter, Moley Sargent said he had little doubt what my views would be. A little later came the text of the Prime Minister's further letter to Blum. This was a warm invitation to visit England. I sent it round to him at once and at 3.30 I visited him at his invitation. He said that Massigli was to come over on Saturday and that if he agreed Blum himself would go to England on Monday, stay Tuesday and Wednesday and return for the presidential election on Thursday. Is it possible that something will be accomplished at last?

January 10, 1947

I lunched with Ghislaine de Polignac at Larue's and it was great fun. My relationship with her is a very happy one, unmarred by jealousy or anything serious.

---

[1] As Secretary of State 1947–9, the former US Army COS gave his name to the Marshall Plan, for which he won the Nobel Peace Prize in 1959.

January 11, 1947

Eric rang up this morning. He had reached the Foreign Office soon after 7. He had seen Sargent and dined with Rumbold. They were still in favour of the visit but not enthusiastically so. Massigli was, as usual, pessimistic, saying that if nothing came of the visit it would be playing into the hands of the Communists. He is coming to Paris today. What he will say to Blum and what will be the result of it we can't say. All today was spent in uncertainty and efforts to find out whether Blum will go to London on Monday. If I knew that he were going I should take the Golden Arrow tomorrow.

January 12, 1947

I got up this morning and dressed in complete uncertainty as to my fate. At last about 10.30 Robin Hooper arrived with the news that Blum had decided this morning that he would go to London. At the same time Massigli, who came over yesterday, telephoned to say that Blum had asked him to inform me accordingly. My preparations were all made. Massigli was on the train, sat opposite to me from Paris to Calais and came to have a talk with me on the boat. He said that I was mainly responsible for the visit and that it was therefore up to me to make a success of it. All that I see we can do is to produce an agreed statement which shall contain a plan and a programme.

January 13, 1947 (London)

At 2.45 I left with Eric to meet Blum at Northolt. On the way there I remembered that he is Head of State, and that the King therefore should have sent somebody to greet him. John Addis was representing the Prime Minister and Cheke the Foreign Secretary so I thought that I had better say I was representing the King. I sent Eric on arrival to telephone to the Foreign Office to get approval for this but of course nobody there was prepared to take the responsibility. So I took the risk and when Blum descended I said that the King had charged me to bid him welcome. Later I got on to Tommy Lascelles who said I had done quite right. At 5 we had a meeting in the Secretary of State's room at the Foreign Office. I thought Bevin seemed more tired than usual. Present were Sargent, Hall-Patch, Hoyer Millar, a private secretary and a coal expert. They had prepared a communiqué to be issued on Blum's departure. I thought it very poor – so did Bevin. I found him full of the most admirable sentiments with regard to France, but to every suggestion he made Hoyer Millar raised some objection. Even Sargent became irritated with Hoyer Millar and insisted that we must give something for Blum to take home. After some inconclusive talk four of us went to another room to redraft the communiqué. I got them to put something in it very definite about the alliance.

January 14, 1947

The revised statement looked quite good this morning. I went to the House of Commons where we lunched, ten only. Bevin was in remarkable form and despite the difficulty of language, for Blum doesn't understand a word of English, he managed to keep the thing going in a wonderful way. He ragged me, telling the Frenchmen that I was more French than English, that I had lost all interest in England and that I never stopped telling him what he ought to do to help France. He said that there was only one point on which he agreed with me, namely that the danger still came from Germany rather than from Russia. This was very satisfactory. He told a number of not very funny vulgar stories which were difficult to translate but at which Blum laughed valiantly. At 5.30 we had a meeting in the Secretary of State's room. I think we shall be able to produce an agreed statement which will be really useful and will look as though something has been accomplished, which it will have been.

January 15, 1947

At one I went to 10 Downing Street for lunch. The lunch was good and the atmosphere very friendly. Mme. Blum asked me if I could find a complete Shakespeare in small compass for Blum to give his granddaughter. I dashed to Hatchards where by great good luck I found the very thing – the 3 vol., india paper edition, very nicely bound. It is almost unobtainable. Back to the F.O. where the final meeting with Blum took place in Bevin's room. After Bevin had changed 'May' to 'towards the end of April' there was complete agreement on the text and I felt that something had indeed been accomplished and that I had myself contributed something towards it. Then to try on a new suit – then to play bridge at White's – then to a reception for the Blums at Claridge's. All the big-wigs of the Labour Party were there. Mme. Blum was delighted with the Shakespeare.

January 16, 1947 (Paris)

Bob Boothby joined us for lunch and was very amusing about Winston's new United States of Europe movement, of which the inaugural lunch took place yesterday. John met me at the Gare du Nord with the news that Vincent Auriol[1] had been elected President, and when I reached the Faubourg St Honoré I saw that the Elysée was illuminated and that a floodlit tricolor was flying over it, for the first time for seven years.

---

[1] Vincent Auriol (1884–1966) represented the Socialists on the CFLN. He presided over the two consultative assemblies that drafted the Constitution of the Fourth Republic, and from 1947 to 1954 was its first President.

January 22, 1947

Ramadier[1] succeeded in forming his government this afternoon. Bidault returns to Foreign Affairs. I wonder if he will hold it against me that I got Blum to London and didn't tell him about it when I met him the Saturday night before I left.

January 24, 1947

Ashley Clarke came back from London today. He said the Foreign Office are being very slow and timid about the French treaty. They are a poor lot – all terrified of something – of the Russians, of the Americans, of the Chiefs of Staff, of the Board of Trade, of the Treasury – with the result that they never want to do anything.

January 25, 1947

I went to see Bidault at 6.30. I was afraid he might resent the Blum episode, but he could not have been more friendly. He said that he might have conducted matters differently himself, that he might have postponed the Treaty of Alliance until after Moscow, but that he accepted entirely what had been agreed and that he was prepared to conclude the Treaty forthwith. This was all very satisfactory. The Oliviers[2] arrived this evening – Vivien looking very beautiful and both of them charming. We dined with Frank Pakenham[3] and went to see *La Nuit de la Colère* – a rather good play about the resistance acted by Jean-Louis Barrault,[4] whom we went round to see afterwards.

January 29, 1947

We were only four for lunch today – Juliet [Lady Juliet Duff] and Louise. I find it difficult not to be rude to the former – she is so foolish and her folly is that of a young girl, not of an old woman. People should try to have the faults of their age. In the afternoon I had to put on my uniform, which I don't think I have worn since the coronation – it was quite comfortable, including the boots which I bought in 1913. We attended Vincent Auriol's first reception of the Diplomatic Corps at the Elysée. After the formalities he came and talked to me in a most friendly way, and said that he had urged Blum to go to London and that he was most anxious for the closest Anglo-French relations. When I

---

[1] Paul Ramadier (1888–1961), French socialist politician, served from Jan.–Nov. 1947 as the first Prime Minister of the Fourth Republic, whose constitution had been approved on 13 Oct. 1946.

[2] Sir Laurence Olivier, Lord Olivier (1907–89), actor and director, married Vivien Leigh (1913–67), actress, in 1940.

[3] Francis (Frank) Pakenham, 7th Earl of Longford (1905–2001). Labour politician and campaigner.

[4] Jean-Louis Barrault (1910–94), French actor known primarily for his theatre work, though he made notable film appearances in Marcel Carné's *Les Enfants du Paradis* and Max Ophuls's *La Ronde*.

got back Diana was beginning a reception for all the literary lights and luminaries for Rosamond[1] [Lehmann]. I tried to dodge it but Loulou came to me in the library and said I must go in, as there was some difficulty because Aragon[2] and Malraux were not on speaking terms and were glaring at one another. I went and talked to both of them and to others. They were all *ébloui* by my uniform – Ashley was also wearing his. We dined – just the house party – and all went to Cocteau's play *L'Aigle a deux Têtes* – I didn't think much of it. I like the Lehmanns. I spent half an hour showing my books when we got back. I also like the Oliviers. It has been a happy house party.

February 7, 1947

I had in the morning to dictate a long letter to Oliver Harvey giving my views on the draft treaty. I feel that our foreign policy is paralysed by fear of doing something that somebody won't like. This fear will be increased by a resolution passed by the French Communist Party and published this morning, against making a treaty with England before settling the German question. A telegram came from London about the signing of the peace treaty, saying they were against any speeches being made. This gave me a reason for going to see Bidault this afternoon. He said he didn't think we need worry about the communist resolution. He seemed cheerful and confident.

February 10, 1947

Today was almost wholly given up to signing the five peace treaties with the satellite powers. It began with a short conference at 10 o'clock in Bidault's room, attended by the Ambassadors of the Big Three – at 10.30 these four signed the Naval Protocol, at 11 the Italian Treaty, and the other four at intervals throughout the afternoon. I did hardly any work but read a thriller – *A Gun for Sale* by Graham Greene[3] – very enjoyable.

February 14, 1947. St Valentine's Day

Those who went to London for the wedding of Christopher Soames and Mary Churchill came back last night. The account they give of the condition of London is gloomy in the extreme. They say also that Attlee was as loudly booed as Winston was cheered at the wedding.

---

[1] Rosamond Lehmann (1901–90), English novelist, was in Paris with her brother John Lehmann (1907–87), writer and critic.

[2] Louis Aragon (1897–1982), French poet, novelist and essayist. A founder of surrealism, he later became a political activist for Communism.

[3] Graham Greene (1904–91), author of many novels including *Brighton Rock* and *The Power and the Glory*. He married Vivien Dayrell-Browning in 1927 and worked in MI6 1941–4. After the war he separated from his wife and began a passionate affair with Catherine Walston (1916–78), a rich, American-born beauty and the inspiration for his novel *The End of the Affair*.

February 27, 1947

I had a row with Louise last night. We went to her room before going to bed. Palewski had been dining with her and had filled her up with a lot of nonsense about de Gaulle, so that she told me I was very silly not to pay more attention to the Gaullists instead of wasting my time with old fools like Blum. I told her she was utterly ignorant of politics and always talked arrant nonsense whenever she got on to the subject. Hence a long, beautiful and most touching letter this morning saying she was leaving the Embassy for ever. But we made it all up over a glass of port before lunch. Diana went out to a concert and I gave a dinner party of 14. Bridge afterwards – great fun. I kissed Susan Mary[1] [Patten] for the first time and find her most attractive.

February 28, 1947

Soon after lunch Ashley came with the definite news that the Treaty was concluded, that Bevin and Bidault would announce it this afternoon and that I was to meet Bevin at Dunkirk on Tuesday, where we would both sign it. I was very pleased. It is just three years since I began working for this at Algiers, and although it would probably have come about somehow some time, I honestly believe it would not have been done now if I had not said what I did say to Blum in our first conversation. Eric and I went to the Chamber. We had been told there would be two speakers before Bidault, but he spoke at once. He never speaks well and this was no exception to the rule. He kept the announcement till the end. The applause was universal, and then gradually the whole house rose. The communists applauded less enthusiastically and rose more slowly than the others, but they all applauded and they all stood. It was an impressive sight. Then Herriot, in the chair, interrupted the speaker and said a few words of congratulation. It was a great moment.

March 1, 1947

March came in like a lamb – or more like a lamb than anything we have seen for a long time. It was still cold but there was bright sunshine and a feeling of spring in the air, or so I thought, being optimistic on account of the Alliance. There are endless preparations to be made for the signature at Dunkirk on Tuesday. Everybody wants to go, including the wives, and Bevin is characteristically in favour of everybody going, but the French are against the wives, as they wish the occasion to be solemn and not turned into what they call a 'picnic'. Personally I am indifferent. Diana will anyhow come in the train with me.

---

[1] Susan Mary Jay (1918–2004) married William (Bill) Patten, an American diplomat, in 1939. He was Financial and Economic Attaché at the US Embassy in Paris. He died of emphysema in 1960 and in 1961 she married Joseph (Joe) Alsop, the well-known American columnist.

March 3, 1947

Bevin insisted on making a statement at the signing of the Alliance to the effect that it doesn't interfere with anything else, especially not with the Four-Power Treaty once proposed by Byrnes. Bidault takes great exception to this, says it will spoil the psychological effect. I went to see him this morning and finally persuaded him to let Ashley and Couve [de Murville] get together and produce a text that both could agree to. This they eventually succeeded in doing.

March 4, 1944

Nunc dimittis – the Alliance [the Treaty of Dunkirk] was signed today. We left Paris at 9.50. There was much ceremony, soldiers and red carpet at the Gare du Nord. Diana and I lunched with the Bidaults in their *coupé*. It was cold and damp at Dunkirk. We had nearly an hour to wait for Bevin, and a further rather awkward wait for the treaties which arrived about a quarter of an hour later. However all went well. Both Bidault and I signed. This was followed by a rather pointless but short excursion to the beaches, where we gazed on the desolate sight of a derelict sea coast under a wintry sky – and shivered. Bevin was as usual very friendly to me, and so was A. V. Alexander who came too. Diana and I hurried back to the warmth of the train where I took a Vieille Cure as a protection against cold and where Diana soon started sneezing.

March 13, 1947

President Truman's announcement concerning future American policy is, to my mind, epoch-making – and should be considered entirely satisfactory by us.[1]

March 20, 1947

General de Lattre came to see me this morning. The excuse for his visit was to convey his condolences on the death of Lord Tyrrell [a former Ambassador to Paris]. The reason for it was to tell me that there is a rumour current in the *salons* of Paris to the effect that the British Embassy possesses the card of his membership of the Communist Party. I assured him that no such rumour emanated from here and that I would deny it. He left consoled. The pre-occupation of the day has been my proposed visit to North Africa. It was thought desirable that I should visit Morocco and Tunis. Diana would like to come with me and bring John Julius. But she won't fly and can't bear that I should. The visit would be very pleasant done by plane and the Air Ministry would put a good one at our disposal, but it would be a *corvée* done by road

---

[1] Truman had said, 'I believe it must be the policy of the United States to support free peoples who are resisting attempted subjugation by armed minorities or by outside pressure.' This became known as the Truman Doctrine and marked the start of the Cold War.

and pressed for time. It is very tiresome, but it is no use making her really miserable so I have decided to call it off.

March 24, 1947

I went to see Chauvel this morning to discuss with him a number of matters – first French slackness in preventing illegal departures of Jews for Palestine, second my postponed visit to North Africa (I couldn't tell him that the real reason was because Diana won't let me fly). Chauvel was as usual very sensible, well-informed and helpful – if only it was easier to hear what he says. We talked English, but despite his excellent knowledge of the language he is just as difficult to understand in English as in French.

At the end of March Duff began a new romance with Susan Mary Patten.

March 27, 1947

I had a very successful dinner party – the Pattens, Dimitri,[1] Teddie, John, Ann [Rothermere],[2] Venetia and Ethel [Russell].[3] We played bridge afterwards. I get fonder every time of Susan Mary.

March 30, 1947

It was a fine morning and we got off at about 10.30. The route to Bruneval [*in Normandy, where de Gaulle was going to inaugurate a war memorial*] was well posted. But as we approached, the narrow lanes were so blocked with traffic that despite help from the police it was nearly two before we approached the rendezvous. Here we found General de Gaulle eating langouste. There was no ceremony. The Vaniers were there and all the Gaullists. The General was in, for him, a very genial mood. At 3.00 the General, flanked by Vanier and me, mounted the hillside to the Monument. Organization there was none. Confusion reigned, de Gaulle delivered his speech. There was quite an amount of politics in it although he had said there would be none – but there was nothing offensive as it seemed to me.[4]

April 1, 1947

We got off at 9.30 [*for a holiday in the Rothermere villa in Monte Carlo*]. Diana, John Julius and I sat in the front seat of the Ford, she driving. René Picot [the Embassy chauffeur], Léon the footman and Jacques the *plongeur*, followed in the Rolls Royce. It was a beautiful spring morning and we were in high spirits.

---

[1] Prince Dimitri Romanov (1901–80), Secretary of the Travellers' Club in Paris.
[2] Ann Charteris (1913–81), married first, in 1932, Lord (Shane) O'Neill (killed in action 1944); then, in 1945, Esmond Harmsworth, 2nd Viscount Rothermere; finally, in 1952, after a divorce, Ian Fleming (1908–64), the creator of James Bond.
[3] Ethel Russell, an American friend of Diana's.
[4] A week after this speech de Gaulle announced the creation of his new mass movement, the *Rassemblement du Peuple Français*, or RPF.

On to Saulieu, where we lunched at the Côte d'Or. Diana thought lunch too expensive, 5,000 francs for us three and the three servants. One bottle of wine for us and one for them, one liqueur for me.

April 3, 1947

We found without difficulty the Rothermere villa, Roc Fleuri, which is the most luxurious, perfectly appointed establishment imaginable. Diana and John Julius can't forgive the bad taste and ostentation. To me, the great comfort makes up for them – and I say that you don't expect good taste at Monte Carlo. The whole place is in bad taste and good taste here would be *mauvais genre*.

April 8, 1947

We had to luncheon Herbert Morrison and his daughter – the *ménage* Schmidt – J.J.'s hosts at Strasbourg[1] – and Willie Maugham.[2] I was dreading it, but it didn't go too badly. Mrs Williams (H.M.'s daughter) has never been taught, I suppose, that people should try to make conversation at meals. She gives a short and doubtless correct answer to every question put to her and leaves it at that. The young Schmidts seem a nice couple. After they had gone I picked up a newspaper but found that I was trembling so violently I couldn't read it. I had a kind of rigor. Diana took my temperature which proved to be 103. I went straight to bed and for three or four days I was very ill. On the second morning when Diana took my temperature early she found it was 104. Not unnaturally she was alarmed. Our doctor, Grasset, with whom we have been very well pleased, brought a Parisian colleague, here on holiday, to see me that morning and from then on I had a nurse who gave me injections of penicillin every three hours day and night. I had over a million units in all. At first I suffered terrible gouty-rheumatic pains in my right foot, but these passed and when, about the fifth day, the fever subsided I was fairly comfortable. I got up for the first time on the 15th and came down to lunch on the 17th. The nurse to my great regret left on the 18th.

April 18, 1947

I still go to bed for dinner. The doctor usually comes about dinner time and gives me an injection in the vein. My illness has been illuminated by letters from Susan Mary. I have had three and received a fourth this morning – long, charming letters, very well written. She obviously likes writing them, but I flatter myself she must like me rather, to write them to me.

---

[1] John Julius was spending six months in Strasbourg, studying at the university. He was staying with a young Alsatian couple, M. and Mme. Paul Schmidt.

[2] Somerset (Willie) Maugham (1874–1965), author and playwright, married Syrie Wellcome, née Barnardo, an interior designer, in 1917; they were divorced in 1929. He lived at the Villa Mauresque, Cap Ferrat.

April 21, 1947

Today we made further progress by going out to lunch at La Réserve at Beaulieu. It is a charming place, but Diana was prejudiced against it because it was smart and expensive. I was prejudiced in favour of it for the same reasons. I must say that the lunch was not particularly good, nor was it very expensive.

April 26, 1947

The doctor came this morning with a *régime* that he wants me to follow for five months. He says that this illness has shown that my liver and kidneys are in a bad state, and that it should serve as a warning. The *régime* is very severe – hardly anything am I allowed to eat except fish, chicken and rabbit, and I should have one or two totally vegetarian days each week. Nothing to drink except a little claret. Three weeks in the summer at Contreville or Vittel. I can't do it and don't believe it is necessary. We took Raimund and Liz to lunch at the Sea Bar at Villefranche. We ate *oeufs sur le plat* (I am only supposed to have one occasionally) and red mullet. I dined alone and wrote to Susan Mary. Her letters to me grow more numerous and more affectionate.

April 29, 1947

On this, our last day in Monte Carlo, the weather was perfect. At 6 we had to go to a cocktail party given by Dr Grasset. The doctor, who has strictly for-bidden me champagne, insisted on my having a glass. He said that one couldn't do me any harm. As we need money for our journey, I went to the Casino to cash a cheque. I took 20,000 of it in counters – sat down at the high *chemin de fer* table – put 5,000 *mille* in my bank, ran it four times, passed the fifth when it immediately went down. I came away in half an hour with a profit of 60,000. I was rather sad to sleep for the last time in the room I had come to know so well – and where, in spite of everything, I had been pretty happy.

May 1, 1947 [Geneva]

I found four letters from Susan Mary awaiting me. They have been getting steadily more affectionate and they are a frank confession of great love – so great that she says it is making her ill. She says she has been fighting against it but that it has proved too strong for her. She has never known anything like it before etc. In fact, she hasn't seen me since it began. It is a strange imaginative affair – very flattering to me, but a little disturbing. She is a very sweet and charming girl whom I find most attractive, but it would be dishonest to pretend that I am madly in love with her. Nor have I the slightest desire to cloud the happiness of what has always seemed to me a perfect *ménage*. In her letters she writes of her love for Bill and his unfailing kindness to her, and she adds that gay and careless as he appears on the surface he is *au fond* a New England puritan, and he has told her that if she was unfaithful to him he would never forgive her.

May 4, 1947. Sunday (Paris)

B. Bullitt came to see me this morning. He said that he hadn't quite made up his mind about Chantilly, but I gathered from what he said that he had – and that he will let us have it. The bargain is a very good one from his point of view. He is getting £4,000 for a lease of a few years of a house in which he has no intention of living and which needs money spent on it. He was extremely friendly. The Pattens and Loelia Westminster who is staying with them came to lunch. Susan Mary seemed constrained, nervous and shy. She never looked at me and avoided any opportunity of having a word with me alone.

May 6, 1947

Massigli came to see me. He was less passionate than usual. He thinks the French zone in Germany should eventually join up with the Anglo-American, but not before the next meeting of Foreign Ministers in November. I looked in at the Travellers', where I found a letter from Gloria in which she said that Kenya didn't suit her. As I came out I met Charlie Grey [an American diplomat], who told me that Gloria had arrived today and was at the Crillon. I was rather appalled. Glad as I shall be to see her, I don't want to start all those troubles again. He said she had told him not to tell anyone she was here.

May 9, 1947

Before lunch I went to the Crillon to see Gloria. I found her full of life and spirits, delighted to have got away from Kenya which she hated, and showing very little sign of the baby which she is to have in three months. She is very happy about the baby and about life in general. Ahmed has inherited a lot of money from his grandmother, and a house in Italy which he has gone to see. She is joining him there and then going to Switzerland to have the baby. I was glad to find that I didn't feel the least in love with her, although I was glad to see her again.

I had to go to meet Winston at Le Bourget at 5 and took Randolph with me. Winston brought Clemmie, the Duncan Sandys and Sarah, who was looking very pretty – also a maid, valet and secretary. He is in excellent health and form. He fulminates against the present government and talks a lot of bosh about the United States of Europe.

May 11, 1947

At lunch yesterday Winston promised to attend the review which was to take place this morning. Later in the day he changed his mind, thinking that it would be too tiring. Last night, therefore, I told all concerned that he would not come. This morning because he saw that it was announced in the press that he was coming he changed his mind again. At 10.30 we drove off. It was a mercifully short *défilé* lasting only half an hour. Winston had a wonderful reception and was very pleased with it. We changed and drove down to Chantilly. Winston was grumpy before lunch but recovered afterwards.

After lunch I had a short and very unsatisfactory conversation with Mr Bullitt, the upshot of which was that the Institut [de France, who owned the Château de St Firmin], according to Germain Martin [an official of the Institut], didn't want me as a tenant. We had already got it direct from Germain Martin that they would be delighted to have me. In any case it is no reason for Bullitt not to make up his mind one way or the other, which he still refuses to do. He was leaving for the U.S.A. today and promised me a decision within a week. I have rarely met a man I dislike so much. He is both stupid and crooked. I drove with Winston and Clemmie to the airport. Winston, since his lunch, was in the highest possible spirits and everything was *couleur de rose*. There was quite a crowd assembled to see him off, which pleased him still further.

I drove back to Chantilly where the others had promised to wait for me, but they had just left. I passed the Pattens, who had Ethel [Russell] with them, on the road. We both stopped and Susan Mary got into my car. It was the first time that we had been alone since she discovered her love for me. She was adorable and was very sad to be going to England on Tuesday for a fortnight.

May 17, 1947. Paris

Three letters from Susan Mary this morning including the first one she wrote addressed to Chantilly. She had forgotten to put 'personal' on the envelope so Miss McEntire opened it. I wonder how much of it she read. That ass Peter Quennell rang her up and said 'I hear Duff Cooper is madly in love with you'. This naturally distressed her.

May 30, 1947 (London)

It was 9.30 before I reached the Dorchester. [The rooms] had been freshly done up – a little dinner table was laid for two – the flowers were prettily arranged on it and all looked very attractive. Presently Susan Mary arrived looking very attractive too and we had a lovely romantic evening together. There was a large moon – I repeated a lot of verse to her and walked her home to Grosvenor Square after midnight.

June 2, 1947. London

Our wedding day. I telegraphed to Diana:

> 'Twenty-eight years ago today
> I heard, or thought I heard, you say
> "I will". I answered "So will I".
> How quickly twenty-eight years fly.'

June 3, 1947

I went at 6 to see Betty Salisbury and found it was a cocktail party for young people and the two Princesses. I was pleasantly surprised by them. Their photographs don't do them justice. They have good eyes, beautiful skins and wonderful teeth. They are both definitely pretty – much slighter than I had imagined. Margaret Rose is too small.

In June the US Secretary of State General George C. Marshall made his historic speech offering economic aid to Europe including countries occupied by the Russians.

June 10, 1947

Last night a 'Most Immediate Top Secret' telegram arrived from Bevin on the subject of Marshall's speech at Harvard, instructing me to see Bidault at once with a view of our getting together in order to take proper advantage of Marshall's offer. I saw Bidault this morning. I hadn't very much to say except to suggest that Alphand, who was in any case going to London next week, should be authorized to discuss the question. Bidault was most forthcoming and helpful. He had already given the matter some thought and had useful suggestions to make.

June 14, 1947

I had a telegram from Bevin proposing that he should come here next Tuesday to discuss the Marshall speech with the French Government. I went to see Bidault, who was of course very pleased with the suggestion, but when I said that Bevin hoped also to see Ramadier he said rather peevishly that he didn't want to make it an 'inter-socialist' affair and he admitted that he had been much irritated by Blum's visit to London last January. He had probably reproached himself for having missed the opportunity.

June 17, 1947

I went to Le Bourget to meet Bevin. [He] had tea with Diana and me. At 6 we had a meeting of the delegation. There was almost entire agreement on the line that we should take. The important thing is the approach to the Russians. They must be invited to participate, and at the same time they must be given no opportunity to cause delay and obstruction. This will not be easy.

On 27 June a conference between Bidault, Bevin and Molotov to discuss the Marshall Plan opened.

June 26, 1947

Caffery came to see me at 11. He was as inarticulate as ever but obviously meant well. He read me passages from a letter and a telegram, which he had received from home and which entirely bore out all that I have said to our own people about the Marshall speech. It is unfortunate that it should be referred to as the 'Marshall Plan'. It is we who have got to make the plan, and unless it is a good one the Americans won't back it.

June 27, 1947

I went to meet Bevin at Le Bourget at 11.15. Bidault was there. He told me that Molotov is very suspicious with regard to previous Anglo-French agreements. Bevin seems in good health and spirits. He sat with me in the glass corridor drinking whiskey until luncheon. We sat in sweltering heat from four till eight. Bidault distributed documents in three languages containing proposed agenda. Molotov then suggested that we should first ask the U.S.A. 1) how much they were prepared to give us and 2) whether Congress would agree. I suggested to Bevin that he should say that anybody could foresee the answer, viz. that both would depend on the scheme we put up. He said this. Argument followed. The meeting was adjourned until tomorrow. It was agreed to tell the press nothing at all.

June 28, 1947

I attended a meeting of the delegation this morning. It seems to me that they waste a good deal of time over details – but that I suppose is the duty and the fate of civil servants. We lunched à quatre, Bevin, Bob [Dixon], Eric and I. It seems to me that Bevin has a great grasp of economic and commercial questions – such as few if any Foreign Secretaries have had. The afternoon meeting was to have been at four. It was postponed until five at the request of the Russians. Molotov produced an agenda which on the face of it differed little from that of the French – but his explanation of it made plain that he didn't contemplate asking the other nations anything except a statement of what they wanted from America. He maintained that the nations of Europe all had their own plans for dealing with their own problems, and implied that they couldn't be expected to change them in order to please America nor in order to fit into a general European scheme. This is going too slow. We have got nowhere so far. I wrote a short memo to the effect that we must make sure that we are all trying to do the same thing before we start discussing how we are going to do it.

June 30, 1947

Hall-Patch, Waley,[1] Dixon and I had a meeting with Bevin. Afterwards I stayed with him and talked for some time. He is now entirely in favour of the Western Bloc, of customs union with France, common currency, etc. – everything in fact which I advocated in my despatch from Algiers in May 1944. How long it has taken! The afternoon meeting was at four. Bidault and Bevin both spoke at some length. Molotov then read out a proposition which he had obviously

---

[1] Sir David Waley (1887–1962), Third Secretary at the Treasury 1946–8.

just received from Moscow, and which had no bearing at all on what the other two had said. Bevin replied that this was asking the United States for a blank cheque. They should have broken then, but Bidault said that while there was obviously much in Molotov's statement to which he couldn't agree he would be glad to see it in writing and they fixed another meeting tomorrow.

We had Harold Macmillan to dinner. He has become somewhat verbose – but it all went all right. Caffery came round afterwards and I got Bevin to see him and tell him all that had happened. Bevin impressed upon him the importance of helping France at this juncture. Caffery said that if the Communists got back into the Government, France wouldn't get a dollar from America.

July 1, 1947 (London)

I thought this morning that I would try to get out of going to London. It seemed foolish to go there only in order to dine with Mrs Bevin and to leave Mr Bevin in Paris. However, when I saw him in the course of the morning I found he wanted me to go, in order to see the Prime Minister and to explain the situation. This gives some point to my journey. He is anxious to go straight ahead with the French tomorrow and to issue invitations to all the nations of Europe to join in. I went to see Bevin before leaving. I found him much put out by the French, who wish to present Molotov with another paper this afternoon and give him another twenty-four hours to get over it. He seemed worried and unhappy.

My plane left at 2.10. I went straight to Downing Street and was shown straight in to the Prime Minister. Attlee wasted no time, agreed entirely with the line Bevin was taking and asked me if I thought there needed to be a further Cabinet decision. I said no, but that I thought it would help Bevin to have a message of approval. This was drafted immediately and sent off.

July 2, 1947

I spoke to Bob Dixon in Paris and learnt that all was going well. Molotov had insisted on a further 24 hours, which they couldn't refuse. There was complete agreement between the English and the French.

July 3, 1947

Eric telephoned from Paris this evening to say that all had gone as expected and that the conference had definitely broken down. It seems that the Russians left at 5 a.m. this morning without a word to anyone. Bevin had said 'We now go straight ahead with the Duff Cooper plan'. He was to see Bidault this morning and the invitations to the other Powers were to go out forthwith. It is an important event. It dates the division of Europe into two groups. We have done all we could to prevent this but have failed, and the Western Bloc which I have always advocated has at last been manufactured in Moscow. *Tant mieux.*

Twenty-two countries in Europe were then invited to a conference in Paris to formulate a plan for consideration by the United States Government.

July 7, 1947

I had to visit M. Bidault to discuss arrangements for Saturday's conference. He had wanted to dissuade Foreign Ministers from attending, but Bevin thinks we had better let them come and is coming himself. All is going well so far: the Ramadier government survives.

July 9, 1947

Burckhardt, the Swiss Minister, came to see me this morning with the good news that Switzerland will take part in the Conference. It helps because it diminishes the 'Western Bloc' aspect of the conference and deprives the other important neutral, Sweden, of any excuse for staying out.

I worked all the afternoon, and when I returned went into the *salon vert* where there was the usual collection. Susan Mary was there and she came into the library with me for a few minutes. When we went back I had it seems the marks of powder on my shoulder which Diana brushed off laughing – but Louise took a less light-hearted view.

July 11, 1947

I went to meet Bevin at Le Bourget. I had a cocktail party for the Cardiff Business Men's Club who are taking part in an organized joy-ride to Paris and Prague. There were about 40 of them. They had played a bridge match last night with a French club, of which the members also were invited to the party. Bevin said he would like to see them so he walked into the party. They all applauded him vigorously although I should think they were most of them extreme conservatives. He made them a little speech in which he paid most generous tribute to France, although he didn't know that there were French people present. The latter were of course delighted – so were the Cardiff men and it was all a great success. Bevin seems in remarkably good form, and when Diana showed him to his room he made violent advances to her and seriously suggested that she should sleep with him. These people are indeed surprising.

July 12, 1947

The first meeting of the conference took place this morning. Bidault opened proceedings and proposed that Bevin should preside. Bevin proposed that each delegation should nominate one member of a working committee and that they should start work at once. The whole thing took hardly an hour. Bevin was very pleased.

I think Bevin is rather in love with Diana. He went for a drive with Bob this afternoon and then went to see Ramadier about the case of the *President Warfield*, a ship with 4,000 illegal Jewish emigrants on board which the

French have allowed to sail although we warned them about it. The Quai d'Orsay are genuinely sorry, but the Ministries of the Interior and Transport refuse to cooperate.

July 14, 1947 [Bastille Day]

Bevin drank a good deal at dinner and got very cheerful. Then we all went out on the town. Diana took Bevin and Bob and the detective. I went with Barley [Alison], [Charles] Ritchie[1] and Hall-Patch who turned up just as we were leaving. It was great fun. We got back about 1.30 and found the other party had got in just before us. Diana had had a wonderful time with Bevin, who had been recognized by the crowd and had made them a speech.

July 15, 1947

At 4 took place the final meeting of the Conference. Everything was agreed, everybody was happy. Bevin and I then went in to see Bidault. Chauvel was there. Bidault was very much distressed about reports which had reached him that we were coming to some sort of agreement about Germany with the Americans without consulting the French. Bevin told him all that had happened, and said that Hall-Patch would discuss the subject with Chauvel. He said also that the Americans had wanted to issue a statement on future German policy but that he had begged them not to. When we got back Bevin thought we had better get Caffery round and tell him what we were doing, as Hall-Patch said that General Clay[2] strongly objected to any communication being made to the French on the subject.

July 16, 1947

I accompanied Bevin to the Quai d'Orsay, where he opened the Cooperation Committee's first *séance*. He and Bidault had a few words before parting, in the latter's room. Bidault seemed sad and tired, but he didn't know the worst. I left Bevin at Le Bourget where he took off at 11 o'clock, and drove back with Ashley. Neither of us knew then what I discovered when Sir Cecil Weir[3] arrived from Berlin, namely that an Anglo-American agreement has been concluded for the raising of the German level of industry, the handing over of management to the Germans and other things. This will not only be a terrible blow to the French, but it may bring down the Government and trip up the Conference. The news was broken this evening to Chauvel, Alphand and Couve by Hall-Patch, Fraser and Cecil Weir. It was very badly received.

---

[1] Charles Ritchie (1906–95), Canadian diplomat and diarist. Canadian High Commissioner to London 1967–71.
[2] General Lucius Clay (1897–1978), US Military Governor of Germany 1947–9.
[3] Sir Cecil Weir (1890–1960), Economic Adviser to the Allied Control Commission for Germany 1946–9.

July 17, 1947

Chauvel rang up Ashley last night after having seen Bidault, who was of course much distressed. I sent a couple of telegrams to London in order to impress upon them there the French reaction. *Humanité* has a headline this morning, *Les mères françaises recommencent à trembler*. Bidault feels that Bevin has let him down and deceived him. He certainly didn't give Bidault or me any impression that an agreement had been concluded. I wonder if he realized this himself on Tuesday afternoon. The agreement was made on Saturday in Berlin. At 5.30 Caffery and I were received by Bidault. He handed us both an official note from the Government and also two private letters written in his own hand addressed respectively to Bevin and Marshall. His main thesis is that if this agreement is maintained it will prove that the Communists were right when they said that the main purpose of the Marshall plan was to build up a strong Germany to fight Russia – in that case he had been wrong and would have to resign. His strongest argument is, why raise the level of industry now when there is no prospect of the Germans reaching within the next twelve months the level already laid down? It was a rather painful interview as Caffery and I had nothing to say.

July 19, 1947

The *President Warfield*, whose name has been changed to *Exodus 1947*,[1] was stopped outside Palestine, boarded, a great deal of fighting took place and the Jews were eventually transferred to three ships which are bringing them back to France. It remains to be seen what the French will do when they arrive. The French are very much to blame, and it is due to the Ministries of Transport and the Interior pursuing an entirely different policy from that of the Quai d'Orsay. A telegram arrived this morning to say that orders had been given that no further announcement was to be made in Berlin, and no step taken to implement the Clay–Robertson agreement pending further instructions. This at least is satisfactory.

July 22, 1947

I [went] to a reception given by the Argentine Ambassador for Señora Peròn [Evita Peròn]. I was disappointed in her looks, but I liked her although she neither spoke nor understood anything but Spanish. We seemed to understand each other – perhaps because she's a tart. She drank to me and we clinked glasses.

---

[1] The *Exodus* carried 4,500 Jewish World War II refugees, who were refused entry into Palestine by the British in July 1947. Forced to return in three British ships to French waters and then to camps in Germany, the passengers went on hunger strike to focus world attention on their situation and the need for a Jewish homeland. The refugees remained in Germany until the State of Israel was founded in May 1948.

July 23, 1947

I had wanted to see Bidault last night about the Jewish emigrants and had counted upon seeing him this morning. I learnt that he had left for Rambouillet at 9 a.m. as a Cabinet meeting was being held there. On the telephone he said that he could see me if I went down there, and would have the discussion of the matter postponed until he had done so. I thought it worthwhile to go there, in order not so much to impress upon him but on his colleagues the importance that we attach to the matter. The French have behaved abominably. They had undertaken to inspect visas with care and to enforce the provisions of the safety of life at sea convention – and they allowed five thousand Jews with obviously forged visas to sail in a ship that was unfit, by their own admission, to carry any passengers. I found that Bidault felt just as strongly as I did on the matter. He attributes the blame to Blum who, he thinks, has encouraged the socialist Ministers of the Interior and Transport to take the line they have taken.

July 24, 1947

My chief preoccupation continues to be the return of the wandering Jews. I have come to the conclusion that it will be a great mistake to attempt to land them by force. The French have undertaken to receive them hospitably. I believe that the best plan will be to put before them the alternatives – freedom and hospitality ashore, or to remain on board in prison conditions until they reach a camp.

July 27, 1947. Sunday

Hall-Patch arrived before lunch. The financial situation in England has become suddenly critical. Our dollars will run out in October and we are assured on the best authority that we shan't get any more till the spring. Therefore we are facing a situation as bad as that of 1931. It is largely the fault of the Government, who insisted on going on with their plans of nationalization although they were warned that this might happen. Now Bevin, in conversation with Lew Douglas,[1] has asked that the United States should advance to us, Great Britain, a billion dollars to tide us over till the spring. He made this request without consulting his colleagues, and if it comes to be known – it may well slip out through the State Department – it will do us irremediable harm with all the fifteen other nations now taking part in the conference. It will look as though we had gone behind their back to do a separate deal with the Americans in defiance of the principle upon which the conference is based, and it may blow the whole thing up.

---

[1] Lewis W. Douglas (1894–1974), American Ambassador to London 1947–50.

July 29, 1947

News from Port de Bouc this morning. The Jews have all refused to disembark.
I knew they would – and now we look silly as I told the Foreign Office we
should. You can't forcibly land 4,500 people of all ages and sexes without
great brutality, especially when there is no cooperation from the land. I sent
a telegram in the afternoon to the F.O. advising them to withdraw the ships
immediately.

July 30, 1947

A telegram came from the Foreign Office this morning instructing me to
insist upon the French Government giving full assistance in landing the Jews
by force. It is astonishing and deplorable that a Government department can
be so utterly ignorant, so entirely remote from realities, as to believe that such
a thing is possible. This morning the French press is solid, from the extreme
left to the extreme right, in attacking Great Britain, and the use of force now
against the emigrants would produce an explosion. Nor would the Government contemplate for one moment the possibility of assisting us in such
a policy. I thought the only thing to do was to send Ashley over to London, in
the hope that he might be able to knock some sense into the addled pates of
these ignorant bureaucrats. I felt ill this morning – giddy. Perhaps I drank
too much yesterday – very little really in comparison with what I was accustomed to, but I suppose I can no longer take a normal or subnormal amount.
I drank nothing but water and orange juice all day.

August 8, 1947

The Jewish children at Port de Bouc are suffering from measles. The French
want to bring them all ashore. The mothers will presumably accompany them.
Nothing could suit us better.

August 10, 1947 [Chantilly]

A misty autumn day. Sun and rain struggled for the mastery and neither
won – a few rays of sun, some heavy drops of rain – not a breath of wind –
equable temperature – an agreeable day. Hall-Patch came down from Paris to
keep me informed of latest developments. The question of the possibility of a
customs union is causing difficulty. It would please the Americans, the French
are for it and our Ministers are willing, but officials of the Treasury and the
Board of Trade – pig-headed as ever – won't hear of it. We need only accept
the principle – the thing itself would not come about for years. Hall-Patch
himself is off to Washington at the end of the week – a deputation of officials
to ask for special treatment for Great Britain when our dollars run out in
October. He agrees with me that this is the wrong way to deal with the
difficulty.

August 15, 1947

Napoleon's birthday, the Assumption of the Blessed Virgin, the end of the British Empire in India. In honour of this last event we were compelled to fly the flags of India and of Pakistan over the Embassy. I was reluctant to do so. It may well be that our rule in India had to come to an end. It may well be that the present Government with the aid of Dickie Mountbatten have handled the situation skilfully and have made an exit with the maximum of dignity, but none the less it is a sad day or should be. A grand thing has come to an end and its last day should be one of mourning. Nor do I personally believe that the new régime will bring good to the peoples of India.

August 17, 1947

A happy day. Diana devoted most of the morning to preparing the picnic while I read Lamartine. They have decided to send the Jews to Hamburg – a decision which I warned them would have a bad reception in France.

August 21, 1947 [Paris]

The decision to send the Jews to Hamburg was communicated to them this morning. We had hoped to combine it with a renewed invitation from the French Government for them to go ashore. The Quai d'Orsay agreed but the Ministry of the Interior held it up. When I called on Bidault [he] turned to the subject of the Jews. He said the French Government had been entirely in the wrong. He couldn't defend them, but what did I want him to do about it? To cause a ministerial crisis would only be to shorten the life of the Government by a few weeks. They would now last over the holidays but could not survive until October. I asked what would follow. He said '*Un gouvernement de combat*' of which he would be the chief. It certainly will have something to combat with if it has a combined Socialist–Communist opposition. He was very friendly, almost affectionate. [*The ships sailed for Hamburg on 23 August.*]

August 25, 1947

Alexander Korda[1] came to see me at my request at 12. I offered him the cinema rights of *David* for a million francs, which he agreed to pay for them. Isaiah Berlin[2] came to see me at 3 and showed me what he had so far written of the Marshall Conference report. I thought it very good. I dined with Korda, Rita Hayworth and Cary Grant at Véfour. Rita Hayworth is very pretty but I don't like dyed yellow hair with a dark skin – and she has pretty hands but the

---

[1] Sir Alexander Korda (1893–1956), Hungarian-born film producer and director, married to the film star Merle Oberon 1939–45.
[2] Sir Isaiah Berlin (1909–97), philosopher and historian of ideas. He drafted the Marshall Plan report.

nails were too long and dirty. Odd that a film star should take so little trouble. I liked Cary Grant.

September 3, 1947

This morning I received a letter from the Secretary of State informing me that I am to leave this embassy at the end of the year. It was a very civil letter saying that 'the service I had rendered was of the highest order', that I would 'certainly be remembered as one of the outstanding British representatives to hold this important post' and that it had been very largely due to me 'personally that in these difficult times the position of H.M. Ambassador in France has been fully restored to its recognized place in French life'. He ends by saying that he owes me a debt of gratitude for my help and loyalty, and that he is sad that this happy association should come to an end. No reason is given for the change except the fact that I have been here for three years. It came as a shock and all shocks are unpleasant. I am sad to go, but perhaps it is better now than later. I am sad to leave the house, but not the pomp and circumstance, which I have always felt as a hindrance and have never enjoyed. I should have time now to do something else before I pack up. Diana took it superbly as she always takes bad news, and said that so long as we can make sure of Chantilly she doesn't mind.

On 4 September Duff and Diana went on holiday.

September 4, 1947 (Basle)

It was a long drive to Basle but I had plenty to think about. I am very glad that Mr Bevin's letter arrived just before my departure – it gives me a greater sense of freedom on my holiday and a clearer prospect to consider. It is also much better that I should leave the post now, when I believe most people say that I have done, and am still doing, well, rather than wait until I make some mistake or until people are saying that it is time I went. It is also pleasant to be able, almost for the first time, to think of the future as something that I can control.

September 5, 1947 (Berne)

I slept rather badly last night. I remember how when I resigned at the time of Munich, although I was quite happy and sure that I had done right, I used to dream that I was very unhappy and, waking, would remain so for a while. So last night I was wretched in my sleep to be leaving the Embassy, and waking about 4 a.m. I began to worry, to think that I had been very ill-treated and to compose letters and speeches on the subject. Everything is out of perspective at 4 in the morning which is, in fact, the middle of the night. I turned on the light, read for a little and fell asleep.

September 22, 1947 (Paris)

I had a busy morning and at 12 I went with the Secretary of State to call on Ramadier. On the way I asked Bevin [*who had arrived the previous day*] whether he could tell me who my successor is going to be. He was obviously embarrassed – said it wasn't quite settled but he thought it would be 'Arvey. This is remarkable promotion for one who has never been head of a mission. He will make a respectable if dull ambassador. The conversation with Ramadier went very well and I was glad to have been present. As we came away Bevin said to me 'We've made the union of England and France this morning'. He would certainly like to – and I believe if it were not for other Government departments he might bring it off. Lunch at the Quai d'Orsay. The final meeting of the Marshall Conference took place at 3.30 and lasted until past six. There were no hitches. The speeches were short and good. Everything went like a marriage bell. I came back and dictated an account of this morning's Bevin–Ramadier conversation. Oliver Franks[1] called to say goodbye to me, which was very civil. I like him and I think he likes me.

September 26, 1947 (Opio, South of France)

I had a letter from Susan Mary again today and I wrote to her. I told her that if Mr Bevin were now to change his mind and to ask me to stay on indefinitely at the Embassy, I should feel disappointed. This is true. I have thought so much of all that I am going to do in the coming year that I should think it dull now to have to continue to carry on as I have for the last three years.

October 2, 1947 (Paris)

A lot of letters were awaiting our arrival – at least four from Susan Mary – and a telegram from Auberon Herbert to say that Eddie Grant was dead. I hadn't seen him for about four years but he was one of my few surviving old friends and his death is a great sadness to me. June Capel[2] with her mother dined. I hadn't seen Diana Westmorland for years. I loved her once. She has changed little except that her hair is white.

October 3, 1947 (Ditchley)

About 4 I set forth for Ditchley and I enjoyed the drive. The house was looking more beautiful than ever and the new hostess, Marietta,[3] is worthy of it. I found her beautiful, not the kind of beauty I admire most – big, blonde, serene like a goddess of the ancient world, serious-minded but with plenty of sense of humour. Staying in the house this evening were only Gerry Koch [de Gooreynd] and Susan Mary who arrived after, and Jeremy [Tree], a most delightful boy who made us six. The arrangement of the rooms was admirable. Susan Mary and I, in the pink and blue bedrooms respectively, had practically a flat to ourselves. Bill is in a nursing home in London.

---

[1] Sir Oliver Franks, Lord Franks (1905–1992), chaired the Committee for European Economic Co-operation, which produced Europe's collective response to the Marshall initiative.

[2] June Capel, the daughter of Diana, Countess of Westmorland, married Jeremy, Lord Hutchinson (b. 1915) in 1966. He was the son of the Coopers' great friend, St John Hutchinson.

[3] Marietta Tree, née Peabody (1917–91), married Ronald Tree MP in 1947.

October 4, 1947

This was one of those heavenly days – the kind that I enjoy most in life – beautiful surroundings, great comfort, good fare, cheerful friends, bridge in the evening and love to crown all. There was no flaw in it. Mrs Douglas, the American ambassadress, and her daughter appeared for lunch and stayed the night. Leo and Edwina d'Erlanger[1] came to dinner. I enjoyed every minute of the day and most of the night.

October 8, 1947 (Paris)

I had a letter from Moley Sargent saying that the King's approval had been obtained for Oliver Harvey's appointment as my successor and that I should take the first opportunity of informing Monsieur Bidault and asking for the *agrément* – by letter if necessary.

I am glad to find that Diana is now just as happy about the change as I am and would not have it different. She and I walked up the hill to the Place du Tertre this morning and lunched there out of doors, walking back afterwards. Good exercise. We have much to talk about concerning our future plans, which are much simplified by the offer of the Guinness flat.[2]

October 13, 1947

At 4.30 I went to see M. Bidault, and after discussing one or two other matters with him informed him of my coming departure. He was genuinely moved and quite eloquent in his expression of regret at my going and gratitude for what I had done. He spoke, he said, not only for himself but for the French Government and the French people. He insisted on accompanying me not only to the door but down the steps to my car and he stood by it, at attention, while I drove away. The *huissiers* must have guessed that something was up – and probably guessed right. He did it all with great dignity and it was almost dramatic. I felt quite moved myself.

Duff hoped that following the Treaty of Dunkirk there would be closer integration on military, economic and colonial policies between Britain and France. He had set up an Anglo-French Economic Committee, but also advocated military staff conversations.

October 14, 1947

I walked back from lunch, and worked till 7.30 on a sort of final broadside at Bevin concerning the Anglo-French alliance. I am doing it in the form of a private letter, which enables me to say things that would be improper in a

---

[1] Leo d'Erlanger (1898–1978), banker and director of companies. His wife Edwina died in 1994.
[2] Group-Capt. Loel Guinness (1906–88), married to Diana's niece Lady Isabel Manners (divorced 1951), had offered to lend the Coopers a flat in his house at 69 rue de Lille.

formal despatch and hardly correct in any communication from an ambassador to a Secretary of State. I am shuffling out of my chains while divesting myself of my grandeur.

October 20, 1947

The Foreign Office telephoned this morning. They are anxious to make the announcement of my departure tomorrow. The elections have produced a great victory for de Gaulle. The situation is complicated. Membership of the Assembly is not affected but the position of M.R.P. Ministers is undermined as the M.R.P. is the party that has lost most heavily. It is hard to see what will happen.

October 21, 1947

The announcement of my leaving appeared in the press this morning. There was a surprisingly friendly paragraph in *The Times* and all the French papers were very complimentary. We both received a number of letters. We dined with the Windsors in a room at the Ritz. Wallis was in good form, very gay, and, Diana thought, slightly tight at the end of the evening. The Duke made a little speech about our leaving the embassy, which was very well meant but very embarrassing. I said a few words in reply. Then Gaston rose and made a very charming speech – saying what I had done for France both over getting the Leclerc division sent to England in 1944 and in saving Strasbourg at the beginning of 1945. I was quite touched.

October 25, 1947

I lunched at the Escargot with Louise, André [de Vilmorin] and André Malraux. The last was dramatic about the situation and said the assassinations would begin next week. The Gaullists are very pleased with the story that when the results of last Sunday's elections were coming out on the radio he [de Gaulle] switched it off and played patience. I went round to see Rosita Winston[1] which I had promised to do last night. Rosita was looking far prettier than on the previous occasions when I had seen her. After the other guests had gone she fell into my arms. Anything might have happened, and certainly would have if she had not been momentarily expecting the arrival of the ex-King [Peter] and Queen [Alexandra] of Yugoslavia. She is returning to America on Monday morning. It is too provoking. We took a passionate farewell.

October 27, 1947

The elections yesterday went even more strongly for de Gaulle than those of last week. This morning the General made a statement demanding a general

---

[1] Rosita Winston, wife of Norman Winston (1899–1977), a rich property developer with a villa in the South of France. She was said to be a Cherokee Indian.

election and the reform of the Constitution. I believe he has been rather premature.

October 28, 1947

In the afternoon I attended the *Assemblée*. It was an extremely stormy meeting. Duclos[1] was on the tribune for two hours. It was a remarkable parliamentary performance. He succeeded in goading everybody else to fury while remaining perfectly calm himself. Ramadier, Bidault and Moch[2] were continually popping up to contradict him furiously. This alone could be thought a triumph for a speaker in the House of Commons.

November 3, 1947

In the afternoon, the Duke of Windsor called to say goodbye. He is off to America for the winter. We dined with the President of the Republic at the Elysée. We were told we could bring friends so we took, besides John Julius, Ashley and Virginia, Eric, Louise and Maria de Gramont. Just before we left Eric told me I was going to be given the *Grande Croix* of the *Légion d'Honneur*. It was a complete surprise. Ramadier and Bidault were there with their wives, the young Auriols and one or two of the staff. We were only about 20. The President made a nice little speech when he presented the cross – but did not put it on me or give me the kiss which he probably thought I shouldn't like. I replied as best I could. Then I went into the next room with Bidault who helped me to put on the sash and the star. I was very pleased.

November 10, 1947 [Paris]

It seems that Chantilly is settled at last. I rather grudge the £2,000 we are paying Bullitt, but it is better than being under an obligation to him.

November 14, 1947

I worked at the books until 11 o'clock this morning – I am most anxious to get the library into order before I leave.[3] I have written another strong letter to Bevin about the reluctance of all Government departments to cooperate with the French. This one was provoked by a letter from the Director of Military Intelligence to Guido Salisbury-Jones, in which he said that the Foreign Office was most anxious to avoid anything in the nature of staff talks with the French at the present time. Why, in heaven's name, when many people think the Russians may march to the channel ports tomorrow?

---

[1] Jacques Duclos (1896–1975), later Deputy Leader of the Communist Party.
[2] Jules Moch (1893–1985), Minister of the Interior and Vice Prime Minister, 1947–9.
[3] When persuading the Government to build the library, Duff had undertaken to stock it with appropriate books from his own collection.

November 18, 1947

We had an agitated morning until 11.30 telephoning, doing bits of work, losing Princess Elizabeth's wedding presents etc. We caught the Golden Arrow at 12. At about 10.30 we went to the party at Buckingham Palace. We seemed to be the last to arrive – but we were by no means too late. There seemed to be nothing happening. Everyone was standing round a vast buffet. Presently all the royalties arrived in a herd. The King and Queen came and talked to us. She has grown very large, but she looked queenly and was very well dressed. They were both very friendly. The King was most outspoken, first aside to me and then aside to Diana, in his criticism of his ministers. He seems to hate and despise them. The only one I saw and talked to was Shinwell,[1] with whom I always get on well. I suppose the others had been asked, but they weren't there. The King said rather resentfully 'Bevin said he would come'. Queen Mary also came and spoke to me, and was full of praise for my work in Paris. The Duchess of Kent was looking very beautiful and Princess Elizabeth was looking really charming – everything that a princess in a fairy tale ought to look like on the eve of her wedding.

November 24, 1947

I had lunch with Clarissa. Her latest admirer is Anthony Eden. She had been to stay for a weekend with him in the country. The only other guest was Massigli. I said how incredible it seemed to me that anybody could ask two such incongruous guests, and only two, to spend a weekend in the country. She said that Anthony was quite incapable of arranging a party. What a curious man he is – he has no friends and no real interests outside politics. Clarissa says that he never stops trying to make love to her. Caroline says she has broken off with him completely. They both concur that he doesn't like me – but also that he loathes Winston. He thinks of nothing except becoming leader of the Conservative Party.

November 28, 1947

During dinner came the shocking news that Leclerc had been killed in an air crash. It is a great loss to France. I had known him very little until that recent day in the Black Forest when we were shooting together. I had then liked him so much. He was only 44.

The autumn of 1947 saw Communist uprisings and widespread strikes. Ramadier had resigned on 19 November. Robert Schuman[2] became Prime Minister and Moch

---

[1] Emanuel Shinwell, Lord Shinwell (1884–1986). Labour Minister of Fuel and Power 1945–Oct. 1947; Secretary of State for War 1947–50; Minister of Defence, 1950–1.

[2] Robert Schuman (1886–1963), French Prime Minister Nov. 1947–July 1948, then Foreign Minister. Elected President of the European Assembly in Strasbourg 1958.

took over as Minister of the Interior. At the end of a marathon three-day session in the Assembly the balance of power swung against the Communists and the unrest subsided.

December 2, 1947

I went to the Assembly. That donkey Emmanuel d'Astier was speaking in support of the Communists. I stayed there for nearly two hours, during which there was continual disorder such as would be unimaginable in the House of Commons. How they ever get any business done I can't understand.

December 3, 1947

The Paris–Lille express was derailed this morning and many were killed. This is, of course, the work of the Communists. This afternoon the streets in the neighbourhood of the Palais Bourbon were deserted. There was no traffic in the Champs Elysées. Police were everywhere. I have received such a miserable reply from the Foreign Office about staff conversations – a letter obviously drafted in the department but signed by Bevin. I wrote a furious rejoinder this afternoon.

December 8, 1947

I left the house soon after 9.30 [*to go to General Leclerc's funeral*] accompanied by Eric and Guido. There was a bit of a scrimmage to get to our places in Notre Dame. We arrived only a few minutes before the President of the Republic. The ceremony was fine and impressive, but the twelve other unhappy coffins detracted from the grandeur of the central figure without adding any themselves. One regretted their presence, yet felt doubly sorry for them on that account. A man's funeral is his last appearance and he ought to have the stage to himself. When we left the cathedral soon after 11, there was a question whether to drive to the Invalides or follow the *cortège* on foot. As I was acting *doyen* I felt it behoved me to walk. The sun was shining and I wanted to look at the crowds. It seemed a very long walk down the Rue de Rivoli but I rather enjoyed it.

December 10, 1947

About 12.30 Winston arrived accompanied by Betty Salisbury, Bill Deakin[1] and Sarah. He had also two secretaries, a valet and a detective with him. In the evening took place our famous ball. [*This was the Coopers' farewell party.*] Diana and I began receiving guests at 10.30. We stood there shaking hands until midnight. Most of the *corps diplomatique* came, with the conspicuous exceptions of the Russian, the Pole and the Yugoslav. Of the Government,

---

[1] F.W., later Sir William, Deakin (1913–2005), historian, who was Churchill's principal literary assistant for his six volumes of war memoirs. Warden of St Antony's College, Oxford, 1950–68.

[Robert] Schuman [Minister of Finance], René Mayer, Moch, Pinaud turned up. They were all very pleased to see Winston. I enjoyed the party – and I think everyone did. The women looked their best and were beautifully dressed. I got to bed at 4.30.

December 17, 1947

I rang up Gloria this morning. I found her in great trouble, poor darling. The police had called on her, said they had *de mauvais renseignements* about her, took her to the prefecture, asked her questions, gave her no indication whatever concerning the nature of the charges against her but merely said that they were acting on instructions from the Ministry of the Interior. Finally they told her she must leave France within 12 days. The arbitrary methods of the police when dealing with foreigners are shocking to us English. I told John to go round to the Ministry and to see the Minister's *Chef de Cabinet*. He spent most of the day on the job. The Minister spent most of his day at Cabinet meetings. We were told that the dossier was on his table awaiting his attention and that nothing could be decided until he had seen it. Finally, late at night, came the message that the Minister had been very happy to be of service to me in this small matter, that the whole affair had been completely wiped out and *annulé*. This was very satisfactory and a great relief to Gloria.

We had naturally a very busy day making final preparations for leaving the house tomorrow. I had a farewell interview with Chauvel at the Quai d'Orsay and a useful talk. Thence I went on to the Travellers' and from there to lunch at the Czechoslovak Embassy. They had a large party. I sat between the Ambassadress and Madame Chauvel. The former was, as usual, astonishingly frank. She said that the position of her husband was becoming more and more impossible. They were spied upon by Communist agents in their own embassy – that Masaryk was a broken reed, hopelessly weak – and of no use to Beneš, who was the last and only hope of the country. It is indeed tragic that the country should have escaped from the German frying pan only to fall into the Russian fire. We drifted back to the Embassy – where we had another drink – our last – in the *salon vert*, and the evening ended in a very happy haze. I felt no melancholy at all at the thought of leaving.

December 18, 1947

There was quite a big crowd at the station. We had what the French call '*une très belle gare*'. The Foreign Office was represented by Chauvel and Dumaine, the *corps diplomatique* by the Canadian and Czechoslovak Ambassadors, the Austrian and South African; there was a representative of the President, of Bidault and of the Turkish Ambassador – and really a host of friends including Susan Mary and Bill, the former looking very sweet and sad. We were met at the station (in London) by the Lord Chamberlain, Lord Clarendon,[1] represent-

---

[1] George Villiers, 6th Earl of Clarendon (1877–1955). Lord Chamberlain 1938–52.

ing the King, and Moley Sargent for the Foreign Office. This was an honour I had not expected. The French Embassy, I learnt later, were very much distressed that they had omitted to send anybody. *À propos* of honours, I forgot to mention that a few days ago I had a letter from Bevin offering me the G.C.M.G., which I have accepted. This means that I shan't get a peerage, to which as an ex-Secretary of State I might consider myself entitled. I should like the platform that it affords but I don't feel strongly about it.

December 19, 1947

I went to see Alexander Korda this morning. He told me of his plan to start a branch of his business in Paris. He wants me to be chairman of it. I am inclined to like the idea. It would not mean much work and he suggests a million francs a year and expenses. I shall think about it. I went to the opening of the [Bertram Mills] circus with Pam Berry[1] and John Julius. The lunch was great fun – there was plenty of champagne – the principal article of food was sausage rolls. I thought the circus very good. Between lunch and circus I went to relieve nature where I met the Prime Minister. While buttoning up his flies he congratulated me on the success of my mission and conveyed to me the thanks of H.M. Government. I while unbuttoning mine expressed my sense of the honour done to me and my gratitude to Ministers for their support and confidence.

December 20, 1947

I went to say goodbye to Bevin. Frank Roberts[2] showed me a copy of Bevin's reply to my last *longa et verbosa epistola*. Although obviously drafted in the department it was quite sympathetic and even flattering in tone. And I have gained my point. Staff talks are to take place when Revers[3] comes here in the new year. Bevin also had a long and to my mind very satisfactory conversation with Bidault before he left. I can feel that I have accomplished something. Our talk was, as talks always are with Bevin, a monologue by him on the subject of his own cleverness. He meant to be very civil and grateful to me, but the Graces were not invited to his christening. I felt a little sad as I left the Foreign Office – probably for the last time as a member of the Service. I was very proud when I first went there in October 1913.

December 21, 1947. Sunday

I caught the train for Oxford to stay with Michael and Nic Hornby.[4] Thirty-four years ago I stayed in the same house – Pusey – with my friend Denis

---

[1] Lady Pamela Berry (1914–82), the daughter of Lord Birkenhead, married Michael Berry, later Lord Hartwell (1911–2001), the newspaper proprietor, in 1936.

[2] Sir Frank Roberts (1907–98), Private Secretary to Bevin 1947–9; Ambassador to Belgrade 1954–6 and Bonn 1963–8.

[3] Gen. Georges Revers (1891–1974), French Army Chief of General Staff 1947–9.

[4] Michael Hornby (1899–1987) and his wife Nicole.

Anson as the guest of his uncle, Sir William. It was in September. Sir William, whom I didn't know, lived there with two old maiden sisters. During dinner I received a telegram from my mother to say that I had passed into the Foreign Office. It was a great moment for me which I longed to celebrate, but I could do nothing about it except inform my host who congratulated me in a courteous stately manner and drank a glass of port to my health. That was the beginning of my connection with the Foreign Office which ended yesterday. The morrow was I remember a beautiful September day. I long looked back upon it as the happiest day of my life. Within a year Sir William, his brother who was Dennie's father and Dennie himself, who had then become the baronet, were all dead.

December 31, 1947

This morning I went to see Harry McGowan,[1] who offered me £500 a year to act as Paris consultant to I.C.I. I accepted. Brendan had arranged this and assures me that there will be other directorships coming along. [Later] I came back and dressed for the Three Arts Ball. I had only a cloak, a mask and a three cornered hat over my ordinary clothes. Diana at the last moment borrowed a Gordon Highlander's bearskin, and a plaid from Scott Adie, and looked quite wonderful. I was in a very happy mood – the brightly coloured scene, the general gaiety and memories of the past all went to my head. I enjoyed myself madly – I felt that being no longer an ambassador I had the right, for once at least, to throw decorum away. I made love to everybody, to Caroline, who was in a heavenly mood, to her sister Rose [McLaren], whom I hardly knew before, to a lady whose name I don't know but with whom I pledged to lunch on Friday – to a very pretty widow called Diana Goldsmith,[2] a relation of the friends I made at Deauville. I also it seems had, at one time, Dick Wyndham's[3] pretty mistress on my knee and this annoyed Diana, who left in anger. But I had a wonderful time.

So ends this year – the third of my term in Paris, the fourth and last of my diplomatic mission. I would not have it otherwise. I have had enough of diplomacy and I am looking forward to a different life.

1948

After leaving the Embassy Duff and Diana settled permanently at the Château de St Firmin at Chantilly, with a pied-à-terre in Paris made available to them by Loel Guinness at 69 Rue de Lille.

---

[1] Harry McGowan, 1st Lord McGowan (1874–1961). Chairman, ICI Ltd, 1930–50.
[2] Diana Goldsmith (1912–99), married first Anthony (Tony) Goldsmith (d. 1943) and second, in 1949, Henry Bleeker, an American.
[3] Maj. Richard (Dick) Wyndham (1896–1948), an artist, was killed in Palestine the following year.

January 1, 1948

I woke up feeling none the worse for the excesses of last night. I called on Korda at noon and we concluded our agreement. I accepted the post of Chairman of the French subsidiary company of London Film Productions. I am to receive for 'my general expenses one million francs per annum, payable quarterly in advance, starting today'. This seems to me very satisfactory. I like and trust Korda.

January 2, 1948

Correspondence begins to accumulate. How I shall get on without a secretary I don't know. There are a lot of letters congratulating me on my G.C.M.G., which is really not much to be congratulated upon. No ambassador in Paris has ever failed to acquire it since the Order was invented, and the Foreign Office have shown how much importance they attach to it by conferring it simultaneously on my successor Oliver Harvey, who is, I suppose, the least distinguished man who has ever been appointed to the post. I cannot think of any previous nominee who had not been at least an ambassador or Permanent Under-Secretary for Foreign Affairs before he is appointed. I want to be known as 'Sir Duff' not 'Sir Alfred' but I'm not sure how that is done.

We dined with Emerald. She had Moley Sargent, the Abingdons, Raimund and Liz. I thought this evening how curious it is that certain marriages succeed and others fail. Nobody who knew them both when they were young would have thought that the Abingdons would have remained happily together all these years.

January 13, 1948

I didn't feel well today. I suppose I have been eating and drinking too carelessly. I went down to Fleet Street this morning to see Mr Watson[1] of the *Daily Telegraph*. It is suggested that I should write articles for them. I said I could do some on foreign affairs – and asked £100 an article. Frank Owen[2] mentioned £125 to me, but I would rather write for the *Telegraph* than the *Mail*.

January 16, 1948

We had a terrible rush to get off this morning. A number of people met us at the Gare du Nord and Tanis[3] was waiting for us at the Rue de Lille, where

---

[1] Arthur Watson (1880–1969), editor of the *Daily Telegraph* 1924–50.

[2] Frank Owen (1905–79), Liberal MP 1929–31, editor of the *Evening Standard* 1938–41 and the *Daily Mail* 1947–50.

[3] Tanis Guinness (1908–93), married first Hon. William Montagu, then in 1937 Howard Dietz. They divorced in 1951, when she married Lt.-Cdr. C. E. H. (Teddie) Phillips, former Comptroller of the Embassy.

everything was arranged charmingly for our reception. Jacques Franck had a cocktail party prepared for us where we met all our old friends, all the denizens of the *salon vert* . . . and it was all very gay and welcoming.

January 17, 1948

We are quite comfortable in our new quarters, although there are no bells and we have to telephone, through the exchange, to the other side of the house in order to get a servant. We gave lunch to Eric Duncannon and Donald Mallet [Press Attaché]. They were full of slightly malicious stories about the new régime at the embassy. We were fortunate when we came in that we succeeded nobody. When I came back [*from seeing the Pattens*] I found Gaston Palewski with Diana. He is entirely occupied with politics these days. The Gaullists are confident.

We set out for dinner on foot. It began to rain. The first two restaurants we tried were shut. We got quite wet before we arrived at Porquerolles, where they gave us an excellent dinner. We ordered white wine but they brought champagne for which they refused to let us pay. I thought it a very pleasant evening, but we got wet again walking home and when we were in bed I found that Diana was crying. She is really unhappy about the fall from grandeur and this evening's walk brought it home to her. I was deeply touched and surprised. I have many weaknesses but have never cared for being grand. I liked living at the Embassy which we made very comfortable, but I always felt there as though I was living in a hotel. I felt the same at Admiralty House. I left both of them with less regret than I shall feel if, as seems not unlikely, we have to leave our cottage at Bognor. I suppose that Diana also enjoyed the position and enjoyed entertaining, although she often complained of it at the time. One always enjoys doing what one does very well. To me the restoration of liberty makes up for everything – but I am sad that she should be sad.

January 18, 1948. Sunday

We had the car and chauffeur of Rufus at our disposal today. We drove down to Chantilly, where we had lunch at the Tipperary Bar. I thought it very good but Diana found it too expensive. She can't get used to present prices or dissuade herself from the conviction that she is being robbed. We went to our house. The sun was shining and the exterior looked lovely – lots of snowdrops and aconites in the garden. The interior is still in great confusion, and not much progress that one can see has been made. We came back. Diana went to get her own car, the Ford, from the Embassy garage. There were more tears at passing by the Embassy again. Later we drove down in her car to Verrières. There was a long and violent argument afterwards, Pierre [de Bénouville] and André [de Vilmorin] being the principal speakers, on the subject of de Gaulle's industrial policy. He has produced some half-baked scheme of profit-sharing and associating the workers with the direction of industry, to which, especially to the second part of it, the Vilmorins are strongly opposed. André certainly had the better of the argument. The truth is that there are people like the Gaullists who think that to defeat Marxism you have got to produce something better. I think this is an error. To begin with they won't produce anything better. Nor are theories defeated by better theories. They die of exposure. I am very glad that Louise, under the influence of her brothers, is turning against the Gaullists because I believe they are a menace.

January 20, 1948

I walked to the Travellers' before lunch. I found a letter there from Rosita Winston complaining of the behaviour of Ghislaine de Polignac who had gone to America as her guest, she paying for her journey and presenting her with a trousseau, for which Ghislaine showed her gratitude by immediately getting into bed with Mr Winston where Mrs Winston eventually found them. Ghislaine returned in ignominy and is now hiding her shame at Rheims and Rosita, so she says, is probably divorcing her husband.

January 21, 1948

We started off this morning about midday for Chantilly – Diana, Rufus and I. We spent the afternoon at our house – Diana interviewing the architect and the plumber, Rufus and I unpacking wine. We unpacked and stacked about 300 bottles of champagne. I have got a supply of wine there that should last me for a long time.

January 27, 1948

Louise came with a car just before luncheon and said she would drop me wherever I was lunching. I was going to meet Susan Mary chez Larue but I couldn't tell her so and had to be driven to the Travellers'. We had a highly successful lunch and Susan Mary was extremely sweet. I am very fond of her. Korda telephoned from London and said that the fall of the franc would of course cancel our previous agreement, which he would change to a similar one adjusting my remuneration in the light of the present rate of exchange. This is very good of him, as I suppose he would have been perfectly justified in holding me to the terms of the agreement recently concluded.

February 8, 1948. Sunday (Paris)

Again this morning I spent from 11 to 1 at my writing table. I wrote short letters to Rose and Daphne[1] [Bath] but most of my time was given to business letters, all of which I could have dictated in ten minutes. Susan Mary told me rather solemnly today that she is going to have a baby and that it will probably

---

[1] The Hon. Daphne Vivian (1904–97), married first, in 1927, Henry Thynne, 6th Marquess of Bath (1905–92), divorced 1953, and second, in 1953, Maj. Xan Fielding (1918–91), divorced 1978.

arrive at the beginning of July. She has been married nine years but this is her first. She was very sweet this evening.

February 13, 1948

I lunched at the Embassy. It was the first time I had been there since I left. Of course I was prejudiced, but I did feel that the Harveys had diffused an atmosphere of dankness and gloom. There were dreadful little green plants dotted about – such flowers as there were seemed faded and ill-arranged – there was no personal touch and the familiar rooms looked like rooms in a hotel – lifeless. I thought the food inferior. After lunch the men were hustled into one corner of the *salon vert*, where they remained seated until Corbin [Charles Corbin, former French Ambassador to London] mercifully got up to go.

February 19, 1948 (London)

I went to White's where I got a message from Buckingham Palace that lunch was at 1 instead of 1.15. Slight panic as there was no means of getting hold of Diana, who had gone shopping. Fortunately however she went back to the Dorchester and got the message and we arrived at the Palace on time. I was taken with the King and was given the accolade and the insignia of the G.C.M.G. Then we had luncheon – only the King and Queen and the two Princesses. We enjoyed it enormously. Conversation never flagged and was really amusing. Margaret Rose is a most attractive girl – lovely skin, lovely eyes, lovely mouth, very sure of herself and full of humour. She might get into trouble before she's finished. The Duchess of Edinburgh will probably make a better Queen.

February 21, 1948 [Paris]

Diana still suffers from nostalgia for the Embassy, I, on the other hand, am glad on returning to Paris not to have to face accumulation of work and appointments.

February 22, 1948

My 58th birthday. It sounds terribly old but I feel as young as ever and enjoy all the pleasures of life as much as I did. I suppose that my political and diplomatic career is over. I feel no regret and rejoice in my liberty. There are three or four books that I should like to write before I die, but it won't matter much if I don't. Diana and I dined in the house off soup and eggs and bacon. We read aloud Evelyn Waugh's latest effort *The Loved One*. It is brilliantly funny, beautifully written and most enjoyable, but he makes to my mind the fault he has made before by introducing real tragedy into a frame of uproarious comic satire. It is typical of his own unhappy character.

February 27, 1948

It occurred to me that my midnight thoughts about Czechoslovakia,[1] which I had been shaping into a letter to *The Times*, might more profitably take the form of an article for the *Daily Mail*. In the afternoon I began the article and then went to see Daisy [Fellowes] at the Ritz. She is living in the most magnificent apartment on the first floor, and *vendeuses* from Dior were showing her dresses and drinking her champagne. It was an exhibition of great wealth.

March 1, 1948 [Piencourt, Normandy, Tanis Guinness's house]

This was an even lovelier day than yesterday – real spring weather and really warm. Diana and I went for a delightful walk in the woods. I think she is a little envious of all the farming facilities here which will be lacking at Chantilly. The charm of amateur farming caught many people in wartime and persists in peace. It makes no appeal to me, and in normal conditions I believe it to be merely a hobby more or less costly in accordance with the scale on which it is undertaken. Normally it must always be cheaper to buy one's agricultural produce.

March 5, 1948

Mr Robertson and a colleague representing I.C.I. came to see me yesterday about the import of something called 'perspex' into France. It is being held up allegedly owing to French lack of sterling, but actually, they suspect, owing to the machinations of a rival French firm called Althom. I went therefore this morning to see Nathan at the Ministry of Finance and found him most sympathetic. I hope I shall be able to fix it and thus earn the £500 a year I get from I.C.I.

March 10, 1948

As I was walking to the Travellers' this fine spring morning I saw the headline of an afternoon newspaper 'M. Masaryk se suicide'. It came as something of a shock. I had been thinking ill of poor Jan Masaryk whom I had always liked. I had suspected him of weakness, and of an inclination to drift with the tide. I must say that suspicions had been confirmed by Madame Norek [the Czech Ambassadress] when we lunched at the Czech Embassy the day before our departure last December. Poor Jan – he was a very likeable man and one who enjoyed life.

March 17, 1948 (London)

I spent an anxious morning worrying about my speech. I went to the Royal Empire Society at 1 o'clock, where I had an unpleasant experience called 'a

---

[1] On 20 Feb. the Communists, under Soviet direction, took over the Czech Government. Duff felt that this was in many ways worse than Munich.

sandwich lunch' which lasted only half an hour. I then made my speech which really went very well. The audience were all most enthusiastic and said it was wonderful. I was glad when it was over.

April 11, 1948. Sunday (Chantilly)

Beautiful sunshine all day long. I finished my work in what I call cellar B. There are in that cellar 799 bottles of champagne plus 10 magnums and 6 rehoboams – and 203 bottles of various kinds of white wine – 1 magnum of *marc du champagne* and 2 magnums of armagnac.

April 22, 1948

The afternoon before we left London Diana saw a doctor who was strongly in favour of drugs. She has always been afraid of sleeping draughts and takes them very rarely. He recommends taking them every night and has given her other things to take. So far the cure is working admirably and she has been quite different and in good spirits ever since we returned, although there have been many tiresome difficulties attendant on *déménagement*. This morning we drove down to Chantilly. Progress has certainly been made with the house and it should really be finished now in a few weeks.

April 27, 1948

We dined with the Rothermeres. I wore my G.C.M.G. for the first time. Magdalen Eldon [Countess of Eldon] told me I had got it on wrong as it should really go over the shoulder but under the arm. I stripped after dinner and she fixed it for me with a safety pin. We went to Buckingham Palace at about 10.30. It was a real dance and was in full fling when we arrived. The first person we ran into was Queen Mary, who was very friendly. Later I had a long talk with the Queen, which is always a great pleasure for me. She was as charming as ever and talked so sensibly about everything. Aneurin Bevan[1] was there in an ordinary blue suit. The Queen intended to say something to him about it if she had the opportunity. I saw him coming towards where we were sitting at one moment, but he must have sensed danger for he swerved off.

April 30, 1948

So ends a third of this year. I have thoroughly enjoyed these four months. I have been glad to be my own master and to be rid of responsibility. Never for a moment have I regretted either the Embassy, the Cabinet or the House of Commons. I am however a little sorry that we shall not be at the Embassy for the visit of Princess Elizabeth next month. We could, I feel sure, have made a great success of it and the best that we can hope for the Harveys is that they will not make a great failure. They are parsimonious, have no imagination and, above all, are so terrified of doing the wrong thing that they can seldom

---

[1] Aneurin Bevan (1897–1960), Labour Minister of Health, 1945–51.

do the right one. The only cloud over my happiness during these months has been Diana's health, or rather her spirits. The latter have improved enormously since she went to the new doctor in London, but I fear that an improvement which depends on drugs can hardly be permanent. We must hope for the best. Although I have done no work during this period on any of the books I mean to write I have not been wholly idle. I have done a little work for I.C.I., a little less for Korda, I have hopes of getting a directorship of the Wagon-Lits and fainter hopes of the Suez Canal. I have written five articles for the *Daily Mail*. I got 400,000 francs for the first four and have demanded 200,000 for the fifth which appeared on Thursday. This I did because Ann Rothermere told me they were re-selling my articles in America and making a profit on them. If my new life goes on as it has started I shall have no cause for complaint.

May 2, 1948. Sunday [Chantilly]

Today the weather was worse than yesterday. It hardly stopped raining. Diana was in very poor spirits. The difficulty of getting into this house combined with the difficulty of getting into the flat in Paris, the number of things lost and broken and above all the incompetence of such servants as we have collected depress her unduly.

May 6, 1948

Barley came to see us. [She] told us that Pierre de Gaulle, the President of the *Conseil Municipal*, sent the Embassy a list of the guests he was inviting to meet the Princess. Oliver Harvey sent it back, objecting to certain names on the ground that they had been collaborators – among others the Brissacs whom we always received. It seems to me the height of impudence for an Englishman to tell a Frenchman, especially a brother of General de Gaulle, whom he should receive of his own compatriots and whom he shouldn't. And surely it shouldn't be our policy to keep alive the divisions and the rancour between the different parties in France, but rather to do all we can to bring them together.

May 7, 1948

I took a taxi to the hairdresser and had my hair cut, thence to the Travellers' Club and thence to lunch with Nancy Rodd [Mitford] in her charming apartment in the Rue Monsieur. The main subject of conversation everywhere seems to be who has and who hasn't been invited to the Embassy to meet the Princess, and stories of the many mistakes the Harveys are making. I have no doubt that people talked in exactly the same way about us when we were at the Embassy. Diana saw Jean, our former *maître d'hôtel*, this afternoon. He did us extremely well for the last three years. He knows how to run a house and he knows our ways. He has agreed to come back to us and to find us a good cook, a good maid and an *homme de ménage*. We shall get rid of the cook, of André and of Thérèse. I hope that Georges will stay. This decision has had a wonderful effect on Diana's spirits.

May 8, 1948. Chantilly

The cow and four pigs arrived this morning. There was naturally great excitement and Diana was much delighted. An equally important event was the sacking of the servants. I told André, who took it well.

Winston made his great speech at The Hague yesterday. I thought it all rather nonsense. They talk of electing a European Parliament at once. But what is the good of a parliament without a government? It can produce nothing but hot air and squabbles. I was disgusted by his making all the delegates give a special cheer for the German delegation.

May 9, 1948. Sunday

Diana heard today that the Harveys have taken up the dark green carpet in the library and cut it up for stairs and passages. They have also changed the dark green curtains in the same room. She was really deeply hurt. It is an extraordinary thing to have done, as neither of the Harveys ever go into the library. The carpet and curtains were in the best of taste and quite new. She thinks it was done entirely out of spite and swears she won't go to the reception for Princess Elizabeth. Eric can hardly contain himself on the subject of Harvey, who he says sees nobody but the socialists, whose political predictions are always wrong and who has no friends here or in England. He tells me that he is cordially disliked by everybody in the embassy. One cannot repress a certain *Schadenfreude*.

May 15, 1948

We dined with Philippe de Rothschild. We were in full evening dress preparatory to the reception at the Embassy for Princess Elizabeth. I was bound to admit it was a good party and well done. Only British colony and French officials were invited – no *corps diplomatique*, no *monde*. Gerry Wellington [the Duke of Wellington] was there. I took him up to see the library. They have quite ruined it with hideous carpet and curtains – and the bust of the great Duke which Gerry presented and which I had put on the mantelpiece has disappeared. Also the Duke's portrait by d'Orsay has gone, nobody seems to know where. The Princess was looking very pretty, I thought, and I was glad to see again some old friends such as Bidault, Moch and Chauvel.

May 18, 1948

The getaway from the dirty, deserted flat this morning was fraught with difficulty and it was one o'clock before we were on the road. When we arrived at Chantilly we found that Jean, our former *maître d'hôtel* in the embassy who has come back to us bringing with him a new cook and an *homme de ménage*, shortly to be followed by a real lady's maid, had already worked a complete change at the Château. We had an excellent lunch and dinner and passed a happy peaceful afternoon and evening. I wish we could stay here indefinitely and had not to go to Paris on Thursday and to Brussels next week. Diana's spirits are a little better.

May 22, 1948

What a fearful muddle we have made in Palestine. It is one of the sorriest chapters in British history. I happened to come across the speech I made on the subject in the House of Commons in 1939. I am still of the same opinion. Had we come down firmly on the side of the Jews we could have made a national home for them. The Arabs would have accepted the situation. But the Foreign Office is always frightened of the Arabs and all our Middle East experts love them. I said then that the policy of giving a fair deal to both sides had failed and would continue to fail. Therefore we had to choose sides. I advocated backing the Jews. But if we had backed the Arabs, although it would have been a breach of the Balfour declaration, it would at least have worked.

May 29, 1948

Alfred Beit and his wife[1] came to lunch. They contrived to let the cow escape from the island and Diana had to pursue through nettles and was terribly stung – suffering all night from it.

May 31, 1948

This morning, as I was writing my diary, Diana arrived in triumph bearing the two missing boxes which contain my diary of three years. She had found them in a cupboard that had not before been opened. This is a great weight off my mind. Diana was rather depressed again today, but we got a lot done. It depresses her to think that our time is so short. She has no philosophy and such religion as she has gives her no comfort.

June 2, 1948

This was our wedding day. We have been married twenty-nine years. I gave Diana the following verses which made her cry.

> Fear not, sweet love, what time can do –
> Though silver streaks the gold
> Of your soft hair, believe that you
> Can change, but not grow old.
>
> Though since we married twenty-nine
> Bright years have flown away

---

[1] Sir Alfred Beit, 2nd Bt. (1903–94), financier, philanthropist and art collector, married Clementine Mitford in 1939.

Beauty and wisdom, like good wine,
Grow richer every day.

We will not weep though spring be past
And autumn shadows fall.
These years shall be, although the last,
The loveliest of all.

June 20, 1948. Sunday [Hatfield House, home of the Salisburys]

I spent most of the morning writing. Only part of the house is open, so that I had to sit in a room which people were constantly passing through. There was no peace. Winston has brought a poodle with him and a detective. In the course of the afternoon the detective lost the poodle and a great dog hunt ensued. It was exceedingly ridiculous and extremely funny. Tea followed and conversation until dinner. After the ladies left Winston became, for the first time during the visit, in admirable form. He and I talked across the table and were both pretty good – nor did we quarrel for once.

June 29, 1948

I met Nancy Cunard at the Gare du Nord and we travelled down to Chantilly. She is in a state of great alarm because she has heard that the police are making enquiries about her. She has the same horror of police that her mother has always had. Is it due to Irish blood? I told her not to worry – that the police always enquire about people in France and that a British subject has nothing to fear. She has of course been mixed up with the Communist party although she swears she hasn't, and they are simply checking up on her. Diana sat up late with Nancy telling her she should go to see her dying mother, and was so far successful as to induce her to say that she would go if her mother wanted to see her.

July 2, 1948

I had my hair cut and went to the Travellers' – thence to lunch at the Embassy where they had a party for the Windsors. I sat between Lady Harvey and Daisy. I must say that the food was admirable, as good as ever we had, and I thought that everything was very well done. I thought the Windsors looked faded and worn, but they were very friendly and I was glad to see them.

July 23, 1948

Diana and John Julius picked me up at the Travellers' and we caught the night ferry. Diana was in a bad unhappy state on going to bed. She is bored – she needs excitement. She misses her admirers. She is sad about Emerald – and about Venetia[1]. She hates old age and she fears death. I wish I could help her – but I don't seem to be able to.

---

[1] Emerald, Lady Cunard, died on 10 July 1948, while Venetia Montagu died on 3 August of that same year.

July 24, 1948 (London)

I went straight to White's and remained there throughout the morning. It is remarkable how quickly the time passes there. I then picked up Diana and John Julius at the Ritz and we drove down to Breccles. It is nearly 30 years since I first went there in November 1918. I was on leave from France, and the Monday of that weekend was Armistice Day. Diana of course was there. It was eight months before we were married. That was the beginning of Breccles – one of the places we have been happiest in – and this perhaps is the end. Venetia is very ill – cannot leave her bed – and probably never will. She is very brave.

July 26, 1948

Having said goodbye to Venetia, perhaps for the last time, Diana and I drove to London taking Isaiah [Berlin] with us. He talked incessantly all the way – two hours and a half. Later we caught the night ferry to Paris. Diana fell into a mood of deep dejection. I tried in vain to cheer her.

August 4, 1948

Today we heard the sad news of Venetia's death. She died yesterday. It is the end of one of my oldest friendships. I remember the evening that I met her at the Desboroughs at Taplow and took her in to dinner. It must have been in 1912. She married in 1915.

August 16, 1948 (Venice)

I felt rather unwell this morning and unwisely told Diana, which further increased her gloom and melancholy. During these days when everything has been perfect she has been getting more and more depressed.

August 17, 1948

The Trees gave us dinner at our hotel – and we went in the gondola after dinner to see Colleoni by moonlight. The moon was almost full. There were a few storm clouds about and the sight was indeed magnificent. Alone worth coming to Venice for. Diana told me she had had today one of the worst days of depression that she remembered. It is very sad and quite inexplicable. I thought she cheered up a little this evening.

September 1, 1948

I am glad that August is over. It is a holiday month and should be one of the happiest, but I have no very pleasant recollections of it – except at Clovelly long ago. I prefer September and October. Nor has this holiday been so far entirely successful. Diana's melancholy has spoilt it. She now attributes it to my health, but the truth is that her spirits have been at their worst when my health was at its best. A minor cause has been the lack of congenial company in Venice. However we were both glad to leave this morning. My health was excellent and Diana's spirits rose.

September 3, 1948 (Portofino)

It is just a year since I received Bevin's letter telling me I was to leave the Embassy. During the last nine months I haven't once wished I was back there. It is four years since we left Algiers for Paris via London. It is eight years since the war began. It is also the day of Cromwell's crowning mercy[1] and the day of his death.

September 14, 1948 (Avignon)

We rang up Winston at the Roy René and found that he was expecting us to dinner. On arriving there we learnt that Clemmie, suffering from a septic tooth, had left for London by air this morning. I'm afraid her absence increased the gaiety of the evening, which was extremely gay. The other guests were Bill Deakin, whom I like very much, and Lord Cherwell, the 'Prof'. Winston was in wonderful form. We had first to inspect his pictures, which I find difficult to judge but with which he himself is delighted. It is wonderful at the age of 74 to be able to say with conviction and gusto 'I have never painted so well'. The dinner was first rate, the drink admirable and plenteous, the conversation highly animated. After dinner Diana and I played Oklahoma with Winston. He is an enthusiastic devotee of the game which he has only recently learnt. 'For a quarter of a century' he said 'I have played six-pack bezique, but since I learnt Oklahoma I have thrown all six packs away and I shall never look at them again.' He plays very badly.

September 16, 1948

We started soon after half-past eight. The first disaster was that shortly after Le Puy we ran out of petrol. At last a small car passed which gave Diana a lift to where she could get help. I remained waiting. Fortunately I had a book to read. Later in the morning the car stopped for no reason that we could discover. We assumed it was bad petrol and after half an hour it went on again. All went well in the afternoon until about 6 o'clock, when, just as we were approaching Montargis, the car showed symptoms of the same malady from which it had suffered in the morning. Further delay and consultation with experts. There was an improvement, but between Montargis and Fontainebleau Diana stopped to clean the windscreen and nothing would persuade the car to start again. Another gloomy expert and a lot of tinkering produced some result and we finally reached Paris a little before 9. So ends a holiday that has upon the whole been very successful. Beginning on August 7th and lasting until now it has been, I think, the longest holiday I ever had. My constant care has been Diana's happiness. She began well. Her spirits soared

---

[1] His victory over Charles II at the battle of Worcester.

at Geneva – sank a little because I wasn't well and then fell below zero during nearly all the time at Venice, reviving only during our short visit to San Vigilio.[1] At Portofino they recovered completely and she says that during the last days she was as happy as she could be. This kept up at Opio and she enjoyed Aix, but today I fear that the prospect of the return is already beginning to depress her. She needs excitement and admiration and occupation without too much responsibility.

September 30, 1948 (London)

At luncheon today Rupert [Hart-Davis] told me about Hugh Walpole's diary. He is writing Hugh Walpole's life. He told me that the diary showed up what a coward he was and how he dreaded in the war of 1914 being compelled to fight. He had no cause to fear it because he was hopelessly short-sighted, but none the less he managed to dodge it until nearly the end of the war when he was passed unfit. 'Why do people keep diaries?' asked Rupert, and I found it difficult to answer. 'Is it because you look forward to re-reading them?' I don't think so. I don't enjoy re-reading mine. 'Are you thinking of posterity reading them?' I don't think I am, but I may be. I don't want Diana to read my diary and she is closer to me than any human being – nor should I particularly like John Julius to. There is much that I shouldn't mention if I wanted them to read it. Perhaps the answer is that people who love life as much as I do want to keep some record of it – because it is all they can keep.

October 5, 1948

A fine morning in Paris. I went to the Café de Paris where I had lunch in a private room with Susan Mary.[2] This was the first occasion that we have been alone for a very long time and we took full advantage of it. But she said we mustn't do anything so dangerous again. She used never to have any sense of danger and was often, I thought, extremely imprudent, coming to lunch with me in her car with the chauffeur driving. It now seems that last spring Bill made her a great scene of jealousy about me. I had no idea of it.

October 24, 1948. Sunday (Rome)

Another beautiful morning. Diana went off with Ned and Joan[3] to do St Peter's and the Vatican. The latter was shut but Diana managed by her method of persistence and persuasion and refusing to take no for an answer not only to get in but to be shown over by a Monsignore and to be admitted to many places that are not open to the public. Nevertheless I am glad I wasn't with

---

[1] The Locanda S. Vigilio on Lake Garda, brilliantly run by a drunken Irishman named Leonard Walsh, was the Coopers' favourite hotel in the world.

[2] Susan Mary Patten had had a son, also called Bill, on 4 July 1948.

[3] Edward Grigg, 1st Lord Altrincham (1879–1955), had married Joan Dickson-Poynder (d. 1987) in 1923.

them. It always embarrasses me when she performs these feats and my presence cramps her style. We dined at the British Embassy. Lady Mallet[1] is charming and everything a British Ambassadress ought to be. She insisted on having a mongrel bitch which has attached herself to the household brought up after dinner, together with her puppy of unknown parentage which promptly made a mess on the carpet. There was no embarrassment, and the servants came in to clear it up as though they were accustomed to it. The house is hideous.

October 25, 1948

Diana had a slight hangover this morning, which was a pity as she has been in such lovely spirits ever since we left Paris that it has enhanced the joy and gaiety of everything. We lunched with the Jack Wards.[2] Luncheon was animated and the food was good. They are a couple who do credit to the Foreign Service. I wish I had completed the paper I was writing last year about conditions in the Service. Ashley and John persuaded me not to. They are driving the best people out and not getting the best people in.

October 30, 1948

At 4 I went to see Monsieur Queuille's *Directeur de Cabinet* at the Hôtel Matignon. Queuille is now both President of the Council and Minister of Finance. I used to known him in Algiers where he had a very small job in de Gaulle's government, and he has had none since until now. His *directeur* treated me with the greatest civility and I hope it may do some good, as I want my job with I.C.I., such as it is, to be continued next year.

This has been a very good month of October. I've enjoyed myself in Paris, London and Rome – not to mention Wilton, Ditchley, Bognor and Chantilly – and I've earned over £350.

November 7, 1948. Sunday

I did some more work on my book[3] this morning. It was a lovely day. Quite a number of people came to lunch [including] Brooks and Hazel Richards, who are over here for a day or two. Brooks is working now in the German Department of the Foreign Office. He tells me that it is as good as settled that the Ruhr, ownership and management, will be restored to Germany. This means, in my opinion, that there will be another war. And I don't believe that we shall beat Germany the third time. All we have to do to make war impossible is to keep control of the Ruhr. It is so simple – but we're not doing it. It's very depressing.

---

[1] Sir Victor Mallet (1893–1969) married Christina Andreae in 1925. Ambassador to Sweden 1940–5, Spain 1945–6 and to Italy 1947–53.

[2] Sir John Ward (1909–91), Ambassador to Argentina 1957–61 and to Italy 1962–6.

[3] Duff's short book *Sergeant Shakespeare* was published the following year. It is a light-hearted attempt to show that Shakespeare had spent some time as a soldier in the Low Countries.

November 30, 1948

My article on the Ruhr appeared last Friday and was extensively quoted in the French press. It has had a great success in France. Even my barber thanked me for having written it, and so have many members of the Travellers'. I had a letter from Adrien Thierry about it. This month of November has been less *mouvementé* than October – the two great events have been the birth of the heir to the throne[1] and the presidential election[2] in America. It has not been an unprofitable one for me. I have received 644,823 francs and £172.

December 5, 1948. Sunday

I arrived at Rambouillet before 10. The President and Madame Vincent Auriol were dispensing delicious hot chocolate and brioches. He was very nice about my last article and solemnly thanked me on behalf of France. He has learnt to shoot since last year which does him great credit. He is slow but pretty accurate. In the first drive he twice wiped my eye. I shot better afterwards.

1949

In 1949 Duff kept a summary diary only.

January 15, 1949

It is nearly three weeks since I wrote in this book. The last days in London, spent between White's and the Dorchester, gave little opportunity for writing, and also I began to wonder whether it was worth while imposing this little burden on myself. Since I no longer hold any office nor play any part in affairs the diary becomes little more than a record of lunches and dinners, pleasures and love affairs, which can be neither entertaining nor edifying to read. My excuse for keeping it from 1944 to 1947 was that it might contribute a footnote to history – but that was only an excuse and not the motive. What the diary writer's true motive is remains mysterious, but I believe it is very like the sportsman's motive in keeping a game book, the desire to record and to remember past happiness.

This past year has been a very happy one for me. Not once have I regretted the important positions I have held in the past. I have been happy at Chantilly, in Paris and in London. I have made no progress with the books I meant to write, but I mean to write them still. I have written a number of articles and made a few speeches so that I can feel that I have justified my existence. Ten

---

[1] Prince Charles was born on 14 Nov. 1948. On 1 July 1969 he was invested as Prince of Wales.
[2] In Nov. 1948 President Truman won the US presidential election in a close race against the Republican candidate, Governor Thomas E. Dewey of New York.

years in the Foreign Office, including more than a year in the army, twenty years in the House of Commons, thirteen of them as a Minister, and four years as Ambassador, four books published, make up a case for a good rest and I shouldn't be ashamed if I did no more work. But I've lost the art of leisure – I don't care much for travel and I am very happy with the few little jobs that come along.

February 28, 1949

During this month I have become 59. It seems a great age to young people. I am an old man. But I feel just as I did twenty years ago. Thirty years ago I had less self-confidence. I was not sure what I could do and what I couldn't, but twenty years ago – the year in which John Julius was born and when I was writing *Talleyrand* – I think I felt just as I do now.

Susan Mary plays a part in my life. She is now in America on a short visit. She writes me the loveliest letters and she loves me far more than I deserve. I love her too, very deeply and tenderly, but not as I love Caroline. I am not 'in love' with her, although there is nothing I wouldn't do for her. I owe her so much.

Maxine[1] is a new star in my firmament. She is only 26. Diana thinks her the most beautiful girl she has ever seen. She is also good and intelligent. She loves her husband who is extremely nice. I like being with her, but I am not in love with her and would never seek to persuade her to do anything she thought wrong. I enjoy the company at the Travellers' but I have no friends there, by which I mean people with whom I am happy to dine alone. I suppose I have no men friends any more. They are all dead, except perhaps Ed [Stanley of Alderley] who is now in Jamaica. I have spent this day, the last day of February, entirely alone – and thoroughly enjoyed it. Fine weather has helped. I have lived very little alone in my life. I cannot remember having passed a day so. I think that the habit might easily grow upon me. I should write more often in this book, with less to say.

May 30, 1949

The weather has been abominable all this month. The much-needed rain has fallen in torrents and there have been no warm days.

Two liaisons have considerably amused me. The first is between Loel Guinness and my Gloria and the second between Tony Marreco[2] and my Louise. Thus two of my mistresses have captured the husbands of two of my nieces – simultaneously. Loel tells me that he has never in his life been so much in love as he is with Gloria. He thinks she is in love with him. She may

---

[1] Maxine Birley (b. 1922), daughter of the artist Sir Oswald Birley (1880–1952) and his wife Rhoda, married Count Alain de la Falaise in 1946.

[2] Lt.-Col. Anthony Marreco (b. 1915) married Lady Ursula Manners, daughter of the 9th Duke of Rutland, in 1943 (divorced 1948).

be – in any case she sees in him the chance of security, which I think she wants above everything.

June 2, 1949

The last day of May we had a pleasant surprise. I went to Paris in the morning to have my hair cut and to attend a meeting of the Travellers' Committee in the afternoon. On arriving there I found a message from Diana to say Princess Margaret was coming in the afternoon to tea. So I drove back after luncheon with Nancy Rodd – and the three of us received the Princess and Lady Mary Harvey. I thought it very kind of her to come all that way to see us and we both found her quite charming. We drove her to the *hameau* and to the stables and she was very appreciative. She had been here for a few days but we had been asked nowhere to meet her – neither to the dance at the Embassy, which didn't surprise me as it was supposed to be only for young people, nor to a party given by Sammy Hood,[1] which did rather surprise me. It made her coming to see us all the more satisfactory.

The month of June has not been eventful. On the first I had an interview with Korda, who suggested that I should become the European representative of the British film industry at a salary of 3,000,000 francs a year. I am not sure what this will involve but it sounds satisfactory. Later in the month he confirmed the offer, and I am to go next week to London to meet Rank and others. This will of course be instead of representing London Films as I have been doing hitherto and it will, I hope, involve more work, for I have been ashamed to get what I was getting for doing nothing at all.

For the Prix du Jockey our racing guests were the young Hartingtons[2] – a charming couple – her sister Nancy, and we had a large luncheon including Aly and Rita.[3] We were all much disappointed by her appearance. Daphne Bath came also to stay and was as heavenly as ever. Then we had Enid Jones,[4] followed by Cecil Beaton, Bob Boothby, Freya Stark,[5] Nancy Cunard – a big lunch for the Achesons and Bruces[6] etc. and finally the David Cecils[7] who arrived for the *grande semaine* which concludes with the Grand Prix. We took them to a dinner party in Paris chez Marie Blanche de Polignac, where Yvonne Printemps sang delightfully after dinner, and the Alphands performed. They also had to come with us to the Hertford Hospital Ball. They seemed to enjoy

---

[1] Samuel Hood, 6th Viscount Hood (1910–81), Counsellor in Paris 1948–51.
[2] Andrew (1920–2004) and Deborah (Debo) Hartington, later 11th Duke and Duchess of Devonshire. Nancy Mitford was her sister.
[3] Prince Aly Khan (1911–60) married Rita Hayworth (1918–70) in 1949; they divorced in 1953.
[4] Enid Bagnold, Lady Jones (1889–1981), the novelist, married to Sir Roderick Jones of Reuters.
[5] Dame Freya Stark (1893–1993), writer and traveller.
[6] Dean Acheson (1893–1971), US Secretary of State 1949–53, and David Bruce, US Ambassador to France 1949–52.
[7] Lord David Cecil (1902–86), writer and don, married Rachel MacCarthy (d. 1982), daughter of Sir Desmond MacCarthy, in 1932.

it all. The Duchess of Kent[1] was the great attraction. She came down to Chantilly the following day and had tea with us.

Diana's friends planned a secret party in her honour.[2] Of course the secret got out before the night. But she was very touched and it was a great success. Maxine, Barley, Nancy, Susan Mary and the Twedes were, I think, the prime movers. They performed a unicorn ballet. Diana drove me home to Chantilly at 4 a.m., a lovely dawn.

During this month, despite the social turmoil, I began again and nearly finished my little book about Shakespeare. I am not very happy about it, but I read a good deal of it to Diana a few evenings ago and she enjoyed it very much. This encouraged me.

December 28, 1949

The end of the year is in sight. I haven't written in this book since August. I think that next year I shall start keeping a daily diary again. It is the only way.

These last months have been happy ones. After our very successful visit to San Vigilio, which we found as lovely as ever, we went on to Venice, where my duties took me on account of the film festival. I have finished working for Korda, for whom by the way I never did any work, and am now the European representative of the British Film Producers Association which has already proved a good deal more strenuous. It is also better paid.

My *Sergeant Shakespeare* appeared at the end of November. I have written 13 articles this year, 9 of them for the *Daily Mail* at £200 each, and I got a new cinema job which is worth 3,000,000 francs a year, but my contract runs only until the end of 1950. It has therefore been a good year financially and I seem to have spent £2000 less than I've made, despite the loss of £500 at Deauville. Even so it is rather alarming to find that I have spent over £4,000. I have no idea how much Diana has spent. She keeps no accounts – but she seems to have plenty. We have paid practically no taxation. How long can that go on?

Tomorrow is the last day of the year. I shall miss White's which is always fun that day – but much more shall I miss the Albert Hall, where I have enjoyed myself so enormously the last two New Year's Eves. And next year I shall be 60. Oh dear!

---

[1] Princess Marina of Greece (1906–68) married Prince George, 1st Duke of Kent, in 1934. He died in an aeroplane accident in August 1942, at the age of forty.

[2] 'There's to be a party given for Diana by all Duffs' mistresses' wrote Nancy Mitford to Lady Pamela Berry (Artemis Cooper and Antony Beevor, *Paris After the Liberation: 1944–1949*).

1950

In 1950 Duff resumed his daily diary.

January 1, 1950 (Paris)

New Year's Day should be devoted to good resolutions. It is more often spent in regretting New Year's Eve. I went to bed at 5.30 this morning. I can't afford these late nights any more. However the day was so beautiful that it made up for much. Frost on the ground and not a cloud in the sky.

January 5, 1950

Diana and I lunched with the Stanislas de Castellanes. The other guests were Sacha Guitry and his new wife, Mondor the biographer of Mallarmé, Sauguet[1] the musician, Marie-Louise and Louise. I had not met Sacha since the war. He was a notorious collaborator and was in prison for a long time, but everything appears now to be forgiven. He told some extremely funny stories and told them beautifully.

January 6, 1950

I cannot drink as much as I used to. The fact has got to be faced. I really didn't have very much last night but I felt very much the worse for it this morning. It may be that my liver is in bad condition, which seems to be the case with most people in France.

January 7, 1950

I am becoming more interested in my book on Venice and less in my novella. I am re-reading Gibbon to give me background for the former and finding it as entrancing as ever. I doubt whether fiction is my affair. Diana thinks my health is in a bad way and talks of our both doing a cruise somewhere for three weeks. I could get on with the novella there and couldn't do anything else.

January 9, 1950

Having written yesterday that I was more interested in my Venetian book than my story, I devoted most of my day to the latter and thought I was getting on better with it. I first had the idea of the book on Venice more than twenty years ago and have always been returning to it. Will it be like Benjamin Constant's comparative history of religions which he worked on all his life and wasn't worth reading when he finished it?

---

[1] Henri Sauguet (1901–89), French composer.

January 11, 1950

In the evening I went to *Othello* with Louise. I gave her caviare and champagne first at the Rue de Lille. It was a new translation in prose by Neveux, not good nor accurate and all the poetry was lost. Othello was a fat old pansy and Desdemona a blowsy middle aged blonde. Yet I enjoyed it enormously. So did Louise although she suffered almost too much. Iago was the best I've ever seen. Louise said that if she had gone behind the scenes and had met him she would have spat in his face. What a compliment! We went on to supper at a nice quiet place in the Champs-Elysées and had a very delightful evening. She is the best companion. It is sad that I cannot be in love with her any more.

January 25, 1950

Diana and I lunched with Graham Greene and his mistress Catherine Walston at the Ritz. I hadn't met her before and found her very attractive. She looks young and beautiful and has six children, which is hard to believe. They are both devout Catholics, both married with children, and living together in open sin. It is odd but perhaps admirable that people should be willing to give up eternal salvation for guilty love.

January 27, 1950 (Aix-les-Bains)

We went to see our doctor in the morning. Terrier is his name. He impressed me favourably. I went on to see another doctor in a laboratory where he took the usual tests. Diana has already started her cure which consists in neither eating nor drinking anything at all. This makes meals, during which she does needlework, not very gay.

January 28, 1950

The doctor called at 9 this morning. He knew some of the results of my tests but not all. I thought him very sensible but Diana was disappointed in him. He was strongly against my giving up all forms of alcohol and strongly in favour of whiskey, which he said was from the point of view of the liver the best drink of all. He was not exaggeratedly in favour of the waters of Aix, said they suited some people and not others – and what this special quality was he really didn't know.

So ends the first month of the year. I have done very little in it. I've only written one short book review and I have not got on as I should have with my story. I have definitely cut myself off from British politics. I had four requests to speak for candidates in the election. Winston and Randolph Churchill, Billy Ednam and Bill Richmond, who is standing for Oldham. Winston asked me to speak in his constituency. I felt that as Leader of the Party he should have invited me to come over to assist the party and do a speaking tour arranged by the Central Office, or else should have left me alone. I felt also that the position of one who lives out of the country and pays no taxation would be open to criticism if I took part in the election. It was not however this that decided me against doing so – it was because I didn't want to.

February 11, 1950 [Aix]

We started off for Toulon. We stopped on the road to open the car, as it was such a lovely morning. Willow [*their golden cocker spaniel, given to them by Gloria*] jumped out, ran across the road, and as she was returning along came a *camion* and passed right over her. I expected to see nothing but blood and fur emerge but she limped yelping to the side of the road and didn't appear to be very badly hurt. Her mouth was bleeding but soon stopped – and her left front leg seems damaged. She was, and is, still suffering from shock – but we hope all will be well. We have been terribly distressed about her.

February 12, 1950

We took Willow, who had been very wretched all day, to a vet. He said she had cracked, not broken her leg, and he put it in a splint. He also gave her a *lavement* [enema]. He seemed capable and was certainly kind.

February 17, 1950

This was a real spring day. It was a pleasure to walk, without an overcoat, in the street. If we do have to leave the Rue de Lille – and it looks as though we shall – we shall have to find something else. We could easily find something more attractive – but it will be very annoying to have to move after the money and time we have spent there. I walked to the Crillon to call on Gloria. She was very sensible about the Rue de Lille and may be helpful.

February 21, 1950

I spoke to Gloria on the telephone this morning. She told me that Loel had now decided, under her influence, to put Tanis and Meraud[1] on the first floor of the Rue de Lille and leave us on the second. Gloria had wisely foreseen that if she had moved in there herself she would have aroused much envy and malice.

February 22, 1950

This is my sixtieth birthday. I hate being sixty. It is old age – undeniably – yet I feel no older than I ever did. I must get used to it. We drove to Paris this morning – very happily. I saw Loel about the house [in Rue de Lille]. I am not to buy it but to rent it at 240,000 francs per annum. This suits me admirably and I now feel secure.

---

[1] Meraud Guinness (1904–93), Loel Guinness's elder sister, married Alvaro Guevara (d. 1951) in 1929.

March 2, 1950

I went to see Gloria, whom I found obsessed by the Pavillon de la Muette, an eighteenth-century hunting lodge in the forest of St Germain, which belongs to the state, which will let her live there for nothing if she will do it up, which would cost 20,000,000. She is mad to have it but Loel, of course, is reluctant to put money into anything which won't be a permanent asset. He telephoned to her from England while I was with her. He is evidently very fond of her and she tells me that she is now in love with him.

March 19, 1950 (Chantilly)

Today I finished *Operation Heartbreak*[1] before luncheon. It is a tremendous relief to have got it done. It is, I feel, the sort of book that might have a great success, or might, equally probably, prove a complete failure – fall quite flat. I walked to the Post Office and back and then started to write the prologue which Rupert [Hart-Davis] suggested. Diana returned for dinner and we read *Little Dorrit* afterwards. Then I finished the prologue, so I felt that I had done a good day's work.

April 24, 1950

A quiet day. Diana is getting depressed again which distresses me. The fact is that she needs excitement, as she admits. The quiet country life bores her. We don't have much of it, but she has tremendous energy which needs an outlet. She has no intellectual occupation. She is not sleeping so well again.

May 16, 1950 [Cruising on Loel Guinness's yacht the Sea Huntress*]*

The weather was perfect and the sun was hot. I read a chapter of *The Decline and Fall*. I have an idea for the production of a Gibbon in one volume. I believe it could be done and I'm sure it would sell. Gloria, Loel and I bathed. Gloria got confidential with Diana today and told her that this was the first time in her life she had had an affair with a married man! In spite of this Diana is beginning to like her.

May 18, 1950

Ed [Stanley] can't stand Gloria – a fact of which she is quite unaware. Nor is he the least attracted by her physically which is surprising, because she is looking her best. I find her rather tiresome at times. Diana sometimes reproaches me for not being nicer to her. I think of four years ago, when I

---

[1] Duff's short novel *Operation Heartbreak* was inspired by the now well-known military operation in 1943 in which a dead body in British officer's uniform was dropped off the Spanish coast with deliberately misleading information on British strategic intentions. The true story, by Ewen Montagu, *The Man Who Never Was*, and the novel were published in one volume in 2004.

really loved her and Diana really believed her to be the personification of evil!

May 28, 1950. Sunday

I went for a walk with Joe Alsop this morning and talked of one thing and another. He thinks it will be impossible for Great Britain to join with France and Germany to work on the Schuman plan on account of the very different standard of wages in our country, which we cannot reduce to the German level. I find him an admirable companion – very sensible and very full of humour.

June 1, 1950

I read through today my diary for the month of May and found it intolerably ill-written. It might well be the work of a child of twelve. I must try to take a little more trouble, or give it up altogether. The fact is that I have very little of interest to record.

This morning Osbert Sitwell arrived from Italy. His appearance is rather disturbing. He limps and his left arm shakes terribly, but he is in a charming mood, very gentle and very amusing.

June 2, 1950. Chantilly

It was hot today and I thought there would be another storm, but it passed over. David Eccles[1] and his wife came to lunch. I had a talk with Eccles. He is strongly in favour of our coming into the Franco-German steel plan, and I am strongly of the same opinion. He said I should be surprised at the amount of opposition there was to it on both sides of the house. He is a clever man, but not attractive.

June 19, 1950

The great event was the birth of Willow's puppies – nine of them – all black. One died almost at once. The vet advised that two should be drowned and another died later, so we are left with three. In the course of the morning Auberon Herbert turned up. He told me that Antony Head[2] got terribly drunk at the party at Windsor Castle on Friday night and had to held up by the Queen when he was dancing with her.

---

[1] David Eccles, 1st Viscount Eccles, Conservative MP and Minister (1904–99), married first the Hon. Sybil Dawson (d. 1977) in 1928, and second the American bibliophile, Mary Hyde (d. 2003).

[2] Antony Head, 1st Viscount Head (1906–83). Conservative MP, married Lady Dorothea (Dot) Ashley-Cooper in 1935. Minister of Defence Oct. 1956–Jan. 1957; British High Commissioner in Nigeria 1960–3 and Malaysia 1963–6. Close friends of the Coopers.

June 21, 1950

We had a lunch party for Berenson who had been spending the morning at the Château. The French were delighted that Berenson had said this morning that there was nothing in Italian art to equal *Les Très Riches Heures du Duc de Berri*. The old man is most astonishing. He is 87. He lay down for half an hour before lunch and again for half an hour afterwards. He looked at my books with great interest. Seeing a set of Pater he said that he was one of the three writers who had influenced him most. He had known him well. I asked him if Pater was very ugly. He said no, except for his absurd moustache. The ugliest man he had ever known was Benedetto Croce – whom I gathered he was not fond of. He is keenly interested in politics. I gave him my views on the Schuman plan. Madame Mariano [Berenson's companion] is very nice, highly educated and easy to talk to. It is a strange relationship. She can never have been beautiful.

I gave up my daily diary at the end of June. Not only had it become a *corvée* but also I found it very uninteresting when I tried to re-read it. Next year I shall try to keep a monthly one.

The remainder of 1950 passed pleasantly. I was somewhat occupied with the publication of *Operation Heartbreak*. Faint resistance was offered by certain branches of the secret service, but I was able to overcome them. The success of the book was instantaneous and surpassed our highest hopes. Nearly 30,000 copies were sold by Christmas. I am hoping it will do as well in America. I am selling the film rights there for 40,000 dollars.

We spent a very happy Christmas and New Year at Vaynol. Diana was happy and I was blissfully so. Diana and J.J. left on the 29th in order that he might spend his New Year's Eve with his beloved Anne [Clifford].[1]

1951

In 1951 Duff kept only a monthly diary.

January 1951

I wrote one article during the month, which appeared in the *Daily Mail* on the 25th. The subject was the danger of war coming about owing to misunderstanding. It had quite a success. I also started writing some sort of an autobiography but didn't make much headway. I mean to deal only with my public life, but I don't find it easy.

John Julius stayed with us until the 11th. He is very much in love with Anne.

---

[1] Anne, eldest daughter of Sir Bede Clifford G CMG, former Governor of the Bahamas, Trinidad and Mauritius. She and John Julius married in 1952. They were divorced in 1985.

Provided they are willing to wait for two or three years I should have no objection.

On the 26th I went to London for a claret dinner given by Harry Rosebery[1] at Berry's. We drank Pichon Longueville 1899, Lafite 1865 and 1864. The last was the best of the lot. It was a pleasant evening. London was much concerned over a recent row at White's. [Air-Marshal] John Slessor brought Aneurin Bevan in one night for a drink. Hugh Stanley, knowing that John [Fox-Strangways] was over the way at Brooks's and was, as usual, pretty drunk, sent over for him. John as was to be expected insulted Bevan and kicked his bottom as he left the Club. Slessor reported the matter to the Committee and John, who had been warned that if he had any more rows in the Club he would have to go, has resigned. There is much sympathy for him. Everybody thinks that Hugh Stanley is most to blame, and many say that Slessor was quite wrong to bring Bevan into the Club. Harry says it is an unwritten rule of every club that members should bring in as visitors only such people as they would put up as candidates, that is to say people whom they think agreeable to other members. Personally I never liked Slessor much and I'm sorry for John.

I saw Winston once during the month when he passed through Paris on his way back from Morocco. We lunched at the Embassy. Schuman was there. Winston was in the best of form and health but he finds it impossible now to listen to anybody else. Schuman tried in vain to talk to him.

February 1951

On the 16th Diana and I set forth for the south. I devoted this holiday to translating a story which Louise has recently written called *Madame De*. It appeared in the *Revue de Paris* and has had an enormous success. I had never tried my hand before at translating prose. I find it fascinating.

(*Monaco*) [We] are staying on board Daisy's yacht. We found Fred Cripps on board. He had come over from the villa at Cap Martin where he is staying with Daisy. We all dined at the villa that evening. It was rather gloomy.

We returned early – about 10.30 – leaving our cars on the quay. We played canasta until 12 when we went to bed. We were woken up with the news that our car had run into the sea. Diana had left the brakes off but even so it was a most astonishing thing to happen, for in order to get into the sea the car had to steer itself between a bollard and a crane. I strongly suspected sabotage, either by communists or drunken sailors. It was a great blow. With the help of divers they hoisted the car up by midday, but it was in a lamentable state. Diana, who took our disaster very philosophically, bought a new car, a Simca, at Nice.

---

[1] Harry Rosebery, 6th Earl of Rosebery (1882–1974).

March 1951

We started off at midday on the 7th in the new Simca. We went to Villeneuve-les-Avignon and had just arranged our luggage in our room when the maid dashed in to tell us the car was on fire. To lose one car by water and another by fire in so short a space of time seemed too bad. The fire was extinguished, but extensive repairs were required.

April 1951

This has been an idle month, much time being occupied by attendance at the Cannes Film Festival. I could at least feel that I was earning my £3,000 a year from the British Film Producers' Association. On the 7th April, Loel and Gloria were married at Antibes. We lunched with them on board their yacht after the ceremony. I feel confident about the success of their marriage. Gloria is a sensible woman. She knows how to make Loel happy, she likes doing the things he likes, she's no longer in her first youth and he gives her and her children wealth and security. Diana has quite come round to her, much against her will. How strange it seems when I think of five years ago.

We paid one or two visits to the Castello at Opio, which was taken by the Ludo Kennedys [Sir Ludovic Kennedy] for April and May. She is Moira Shearer, the dancer. They have just married and I thought them a charming couple. She performs in the film Korda was showing at the festival *Tales of Hoffman* which is most disappointing. He was there himself. I cannot think he's pleased with it.

The great events of the month have been the sacking of MacArthur[1] and the resignation of Bevan. My feeling about MacArthur is that his views are right but his conduct has been wrong. One can't fight a war with one arm tied behind one's back, but neither can one allow a military leader to defy the civil superior authority. Bevan's going must greatly weaken if not split the Labour Party, and must surely hasten the advent of the General Election.

May 1951

Although this month of May has been the coldest and wettest recorded it has been a happy month for me. On May 2nd I went to a sale of books at Sotheby's and bought for £125 a first edition of Keats which belonged to Browning's father. This is the largest sum I have ever paid for a book. l had luncheon with Winston next day. He was in excellent form. We drank champagne and I drove down to the House of Commons with him afterwards. Randolph brought little Winston in during lunch to say goodbye as he was going to school at Ludgrove for the first time. The child interrupted his grandfather in the middle of a

---

[1] General Douglas MacArthur (1880–1964), Supreme United Nations Commander at the start of the Korean War in 1950. He was relieved of his command in April 1951 for disagreeing with Truman's Government.

discourse on the situation in Persia to tell him what a beautiful little motorcar he had recently been given. 'Indeed', said Winston, 'and who gave you that?' 'Mummy's great friend, Gianni Agnelli[1] who owns the Fiat company' was the reply in ringing tones. That evening I dined with Pam Berry. Her house is the most amusing in London. It is always fun there.

On May 24th we went with Liz and Raimund to see Larry and Vivien in *Antony and Cleopatra*. I thought it an amazingly good performance. I had doubted whether Vivien would be up to the part. She was really wonderful and I enjoyed it enormously. We had a very gay supper party afterwards chez the Hoffs. Pam and Michael Berry and Larry and Vivien, who was looking lovely. I drank a good deal and did a lot of kissing.

June 1951

After Ascot I returned to Chantilly. Evelyn Waugh was staying at the Hôtel du Château. Diana had taken him rooms as he wanted somewhere quiet where he could write a book. We saw a great deal of him during the rest of the month, and he eventually moved from the hotel, where he wasn't comfortable, into our house. I have nearly always quarrelled with him in the past, but, whether it is he or I whom the years have mellowed I can't say, we now seem to get on extremely well together and there hasn't been a cross word between us.

The Windsors whom I hadn't seen since their return from America were [at the Travellers' Ball]. She is causing a great deal of scandal here, as she did there. The Duke said he wanted to have a talk with me and we fixed a date for the following week. I feared he might be going to discuss his domestic difficulties, but all he wanted was that I should help him over a speech he has to make in the autumn at some publishers' dinner in London.

July 1951

On July 9th we dined, Diana, John Julius, Evelyn and I, and travelled by the night ferry to London. There was a party that evening at Buckingham Palace. I enjoyed it very much as I always do, but it was not such a good party as the winter one, no general sit-down supper, only one table for the royalties. I had a pretty long innings there with the Queen. I told her the whole saga of Freda's affair with the Duke of Windsor as Freda once told it to me.

August 1951 (Chantilly)

I dined with Susan Mary and her mother. The latter went to bed soon after dinner. In the course of the evening my nose started bleeding. I had little difficulty in stopping it, but the next day as I was driving to Paris it started again. Nothing would stop it. Letty and Guy [Benson] arrived at the Rue de Lille while I was still bleeding profusely. After some time Letty's ministrations

---

[1] Gianni Agnelli was Pamela Churchill's lover.

'succeeded in stemming the flow. I took them to lunch at the Berkeley but had hardly sat down before the bleeding started again. The *gérant* had been an *infirmier* in the war and sent out for some special preparation which is made for the prevention of nose bleeding. We stuffed it up with this which I was told should be removed by a doctor, so in the afternoon I went to the Hertford Hospital where the doctor removed it and gave me an injection. He said my blood pressure was rather too high.

I reached La Reine Jeanne[1] early on Saturday morning. My short stay there was spoilt by a return of the nose bleeding. The local doctors coped with it quite ineffectually so that on Wednesday afternoon we drove to Cannes, where an admirable doctor came round to the Carlton at five minutes notice and cauterised the nose, quite painlessly. I had one or two alarms afterwards but no more real trouble.

I had to go to Venice on account of the film festival. I found Winston and Clemmie staying at the Lido. I lunched with them one day and we all three [with John Julius] dined with them on another. After dinner I persuaded Winston to come to the film. It was an Irish film called *No Resting Place*. He happened to be in a receptive mood and enjoyed it enormously, saying it was the best film he had ever seen. It did me good from the point of view of my job with the B.F.P.A. to have been able to get him to see a British film. He had refused hitherto. I found him much older and very deaf. He depends on champagne and is morose and gloomy until he has had a good deal. He then becomes transformed and is as brilliant and charming as ever.

[December 1951]

Today is Christmas Eve, and I have added nothing to my account of 1951 since the end of August. I intend to begin again next year keeping a daily chronicle. Two reasons have persuaded me to do so. The first is that since I have been trying to write an autobiography[2] I have been obliged to read the diaries I have kept in the past, which I have done with more pleasure than I expected. They will be of course of very great use to me as the book goes on and have been of use already, especially when dealing with the war of 1914–1918. An account of a battle written the day after the event must be both of greater value and of greater interest than any account, however painstaking, accurate and eloquent, written years later. I am not very well pleased with this autobiography as far as it has gone. The first chapter is the worst. Perhaps the reason is that I don't recall my childhood with interest or affection. In the course of this work I have re-read many of my old letters. During the six months that I was at the war I wrote to Diana every day and she wrote to me as often. I believe that these letters well-edited would make a better book than the autobiography.[3]

---

[1] A house near Le Lavandon in the South of France owned by Paul-Louis Weiller, a rich French industrialist and a great friend and admirer of Diana's.

[2] *Old Men Forget*, published in 1953.

[3] They were edited by Duff's granddaughter Artemis Cooper and published in 1983.

The other reason for my decision to resume diary-keeping has been the reading of Gide's journal which I am doing now. I certainly like it better than any of his novels, and it is difficult I find not to like him, though I should have thought it impossible to like a septuagenarian who boasts of his sexual adventures with little boys.

The month of September I passed in Italy. Venice was more gay and agreeable even than usual owing largely to the presence of a great number of English and French people who had come for Charlie Beistegui's famous fancy dress ball. The press of all countries made a great fuss about it and behaved abominably. It seems that everybody who is prepared to entertain nowadays must keep a public relations officer to protect himself from the vulgar abuse of a gang of journalists who will write anything they are told to for money. It was really a very beautiful party and great fun besides. Diana, as Tiepolo's Cleopatra, looked more beautiful than anybody. I thoroughly enjoyed the evening.

Winston was staying at the Lido and we saw a great deal of him and Clemmie. We had one very pleasant evening when he dined with us at the Gritti. He was in ill humour at first and would hardly speak but under the benign influence of the grape he soon came into wonderful form and was singing old music hall songs at the end and fearing that he would be re-proached by Clemmie on the way home for lacking in dignity.

When I got back to Chantilly I started the autobiography but we returned to London for the General Election.[1] I thought the result disappointing. The conditions could not have been more unfavourable for the Labour Party and yet more people voted Labour than ever before. I can see little hope for the Conservatives in the future. Never for one moment do I regret my decision to give up politics.

The chief event of November was the visit of Princess Margaret to Paris. She came to dinner with us at Chantilly. It was a very successful evening. We tried to get as many young people as possible. John Julius came over and brought Denys Dawnay, a friend of his and of Princess Margaret's. She brought Miss Bevan and Miss Beaumont-Nesbitt. Cecil Beaton and Greta Garbo came and the Pattens and Alain and Mary de Rothschild.[2] Mark Bonham Carter,[3] another friend of the Princess's, came and stayed with us. I liked him very much. We had two men sing after dinner and John Julius sang and the Princess finally went to the piano and remained there singing and playing for about an hour. I thought her wonderful and was quite in love with

---

[1] At the general election on 25 Oct. 1951, the Conservatives won 321 seats, Labour 295 and other parties 9.

[2] Baron Alain de Rothschild (1910–82) married Mary Chauvin du Treuil (b. 1916) in 1938.

[3] Mark Bonham Carter, Lord Bonham-Carter (1922–94), son of Sir Maurice and Lady Violet Bonham Carter, married Leslie Grenfell, daughter of Condé Nast, in 1955. Liberal MP 1958–9, Chairman of the Race Relations Board 1966–70 and of the Community Relations Committee 1971–7.

her. Diana had arranged everything beautifully. We had the grounds floodlit, showing up the waterfall, and a brazier in the garden with hot chestnuts. Princess Margaret stayed until nearly 4 and I've heard since on good authority that she never enjoyed a party so much.

Though Duff writes that he intends to resume a daily chronicle in 1952, there is no trace of it. In May of that year he was offered a peerage by Churchill and became Viscount Norwich of Aldwick. By this time his health was failing fast. In May 1953 he had a violent haemorrhage, but by the end of the year – after the publication in November of his autobiography, Old Men Forget *– he had recovered enough to sail for Jamaica to stay with his friend Lord Brownlow. On the second day of the crossing he suffered another haemorrhage, which proved fatal. He died at sea on New Year's Day 1954.*

ACKNOWLEDGEMENTS

In the editing of this book I am above all indebted to the work of my wife, Mollie. It is she who has shouldered the immense labour of transcribing the bulk of my father's diaries from his manuscript notebooks to computer; she who has done virtually all the cutting and has taken on the immense burden of the footnotes. I cannot thank her enough.

I am also more than grateful to my daughter, Artemis, whose edition of my parents' correspondence, *A Durable Fire*, has been invaluable, as has *Paris After the Liberation 1944–49*, written jointly by her and my son-in-law, Antony Beevor. Many thanks, too, to my step-daughter, Kate Juteau, for her help in tracking down forgotten Frenchmen and to Hugo Vickers, whose encyclopaedic knowledge of the period has solved many a problem.

INDEX